OXFORD WORLD'S CLASSICS

PLATO

Republic

Translated with an Introduction and Notes by
ROBIN WATERFIELD

OXFORD
UNIVERSITY PRESS

Oxford University Press, Great Clarendon Street, Oxford OX2 6DP

Oxford New York
Athens Auckland Bangkok Bogota Bombay Buenos Aires
Calcutta Cape Town Dar es Salaam Delhi Florence Hong Kong Istanbul
Karachi Kuala Lumpur Madras Madrid Melbourne Mexico City
Nairobi Paris Singapore Taipei Tokyo Toronto Warsaw
and associated companies in
Berlin Ibadan

Oxford is a trade mark of Oxford University Press

First published as a World's Classics paperback 1994
Reissued as an Oxford World's Classics paperback 1998

British Library Cataloguing in Publication Data
Data available

Library of Congress Cataloging in Publication Data
Data available
ISBN 0–19–283370–7

3 5 7 9 10 8 6 4

Printed in Great Britain by
Cox & Wyman Ltd,
Reading, Berkshire

FOR MY PARENTS

PREFACE

I SHOULD say a few words about the strategy of the book. The translation is intended to be readable—as readable as I can make it and still remain true to Plato's Greek. We can only speculate on what kind of audience Plato wrote the book for: was it aimed at an intelligent lay readership or 'professional' philosophers? At any rate, his Greek is invariably readable and fluent, so I have tried to write the same kind of English.

Plato did not furnish his works with notes. Of course, his original audience would have detected more of his implicit references than most people will today; so it is incumbent on a translator to provide notes to explain as many of those obscurities as he can. But it is a virtue of end-of-book notes (as used in the World's Classics series) that one can read the translation without constantly feeling the need to interrupt one's reading to refer to what is printed at the foot of the page. In this sense one can simulate Plato's original audience, and that is for the best: like any great work, *Republic* has many facets, and a reader should enjoy it in the first instance for what he or she happens to get out of it.

Apart from the kind of explanatory notes mentioned in the previous paragraph, I have also occasionally indulged in critical and philosophical commentary. The chief purpose of this kind of note is to stimulate the reader to think more deeply about what he or she is reading; paradoxically, however, such notes in a volume like this are bound, for reasons of compass, to be rather dogmatic. A highly selective bibliography has been provided in case a reader *is* prompted to read further. These notes, then, should be understood to skim the surface of current scholarship on *Republic*. One thing I have avoided in the notes is cross-reference to other Platonic dialogues: *Republic* is so central within Plato's corpus that there would have been no end to it.

The Introduction is intended to provide some kind of overview of *Republic* and to develop one or two lines of thought at greater length than the notes would allow.

The two books I most frequently consulted were Sir Desmond Lee's translation, which always urged me to try to do better, and Julia Annas's modestly entitled 'Introduction', which constantly prompted me to think more deeply about what I was reading.

In addition, there are a number of personal debts which should be acknowledged. The overriding one is to my wife Briji. This translation has been completed on schedule, and the time spent over it has been as wonderful as it should be, when things could have been so different: in the face of life-threatening disease, her courage and lack of self-indulgence have been astounding.

Talking of schedules, Catherine Clarke of Oxford University Press has been an excellent editor—patient and firm in the right proportions. The assiduous work of the Press's anonymous reader and my father Peter Waterfield's fine tuning resulted in many changes to earlier drafts of the translation. Trevor Saunders was gracious and benevolent at a crucial stage, and Peter Kingsley was always at the end of the phone when I needed his advice.

R. A. H. W.

CONTENTS

INTRODUCTION

REPUBLIC is a sprawling work. It is written as if it were the record of an actual conversation, and to a certain extent it meanders like a true conversation. The topic of morality unifies it, but it also takes in a number of other major philosophical areas, and throws out a huge number of lesser ideas. Reading Plato should be easy; understanding Plato can be difficult. He wrote philosophical literature, not philosophical textbooks. Sometimes he stresses things which are fairly unimportant; sometimes he underplays vital philosophical issues. Not everything is sewn up tight; issues emerge and then go underground, sometimes never to reappear. This procedure raises half-questions in the reader's mind. There often seems to be slightly more going on than one can immediately grasp.

The best possible benefits of this Introduction would be to provide a unified picture of the overall scope of the book, and to help the reader deepen his or her thinking about the major topics. This is what I hope to do, but with the following qualification. There are so many diverse topics to cover that it is impossible to treat them all, without considerable awkwardness, under a single heading. If *Republic* is a huge estate, we have to explore the areas within it one by one and on foot, rather than looking at the whole estate at once from the air. The very nature of the book makes this approach necessary, and some topics have also been covered in the notes. In any case, it is to be hoped that the end result will still be an overall picture. If before reading this Introduction a reader wants a summary of the whole book, I recommend the following procedure. Every chapter and section has been introduced with an italicized summary. These are easy to pick out by flicking through the pages of the book; read consecutively, they add up to a detailed summary of the work.

The title *Republic* is a bad translation of the Greek *politeia*. The Greek word does occur a number of times in the book, as well as forming the title, and in this translation it has invariably been rendered as 'political system'. *Politeia* is the public and political life of a community; in Latin this is *res publica*, 'public business'; Greek works used to be referred to by their Latin or Latinized titles: hence *Republic*. The book, however, is not by any stretch of the imagination a treatise on republicanism or Republicanism. Nevertheless, the title is immovable.

In this translation, *Republic* is about morality—what it is and how it fulfils one's life as a human being. Some readers, however, may have encountered translations which make it a treatise on 'justice'. But Aristotle says (*Nicomachean Ethics* 1129^b–1130^a) that *dikaiosunē*—the Greek word involved—refers to something which encompasses all the various virtues and is almost synonymous with 'virtue' in general; my own experience of the relevant Greek words confirms that Aristotle is not indulging in special pleading to make some philosophical point. To most people, 'justice' means (roughly) 'acting fairly and impartially towards others': this is a part, but not the whole, of *dikaiosunē*. There were times when the translation 'justice' would have sat better in the text, but I found it preferable to use a single equivalent throughout, so as not to mislead a Greekless reader.

Plato's Life in its Contemporary Political Setting

Plato was born in Athens in 427 BC and died there in 347. Although the sources for details of his life are unreliable, the story that he considered a political career is not implausible, since many high-born young men like him did just that. His formative political experiences, however, soon put him off. He grew up during the Peloponnesian War (431–404), in which Athens took on her long-standing rival Sparta and lost. This was a 'world war' in the sense that—what with Athens' and Sparta's allies and subjects—it involved almost all the known civilized world; and it was a war in which Plato's native city excelled in the kinds of stupidities and atrocities that are usual in war.

For most of the conflict, Athens was a democracy. If a modern liberal were to accuse Plato of betraying signs of contempt for the masses and for their power-hungry leaders, Plato would respond that he knew what they were capable of. Reading Thucydides' account of the war, one is occasionally reminded of the worst excesses of the French Revolution or of Pol Pot's regime.

Of course, Plato also saw democracies enact sensible laws, but he knew that the system was capable of terrible abuse, and he knew the instability of a system where decrees could be repealed almost as soon as they were made. There is a joke about a distressed would-be philanthropist who found that although he loved humanity, he loathed people. In Plato's case, the tale might be inverted: although it is clear that he disliked the masses as a mass, there is little evidence that he felt the same about individuals just because of their class. In a famous episode in *Meno*, he demonstrates that in terms of intellectual capacity Meno's slave is the equal of Meno.

In Britain in the 1930s political opinions became highly polarized between fairly extreme versions of right-wing and left-wing thought. A great many people—including Philby, Burgess, Maclean, and Blunt—felt that they had to side with one extreme or the other. In the Athens of Plato's time it was equally difficult to be neutral: the choice lay between democracy and Athens on the one hand, oligarchy and Sparta on the other. By birth and upbringing, Plato would have been inclined towards oligarchy.

Oligarchy twice had an opportunity to show its colours in Athens during Plato's youth. In 411 a moderate oligarchy was established, but was overthrown just as it was drifting towards extremism, and before too many allies seized the chance to secede. More importantly, in 404, immediately following Athens' downfall in the war, a government of thirty leaders took control, who counted among their number several relatives and many friends of Plato's family. The Thirty embarked upon a reign of terror, however, until they were overthrown the following year in a democratic counter-revolution.

Some time in the dying years of the fifth century Plato joined the circle of followers of Socrates, and Socrates became the decisive philosophical influence on Plato's life and thinking. The details and extent of that influence cannot be gone into here; there are, in any case, a number of good and available accounts of Socratic thought and Plato's intellectual development. Suffice it to say, in the present context, that Plato loved and admired Socrates above all others—and that in 399 the restored democracy of Athens put Socrates to death on charges of irreligion and corrupting the minds of the city's youth.

Plato's disillusionment with politics was now complete, and he devoted the rest of his life to philosophy. He began—along with others from Socrates' circle—to write dialogues with Socrates as the protagonist. To what extent the historical Socrates is accurately reflected in these works is a matter of endless and fascinating debate. It is certain, however, that by the time he wrote *Republic* Plato had already gone beyond history and was using 'Socrates' to voice views which were increasingly taking on a distinctive Platonic hue.

This carries us ahead of our story, however. During the 390s Plato's reputation as a writer and thinker was spreading through the Greek world. In those days powerful 'tyrants' (the word did not necessarily mean that they ruled unpopularly and by force) liked to embellish their own and their state's prestige by inviting famous artists to live in their territory under their patronage. In 388 Plato accepted such an invitation from Dionysius I of Syracuse in Sicily. We do not know details of the sojourn, which was short and bitter. Did he hope to use philosophy to influence politics? His friend the Pythagorean philosopher Archytas was a powerful political figure in Tarentum in southern Italy, and may have been a model.

Some time after returning from Sicily, Plato established a philosophical community in Athens, which came to be called the Academy since it occupied a grove sacred to the local hero Academus. Philosophers and budding philosophers from all over the Greek world came and lived here, sometimes for much of their life. In modern terms, it was part research university, part religious community.

As near as we can estimate, *Republic* was written in the 370s, when Plato had already completed getting on for twenty shorter works. *Republic* was to be far more ambitious, in scope and in length. Subsequent visits to Syracuse in 367 and 361, to tutor the new young king Dionysius II, may have briefly kindled some hopes that the other-worldly political ideas of the book might be partially realizable; but if so, such hopes were soon dashed. Plato's interest in real politics resurfaced in later works such as *Statesman* and *Laws*, but it is arguable that at the time of writing *Republic* he was thoroughly disillusioned with real politics.

Reading Republic

Plato was a genius as a thinker and as a writer. Few would dispute this, even if they disagree with all or any of his views. All great works of literature contain more than one layer: they gain depth as the more hidden layers resonate with parts of the reader's mind that are not directly being used while focusing on the immediate words of the text: this is where reading even a work of philosophy becomes a subjective exercise. I call the 'immediate words of the text' the 'hard' aspects of a book, and the other layers the 'soft' aspects.

Like any great work of literature, then, *Republic* is a difficult book to discuss. A commentator may go on at length about certain aspects of the book, and be left with the uneasy feeling that he or she has neglected other rich veins. Let us put these considerations in the context of the claim that at the time of writing *Republic* Plato was disillusioned with politics. The one thing that everyone knows, even before picking the book up, is that in it Plato envisages a community ruled by philosophers; and as soon as one gets into the meat of the dialogue, it is clear that it is thoroughly infused with politics. How can this paradox be explained? Did Plato somehow not mean us to take these proposals seriously? These questions are answerable with some plausibility, if one follows up one of the half-submerged threads mentioned earlier.

The Greek world of Plato's time was divided essentially into more or less independent city-states (*poleis*, singular *polis*), each with influence over the immediately surrounding territory, and with friendships and enmities abroad. Accurate population figures are a matter of unreliable conjecture, but the largest of these states was a mere town by modern standards. Politics, therefore, was not some remote game played by your chosen representatives in a distant place. Politics permeated your life and was acted out on your doorstep. In Athenian-style democracies every male citizen had the right and the duty to participate directly in the decision-making processes.

One result of this was that the Greeks had, in certain respects, a far less fully formed concept of the individual than we do today. Mystics and philosophers were suspected of peddling private salvation, when religion was a state matter. It was your duty as a citizen to keep the gods smiling on your community—and that was the end of religion. The notion of an individual's 'rights' was more or less unknown; an individual's happiness was scarcely relevant compared with that of the state. The good life was the political life, or at least it was guaranteed for you by the state rather than by your own efforts. In the relatively early dialogue *Euthydemus*, for instance, at 288b–292e, Plato portrays Socrates searching for the branch of knowledge which will bring individual happiness. The closest he can get is to argue that it is the best kind of political system which can do this.

Yet Socrates was a great individualist, and was killed for promoting individualism and therefore subverting the traditional state-centred values. And it is clear that Plato inherited this tendency from his master. *Republic* is Plato's main attempt to define in non-abstract terms how an individual can fulfil himself, can attain happiness or 'live the good life', as a Greek would have said. A Greek would have expected such a discussion to be couched in political terms—and that is what we get, though not entirely in the way a Greek would have expected.

Overt discussion of political and other external issues would be a 'hard' aspect of the book; in *Republic* there are also 'soft' aspects to this discussion. It is possible to read the book as a predominantly individualist approach to the issues, with the traditional political terminology of the debate suborned and largely turned over to metaphorical purposes, to describe the inner state of the individual. Metaphor is a familiar method for turning hard aspects into soft aspects; and it is typical of Plato's sense of humour that he would turn the usual terms of debate on their head in this way.

This is not to say, of course, that the soft aspects of the book (those concerned with the inner state of an individual) are all the book consists of. As Plato projects the inner life of an individual out on to the larger screen of a mythical world where political factors play a part, he does also make some proposals which are more concerned with outer politics than the inner politics of the individual—which are hard rather than soft. In fact, because he is such a skilful writer, he often writes for both layers simultaneously. But the hard aspects of the book are less than one might expect: the outside world takes on a half-life, but the inner life of the individual is the primary concern of the book. As a metaphor, the politics of *Republic* is stimulating and coherent; as a manifesto, it is naïve and fragmentary. Anyone reading the book with a view to finding a political philosophy to follow or to criticize is going to be disappointed and will be forced to supply a lot of the evidence.

The ambitious project of the book is to demonstrate that morality is beneficial to its possessor—that, in fact, an individual gains in happiness by being moral whether or not any external advantages accrue to him. At the beginning of Chapter 3 Plato says that this is a tough task, since it is difficult to look inside a person's mind and see what is good or bad there. He therefore proposes to work with a political analogy: perhaps morality will be easier to see if we construct a community, describe its political system, and look for morality in this imaginary community. If the analogy with an individual is exact, we shall then be able to discover the features of the 'political' state of affairs in an individual.

There is nothing ambiguous about this. In *Republic* Plato is not primarily interested in politics in the real world: he is constructing an *imaginary* community, to serve as a paradigm. The primary purpose for any political exploration that will occur in the book is a 'soft' purpose—to help us understand an individual. And Plato constantly reminds us that this is the point of the 'politics': time and again he mentions the individual who is supposed to correspond to the imaginary state. These reminders can be found at 351e, 369a, 432b, 434d, 441c, 445c, 472c–d, 541b, 543d–544a and throughout Chapters 11 and 12, 605b, and 608a–b.

Despite so much unequivocal evidence, this way of reading *Republic* is not the one which is usually found in scholarly books on the subject. There are a number of reasons for this, not the least of which is that psychology is a softer science than political theory, and therefore less susceptible to the traditional tools of scholarly exegesis. The possible extent of the analogy has, of course, been noticed, but it has never been fully followed through. For instance, Guthrie says (p. 561), 'Essentially, however, the *Republic* is not a piece of political theory, but an allegory of the individual human spirit.' And Murphy says (p. 76), responding to those who accuse Plato of political totalitarianism: 'It seems fair to remember that the study of the *polis* is subsidiary ... To some extent this consideration may be taken to explain the many noticeable gaps in the account of the city; much of its actual institutions and working (not being necessary to the analogy) is simply left to the reader's imagination—an imagination very differently exercised by different readers!'

It is in my view not just a case of 'gaps', as Murphy puts it, though those are startling enough (he could have added the lack of mention of foreign policy). It is also that a great deal of the book is simply absurd if read as serious political philosophy. An often-quoted remark by Trevor Saunders sums it up: 'To suppose that Plato ever thought that the *Republic* was attainable would be to suppose him capable not merely of optimism or idealism, but of sheer political *naiveté*' (*Plato*: The Laws (Penguin Books, 1970), 27–8). A number of the most blatant oddities and absurdities which point in the same direction, and support the notion that in *Republic* Plato is considerably less interested in external politics than in individual psychology, have been mentioned in the notes (on 370b, 407a, 428d, 432a, 460c, 472e, 537a, 575d).

In short, then, attention to the soft aspects of the book, as well as the hard, explains how Plato could have written a 'political' work while not being interested in real politics; and it can also explain or mitigate some of the peculiar features of the book. I shall give one more example of this latter point, because it does not occur in the notes mentioned above. It has been claimed that the whole analogy is radically mistaken, because people are unlike parts of the mind in important ways. Plato uses the analogy to claim that just as there are three different kinds of people in his community, so there are three equivalent parts of the mind. But while it makes sense to say that an appetitive part of the mind is hardly rational, it does not make sense to say that a worker is hardly rational, just because he is a worker. This whole issue begins to evaporate if it is borne in mind that the main reason for dividing the paradigmatic community into three parts is to provide a parallel with the mind. No one supposes for one minute that Plato thought up the tripartite state and the tripartite mind independently and then noticed, to his surprise, that they were equivalent. Of course the political proposals will appear unrealistic or even unsavoury at times: they may not be destined for the real world, but their primary function is to illustrate the workings of the human mind.

The Soft Republic

It is perfectly possible, then, to read a great deal of the book as an extended metaphor; not only is it possible, but there is good textual authorization for that reading. However, I will not develop an extensive interpretation of *Republic* along those lines. There are two reasons for this. In the first place, this soft layer of the book is, as I have said, somewhat subjective, and therefore it is up to every reader to pursue it as he or she sees fit; in the second place, it would ultimately be only a partial interpretation—it would deal with one main layer of the book to the exclusion of the other. However, it is important to draw the reader's attention to the fact that the book has more than one layer.

Here, then, briefly and dogmatically, is one possible reading of some passages of the book, in accordance with the soft interpretative approach Plato invites us to take: he invites us, as we read, to use features of the community he constructs as a map or key for understanding our own psyches. If any of what follows strikes a modern reader as banal, it should be remembered that we live in an age which has far more theoretical psychological knowledge than was available in Plato's time; if any of it strikes a reader as odd, then it should be said that it is no more odd in its way than many of Plato's political proposals are in their way.

We could learn from 369b–376c that an individual is complex and consists of a range of needs, not all of which are concerned with the mere maintenance of physical life. Desires are fundamental (perhaps as in Abraham Maslow's psychology). As individuals interact, they threaten one another's integrity. They therefore have innate means for preserving their integrity. These mechanisms are passion and intelligence, distinct from the general run of faculties, which cater to our various needs or desires.

The external educational directives Plato gives in 367c–412a are also easy to internalize: proper psychological development needs to be nourished by the right kind of information and impressions. The 'right' kind means (*a*) that it corresponds with our natures—we should not try to be other than what we are; and (*b*) that it increases our psychic harmony. Immorality breeds internal dissension. Rotten parts of the mind—parts which damage its unity—should be eliminated. The net result of correct nourishment is a harmonious fusion of passion and intelligence: our inner guardians function correctly.

There are three parts of the mind (412a–427c). The 'workers' are one's contact with the outside world; they must continue to do their jobs, which is to say that contact with the outside world is vital for psychological health. The passionate part defends one's integrity, while the intellectual part supervises it. Both these two higher parts work abstractly (they have no 'possessions').

From 427d–449a Plato spells out the analogy himself, as it applies to morality. Then, with Chapter 7, we enter some fascinating and highly speculative areas. If the guardians are to have no possessions, then they must have no wives or children. Since we are reading lack of possessions as abstraction of thought, then what are wives and children? Children could be formulated concepts, and wives the means or 'matrix' for formulating them. The female function of formulating ideas (children) is just as important as the male function of seeding ideas, and requires just as much attention. But neither faculty should regard the formulations as its own, otherwise they lose the abstract ability to stand back and be creative. Worthless formulations are to be rejected. All the parts of the mind have their work to do, and should be allowed to get on with it, without interference: in that way one becomes a single, unified individual (which is also, interestingly enough, the goal of Jungian psychology).

These suggestions for an interpretation of some of the soft aspects of the book must not be taken to be more than they are—speculative and subjective. A reader can reject or accept or alter them as he or she sees fit. But it would not be doing justice to Plato's genius to discuss only the hard aspects of the book. If *Republic* was monochrome—if it consisted only of hard aspects—it would not (I dare say) have been acclaimed so long and so loud by so many different kinds of reader; the work is many-hued, and it is incumbent upon commentators not to exclude facets with which they feel uncomfortable. But now we can turn from the soft aspects of the book to the more familiar ground of the hard aspects.

The Objective of Republic

Plato gets down to the task of demonstrating that morality is the major cause of happiness in an individual's life by trying to define morality, or its psychological parameters, and then by proving that anyone with this psychological state is better off than anyone without it. Towards the end of the book, at 613a–b, we are also told that morality is assimilation to God. By now we know quite a lot about God, especially from 379a–383b. We know that God is single, uniform, stable, unchanging, and eternal. These same attributes are also applied to God in other dialogues. So an ideally moral person would have them too.

Now, this set of attributes is bound to set off echoes in the mind of a reader. It is not only God and an ideally moral person who have them; Plato's metaphysics and epistemology (theory of knowledge) depend crucially on the existence of entities called 'characters' or 'types' which have these attributes; and the community he has spent so much of the book constructing also has these qualities. In other words, all the major elements of *Republic* have the same features.

Plato's purpose in *Republic*, then, is to provide a kind of unified-field theory, in which all the elements which make human life good are tied together in a vision of eternal unity, orderliness, and stability. But why do this? Is it just the obsessive desire to have everything tied neatly together, or to paint a pretty picture? Actually, Plato's objective is to paint a *compelling* picture. He does not care whether an ideally moral person can ever exist in the real world (472b–d); despite some prevarication (see the note on 472e), he does not care ultimately whether or not the model community could ever exist in the real world. The point is that they exist as paradigms to urge us to approximate to them as best we can in our lives—which is to say, to assimilate ourselves to God. As long as we are not assimilated to God, we are in exile (592b; cf. *Theaetetus* 176a–b). It is important to remember that philosophy for Plato was not, or not just, confined to lectures and books: it was a way of life. The modern distinction between the rational activity of philosophy and the emotional engagement of religion and mysticism would have struck Plato as outlandish. His purpose was to get his readers to change their lives, to undertake the pursuit of assimilation to God.

These powerful and heartfelt ideas are central to the book. As we go through the principal issues and ideas that arise in the work, we shall from time to time notice the traces left on Plato's thinking by this nest of notions surrounding unity and assimilation to God.

The Principle of Specialization

Apart from the community–individual analogy, the implications of which have already been followed through, the important feature of Chapter 3 is that at 370a–c it introduces the Principle of Specialization (PS). In fact, it is probable that the main reason for the discussion of the 'community fit for pigs' in this chapter is to introduce PS in a plausible context. Each person has a single talent and single way of contributing towards the welfare of the whole community; he is to perform that function, and that function alone (without interfering in the domains of others), throughout his life. This is not argued for: it is taken to be self-evident, and is made into an axiom. The use to which it is put in the book is extensive. It is constantly alluded to, and is just under the surface throughout much of the work. Here are some of its more important uses.

At the political level it leads directly to the structure of the paradigmatic community as consisting of separate classes: the classes are defined by PS (374a ff., 375a–376c). It forms an important criterion for the exclusion of some poetic themes: if each individual is unified by PS (because of having a unique talent), that unity must not be compromised by bad poetry (394e–398b). Complying with PS is the foundation of individual happiness and fulfilment (406c–407a, 421c), the foundation of the unity of the community (423d), and is social morality (433a ff.), because it involves co-operating with others and contributing to the welfare of the whole. And this has a psychological counterpart: if each part of one's mind conforms to the internal equivalent of PS, then one is unified and moral (Chapter 6).

Returning to the political level, PS allows Plato to argue for the equality of female guardians (453b–456b); it is the cause of political provisions such as the avoidance of excessive wealth and poverty (421d–422a), because these damage the unity of the community. It is used to explain the degeneration of society and the end of community unity (547b–c), and it underlies his vehement attack on democracy, as a system where anyone can do any job he likes (555b–556c).

These are all overt uses of PS—places where the use to which it is being put is signalled or all but signalled by Plato. There are other passages where it is employed more subtly, however. For instance, PS helps to explain the bad reputation which philosophy has, in Plato's view (p. 207). In short, this is clearly a very important principle for Plato. It is a pity, therefore, that he made it a self-evident axiom rather than arguing for it.

We have to supply some points which Plato takes for granted. The connection between PS and the unity of the community is easy to explain: if all individuals are conforming to PS, then they are co-operating with their fellows. Co-operation is the basis of political unity. The connection between PS and human happiness and fulfilment is somewhat less clear. It seems that we are supposed to remember the argument from Chapter 1 (352d ff.) that happiness depends on fulfilling one's function: I only create problems for myself by suppressing my talent and failing to co-operate with others. Moreover, if I do not co-operate with others I have to do more than one job; and, of course, doing more than one job makes me more than one person (423d), and a divided person is an unhappy person.

Education: Moulding Minds

The educational programme of Chapter 4 is entwined with the notion of unity chiefly through the fact that it is introduced as a means of preserving the guardian function within the community, and at the conclusion it is announced that this has been achieved: they have found a way of training guardians within the community who will protect it rather than turn against it (410b ff.). So this links the programme with PS, and thus with the unity of the community.

This aspect of the educational programme is easy to state. Another topic that claims our attention is that of the notorious deficiencies in Plato's educational system. It seems at times to be little more than indoctrination in the moral values of the community; and it is therefore critically unclear how, after a childhood spent in this kind of schooling, a few candidates are to be equipped for the kind of investigative further education described in Chapter 10. Their investigative faculty will have atrophied, it has been argued. In any case, it is not just a question of childhood schooling. It is true that this is the primary topic of the chapter, and it is true that, since Plato (like his contemporaries) believed that children were not fully rational, some authoritarianism may be more justified. It is also clear, however, that the chapter raises wider issues. Prohibited kinds of poetry are not just prohibited until the age of seventeen: they are banned from the community altogether. Therefore, we are faced not just with authoritarianism in devising a school curriculum, but also in enforcing uniformity of thought through social conditioning.

I believe that these points are valuable in themselves, but are not altogether germane to Plato's enterprise. Plato is not trying to provide a philosophy of education: the educational programme of Chapter 4 is specifically designed within a paradigmatic community. The unity and stability of that community are important, and therefore Plato devises a curriculum which is expressly supposed to prevent innovation (424a–c) and support PS in the ways mentioned above. Plato does not expect this community ever to be realized; but he does expect those who want to be assimilated to God to be very careful about what kinds of impressions they take in, and what kinds of roles they play. He believes that impressions are a kind of food, and may therefore poison the system (401c).

Anyway, in the imaginary community how much control would the rulers exercise over the private lives of the inhabitants? It is clear that those who are destined for rulership are to have almost no private life; but there are very few of them. What about the vast majority of the citizen body? The government of the community is entirely out of their hands, and the overall pattern of their life is set by their talents and jobs; but their daily lives and thoughts are not legislated for at all, since the educational programme of Chapter 4 is not designed for them (see the note on 376c), and Plato's focus throughout is on the ruling class. Nevertheless, what we find is that, despite their lack of schooling, the workers are not expected to disagree with the values of the community, and this is partly a result of their social conditioning.

Even these kinds of comments, however, rely to some extent on filling gaps in Plato's text. In short, he does not give us many clues. What he says is compatible with a wide variety of positions on the scale which runs from outright control to outright self-determination. So little is mentioned concerning slavery, for instance, that it is a matter of hot debate even whether there would be slaves in the community (see the note on 431b). Almost anything we say about the third class is speculative, since the fact is that once they have played their role of paralleling the acquisitive psychological part, they drop out of the discussion altogether. If their happiness is assumed to depend on the provisions of the rulers, that is no more than a Greek would expect (pp. xv–xvi). Even the second class, the auxiliaries, are rather shadowy, since they are presumed to side willingly with the guardians. Almost all we can say for certain applies to the guardians, and there may be no more than a few dozen of them at any one time in the community. They have little private life and few possessions, they are to undergo a long educational programme (but being budding philosophers, they want this), and then they are 'forced' to rule; but even the *kind* of power they enjoy remains unclear. Are they civil servants or do they have absolute power? While it might appear that they sacrifice individual happiness to the welfare of the community as a whole (419a–421c), the validity of the response (421b) that they are actually very happy indeed is borne out, in Plato's view, by the end of the book (see further pp. lvi–lviii).

Authoritarianism

The remaining impression of a somewhat authoritarian state is derived, I believe, from two main sources. In the first place, Plato clearly believes (as did Socrates before him, apparently) that government should not be left to just anyone, but to the experts; and it turns out that only philosophers are such experts because only they can know what goodness is and therefore guarantee its perpetuation in the state. The second source (discussed in the following section) is what we might call the rigidity of the state: it is supposed to come into being at a stroke, rather than evolving through consensus over a period of time, and everything possible is done to ensure its stability and unity.

Plato would undoubtedly be surprised to come across reservations about the first point. He would accuse us of confusing authoritarianism with authority. He takes it as self-evident that we would be willing to obey someone who speaks with the authority of knowledge: we somehow recognize that knowledge and appreciate that the person is therefore recommending what is in our best interests (the topic of acquiescence recurs below, p. xxxiv). Problems arise only when someone is incapable of that recognition; and in extreme cases even coercion may become necessary.

A constant and important aspect of modern liberal views is that all people know what is best for themselves: they are responsible for themselves and should be allowed a very large measure of self-determination. Plato believes that there is a sense in which people may need saving from themselves. He believes that, if one were to be ruled by one's desirous part, it would bring one into conflict with others (586a–b) and would not lead to true satisfaction (583b ff.). He also believes that the natural state of the desirous part is one of *pleonexia*: it goes on wanting more and more (442a, 562b, 586b), and will inevitably degenerate. If left to its own devices, it will lead a person from being an oligarchic type at best to being a dictatorial type at worst (see Chapter 11). This nightmarish situation is not one anybody could wish on his or her worst enemy; but it is exactly, in Plato's view, the risk one runs.

Plato does not believe that people are usually like this: there are systems of checks, supplied by convention (571b). In extreme cases, however, someone may be deaf to his own reason; and then one should step in. Extreme cases aside, however, Plato does believe that all of us have the *tendency* towards excess within us. It is therefore important for him to ensure that the tendency is checked. The guardians' rule is designed to provide those checks; social conditioning is a valuable tool in this context (Plato's estimate of the importance of social conditioning is clearly shown by 492a ff.). If Plato is wrong in this, he is at least wrong for the right reasons; and since all states engage in some social engineering (they all have aims and objectives to fulfil), then overhasty condemnation of Plato on this score may well be a case of sinners casting the first stone.

It should also be clear that the unity of the individual and that of the community are again prime concerns. Immoral behaviour brings one into conflict with others, and so is disruptive of external unity; and immoral behaviour is an external manifestation of internal disunity (351c–352a).

Politics

In the heady political days of the 1930s it was fashionable to pin a political position on Plato, and then side with it or against it. Sir Karl Popper's book, which paints Plato as an evil totalitarian, is only the most extreme example of the tendency. Nowadays scholars recognize that what Plato says is compatible with a number of views, in the sense that, depending on which set of passages is stressed, Plato can be portrayed as a totalitarian or a utilitarian. We are not dealing so much with a political position as a number of political provisions; and in the case of *Republic* we have already seen to what extent talk of Plato's politics must constantly be weighed against the ever-present psychological analogy.

It is even surprisingly hard to pinpoint exactly what political systems Plato is opposed to. The four corrupt systems described in Chapter 11 are all, in various ways, exaggerations. In each case a seed of truth and insight has been made to create more or less of a monstrosity, as an excuse for Plato to exercise his literary skills (a task he undertakes at this point with considerable relish) and as a backdrop for the vignettes of the equivalent psychological types. It is in the nature of our sources for the ancient world that we know the most about Athenian democracy; and it is clear that only some of the features Plato attributes to democracy are drawn from life. We are safe in assuming that the same goes for the other three systems.

Nevertheless, two points are clear: that the exemplary community is supposed to be a benevolent, enlightened dictatorship (as we would call it), and that this feature, as well as every other feature of the community (see 421e–424c), is supposed to contribute directly or indirectly towards the preservation of the community's unity and stability.

This latter point is one of the chief features which raise our hackles. We are deeply suspicious of appeals to 'the state' as some kind of super-entity, since they so often seem to occur in totalitarian contexts such as the former USSR or National Socialist Germany, or in times of national madness such as war, when they crop up as Wilfred Owen's 'old lie'. Some of this hackle-raising is quite anachronistic. I have already mentioned that the Greeks had a less developed view of the individual than we do, especially in his relation to the state. When I described Plato as an individualist, I did not mean that this was some kind of political position for him. He would have thought civic liberty a sham without inner liberty: the kind of freedom we find stressed in *Republic* and elsewhere is detachment from the material world, not a set of political rights.

Some of the hackle-raising is even wrong. Plato does not—or does not *quite*—seem to regard the community as an organic entity in its own right, to which the rights of individuals are subordinated. On the contrary, when he talks about the happiness of the whole community (as at 412c–413c, 420b, and 462a ff.), he seems to mean the happiness of all the inhabitants. Philosophers have to become rulers because they, with their knowledge of goodness, are the only ones who can produce goodness and happiness in everyone in a community (519e–520a).

Still, from our point of view, we require very strong arguments in support of the view that the unity of the political state is such a good thing that it justifies loss of what we are bound to regard as individual freedom. We never get these kinds of arguments in Plato, however, and we get few hints from which we could construct such an argument. Plato simply takes the value of the unity of the state as self-evident. Perhaps it is more accurate to say that what he takes as obvious is that dissension or disruption of unity is bad, and a cause of misery. The main relevant passages are 422e–423a (where any community which lacks unity is even said to be not really a community), 462a–466d, 519e–520a, 547b–c, and 551d.

Plato's contention that dissension, or even any kind of pluralism, must be ruled out in a community worthy of the name leads to all his most notorious political provisions. The common possession of wives and children is a direct result of the desire for unity (462a ff.). The philosophers are to rule because only they have the kind of overview which enables them to regulate the happiness of the state as a whole and to preserve its stability and unity. The community will only remain a unity if every member of it sticks to PS (423d)—that is, keeps to his or her natural class. In short (in the case of the guardians, at any rate), individuality of thought is to be excluded by the education, and individuality of expression thereafter. Education and politics are mutually maintaining: both exist to keep the other stable, unified, and unchanging (423c–427a); legislative reform without a proper programme of social engineering is like an invalid trying out various remedies.

Now, if politics is the art of achieving what is possible, and accordingly involves compromise, it is clear that these are not really political proposals. Compromise takes place between parties with different views; but parties with different views can only exist in a community which is not really, in Plato's view, a community. Plato's proposals are better described as fanciful or idealistic. The unity of the community is precisely what makes it an impossible paradigm (472d ff., 592b).

Those who are so inclined will remember the instability of the political world of Greece during Plato's formative years, and will speculate that this is why he favours political unity and stability so highly. This is not impossible, but it is also important to remember the ever-present psychological analogy: the desirability of unity and stability of personality and character is not an unreasonable axiom, and it is one which Plato stresses (see especially 423d, 443d–e, and Chapter 11 as a whole).

Poetry, Morality, and Education

In Chapters 4 and 13 Plato proscribes, on various grounds, certain kinds of 'representational' poetry. There are apparent discrepancies between the two chapters (see the note on 595a), and quite a bit of scholarly work has gone into attempting to bring the various arguments into line with one another. Here, however, we should merely take an overview of some aspects of the discussion, to act as a kind of broad framework within which Plato's comments should be read.

What Plato has to say about poetry is mostly transparent, although his *reasons* for saying it are not. But the most important suggestion I can make to a reader at this point is to try to avoid the natural tendency to mitigate Plato's words. When he claims that representational poetry can deform minds (595b), he means it; when he says that avoiding such poetry is critical if one wants to be a good person (608b), he means that too.

Poetry is Plato's main target in these chapters; painting gets swept in as well (596a–598b, 601b–602b), but chiefly because it is a clearer case of a kind of representation than poetry, so that conclusions drawn with regard to it can be applied to poetry (even though the fit is awkward in some respects: see the notes on 597e and 605a).

Why this hostility to poetry? Why is it the enemy? Because the poets were the educators of Greece (606e). They were used as such in the schools and played a central role in a Greek's general cultural conditioning. The poets (even the comic poets) thought of themselves as teachers, and their audience took them to be teachers. Looking at some of the works of Greek art, it is impossible not to think that they did have a conception of art for art's sake (as well as for the sake of religion, decoration, or whatever context the piece was produced for); but the overriding purpose of poetry was didactic, and so Plato may not be too cavalier in dismissing its aesthetic aspect as not an end in itself but rather a vehicle for getting the message across (601a–b; see also 568c).

Now, Plato's criticisms of poetry are overwhelmingly moral in tone, even when he is adducing metaphysical grounds for mistrusting its value. Representation is taken from the start to be assimilation to something or someone else (393c), and a great deal of Plato's worry has to do with people assimilating themselves to the wrong kind of model, since one becomes like one's role models (395d; see also 606b). We know, however, that the one true model is God—that morality is assimilation to God (see p. xxi). The more moral a person is, the closer he is to being unified, stable, and so on.

Plato's criticism of poetry develops within this perfectionist and educational context. It is immediately noticeable that Chapter 4 begins by excluding certain kinds of statement about God—statements which deny his unity and so on—and then goes on to censor certain kinds of statement about the heroes of myth and legend. These heroes were precisely the people whom the Greeks took as their models of virtue. Plato wants them to feature in poetry in ways which portray them as having the virtues and do not therefore encourage others to behave immorally. In other words, poetry should encourage the mental concord and stability which is morality (441d ff.).

It was hard for the Greek language to distinguish between storytelling and lying. So when Plato asks what kinds of story-telling are legitimate, he is asking what kinds of lies are acceptable. If we tell a lie, but are aware that we do not know the truth, that is not a 'true lie' (382a–d). A conscious lie may still be morally right or wrong, however. It is acceptable if it is wielded with knowledge and for moral purposes: two examples are the Myth of Metals (414c ff.) and the Myth of Er (Chapter 14). Indeed, the whole sketch of the model community is a word-picture (472d–e; cf. 376d and 501e) with the purpose of prompting readers to try to become moral themselves. But some of the poets' portraits do not satisfy Plato's moral criteria.

Moreover, Plato includes the intention to deceive as part of his *definition* of representational poetry (393a). The audience is expected to take the stories to be true, while the poets are laying claim to knowledge they cannot possibly have. That is why Plato argues, in Chapter 13, that the poet (who lacks true belief, let alone knowledge: 598e–602b) creates things that are far removed from the truth. The metaphysical argument of Chapter 13 is an expansion of the point adumbrated in 393a. And the moral point of this is clear: if the chief purpose of representation is to create an impression, then a representer does not have to know about the moral value of his work (599d). He lacks knowledge, and knowledge is always in some sense knowledge of goodness.

Apart from the metaphysical argument, the other main argument of Chapter 13 is psychological: representational poetry feeds the base part of the mind. (This again picks up and expands a point from Chapter 4, at 397d.) These two main arguments of Chapter 13 converge. The metaphysical argument says that the products of representation are far removed from the truth, and the psychological argument says that they feed the base part of the mind. Since only reason can grasp and understand the truth, then feeding the base part of the mind will take energy away from reason and lessen one's ability to grasp the truth (606a–b; see p. xxxviii).

Since reason, truth, unity, and stability are so closely connected in Plato's thought, and since we know that the desirous part of the mind disrupts psychic harmony (p. xxvi), then it is again clear that the nest of ideas surrounding the objective of assimilation to God are at the back of Plato's mind. The same goes for the fact that in Chapter 4 one of the problems with representation is that it imitates any number of things. It directly conflicts, then, with

PS (see p. xxii). The same thought probably underlies the point emphasized in Chapter 13, that representers can 'make' anything in the world (596c–e), unlike true craftsmen.

In short, Plato interrogates representation from several different angles, which are loosely combined in the two relevant sections of the book. Is the object represented the kind of object it is morally sound to represent? Do poets represent the truth, wherever possible? Are we expected to believe their lies, or are they just for entertainment (396e)? Are there grounds for thinking that poets have knowledge? If there is a unifying thread tacitly linking these various approaches, it is that of the desirability of assimilation to God.

We know, however, that true unity is impossible for a living human being (472b ff.). Assimilation to God is an ideal in the sense that, though unattainable, it must still be striven for (Tolstoy is this kind of idealist too, in the epilogue to *The Kreutzer Sonata*). Therefore, it is not surprising to find that Plato's provisions concerning poetry are unrealistic: the only kinds of poetry to survive his critique are portraits of good people (395c, 397d, 604e, 607a) and hymns to the gods (607a). When he offers the olive-branch of poetry being reinstated if it can come up with evidence that it is of benefit to humanity (607b ff.), that is clearly considered to be a remote possibility.

So the final guideline I want to recommend to readers of Plato's assault on poetry is that he is talking about poetry within an ideal community, not in real life. Although it somehow seems trite, a comparison with television today is instructive. In some moods, most thinking people must have occasionally wished that television had never been invented, or that its output could be restricted (even if not to documentaries about good people and to religious programmes!). But at the same time one knows it cannot be done. There is no room in Plato's ideal state for literature which serves pleasure rather than goodness; but then there is no room in Plato's community for Pericles either—or even for Socrates, who had little to do with politics. And yet opponents of Plato's critique of poetry rarely get hot under the collar about Pericles' and Socrates' exclusion from the community.

All art is food (401b–402a). Some art—poetry is singled out because of its pervasive educational role—puts us to sleep, however, by preventing the rule of reason and thereby condemning us to the dream-world of illusion (476c, 534c–d). It gives us conditioned moral answers, whereas we should continue the quest for moral truth and perfection. In this sense, poetry is an impostor (see the note on 598c).

Class Division

A very odd feature of Plato's community is that even while providing for its unity he seems to undermine it. The sharing of wives, children, and property is, as we have noted already, designed to ensure the unity of the state, since possessiveness tends to cause dissension. However, only the guardians and auxiliaries will be subject to this system; everyone else will live a normal life. Therefore, the state will be split between those who do and those who do not live a normal life, those who have no political power and those who have it all, and who are revered by the rest (e.g. 465d).

Plato's problem here derives from his devotion to PS: everyone has different talents and a different contribution to make to the state. These talents and jobs fall into three broad bands, which define the three classes of the state. Therefore, no absolute unity is possible, but only the lesser unity of harmony between the classes. (There is an interesting parallel with his view on the mind: in itself, this is a sheer unity—see 611cff.—but tripartition is an inevitable consequence of incarnation.) At the same time, he is convinced that it is dissension or concord within the ruling class of a state which determines whether or not the state as a whole has unity (545d); hence all his efforts throughout the book are designed to ensure the unity of the state as a result of the unity of the rulers.

The dominant features of the imaginary state are all based on the division into three classes. The unity of the state depends on people keeping to their classes (there is little room for movement between them), and social morality is defined in these terms (432b–434d; see 415a–c). The workers are the body and limbs of the state, the auxiliaries its heart, philosophers its head. It is the philosophers' job to rule.

Juvenal asks a famous question (6. 346–7): *Quis custodiet ipsos custodes?* 'Who will guard the guardians?' We can apply the question to *Republic*. What is to stop the guardians becoming tyrants? Plato again trusts in the educational programme (and a bit of natural inclination). As far as the auxiliaries are concerned, education will prevent them being harsh to their fellow citizens (410c–412a, 416b). And the philosophers' education nurtures their innate love of abstract knowledge so much that they are not interested in the material world and power within it. Paradoxically, then, they are the perfect rulers because they do not want to rule; and this guarantees that they will not abuse their power. The question as to why they should want to rule at all is discussed on pp. lvi–lviii.

Another important question we need to ask is why the workers should acquiesce in the philosophers' rule. As noted (on 432a and 485e), there is some ambivalence in Plato's assumptions on this score, but the underlying expectation is that the workers can appreciate the value of the philosophers ruling (and by the same token of themselves keeping to their class). However, this would only be possible if the workers were capable of some degree of rational discrimination, and since it has sometimes been claimed that Plato dismisses them as incapable in this respect, then we need to assess the evidence. This is not as easy as it might be, since (as already mentioned) Plato hardly mentions the third class at all, let alone discussing them.

That Plato does not think artisans incapable of reason is clear in the first instance from the general consideration that they would be incapable of doing their jobs if they were. Moreover, it is clear from 553c–d that even someone dominated by desire possesses and employs reason: he uses it to work out how to fulfil his desires. People differ not in having only one mental part out of a possible three (that would be absurd), but in which part is dominant over the other two. So the fact that the third class consists of money-minded people (581b–c) is insufficient evidence that Plato denied them any rationality. Moreover, everyone aims for goodness (505d–e), and it is reason which assesses goodness (p. xxxvii); therefore everyone has reason.

Furthermore, nothing in the analogy between the mind and the state need make one regard artisans as lacking in reason. If the desirous part were not capable of some degree of reasoning, it would make no sense for Plato to talk of it agreeing to the rule of reason (442c–d) or interfering in the jobs of the other parts

(443d). The psychological half of the analogy will be more fully discussed in the next section.

That artisans have some rationality, then, is clear enough. There is nothing to prevent us from thinking that they can appreciate the value of the philosophers' rule. Their minds can assess what is good for themselves, if not for the community as a whole, and that should be enough for them to acquiesce in being ruled, Plato supposes. They do not have to be forced to toe the line, and nothing prevents us understanding Plato's talk of compulsion as the compulsion of rational argument (as suggested in the note on 432a). If we do not understand it in this way, then passages like 590c–d make no sense: in the same breath, Plato talks of external control having, in some circumstances, to be imposed on the third class, and of the relation between the classes being one of loyalty and affection (see also 415a, 431d–e, 463b, 547c).

If the artisans do not have fully developed philosophic rationality, this need not worry us; that is not their function within the state. But it has sometimes been claimed that only philosophers can be moral, and that Plato denies this possibility to anyone else, since inner morality is defined as the rule of reason over the other parts of the mind. Again, it seems clear (despite the paucity of evidence) that Plato not only expects the third class to be capable of morality, but also wants their morality to be definable in the same terms as philosophic morality. This follows from the fact that the artisans can obviously achieve social morality, since that is defined as keeping to one's job (433a ff.), and from the assertion that social morality contributes towards the inner morality which is mental harmony under reason (443e). It is also an implication of 353d–e that every human being can attain morality by performing his or her function, which is to say by fulfilling himself or herself. If we attribute to the third class the kind of rationality which assesses ways and means (so that they can achieve their money-oriented goals), this does not exclude them from being moral. In a difficult passage of another dialogue which was written at roughly the same time (*Phaedo* 68c–69c), Plato distinguishes between philosophic virtues and ordinary virtues, on the grounds that the former depend on understanding whereas the latter depend on weighing up personal advantages and disadvantages. There is nothing to prevent the third class of Plato's state having this kind of morality. It is still morality—it is not bogus—but it is not as deep or thorough or unshakeable as philosophic morality. In the terms of 485d–e, only philosophers have channelled all their energy towards pure reason and thereby lessened the grip of the other parts.

In short, in the context of Plato's constant claim that his community is a unity, it is hardly likely that he would have pictured it as a class society where the rational, moral rulers have to be constantly repressing the unruliness of the irrational, immoral majority. Nevertheless, there are traces of an ambivalence in Plato's mind. He sometimes wants to talk of mere difference of function, where no function is better than another and all are rated by the fact that the whole could not exist without them all; at the same time he finds it hard to resist the notion that philosophy is in fact the better course.

A Tripartite Psychology

Parallel to the three classes in the state, there are three parts to the mind. Plato's views on morality depend crucially on his psychology: morality and other kinds of virtue are special states of mind, in which the parts of the mind are disposed and related in certain ways (441c–444a). Plato's psychology is therefore of prime importance in the book. Even apart from its connection to morality, however, it is interesting as an independent theory of motivation and desire. The theory sprawls between Chapters 6, 11, and 13; what follows is, accordingly, a synthesis.

Plato thought he detected three main sources of motivation in people. There is the desire to satisfy one's instincts and those perceived lacks which are related to one's instincts; there is the desire (which often manifests as anger or outrage) for preservation of one's 'sense of I'; and there is the desire for understanding and truth. There are fascinating resonances here with modern discoveries in neurology (let alone with other psychological theories such as those of W. H. Sheldon and the later Freud): the functions of Plato's three parts correspond quite closely to those of the so-called reptilian, mammalian, and neo-mammalian parts of the brain.

It will immediately be noticed that I have spoken of what Plato calls the 'rational' and 'passionate' parts of the mind desiring, as well as the 'desirous' part. The justification for this is less clear in Chapter 6 than in Chapter 11. If Chapter 6 were taken on its own, one might be tempted to think that *all* the desirous part does is desire, and *all* the rational part does is reason, so that no desires should be attributed to reason. But even in Chapter 6 the desire for food or drink which is of overall benefit is attributed to reason. Then in Chapter 11 it becomes even more clear that each part can motivate a person: at 554d, for instance, the desire for respectability (the passionate part) is said to motivate one to repress certain base desires, and each part is portrayed as aiming at certain goals (see especially 580d ff.).

Not only can each part of the mind be said to desire, but each part of the mind can also be seen to have some cognitive ability. At the very least, the desirous part has to be able to recognize a drinkable object; and at 602e–603a Plato expressly talks about the 'non-rational' parts of the mind having 'beliefs' or 'views'. It also seems as though it is the job of reason, whether in its highest manifestation or when it is the reasoning power of desire, to perceive goodness. For instance, in Chapter 11 each of the degenerate types is motivated by a belief that something is good for him; but Plato clearly wants us to think that if they had followed the dictates of a true understanding of goodness they would not have gone astray. The 'timocratic' type in particular illustrates conflict between different manifestations of reason: he is torn between true reason and the passionate part's belief that it is good for him to be a 'real man' (549c–550b). This kind of situation cannot be a conflict within the rational part of the mind alone, since that would violate the principle of opposition which enabled Plato to distinguish the mind's parts in the first place (436b–437a). Therefore, it is a conflict between different manifestations of reason. It makes sense, in fact, to say that the unsullied rational part perceives and knows what is good for a person overall, while the other parts recognize goods which are more restricted (they are short-term, non-altruistic, and so on—442c), and are limited to instrumental calculation of how to achieve them (553d, 562b).

These considerations enable us to cast an interesting light on Plato's notion that one can be 'ruled' by a part of the mind. He clearly believes that to perceive goodness is to act on it; he never quite articulates this belief, though it is close to the surface at

505d. (It will be objected that this cannot always be the case, since even philosophers, for all their vision of goodness, have to be *compelled* to take up the reins of government. But on this issue see pp. lvi–lviii: it is not a clear counter-example.) In any case, when it is a question of what is good *for oneself*, the idea is plausible. Since it is the rational or cognitive element within one of the mind's parts which enables it to recognize goodness, then it is the rational part which motivates it to act on it. All desires are in this sense rational desires.

Of course, the fact that his full position includes acknowledging that reason desires and that desires reason poses a problem for Plato, since he needs to distinguish the parts clearly from the start. This is surely why in 434e–442d Plato goes to such elaborate lengths to establish the distinctness of these parts. In order to do so, he has to rely chiefly on extreme cases—cases where desire arguably has no element of reasoning, no contact with goodness (see the note on 439a). These extreme cases are thirst experienced during illness (see the mention of 'afflictions and diseased states' at 439d) and Leontius' perversion. Once he has established, by the principle of opposition, the existence of different sources for different desires and motivations, he can then add what would only have obscured the argument earlier—that all of these sources also recognize goodness in their own way.

We have already had occasion to refer to 485d–e and its importance within Plato's psychology (p. xxxvi). The more someone is devoted to something, the less energy he has available for other things. The application of this principle in the context of the tripartite psychology is obvious. The more I subordinate the rational part to the desirous part of my mind, the more I weaken it and the more energy I divert to the desirous part—the more it becomes my 'ruler' and the other parts are 'enslaved'. This again helps to explain Plato's emphasis on education. People must be prevented from feeding their baser parts too often; if there are aspects of poetry which do feed these parts, then censorship is desirable. Without proper education, the baser parts of the mind will be fattened up on so many occasions that they become the dominant parts in one's life in general. This is how one becomes one of the degenerate types of Chapter 11 (see 554b).

Most of us, most of the time, are not in such an extreme situation, but we have not achieved the stability of the dominance of reason. We still suffer from conflict between the parts of our mind. Although we aim for goodness in everything we do (505d–e), we can make mistakes about what is *really* good for us; in the terms of Plato's epistemology, we lack the stability of knowledge, so that there can be conflict between what the various motivating parts of our mind take to be good. In particular, the self-centred beliefs of the desirous and passionate parts, about what is good for oneself immediately or in the short term or in part, can conflict with the rational part's knowledge of what is good for us overall.

However, if the rational part becomes my overall dominant part, then I can perceive true goodness (for myself and for others), which puts me in control of my own life, affords me all the virtues, and gives me the authority to rule over others.

Morality

In Chapter 6 Plato defines social morality as every member of the community adhering to PS (433a–434c; see the note on 433a), and inner morality, which is the real objective, as the three parts of the mind adhering to PS in the sense of ruling or being ruled; inner morality is harmony or concord between the three parts of the mind under the rule of reason.

Before we explore some aspects of this idea, there is an important side-issue to dispose of. In the last thirty years a great deal of scholarly effort has gone into exploring and trying to resolve a single particular issue. Thrasymachus assumed that morality involved the performance or non-performance of certain actions; the task Socrates took on was to show that *this* morality ('ordinary morality') is good for a moral person. If he ends up defining morality as psychic harmony and demonstrating that *this* is good for a person, then the argument is crucially incomplete. He has to show also that psychic harmony and ordinary morality entail and are entailed by each other. Otherwise, whatever its interest, the whole argument would be beside the point: Plato would tacitly have changed the subject.

It is true that Plato has Glaucon and Adeimantus, in Chapter 2, specifically ask for an encomium of morality in terms of the inner state of a moral individual; but all the same, Plato obviously feels that a person's inner psychological state will be reflected in his external behaviour. Therefore, however revisionary Plato is being in offering an account of morality in terms of an inner state, he should not violate all our basic intuitions about what morality is or entails in terms of behaviour, and indeed it is clear that he does not intend to: on several occasions (cited below) he relates ordinary morality and psychic harmony. If the gap cannot be filled, then these are occasions when Plato is simply being dogmatic and is insisting, without good grounds, that the relationship exists.

Several ingenious ways of filling the gap have been proposed, but the matter is actually fairly straightforward. This is as it should be, since if Plato needs the kind of lengthy gap-filling arguments some scholars have supplied him with, their very complexity would tend to show that he would be wrong merely to assume the relationship between the two conceptions of morality. However, I would go so far as to claim that the factors are so close to the surface that Plato is entitled to take them for granted, and that to a Greek of his time they would not even constitute a serious gap.

All the parties to the discussion agree implicitly or explicitly to the common Greek assumption that immoral behaviour involves *pleonexia* (trying to get more than your fair share) and that morality is to be thought of, negatively, as the avoidance of *pleonexia*, and positively as attending to others' goods (343a, 372a). It is just that Thrasymachus thinks *pleonexia* is a good thing (343b–344c), as opposed to ordinary morality's proscription of it.

In Plato's analysis *pleonexia* is a result of the desirous part of the mind being unchecked (see p. xxvi and the note on 443b). Therefore, since the state of psychic harmony involves checking the desirous part by the rulership of reason, it will involve the checking of *pleonexia*. Moreover, on the positive side, if I do my job in society I am bound to pay attention to others' goods, since societies are essentially co-operative (369b–c). Therefore, Platonic psychic harmony does entail ordinary morality and Plato is entitled to assert that it does (442e–443b, 485d ff., 554e), and as for the opposite entailment, it is true to say, on these terms, that ordinary immorality disrupts psychic harmony by feeding the pleonectic part of the mind (443e, 589d–590c). See also the notes on 443b, 443d, 443e, and 589d.

What Plato has to say on morality is relevant, then, to the ordinary conception of morality, and he makes its relevance clear as well. Moreover, the approach Plato takes in *Republic* is important and valuable, in that for the first time in Western philosophical history he provides detailed arguments for an agent-centred theory of morality rather than an act-centred one. It is really only this shift of emphasis that has created the 'gap' we have just had to fill: for Plato the inner dimension of morality was primary.

For such a theory, one needs independent criteria for assessing the agent's morality. 'It is clearly unhelpful to say that just acts are those the just person would do, if all you can say then about the just person is that he or she is the kind of person who would be likely to do just acts' (Annas, p. 159). The psychology discussed in the previous section is supposed to provide these independent criteria. A moral person is one with psychic harmony under the rule of reason.

This formula must, however, be spelt out somewhat differently in the case of different kinds of people. It applies with full force only to those few with inherent philosophic characteristics who survive the further-education programme of Chapter 10 and attain the vision of goodness. They are moral experts because they know what is good, and because they are best equipped to educate others in morality (412a, 500d, 540b).

Those who have been correctly brought up under the conditions of Chapter 4 lack full knowledge, but have true belief about morality (see the notes on 441e and 544a). Their touchstone is not absolute goodness, but the preservation of their own and their community's integrity (e.g. 412c ff.). This is what Plato appears to call 'ordinary' morality (500d). A person with this morality is not infallible, and cannot justify his behaviour by reference to an absolute standard.

Everyone else can at the most hope for moral behaviour based on the dictates of an external rationality (590c–d). The laws and conventions of a community can provide this kind of external rational setting (619c–d), but only a proper educational programme can convert blind adherence to law into morality founded on true belief; and then only a philosopher's education can convert this true belief into knowledge.

The mechanism of reason's rule is in all cases the same. To

express it in terms of the analogy with the state, even the lower orders have enough rationality to listen to the voice of reason (p. xxxiv). In psychological terms, there is not such radical dissimilarity and incompatibility between the various aspects of oneself that what I know or believe to be good will simply fail to impinge on my conduct. (Owing to the lack of any conception of neurology, it is a recurrent puzzle in Greek philosophy how ideas can cause actions.) All these three kinds of morality can be described loosely as the control of reason. What Plato does is establish this definition in Chapter 6, and then spend the rest of the book deepening our understanding of it and its possible meanings.

Knowledge and Belief: A Sketch

Thanks to their knowledge, I have suggested, philosophers are capable of more perfect morality than others. Why does Plato think this is the case? They have an impressive array of natural talents (484a–487a), which get them off to a good start; but above all they have knowledge.

A passage in Chapter 8 (474b–480a) is of great importance, because there Plato tries to meet the man on the street on his own terms and persuade him that there is something special about knowledge. The passage has been endlessly discussed, and some details of my interpretation of it are contained in the notes to that section. Broadly, Plato claims to establish the thesis that there are degrees of reality, falling into three bands, and that each of the three bands of reality forms the domain of a different cognitive state. Perhaps the most startling aspect of the thesis is that, despite the fact that as human beings our hard evidence about things is provided by our senses, Plato wants to deny full reality to the world of the senses. What are his grounds for this?

In order for us to identify something, it has to have some quality or attribute. Of course, most things have a number of attributes: they are not *just* big, but they are big, hard, white, buildings (or whatever). If we were faced, *per impossibile*, with a quality-less thing, our mental response would be one of blankness or incomprehension. Plato establishes this impossibility for the sake of completeness and contrast.

At the other extreme, since knowledge is a cognitive state

involving certainty, it is only if something securely and absolutely possesses an attribute that we can be said to know it. If I say 'I know that x is white', then x must be white. The more securely it is white, the more its whiteness can be known by me.

In between (Plato uses this expression because he is thinking of a range of relative clarity and certainty) there is belief and its domain of things which do not reliably have their attributes. It makes sense to think of belief as an intermediate state, because it does not have the degree of certainty of knowledge. We say 'I believe the building is white' when we mean that we are not quite sure.

What is the domain of belief? Keeping more literally to the Greek, what is belief 'set over'? Plato says it is the plurality of white (etc.) things—the things of our everyday world. These are the domain of belief, not knowledge, because they cannot supply our minds with the kind of certainty required for knowledge: a white building does not seem white at night, its colour will fade over time, it can be repainted, and so on (see the note on 479b). Nor is it just white: it is hard, tall, and so on and so forth. It does not present our mind with unmitigated whiteness. In short, it is not absolutely, unchangingly, and eternally white in all respects (479a–b; see *Symposium* 210e–211b). In the light of 597c, these things are probably also deficient just in the sense that there are many of them, not one absolute.

What, on the other hand, is knowledge 'set over'? The domain of knowledge consists of things Plato calls 'types' or 'characters'. These are what enable us to identify the properties things bear. Every time I see a white table or a white building or white hair, I am seeing the character 'whiteness' in these things, or (to put it another way) I am seeing that this property of these things belongs to the type or category 'whiteness'.

Now plainly, given this analysis, Plato will think of each type as single. It must be single, because if there was more than one whiteness, which one of them would I be referring to when I identify something as white? It must also enable me to identify things as white tomorrow as well as today; in short, it must be perfect in all the ways in which the things of this world are deficient—it is eternally and unvaryingly what it is. This is what makes it an object of knowledge. Plato is not saying (as he has occasionally been thought to) that even the objects I see as white are not white for me as long as they are white for me; it is just that by Plato's strict criteria they cannot stand as objects of knowledge, because there will always be a point of view or a respect from which a white thing can legitimately be said to be not-white.

So there is a clear line of thought in this passage, which the man on the street can follow, because no abstruse or specialist moves appear to have been made. To say that something 'partakes of whiteness' is, initially, just a long-winded way of saying that it is white. This is why Plato nowhere in his works directly addresses the question as to what exactly a type is: they are always introduced as familiar. How else would we identify something as big, if it did not have bigness in it? The man has been led to think about how he identifies things, and to conclude that there must be some single standard which enables him to do so. This standard may appear in the world, but it is somehow not of the world. Types have the stability required for knowledge, and in so far as they are the objects of philosophic endeavour, whereas no one else acknowledges their existence, then philosophers are concerned with knowledge and are different from the general run of mankind.

However, some of this glosses over an interesting problem. If types are what enable us to identify the properties of things (an analysis which is borne out by the other main exposition of Plato's middle-period metaphysics in *Phaedo*), then aren't we all philosophers? Even granted that a given building is only white for a limited time and in certain respects and so on, nevertheless it is white in these respects for me, and it must be the presence of a type which enables me to identify it as white. Plato's metaphysics seems to be self-defeating: even while differentiating two realms, he aligns them.

A later passage in *Republic* provides a solution. In 523a–524d (a passage which deliberately echoes 474b–480a) Plato distinguishes between the straightforward identification of things like fingers and the more contentious identification of things like hardness and softness. The difficulty with the latter kind of identification, he says (523e–524a), is that both hardness and softness are the domain of the same faculty (in this case, touch). Each such domain is, so to speak, an infinitely divisible continuum. I break it at one point and say 'soft'; I break it at another point and say 'hard'. But because it is infinitely divisible, what I call 'hard' is not absolutely hard and there will always be further points at which to break it, further up the scale of hardness.

This is a far more radical thought. It is not that a stone is simply hard in some respects, or for certain people, or for a certain time. It is that it is simultaneously no more hard than not-hard. This does not invalidate the *Symposium*-style reading of 479a–b (that things only have their properties in certain respects and so on), but it makes this feature of things a symptom rather than a cause. Things are liable to be only relatively hard because they are in themselves no more hard than not-hard. Therefore, even though the building is white for me, for as long as it is white for me, I have not got a grasp on anything reliable.

There is, then, a clear distinction between types, which are absolutely and unfailingly what they are, and the things of this world, which are utterly defective in this respect. It may be the case that a non-philosopher's ascription of a given property is correct, but he has no way of knowing.

Since we have had to clarify the argument in Chapter 8 by importing a more explicit passage from later in the dialogue, one may legitimately wonder whether Plato's man on the street would have been as meek as Glaucon and would have been persuaded by the argument; nevertheless, in the book as a whole the distinction is clear. And given the nature of Plato's doctrine on this issue, his distinction between philosophers and the rest of us is also clear. We do spend our lives attributing properties to things and assuming that we are justified in doing so; a Platonic philosopher, however, reflects on his sense-experience and can justify his views by argument. There is a plausible argument in the study of the mind which suggests that it is to some extent a hopeless project: it is impossible for the mind to understand itself as a whole. Likewise, Plato argues, it is only by withdrawing from the evidence of the senses that we can begin to understand and explain the evidence.

The Work of Types

In considering types, the first idea that probably comes to mind is that they are what we call concepts. I carry in my mind a concept, whiteness, which I have gained by attending to various instances of whiteness throughout my life; this concept enables me to apply the term 'white' every time I receive the same or closely similar sense-impressions again.

In his middle period Plato would want to qualify this to a certain, important extent. Instead of each of us being born with a mental *tabula rasa* and acquiring concepts such as whiteness, Plato wants to say that we already have latent knowledge of whiteness (518b ff.), of which we are reminded by particular perceived instances of whiteness. This is an important qualification because it takes concepts out of our minds, so to speak, and awards them some kind of independent existence. We do not invent them; we discover them. They are properties, external to our minds, although they may function in our minds as concepts.

The logical correlate of a concept is a 'universal'. In the sentence 'Socrates is a human being', 'Socrates' refers to the particular individual, but 'human being' can be applied to others as well as to Socrates. 'Human being' is a universal: it applies universally over the range of actual human beings. There is no doubt that some of the work of 'types' coincides with some of the work of universals; but there is also no doubt that Plato did not expect types to function solely as universals. If the types function as universals—if a given type is named in a number of different sentences (596a)—that would not to Plato's mind make the types mere universals. He thinks that the existence of the type is prior and enables us to use the same name in different sentences.

The linguistic root of the words Plato uses to refer to types (see the note on 479a) shows that the problem of identification is uppermost in his mind. As a matter of fact, no two of the infinite instances of whiteness are identical: the light is playing differently on it, it has faded a minute amount since yesterday, this patch is a shade darker than that patch, and so on and so forth. Yet something makes us want to call them all by the same name. Given their differences, we cannot (to Plato's mind) have acquired this awareness of some common character from the instances alone; it is by reflecting on our sense-experience that we discover (or remember) these common natures. Then we can securely identify other things as white, and make true assertions about the world.

So the main job that types have to do in *Republic* is to act as paradigms. It is because they really are what they are (see the notes on 476e, 479b, and 480a) that they can act as reference-points (e.g. 484c, 596b). It is not surprising that their paradigmatic role is prominent in *Republic*, since the book is an ethical enquiry, in which metaphysics and logic play only a supporting role. In an ethical enquiry these metaphysical entities of Plato's serve as sources of objective standards.

In another dialogue of roughly the same period of Plato's writing (*Phaedo* 99c–105c) Plato adds what might seem to be a third job for types to do: they cause things to have their properties. But we need take this to be no more than a way of expressing their function as paradigms: they are what enable us to identify the properties of things.

Last, but not least, types and their interrelations are what feature in true accounts (533b ff.). This presumably means that statements about types are essentially true, whereas true statements about the things of this world are only contingently true (because of their deficient nature, as analysed above). If I ascribe hardness to a particular stone, I may be right, but I have no way of knowing whether or not I am right without referring to the type, the paradigm. (If at this point it strikes a reader as peculiar that an immaterial entity such as a type can serve as a paradigm of hardness, please see the first note on 479b.)

Plato actually makes it a requirement of knowledge that one is able to give an account of things (531e, 534b). Two different kinds of account seem to be involved, in a compressed form. In the first place, I have to be able to explain why things are as they are, which involves not just truly identifying things, but also explaining them in terms of their broader context, which is to say their interconnections with other types; secondly, I have to be able to justify any belief I may have by understanding why it is right—which comes down to knowing why the things that feature in my beliefs are as they are and having the ability to explain them.

Two Worlds?

I have said that types enjoy independent existence of some kind. But of what kind? Plato clearly thinks that they are genuine features of reality, whose existence is not determined by or reducible to the existence of the things of this world: morality would exist even if no moral people or behaviour could ever exist (472b–473a).

Plato is committed to there being in some sense two worlds—the real world of types and the clarity of knowledge, and the 'dream' world of the workaday world and the ambivalence of belief. But the extent of separation between the two worlds should not be exaggerated. After all, it is the presence in things of types which gives things their properties: the types *are* the properties of things. Nevertheless, they are distinct enough for the philosopher to be able to work with types alone, with no reference to examples of their instantiation in the world.

Plato leaves us in no doubt in *Republic* that the difference between the two realms depends not just on the different nature of their inhabitants, but on a shift of mental attitude or state. That this is the main point of the Cave analogy is made absolutely plain in the discussion following it: see especially 518b ff. and the general emphasis on reorienting the mind. The more one withdraws from reliance on the senses, and from adherence to conventional views (479d, 517d–e), the more one approaches types and the possibility of knowledge. A philosopher rids himself of the relative viewpoint and is thereby enabled to see things as they are. There is a strong pre-Platonic epistemological tradition to this effect as well.

The philosophers' mental reorientation does not take them out of this world. There is nothing in what Plato says that rules out knowledge of things in this world (see also Julia Annas's book, and Gail Fine's series of articles, all mentioned in the bibliography). Since this is still not the orthodox view of Plato's metaphysics, we ought to be clear, in the first place, about the general plausibility of the claim. The point is (to repeat) that it is a firm part of Plato's theory that things gain their properties as a result of their connection with types. To see something as white is to see the presence of whiteness in it. In this sense, types are immanent in the world; and since types are the objects of knowledge, then the world can become the object of knowledge. To believe that something is white, and to be able to justify that belief, is to have knowledge of it as white.

There is nothing in the passage of *Republic* we are chiefly concerned with (474b–480a) which tells against this interpretation. A number of translators and commentators have taken the passage to be claiming that knowledge and belief have different 'objects' rather than different 'domains', as if there could be no overlap between the two sets of objects. I maintain that an unbiased reading of the passage could never produce this interpretation. It is not incompatible with the text, but it is not the first interpretation that comes to mind since it is on the face of it outrageous. We commonly say things like 'John only believes that smoking is bad for him, whereas Dr Smith knows it is.' In other words, we imply that belief and knowledge have the same objects. And apart from his ignorance of smoking, this statement of ours would also have been perfectly normal to a Greek. Plato in this passage is explicitly (476d–e) trying to convince the man on the street of his views, so he should not be making too many outrageous assumptions. It is better to talk of domains rather than objects, because it is easier to understand that domains can overlap (as in William Blake's 'To see a world in a grain of sand'). It is not overlap that is denied in the emphatic statements of 478a–b, but belief's access to reality—and that at first sight would be understood as the reality of everyday things, not the reality of some other-worldly region.

Plato describes knowledge and belief as 'faculties', with each faculty being 'set over' a particular 'domain'. Different faculties are defined by their different abilities, by the different effects they have (477c–d). In Greek terms (compare *Theaetetus* 153e–154a, for instance), the faculty of sight, in conjunction with a potentially visible object, *produces* seeing. So here in *Republic* the capacity for knowledge is realized in a grasp of reality, while the capacity for belief is liable to be realized in illusion. There is no reason not to think that the same objects may be involved in both cases.

Notice that this is not to say that knowledge does not have its own proper objects—the types. But it is to say that although types can be known on their own (511b–c), they can also be known in the material world. I can see the beauty in Helen as beauty in itself provided I do not compare it with that of others and provided I just see it for what it is, and provided I can justify my belief. Just as in Plato's early dialogues Socrates is often portrayed as searching for definitions of concepts, precisely to enable him to recognize and understand cases of their instantiation in this world, so Socrates continues this quest in the middle-period dialogues.

There is also clear textual evidence for this overlap between the two worlds. At 506c, for instance, Socrates says that he has belief without knowledge of goodness, and at 520c philosophers who return to the cave are said to have knowledge of the shadowy things down there. This is just as well: if it were flatly impossible to have knowledge of this world, just because it is this world, then philosophers would be no better at ruling than anyone else, and the whole political point of Plato's enquiry into knowledge would collapse.

One of the more important consequences of this reinterpretation of *Republic* is that it brings it in line with what is said in other dialogues (as well as with common sense, since those other dialogues reflect common sense). In the early-ish dialogue *Meno* (97e–98a), and again at *Symposium* 202a (which is more or less contemporary with *Republic*), Plato floats the possibility of converting belief into knowledge (by understanding and being able to justify the truth of a true belief); the same idea recurs in the late dialogue *Theaetetus* (201c–d). These dialogues bracket *Republic*, so to speak, which on the usual interpretation excludes the possibility of converting belief into knowledge by radically separating them. At the same time, our interpretation also makes sense of the impression one gains from reading *Republic* that Plato allows for gradual progress and conversion from a state of ignorance to one of knowledge (see especially Chapters 9–10). In this context one should note a prime use to which paradigms are typically put: if challenged about my belief that *x* is F, I can refer to the paradigm of F-ness to check. So it is well in keeping with the paradigmatic interpretation of types that belief and knowledge should not be utterly divorced.

Types of Substances

A fascinating problem is raised in a particularly acute way by *Republic*. This is the question of whether or not there are types of only a restricted range of things, or whether there are types of everything—that is, everything which is not a unique individual (such as Socrates).

In Chapters 8 and 10 Plato constructs, as we have seen, an argument for the existence of types based on the fact that the properties of things exist on a continuum which includes both of a pair of opposites. The argument in Chapter 8, however, does not look as though it is supposed to be an argument about a restricted range of predicates (those with opposites); it reads as though we are meant to contrast the 'dream' world of the senses as a whole with the reliable world of knowledge as a whole.

It is quite a surprise, then, to find in Chapter 10 that our perception of hardness, softness, and so on is contrasted with the reliability of identifying a finger as a finger. For surely a finger is just as much a part of the 'dream' world as its hardness is; and surely the *only* things we have been led to expect we can reliably identify are types.

Perhaps, one might think, there need only be types of disputed properties, not of things like fingers. If one thinks like this, however, one is going to be taken aback on turning to 596a ff. (in Chapter 13) and finding bed-hood and table-hood trotted out as if they were standard types, easy for one to accept. But surely particular beds and tables in this world are just as easy to identify as fingers: they do not puzzle the mind either.

As far as evidence internal to *Republic* is concerned, it is impossible to deny that Plato held that there were types of beds and tables—and if so, also (presumably) of fingers. We should note that at 523c Plato is at pains to ensure that the finger he is talking about is a finger seen close to. In other words, he specifically excludes the possibility of 'finger seen at dusk' and 'finger seen at a distance'. Under these kinds of circumstances, people can in fact seem like statues (*Philebus* 38c–39a). So perhaps Plato does allow that even fingers and beds can under some circumstances be unreliable. But even if he is making this allowance, he is still also trying to distinguish between properties which (for whatever reason) are perceived reliably and those which (for whatever reason) are not, and we ought to try to understand the basis for the distinction.

The following scenario seems to me to be plausible. The central premise of my interpretation of the metaphysics of *Republic* is that the function of types is to enable us to identify things. This must go for bed-hood as much as for hardness and whiteness and so on. Therefore, supposing (for the sake of the argument) that there is never any doubt about my identification of beds, tables, and fingers, we are forced to conclude that these types are always correctly identifiable, whereas others are not. In the *Philebus* passage just referred to Plato talks of uncertainty in identification provoking an internal conversation—a series of questions and answers leading to an identification. However, it is obvious that some situations and some objects do not require the mediation of this process: they are immediately identified. It is likely, then, that Plato assumes two kinds of types: some are instantiated directly in the physical world (which is a way of saying that the human mind rarely needs to doubt the identification); others are instantiated first in the human mind, and then projected out on to the physical world.

This is obviously not a complicated distinction to attribute to Plato. He gives us the reasons for making it—doubt and dispute—without actually making it explicitly. We can safely conclude that there is nothing to prevent his maintaining that there are types of things like bed-hood just as much as there are types of things like whiteness, but that some types require (so to speak) the mediation of the human mind. The ascription of certain properties requires a higher degree of human judgement than that of other properties.

Consider the strategy. Plato wants to argue that philosophers have access to something the rest of us do not—that which enables true identification in all important cases. In the first place, he would have a hard time arguing this point if he started by talking about cases of straightforward identification: it does not take a philosopher to identify a finger. In the second place, in the moral sphere which is the ultimate context of the argument it is disputed cases that are of the most interest and importance. For both reasons, Plato emphasizes disputed cases more than the others. The strategy is comprehensible.

Goodness, Morality, and Metaphysics

The ultimate purpose of the higher training of philosophers is that they should know goodness and be able to duplicate it, as much as is possible, here on earth (540a–b). They are able to attain knowledge of goodness because the whole domain of types is structured under goodness. In the image of the Sun (507b–509c) goodness is said to be responsible for the knowability of the types. This puzzling claim is to be understood as meaning that goodness is responsible for their possession of properties like being, unity, stability, and eternity, in the sense that these are the properties which make them 'good' (perfect, in fact) cases of what they are. And by the standard axiom of Platonic metaphysics, their goodness must be due to their participation in the type 'goodness'. Hence it is the supreme type.

Now, this synoptic knowledge of goodness, which enables one to know the whole realm of types as the sun enables us to see the whole visible world (507d ff.), is supposed to bear on the moral enquiry which Plato undertook in Chapters 1–6. When the moral enquiry resumes at the start of Chapter 11, a link is expressly effected between the two aspects of the book—morality and metaphysics. The same point is an implication of 540a–b, cited just above. Knowledge of goodness would make philosophers good rulers, capable of benefiting the community as a whole and all its members (505d–506b). Thus, as well as being the metaphysical acme, goodness is also the moral and political acme.

Aristotle (in *Nicomachean Ethics* 1. 6) and Sir Karl Popper are only the two most famous commentators to have charged Plato with empty formalism. While making these grand claims for knowledge of goodness, Plato declines to provide a proper account of what goodness is, and instead resorts to image and metaphor (506c–e). However, we can speculate about the background to the claims.

In the first place, we should recall some aspects of the Principle of Specialization (pp. xxii–xxiii). If all members of a community perform their proper functions, they are not only behaving morally (433a–434c), but are also enabling the community as a whole to perform its function of benefiting all of its members (369b–c, 420b–421c). Such a community is a good community (427e) because fulfilling one's function is good (352e–353c).

Whatever one might think of all this, it does not consist of empty claims, but has been backed up by extensive argument. We can immediately rephrase our question. Instead of asking 'What use is knowledge of goodness?', we can ask 'How does Plato think that knowledge of goodness helps philosophers to organize society in such a way that every member performs his or her proper function?'

It seems likely that Plato would more or less equate knowledge of a thing's goodness with knowledge of its function. The connection between goodness and function is clear in 352e–353c (just referred to). It is also worth reflecting on 601c–602a: the goodness of anything is to be assessed by its function, and anyone who knows a thing's proper function also knows how it is good for that thing to be.

Therefore, there is no gap in theory between knowledge of goodness and knowing a person's function in society. The practical gap is to be filled by fifteen years' experience of human management (539e–540a). The metaphysical aspect of this is that since every type is good, then instances of types in the world are good to the extent that they participate in types. Since it is philosophers above all who are capable of seeing types in the world, then philosophers can see the good in the world—see everything's function—and work towards improving matters in general.

Some plausibility can be given, then, to Plato's claims about the moral and political importance of knowing goodness. And this in turn gives added meaning to his definition of morality in Chapter 6. Morality involves the rule of reason, and reason knows what is good for the various strata of society and for a community as a whole, whether this is understood at the individual or at the political level (428c–d, 442c, 484c–d, 488a–489a, 520c). Hence morality requires knowledge of goodness.

It is important to bear in mind in all of this that Plato does not mean by goodness some one thing, which philosophers get to know and then seek to instantiate. It is not the philosophers' job to make everything altogether uniform. Goodness is more like the structure of things, to which everything and everyone may contribute (as in the model community everyone contributes to its goodness by conforming to PS).

One should also note that morality entails the harmony or structure of the mind under reason, and that the realm of types, and thus the sensible world too, are made rational and knowable under goodness. Knowledge of goodness involves the vision of the whole rational ordering of the universe, in which morality plays its part. So a philosopher, one may presume, wants to 'advance the reign of rational order in the world as a whole' (Cooper, 'Psychology of Justice', 155). Knowledge is impossible without rational order (hence *all* knowledge is of goodness), and the philosopher seeks always to extend and improve his knowledge (475b–c).

It is true, then, that Plato does not provide us with an argument to demonstrate how a philosopher's knowledge of goodness translates into practical skills like resourcefulness, decision-making, and understanding human nature (which are the kinds of skills the guardians of Chapter 6 possess). But if one who knows goodness knows how it structures not only the realm of types, but also the sensible realm, then the philosopher's vision of rational order is not confined to remote, other-worldly regions, although they are its source. The pursuit of the structure of goodness within the world is all the practical intelligence a philosopher-ruler requires. Overall, and moment by moment as well, he has a reference-point (484c–d, 500d, 517c, 519c, 520c, 540a–b) by which to guide his thinking and his decisions.

In short, Plato's vision is of a rationally ordered, teleological universe, where everything has its place and its purpose. This vision of order is given vivid expression in the Myth of Er with which the book concludes. Some may find the vision too impersonal for their tastes. In the long run, even evil seems to serve some purpose within the ordered cosmos, if only when its inevitable punishment deters future wrong. But to complain that in such an impersonal universe my morality makes no difference is to miss the point: apart from the fact that it provides one with a weak excuse for not trying, the point is that the universe is good because it is rationally ordered. Therefore, by maintaining and enhancing the rational order within our minds, and (as much as may be possible) within our societies, we maintain and enhance it at large in the universe, Plato seems to suggest. As above, so below.

Plato's predecessors had been mightily impressed with the apparent orderliness of the universe and had boldly extended the everyday Greek word *kosmos* ('elegant order') to apply to it. But while many have admired the structure of the heavens, few have included the whole of human life too, which is more commonly deplored as chaotic. Alexander Pope shares Plato's vision (*An Essay on Man* 1. 289–94):

> All nature is but art, unknown to thee;
> All chance, direction which thou canst not see;
> All discord, harmony not understood;
> All partial evil, universal good;
> And, spite of pride, in erring reason's spite,
> One truth is clear: Whatever is, is right.

Moral Egoism

How should one live? What is it to be a human being and to fulfil one's potential as a human being? What is human happiness and the good life? These are central questions for Plato; he is in many respects concerned above all with ethics. He answers the questions with a remarkable degree of consistency throughout his life, considering that his views on other major topics change and evolve over time. In the concluding sections of this Introduction we shall try to pull some threads together from the preceding discussions and to spell out Plato's answer in *Republic*.

First, does he recommend the same kind of life for everyone? Yes and no. He recognizes that people have different natures and therefore different parts to play (370a, 415a, 453e), but he thinks that being moral and being happy (fulfilling one's nature) go hand in hand (Chapter 12), and he thinks that morality can always be described as psychic harmony under the rule of reason (Chapter 6). If one cannot achieve this harmony on one's own, then it is best if it is imposed from outside (590d); and artisans and auxiliaries have less stable and perfect kinds of morality (pp. xli–xlii).

Clearly, however, it is best to do it on one's own, if possible, and to have full morality. And this is to say that it is best to be a philosopher, in Plato's terms. Within the context of the political fantasy of *Republic*, happiness is discussed as an attribute of the philosopher-rulers. However, outside of that fantasy we too are supposed to find ourselves attracted towards philosophy; we are supposed to strive to know goodness and to instantiate it in our own and in others' lives.

I have begged a question here. An argument could be and has been constructed to the effect that the philosophers are *not* in fact happy. They are happiest contemplating the immaterial realm of types and goodness; they have to be *compelled* to return to earth (to the cave) and undertake ruling (499b, 519c–521b, 539e–540b).

The first point to note is that the talk of compulsion is a conceit, within the grand conceit of the foundation of an imaginary community. It is Socrates and his interlocutors, apparently, who will force philosophers to return. In these terms, the rulers have been selected specifically to be those who see their own good and that of the community as coinciding (see the note on 520e for this and other possible reasons for the philosophers' return to the cave); and Plato has argued extensively that the good of the community depends on philosophic rule.

However, the fact that philosophers will see the two kinds of good coinciding was merely asserted. Has Plato provided us with the elements of an argument to support the assertion? I think he has. In order to be happy, one has to be moral; in order to be moral, one has to conform to PS—to carry out one's proper function within the community. It is not merely that a trained ruler's function is evidently to rule (520b–d). It is that it is an intrinsic part of PS from the outset (369e, 420b, 421c, 433c–d, 465d) that one contributes in one's own way towards the welfare of the community (see the note on 433a). Therefore, philosophers will not be fully happy unless they rule; and since happiness and morality increase and decrease together, they will not be fully moral either.

Perhaps the most telling application of this aspect of PS is as follows. Plato is so firmly wedded to the requirement that everyone contributes that he describes a situation where it is possible for people not to contribute as 'the ultimate evil' (552a). So it is actually evil for philosophers to live only a contemplative life, and not to undertake the task of ruling as well.

It turns out, in fact, to be rather hard to find any real implication in the text that the philosophers would not be happy if they ruled, beyond the conceit of 'compulsion'. *If* ruling were not part of what it is for a philosopher to be happy, *then* we could infer from the interchange between Socrates and Glaucon at 519d that ruling would decrease the quality of the philosophers' lives. But all Socrates need be taken as saying here is that *even if* it were to decrease their happiness, still the happiness of the whole would be of paramount importance. As a matter of fact, however (the inference is), it does not decrease their happiness, as Socrates asserts in 420b, which 519e echoes and recalls.

Ultimately, then, if a philosopher were not to get involved in human affairs to some extent (not to the extent of petty details, 500b–c), he would simply be making a mistake—as in real life some philosophers do, Plato implies at 519c–d. The attraction of the world of eternal perfection is enormous (see the sexual imagery of 490b, 496a, 611e), and Plato clearly found it so himself. Any lingering impression we receive that Plato is some-how reluctant to admit that philosophers must be rulers is a reflec-tion simultaneously of his own ambivalence, and of the situation outside the ideal world of his imagination (see 496b–497a, 520b). Almost despite himself, he concedes that philosophers have to descend from their ivory towers.

Plato, like Socrates before him, is a moral egoist—that is, an egoist who holds that it is good for me to do good for others. My happiness increases by increasing others' happiness. A major purpose of the Myth of Er is to depict this point by comparing the post-mortem experiences of good and bad people; and we have seen (p. xl) that Plato's idiosyncratic definition of morality as psychic harmony, which seems at first sight very introverted and self-centred (e.g. at 443d–e and 592a), coincides with common conceptions of morality.

Real and Ideal

Translated out of its political metaphor, then, Plato's recom-mendation is that we spread the rational orderliness of goodness by pursuing philosophy and helping our neighbours. I have suggested in this introduction that Plato was not interested in real politics, and his pessimism in this regard is striking in passages such as 496b ff. So I suggest that 'philosophic rule' is primarily translated not as a serious political ideal, but as a recommenda-tion not to ignore whatever benefit we can give to those around us.

If all this is right, it goes some way towards closing an impor-tant gap in *Republic*. At first sight Plato's defence of morality has turned out to be very odd. What started life as a discussion of why it benefits you and me to be moral has turned into a reservation of true morality for the few. The notion that psychic harmony under reason is morality (which is an obscure but ultimately compre-hensible notion of common morality) was developed in Chapters 3–6 and re-emerges in Chapters 11–12; but, it might be objected, the intermediate chapters have presented us with something altogether different—an élitist morality. Psychic harmony involves all the parts of the mind, even the worldly parts; but in Chapters

7–10 the world and all its aspects are presented as so much trash to be escaped from (e.g. 500b–c, 517c–d, 519a–b). The mood at times seems to be that of the asceticism we find in *Phaedo*.

We are obviously seeing traces here of the same ambivalence in Plato's mind that we noted a short while ago. He is torn between eternalism and practical reality. But it is too harsh to say that asceticism and psychic harmony are actually incompatible.

We should recall, first, that we have already closed the gap in two other contexts—the metaphysical context (pp. xlvii–l) and the political one (pp. liii–liv). The general metaphysical background is that the two worlds, real and ideal, overlap; it is less misleading to say that there are two ways of approaching the world, rather than that there are two separate worlds. And it is possible to claim that the philosophers' 'remote' knowledge of goodness can be translated into practical benefit.

Rather than there being an incompatibility, unnoticed by Plato, between the notion of psychic harmony and the contemplative ideal of the central chapters, it is arguable that he intends the contemplative ideal to supplement and deepen the notion of psychic harmony. We should recall that the kind of reason which is taken for granted up to and including the introduction of the notion of psychic harmony in Chapter 6 is a second-rate kind of intelligence. It is the intelligence of auxiliaries, not philosophers (see the note on 544a); its chief function is to understand commands and carry them out (429b ff.). This of course raises the question of where these commands are to come from; and the answer, obviously, is that they derive from higher philosophic reason. 'Whereas the first phase of education trains the mind to listen to the voice of reason, the second phase provides the mind with its own authoritative voice' (Gill, p. 17).

This means that the talk of psychic harmony under reason in Chapter 6 is promissory, in the sense that the full 'reason' which the mind should be 'under' to be moral has not yet emerged. Nevertheless, it is likely that all along Plato intended philosophic reason to play so crucial a role; and given the paltriness and passivity of what is described as reason in the earlier phase of the book (see 522a and the notes on 414b, 441e, 484d), it is difficult to champion it as if it were a more realistic conception of morality than rule by philosophic reason.

The Good Life

The definition of morality as psychic harmony in Chapter 6 is rather formal. Understanding its content involves reference to philosophic knowledge, because Plato wants us to see that 'reason' in the formula 'psychic harmony under reason', properly understood, inherently loves truth, goodness, unity, and stability. What other ingredients are there in the good life? What other criteria distinguish the good life from other lives which might satisfy the formal terms? For an answer we need to turn to Chapter 12, where Plato argues that the philosopher's life—the moral life—is the good life. The chapter is important because it attempts to establish exactly what is needed—criteria for selecting the good which are independent of the formal requirements of Chapter 6 and whose results can therefore legitimately be applied to those formal requirements.

In an abstract manner (583b–587b) Plato argues that the pleasures which accompany a philosopher's life are more 'true' than those of others. What he means (see also the notes on the passage) is that other pleasures merely satisfy lacks: the pleasure and the lack cancel each other out. Filling an empty stomach has no value beyond what it does. There are some pleasures, however (which are or include the pleasures of philosophic activity such as contemplation), which do not merely remedy a lack, and therefore may be said to have 'intrinsic value' (the phrase is Nussbaum's). Everyone wants what is good (505d–e), but most of the pleasures thought to be good have no value except as remedies. A life ruled by the desirous or passionate parts of the mind, then, is simply some kind of mistake.

So far, however, the ideal Plato is establishing is rather too remote and effete—an ivory-tower existence of contemplation interspersed with periods of listening to Gregorian chants and smelling roses (see the note on 584b for these as 'true' pleasures). What about the rest of life? We do have to eat, sleep, and interact with others. Should we avoid all this as much as possible? This is the teaching of *Phaedo*, and it is echoed in *Republic* 581e.

It is easy to misunderstand Plato's asceticism, however. He is not recommending hair-shirts and frequent scourging with barbed-wire whips. There is a vital difference between denying feelings and being detached from feelings (a difference which the Stoics were to explore in greater depth): it is the difference between not experiencing and experiencing the feelings. Yet even while experiencing them, someone who is detached chooses not to find them valuable; they are not his or her standards of goodness.

Plato's philosopher is detached, not denying: he does experience other pleasures (582a–e). We have seen that the ideal of Chapter 6 is a life involving all the parts of the mind (i.e. a full range of worldly activities); but Plato says precisely the same in Chapter 12, at 586e–587a and 589a–b. In the political terms of the book we know that the workers and auxiliaries are essential for a properly functioning community. The philosopher's life, we are supposed to think, is a rounded life.

In 558d–559d (and 571b–572b) Plato distinguishes between necessary and unnecessary desires and their subsequent pleasures. Necessary desires are 'those which we're incapable of stopping and any whose satisfaction is beneficial to us'. An example is eating as much as is required for health. The immediate use to which the distinction is put is to condemn the niggardliness of attending only to necessary pleasures, and the extravagance of attending to unnecessary ones. But this is not the only use to which the distinction may be put. What is deplorable about attending to necessary pleasures is being *ruled* by them (559d). But Plato uses the strong word 'necessary' because that is exactly what they are: life is impossible without them.

That these desires and pleasures will feature in the philosopher's life is clear from their mention at 581e. It follows that the philosopher will assign some value to things like health. Only philosophic activity and morality are good in themselves and for their consequences. Other things like health are good if their consequences are good. Their value is instrumental. The criterion for value is whether or not a thing promotes philosophic activity and morality—whether it distracts the mind to such an extent that reason is dislodged from its position as ruler (455b, 498b, 591b–592a). As always, it is important to recall that this is not merely an internal aim: psychic harmony is what enables one to do good to others. Therefore, the philosopher's criterion can be expressed as what promotes not only his own good, but also that of others (see above on moral egoism).

Plato has no difficulty in finding terms to describe this attitude and approach to the 'necessary' worldly desires. He helps himself to the conventional Greek virtues—self-control, courage, and wisdom, above all. The terms may need a little redefinition or clarification (see also *Phaedo* 68c ff.) before they completely fit in, as Plato wants them to, as instrumental means to preserving morality and goodness. But this is how they figure not only in Chapter 6, but also at 591c ff. (self-control) and within the central chapters at 485d–486b (self-control and courage).

There is, it is worth noting in passing, no significant difference between all this and Plato's more abstract recipe for the good life in *Philebus*. We are ideally to be devoted above all else to the perpetuation of morality, goodness, and rational orderliness in ourselves and in the world, against the nightmare forces of chaos and evil. To help us in this task, we live lives of simple virtue. This is not grim asceticism: we live in the material world and we serve the world. But Plato would agree that it is not an easy life: for a start, it takes many years of preparation (Chapter 10). Finally, we pursue and carry out this task not because we expect rewards (even though in fact it is arguable that they are worth while), but because it is good in itself to do so, and to do less is to fail, to a greater or lesser degree, to fulfil one's human nature.

SELECT BIBLIOGRAPHY

THIS bibliography serves two purposes: it shows a portion of the debts I incurred while writing the book; and it introduces the reader to what I consider the most enjoyable and illuminating of the modern scholarly literature on the subject. It is meant to be thorough enough to help with further study, but not with intense study: many of the works cited have fuller bibliographies for a reader to follow up particular fields of interest. Quite a number of academic articles are written every year on *Republic*, so I am particularly aware of having included only a tiny proportion of this category of work (some others, however, have been mentioned from time to time in the notes). I have included only works written in English; some require knowledge of Greek, some are in other respects hard going, but all are valuable.

Translations

There have been many previous translations of *Republic*. The following have achieved the widest circulation:

Cornford, F. M., *The* Republic *of Plato* (London: Oxford University Press, 1941).

Grube, G. M. A., *Plato*: Republic, 2nd edn., revised by C. D. C. Reeve (Indianapolis: Hackett, 1992).

Lee, H. D. P., *Plato*, The Republic, 2nd edn. (Harmondsworth: Penguin, 1974).

Editions

These are all scholarly works and include the Greek text:

Adam, J., *The* Republic *of Plato* (2 vols.; Cambridge: Cambridge University Press, 1902; 2nd edn., with introduction by D. A. Rees, 1963).

Allan, D. J., *Plato:* Republic Book I (London: Methuen, 1940).

Ferguson, J., *Plato:* Republic Book X (London: Methuen, 1957).

Halliwell, S., *Plato:* Republic *10* (Warminster: Aris & Phillips, 1988).

Plato in General

The best introduction to Plato is, of course, to find reliable and readable translations and immerse yourself in them. Plato is set in his general ancient philosophical context, with admirable concision, by:

Irwin, T., *Classical Thought* (Oxford: Oxford University Press, 1989).

The most accessible good introductions to Plato's work as a whole are:

Field, G. C., *The Philosophy of Plato*, 2nd edn. (London: Oxford University Press, 1969).

Grube, G. M. A., *Plato's Thought* (London: Methuen, 1935).

Hare, R. M., *Plato* (Oxford: Oxford University Press, 1982).

Rowe, C. J., *Plato* (Brighton: The Harvester Press, 1984).

Harder work, but rewarding, are:

Crombie, I. M., *An Examination of Plato's Doctrines* (2 vols.; London: Routledge & Kegan Paul, 1962–3).

Demos, R., *The Philosophy of Plato* (London: Charles Scribner's Sons, 1939).

Gosling, J. C. B., *Plato* (London: Routledge & Kegan Paul, 1973).

Vlastos, G., *Platonic Studies*, 2nd edn. (Princeton: Princeton University Press, 1981).

Republic *in General*

The single most important book on *Republic*, and the essential starting-point for further work, is:

Annas, J., *An Introduction to Plato's* Republic (Oxford: Oxford University Press, 1981).

And there is plenty of value in:

Cross, R. C., and Woozley, A. D., *Plato's* Republic: *A Philosophical Commentary* (London: Macmillan, 1964).

Guthrie, W. K. C., *A History of Greek Philosophy*, iv. *Plato, the Man and his Dialogues: Earlier Period* (Cambridge: Cambridge University Press, 1975).

Murphy, N. R., *The Interpretation of Plato's* Republic (London: Oxford University Press, 1951).

White, N. P., *A Companion to Plato's* Republic (Oxford: Basil Blackwell, 1979).

Politics

By far the best book on the subject (and after Annas's book, the next book to read) is:

Klosko, G., *The Development of Plato's Political Theory* (London: Methuen, 1986).

The classic accounts, and still worth reading, are:

Barker, E., *Greek Political Theory: Plato and his Predecessors* (London: Methuen, 1918).

Sinclair, T. A., *A History of Greek Political Thought* (London: Routledge & Kegan Paul, 1951).

Plato's political pronouncements used to arouse passionate denunciations and counter-argument. One should start with Plato's most strident enemy:

Popper, K. R., *The Open Society and its Enemies*, i. *The Spell of Plato* (London: Routledge & Kegan Paul, 1945).

The rest of the debate can be satisfactorily followed through the essays in two collections:

Bambrough, R. (ed.), *Plato, Popper and Politics* (Cambridge: W. Heffer & Sons, 1967).

Thorson, T. L. (ed.), *Plato: Totalitarian or Democrat?* (Englewood Cliffs: Prentice-Hall, 1963).

Education

An unusual defence of some of Plato's educational ideas (and a counter-attack against Popper) is undertaken by:

Barrow, R., *Plato, Utilitarianism and Education* (London: Routledge & Kegan Paul, 1975).

Plato's educational proposals, such as they are, are most usefully studied in:

Gill, C. J., 'Plato and the Education of Character', *Archiv für Geschichte der Philosophie*, 67 (1985), 1–26.

Ethics

It is invaluable to start by knowing something of the background. For everyday ethics, two books stand out:

Dover, K. J., *Greek Popular Morality in the Time of Plato and Aristotle* (Oxford: Basil Blackwell, 1974).

Pearson, L., *Popular Ethics in Ancient Greece* (Stanford: Stanford University Press, 1962).

The best introduction to the history of ethical thought is:

MacIntyre, A., *A Short History of Ethics* (London: Routledge & Kegan Paul, 1967).

Useful introductions to Greek philosophical ethics are:

Prior, W. J., *Virtue and Knowledge: An Introduction to Ancient Greek Ethics* (London: Routledge, 1991).

Rowe, C. J., *An Introduction to Greek Ethics* (London: Hutchinson, 1976).

Plato's views on everyday ethical issues which trouble us today are discussed in:

Huby, P., *Plato and Modern Morality* (London: Macmillan, 1972).

Rankin, H. D., *Plato and the Individual* (London: Methuen, 1964).

A tough, controversial, and outstanding book on Plato's moral theories (and more besides) is:

Irwin, T., *Plato's Moral Theory: The Early and Middle Dialogues* (Oxford: Oxford University Press, 1977).

A starting-point for the scholarly debate on the moral theories of *Republic* is provided by articles collected in:

Vlastos, G. (ed.), *Plato: A Collection of Critical Essays*, ii (Garden City: Anchor Books, 1971).

Apart from essays in that collection, the following articles, of the many that focus on the central moral ideas of the book, may be singled out:

Kraut, R., 'Reason and Justice in Plato's *Republic*', in E. N. Lee *et al.* (eds.), *Exegesis and Argument* (*Phronesis* suppl. 1; 1973), 207–24.

White, F. C., 'Justice and the Good of Others in Plato's *Republic*', *History of Philosophy Quarterly*, 5 (1988), 395–410.

Wilson, J. R. S., 'Reason's Rule and Vulgar Wrongdoing', *Dialogue*, 16 (1977), 591–604.

The role of Plato's conception of goodness, or 'the good', in his moral thinking in the dialogue, is rightly stressed (in very different ways) by:

Cooper, J., 'The Psychology of Justice in Plato', *American Philosophical Quarterly*, 14 (1977), 151–7.

Santas, G. X., 'Two Theories of Good in Plato's *Republic*', *Archiv für Geschichte der Philosophie*, 67 (1985), 223–45.

Apart from the inner psychological state which Plato calls morality, his views on what we may more immediately recognize as morality or justice have been discussed in:

Lee, E. N., 'Plato's Theory of Social Justice in *Republic* II–IV', in J. P. Anton and A. Preus (eds.), *Essays in Ancient Greek Philosophy*, iii (Albany: State University of New York Press, 1989), 117–40.

Vlastos, G., 'The Theory of Social Justice in the *Polis* in Plato's *Republic*', in H. North (ed.), *Interpretations of Plato* (*Mnemosyne* suppl.; 1977), 1–40.

Various aspects of the structure and nature of Plato's main moral arguments in *Republic* have been interestingly analysed in:

Neu, J., 'Plato's Analogy of State and Individual: The *Republic* and the Organic Theory of the State', *Philosophy*, 46 (1971), 238–54.

Wilson, J. R. S., 'The Argument of *Republic* IV', *Philosophical Quarterly*, 26 (1976), 111–24.

Plato sets out in *Republic* to prove that morality pays. Does he succeed? And whether or not he does, what are the parameters of his arguments?

Aronson, S. H., 'The Happy Philosopher: A Counterexample to Plato's Proof', *Journal of the History of Philosophy*, 10 (1972), 383–98.

Brickhouse, T. C., 'The Paradox of the Philosophers' Rule', *Apeiron*, 15 (1981), 152–60.

Kraut, R., 'Egoism, Love and Political Office in Plato', *Philosophical Review*, 82 (1973), 330–44.

Nussbaum, M., 'The *Republic*: True Value and the Standpoint of Perfection': ch. 5 (pp. 136–64) of M. Nussbaum, *The Fragility of Goodness: Luck and Ethics in Greek Tragedy and Philosophy* (Cambridge: Cambridge University Press, 1986).

Psychology

A sound general introduction to Plato's views on the nature of the mind is:

Lovibond, S., 'Plato's Theory of Mind', in S. Everson (ed.), *Companions to Ancient Thought*, ii. *Psychology* (Cambridge: Cambridge University Press, 1991), 35–55.

The famous tripartite division of the mind in *Republic* is discussed in:

Lesses, G., 'Weakness, Reason and the Divided Soul in Plato's *Republic*', *History of Philosophy Quarterly*, 4 (1987), 147–62.

Stalley, R. F., 'Plato's Arguments for the Division of the Reasoning and Appetitive Elements within the Soul', *Phronesis*, 20 (1975), 110–28.

Woods, M. J., 'Plato's Division of the Soul', *Proceedings of the British Academy*, 73 (1987), 23–47.

Wider-ranging, though still of course centring on tripartition, are the following important pieces:

Cooper, J., 'Plato's Theory of Human Motivation', *History of Philosophy Quarterly*, 1 (1984), 3–21.

Kahn, C. H., 'Plato's Theory of Desire', *Review of Metaphysics*, 44 (1987), 77–103.

Kenny, A., 'Mental Health in Plato's *Republic*', repr. in A. Kenny, *The Anatomy of the Soul: Historical Essays in the Philosophy of Mind* (Oxford: Basil Blackwell, 1973), 1–27.

Moline, J., 'Episteme and the Psyche': ch. 3 (pp. 52–78) of J. Moline, *Plato's Theory of Understanding* (Madison: University of Wisconsin Press, 1981).

Penner, T., 'Socrates on Virtue and Motivation', in E. N. Lee *et al.* (eds.), *Exegesis and Argument* (*Phronesis* suppl. 1; 1973), 133–51.

Socrates and Thrasymachus

The opening shots of *Republic* have been extensively studied on their own. The following articles give some taste of the variety of views:

Boter, G. J., 'Thrasymachus and *Pleonexia*', *Mnemosyne*, 39 (1986), 261–81.

Kerferd, G. B., 'The Doctrine of Thrasymachus in Plato's *Republic*', *Durham University Journal*, 9 (1947), 19–27.

Maguire, J. P., 'Thrasymachus...or Plato?', *Phronesis*, 16 (1971), 142–63.

Nicholson, P. P., 'Unravelling Thrasymachus' Arguments in the *Republic*', *Phronesis*, 19 (1974), 210–32.

Poetry

Attempts to argue for some coherence in Plato's scattered remarks about art include:

Belfiore, E., 'A Theory of Imitation in Plato's *Republic*', *Transactions of the American Philological Association*, 114 (1984), 121–46.

Tate, J., ' "Imitation" in Plato's *Republic*', *Classical Quarterly*, 22 (1928), 16–23.

There is a good collection of essays:

Moravcsik, J. M. E., and Temko, P. (eds.), *Plato on Beauty, Wisdom and the Arts* (Totowa: Rowman and Littlefield, 1982).

And valuable contributions to the debate are made by:

Belfiore, E., ' "Lies Unlike the Truth": Plato on Hesiod, *Theogony* 27', *Transactions of the American Philological Association*, 115 (1985), 47–57.

Gallop, D., 'Image and Reality in Plato's *Republic*', *Archiv für Geschichte der Philosophie*, 47 (1965), 113–31.

Havelock, E. A., *Preface to Plato* (Oxford: Basil Blackwell, 1963), ch. 1 and 2; repr. without notes in A. Sesonske (ed.), *Plato's* Republic: *Interpretation and Criticism* (Belmont: Wadsworth, 1966), 116–35.

Moravcsik, J. M. E., 'On Correcting the Poets', *Oxford Studies in Ancient Philosophy*, 4 (1986), 35–47.

An instructive stroll through some aspects of Platonism, based loosely on the criticism of poetry, can be found in:

Murdoch, I., *The Fire and the Sun: Why Plato Banished the Artists* (Oxford: Oxford University Press, 1977).

Metaphysics

The reader can perhaps imagine the vast amount of debate that goes on about Plato's metaphysical views. The standard account is that of:

Ross, W. D., *Plato's Theory of Ideas* (London: Oxford University Press, 1951).

Two collections of essays are extremely valuable:

Allen, R. E. (ed.), *Studies in Plato's Metaphysics* (London: Routledge & Kegan Paul, 1965).

Vlastos, G. (ed.), *Plato: A Collection of Critical Essays*, i (Garden City: Anchor Books, 1971).

Two recent specialist book-length studies are worth mentioning for their interest, for their good bibliographies—and to illustrate the widely diverging conclusions scholars reach on these matters:

Malcolm, J., *Plato on the Self-Predication of Forms* (Oxford: Oxford University Press, 1991).

Patterson, R., *Image and Reality in Plato's Metaphysics* (Indianapolis: Hackett, 1985).

Of the many scholarly articles which are also concerned with various aspects of Plato's metaphysics, I would single out the following:

Brentlinger, J., 'Particulars in Plato's Middle Dialogues', *Archiv für Geschichte der Philosophie*, 54 (1972), 116–52.

Fine, G., 'The One over Many', *Philosophical Review*, 89 (1980), 197–240.

—— 'Separation', *Oxford Studies in Ancient Philosophy*, 2 (1984), 31–87.

—— 'Immanence', *Oxford Studies in Ancient Philosophy*, 4 (1986), 71–97.

Heinaman, R., 'Self-Predication in Plato's Middle Dialogues', *Phronesis*, 34 (1989), 56–79.

Irwin, T., 'Plato's Heracleiteanism', *Philosophical Quarterly*, 27 (1977), 1–13.

Ketchum, R. J., 'Plato on Real Being', *American Philosophical Quarterly*, 17 (1980), 213–20.

—— 'Plato on the Unknowability of the Sensible World', *History of Philosophy Quarterly*, 4 (1987), 291–305.

Nehamas, A., 'Plato on the Imperfection of the Sensible World', *American Philosophical Quarterly*, 12 (1975), 105–17.

—— 'Self-Predication and Plato's Theory of Forms', *American Philosophical Quarterly*, 16 (1979), 93–103.

—— 'Participation and Predication in Plato's Later Thought', *Review of Metaphysics*, 36 (1982), 343–74.

White, N. P., 'Perceptual and Objective Properties in Plato', in T. Penner and R. Kraut (eds.), *Nature, Knowledge and Virtue* (Edmonton: Academic Printing & Publishing, 1989 = *Apeiron* 22.4), 45–65.

Ideas expressed in *Republic* play an important part in the general debate about Plato's metaphysical views. Here again a number of articles may be mentioned:

Allen, R. E., 'The Argument from Opposites in *Republic* V', *Review of Metaphysics*, 15 (1961), 325–35.

Parry, R. D., 'The Uniqueness Proof for Forms in *Republic* X', *Journal of the History of Philosophy*, 23 (1985), 133–50.

White, F. C., 'The "Many" in *Republic* 475a–480a', *Canadian Journal of Philosophy*, 7 (1977), 291–306.

A particularly important article, which clarifies the role of goodness within Plato's metaphysics, is:

Santas, G. X., 'The Form of the Good in Plato's *Republic*', *Philosophical Inquiry*, 2 (1980), 374–403; repr. in J. P. Anton and A. Preus (eds.), *Essays in Ancient Greek Philosophy*, ii (Albany: State University of New York Press, 1983), 232–63.

Epistemology

Plato's views on knowledge are intrinsically bound up with his metaphysics, so the following works will all contribute to the debates covered in works mentioned in the previous section (and vice versa). A general survey of Plato's views on knowledge can be found in:

White, N. P., *Plato on Knowledge and Reality* (Indianapolis: Hackett, 1976).

An outstanding pair of articles on the general nature of Plato's approach to epistemology is:

Hintikka, J., 'Knowledge and its Objects in Plato', in J. M. E. Moravcsik (ed.), *Patterns in Plato's Thought* (Dordrecht: D. Reidel, 1973), 1–30; repr. in J. Hintikka, *Knowledge and the Known* (Dordrecht: D. Reidel, 1974), 1–30.

Santas, G. X., 'Hintikka on Knowledge and its Objects in Plato', in J. M. E. Moravcsik (ed.), *Patterns in Plato's Thought* (Dordrecht: D. Reidel, 1973), 31–51.

On the subject as a whole as it manifests in *Republic*, see:

Cooper, N., 'Between Knowledge and Ignorance', *Phronesis*, 31 (1986), 229–42.

Fine, G., 'Knowledge and Belief in *Republic* V', *Archiv für Geschichte der Philosophie*, 60 (1978), 121–39.

——— 'Knowledge and Belief in *Republic* V–VII', in S. Everson (ed.), *Companions to Ancient Thought*, i. *Epistemology* (Cambridge: Cambridge University Press, 1990), 85–115.

Gosling, J. C. B., '*Doxa* and *Dunamis* in Plato's *Republic*', *Phronesis*, 13 (1968), 119–30.

White, F. C., 'The Scope of Knowledge in *Republic* V', *Australasian Journal of Philosophy*, 62 (1984), 339–54.

The three striking images in Chapter 9 (the Sun, the Line, and the Cave) have been much discussed. Notable recent papers covering a range of views are:

Karasmanis, V., 'Plato's *Republic*: The Line and the Cave', *Apeiron*, 21 (1988), 147–71.

Malcolm, J., 'The Line and the Cave', *Phronesis*, 7 (1962), 38–45.

Morrison, J. S., 'Two Unresolved Difficulties in the Line and the Cave', *Phronesis*, 22 (1977), 212–31.

Strang, C., 'Plato's Analogy of the Cave', *Oxford Studies in Ancient Philosophy*, 4 (1986), 19–34.

Wilson, J. R. S., 'The Contents of the Cave', in R. Shiner and J. King-Farlow (eds.), *New Essays on Plato and the Presocratics* (*Canadian Journal of Philosophy* suppl. 2; 1976), 117–27.

And Plato's epistemological methodology is discussed in:

Hare, R. M., 'Plato and the Mathematicians', in R. Bambrough (ed.), *New Essays on Plato and Aristotle* (London: Routledge & Kegan Paul, 1965), 21–38.

Robinson, R., *Plato's Earlier Dialectic*, 2nd edn. (London: Oxford University Press, 1953).

Taylor, C. C. W., 'Plato and the Mathematicians: An Examination of Professor Hare's Views', *Philosophical Quarterly*, 17 (1967), 193–203.

REPUBLIC

Note

At some time in the early history of the transmission of the Greek text of *Republic* it was divided into ten 'books'; this was the work of a Greek scholar, not of Plato himself, and his criteria were, as much as anything, what would fit on to a single papyrus roll. The beginnings and endings of these books only partially coincide with major breaks in the sequence of arguments. Book I, for instance, ends where it should, at the end of Socrates' discussion with Thrasymachus; but Book IX begins in the middle of the discussion of the dictatorial type of person. In this translation I have dispensed with the division into books and have broken up the text into chapters whose beginnings and endings are dictated by the arguments themselves. I have given each chapter a title, for convenience.

For those who are interested, here is a list of the extents of the traditional ten books:

I. 327a–354c
II. 357a–383c
III. 386a–417b
IV. 419a–445e
V. 449a–480a
VI. 484a–511e
VII. 514a–541b
VIII. 543a–569c
IX. 571a–592b
X. 595a–621d

These ciphers, and those which appear throughout the book in the margins of the translation, are the standard means of precise reference to passages in Plato: they refer to the pages and sections of pages of the edition of Plato by Stephanus, or Henri Estienne (Geneva, 1578).

For the use of asterisks (*) and obelisks (†) in the course of the translation see the footnotes on pp. 3 and 27 respectively.

Chapter 1

Convention under Attack

The first chapter consists of a typical early Platonic dialogue: it was possibly originally written separately from the rest of the book. No firm conclusions are reached about the ostensible purpose of the enquiry—to discover the nature of morality—but the arguments are lively and interesting, and raise themes which will recur later in the book. Once the scene has been set, Socrates whittles away at the unthinking acceptance of conventional views on morality (represented by Cephalus and Polemarchus), before dealing more vigorously with the robust assault on convention (and on Socrates himself) delivered by the sophist Thrasymachus. Socrates accepts neither conventional nor unconventional views unless they survive his logical scrutiny; the ground is prepared for Plato's stress throughout Republic *on the importance of reason for morality.*

SOCRATES

Yesterday I went down to the Piraeus with Glaucon the son of 327a
Ariston to worship the goddess* and also because I wanted to see how they would conduct the festival on this, its first performance.* I was certainly impressed with the splendour of the procession made by the local people, but I have to say that the Thracians rose to the occasion just as well in their procession. Once our worshipping and watching were over, b
we were starting to make our way back to town, when Polemarchus the son of Cephalus spotted us from a distance setting off home, and he told his slave to run over to us and tell us to wait for him. The boy came up behind me, caught hold of my coat, and said, 'Polemarchus wants you to wait.'

I turned around and asked where his master was. 'There,' he said, 'coming up behind you. Please wait.'

'All right, we will,' said Glaucon.

Polemarchus soon caught up with us, and so did Glaucon's c

---

* An asterisk in the text indicates that there is a note in the section beginning on p. 380.

brother Adeimantus, Niceratus the son of Nicias, and some others; they had all apparently been at the procession.

'Socrates,' Polemarchus said, 'it looks to me as though the two of you are setting off back to town.'

'That's right,' I replied.

'Well,' he said, 'do you see how many of us there are?'

'Of course.'

'You'd better choose, then,' he said, 'between overpowering us and staying here.'

'Well, there *is* one further possibility,' I pointed out. 'We might convince you to let us leave.'

'Can you convince people who don't listen?' he asked.

'Impossible,' Glaucon replied.

'Then I think you should know that we won't be listening to you.'

328a 'Anyway,' Adeimantus added, 'don't you realize that there's going to be a horseback torch-race this evening for the goddess?'

'Horseback?' I said. 'That's unusual. Do you mean there'll be a horse-race in which they'll carry torches and pass them on to one another?'

'Precisely,' Polemarchus said. 'And they're also putting on an all-night celebration, which should be worth seeing.* We're going to go out to watch it after dinner, and lots of young men will be there too, whom we shall be talking to.* So you must b do as we suggest and stay.'

'It looks as though we'd better stay,' said Glaucon.

'Well, if you think so,' I said, 'then that's what we should do.'

So we went to Polemarchus' house, and there we found his brothers Lysias and Euthydemus, and also Thrasymachus of Chalcedon, Charmantides of Paeania, and Cleitophon the son of Aristonymus. Polemarchus' father Cephalus was in the house too; I thought he looked very old, but then I hadn't seen him c for quite a while. He was sitting on a chair with a cushion, and wearing a chaplet, since he had just been making a ritual offering in the courtyard.* Some other chairs had been placed in a circle there, so we sat down beside him.

As soon as Cephalus saw me, he said hello and then went on, 'Socrates, unfortunately for us, you're not in the habit of coming down to the Piraeus. You should, you know. I mean, if I still had the strength to make the journey up to town easily, you wouldn't have to come here, because I'd be visiting you. But as things are, you should come here more often. In my case, d you see, declining interest in physical pleasures is exactly matched by increasing desire for and enjoyment of conversation.* So please do as I ask: by all means spend time with these young men who are your companions, but treat us too as your friends—as your very close friends—and come here to visit us.'

'I certainly will, Cephalus,' I replied. 'I do in fact enjoy talking with very old people, because I think we ought to learn e from them. They've gone on ahead of us, as it were, on a road which we too will probably have to travel, and we ought to find out from them what the road is like—whether it is rough and hard, or easy and smooth. And I'd be especially glad to ask you your opinion about it, since you've reached the time of life the poets describe as being "on the threshold of old age".* Is it a difficult period of one's life, would you say, or what?'

'Of course I'll tell you my opinion, Socrates,' he said. 'You 329a see, it's not uncommon for some of us old men of approximately the same age to get together (and so vindicate the ancient proverb!).* These gatherings are invariably used for grumbling, by those who miss the pleasures of youth. They remind themselves of their love lives, drinking, feasting, and the like, and consequently complain of having been robbed of things that are important and claim that in those days they used to live well, whereas nowadays they aren't even alive. Others bleat about how their families treat old age like dirt; in fact, b this is the main reason they go on and on about all the evils for which old age is responsible. But to my mind, Socrates, they are holding an innocent responsible. If old age were to blame, then I too would have had the same experiences as them—at least as far as old age is concerned—and so would everyone else who has reached this age. But in the past I, at any rate, have met others like myself who do not feel this way. In particular, I was once with Sophocles the poet when someone asked him, "How c do you feel about sex, Sophocles? Are you still capable of having sex with a woman?" He replied, "Be quiet, man! To my great delight, I have broken free of that, like a slave who has got away from a rabid and savage master." I thought at the time that this was a good response, and I haven't changed my mind. I mean, there's no doubt that in old age you get a great deal of peace and freedom from things like sex. When the desires lose their intensity and ease up, then what happens is absolutely as Sophocles described—freedom from a great many

d demented masters. However, the one thing responsible for this, and for one's relationship with relatives as well, is not a person's old age, Socrates, but his character. If someone is self-disciplined and good-tempered, old age isn't too much of a burden; otherwise, it's not just a question of old age, Socrates—such a person will find life difficult when he's young as well.'

I was filled with admiration for him and his words, and
e because I wanted him to continue, I tried to provoke him by saying, 'Cephalus, I think that most people would react to what you're saying with scepticism; they'd think that you're finding old age easy to bear not because of your character, but because of your great wealth. The rich have many consolations, they say.'

'You're right,' he said, 'they are sceptical. And they do have a point, though not as important a point as they imagine. The story about Themistocles* is relevant here—how when the man from Seriphus was rudely saying that his fame was due not to

330a his own merits but to his city, he replied, "It's true that I wouldn't have become famous if I were a Seriphian, but it's also true that you wouldn't if you were an Athenian." The same principle applies to people who aren't rich and are finding old age hard to bear. It's true that a good man wouldn't find old age particularly easy to bear if he were poor, but it's also true that a bad man would never be content with himself even if he were wealthy.'

'Did you inherit most of your wealth, Cephalus,' I asked, 'or did you make it yourself?'

b 'What's that you say, Socrates?' he asked. 'Make it myself? As a businessman, I come between my grandfather and my father. My grandfather (after whom I'm named) inherited assets approximately equal to what I have now, and increased them considerably; my father Lysanias, however, decreased them to less than they are now. It'll make me happy if I leave these sons of mine not less, but a little more than I inherited.'*

6

'I'll tell you why I asked,' I said. 'It was because I got the impression that you don't particularly care for money, and this c is usually the mark of someone who hasn't made it himself, whereas people who have made it themselves are twice as attached to it as anyone else. Poets are attached to their own compositions, fathers to their sons; in the same way, business-men are concerned about money not only because it's useful (which is why everyone else is interested in it), but also because it is the product of their own labours. This makes them irritating to be with, since money is the only thing they're prepared to think highly of.'

'You're right,' he said.

'Yes,' I said. 'But there's another question I wanted to ask d you. What do you think is the greatest benefit you've gained from being rich?'

'Something which many people might find implausible,' he answered. 'You see, Socrates, when thoughts of death start to impinge on a person's mind, he entertains fears and worries about things which never occurred to him before. In the past he used to laugh at the stories that are told about what goes on in Hades—about how someone who has done wrong here is bound to be punished there—but now they trouble his mind, in e case they might be true. This might be due to the weakness of old age or it might be because, now that he's closer to the next world, he sees it more clearly; the result is that he becomes filled with anxiety and fear, and starts to make calculations and to see if he has wronged anyone in any way. Anyone who discovers that during his life he has committed a lot of crimes wakes up constantly in terror from his dreams, as children do, and also lives in dread; on the other hand, anyone who is 331a aware of no wrong in himself faces the future with confidence and optimism which, as Pindar* says as well, "comforts him in old age". To my mind, Socrates, he expresses it beautifully when he says that anyone who has spent his life behaving morally and justly has "Sweet hope as a companion, joyfully fostering his heart, comforting him in old age—hope which steers, more than anything else does, men's fickle intention." This is incredibly well put. And this is the context in which I value the possession of money so highly—at least for a decent, orderly person. I mean, the possession of money has a major b

7

role to play if one is to avoid cheating or lying against one's better judgement, and also avoid the fear of leaving this life still owing some ritual offerings to a god or some money to someone. It serves a lot of other purposes too, but all things considered I'd say that for an intelligent person, Socrates, wealth is particularly useful in this far from insignificant context.'*

c   'A thoroughly commendable sentiment, Cephalus,' I said. 'But what about this thing you mentioned, doing right?* Shall we say that it is, without any qualification, truthfulness and giving back anything one has borrowed from someone? Or might the performance of precisely these actions sometimes be right, but sometimes wrong? This is the kind of thing I mean. I'm sure everyone would agree that if you'd borrowed weapons from a friend who was perfectly sane, but he went insane and then asked for the weapons back, you shouldn't give them back, and if you were to give them back you wouldn't be doing right, and neither would someone who was ready to tell the whole truth to a person like that.'

d   'You're right,' he agreed.

'It follows that this isn't the definition of morality, to tell the truth and to give back whatever one has borrowed.'

'Yes, it is, Socrates,' Polemarchus interjected. 'At least, it is if we're to believe Simonides.'

'Well now,' said Cephalus, 'I shall pass the discussion on to you two, since it's time for me to attend to the ceremony.'*

'And shall I be your heir?' asked Polemarchus.

'Of course,' he said with a chuckle, and promptly left for the ceremony.

In a manner strongly reminiscent of Plato's earlier dialogues, Socrates draws inferences about morality by assuming that it is an area of expertise, and that what holds good for other areas of expertise will hold good for morality as well. Polemarchus could have denied that morality has a single field of operation, as crafts do: morality might have some broader function in human relationships, or its purpose might be something general, like promoting happiness. Lacking this insight, Polemarchus is tied into paradoxical knots. In a startling anticipation of Christian ethics (prefigured in the dialogues Crito *and* Gorgias), *Socrates finally concludes that it is never right to harm anyone under any circumstances.*

8

'Well then,' I told him, 'now that you've inherited the dis- e
cussion, tell us what it is that Simonides says which you think
is an accurate statement about morality.'

'That it is right to give anyone back what you owe them,' he
said. 'In my opinion, this is a fine remark.'*

'Well,' I said, 'it isn't easy to disagree with Simonides: he's a
clever man—superhumanly so. But while *you* may understand
what he means by this, Polemarchus, I don't. I mean, he
obviously doesn't mean what we were talking about a moment
ago, the returning of something one has been lent to someone
insane who's asking for it back. And yet something lent is 332a
owed, wouldn't you say?'

'Yes.'

'And if the person asking for it back is insane, it's
inconceivable that it should be given back, isn't it?'

'True,' he replied.

'Then apparently it wasn't this, but something else, that
Simonides meant by the assertion that it is right to give back
what is owed.'

'Yes, of course it was something else,' he said. 'His view is
that friends owe friends good deeds, not bad ones.'

'I see,' I said. 'So if someone gives money back to someone
who lent it to him, and this repayment and returning turns out
to be harmful, and both the giver and the receiver are friends, b
then this is not a case of giving back what is owed: is this
Simonides' meaning, according to you?'

'Yes, exactly.'

'Now, should we give back what is owed to our enemies?'

'Oh, yes,' he said. 'What is owed to them—yes, absolutely.
And what an enemy owes an enemy, I think, is also what is
appropriate—something bad.'*

'There was apparently a certain obscurity, then, in Simonides'
definition of morality,' I remarked. 'How typical of a poet! c
Although, as it turns out, he meant that it is right to give back
to people what is appropriate for them, he called it what is
owed to them.'

'I'm surprised you thought any different,' he said.

'But listen,' I said, 'suppose he were asked, "So, Simonides,
take the art that we know as medicine. What is it? What does it

give that is owed and appropriate, and to what does it give it?"
What do you suppose his reply to us would be?'

'Obviously,' he answered, 'he'd reply that it is the art of
giving drugs, food, and drink to bodies.'

'What about cookery? What art do we say it is? What does it
give that is owed and appropriate, and to what does it give it?'

d 'It gives taste to cooked food.'

'All right. So which art—the art of giving what to what—
might we call morality?'

'In order to be consistent with what was said earlier,
Socrates,' he replied, 'it has to be the art of giving benefit and
harm to friends and enemies respectively.'

'So Simonides claims that morality is doing good to one's
friends and harm to one's enemies, does he?'

'I think so.'

'Now, where sickness and health are concerned, who is best
able to do good to his friends and harm to his enemies when
they aren't well?'

'A doctor.'

e 'And where the risks of a sea voyage are concerned, when
friends are on board a ship?'

'A ship's captain.'

'And what about a moral person? In which walk of life or for
what activity is he best able to benefit his friends and harm his
enemies?'

'In fighting against enemies and in support of friends, I'd
say.'

'All right. Now, my dear Polemarchus, a doctor is no use
unless people are ill.'

'True.'

'And a captain is no use unless people are on a sea voyage.'

'Quite so.'

'Is a moral person, then, no use to anyone who is not at
war?'

'No, I don't agree with that.'

'So morality is useful during times of peace too?'

333a 'Yes.'

'And so is farming. Yes?'

'Yes.'

'To provide us with crops?'

'Yes.'

'And shoemaking too?'

'Yes.'

'To provide us with shoes, I imagine you'd say?'

'Exactly.'

'All right, then. What can we use morality for? What does it provide us with? What would you say morality is good for in times of peace?'

'For business contracts, Socrates.'

'By business contracts do you mean when people enter into association with one another, or what?'

'Yes, when people enter into association with one another.'

'So when there's a move to make in backgammon, is it a b moral person, or an expert backgammon player, who is a good and useful associate?'

'An expert backgammon player.'

'And when it's a question of the positioning of bricks and stones, is a moral person a better and more useful associate than a builder?'

'Not at all.'

'Well, what kind of association is it that people enter into for which a moral person is a better associate than a builder or a musician? I mean, analogously to how a musician is better than a moral person when it comes to an association over melodies.'

'An association involving money, in my opinion.'

'Yes, Polemarchus, but what about when money is put to use? When you jointly need to buy or sell a horse, for instance, then I suppose an expert in horses is a better associate, don't c you think?'

'I suppose so.'

'And if you need to buy or sell a ship, then it's a shipwright or a sailor?'

'You could be right.'

'For what joint usage of money, then, is a moral person more useful than anyone else?'

'When we want to put it on deposit and have it in safe keeping, Socrates.'

'You mean when you don't want to put it to use, but just to have it in store?'

'Yes.'

'So morality is useful in relation to money at precisely the
d time when money is not in use?'

'So it seems.'

'Furthermore, when a pruning-knife needs to be kept safe,
then morality is useful (whether you're on your own or have an
associate); but when it needs using, then it's viticulture that is
useful. Yes?'

'I suppose so.'

'And would you also say that when a shield or a lyre needs to
be protected and kept unused, then morality is useful, whereas
when they need using, then military or musical expertise is
useful?'

'Of course.'

'In every instance, then, morality is useless when anything is
being used, and useful when anything is not being used.'

'So it seems.'

e   'Morality can't be a very important thing, then, can it, my
friend, if it is useful for useless objects. And there's another
point for us to consider. In a fight—a boxing-match or any
other kind of fight—isn't it the person who is expert at hitting
who is also expert at protecting himself?'

'Yes.'

'And isn't it the person who knows how to give protection
from a disease who is also the expert at secretly inducing the
disease?'

'I would say so.'

334a   'Moreover, it's one and the same person who's good at
protecting an army and at stealing the enemy's plans and out-
witting the rest of his projects, isn't it?'

'Yes.'

'So anything one is good at protecting, one is also good at
stealing.'

'So it seems.'

'If a moral person is good at protecting money, therefore,
he's also good at stealing it.'*

'That's what the argument suggests, anyway,' he said.

'Morality has been exposed, then,' I said. 'A moral person is
a kind of thief, apparently. You probably got this notion from
b Homer. He speaks warmly of Autolycus, Odysseus' grandfather
on his mother's side, and also says that he surpassed everyone

12

"at theft and perjury".* So the view that morality is a kind of stealing is yours, Homer's, and Simonides'—with the qualification that it must be done to benefit friends and harm enemies. Was this what you meant?'

'It most certainly was not,' he said, 'but I'm no longer sure what I meant. I do still think this, however—that morality lies in helping one's friends and harming one's enemies.'

'When you say "friends", do you mean those who appear to c a person to be good, or those who genuinely are good (even if they don't appear to be)? And likewise for enemies.'*

'It seems plausible to suggest', he said, 'that one treats as friends those one regards as good, and as enemies those one regards as bad.'

'Isn't it common to make mistakes about this, and think that people are good when they aren't, and vice versa?'

'Yes.'

'When this happens, then, doesn't one regard good people as enemies and bad people as friends?'

'Yes.'

'But all the same, in these circumstances it's right for one to help bad people and harm good people, is it?' d

'Apparently.'

'But good people are moral and not the kind to do wrong.'

'True.'

'On your line of reasoning, then, it's right to harm people who do no wrong.'

'Not at all, Socrates,' he said. 'My reasoning must be flawed, I suppose.'

'It's right to harm wrongdoers, then,' I said, 'and to help those who do right?'

'That sounds better.'

'But since there are lots of people who are completely mistaken, Polemarchus, then it will commonly turn out to be e right for people to harm friends (whom they regard as bad) and to help enemies (whom they regard as good). And in affirming this, we'll be contradicting what we said Simonides meant.'

'Yes,' he said, 'that is a consequence of what we're saying. Let's change tack, however: we're probably making a wrong assumption about friends and enemies.'

'What assumption, Polemarchus?'

'That someone who appears good is a friend.'

'What shall we change that to instead?' I asked.

'That someone who doesn't just appear good, but actually *is* good, is a friend; and that someone who seems good, but 335a actually isn't, is an apparent friend, not a genuine one. And the same goes for enemies.'

'So on this line of reasoning, it's a good man who is a friend, and a bad man who is an enemy.'

'Yes.'

'You're telling us, then, that our original description of morality, when we said that it was right to do good to a friend and harm to an enemy, was incomplete. Now you want us to add that it is right to do good to a friend, provided he is good, and to harm an enemy, provided he is bad. Is that right?'

b 'Yes,' he said, 'I think that's a good way to put it.'

'Can a moral person harm *anyone*?' I asked.*

'Yes, he can,' he replied. 'He has to harm bad men, people who are his enemies.'

'When horses are harmed, do they improve or deteriorate?'

'Deteriorate.'

'In respect of a state of goodness for dogs or of a state of goodness for horses?'

'In respect of a state of goodness for horses.'

'So the same goes for dogs too: when they are harmed, they deteriorate in respect of what it is to be a good dog, not in respect of what it is to be a good horse. Is that right?'

'No doubt about it.'

c 'And where people are concerned, my friend, shouldn't we say that when they're harmed they deteriorate in respect of what it is to be a good human?'

'Yes.'

'And isn't a moral person a good human?'

'There's no doubt about that either.'

'It necessarily follows, Polemarchus, that people who are harmed become less moral.'

'So it seems.'

'Now, can musicians use music to make people unmusical?'*

'Impossible.'

'Can skilled horsemen use their skill to make people bad horsemen?'

'No.'

'So can moral people use morality to make people immoral? Or in general can good people use their goodness to make d people bad?'*

'No, that's impossible.'

'I imagine this is because cooling things down, for instance, is not the function of warmth but of its opposite.'

'Yes.'

'And moistening things is not the function of dryness but of its opposite.'

'Yes.'

'So harming people is not the function of a good person, but of his opposite.'

'I suppose so.'

'And is a moral person a good person?'

'Of course.'

'It is not the job of a moral person, then, Polemarchus, to harm a friend or anyone else; it is the job of his opposite, an immoral person.'

'I think you're absolutely correct, Socrates,' he said.

'So the claim that it's right and moral to give back to people e what they are owed—if this is taken to mean that a moral person owes harm to his enemies and help to his friends—turns out to be a claim no clever person would make. I mean, it's false: we've found that it is never right to harm anyone.'

'I agree,' he said.

'You and I will join forces, then,' I said, 'to combat anyone who asserts that it is the view of Simonides or Bias or Pittacus or anyone else who is so sublimely clever.'

'Yes,' he said, 'I'm ready to play my part in the battle.'

'Do you know whose view I think it is,' I said, 'that it's right 336a to help one's friends and harm one's enemies?'

'Whose?' he asked.

'I think it was Periander or Perdiccas or Xerxes or Ismenias of Thebes or someone else like that—a rich man who fancied himself to be vastly powerful.'*

'You're quite right,' he said.

'All right,' I said. 'Now that we've found that being moral and doing right don't consist in this, can we come up with an alternative definition?'

15

Thrasymachus now bursts into the picture. Plato's portrait of Thrasymachus is patently unfavourable, but his position is at least forcefully argued and defended. Socrates first shows that his position—that morality is a convention to enable the stronger party to get the weaker party to act to the stronger party's advantage—cannot be universally true. Thrasymachus intends his view to be a cynical comment on the dog-eat-dog nature of the real world, but is now forced to admit that his views only really apply to ideal, infallible rulers. With a weak inference based on the art of medicine, Socrates concludes that no arts, including morality, are self-serving, but that they all look out for their subjects' interests.

b   Now, Thrasymachus had often made as if to interrupt us in mid-sentence and pounce on the argument, but he'd always been restrained by his neighbours, who had wanted to hear the discussion out. But when we did come to a break, and I'd asked this question, he could no longer remain silent: like a wild animal, he crouched and hurled himself at us as if to tear us apart.

Polemarchus and I were terrified and panic-stricken, but Thrasymachus bellowed out for all to hear, 'What a lot of
c drivel, Socrates! Why are you deferentially bowing and scraping to each other like simpletons? If you really want to know what morality is, then don't just ask questions and look for applause by refuting any and every answer you get, because you've realized that it's easier to ask questions than it is to answer them. No, state an opinion yourself: say what you think morality is. And make sure you state your view clearly and
d precisely, without saying that it is duty or benefit or profit or gain or advantage; I won't let you get away with any rubbish like that.'

I was scared stiff at his words, and I looked at him in fear. I think that if I hadn't seen him before he saw me, I'd have been unable to speak.* But in fact I had got in the first look, when he originally began to get furious at the discussion, and so I
e was able to respond to him. 'Thrasymachus,' I said, trembling with fear, 'please don't be cross with us. If Polemarchus and I are going wrong anywhere in the course of investigating the ideas, I assure you that we don't mean to. You can imagine that, if we were looking for money, we wouldn't under any circumstances choose to defer to each other in the course of the

search and ruin our chances of finding it. It is morality we are looking for, however, and this is more valuable than pots of money; so you shouldn't think that we'd be so stupid as to give in to each other and not do our level best to discover it. Believe me, Thrasymachus, we're doing all we can. If we lack competence—which I suppose is the case—then pity is a far more reasonable feeling for you experts to have for us than impatience.' 337a

He erupted into highly sarcastic laughter at my words and said, 'God, there goes Socrates again, pretending to be an ignoramus! I knew this would happen; I even told the others here some time ago that you wouldn't be prepared to express opinions, and would feign ignorance and do anything rather than answer a question put to you.'

'That's because you're clever, Thrasymachus,' I said. 'You were well aware of the fact that if you were to ask someone what twelve is, and were to add as a rider to the question, "And just make sure you avoid saying that twelve is two times b six, or three times four, or six times two, or four times three. I won't let you get away with any nonsense like that"—well, I'm sure it was obvious to you that no one would answer a question phrased like that. But suppose this person said, "What do you mean, Thrasymachus? You don't want me to give any of the answers you've mentioned? But what if twelve really is one of those things, Thrasymachus? Shall I still avoid that answer— that is, not tell the truth? Or what would you have me do?" How would you respond to this?' c

'Well,' he said, 'it's not as if the two cases were similar.'

'Why not?' I replied. 'Anyway, even if they aren't, and it's only that the person you've asked thinks they are, do you think that makes any difference? Won't he still state his opinion, whether or not we rule it out?'

'That's what you're going to do as well, is it?' he asked. 'Respond with one of the answers I ruled out?'

'I wouldn't be surprised if I decided to do that, once I'd looked into the matter,' I said.

'What if I were to demonstrate that there's another answer d you can give about morality,' he asked, 'which isn't any of those answers and is better than any of them? What penalty would you expect?'*

17

'The penalty which is appropriate for ignorance, of course,' I said, 'which is learning from an expert. That's the penalty I expect.'

'Don't be naïve,' he said. 'You can't just learn: you must pay for it too.'

'If I ever have the money,* I will,' I said.

'He has it,' said Glaucon. 'We'll all help Socrates out financially, so as far as the money is concerned, Thrasymachus, go ahead and speak.'

e   'Oh yes, sure!' he said. 'So that Socrates can get his way and not make any claims himself, while he attacks and criticizes someone else's claims.'

'That's because I have no choice, Thrasymachus,' I explained. 'How can anyone express a view when he's not only ignorant, but also admits his ignorance? Moreover, when he's been forbidden to mention any opinion he might happen to hold by a man of considerable calibre? No, it's you who ought to

338a speak, really, since you do claim to have knowledge and to be able to express it. So please do what I'm asking: if you state your view, you'll be doing me a favour, and also generously teaching Glaucon here and all the others too.'

My words prompted Glaucon and the others to urge him to do what I was asking, and although it was clear that Thrasymachus wanted to be heard (since he thought he had an impressive position to state, which would win him acclaim), yet he continued to dissemble and to argue that it should be me who stated my position. Eventually, however, he gave

b in, and then added, 'Now you can see what Socrates is good at—he refuses to do any teaching himself, but he goes around learning from other people and doesn't even give them thanks in return.'

'You're quite right to say that I learn from other people, Thrasymachus,' I said, 'but quite wrong to say that I don't repay them with gratitude. I pay what I can—and compliments are all I can give, since I don't have money. If I think someone has a good idea, I'm quick to applaud it—as you'll find out very soon when you tell us your opinion, since I'm sure it will be a good one.'

c   'All right, then, listen to this,' he said. 'My claim is that morality is nothing other than the advantage of the stronger party . . . Well, why aren't you applauding?* No, you won't let yourself do that.'

'First I need to understand your meaning,' I told him. 'I don't yet. You say that right is the advantage of the stronger party, but what on earth do you mean by this, Thrasymachus? Surely you're not claiming, in effect, that if Poulydamas the pancratiast* is stronger than us and it's to his advantage, for the sake of his physique, to eat beef, then this food is advantageous, and therefore right, for us too, who are weaker d than him?'

'Foul tactics, Socrates,' he said, 'to interpret what I say in the way which allows you unscrupulously to distort it most.'

'No, you've got me wrong, Thrasymachus,' I said. 'I just want you to explain yourself better.'

'Don't you know, then,' he said, 'that some countries are dictatorships, some are democracies, and some are aristocracies?'

'Of course I do.'

'And that what has power in any given country is the government?'

'Yes.'

'Now, each government passes laws with a view to its own e advantage: a democracy makes democratic laws, a dictatorship makes dictatorial laws, and so on and so forth. In so doing, each government makes it clear that what is right and moral for its subjects is what is to its own advantage; and each government punishes anyone who deviates from what is advantageous to itself as if he were a criminal and a wrongdoer. So, Socrates, this is what I claim morality is: it is the same in every country, and it is what is to the advantage of the current government. 339a Now, of course, it's the current government which has power, and the consequence of this, as anyone who thinks about the matter correctly can work out, is that morality is everywhere the same—the advantage of the stronger party.'

'Now I see what you mean,' I said. 'And I'll try to see whether or not your claim is true. Your position too, Thrasymachus, is that morality is advantage—despite the fact that you ruled this answer out for me—except that you immediately add "of the stronger party".'

'Hardly a trivial addition,' he said.   b

'Whether or not it is important isn't yet clear. What *is* clear is that we must try to find out whether your claim is true. The point is that I agree that morality is some kind of advantage,* but you are qualifying this and claiming that it is the advantage of the stronger party; since I haven't made up my mind about this qualified version, we must look into the matter.'

'Go ahead,' he said.

'All right,' I said. 'Here's a question for you: you're also claiming, I assume, that obedience to the government is right?'

'Yes, I am.'

c 'And is the government in every country infallible, or are they also capable of error?'

'They are certainly capable of error,' he said.

'So when they turn to legislation, they sometimes get it right, and sometimes wrong?'

'Yes, I suppose so.'

'When they get it right, the laws they make will be to their advantage, but when they get it wrong, the laws will be to their disadvantage. Is that what you're saying?'

'Yes.'

'And you're also saying that their subjects must act in accordance with any law that is passed, and that this constitutes doing right?'

'Of course.'

d 'Then it follows from your line of argument that it is no more right to act to the advantage of the stronger party than it is to do the opposite, to act to their disadvantage.'

'What are you saying?' he asked.

'Exactly the same as you, I think; but let's have a closer look. We're agreed that sometimes, when a government orders its subjects to do things, it is utterly mistaken about its own best interest, but that it's right for the subjects to act in accordance with any order issued by the government. Isn't that what we agreed?'

'Yes, I suppose so.'

e 'Then you must also suppose', I continued, 'that you have agreed that it is right to do things which are not to the advantage of the government and the stronger party. When the rulers mistakenly issue orders which are bad for themselves, and since you claim that it is right for people to act in conformity with all the government's orders, then, my dear

Thrasymachus, doesn't it necessarily follow that it is right to do the opposite of what your position affirmed? I mean, the weaker party is being ordered to do what is disadvantageous to the stronger party, obviously.'

'Yes, Socrates,' said Polemarchus, 'that's perfectly clear.'   340a

'Of course,' Cleitophon interrupted, 'if you're going to act as a witness for Socrates.'

'There's no need for a witness,' Polemarchus replied. 'Thrasymachus himself admits that rulers sometimes issue orders which are bad for themselves, and that it's right for people to carry out these orders.'

'That's because Thrasymachus maintained that it was right to carry out the rulers' instructions, Polemarchus.'

'Yes, Cleitophon, and he also maintained that right is the advantage of the stronger party. And once he'd affirmed both b of these propositions, he also agreed that sometimes the stronger party tells the weaker party, which is subject to it, to do things which are disadvantageous to it. And from these premises it follows that morality is no more what is advantageous to the stronger party than it is what is disadvantageous to the stronger party.'

'But,' Cleitophon said, 'what he meant by the advantage of the stronger party was what the stronger party *thinks* is to its advantage. This is what he was maintaining the weaker party ought to do, and this is what he was maintaining morality is.'

'But that's not what he said,' Polemarchus remarked.

'Never mind, Polemarchus,' I said. 'If this is what c Thrasymachus is saying now, then let's accept it as his view. But do please tell me, Thrasymachus: *did* you mean to define morality as what appears to the stronger party to be to its advantage, whether or not it really is to its advantage? Is that how we are to understand your meaning?'

'Absolutely not!' he protested.* 'Do you suppose I would describe someone who makes mistakes as the stronger party when he is making a mistake?'

'Yes,' I replied, 'I did think you were saying this, when you agreed that rulers are not infallible, but also make mistakes.'

'That's because you're a bully* in discussions, Socrates,' he d said. 'I mean, to take the first example that comes to mind, do you describe someone who makes mistakes about his patients

21

as a doctor in virtue of the fact that he makes mistakes? Or do you describe someone who makes mistakes in his calculations as a mathematician, at precisely the time when he is making a mistake, and in virtue of the mistake that he is making? It's true that the expression is in our language: we say that a doctor or a mathematician or a teacher makes mistakes; but in fact, in my
e opinion, to the extent that each of them is what we call him, he never makes mistakes. And the consequence of this is that, strictly speaking—and you're the stickler for verbal precision— no professional makes mistakes: a mistake is due to a failure of knowledge, and for as long as that lasts he is not a professional. Professional, expert, ruler—no ruler makes a mistake at precisely the time when he is ruling, despite the universal usage of expressions like "The doctor made a mistake" or "The ruler made a mistake". So, when I stated my position to you recently, you should appreciate that I too was speaking like that; but the most precise formulation is in fact that a ruler, to
341a the extent that he is a ruler, does not make mistakes; and in not making mistakes he passes laws which are in his best interest; and any subject of his should act in conformity with these laws. Consequently, as I said in the first place, my position is that morality is acting to the advantage of the stronger party.'

'Well, Thrasymachus,' I said, 'so you think I'm a bully, do you?'

'Yes, I do,' he said.

'And that's because you think my questions were premeditated attempts to wrong you?'

'I'm certain of it,' he said. 'And you won't gain any advantage
b from it, firstly because I'm aware of your unscrupulous tactics, and secondly because as long as I am aware of them, you won't be able to use the argument to batter me down.'

'My dear Thrasymachus,' I protested, 'the idea would never even occur to me! But we must make sure that this situation doesn't arise again, so please would you make something perfectly clear? Is it, according to you, the ruler and the stronger person in the loose sense, or in what you were just calling the precise sense, whose interest, since he is the stronger party, it is right for the weaker party to act in?'

'I'm talking about the ruler in the most precise sense possible,' he replied. 'You can do anything you like, as far as I'm concerned, so try your unscrupulous and bullying tactics on that, if you can! But you don't stand a chance.'

'Do you think I'm crazy enough to try to shave a lion* and c bully Thrasymachus?' I asked.

'Well, you tried just now,' he said, 'even though you're a nonentity at that too.'

'That's enough of that sort of remark,' I said. 'But let's take this doctor you were talking about a short while ago—the one who's a doctor in the strict sense of the term. Is he a businessman, or someone who attends to sick people? Think about the genuine doctor, please.'

'He attends to sick people,' he replied.

'What about a ship's captain? Is the true captain in charge of sailors or a sailor?'

'In charge of sailors.'

'In other words, we shouldn't take any account of the fact d that he is on board a ship and describe him as a sailor. I mean, it isn't because he's on a ship that he's called a captain, but because of his expertise and because he has authority over the sailors.'

'True,' he said.

'Now, does each of the various parties in these situations have a particular advantage to gain?'

'Yes.'

'And isn't it the case,' I went on, 'that the *raison d'être* of a branch of expertise is to consider the welfare and interest of each party and then procure it?'

'Yes, that is what expertise is for,' he answered.*

'Is there anything which is in the interest of any branch of expertise except being as perfect as possible?'

'I don't understand the question.'   e

'For instance,' I said, 'suppose you were to ask me whether it's enough for the body just to be the body, or whether it needs anything else. I'd reply, "There's no doubt at all that it needs something else. That's why the art of medicine has been invented, because the body is flawed and it isn't enough for it to be like that. The branch of expertise has been developed precisely for the purpose of procuring the body's welfare." Would this reply of mine be correct, do you think, or not?' I asked.

'Yes, it would,' he said.

342a 'Well now, is medicine itself flawed? Are all branches of expertise imperfect? For instance, eyes need sight and ears need hearing, and that's why they need a branch of expertise* to consider their welfare in precisely these respects and to procure it. Is expertise itself somehow inherently flawed as well, so that each branch of expertise needs a further branch to consider its welfare, and this supervisory branch needs yet another one, and so on *ad infinitum*? Or does every art consider its own interest

b and welfare? Or is the whole question of it, or another art, being needed to consider its welfare in view of its flaws irrelevant, in the sense that no branch of expertise is flawed or faulty in the slightest, and it's inappropriate for any branch of expertise to investigate the welfare of anything other than its own area of expertise? In other words, any branch of expertise is flawless and perfect, provided it's a genuine branch of expertise—that is, as long as it wholly is what it is, nothing more and nothing less.* Please consider this issue with the same strict use of language we were using before, and tell me: am I right or not?'

'I think you're right,' he said.

c 'It follows, then,' I said, 'that medicine does not consider the welfare of medicine, but the welfare of the body.'

'Yes,' he said.

'And horsemanship considers the welfare of horses, not of horsemanship. In short, no branch of expertise considers its own advantage, since it isn't deficient in any respect: it considers the welfare of its area of expertise.'

'So it seems,' he said.

'But surely, Thrasymachus, the branches of expertise have authority and power over their particular areas of expertise.'

He gave his assent to this with extreme reluctance.

'So no branch of knowledge considers or enjoins the advantage of the stronger party, but the advantage of the weaker

d party, which is subject to it.'

Eventually, he agreed to this too, although he tried to argue against it. Once he'd agreed, however, I said, 'Surely, then, no doctor, in his capacity as doctor, considers or enjoins what is advantageous to the doctor, but what is advantageous to the patient? I mean, we've agreed that a doctor, in the strict sense of the term, is in charge of bodies, not a businessman. Isn't that what we agreed?'

He concurred.

'And a ship's captain too is, strictly speaking, in charge of sailors, not a sailor?'

He agreed.

'So since captains are like this and wield authority in this way, they won't consider and enjoin the interest of the captain, but what is advantageous to the sailor, the subject.'

He reluctantly agreed.

'Therefore, Thrasymachus,' I said, 'no one in any other kind of authority either, in his capacity as ruler, considers or enjoins his own advantage, but the advantage of his subject, the person for whom he practises his expertise. Everything he says and everything he does is said and done with this aim in mind and with regard to what is advantageous to and appropriate for this person.'

Socrates has tried to reduce Thrasymachus' position to the relatively trivial claims that rulers rule in their own interest, and that morality is obeying rulers. Thrasymachus therefore changes his formulation, but not his tack. The important thing about morality being to someone else's advantage, he says, is that it shows that morality is a bad thing, and weak, and unprofitable to its possessor. Socrates' inability (or possibly artificial refusal) to distinguish higher-order arts from lower-order ones (see p. 8) results in the strange position that profit-making is a separate art, so that (again) no art—or at least no art other than profit-making—seeks the profit or advantage of the artisan.

Once we'd reached this point in the discussion, it was 343a perfectly clear to everyone that the definition of morality had been turned upside down. Thrasymachus didn't respond to my last remarks, but instead said, 'Tell me, Socrates, do you have a nurse?'

'What?' I asked. 'Shouldn't you come up with some response rather than this question?'

'The point is,' he said, 'that she takes no notice of your runny nose and lets it dribble on when it needs wiping, when you can't even tell her the difference between sheep and shepherd.'

'I haven't the faintest idea what you're getting at,' I said.

b 'What I'm getting at is your notion that shepherds or cowherds consider what is good for their sheep or their cows, and fatten them up and look after them, with any aim in mind other than what is good for their masters and for themselves; and also at your supposition that the attitude which people with political authority—who are the real rulers*— have towards their subjects differs in the slightest from how one might feel about sheep, and that what they consider day and night is anything other than their own advantage and how

c to gain it. You're so far off understanding right and wrong, and morality and immorality, that you don't even realize that morality and right are actually good for someone else—they are the advantage of the stronger party, the ruler—and bad for the underling at the receiving end of the orders. Nor do you realize that the opposite is true for immorality: the wrongdoer lords it over those moral simpletons—that's what they are, really—while his subjects do what is to his advantage, since he is stronger, and make him happy by doing his bidding, but don't further their own happiness in the slightest.

d 'You fool, Socrates, don't you see? In any and every situation, a moral person is worse off than an immoral one. Suppose, for instance, that they're doing some business together, which involves one of them entering into association with the other: by the time the association is dissolved, you'll never find the moral person up on the immoral one—he'll be worse off. Or again, in civic matters, if there's a tax on property,* then a moral person pays more tax than an immoral one even when they're both equally well off; and if there's a hand-out, then the

e one gets nothing, while the other makes a lot. And when each of them holds political office,* even if a moral person loses out financially in no other way, his personal affairs deteriorate through neglect, while his morality stops him making any profit from public funds, and moreover his family and friends fall out with him over his refusal to help them out in unfair ways; in all these respects, however, an immoral person's experience is the opposite.

'I'm talking about the person I described a short while ago,

344a the one with the power to secure huge advantages for himself. This is the person you should consider, if you want to assess the extent to which immorality rather than morality is personally advantageous—and this is something you'll appreciate most easily if you look at immorality in its most perfect form and see how it enhances a wrongdoer's life beyond measure, but ruins the lives of his victims, who haven't the stomach for crime, to the same degree. It's dictatorship I mean, because whether it takes stealth or overt violence, a dictator steals what doesn't belong to him—consecrated and unconsecrated objects, private possessions, and public property—and does so not on a small scale, but comprehensively. Anyone who is caught com- b mitting the merest fraction of these crimes is not only punished, but thoroughly stigmatized as well: small-scale criminals who commit these kinds of crimes are called temple-robbers,* kidnappers, burglars, thieves, and robbers. On the other hand, when someone appropriates the assets of the citizen body and then goes on to rob them of their very freedom and enslave them, then denigration gives way to congratulation, and it isn't only his fellow citizens who call him happy, but anyone else c who hears about his consummate wrongdoing does so as well. The point is that immorality has a bad name because people are afraid of being at the receiving end of it, not of doing it.

'So you see, Socrates, immorality—if practised on a large enough scale—has more power, licence, and authority than morality. And as I said at the beginning, morality is really the advantage of the stronger party, while immorality is profitable and advantageous to oneself.'

After flooding our ears, like an attendant in the baths, with d this torrential gush of words, Thrasymachus was thinking of leaving. No one there would let him go, however: they forced him to stay and justify what he'd been saying. I myself was particularly insistent. 'My dear Thrasymachus,' I said, 'you surely aren't thinking of leaving? You can't just pelt us with words, so to speak, and then leave before adequately demonstrating—or before finding out yourself—whether or not they're true. Or do you think that what you're attempting to define is a trivial matter, and not† how anyone can live his life e in the most rewarding manner?'

'Am I disagreeing with you?' Thrasymachus protested.

'You do give that impression,' I replied, 'unless it's just us

---

† An obelisk indicates a textual note in the section starting on p. 460.

you don't care about in the slightest, and you don't spare a thought for whether our ignorance of what you're claiming to know will make us live better or worse lives. No, Thrasymachus, 345a please do your best to enlighten us too: it won't turn out badly for you to do so many of us a favour. I'll tell you my position: I'm not convinced. I do not think that immorality is more profitable than morality, not even if it is given free rein and never prevented from getting its own way; and even if I grant you your immoral person, Thrasymachus, with the power to do wrong either by stealth or by brute force, for my part I'm still not convinced that it is more profitable than morality. It's b possible that someone else here feels the same, and that I'm not alone; so, Thrasymachus, you must come up with a good enough argument to convince us that rating morality higher than immorality is a mistake.'

'How do you expect me to do that?' he asked. 'If what I've just been saying doesn't convince you, what else can I do? Do you want me to spoonfeed the argument into your mind?'

'No, I certainly don't want you to do that,' I said. 'Above all, I'd like you to be consistent; or if you do change your mind, I'd like you to do so openly, without trying to deceive us. What's happening, you see, Thrasymachus—I mean, we haven't com- c pleted our investigation of what you were saying before—is that although you started by trying to define the true doctor, you didn't maintain the same level of precision when you sub- sequently turned to the true shepherd. You don't think that the reason a shepherd, in his capacity as shepherd, herds sheep[†] is what is best for the sheep; you think he's like a dinner- guest when a meal is due, and is interested only in indulging himself—or alternatively that he behaves like a businessman d rather than a shepherd, and is interested only in making money. But of course the sole concern of shepherding is to procure the best for what is in its charge, since its own best state has been sufficiently procured, as we know,[*] as long as it wholly and entirely is shepherding. The same reasoning, I thought, was what compelled us not long ago to conclude that all authority (whether political or non-political), *qua* authority, considers e what is best for nothing except its subjects, its wards. But do you think that people with political authority—the "real" rulers—exercise authority willingly?'

'I most definitely do not *think* so,' he replied. 'I'm absolutely certain of it!'

'But, Thrasymachus,' I said, 'don't you realize that no other form of authority is willingly exercised by its holder? People demand wages, on the grounds that the power isn't going to benefit *them*, but those who are in their charge. I mean, tell me this: when we want to distinguish one branch of expertise from 346a another, don't we do so by distinguishing what it is capable of doing? And please, Thrasymachus, make sure that your reply expresses what you really believe; otherwise, we won't make any progress.'

'Yes, that's how we distinguish it,' he said.

'And doesn't every branch of expertise have its own particular benefit to bestow as well, rather than one which it shares with other branches of expertise? For instance, medicine confers health, naval captaincy confers safety at sea, and so on.'

'Yes.'

'And isn't an income conferred by expertise at earning b money? I mean, this is what it is capable of doing. You surely don't identify medicine and captaincy, do you? We must do as you suggested and make precise distinctions, so if a ship's captain recovers from illness because seafaring is good for him, does this lead you to call what he does medicine?'

'Of course not,' he said.

'Nor, I imagine, if someone recovers from illness while earning money, do you describe moneymaking skill as medical skill.'

'Of course not.'

'Well, suppose someone earns money while restoring health? Does this make you describe medicine as moneymaking?'*

'No.'   c

'We've agreed that every branch of expertise has its own particular benefit to bestow, haven't we?'

'Yes, I grant you that,' he said.

'So if there's any benefit which the practitioners of every branch of expertise share, then obviously this benefit must come from something which is the same for all of them, and which they all equally make use of, over and above making use of their own particular expertise.'

'I suppose so,' he said.

'And it's our view that practitioners of branches of expertise benefit by earning money because they make use of the skill of moneymaking in addition to their own particular skill.'

He reluctantly agreed.

d 'It follows that no one benefits, in the sense of earning money, as a result of practising his own branch of expertise. Instead, given that our enquiry has to be conducted with precision, we should say that medicine creates health, while moneymaking creates an income, and that building creates a house, while moneymaking may accompany building and create an income, and so on for the other branches of expertise: each of them has its own job to do and benefits what is in its charge. But leaving wages aside, is there any benefit which a practitioner gains from his expertise?'

'Apparently not,' he said.

e 'And what about when he works for free? Does he in fact fail to confer any benefit at that time?'

'No, I think he does.'

'So, Thrasymachus, it's now clear that no branch of expertise or form of authority procures benefit for itself; as we were saying some time ago, it procures and enjoins benefit for its subject. It considers the advantage of its subject, the weaker party, not that of the stronger party. That, my dear Thrasymachus, is why I was proposing just now that no one willingly chooses authority and the task of righting other 347a people's wrongs; they ask to be paid for it, because anyone who works properly with his expertise consistently fails to work for his own welfare, and also fails to legislate for his own welfare when he gives instructions as a professional. It isn't *his* welfare, but that of his subject, which is his concern. This presumably explains why it is necessary to pay people with money or prestige before they are prepared to hold authority, or to punish them if they refuse.'

'What do you mean, Socrates?' asked Glaucon. 'I recognize your two modes of payment, but I don't know what punishment you are referring to and how it replaces payment.'

'Then you don't know what kind of payment is needed to b induce truly excellent people to be prepared to rule,' I said. 'Don't you realize that to say that someone is interested in prestige or money is thought—and rightly thought—to be insulting?'

'Yes, I know that,' he said.

'Well,' I explained, 'that's why neither money nor prestige tempts good people to accept power. You see, if they overtly require money for being in charge, they'll be called hired hands, and if they covertly make money for themselves out of the possession of power, they'll be called thieves; and they don't want either of these alternatives. On the other hand, they won't do it for prestige either, since they aren't ambitious. So one has to pressurize them and threaten them with punishment, c otherwise they'll never assume power; and this is probably the origin of the conventional view that it's shameful to *want* to take power on, rather than waiting until one has no choice. The ultimate punishment for being unwilling to assume authority oneself is to be governed by a worse person, and it is fear of this happening, I think, which prompts good men to assume power occasionally.* On these occasions, they don't embark upon government with the expectation of gaining some advantage or benefit from it: their attitude is that they have no choice in the matter, in the sense that they haven't been able to d find people better than themselves, or even their equals, to whom they might entrust the task. The chances are that were a community of good men to exist, the competition to avoid power* would be just as fierce as the competition for power is under current circumstances. In such a community, it would be glaringly obvious that any genuine ruler really is incapable of considering his own welfare, rather than that of his subject, and the consequence would be that anyone with any sense would prefer receiving benefit to all the problems that go with conferring it. So anyway, I utterly disagree with Thrasymachus' assertion that morality is the advantage of the stronger party; e but we've examined that topic enough for the time being.'

Thrasymachus has also claimed that immorality is more rewarding than morality. Socrates now attacks this claim, which is also the target of much of the rest of Republic. *In an argument which is rather too clever for its own good, Socrates first argues that an immoral person's behaviour resembles that of bad, stupid people in other areas of expertise, rather than that of good, intelligent people. The argument exploits an ambiguity in superiority, which can mean 'doing better than' or 'having more than'; and, by means of the analogy between*

31

morality and skill, it assumes that an immoral person is a failure where a moral person succeeds. In fact, however, moral and immoral people have different goals.

'Thrasymachus' current claim, however, is that a life of crime is better than a life of integrity, and this seems to me to be a far more important assertion. Do you have a preference, Glaucon?' I asked. 'Which view do you think is closer to the truth?'

'I think a moral life is more rewarding.'

348a 'Did you hear Thrasymachus' recent long list of the advantages of an immoral life?' I asked.

'I did,' he answered, 'but I'm not convinced.'

'Shall we try to convince him, then, if we possibly can, of the falsehood of his claim?'

'Yes, of course, let's,' he said.

'Well,' I said, 'if we counter his claim by drawing up an alternative list of all the advantages of morality, and then he responds to that, and we respond to his response, we'll find ourselves in the position of having to add up advantages and b measure the lengths of our respective lists, and before we know it we'll need jurors to adjudicate for us. On the other hand, if we conduct the investigation as we did just now, by trying to win each other's consent, then we'll be our own jurors *and* claimants.'

'Quite so,' he said.

'Which plan do you like, then?' I asked.

'The latter,' he said.

'All right, then, Thrasymachus,' I said, 'let's go back to the beginning. Could you please confirm for us that your claim is that perfect immorality is more profitable than perfect morality?'

c 'Yes, that's my claim,' he said, 'and I've explained why too.'

'And here's another question about them: do you think that one of them is a good state and the other is a bad one?'

'Of course.'

'That is, morality is a good state, and immorality a bad one?'

'Don't be so naïve, Socrates,' he said. 'Would I say that when I'm claiming that it's immorality which is profitable, not morality?'

'What *is* your position, then?'

32

'The opposite of what you said,' he replied.

'That morality is bad?'

'No, it's sheer simplicity.'

'So you're saying that immorality is duplicity, are you?'   d

'No, it's sound judgement,' he said.

'Do you really think that criminals are clever, good people, Thrasymachus?'

'Yes, if their criminality is able to manifest in a perfect form and they are capable of dominating countries and nations. I suppose you think I was talking about pickpockets. Actually,' he added, 'activities like that are rewarding too, if you can get away with them, but they're insignificant—unlike the ones I've just mentioned.'

'Yes, I see what you mean,' I said. 'But I'm surprised you e count immorality as a form of goodness and cleverness, and morality as the opposite.'

'Nevertheless, that's exactly what I do.'

'You've come up with a rather intractable idea this time,' I commented. 'It's not easy to know how to respond to it.* If you were proposing that immorality is profitable, but also conceding (as others do)* that it's contemptible and bad, then our conversation could proceed against a background of convention. However, since you've made the enterprising suggestion that it's to be classified along with goodness and cleverness, you're obviously going to say that it is a fine, effective quality, 349a and will attribute to it all the other properties which we tend to ascribe to morality.'

'Your prophecy couldn't be more accurate,' he said.

'All the same,' I said, 'I mustn't be put off. I must continue with the discussion and carry on with the investigation, as long as I feel that you're speaking your mind. I mean, I get the impression, Thrasymachus, that now you aren't toying with us in the slightest, but are expressing your beliefs about the way things truly are.'

'What does it matter to you whether or not it's what I believe?' he said. 'Why don't you just tackle what I'm saying?'

'It doesn't matter to me at all,' I said. 'But here's another b question I'd like you to try to answer, over and above what you've already said. Do you think a moral person would wish to set himself up as superior to another moral person?'

'Of course he wouldn't,' he replied. 'Otherwise he wouldn't be the civilized simpleton he is.'

'Well, would he want to set himself up as superior to moral behaviour?'

'Again, no,' he replied.

'Would he, or would he not, want and intend to set himself up as superior to an immoral person?'

'He would intend to,' he replied, 'but he wouldn't be able to.'

'I'm not asking whether he'd be able to do it,' I said. 'My question is: isn't it the case that a moral person does not intend c or wish to set himself up as superior to another moral person, but only to an immoral person?'

'That's correct,' he said.

'What about an immoral person? Does he want to set himself up as superior to a moral person and to moral behaviour?'

'Of course,' he replied. 'He wants to gain the upper hand in everything.'

'So will an immoral person also try to set himself up as superior to another immoral person and to immoral behaviour? In short, will he struggle to gain the upper hand over everyone else in everything?'

'Yes.'

'Let's put it this way,' I said. 'A moral person doesn't set himself up as superior to people who are like him, but only to people who are unlike him; an immoral person, on the other hand, sets himself up as superior to people who are like him as d well as to people who are unlike him.'

'You couldn't have put it better,' he said.

'Now, an immoral person is clever and good, and a moral person is neither clever nor good. Isn't that right?'

'Yes, you've put that well too,' he said.

'So is it the case that an immoral person also *resembles* a clever, good person, while a moral person does not?' I asked.

'Naturally,' he replied. 'Since that's the type of person he is, then of course he resembles others of the same type; and of course a moral person does not resemble them.'

'Fine. So each of them is of the same type as people he resembles?'

'That goes without saying,' he said.

'All right, Thrasymachus. Do you acknowledge that some e people are musical and some aren't?'

34

'I do.'

'Which ones are clever and which aren't?'

'The musical ones are clever, of course, and the unmusical ones aren't.'

'And if someone is clever at something, isn't he also good at it, and bad at it if he isn't clever at it?'

'Yes.'

'And doesn't the same apply to medicine?'

'Yes.'

'Do you think, then, Thrasymachus, that when a musical person is tuning a lyre—tightening and slackening the strings— he would want to set himself up as superior to, and gain the upper hand over, another musical person?'

'No, I don't think so.'

'As superior to an unmusical person, then?'

'Inevitably,' he said.

'And what about a doctor? Do you think that in dietary 350a matters he would have the slightest desire to set himself up as superior to another doctor or to medical practice?'

'Of course not.'

'But as superior to non-medical people and practice?'

'Yes.'

'Consider any instance of knowledge or ignorance. Do you think that the actions or words of anyone who is knowledgeable in anything are motivated by a desire to surpass the actions or words of another person with the same knowledge? Don't you think that his actions and words would be identical to those of someone like him in the same circumstances?'

'Yes, I suppose that's bound to be the case,' he said.

'What about an ignoramus? Wouldn't he try to set himself up as superior to knowledgeable people and to ignorant people b equally?'

'I suppose so.'

'A knowledgeable person is clever, isn't he?'

'Yes.'

'And a clever person is good?'

'Yes.'

'So it's if someone is good and clever that he won't want to set himself up as superior to people who are like him, but only to people who are unlike him and have nothing in common with him.'

'So it seems.'

'If someone is bad and ignorant, however, he'll want to set himself up as superior to people who are like him as well as to people who are unlike him.'

'I suppose so.'

'Well, Thrasymachus,' I said, 'we found that it was an immoral person who sets himself up as superior to people who are like him as well as to people who are unlike him, didn't we? Isn't that what you said?'

'I did,' he replied.

c   'And a moral person won't set himself up as superior to people who are like him, but only to people who are unlike him?'

'Yes.'

'It follows,' I said, 'that it is a moral person who resembles a clever, good person, and an immoral person who resembles a bad, ignorant person.'

'It looks that way.'

'And we agreed that each of them is of the same type as people he is like.'

'Yes, we did.'

'We've proved, then, that it is a moral person who is good and clever, whereas an immoral person is ignorant and bad.'

Socrates launches an attack on the effectiveness of immoral behaviour. Criminals fall out with one another, and therefore cannot act in concert; an immoral individual, such as Thrasymachus' dictator, falls out with himself. Thrasymachus meekly accepts this idea (which prefigures the psychology and the definition of morality which will occur later in Republic*) because he accepts that immorality is essentially destructive of concord.*

Now, although Thrasymachus did concede all these points, it wasn't as easy as I'm making it sound by describing it: he was
d hauled along with great reluctance, sweating profusely (since it was the hot season). And I also saw then something I'd never seen before—a red-faced Thrasymachus.*

So anyway, we agreed that morality was a good state and was knowledge, and that immorality was a bad state and was ignorance. Next I said, 'All right. We may have settled that issue, but we also have before us the claim* that immorality is effective. Do you remember, Thrasymachus?'

'Yes, I remember,' he replied. 'But I'm not satisfied with the statements you've just been making. I could address them, but I'm sure that if I did, you'd claim that I was holding forth like an orator. So either let me say what I want and for as e long as I want, or go on with your questions, if you insist on doing that, and I'll go on saying "All right" and nodding and shaking my head as if I were listening to old women telling stories.'

'But you must never go against what you actually believe,' I said.

'Why shouldn't I?' he said. 'It makes you happy. You won't let me speak—do you want more from me than that?'

'No, not at all,' I replied. 'If you'll do what you said, that's fine, and I'll ask the questions.'

'Go ahead, then.'

'Well, here's the question I was getting at just now; I think it's the logical next one for our investigation. When morality is 351a compared with immorality, what do we learn about morality? I mean, the suggestion was made that immorality is more powerful and more effective than morality; but the fact that we've now established that morality is a good state and is knowledge will make it easy to prove, I think, that it's also more effective than immorality, given that immorality is ignorance, as everyone knows by now. However, I don't want our investigation to be couched in such abstract terms, Thrasymachus, but rather as follows: would you agree that it is wrong for a community to b undertake the domination of other communities, to deprive other communities of their freedom, and to keep a number of other communities subservient to itself?'

'Of course it is,' he said. 'And the better the community—the more perfectly immoral—the more it will act in exactly that way.'

'I appreciate that this is your position,' I said, 'but what I'm doing is exploring an aspect of it and asking whether a community which is stronger than another community will retain its power if it doesn't have morality, or whether it can do so only if it has morality.'

'If your recent assertion was correct,' he replied, 'that morality c is knowledge, then it will take morality; but if I'm right, it takes immorality.'

'Thrasymachus,' I said, 'I'm really pleased that you're not just nodding and shaking your head, but are giving these excellent answers.'

'I'm doing it to make you happy,' he said.

'Thank you. You'll carry on making me happy if you answer this question of mine. Do you think that a community or an army or pirates or thieves or any other band which forms for the purpose of wrongdoing would be capable of doing anything if the members of the band wrong one another?'

d   'Of course not,' he said.

'But if they don't wrong one another, then they stand a better chance of success?'*

'Yes.'

'Because immorality makes for mutual conflict, hatred, and antagonism, while moral behaviour makes for concord and friendship. Is that right?'

'I'll grant you that: I don't want to quarrel with you,' he said.

'Thank you, Thrasymachus. Now here's another question for you. If it's a function of immorality to generate hatred in its train, then whenever it arises among people—people from any walk of life—won't it make them hate one another and clash

e with one another and be incapable of doing things together?'

'Yes.'

'What about when it arises between two people? Won't it make them quarrel with and feel hatred and hostility towards not only each other but also moral people?'

'It will.'

'And, Thrasymachus, if immorality arises within a single person, it won't lose its power, surely, will it? Won't it retain it in an undiminished form?'

'I dare say it does,' he said.

'Evidently, then, its power is twofold. First, its occurrence makes things incapable of co-ordinated action, because of their internal conflict and dissension; second, as well as generating

352a internal hostility, it generates hostility between them and anything which is completely different from them—that is, anything which is moral. And this is the case whether it arises in a community, a family, an army, or anything else. Isn't this right?'

'Yes.'

'And when it arises within a single individual, it will, I suppose, produce exactly the same results—the results it is inherently bound to have. First, it will make him incapable of action, because of internal dissension and discord; second, as well as generating internal hostility, it will generate hostility between him and moral people. Right?'

'Yes.'

'Now, my friend, aren't the gods moral beings?'

'I dare say.'

'Therefore, an immoral person will be an enemy of the gods, b Thrasymachus, and a moral person will be in their favour.'

'That's right, indulge yourself,' he said. 'And don't worry: I won't contradict what you're saying. I mean, I don't want to fall out with our friends here.'

'All right, then,' I went on. 'You'll treat me to all the food I still need to be satisfied, if you continue to answer my questions as you have been just now. I mean, we've found that moral people are more expert at getting things done, are better at it, and are more capable of it, and that immoral people are not capable of acting together at all. Moreover, if we ever claim that immoral people have been effective and have performed c some concerted action together, then we are not telling the whole truth, because if they were absolutely immoral, they'd have been at one another's throats; there was obviously a degree of morality in them, which enabled them to refrain from wronging one another as well as their victims and which allowed them to do what they did. Immorality had only half perverted them when they embarked upon their misdeeds, since people who are rotten through and through and are perfectly immoral are perfectly incapable of doing anything either. I now see that all this is correct, and that your original position was d quite wrong.'

At last Socrates turns to a direct refutation of Thrasymachus' claim that immorality is rewarding. Everything has a particular job to do, and the good state of anything is what enables it to do its job well. Therefore, if morality is a good state, it enables one to do a good job at life—to live well, and be happy and fulfilled. The argument is, as with most of the arguments in this chapter, as weak or as strong as the pervasive analogy between morality and skill or being good at something.

'However, we must also look into the postponed* issue of whether moral people have a better and a more fulfilled life than immoral people. I must say that at the moment it does look to me as though they do, on the basis of what we've been saying. All the same, we must look more closely at the matter, since what is at stake is far from insignificant: it is how one should live one's life.'

'Go ahead with your investigation, then,' he said.

'All right,' I said. 'Tell me, please: do you think that a horse has a function?'

e   'Yes.'

'And would you say that a horse's function, or anything else's function, is what can be done only with that thing, or can be done best only with that thing?'

'I don't understand,' he said.

'Look at it this way: can you see with anything except eyes?'

'Of course not.'

'And can you hear with anything except ears?'

'No.'

'Would it be right, then, for us to say that these are their functions?'†

'Yes.'

353a   'Now, you could cut a vine-twig with a shortsword or a cobbler's knife or plenty of other things, couldn't you?'

'Of course.'

'But I should think that the best tool for the job would be a pruning-knife, the kind made especially for this purpose.'

'True.'

'Shall we say that this is its function, then?'

'Yes.'

'No doubt you can now see the point of the question I asked a moment ago, whether the function of anything is what it alone can do, or what it can do better than anything else.'

'Yes, I can,' he said. 'And I agree that this is anything's

b   function.'

'All right,' I said. 'Now, don't you think that anything which has been endowed with a function also has a state of being good? Let's go back to the same examples. We're saying that eyes have a function?'

'Yes.'

'And do eyes also have a state of being good?'

'Yes, that too.'

'And do ears have a function?'

'Yes.'

'And a state of being good as well?'

'Yes, that too.'

'And does the same go for everything else?'

'Yes.'

'Now then, could eyes do a good job if they weren't in their   c own special good state, but were instead in a bad state?'

'Of course not,' he replied. 'I suppose you mean if they were blind instead of capable of seeing.'

'I mean whatever their good state is,' I said. 'You've answered a question I haven't yet asked. At the moment I'm asking only whether it is thanks to its own special state of goodness that anything with a job to do performs its function well, and thanks to badness that it does its job badly.'

'Well, that's true,' he said.

'And in the absence of their goodness, will ears do their job badly?'

'Yes.'

'And so on, on the same principle, for everything else?'   d

'I think so.'

'All right, now here's the next point to think about. Does the mind have a function—something you couldn't do with anything else? Consider, for instance, management, the exercise of authority, planning, and so on: would it be right for us to ascribe them to anything except the mind or to say that they were the particular province of anything except the mind?'

'No.'

'And what about one's way of life? Won't we say that this is a function of the mind?'*

'Absolutely,' he said.

'And do we also think that the mind has a good state?'

'Yes.'

e   'Will the mind, then, Thrasymachus, ever perform its functions well in the absence of its own special goodness? Or is that
impossible?'

'Yes, it's impossible.'

'Therefore, management and authority will inevitably be
handled badly by a bad mind, whereas a good mind will do all
these things well.'

'Inevitably.'

'Now, we agreed* that morality is a good mental state, and
that immorality is a bad state.'

'We did.'

'So a moral mind and a moral person will live a good life,
and an immoral person will live a bad life.'

'Apparently,' he said, 'on your line of reasoning.'

'Now, anyone who lives a good life is happy and fulfilled,
and anyone who doesn't is the opposite.'

'Of course.'

354a   'Therefore, a moral person is happy, whereas an immoral
person is unhappy.'

'I dare say,' he said.

'Now, no one is well off because they're unhappy, but
because they're happy.'

'Of course.'

'Therefore, my dear Thrasymachus, immorality is never more
rewarding than morality.'

'There's your treat, Socrates,' he said, 'for this festival of
Bendis.'

'And the meal was provided by you, Thrasymachus,' I said,
'since you were kind to me and stopped being cross. I've not
b   had a proper meal, however—but that's my fault, not yours. I
think I've behaved like those gluttons who can't wait to taste
every dish that's served up, before they've given themselves
a proper chance to enjoy the previous one. I gave up before
we discovered what we set out to discover—the nature of
morality—and I embarked instead on an investigation into
whether it was a bad state and ignorance, or whether it was
knowledge and a good state; then later, when the idea cropped
up that immorality was more profitable than morality, I
couldn't resist turning to that next. Consequently, the effect of
our discussion on me has been ignorance. I mean, if I don't

42

know what morality actually is, it's going to be difficult for c
me to know whether or not it is good, and whether its possession makes someone unhappy or happy.'*

Chapter 2

The Challenge to Socrates

Glaucon and Adeimantus (Plato's brothers) now become Socrates' interlocutors for the rest of the book. Socrates has claimed (352d– 354a) that morality enables us to prosper; they demand a full justification of this claim. Instead of the more usual views that morality is (a) not good, but a lesser evil (Glaucon), and (b) valued only for its external rewards (Adeimantus), they challenge Socrates to prove that morality is intrinsically good and rewarding, and that it contributes towards a moral person's happiness.

357a At this point, I thought I'd be exempt from further talking, but apparently that was only the preamble. You see, it's not in Glaucon's nature to cut and run from anything, and on this occasion he refused to accept Thrasymachus' capitulation, but
b said, 'Socrates, do you want us *really* to be convinced that in all circumstances morality is better than immorality or merely to pretend to be?'

'If it were up to me,' I replied, 'I'd prefer your conviction to be genuine.'

'Well,' he remarked, 'your behaviour is at odds with your wishes, then. I mean, here's a question for you. Don't you describe as good something which is welcomed for its own sake, rather than because its consequences are desired? Enjoyment, for instance, and all those pleasures which are harmless and whose future consequences are only enjoyable?'

'Yes,' I agreed, ' "good" seems to me the right description for that situation.'

c 'And what about things which are welcome not just for their own sakes, but also for their consequences? Intelligence, sight, and health, for instance, are evidently welcomed for both reasons.'

'Yes,' I said.

'And isn't there, in your experience,' he asked, 'a third category of good things—the category in which we find exercise, medical treatment, and any moneymaking job like being a doctor? All these things are regarded as nuisances, but beneficial, and are not welcomed for their own sakes, but for their financial rewards and other consequences.'   d

'Yes,' I agreed, 'there is this third category as well. What of it?'

'To which category do you think morality belongs?' he asked.

'In my opinion,' I replied, 'it belongs in the best category—   358a the category which anyone who expects to be happy should welcome both for its own sake and for its consequences.'*

'That's not the usual view,' he said, 'which consigns morality to the nuisance category of things which have to be done for the sake of financial reward and for the prospect of making a good impression, but which, taken in isolation, are so trying that one should avoid them.'

'I'm aware of this view,' I said, 'and it's the reason why Thrasymachus has been running morality down all this time, and praising immorality. But I'm slow on the uptake, apparently.'

'All right, then,' he said, 'listen to what I have to say too, and   b see if you agree with me. The point is that Thrasymachus gave up too soon, in my opinion: you charmed him into docility as if he were a snake. The arguments that have been offered about both morality and immorality leave *me* unsatisfied, however, in the sense that I still want to hear a definition of them both, and to be told what the effect is of the occurrence of each of them in the mind—each of them in isolation, without taking into consideration financial reward or any other consequence they might have.*

'So if it's all right with you, what I'll do is revive Thrasymachus' position. First, I'll explain the usual view of   c the nature and origin of morality; second, I'll claim that it is only ever practised reluctantly, as something necessary, but not good; third, I'll claim that this behaviour is reasonable, because people are right to think that an immoral person's life is much better than a moral person's life.

'Now, I don't agree with any of this, Socrates, but I don't know what to think. My ears are ringing from listening to Thrasymachus and countless others, but I've never yet heard

the kind of support for morality, as being preferable to
d immorality, that I'd like to hear, which is a hymn to the virtues
it possesses in and of itself. If I can get this from anyone, it'll be
you, I think. That is why I'll speak at some length in praise of
the immoral life; by doing so, I'll be showing you the kind of
rejoinder I want you to develop when you criticize immorality
and commend morality. What do you think of this plan?'

'I thoroughly approve,' I replied. 'I mean, I can't think of
another topic which any thinking person would more gladly see
cropping up again and again in his conversations.'

e 'That's wonderful,' he said. 'Well, I promised I'd talk first
about the nature and origin of morality, so here goes. The idea
is that although it's a fact of nature that doing wrong is good
and having wrong done to one is bad, nevertheless the disadvantages of having it done to one outweigh the benefits of
doing it. Consequently, once people have experienced both
committing wrong and being at the receiving end of it, they see
that the disadvantages are unavoidable and the benefits are
359a unattainable; so they decide that the most profitable course is
for them to enter into a contract with one another, guaranteeing
that no wrong will be committed or received. They then set
about making laws and decrees, and from then on they use
the terms "legal" and "right" to describe anything which is
enjoined by their code. So that's the origin and nature of
morality, on this view: it is a compromise between the ideal
of doing wrong without having to pay for it, and the worst
situation, which is having wrong done to one while lacking
the means of exacting compensation. Since morality is a compromise, it is endorsed because, while it may not be good, it
does gain value by preventing people from doing wrong. The
b point is that any real man with the ability to do wrong would
never enter into a contract to avoid both wronging and being
wronged: he wouldn't be so crazy. Anyway, Socrates, that is
what this view has to say about the nature and origin of
morality and so on.*

'As for the fact that morality is only ever practised reluctantly, by people who lack the ability to do wrong—this would
become particularly obvious if we performed the following
c thought-experiment. Suppose we grant both types of people—
moral and immoral—the scope to do whatever they want, and

46

we then keep an eye on them to see where their wishes lead them. We'll catch our moral person red-handed: his desire for superiority will point him in the same direction as the immoral person, towards a destination which every creature naturally regards as good and aims for, except that people are compelled by convention to deviate from this path and respect equality.

'They'd have the scope I'm talking about especially if they acquired the kind of power which, we hear, an ancestor of Gyges of Lydia* once acquired. He was a shepherd in the service of the Lydian ruler of the time, when a heavy rainstorm occurred and an earthquake cracked open the land to a certain extent,* and a chasm appeared in the region where he was pasturing his flocks. He was fascinated by the sight, and went down into the chasm and saw there, as the story goes, among other artefacts, a bronze horse, which was hollow and had windows set in it; he stooped and looked in through the windows and saw a corpse inside, which seemed to be that of a giant. The corpse was naked, but had a golden ring on one finger; he took the ring off the finger and left.† Now, the shepherds used to meet once a month to keep the king informed about his flocks, and our protagonist came to the meeting wearing the ring. He was sitting down among the others, and happened to twist the ring's bezel in the direction of his body, towards the inner part of his hand. When he did this, he became invisible to his neighbours, and to his astonishment they talked about him as if he'd left. While he was fiddling about with the ring again, he turned the bezel outwards, and became visible. He thought about this and experimented to see if it was the ring which had this power; in this way he eventually found that turning the bezel inwards made him invisible and turning it outwards made him visible. As soon as he realized this, he arranged to be one of the delegates to the king; once he was inside the palace, he seduced the king's wife and with her help assaulted and killed the king, and so took possession of the throne.

'Suppose there were two such rings, then—one worn by our moral person, the other by the immoral person. There is no one, on this view, who is iron-willed enough to maintain his morality and find the strength of purpose to keep his hands off what doesn't belong to him, when he is able to take whatever

he wants from the market-stalls without fear of being dis-
c covered, to enter houses and sleep with whomever he chooses,
to kill and to release from prison anyone he wants, and
generally to act like a god among men. His behaviour would be
identical to that of the other person: both of them would be
heading in the same direction.

'Now this is substantial evidence, it would be claimed, that
morality is never freely chosen. People do wrong whenever they
think they can, so they act morally only if they're forced to,
because they regard morality as something which isn't good for
one personally. The point is that everyone thinks the rewards of
d immorality far outweigh those of morality—and they're right,
according to the proponent of this view. The sight of someone
with that kind of scope refusing all those opportunities for
wrongdoing and never laying a finger on things that didn't
belong to him would lead people to think that he was in an
extremely bad way, and was a first-class fool as well—even
though their fear of being wronged might make them attempt
to mislead others by singing his praises to them in public.

'That's all I have to say on this. As for actually assessing the
e lives of the people we're talking about, we'll be able to do that
correctly if we make the gap between a moral person and an
immoral person as wide as possible. That's the only way to
make a proper assessment. And we should set them apart from
each other by leaving their respective immorality and morality
absolutely intact, so that we make each of them a consummate
professional. In other words, our immoral person must be a
true expert. A top-notch ship's captain, for instance, or doctor,
recognizes the limits of his branch of expertise and undertakes
361a what is possible while ignoring what is impossible; moreover,
if he makes a mistake, he has the competence to correct it.
Equally, our immoral person must get away with any crimes he
undertakes in the proper fashion, if he is to be outstandingly
immoral; getting caught must be taken to be a sign of incom-
petence, since the acme of immorality is to give an impression
of morality while actually being immoral. So we must attribute
consummate immorality to our consummate criminal, and if we
are to leave it intact, we should have him equipped with a
b colossal reputation for morality even though he is a colossal
criminal. He should be capable of correcting any mistakes he

makes. He must have the ability to argue plausibly, in case any of his crimes are ever found out, and to use force wherever necessary, by making use of his courage and strength and by drawing on his fund of friends and his financial resources.

'Now that we've come up with this sketch of an immoral person, we must conceive of a moral person to stand beside him—someone who is straightforward and principled, and who, as Aeschylus says, wants genuine goodness rather than merely an aura of goodness.* So we must deprive him of any such aura, since if others think him moral, this reputation will c gain him privileges and rewards, and it will become unclear whether it is morality or the rewards and privileges which might be motivating him to be what he is. We should strip him of everything except morality, then, and our portrait should be of someone in the opposite situation to the one we imagined before. I mean, even though he does no wrong at all, he must have a colossal reputation for immorality, so that his morality can be tested by seeing whether or not he is impervious to a bad reputation and its consequences; he must unswervingly follow his path until he dies—a saint with a lifelong reputation d as a sinner. When they can both go no further in morality and immorality respectively, we can decide which of them is the happier.'

'My dear Glaucon,' I said, 'I'm very impressed at how industriously you're ridding each of them of defects and getting them ready for assessment. It's as if you were working on statues.'

'I'm doing the best I can,' he replied. 'And now that we've established what the two of them are like, I'm sure we won't find it difficult to specify what sort of life is in store for either of them. That's what I must do, then—and if my words are e rather coarse, Socrates, please remember that the argument is not mine, but stems from those who prefer immorality to morality.

'Here's what they'll say: for a moral person in the situation I've described, the future holds flogging, torture on the rack, imprisonment in chains, having his eyes burnt out, and every ordeal in the book, up to and including being impaled on a 362a stake. Then at last he'll realize that one's goal should be not actual morality, but the appearance of morality. In fact, that

phrase of Aeschylus' has far more relevance for an immoral person, in the sense that, as they will claim, it is really an immoral person who wants genuine immorality rather than merely an aura of immorality, because his occupation takes account of the way things are and his life is not concerned with appearances. He is the one who "reaps the harvest of wise
b plans which grow in his mind's deep furrow"*—and what he plans is first to use his reputation for morality to gain control over his country, and then to marry a woman from any family he wants, to have his children marry whomever he wants, to deal and do business with whomever he wants, and, over and above all this, to secure his own benefit by ensuring that his lack of distaste for crime makes him a financial profit. If he's challenged privately or publicly, he wins the day and comes off better than his enemies; because he gains the upper hand, he
c gets rich; he therefore does good to his friends and harm to his enemies, and the religious rites he performs and the offerings he makes to the gods are not just adequate but magnificent; his service to the gods and to the men he favours is far better than a moral person's; and consequently it is more appropriate for the gods to smile on him rather than on a moral person, and more likely that they will. And this, Socrates, is why both gods and men provide a better life for an immoral person than for a moral person, according to this view.'

d   After Glaucon's speech, I was intending to make some reply to what he'd been saying, but his brother Adeimantus asked, 'Surely you don't consider that an adequate treatment of the issue, do you, Socrates?'

'Why shouldn't I?' I said.

'It's precisely the most important point which has been omitted,' he said.

'Well,' I said, 'as the saying goes, a man and his brother should stick together. So if Glaucon here has left anything out, you should back him up. As far as I'm concerned, however, even what he's already said is enough to floor me and make me a totally ineffective ally of morality.'

e   'Rubbish,' he said. 'But don't let that stop you listening to what I have to say as well. In order to clarify Glaucon's meaning, we also have to go into the arguments for the opposite of his point—the arguments in favour of morality and against immorality. As you know, fathers point out to their sons the importance of morality and impress it upon them (as every guardian impresses it upon his ward) by singing the praises not of morality itself but of the good reputation it brings. The inducement they offer is that power, good marriage, and all the things Glaucon mentioned a moment ago come to someone who is thought to be moral as a result of this reputation: if a moral person gets them, it is because he is well thought of. 363a

'They have more to say about the consequences of reputation. They adduce being well thought of by the gods, and then they have benefits galore to talk of, all the ones the gods are said to award to just people. There are, for instance, the statements of noble Hesiod and of Homer. Hesiod says* that the gods make "oaks bear acorns on their outsides and bees in their centres" for moral people; and he says that "their woolly sheep are weighed down by their fleeces", and that they gain many other advantages. Homer makes very similar claims:* "As of some righteous king," he says, "who pleases the gods by upholding justice, and the dark earth bears wheat and barley, the trees hang heavy with fruit, the sheep steadily give birth, and the sea-waters yield fish." b

c

'Musaeus and his son* claim that the gods give moral people even more exciting advantages. Once they've transported them, in their account, to Hades and got them reclining on couches for the party they've laid on for just people, they next have them spending eternity wearing chaplets on their heads and drinking, on the assumption that the best possible reward for goodness is perpetual intoxication. Others* have the gods' rewards for morality lasting even longer: they say that the legacy left behind by a person who is just and keeps his promises is that his children's children are better people.† d

'These, and others like them, are the glowing terms in which they speak of morality. As for unjust and immoral people, they bury them in Hades in a kind of mud* and force them to carry water in sieves,* and they make sure that while they remain alive they are thought badly of; and they claim that all the punishments which Glaucon specified for people who, despite being moral, are thought to be immoral are destined for immoral people. They have no novel punishments to add to this list, however. e

'Anyway, that's how morality is commended and immorality

51

condemned. But there's also another point for you to take into consideration, Socrates. It's the sort of thing ordinary people say to one another about morality and immorality, but 364a it occurs in the poets as well. They all unanimously go on and on about how self-discipline and morality may be commendable, but are also difficult and troublesome, whereas self-indulgence and immorality are enjoyable and easily gained, and it's only in people's minds and in convention that they are contemptible. They also say that, on the whole, immorality is more rewarding than morality; and whereas they're perfectly ready to admire bad men, if they're affluent and powerful in other respects as well, and to award them political office and personal prestige, they have disrespect and look down on people who are in any way powerless or are poor, even while b admitting their moral superiority to the others.

'The most astonishing thing of all, however, is what gets said about the gods and goodness—that the gods often assign misfortune and a terrible life to good people, and the opposite to the other type of person.* Beggar-priests and soothsayers knock on the doors of wealthy households and try to persuade the owners that (as long as there's some enjoyable feasting involved) the gods have granted them the power to use rituals and spells to expiate any sin committed by a person or by any c of his ancestors, and that if anyone has an enemy he'd like to hurt, then it'll cost hardly anything to injure him—and it makes no difference whether the target is a moral or an immoral person—by means of certain incantations and formulae, since they can persuade the gods, they say, to do their bidding.

'The poets are called on to support all these claims. Some people concede that vice involves nothing arduous, on the grounds that "There's no difficulty in choosing vice in abun- d dance: the road is smooth and it's hardly any distance to where it lives. But the gods have put sweat in the way of goodness",* and a long, rough, steep road. Others cite Homer in support of the idea that humans can influence the gods, pointing out that he too said,* "Even the gods themselves can be moved by entreaty: men appeal to them by means of rites and softly spoken prayers, libations and sacrifices, and influence them, e when a crime has been committed and a wrong has been done." They come up with a noisy mob of books written by

52

Musaeus and Orpheus (who are descended from the Moon and the Muses, they say), which are source-books for their rituals; and they convince whole countries as well as individuals that there are in fact ways to be free and cleansed of sin. While we remain on earth, this involves rituals and enjoyable diversions, 365a which also work for us after we have died and which they call initiations.* These initiations, they say, free us from all the terrors of the other world, but ghastly things await anyone who didn't take part in the rituals.

'This, my dear Socrates,' he went on, 'is the kind of thing that gets said—and at this kind of length—about how highly gods and men regard virtue and vice. Can we tell what the effect of being exposed to all this is on a young mind which is naturally gifted and is capable of working out, as a result of flitting (so to speak) from one idea to another and dipping into them all, what type of person he has to be and what road he has to take to have as good a life as possible? He would b probably follow Pindar* and ask himself, "'Is it honesty or crooked deceit that enables me to scale the higher wall' and so live my life surrounded by secure defences? What I hear is people telling me that, unless I also gain a reputation for morality, my actually being moral will do me no good, but will be a source of private troubles and public punishments. On the other hand, an immoral person who has managed to get a reputation for morality is said to have a wonderful life. There- fore, since the experts tell me that 'Appearance overpowers c reality'* and is responsible for happiness, I must wholeheartedly devote myself to appearance. I must surround myself with an illusion of goodness. This must be my front, what people see of me, but behind me I must have on a leash that cunning, subtle fox of which Archilochus,* the greatest of all experts, speaks. Someone might object, 'But it's not easy to cloak one's badness for ever.' That's because no important project is easy, we shall reply; nevertheless, everything we hear marks this as the road d to take if we are to be happy. To help us with our disguise, we shall form clubs and pressure-groups,* and we can acquire skill at political and forensic speaking from teachers of the art of persuasion. Consequently, by a combination of persuasion and brute force, we shall dominate others without being punished for it."

'"But you can't hide from the gods, or overpower them."*
"Well, suppose there are no gods, or suppose they aren't
bothered in the slightest about human affairs: then why should
we in our turn bother about hiding from them? On the other
e hand, if the gods do exist, and do care for us, then our only
sources of knowledge and information about them are tradition
and the poets who have described their lineage.* And these are
precisely the people who are telling us that the gods can be
persuaded and influenced by 'rites and softly spoken prayers'
and offerings. Their credibility in one respect stands or falls
with their credibility in the other respect. So if we listen to
them, our course is to do wrong and then make offerings to
the gods from the proceeds of our crimes. The point is that if
366a we behave morally, then the most that we'll avoid is being
punished by the gods, but we'll also pass up the opportunity
for making a profit from our immorality; if we are immoral,
however, we'll not only get rich, we'll win the gods over
with our entreaties and get off scot-free, for all the crimes we
commit and wrong we do."

'"But we'll pay in Hades for the crimes we've committed
here on earth—or if we don't ourselves, then our children's
children will." He'll think about it and then reply, "No, my
friend, we won't. Initiations are very effective and the gods
whose domain is exoneration have a great deal of power: that
is the message we are given by very important countries and by
b the offspring of the gods, who have become poets and the gods'
interpreters, and who reveal that this is so."

'Is there any argument left, then, which might persuade us
not to choose out-and-out immorality, but to prefer morality?
I mean, if we combine immorality with a fraudulent, but
specious, façade, then we can do as we please in this world and
in the next, in the presence of both gods and men. This is what
both ordinary people and outstanding people are telling us. So
c after all these arguments, Socrates, is there any strategy to
enable someone with potential—whether it is due to mental
attributes or wealth or physique or lineage—to be prepared to
rate morality highly, rather than laugh when he hears it being
praised?

'I tell you, if there's anyone who can not only refute the
arguments I've been stating, but is also secure in his knowledge

that morality is best, then what he feels for immoral people is not anger but a large measure of forgiveness. He knows that people abstain from wrong either because, by divine dispensation, they instinctively find it distasteful, or because of some realization they've come to, and that otherwise no one chooses d to be moral, although people find fault with immorality when cowardice or old age or some other form of weakness prevents them from doing wrong. This is obviously the case: the first of these people to gain power is the first to behave immorally— and as immorally as he possibly can.

'One thing is responsible for all this, and it is the same thing which constituted the starting-point of this whole discussion. Both Glaucon and I, Socrates, are saying to you, "My friend, we can start with those original heroes whose writings are e extant and end with our contemporaries, but we find that not a single one of you self-styled supporters of morality has ever found fault with immorality or commended morality except in terms of the reputation, status, and rewards which follow from them. What each of them does on its own, however, and what the effect is of its occurrence in someone's mind, where it is hidden from the eyes of both gods and men, has never been adequately explained either in poetry or in everyday conversation; nor has it ever been proven that the worst possible thing that can occur in the mind is immorality, and that morality is the best. If this is how all of you had approached the matter 367a from the outset, and if you had started trying to convince us when we were young, then we wouldn't now be defending ourselves against one another's wrongdoing, but everyone would be his own best defender, since he'd be afraid that if he did wrong he'd be opening his doors to the worst of all possible residents."

'That, Socrates, is what Thrasymachus—though he's not the only one, of course—might say on the subject of morality and immorality, and he'd probably have even more to add.* Now, I think he's crudely misrepresenting their functions, but the reason I've taken his argument as far as I can is, to be perfectly candid, because I want to hear you making the opposite claims. b It's not enough just to demonstrate that morality is better than immorality. Why does one of them, in and of itself, make anyone who possesses it bad, while the other one, in and of

itself, makes him good? And, as Glaucon suggested,* don't bring reputation into it. You see, if you leave them with reputations which genuinely reflect their natures, and don't attribute to each of them reputations which fail to do justice to them, then we'll accuse you of praising a reputation for morality rather than morality itself, and of criticizing a reputation for immorality rather than immorality itself; and
c we'll claim that what you're recommending is being immoral and getting away with it, and that you actually agree with Thrasymachus that morality is good for someone else—that it is the advantage of the stronger party—while it is immorality that is to one's own advantage and profit, but is disadvantageous to the weaker party.

'So, since it is your expressed opinion that morality is one of those paramount good things which are worth having not just for their consequences, but also and especially for themselves (like sight, hearing, intelligence—health, of course—and any
d other good things which are not just thought to be worth while,† but are inherently so), then this is the aspect of morality which you should pay tribute to. You should show how morality is worth while in and of itself for anyone who possesses it and how immorality harms him, and leave others to praise rewards and reputations. I mean, I can accept the fact that others praise morality and criticize immorality in these terms, by eulogizing or abusing their reputations and rewards, but I won't put up with that from you (unless you insist),
e because this and this alone is what you've spent your whole life investigating. So it's not enough just to demonstrate that morality is better than immorality: show us why one of them, in and of itself, makes anyone who possesses it good, whether or not it is hidden from the eyes of gods and men, while the other one, in and of itself, and whether or not it is hidden from the eyes of gods and men, makes him bad.'

Chapter 3

Fundamentals of Inner Politics

In order to meet the challenge issued in the last chapter, Plato begins to imagine the constitution of a community which will correspond to human psychology and make it easier to understand morality. On this analogy and its implications, see pp. xvii–xx. The first community consists of workers alone living a life of rude and primitive health, each with a single talent and therefore a single job, responding co-operatively to one another's selfish needs. In political terms, economics underpins society; in psychological terms, our desires or needs are fundamental.

Now, I've always admired Glaucon's and Adeimantus' temperaments, but I was particularly delighted with them on this occasion, once I'd heard what they had to say. 'Like father, like 368a sons,' I remarked. 'The first line of the elegiac poem which Glaucon's lover composed when you distinguished yourselves at the battle of Megara wasn't wrong in addressing you as "sons of Ariston, godlike offspring of an eminent sire".* I think this is quite right: "godlike" is certainly the word for your state, if you can speak like that in support of immorality, and yet remain unconvinced that it is better than morality.* I *do* think that you really are unconvinced; my evidence is what I b know of your characters from other occasions. If I'd had to judge from your words alone, I would have doubted it. But it's precisely because I don't doubt it that I'm in a quandary. On the one hand, I can't come to the assistance of morality, since I am incompetent—as is proven by the fact that although I thought the points I'd made to Thrasymachus had shown that morality was better than immorality, you weren't satisfied. On the other hand, I can't not come to morality's assistance, since I'm afraid that it might actually be sacrilegious to stand idly by while morality is being denigrated and not try to assist as long as one has breath in one's body and a voice to protest with. c

Anyway, the best thing is for me to offer it whatever help I can.'

Glaucon and the others begged me to do everything I could to help; they implored me not to abandon the discussion, but to make a thorough enquiry into the nature of both morality and immorality, and to search out the truth about their expediency. I told them what occurred to me: 'We're undertaking an investigation which, in my opinion, requires care and sharp eyesight. Now, we're not experts,' I pointed out, 'so I suggest we conduct the investigation as follows. Suppose we were rather short-sighted and had been told to read small writing from a long way off, and then one of us noticed the same letters written elsewhere in a larger size and on a larger surface: I'm sure we'd regard this as a godsend and would read them there before examining the smaller ones, to see if they were really identical.'*

'Of course we would,' said Adeimantus. 'But how is this analogous to our investigation into morality, Socrates, in your view?'

'I'll tell you,' I replied. 'Wouldn't we say that morality can be a property of whole communities as well as of individuals?'*

'Yes,' he said.

'And a community is larger than a single person?'

'Yes,' he said.

'It's not impossible, then, that morality might exist on a larger scale in the larger entity and be easier to discern. So, if you have no objection, why don't we start by trying to see what morality is like in communities? And then we can examine individuals too, to see if the larger entity is reflected in the features of the smaller entity.'

'I think that's an excellent idea,' he said.

'Well,' I said, 'the theoretical observation of a community in the process of formation would enable us to see its morality and immorality forming too, wouldn't it?'*

'I should think so,' he said.

'And once the process is complete, we could expect to see more easily what we're looking for?'

'Yes, much more easily.'

'Are we agreed, then, on the necessity of trying to see this plan through? I'm asking because I think it'll take a lot of work. So are you sure?'

'Yes, we are,' said Adeimantus. 'Please do what you're proposing.'

'Well,' I said, 'a community starts to be formed, I suppose, when individual human beings find that they aren't self-sufficient, but that each of them has plenty of requirements which he can't fulfil on his own. Do you have an alternative suggestion as to why communities are founded?'

'No,' he said.

'So people become involved with various other people to fulfil various needs, and we have lots of needs, so we gather lots of people together and get them to live in a single district as our associates and assistants. And then we call this living together a community. Is that right?'

'Yes.'

'And people trade goods with one another, because they think they'll be better off if each gives or receives something in exchange,* don't they?'

'Yes.'

'All right, then,' I said. 'Let's construct our theoretical community from scratch. Apparently, its cause is our neediness.'

'Of course.'

'And the most basic and most important of our needs is that we are provided with enough food for existence and for life.'

'Absolutely.'

'The second most important is our need for somewhere to live, and the third is our need for clothing and so on.'

'True.'

'All right,' I said. 'How will our community cope with all this provisioning? Mustn't one member of it be a farmer, another a builder, and another a weaver? Is that all the people we need to look after our bodily needs? Shall we add a shoemaker to it as well?'

'Yes.'

'And there we'd have our community. Reduced to its bare essentials, it would consist of four or five people.'

'So it seems.'

'Well now, should each of them make what he produces publicly available for everyone? For instance, although the farmer is only one person, should he supply all four people with food? Should he spend four times as long and work four times as hard on supplying food and share it out, or should he ignore everyone else and spend a quarter of his time producing only a quarter of this amount of food for himself, and divide 370a the other three-quarters between getting a house and clothes and shoes for himself, and not have all the bother of associating with other people, but look after his own affairs on his own?'

Adeimantus said, 'It looks as though the first alternative is simpler, Socrates.'

'That's not surprising, of course,' I said. 'I mean, it occurred to me while you were speaking that, in the first place, different people are inherently suitable for different activities, since b people are not particularly similar to one another, but have a wide variety of natures. Don't you agree?'

'I do.'

'And is success a more likely consequence of an individual working at several jobs or specializing in only one?'*

'Of his specializing in only one,' he said.

'Now, here's another obvious point, I'm sure—that missing the critical opportunity has a deleterious effect.'

'Yes, obviously.'

'The reason being that the work isn't prepared to wait for the worker to make time for it. No, it's crucial for the worker to c fall in with the work and not try to fit it into his spare time.'

'Yes, that's crucial.'

'So it follows that productivity is increased, the quality of the products is improved, and the process is simplified when an individual sets aside his other pursuits, does the one thing for which he is naturally suited, and does it at the opportune moment.'

'Absolutely.'

'We need more than four citizens, then, Adeimantus, to supply the needs we mentioned. I mean, if the farmer's going to have a good plough, he will apparently not be making it d himself, and the same goes for his hoe and all the rest of his farming implements. Moreover, the builder won't be making his own tools either, and he too needs plenty of them; nor, by the same token, will the weaver and the shoemaker. True?'

'True.'

'So plenty of other craftsmen—joiners, metalworkers, and so on—will join our little settlement and swell its population.'

'Yes.'

'It still won't be very big, though, even when we've added shepherds and other herdsmen—who are also needed, otherwise the farmers won't have oxen to plough with, and there'll e be no draught-animals for them and the builders to use for pulling things, and no leather or wool for the weavers and shoemakers.'

'No,' he said, 'but it won't be small either with all that lot.'

'Now, it's practically impossible to build the actual community in a place where it will have no need of imports,' I pointed out.

'Yes, that's too much to expect.'

'Then they'll need more people, to bring in what it needs from elsewhere.'

'Yes.'

'But if their man goes empty-handed, in the sense of taking nothing with him which satisfies the requirements of the people from whom they're trying to get what they need, then he'll 371a depart empty-handed, won't he?'

'I should say so.'

'Then their home production must not only be enough to satisfy their own requirements, but must also be of a type and a quantity which satisfies the requirements of the people they need.'

'Yes, it must.'

'So our community had better increase the number of its farmers and other craftsmen.'

'Yes.'

'And also the number of its workers, I suppose, who import and export all the different kinds of goods—which is to say, merchants. Don't you agree?'

'Yes.'

'We'll need merchants too, then.'

'Certainly.'

'And if they deal with overseas countries, then a great many other people will be needed—experts in all sea-related work.' b

'Yes, we'll certainly need a lot of them.'

'Now, within the actual community, how will people trade their produce with one another? I mean, that was why we established an association and founded a community in the first place.'

'They'll trade by buying and selling, obviously,' he said.

'Then a consequence of this is that we'll have a market-place and coinage as a system of trading.'

'Yes.'

c 'So if a farmer or one of the other producers brings some of his produce to the market-place, but doesn't arrive at the same time as the people who want to trade with him, won't he be sitting in the market-place neglecting his own work?'

'No,' he replied, 'because there are people who notice the situation and take it on themselves to supply this service; in properly organized communities, they tend to be those who are physically the weakest and who are therefore unsuited for any other kind of work. Their job is to stay there in the market-

d place and to give people who want to sell something money in exchange for their goods, and then to give goods in exchange for money to people who want to buy something.'

'So this need', I said, 'gives rise to stallholders in our community. I mean, aren't people who stay put in a market-place and do the job of buying and selling called "stallholders", as distinct from those who travel from community to community, who are called "merchants"?'

'Yes, that's right.'

e 'I think there's another category of worker too, consisting of people who don't really deserve to join our community for their mental abilities, but who are physically strong enough to undertake hard labour. They sell the use of their strength, "pay" is the name of the reward they get for this, and that is why they're called "paid hands", I suppose, don't you?'

'Yes.'

'With paid hands as well, then, our community has reached its limit, I should think.'

'I agree.'

'Well, Adeimantus, our community has certainly grown. Is it now just right?'

'I suppose so.'

'Does it contain morality and immorality, then? If so, where and thanks to which of the people we've considered?'

372a 'I've no idea, Socrates,' he said, 'unless it has something to do with how these people treat one another.'

'You might be right,' I said. 'We must look into your idea: it deserves to be taken seriously. Let's start by considering how people who've been provided for like this will live. Surely they'll spend their time producing food, wine, clothes, and shoes, won't they? Once they've built their houses, they'll turn to production, which they'll invariably work at in the summer naked and with bare feet, and in the winter with adequate protective clothing and footwear. Their food will be barley- b meal and wheat-meal, which will sometimes be cooked and sometimes pulped, and the resulting honest fare of barley-cakes and wheat-cakes will be served up on reeds or on clean leaves, as they and their children, wearing chaplets and singing hymns to the gods, recline on carpets of bryony and myrtle and eat their fill, while drinking wine. They'll enjoy having sex, except that concern about poverty or war* will stop them procreating c beyond their means.'

At this point Glaucon interrupted and said, 'This diet you're giving them dispenses with savouries,* apparently.'

'You're right,' I said. 'I was forgetting that they'll also have savouries—salt, obviously, and olives and cheese—and they'll boil up the kinds of roots and vegetables which country stews are made of. We'll serve them with desserts too, I suppose, of figs, chick-peas, and beans; and they'll roast myrtle-berries and acorns in the fire as they sip their drinks. And so, it seems, their d life will pass in peace and good health, and at their death in old age they will pass on a similar way of life to their offspring.'

'Socrates,' he remarked, 'isn't this exactly the fodder you'd lay on if you were devising a community for pigs?'

'What would you suggest, then, Glaucon?' I asked.

'Nothing abnormal,' he replied. 'I think they should recline on couches, if they're to be comfortable, and eat from tables, and have the kinds of savouries and desserts which are in e current usage.'

Realistically, there is more to human life than the first community can provide—more to the human psyche than mere needs. The community is expanded to include non-necessary needs, until it threatens the integrity of others with which it comes into contact, and is itself threatened in the same way. It therefore needs guardians, to protect its integrity. The job of protection requires passion and love of knowledge.

'All right,' I said. 'I see. We're not just investigating the origins of a community, apparently, but of an indulgent community. Well, that may not be wrong: if we extend our enquiry like that, we might perhaps see how morality and immorality take root in communities.* Now, I think that the true community—the one in a healthy condition, as it were—is the one we've described;* but if you want us to inspect an inflamed community as well, so be it. There's no reason not to. I mean,
373a some people apparently won't be satisfied with the provisions and the lifestyle we've described, but will have all sorts of furniture like couches and tables, and a wide selection of savouries, perfumes, incense, prostitutes, and pastries. Moreover, the essential requirements can no longer be restricted to the houses and clothing and shoes we originally mentioned; no, we have to invent painting and ornamentation, and get hold of gold and ivory and so on. Don't you agree?'

b 'Yes,' he said.

'So we have to increase the size of our community once again. That healthy community will no longer do; it must become bloated and distended with occupations which leave the essential requirements of a community behind—for instance, with all kinds of hunters and imitators.* Among the latter will be hordes of people concerned with shapes and colours, and further hordes concerned with music (poets and their dependants—rhapsodes,* actors, dancers, producers), and manufacturers of all kinds of contraptions and all sorts of
c things, especially women's cosmetics. Furthermore, we'll need a larger number of workers—don't you think?—such as children's attendants,* nurses, nannies, hairdressers, barbers, and savoury-cooks and meat-cooks too. And that's not the end of it: we'll need pig-farmers as well—a job which didn't exist in our previous community, since there was no need of it, but which will be needed in the present one—and huge numbers of cows and sheep, if they are to be eaten, won't we?'

'Of course.'

d 'And with this lifestyle won't we be in far greater need of doctors than we were before?'

'Yes.'

'And, of course, although the inhabitants of our former community could live off the produce of the land, the land will be too small now, don't you think?'

'I agree.'

'So we'll have to take a chunk of our neighbours' land, if we're going to have enough for our herds and our crops, won't we? And suppose they too have stopped limiting themselves to necessities and have gone in for the uncontrolled acquisition of innumerable possessions: then they'll have to take a chunk of our land too, won't they?'

'That's more or less inevitable, Socrates,' he replied. e

'And the next step will be war, Glaucon, don't you think?'

'I agree,' he said.

'Now, let's not commit ourselves yet to a view on whether the effects of war are good or bad,' I said. 'All we're saying at the moment is that we've now discovered the origin of war. It is caused by those factors whose occurrence is the major cause of a community's troubles, whether it's the community as a whole which is afflicted or any individual member of it.'

'Yes.'

'We need another sizeable increase in our community, then, Glaucon—an army-sized increase. We need an army to go out 374a and defend all the community's property and all the people we were talking about a moment ago against invaders.'

'But can't the inhabitants do this themselves?' he asked.

'No,' I replied. 'At any rate, they can't if the proposition we all—including you—agreed to when we were forming our community was correct. The proposition was, if you remember, that it is impossible for one person to work properly at more than one area of expertise.'

'You're right.'

'Well,' I said, 'don't you think that warfare requires expertise?' b

'I certainly do,' he answered.

'So should we take more trouble over our shoemakers than we do over our soldiers?'

'Not at all.'

'Well now, we prohibited a shoemaker from simultaneously undertaking farming or weaving or building, but had him concentrating exclusively on shoemaking, to ensure quality achievements in shoemaking; and we similarly allotted every single person just one job—the one for which he was naturally suited, and which he was to work at all his life, setting aside his other pursuits, so as not to miss the opportunities which c are critical for quality achievement. Isn't it crucial, however,

that the achievements of warfare are of a high standard? Or is soldiering so easy that someone can be expert at it while carrying on with his farming or shoemaking or whatever his profession might be, despite the fact that no one could even become a competent backgammon-player or dice-player if he took it up only in his spare time and didn't concentrate on it for years, starting when he was a young man? Does someone
d just have to pick up a shield (or whatever military implement or instrument it may be) and he instantaneously becomes a competent fighter in a heavy infantry engagement (or in whatever form of armed conflict it may be)? This would be unique, since no other implement makes a person a craftsman or an athlete if he just holds it, and no other implement is the slightest good to anyone unless he's acquired the knowledge of how to use it and has devoted sufficient attention to it.'

'Yes,' he said, 'if tools could do that, they'd be highly prized.'

'Now,' I said, 'the amount of time allotted just to it, and also
e the degree of professionalism and training, should reflect the supreme importance of the guardians' work.'

'I certainly think so,' he said.

'And a natural talent for the job would help too, wouldn't it?'

'Of course.'

'Our job, then, if we're up to it, would seem to be to select which people and what types of person have a natural gift for protecting our community.'

'Yes, it is.'

'We've certainly taken on an awesome task, then,' I said. 'Still, we mustn't be intimidated; we must do the best we can.'

375a 'I agree.'

'Well,' I went on, 'do you think there's any difference, as far as suitability for guarding is concerned, between the nature of the best type of dog and that of a well-born young man?'

'What are you getting at?'

'That both of them have to be acutely perceptive, quick on their feet (so as to chase after anything they do perceive) and strong as well, in case they have to fight someone they've cornered.'

'Yes,' he said, 'they need all these qualities.'

'And a good fighter must be brave, of course.'

66

'That goes without saying.'

'Now, you'll never find courage without passion, in a horse or a dog or any other creature, will you? I mean, you must have noticed how indomitable and invincible passion is. It always takes passion in a mind to make it capable of facing any b situation without fear and without yielding, doesn't it?'

'Yes.'

'It's obvious what physical attributes a guardian must have, then.'

'Yes.'

'And the importance of a passionate temperament is also clear.'

'Again, yes.'

'Well, aren't people of this type bound to behave like brutes to one another and to the rest of their fellow citizens, Glaucon?' I asked.

'Yes, it certainly won't be easy to stop them,' he replied.

'However, they should really behave with civilized gentleness c towards their friends and neighbours and with ferocity towards their enemies. Otherwise, it won't be a question of waiting for others to come and destroy them: they'll do the job first themselves!'

'True,' he said.

'What shall we do, then?' I asked. 'Where are we going to find a character that is simultaneously gentle and high-spirited, when gentleness and passion are opposites?'

'Yes, they do seem to be mutually exclusive.'

'And yet if a guardian is deprived of either of them he can't be a good guardian. We seem to be faced with an impasse; it turns out that a good guardian is an impossibility.'   d

'I suppose so.'

I was stuck. I surveyed the course of the discussion and then said, 'We deserve to be stuck, Glaucon. We haven't kept to the analogy we proposed.'

'What do you mean?'

'We've overlooked the fact that the supposedly impossible type of character, which contains these opposite qualities, does exist.'

'Where?'

'In animals. You could find the combination primarily—

e though not exclusively—in the animal we used as an analogy for our guardian. I mean, as I'm sure you know, there's no creature more gentle towards people it knows and recognizes, and no creature more savage towards strangers, then the best type of dog; and this is due to its innate character.'

'Yes, I'm aware of that.'

'So it *is* a possibility, then,' I said. 'We're not looking for something unnatural in looking for a guardian of this type.'

'No, I suppose not.'

'Now, don't you think there's another quality which a would-be guardian needs as well? Don't you think that in addition to being naturally passionate he should also have a philosopher's love of knowledge?'*

376a   'Why?' he asked. 'I don't see why.'

'Take dogs again,' I said. 'It's noticeable that they have a remarkable feature.'

'What?'

'They get fierce with strangers even before the slightest harm has been done them, and they welcome familiar people even if they've never been benefited by them. Has this never struck you as surprising?'

'I hadn't really thought about it until now,' he said. 'But yes, they do clearly do that.'

'But don't you think that this feature shows how naturally b smart they are and how genuinely they love knowledge?'

'How?'

'Because', I explained, 'their sole criterion for the friendliness or hostility of what they see is whether or not they have learnt to recognize it. Now, anything that relies on familiarity and unfamiliarity to define what is congenial and what is alien must prize learning, mustn't it?'

'Yes,' he said, 'inevitably.'

'Well,' I went on, 'isn't loving learning the same thing as loving knowledge?'

'Yes, it is,' he said.

'So why don't we stick our necks out and suggest that the same goes for a human being too—that if he's going to be c gentle with his friends and acquaintances, he must be an innate lover of knowledge and learning?'

'All right,' he said.

'Anyone who is going to be a truly good guardian of our community, then, will have a philosopher's love of knowledge, and will be passionate, quick on his feet, and strong.'*

'Absolutely,' he said.

Chapter 4

Primary Education for the Guardians

The would-be guardians have natural aptitude, but how should their characters be moulded? (Academic education is reserved for the few, and for when they are older.) Plato begins with the stories they hear from childhood onwards. These inculcate values, so they must hear only morally sound stories, which will help them gain the appropriate social attitudes, such as respect for their parents, the desire for political unity, and, above all, correct beliefs about God, who is good, straightforward, and unchanging. Any stories which could inculcate the wrong attitudes in any of these respects is to be censored.

'So those are his attributes. But how are we going to bring these people up?* What education shall we give them? If we look into these issues, does it further the overall purpose of our enquiry, which is to see how morality and immorality arise in society? We have to be careful not to leave out any relevant argument or to swamp the discussion with too many topics.'

376d

It was Glaucon's brother who said, 'I expect the consideration of these issues will substantially further it.'

'In that case, my dear Adeimantus,' I said, 'we must certainly not give up, even if the investigation turns out to be rather lengthy.'

'No, we mustn't.'

'All right, then, let's devise a theoretical education for these people, as if we were making up a story and weren't worried about time.'

e

'Yes, that's a good idea.'

'How shall we educate them, then? Or is it hard to improve on the educational system which has evolved over a long period of time? This, as you know, consists of exercise for the body and cultural studies for the mind.'*

'Yes.'

'And shall we begin the cultural programme before the physical one?'

'Of course.'

'Cultural studies include literature, don't you think?' I asked.

'I do.'

'Aren't there two kinds of literature, true and false?'*

'Yes.'

'Should we include both kinds in our educational system, and 377a start with the untrue kind?'

'I don't understand what you're getting at,' he said.

'Don't you realize,' I asked, 'that we start by telling children stories which are, by and large, untrue, though they contain elements of truth? And stories precede physical exercise in our education of children.'

'True.'

'Which is why I suggested that cultural studies should be taken up before physical exercise.'

'It was a good suggestion,' he said.

'Now, do you appreciate that the most important stage of any enterprise is the beginning, especially when something young and sensitive is involved? You see, that's when most of b its formation takes place, and it absorbs every impression that anyone wants to stamp upon it.'

'You're absolutely right.'

'Shall we, then, casually allow our children to listen to any old stories, made up by just anyone, and to take into their minds views which, on the whole, contradict those we'll want them to have as adults?'

'No, we won't allow that at all.'

'So our first job, apparently, is to oversee the work of the story-writers, and to accept any good story they write, but c reject the others.* We'll let nurses and mothers tell their children the acceptable ones, and we'll have them devote themselves far more to using these stories to form their children's minds than they do to using their hands to form their bodies.* However, we'll have to disallow most of the stories they currently tell.'

'Which stories?' he asked.

'If we examine the grander kind of story,' I said, 'that will give us insights into the more lightweight kind as well, because the same principle must be involved and both kinds are bound to have the same effect, don't you think?' d

71

'That sounds fine to me,' he replied, 'but I don't even understand which stories you're describing as grander.'

'The ones which Hesiod, Homer, and their fellow poets tell us. In the past, it's always been the poets who've composed untrue stories to tell people, and it's no different nowadays.'

'Which stories?' he asked. 'And what's their defect, in your view?'

'There is no defect which one ought to condemn more quickly and more thoroughly,' I replied, 'especially if the lies have no redeeming feature.'

'Yes, but what *is* this defect?'

e 'Using the written word to give a distorted image of the nature of the gods and heroes, just as a painter might produce a portrait which completely fails to capture the likeness of the original.'

'Yes,' he said, 'it's quite right to find fault with that sort of thing. But how do they do that? What kinds of things do they say?'

'First and most important, since the subject is so important,' I said, 'there is no redeeming feature to the lies which Hesiod 378a repeats, about Uranus' deeds and Cronus' revenge on Uranus.* Then there are Cronus' deeds and what his son did to him.* Now, I think that even if these stories are true, they oughtn't to be told so casually to young people and people who lack discrimination; it's better to keep silent, and if one absolutely has to speak, to make them esoteric secrets told to as few people as possible, who are to have sacrificed no mere piglet,* but something so large and rare that the smallest conceivable number of people get to hear them.'

'Yes,' he said, 'these stories are definitely dangerous.'

b 'And we must censor them in our community, Adeimantus,' I said. 'No young person is to hear stories which suggest that were he to commit the vilest of crimes, and were he to do his utmost to punish his father's crimes, he wouldn't be doing anything out of the ordinary, but would simply be behaving like the first and the greatest gods.'

'No, I absolutely agree,' he said. 'I share your view that these stories are unsuitable and shouldn't be repeated.'

'And that's not all,' I said. 'The stories which have gods c fighting and scheming and battling against one another are utterly unsuitable too, because they're just as untrue. If the prospective guardians of our community are to loathe casual quarrels with one another, we must take good care that battles between gods and giants* and all the other various tales of gods and heroes coming to blows with their relatives and friends don't occur in the stories they hear and the pictures they see. No, if we're somehow to convince them that fellow citizens never fall out with one another, that this is wrong, then that is the kind of story they must hear, from childhood onwards, from the community's elders of both sexes; and the poets d they'll hear when they're older must be forced to tell equivalent stories in their poetry. But we'd better not admit into our community the story of Hera being tied up by her son, or the episode when Hephaestus is hurled away by his father for trying to save his mother from a beating, or any of the battles between the gods which Homer has in his poetry, whether or not their intention is allegorical.* The point is that a young person can't tell when something is allegorical and when it isn't, and any idea admitted by a person of that age tends to become almost ineradicable and permanent. All things con- e sidered, then, that is why a very great deal of importance should be placed upon ensuring that the first stories they hear are best adapted for their moral improvement.'

'Yes, that makes sense,' he said. 'But suppose we were once again to be asked,* in this context as well, what stories we meant, how would we respond?'

'Adeimantus,' I said, 'you and I are not making up stories at the moment; we're founding a community. Founders ought 379a to know the broad outlines within which their poets are to compose stories, so that they can exclude any compositions which do not conform to those outlines; but they shouldn't themselves make stories up.'

'You're right,' he said. 'But that's precisely the point: what are these guidelines for talking about the gods?'

'They'd be something like this,' I said. 'Whatever the type of poetry—epic, lyric, or tragic—God must of course always be portrayed as he really is.'*

'Yes, he must.'

'Well, isn't God good, in fact, and shouldn't he be described b as such?'

'Of course.'

'And nothing good is harmful, is it?'

'I don't think so.'

'Now, can anything harmless cause damage?'

'No, of course not.'

'Can anything incapable of causing damage do anything bad?'

'Again, no.'

'And something which never does bad couldn't be responsible for bad, could it?'

'Of course not.'

'Well now, is goodness beneficial?'

'Yes.'

'And it's responsible for doing good, then?'

'Yes.'

'So goodness is not responsible for everything: it's responsible for things that are in a good state, but bad things cannot be attributed to it.'

c   'Exactly,' he said.

'The same goes for God too, then,' I said. 'Since he is good, he cannot be responsible for everything, as is commonly said. He is responsible only for a small part of human life, and many things cannot be attributed to him—I mean, there's far more bad than good in the world. He and he alone must be held responsible for the good things, but responsibility for bad things must be looked for elsewhere and not attributed to God.'

'I think you're absolutely right,' he said.

'So,' I said, 'we shouldn't connive at Homer or any other

d   poet making the stupid mistake of saying about the gods, "Two jars sit on Zeus' threshold: one is full of good destinies, but the other is full of wretched destinies",* and that if Zeus mixes the two up together and doles them out to someone, that person "sometimes meets with bad, sometimes with good", whereas if he doesn't mix them up, but allots the pernicious ones to someone in an unadulterated form, that person "is driven over the glorious earth by the evil of poverty". Nor will we connive

e   at them claiming that "Zeus is the dispenser of both good and evil".*

'Moreover, we'll disapprove of the attribution of Pandarus' perjury and truce-breaking to the agency of Athena and Zeus,* and of the gods' quarrel and its resolution to Themis and Zeus;* and we'll not allow the younger generation to hear the 380a idea which Aeschylus* expresses as "When God wants to visit utter ruin on a household, he implants the cause in men." No, if plays are composed (such as the one these lines are from) about Niobe's afflictions, or about the trials and tribulations of the descendants of Pelops,* or about the Trojan War, the playwrights must either be prohibited from saying that God was responsible for these events, or if they do attribute them to God, they have to come up with an explanation which approximates to the one we're looking for at the moment, and say that what God did was right and good, in the sense that the b people in question were being punished and therefore benefited; but poets should be prohibited from saying that these people were in a *bad* way as a result of being punished and that this was God's doing. The claim that the sinners were badly off because they were in need of punishment, and that in punishing them God was benefiting them, is permissible; but the claim that God, who is good, is responsible for any instance of badness is to be resisted as forcefully as possible by anyone who wants a well-regulated community, until it is never spoken and never heard by anyone, of whatever age, whether the tale is c told in verse or in prose. And the reasons are that the voicing of these views is sacrilege, they do us no good, and they are inconsistent with one another.'

'I approve of this law,' he said. 'I'll be right behind you when you cast your vote for it.'

'So now we have the first of the laws and guidelines which pertain to the gods,' I said. 'Any spoken words or composed works will have to conform to the principle that God is not responsible for everything, but only for good.'

'Well, I'm certainly happy with it,' he said.

'All right, then. What about a second principle, as follows? d Do you think that God is a sorcerer and can by exercising his will vary his appearance from time to time, sometimes by actually changing and† transforming his appearance into a large number of forms, and at other times by deluding us into thinking that's what he's done? Or do you think he's uniform and extremely unlikely to abandon his own appearance?'

'I'm not in a position to say just at the moment,' he replied.

'Look at it this way. Isn't it inevitable that if anything sheds
e its form, the change is due either to itself or to something else?'

'Yes.'

'Now, really good things are extremely unlikely to be altered
or moved by an external agent, aren't they? For instance, a
human body is altered by food, drink, and exercise, and plants
are altered by the heat of the sun and by wind and phenomena
like that; but the more healthy and strong a thing is, the less
381a likely it is to be altered.'

'Of course.'

'And the more courageous and intelligent a mind is, the less
likely it is that an external agent would disturb it and alter it?'

'Yes.'

'Moreover, the same principle applies universally even to
manufactured items, such as utensils, houses, and clothes:
things which are well made and are in good condition are less
likely to be altered by time and other phenomena.'

'True.'

b   'So anything which is in a good state—whether that is due to
nature or human skill or both—can hardly be changed at all by
an external agent.'

'That sounds right.'

'But God and the divine realm are of course in all respects as
perfect as anything can be.'

'Of course.'

'From this point of view, then, God is extremely unlikely to
have at his disposal a large number of forms.'

'Yes, extremely unlikely indeed.'

'Would he, however, change and alter himself internally, by
his own resources?'

'If he changes in the first place,' he said, 'then obviously this
must be how.'

'Well, does he enhance and improve himself, or does he
worsen and debase himself?'

c   'If he changes,' he said, 'then it must be for the worse, since
it's unthinkable that God's goodness and excellence are
anything less than perfect.'

'You're absolutely right,' I said. 'And, Adeimantus, in
this context, do you think that anyone—human or divine—
deliberately makes himself deteriorate in any respect?'

'That's impossible,' he said.

'It is equally impossible, then,' I said, 'for God to want to change himself. Since, as we have found, the divine nature is as perfect and as good as anything could be, then any god retains his own form in a uniform, direct fashion for ever.'

'I think that's absolutely inevitable,' he said.

'It follows, Adeimantus,' I said, 'that none of our poets is to d say, "The gods travel around human habitations disguised as all sorts of visitors from other lands."* Nor are they to tell lies about Proteus and Thetis,* or present Hera in a tragedy or any other kind of poem in an altered form, as a mendicant holy woman begging alms "for the life-giving children of the Argive river Inachus",* or repeat the mass of other similar lies that have been told. Furthermore, we should neutralize the poets' e influence on mothers, which makes them scare their children with terrible stories about how some gods tend to prowl around during the hours of darkness in a wide variety of unfamiliar human guises, so that we stop the mothers blaspheming against the gods, and at the same time stop them making their children too timid.'

'Yes, we should,' he said.

'But even if it isn't in the gods' nature actually to change,' I said, 'do they magically delude us into seeing them appear in all kinds of guises?'

'It's not inconceivable,' he said.

'Well, would God willingly mask the truth behind appear- 382a ance and deceive us by his words or actions?' I asked.

'I don't know,' he answered.

'Don't you know that a true falsehood (if you'll allow me the phrase) is loathed by everyone, divine or human?' I asked.

'What do you mean?' he asked.

'I mean', I said, 'that no one chooses and wants to be deceived in the most important part of himself and about the most important things. The presence of falsehood there is his worst fear.'

'I still don't understand,' he said.

'That's because you think I'm trying to make a high-powered b point,' I said. 'But all I'm saying is that no one is at all happy at being lied to and deceived in his mind about the facts; no one likes being ignorant, and the existence and presence of falsehood there are extremely unwelcome to everyone; they particularly hate it there.'

'They certainly do,' he said.

'Well, I might have been perfectly correct when I described this state a moment ago as true falsehood—the state of misapprehension caused by falsehood in the mind. I mean, a spoken lie is a kind of copy and subsequent reflection of the
c mental condition, and no pure lie, don't you think?'

'Yes.'

'Now, a genuine lie is hated by men as well as gods.'

'I think so.'

'What about a spoken lie? Aren't there occasions and situations when telling lies is helpful and doesn't therefore warrant hatred? What about when we're dealing with enemies, or with people we count as friends, but who are trying to do something bad because they've gone mad or have somehow taken leave of their senses? Isn't telling lies helpful under these circumstances as a preventative medicine? Moreover, consider those stories
d we were discussing not long ago: we cannot know the truth about events in the past, so we make something up which approximates as closely as possible to the truth, and that helps us, doesn't it?'

'Yes,' he said, 'you're quite right.'

'Which of these reasons, then, makes telling lies helpful to God? Would he make up something which resembles the truth because he doesn't know the past?'

'That's a ridiculous suggestion,' he said.

'So there's nothing of the lying poet in God.'

'I don't think so.'

'Would he lie out of fear for his enemies?'
e 'Hardly.'

'Because his friends have taken leave of their senses or gone mad?'

'Anyone witless or insane is no friend of God,' he said.

'So God has no reason to lie.'

'No.'

'So it is not in the nature of deities or gods to deceive.'

'Absolutely not,' he said.

'Whether acting or speaking, then, God is entirely uniform and truthful. He doesn't actually change himself, and he doesn't delude others either, during their sleeping or their waking hours, in how he appears or in what he says or in the signs he sends.'

'Listening to you speak,' he said, 'I find myself agreeing with 383a you.'

'So do you agree,' I said, 'that this is the second principle to which religious discussions and literature must conform—that the gods are not shape-shifting wizards and do not mislead us by lying in what they say or do?'

'I agree.'

'Although there is much to commend in Homer, then, we won't approve of the passage when Zeus sends the dream to Agamemnon.* Likewise, we won't approve of the bit of Aeschylus* where Thetis says that at her wedding Apollo "celebrated in song how happy my children would make b me—how they wouldn't know sickness and would live for many long years—and went on and on about how lucky I was and how the gods smiled on me, until he made my heart glad. And since Phoebus is a god and abounds in prophetic skill, I expected his words to be true. But for all his singing, for all his sharing of our feast, for all these claims of his, it is he who has now killed my son." We'll come down hard on anyone who says anything like this about the gods: we'll refuse him a c chorus* and ban teachers from using his works to educate our children. Otherwise, our guardians won't grow up to be religious people, or to be as godlike themselves as is humanly possible.'

'I'm in complete agreement with these principles,' he said, 'and would want them enshrined as laws.'

Poets—especially Homer—also carelessly promote cowardice, servility, lying, over-indulgence in emotion and sensual desire, avarice, and disrespect. To the extent that story-telling, which was the domain of the poets, is an important psychological influence (and it formed a major part of a child's education in Plato's Athens), we must prevent poets from promoting these values, and permit only the opposite values to be inculcated in the community.

'All right, then,' I said. 'If people are going to revere the 386a gods, respect their parents, and not belittle friendship with one another, then apparently those are the kinds of stories they should and shouldn't hear about the gods, from childhood onwards.'

'I'm sure we're right about this,' he said.

'What about if they are to be brave? Won't they also need stories which are designed to make them fear death as little as b possible? I mean, don't you think that courage and fearing death are mutually exclusive?'

'Yes, I certainly do,' he answered.

'What about the idea that Hades doesn't just exist, but is terrifying? Do you think this goes with facing death fearlessly and with preferring death in battle to defeat and slavery?'

'Of course not.'

'So here's another aspect of story-telling for us to oversee, apparently. We must ask those who take on the job of telling stories not to denigrate Hades in the simple fashion they have been, but to speak well of it, because otherwise they'll not only be lying, but also not speaking in a way that is conducive to c courage in battle.'

'Yes, we must,' he said.

'Then we'll start with the following lines,' I said, 'and delete everything which resembles them: "I'd rather be a slave labouring for someone else—someone without property, who can hardly make a living—than rule over all the spirits of the dead";* and "The vile, dank halls, which even the gods hate, d might appear to men and gods"; and "Amazing! The soul, the likeness of a person, really does exist in Hades' halls, but it is completely witless"; and "He alone had consciousness, while the rest were darting shadows"; and "His soul flew from his body and went to Hades bewailing its fate, forfeiting courage 387a and the glory of young manhood"; and "Like a wisp of smoke, his soul went down to the underworld with a shrill cry"; and "As when bats flit about squeaking in the depths of an awful cave, when one of them loses its perch on the crowded rock, and they cling to one another, so the flock of souls went with b shrill cries." We'll implore Homer and the rest of the poets not to get cross if we strike these and all similar lines from their works. We'll explain that it's not because the lines are not good poetry and don't give pleasure to most people; on the contrary, the better poetry they are, the more they are to be kept from the ears of children and men who are to be autonomous and to be more afraid of losing this freedom than of death.'

'Absolutely.'

'Now, we'd better get rid of all the frightening and terrifying names which crop up here. I mean names like Cocytus and Styx,* ghost and wraith, and so on—all the names which c are designed to make everyone who hears them shudder.† In another context, they may have a useful purpose to serve; but our worry is that this shivering might make our guardians too feverish and enervated.'

'It's a legitimate worry,' he remarked.

'Should we ban them, then?'

'Yes.'

'It's names which have the opposite effect that should be used in both prose and poetry, isn't it?'

'Clearly.'

'Shall we also remove the passages where eminent men weep d and wail in mourning, then?'

'We have to,' he said. 'It follows from what we've already done.'

'Let's see whether or not we're right to remove them,' I said. 'We can agree that one good man will not regard death as a terrible thing for another good man—a friend of his—to suffer.'

'Yes, we can.'

'So a good man won't mourn as if the other person had suffered something terrible.'

'No.'

'Moreover, we can also agree that a good man is pre-eminently capable of providing himself with a good life entirely from his own resources, and is absolutely the last person to need anyone or anything else.' e

'True.'

'So he'd be the last person to be overwhelmed by the loss of a son or a brother or some money and so on and so forth.'

'Yes, definitely.'

'He'll also be the last person to mourn, then, when some such disaster overtakes him: no one will endure it with more equanimity than him.'

'Very true.'

'We'd be right, then, not to have famous men mourning. We can allow women to do that (as long as they aren't admirable women) and any bad men there might be, so that the people we 388a claim to be training for guardianship of our land find all that sort of behaviour distasteful.'

'That's right,' he said.

'So we have a further request to make of Homer and the rest of the poets. We'll ask them not to portray Achilles, who was the son of a goddess,* "at one point lying on his side, then later on his back, and then on his front; and then getting to his feet b and sailing, crazed with grief, over the sands of the bitter sea", or as "pouring handfuls of filthy ashes over his head", or generally as weeping and wailing to the extent and in the fashion that the poet portrays him. And we'll ask them not to have Priam, a close relative of the gods by birth,* "begging, and rolling in the dung as he calls out to each man by name". We'll be even more forceful, however, in our request that they don't portray the *gods* lamenting and saying things like, "Oh, c poor me! How wretched I am to have borne the noblest of children!"; or at the very least they ought to stop short of giving such an inaccurate portrait of the greatest of the gods that they have him saying, "Alas! The man I now see being chased around Troy is dear to me, and my heart grieves", and "Alas that Sarpedon, the dearest of men to me, is destined to d fall at the hands of Patroclus the son of Menoetius."

'The point is, my dear Adeimantus, that if the young men of our community hear this kind of thing and take it seriously, rather than regarding it as despicable and absurd, they're hardly going to regard such behaviour as despicable in human beings like themselves and feel remorse when they also find themselves saying or doing these or similar things. Instead, they won't find it at all degrading to be constantly chanting laments and dirges for trivial incidents, and they won't resist doing so.'

e 'You're quite right,' he said.

'And what we've just been arguing, in effect—and at the moment no one's come up with a better argument, so we should stick to this one—is that we must prevent this happening.'

'Yes, we must.'

'Now, they'd better not be prone to laughter either.* I

82

mean, the stronger the laughter, the stronger the consequent emotional reaction too—that's almost inevitable.'

'I agree,' he said.

'We should, therefore, refuse admittance to any poetry which portrays eminent humans as being overcome by laughter, and do so even more vigorously if it shows gods in that state.'   389a

'Yes, indeed,' he said.

'So we'll also reject the lines of Homer where he says about the gods,* "Unquenchable laughter arose among the blessed gods as they watched Hephaestus bustling about the house." According to your argument, we should disallow this type of passage.'

'Yes, if you want to attribute the argument to me,' he said. 'At any rate, we should disallow it.'   b

'Next, they must rate honesty highly. You see, if we were right in what we were saying a short while ago,* and the gods really have no use for falsehood, although it can serve as a type of medicine for us humans, then clearly lying should be entrusted to doctors, and laymen should have nothing to do with it.'

'Clearly,' he said.

'If it's anyone's job, then, it's the job of the rulers of our community: they can lie for the good of the community, when either an external or an internal threat makes it necessary. No one else, however, should have anything to do with lying. If an ordinary person lies to these rulers of ours, we'll count that as c equivalent in misguidedness, if not worse, to a patient lying to his doctor about his physical condition, or an athlete in training lying to his trainer about his physical condition, or someone misleading a ship's captain, with respect to his ship or crew, by telling him lies about his own state or that of one of his fellow crewmen.'

'You're absolutely right,' he said.

'So if anyone else is caught lying in our community—"any d artisan, whether diviner or healer of ills or carpenter"*—he is to be punished on the grounds that he's introducing a practice which is just as liable to wreck and ruin a community as a ship.'

'Yes, it would,' he said, 'if what people did was influenced by what he had said.'

83

'Now, won't the young men of our community need self-discipline?'

'Of course.'

'And aren't the most important aspects of self-discipline, at least for the general rank and file, obedience to those
e in authority and establishing one's own authority over the pleasures of drink, sex, and food?'

'I think so.'

'So I'm sure we'll approve of the kind of thing Homer has Diomedes say*—"Sit down, shut up, and listen to me"—and related passages, like "Exuding an aura of courage, the Greeks advanced in silence, respecting their leaders", and so on and so forth.'

'Yes, we will.'

'Well, what about lines like "You're groggy with wine, you have the eyes of a dog and the heart of a deer"* and the next
390a few lines? Are they all right? And what about all the other impertinent things people have said to their rulers in works of prose or poetry?'

'We won't approve of them.'

'That, I suppose, is because they don't encourage self-discipline in their audience, though they may well be enjoyable from another point of view. What do you think?'

'I agree,' he said.

'What about having your cleverest character saying that in his opinion the best thing in the world is when "The nearby
b tables are laden with bread and meat, and the steward draws wine from the mixing-bowl, brings it, and pours it into the cups"?* Do you think this is the right material for a young man to hear if he is to be self-controlled? Or "There is no death worse than death by starvation, no more wretched fate to face"?* And then there's the passage* where, while everyone else—mortal and immortal—is asleep, Zeus stays awake to do some planning, but in no time at all it is driven completely out
c of his mind by his sexual desire, and he is so overwhelmed by the sight of Hera that he doesn't even want to go to their room, but wants to have sex with her there and then, on the ground, and he says that he's feeling more desire for her even than the first time they slept together, "without our parents knowing". And the story of how Hephaestus ensnared Ares and Aphrodite

for similar reasons is equally inappropriate material for them to hear.'*

'I couldn't agree with you more,' he said. 'It's quite unsuitable.'

'On the other hand,' I said, 'it's worth their paying attention d to the portrayal on stage or in writing of occasions when famous men express, by their words or actions, resistance to all kinds of temptations. For instance, there are the lines,* "He struck his breast and spoke sternly to his heart: 'Patience, heart—you've put up with worse in the past.'"'

'Absolutely,' he said.

'Then again, we shouldn't let them be mercenary or avaricious.'

'Of course not.'   e

'So they shouldn't repeat the verse "Gifts win over even gods and magnificent kings".* And we won't compliment Achilles' attendant Phoenix on his restraint in advising Achilles to accept the gifts he was being offered and help the Greeks in their fight, but not to refrain from his "wrath"* unless he was bribed. It will also go against our wishes and our convictions for Achilles himself to be mercenary enough to accept Agamemnon's gifts and to refuse to release a corpse until he'd been given a ransom.'*   391a

'Yes, it would be wrong to approve of that kind of behaviour,' he said.

'Now, the fact that it's Homer makes me hesitate,' I said, 'but I'm not sure it's not actually sacrilegious for us to say things like this about Achilles and accept them when others say them. The same goes also for when Achilles says to Apollo,* "There's no god more baneful than you—you with your aloofness. You misled me, and I'd pay you back if I could." We shouldn't believe that he refused to obey the river-god either, b and was ready to fight him,* and that he said of his hair, which was dedicated to another river, the Spercheius, "I hereby give my hair to the hero Patroclus: may he take it with him",* when Patroclus was dead—we shouldn't believe that he did this. And we'll deny the truth of the stories that he dragged Hector around Patroclus' tomb and slaughtered prisoners on his funeral pyre.* And we won't allow our citizens to believe that Achilles—the child of a goddess and of Peleus (who was him- c self a model of self-discipline and a grandson of Zeus) and tutored by the sage Cheiron—was so full of turmoil that he suffered from the two conflicting diseases of mean-spirited avarice and disdain for gods and men.'*

'You're right,' he said.

'Moreover,' I went on, 'we won't believe or tolerate the story about those horrific kidnap projects by Theseus and Peirithous,* who were respectively the sons of Poseidon and

d Zeus; and in general, we find it unthinkable that anyone with a god as a parent, or any hero, would be unscrupulous enough to do the terrible, sacrilegious things people falsely attribute to them. No, we should force the poets to deny either that the heroes did these things or that their parents were gods, but not to say both; and they should also be forcibly prevented from trying to persuade the young men of our community that the gods are the source of evil and that the heroes are no better than ordinary people. We demonstrated earlier the impossibility

e of bad things originating with the gods; so, as we said then, these stories are not only sacrilegious, but also false.'*

'Of course.'

'And they have a pernicious effect on their audience as well, in the sense that no one will find his own badness reprehensible once he's been persuaded that these things are and always have been done by "immediate descendants of the gods, close relatives of Zeus, people whose altar to Zeus, their father-protector, is high on Mount Ida, above the clouds" and "in whom the blood of deities is still fresh".* That's why we must put an end to stories of this nature: if we don't, they will

392a engender in the young men of our community a casual attitude towards badness.'

'I quite agree,' he said.

'Now,' I said, 'if we want to distinguish what in literature should be allowed and what should be censored, there's one further type of writing we should still look at, isn't there? I mean, we've discussed how gods must be portrayed—and deities, heroes, and the dead.'*

'Yes.'

'So wouldn't we be left with writing which has human beings as its subject?'

'Yes, obviously.'

'In fact, though, we can't evaluate this kind of writing at the moment.'

'Why not?'

'Because what we'd claim, I imagine, is that poets and prose-writers misrepresent people in extremely important ways, b when—as they often do—they portray immoral people as happy and moral people as unhappy, and write about the rewards of undiscovered immorality and how morality is good for someone else, but disadvantageous to oneself. I suppose we'd proscribe assertions of that kind, and tell them that their poems and stories are to make the opposite points, don't you think?'

'I'm certain we would,' he said.

'Well, if you concede this, then won't I claim that you've conceded the original purpose of the enquiry?'*

'Yes, I take your point,' he said.

'So we'll postpone our conclusion that these are the types of c stories that should be told about people until we've got to the bottom of morality and found out how, given its nature, it rewards its possessor whether or not he gives an impression of morality.'*

'You're quite right,' he said.

Turning from content to form, Plato classifies poetry according to how much 'representation' or 'impersonation' it uses—how much the poet speaks for himself as opposed to having characters speak in their persons. This is a form of dishonesty, but more importantly, it allows people to take on characteristics which may be alien to what they themselves actually are, and undesirable. This habituation would warp their true natures, whereas the principle of 'one man, one job' requires adherence to one's own nature.

'Let's take our discussion of stories no further, then. But the next thing we should look at, in my opinion, is style. Then we'll have considered not only the content, but also the form the stories should have, and our enquiry will be complete.'

'I don't understand what you're getting at here,' said Adeimantus.

'But it's important that you do,' I responded. 'Maybe this d will clarify matters for you: isn't everything told by story-tellers or poets actually a narrative of events in the past, present, or future?'

'Of course,' he said.

'And don't they achieve their effect by making use either of pure narrative, or of representational narrative, or of both?'

'I'm still finding this very obscure,' he said.

'What a ridiculous teacher I seem to be!' I said. 'I don't make things plain at all. I'll stop trying to behave like a professional speaker, and instead of talking in general terms, I'll take a
e particular example and use that to try to explain my meaning. So here's a question for you. You know the very beginning of the *Iliad*, where Homer has Chryses ask Agamemnon to release his daughter, and Agamemnon gets annoyed, and Chryses
393a doesn't get his way and so calls on his god* to curse the Greeks?'

'Yes.'

'Well, as you know, Homer starts by speaking in his own voice and doesn't try to lead us astray by pretending that anyone else is the speaker; this goes on up to the lines* "He implored all the Greeks, but especially their leaders, the two sons of Atreus." Next, however, he speaks in Chryses' voice
b and tries his very hardest to make us believe that it isn't Homer who is speaking, but the old priest. And the same method of composition is employed throughout nearly all his narrative of events in Troy and Ithaca and in the *Odyssey* in general.'

'Quite so,' he said.

'Now, the term "narrative" covers all the speeches as well as the passages in between the speeches, doesn't it?'

'Of course.'

c 'And when he assumes someone else's voice to make a speech, don't you think that on those occasions he does his very best to adapt his own style to whoever he tells us is about to do the talking?'

'Yes, certainly.'

'Now, to adapt oneself—one's voice or one's appearance— to someone else is to represent that person, isn't it?'

'Of course.'

'So this turns out to be a case of Homer and the rest of the poets composing representational narrative.'

'Yes.'

'And if Homer were to remain undisguised throughout, then
d all his poetry and all his narrative would be free of representa-

tion. But I don't want you saying that you don't understand again, so I'll tell you how this might happen. If Homer had described Chryses as coming with his daughter's ransom to appeal to the Greeks, but especially their kings, and had then gone on to continue speaking in his own voice rather than taking on the role of Chryses, then it would be pure narrative, not representation. It would go something like this, in my prose version—I'm no poet. "The priest came and prayed that the gods would allow the Greeks to take Troy and come through e unscathed, and also prayed that the Greeks would accept the ransom and, out of reverence for Apollo, release his daughter. Although everyone else gave their assent and approval to what he said, Agamemnon became incensed and ordered him to leave immediately and not to return, or else he would find that his staff and its Apolline garlands* were insufficient protection; he said that his daughter would grow old in Argos with him sooner than be released, and he told him to leave and not to make him angry, if he wanted to get home safe. The old man 394a was frightened by what Agamemnon had said, and left without a word, but once he was away from the encampment he prayed over and over to Apollo. He invoked the god's titles, reminded him of all favours he had done him, and asked to be recompensed for any shrine he had built or ritual sacrifice he had performed which had pleased the god. He prayed that, in recognition of these favours, the Greeks would be made to pay for his tears with Apollo's darts." That, my friend,' I concluded, 'is how we get pure narrative, which is free of b representation.'

'I see,' he said.

'Well,' I went on, 'do you also appreciate that we get the opposite when all the passages which the poet composed in between the speeches are excised and only the dialogue is left?'

'Yes,' he said, 'I understand this as well: this is what happens in tragedies, for instance.'

'You've grasped my meaning perfectly,' I said. 'I think I'm now getting across to you what I couldn't explain before. There are several varieties of poetry and story-telling. Some—tragedy and comedy, as you say—is entirely representational; some c is in the poet's own voice—you'd find this particularly in dithyrambic poetry;* finally, the kind which employs both methods is what we find in epic poetry, but also in many other types of poetry too. Do you see what I mean?'

'Yes,' he said, 'and I understand what you were trying to tell me earlier.'

'Now cast your mind back to what we were saying even before that—that we had discussed the required content of stories, but still had their form to consider.'

'I remember.'

d 'What I was getting at, then, was just this: we have to decide whether to allow our poets to compose representational narratives, or to compose narratives which are partly representational and partly not (and if so, we have to decide what kinds of subjects should be treated in either of these ways), or to insist that they avoid representation altogether.'

'The underlying point of your enquiry seems to me', he said, 'to be whether or not we'll allow tragedy and comedy into our community.'

'It could be,' I said, 'but it may be far broader. I certainly don't know yet; we must let our destination be decided by the winds of the discussion.'

'Well said,' he commented.

e 'What I want you to consider carefully, Adeimantus, is whether or not our guardians should be good at representation. Or do you think the answer follows from what we've already established—that whereas an individual can do one job well, he cannot do lots of jobs well, and if he were to try to do so, he would fail to achieve distinction in any occupation, despite undertaking a lot of them?'

'Of course it does.'

'So the same principle applies to representation too: it's impossible for a single individual to play lots of roles as successfully as he plays a single role.'*

'That's right.'

395a 'It would be unreasonable, then, to expect a single individual to work at one of the commendable pursuits and at the same time play lots of parts and be good at representation. I mean, as you know, it isn't possible for the same people simultaneously to be successful in two representational spheres at once, even when those spheres are arguably closely related. Witness, for example, the composition of comedy and the composition of tragedy. Didn't you just describe them as representational?'

'I did—and you're right: people are incapable of doing both at once.'

'And they can't be competent rhapsodes* and competent actors at the same time either.'

'True.'

'In fact, the same people can't be competent comic actors and also competent tragic actors. These are all representational, b wouldn't you say?'

'Yes.'

'And the totality of human nature seems to me, Adeimantus, to have been broken down into even smaller slivers than this, until an individual is incapable of successfully playing more than one representational role, or of doing more than one of the actual things which the roles represent.'

'You're absolutely right,' he said.

'Our original position was that our guardians ought to be released from all other sorts of work: they are to be precision craftsmen of the community's autonomy, and must not engage c in any work which does not tend towards this goal. If we're not to undermine this position, then, our guardians have to concentrate exclusively on this work and on this role. Any representational roles they do take on must, from childhood onwards, be appropriate ones. They should represent people who are courageous, self-disciplined, just, and generous and should play only those kinds of parts; but they should neither do nor be good at representing anything mean-spirited or otherwise contemptible, in case the harvest they reap from representation is reality. I mean, haven't you noticed how if d repeated representation continues much past childhood, it becomes habitual and ingrained and has an effect on a person's body, voice, and mind?'

'I certainly have,' he replied.

'So,' I said, 'we won't allow people we claim to care for, and who we're saying have to be good men, to represent (despite being men) a woman, young or old, as she hurls insults at her husband, or pits herself against the gods and arrogantly imagines herself to be happy, or is gripped by catastrophe, e grief, and sorrow;* and it goes without saying that the same goes for representing a woman who's ill or is suffering pangs of love or labour.'

'I couldn't agree more,' he said.

'And the same prohibition applies to representing slaves of either sex going about their servile duties.'

'I agree.'

'And also, I suppose, to representing bad men who are cowards and whose conduct is the opposite of what we mentioned a short while ago—who abuse and mock and revile one another when they're drunk, or even when they're sober, or 396a who in general, by their words and their actions, sin against themselves and others. Moreover, I'm sure they shouldn't get into the habit of adapting their behaviour to the words and actions of mad people; they must be able to recognize madness and badness in men and women, but they mustn't do or represent any of these things.'

'You're absolutely right,' he said.

'And should they represent artisans like metalworkers,' I asked, 'or oarsmen on a trireme or the petty officers in charge of them, or the like?'

'There'll be no chance of that,' he said, 'since there won't b even be the opportunity for any of these concerns to occupy their attention.'

'And will they represent horses neighing, bulls bellowing, rivers splashing, the sea crashing, thunderclaps, and so on and so forth?'*

'No,' he said. 'We've already forbidden them to behave abnormally or like madmen.'

'So what you're saying, if I'm getting it right,' I said, 'is that there are two kinds of style, two kinds of narrative. There's one kind which a truly good person would use, when called upon to c deliver a narrative; and then there's another, quite different kind, which would be the staple narrative method of someone who by nature and upbringing was the opposite of truly good.'

'What are they?' he asked.

'My impression', I said, 'is that when a moderate man comes in the course of a narrative to something said or done by a good man, he'll happily assume the role of that good man and read it out. He won't find representation of this kind ignominious. He'll concentrate on representing a good man

who is acting reliably and in full possession of his senses, d
but he'll be less enthusiastic about and will tend to avoid
representing a good man who has become unreliable as a result
of illness, love, drink, or in general some catastrophe. However,
when he comes across a degrading character, he won't be
prepared to assimilate himself seriously to this inferior person,
except on the few occasions when this character does something good. He'd be ashamed to do so, not only because he's
untrained in representing this type of person, but also because
he finds it distasteful to mould and conform himself to an
inferior stamp, which his mind finds contemptible, except for e
fun.'

'Yes, that's likely,' he said.

'So the sort of narrative he'll use will be the kind we described
a short while ago when we were discussing the Homeric epics:
he'll employ the style which incorporates both representation
and narrative, but the proportion of representation in the
text will be small. Do you think I'm right, or am I talking
nonsense?'

'What you're talking is certainly not nonsense,' he replied.
'You're describing the principle that kind of person is bound to
follow when speaking.'

'All right, then,' I said. 'Now, what about the other kind of 397a
person? The less good he is, the less he'll be inclined to omit
any of the narrative and regard anything as degrading. We'll
end up with someone who's prepared to represent anything and
everything, and to do so seriously and publicly. He'll even
represent sounds and noises and cries like those of the things
we mentioned just now—thunder, wind and hail, axles and
pulleys, trumpets, reed-pipes, wind-pipes, and every single
musical instrument, and also dogs, sheep, and birds. His style
will be the one which relies entirely on vocal or bodily repre- b
sentation (though it may contain a small amount of narrative),
won't it?'

'Yes, it's bound to be,' he said. 'You're right again.'

'Well, that's what I meant when I said that there were two
kinds of style,' I said.

'And there are,' he said.

'Now, one of them involves little variation. Suppose a suitable musical mode and rhythm is assigned to a speaker's style:

it turns out that anyone who uses this style correctly is not far off speaking in one and the same mode (given that the variation is only slight), and also with a rhythm that is similarly almost

c constant. Do you agree?'

'Yes, that's exactly how it is,' he said.

'What about the other speaker's style? Won't it be the opposite? For it to be used properly, won't it need every mode and every rhythm there is, since it involves every conceivable kind of variation?'*

'Yes, that's an excellent description of it.'

'Now, doesn't every poet—everyone who expresses himself in any way at all, in fact—conform to one of these two styles or to one which he concocts by mixing the two together?'

'Necessarily,' he said.

d 'What shall we do, then?' I asked. 'Shall we allow all these styles into our community, or one of the two unmixed styles, or the mixed one?'

'I'd vote for the unmixed style which represents the good man,' he said.

'But the mixed style does at least give pleasure, Adeimantus; and the one which gives by far the most pleasure to children and their attendants, and the general run of people, is the one which is the opposite of your choice.'

'Yes, that's because it *is* very enjoyable.'

'But perhaps you'd say that it isn't compatible with our community's political system,' I went on, 'because each of our

e people has a single job to do, and therefore none of them is two-sided or many-sided.'

'That's right: it's incompatible.'

'And this was the principle which meant that ours is the only kind of community where we'll find a shoemaker who is a shoemaker and not a ship's captain as well, and a farmer who is a farmer and not a judge as well, and a soldier who is a soldier and not a businessman as well, and so on, wasn't it?'

'True,' he said.

398a 'So it follows that were a man who was clever enough to be able to assume all kinds of forms and to represent everything in the world to come in person to our community and want to show off his compositions, we'd treat him as an object of reverence and awe, and as a source of pleasure, and we'd prostrate ourselves before him; but we'd tell him that not only is there no one like him in our community, it is also not permitted for anyone like him to live among us, and we'd send him elsewhere, once we had anointed his head with myrrh and given him a chaplet of wool.* Left to ourselves, however, with benefit as our goal, we would employ harsher, less entertaining b poets and story-tellers, to speak in the style of a good man and to keep in their stories to the principles* we originally established as lawful, when our task was the education of our militia.'

'Yes,' he said, 'that's certainly what we'd do, if it were up to us.'

'So now, Adeimantus,' I said, 'I should think we've exhausted the aspect of cultural studies which relates to stories and fables. I mean, we've discussed both the content and the form which the stories should have.'

'I agree,' he said.

A great deal of Greek poetry was chanted or sung, so Plato has to deal with music too. Only certain modes and rhythms are to be allowed: they are the ones which do not titillate or indulge one's emotions.

'Next, we still have to discuss the procedure for singing and c music,' I said.

'Evidently.'

'Well, what we have to say about them—about which types are permitted—if we are to be consistent with what has already been said, must by now be universally obvious, surely?'

Glaucon laughed and said, 'It looks as though I don't belong to this universe, then, Socrates. It's not sufficiently clear to me at the moment what we ought to say, though I have a vague idea.'

'Well,' I said, 'I'm sure that here, in the first place, is a notion you have a perfectly adequate grasp of: that a song is a blend of d three ingredients—words, music, and rhythm.'

'Yes,' he said, 'I understand that.'

'Now, surely the verbal component doesn't differ at all from words which are not part of a song, in the sense that the words still have to conform to those same principles we mentioned a moment ago and to the same style, don't they?'

'True,' he said.

'And the music and the rhythm must be in keeping with the words.'

'Of course.'

'Well, we said* that laments and dirges need never be voiced.'

'That's right.'

e 'So which are the plaintive musical modes?* You must tell me—you're the musician.'

'The Mixed Lydian', he replied, 'and the Taut Lydian, and any others like them.'

'We should exclude them, then,' I said. 'They don't help even women achieve the required goodness, let alone men.'

'Right.'

'Now, it's utterly inappropriate for our guardians to be drunk and soft and idle.'

'Of course.'

'Well, which modes are soft and suitable for drinking-parties?'

'There's an Ionian mode which is called "loose",' he answered, 'and another Lydian one as well.'

399a 'Can you find any use for them, Glaucon, when you're dealing with military men?'

'None at all,' he replied. 'It looks as though you're left with the Dorian and Phrygian modes.'

'I'm no expert on the modes,' I said, 'but please leave me with a mode which properly captures the tones and variations of pitch of a brave man's voice during battle or any other enterprise he'd rather not be involved in—the voice of a man b who, even when he fails and faces injury or death or some other catastrophe, still resists fortune in a disciplined and resolute manner. And leave me another mode which captures his voice when he's engaged in peaceful enterprises, where there's no lack of will and he can choose what to do; or when he's trying to win someone over to his point of view and is appealing to him, whether this involves praying to a god or explaining to a human being where he has gone wrong; or alternatively when he patiently submits to others' appeals or explanations or arguments, and when he has subsequently completed an action to his satisfaction, and doesn't get big-headed, but acts with self-discipline and restraint throughout

and accepts whatever outcome there may be. Leave me these c
two modes, then—the voluntary and the involuntary ones—
which perfectly capture the tones of self-disciplined and
courageous men in failure and success.'

'But you're asking to be left with exactly the modes I just
mentioned,' he said.*

'We'll not need in our songs and music a wide range of notes
and the full range of modes, then,' I remarked.

'No, I suppose not,' he said.

'Then we won't keep artisans to make psalteries and harps
and any other instruments which are designed to produce a
wide range of notes and modes.' d

'I suppose we won't.'

'Well, will you allow into our community people who make
reed-pipes or people who play them? I mean, doesn't this produce a wider range of notes than any other instrument? Don't
all instruments† which can play the full range of modes† in fact
take after the reed-pipe in this respect?'

'Obviously they do,' he said.

'So you're left with the lyre and the cithara', I said, 'as
instruments which serve some purpose in an urban setting; and
then in the countryside the herdsmen can have wind-pipes.'

'That's what the argument suggests, anyway,' he said.

'It's not as if we were doing anything startlingly original', e
I pointed out, 'in preferring Apollo and Apollo's kind of
instrument to Marsyas and his kind of instrument.'*

'How interesting!' he said. 'I suppose we aren't.'

'You know what strikes me?' I said. 'Without realizing it,
we've been re-purging the community of the indulgence we
mentioned a while back.'*

'That just shows how disciplined we are!' he said.

'All right, then, let's finish the purging. We should discuss
rhythm next, after music, and make sure we avoid chasing after
complexity of rhythm and a wide variety of tempos. We should
try to discern the rhythms of a life which is well regulated and
courageous. When we've done so, we'll force the metre and the
tune to conform to the words which express such a life, rather 400a
than forcing the words to conform to the metre and the tune.
And it's up to you to tell us what those rhythms are, just as you
did with musical modes.'

'Good heavens, no!' he said. 'I can't do that. Because of my

studies, I could tell you that there are three elements of tempo, just as in the case of sound there are four basic constituents of all the musical modes.* But I can't tell you which rhythmic
b elements represent which lifestyle.'

'Well,' I said, 'we'll have to bring in Damon too, and consult him about which tempos suit meanness and promiscuity or derangement, and other forms of badness, and which rhythms should be reserved for the opposite qualities. I remember having heard a difficult talk of his in which he described one compound rhythm as martial, finger-like,† and heroic, and he somehow divided it into ordered parts and made it equal in its rise and its fall;* and, as I recall, he described an iamb as involving a short period and a long period,† and he described a trochee too;* and he assigned to all of these their long and
c short quantities. And I think he condemned and commended the cadences of some of these rhythms just as much as he did the rhythms themselves; or perhaps it was the combination of cadence and rhythm he was talking about—I can't say. As I said, let's put this on one side for Damon, since it would take us ages to resolve the issue. What do you think?'

'I couldn't agree more,' he said.

The arguments of the previous sections are now generalized and expanded. Not only poetry, but every artefact and every natural entity can display grace or inelegance, and so be poor food for the guardians. Moreover, not only do inelegant things harm a person's character, but they are also products in the first place of a bad character. This could create a downward spiral of increasing badness in a community, whereas a spiral of increasing appreciation of goodness and beauty is possible through proper education. And this appreciation in turn binds the members of a community together in shared authentic (non-sexual) love.

'But at least you're sure that grace and inelegance depend on good and bad rhythm, aren't you?'

'Of course.'
d 'Furthermore, good and bad rhythm depend, respectively, on assimilation to a good speaking style or its opposite, and the same goes for harmony and disharmony. This follows from what we were just saying—that rhythm and the harmony of music should conform to language, not vice versa.'

'Yes, they should,' he said.

'As for speaking style and language,' I said, 'they depend on a person's character, don't they?'

'Of course.'

'And everything else depends on speaking style?'

'Yes.'

'It follows, then, that good use of language, harmony, grace, and rhythm all depend on goodness of character. I'm not talking e
about the state which is actually stupidity, but which we gloss as goodness of character;*† I'm talking about when the mind really has equipped the character with moral goodness and excellence.'

'Absolutely,' he said.

'And shouldn't the young people of our community take every opportunity to cultivate these qualities, if they are to do their jobs?'

'Yes, they should.'

'Now, painting and related arts, and weaving, embroidery, 401a
architecture, and the manufacture of utensils in general, and also the physical structures of creatures and plants, are all pervaded by these qualities, in the sense that they may display grace or inelegance. And inelegance, lack of rhythm, and disharmony are allied to abuse of language and a corrupt character, whereas their opposites are allied to and reflect a disciplined and good character.'

'Absolutely,' he said.

'Is it only the poets we should oversee, then, and compel to b
choose between imbuing their compositions with the image of goodness of character or not practising their art in our community? Don't we also have to oversee artisans in general and stop them imbuing their portraits of animals, their edifices,*
and whatever else they may produce, with corruption, lack of self-restraint, meanness of spirit, and inelegance, and punish failure to comply with a ban on working in our community? Otherwise, during their upbringing our guardians will be surrounded by the pernicious pasturage of images of badness, c
which will be so common that they'll often be nibbling and feeding on them, day in and day out, a little at a time, until without realizing it they'll amass badness in their minds. No, we must look for craftsmen who have the innate gift of tracking

down goodness and grace, so that the young people of our community can live in a salubrious region where everything is beneficial and where their eyes and ears meet no influences except those of fine works of art, whose effect is like a breeze which brings health from favourable regions, and which

d imperceptibly guides them, from childhood onwards, until they are assimilated to, familiar with, and in harmony with the beauty of reason.'*

'Yes, that would be an outstandingly fine upbringing for them,' he said.

'Now, Glaucon,' I said, 'isn't the prime importance of cultural education due to the fact that rhythm and harmony sink more deeply into the mind than anything else and affect it more powerfully than anything else and bring grace in their train? For someone who is given a correct education, their product is

e grace; but in the opposite situation it is inelegance. And isn't its importance also due to the fact that a proper cultural education would enable a person to be very quick at noticing defects and flaws in the construction or nature of things? In other words, he'd find offensive the things he ought to find offensive. Fine things would be appreciated and enjoyed by him, and he'd accept them into his mind as nourishment and would therefore

402a become truly good; even when young, however, and still incapable of rationally understanding why, he would rightly condemn and loathe contemptible things. And then the rational mind would be greeted like an old friend when it did arrive,* because anyone with this upbringing would be more closely affiliated with rationality than anyone else.'

'Yes,' he said, 'to my mind those are the kinds of reasons for cultural education.'

'It's analogous to the process of becoming literate, then,' I said. 'We weren't literate until we realized that, despite being few in number, the letters are fundamental wherever they occur, and until we appreciated their importance whether the word which contained them was great or small, and stopped

b thinking that we didn't need to take note of them, but tried hard to recognize them everywhere, on the grounds that literacy would elude us until we were capable of doing so.'

'True.'

'And we won't be able to tell which letters are which when

they're reflected in water or a mirror either, until we can recognize the letters themselves, will we? It takes the same expertise and training, doesn't it?'

'Absolutely.'

'Then this is incredibly similar to what I've been saying. We won't be cultured either (and this doesn't apply only to us, but c to the people we're claiming to educate for guardianship) until we recognize the types—self-discipline, courage, generosity, broadness of vision, and all the qualities which are allied and opposed to them—wherever they occur, and notice instances of their presence, whether it is the qualities themselves or their reflections that we are noticing, and don't underestimate them whether the situation in which they're occurring is great or small, but bear in mind that it takes the same expertise and training. Right?'

'Definitely,' he said.

'Now,' I went on, 'imagine a situation where someone d combines beautiful mental characteristics with physical features which conform to the same principle and so are consistent and concordant with the beauty of his mind. Could there be a more beautiful sight for anyone capable of seeing it?'

'Hardly.'

'And the more beautiful a thing is, the more lovable it is?'

'Naturally.'

'Therefore, the more people are of this type, the more a cultured person will love them. If they're discordant, however, he will not love them.'   e

'No, he won't,' he said, 'if they have a mental defect; but if their flaw is physical, he'll put up with it and not refuse his affection.'

'I appreciate what you're saying,' I said. 'I know you are or were in love with someone like that, and I concede the point. But answer me this: can self-discipline and excessive pleasure go together?'

'Of course not,' he said. 'Pleasure deranges people just as effectively as distress.'

'Can excessive pleasure partner any of the other virtues?'

'No.'   403a

'What about promiscuity and dissoluteness?'

'Yes, they're its chief partners.'

'Can you think of any pleasure which is greater and more intense than sexual pleasure?'

'No, I can't,' he said, 'and I can't think of any pleasure which is more manic either.'

'And authentic love is a disciplined and cultured love of someone who is restrained as well as good-looking. Yes?'

'Definitely,' he said.

'Authentic love should have no involvement, then, with anything manic or anything which bears the trace of dissoluteness, should it?'

'No, it shouldn't.'

b   'Doesn't it follow, then, that lovers and their boyfriends who love and are loved authentically should have no involvement with this pleasure and should have nothing to do with it?'

'That's right, Socrates,' he said. 'They most certainly should not.'

'So you'll apparently be making a regulation in the community we're founding to the effect that although a lover can (if he can persuade his boyfriend to let him) kiss and spend time with and touch his boyfriend, as he would his son—which is to say, for honourable reasons—still his relationship with anyone he cares for will basically be such that he never gives the impression that there is more to it than that. Otherwise,

c he'll be liable to condemnation for lacking culture and moral sensibility.'

'Exactly,' he said.

'Now, do you join me in thinking that we've completed our discussion of cultural studies?' I asked. 'At any rate, we've reached a good place to finish: I mean, it's good for cultural studies to lead ultimately to love of beauty.'

'I agree,' he said.

The sketch of physical training which follows stresses moderation of diet. Neglect of moderation in diet is the cause of a great deal of ill health, as the neglect of discipline in emotion is the cause of crime (and the legal profession). Hypochondria is an indulgence born of idleness, and interferes with life. Incurably ill people should accept death gracefully (just as incurable criminals should be executed), because they cannot exercise their talents.

'Well, after their cultural education, our young men should receive physical training.'

'Of course.'

'And this too should be a precise course of training which starts in childhood and continues throughout a person's life. See what you think too, but my thinking is that this is the way d things are: I am not of the opinion that if the body is in a good condition, then this state of physical excellence makes the mind good too. I think it's the other way round: a good mind, by being in a state of excellence, allows a body to maximize its potential for physical goodness. What about you? What do you think?'

'I agree with you,' he replied.

'So if the education we've provided for the mind is adequate, then wouldn't it be best for us to leave the mind to attend to the details of the physical training, and steer clear of a lengthy e discussion by just outlining the principles?'

'Yes, certainly.'

'Now, we've already said* that they should avoid getting drunk. I mean, a guardian is, of course, the last person who should get so drunk that he doesn't know where on earth he is.'

'Yes,' he said, 'because then our guardians would need guardians, and that would be ridiculous.'

'What about their food? These men are competitors in the greatest contest of all,* aren't they?'

'Yes.'

'So would the condition of one of today's athletes be suitable 404a for them?'

'Maybe.'

'But it's a sluggish condition, and makes health precarious. Can't you see how these athletes spend their lives sleeping and only need to deviate a tiny bit from their prescribed regimen to come down with serious and severe illnesses?'

'Yes, I can.'

'Then our warriors need a less crude form of training,' I said. 'It's essential for them to be as vigilant as watchdogs, with the best possible eyesight and hearing, and for their health to be not so precariously balanced that it is affected by changes in their drinking-water and their diet generally, and in the heat b or cold of the weather, because these changes are commonly encountered during warfare.'

'I agree.'

'Doesn't it follow that the best physical training for them would be comparable in simplicity to the cultural education we described a short while ago?'

'In what sense?'

'I mean a simple and moderate form of physical training, and one designed particularly for warfare.'

'How?'

'Even Homer's a good source for the sort of thing I mean,' I said. 'As you know, when he portrays the heroes eating, he doesn't feed them, while they're campaigning, either on fish

c (despite the fact that they are in the Hellespont by the sea) or on boiled meat, but only on roasted meat. This is the diet which would be particularly convenient for soldiers, in the sense that they can cook on an open fire almost anywhere, whereas it's less easy for them to carry cooking-pots around wherever they go.'

'Quite so.'

'Nor, I think, does Homer ever mention savoury sauces. In fact, the necessity of avoiding this kind of food if you want to be physically fit is common knowledge among athletes, isn't it?'

'Yes, it is,' he said, 'and they're right to avoid it.'

d 'If you think they're right to do this, my friend, I suppose you disapprove of Syracusan rations* and the wide variety of savouries that can be found in Sicily.'

'Yes, I think I do.'

'Then you also take exception to anyone having a Corinthian lady friend, if he intends to get fit.'

'Absolutely.'

'And to him enjoying the apparent delights of Attic pastries?'

'No doubt about it.'

'And the reason for your disapproval, I imagine, is because we'd be right to draw an analogy between everything that constitutes this kind of diet and lifestyle, and the composition

e of songs and ballads which use the full range of modes and rhythms.'

'Of course that would be a fair analogy.'

'Now, although in the case of music variety tends to engender lack of discipline, in the present case it engenders illness. Simplicity in music, however, engenders self-control, and simplicity in physical training gives rise to bodily health. Right?'

'Perfectly true,' he said.

'When dissoluteness and disease proliferate in a community, 405a then lawcourts and doctors' surgeries open up all over the place, and the professions of lawyer and doctor have high opinions of themselves, when even large numbers of free men regard them as extremely important.'

'That's inevitable.'

'Could you produce more telling evidence of when a community's educational system is bad and contemptible than when top-notch doctors and lawyers are needed not only by low-ranking people and labourers, but also by those who pride themselves on their privileged upbringing? I mean, don't you think it's despicable, and highly indicative of lack of culture, b to feel compelled to rely on a moral code which has been imported from others, as if they were one's masters and judges, and to lack one's own moral sense?'

'Nothing could be more contemptible,' he replied.

'Really?' I asked. 'Don't you think that it's more contemptible to waste most of one's life* in the lawcourts as a prosecutor or defendant, and moreover to be so lacking in moral sensibility that one confidently preens oneself on this fact, and regards oneself as a skilful criminal, accomplished in every manoeuvre, c in dodges and subterfuges for slipping through every loophole which enables one to avoid being punished, and to do all this for the sake of matters which are trivial and of no importance, because one is ignorant of how much finer and better it is to arrange one's life so that one has no need of a drowsy juror?'

'Yes, you're right,' he said. 'This ranks even higher on the scale of contemptibility.'

'What about needing the art of medicine', I continued, 'for anything except serious injuries and when infected by certain of the seasonal epidemics? What about when it's needed instead because people are, thanks to inactivity and the diet we d described, as full of fluids and gases as a marsh, and leave the ingenious Asclepiadae* no choice but to come up with names like flatulence and catarrh for their disorders? Doesn't this strike you as contemptible?'

'Yes,' he said, 'these words certainly are really unfamiliar and odd when used as the names of diseases.'*

'And I don't think they were used like that in Asclepius' time,' I said. 'The reason I think this is because when Eurypylus e was wounded at Troy* and was treated with Pramnian wine which had lots of pearl barley and grated cheese stirred in it 406a (which is supposed to be an inflammatory brew), Asclepius' sons didn't tick the woman off for giving it him to drink, and didn't criticize Patroclus' treatment of him either.'

'Well, it *was* an odd drink for someone in his condition,' he remarked.

'Not if you bear in mind the fact that doctors didn't use this modern medical technique of pampering illness until Herodicus' time,' I said. 'Herodicus was a physical-education instructor who became chronically ill and combined the arts of physical exercise and medicine into a means of tormenting first b and foremost himself, and then subsequently a lot of other people.'

'How?' he asked.

'By prolonging his death,' I answered. 'Although he danced attendance on his illness, it was terminal, and there was no way he could cure himself, of course. He was so busy doctoring himself that for the rest of his life he had no time for anything else and suffered torments every time he deviated in the slightest from his usual regimen; thanks to his cleverness he reached old age, but had one foot constantly in the grave.'

'His expertise earned him a fine reward, then!' he said.

c 'A suitable one for someone who didn't realize that Asclepius' omission of this type of medical method in the art he invented and handed down to his successors was not due to his being ignorant and unaware of it,' I said. 'It was because he knew that every citizen of a well-regulated community is assigned a single job which he has to do, and that no one has the time to spend his life ill and doctoring himself. Ridiculously enough, it is noticeable today that while the working class conform to this principle, people who are rich and supposedly happy do not.'

'What do you mean?' he asked.

d 'If a joiner gets ill,' I explained, 'what he expects from his doctor is an emetic drug to drink to vomit up the illness, or an aperient for his bowels, or to resort to cautery or surgery to get

rid of the affliction. If he's prescribed a long course of treatment, and told to wrap his head in dressings and so on, then his
immediate response is to say that he has no time to be ill, and
that this way of life, which involves concentrating on his illness
and neglecting the work he's been set, holds no rewards for
him. Then he takes his leave of this type of doctor, returns to e
his usual regimen, regains his health, and lives performing his
proper function; alternatively, if his body isn't up to surviving,
he gets rid of his troubles by dying.'

'That's the right way for an artisan to approach medical
science, I think,' he said.

'Isn't that because he has a job to do,' I asked, 'and because 407a
if he doesn't do it, his life is unrewarding?'*

'Obviously,' he said.

'But a rich person, by definition, has no job assigned to him
such that if he were forced to abstain from it his life would
become intolerable.'

'He isn't said to, anyway.'

'If you say that, then you haven't heard what Phocylides said
about how as soon as one's livelihood is secure, one should
practise goodness.'

'I think one should do so even earlier,' he said.

'Let's not quarrel with him about this,' I said. 'Let's be our
own teachers, and find out whether a rich person ought to
practise what Phocylides says and whether life becomes intolerable for a rich person if he doesn't practise it. Let's see
whether despite the fact that pampering an illness prevents a b
person applying himself to joinery and all the other branches
of expertise, it is no impediment to anyone carrying out
Phocylides' injunction.'

'Of course it is,' he exclaimed. 'It's hard to think of any
impediment greater than this excessive attention to the body,
this attempt to improve on physical exercise. It's a nuisance in
the context of estate-management, of military service, and of
sedentary political office too.'

'Its worst aspect, however, is that it makes it difficult to
study anything and to think and concentrate, since one is c
constantly worried about headaches and dizziness, and blaming
philosophy* for their occurrence. So if you're practising this
philosophical type of goodness, then excessive attention to the

body is a thorough hindrance, since it constantly makes you imagine that you're ill and you're always agonizing about your body.'

'Yes, that's likely,' he said.

'Well, shall we say that Asclepius realized this as well? He invented the art of medicine for people who are physically healthy, thanks to both their constitutions and their lifestyles, d but who contract some isolated illness. This is the type of person and condition he had in mind. He used drugs and surgery to get rid of their illnesses, and then he told them to continue with their usual lifestyles, because he didn't want to damage the functioning of the community. However, he didn't try to use diet gradually to drain and fill bodies which were diseased to the core, and so be responsible for the person having a long and horrible life and in all probability producing children with the same afflictions. He didn't see any point in treating anyone who was incapable of living a normal life, e because such a person does neither himself nor his community any good.'

'Asclepius was a public-spirited person, according to you,' he remarked.

'Obviously he was,' I said. 'And look at his sons too: it 408a was because this was his nature that at Troy they proved themselves to be good fighters and practised the kind of medicine I'm describing. Don't you remember how when Pandarus wounded Menelaus, "they sucked the blood" from the wound "and applied soothing medicines",* but didn't tell him (any more than they did Eurypylus) what to eat and drink after this treatment? They were acting on the assumption that the medicines were enough to cure men who had, before being b wounded, been healthy and had led orderly lives, even if they happened to be drinking potions at that precise moment. But they didn't think that the people themselves or anyone else would gain by someone who was constitutionally sickly and who lacked self-discipline remaining alive; they didn't want to waste their art on these people or treat them, even if they were richer than Midas.'

'Asclepius' sons were very clever, according to you,' he said.

'Just as clever as they should be,' I responded. 'And yet the tragedians and Pindar don't see things the way we do, and they claim that Asclepius, despite being the son of Apollo, was bribed to treat a rich man who was already at death's door, and that this is why he was struck by lightning.* However, c we'll stick to the principles we formulated earlier and therefore not let them convince us of the truth of both assertions: either he was the son of a god, in which case (we'll claim) he wasn't attracted by dirty money; or he was attracted by dirty money, in which case he wasn't the son of a god.'*

'Yes, you're quite right,' he said. 'But here's a question for you, Socrates: surely we need to have good doctors in our community, don't we? And, I suppose, the more healthy and sick people they've dealt with, the more likely they are to be d good. The same goes for legal experts too: it's those who've been involved with people of all sorts and characters who are most likely to be good.'

'I am certainly saying that we need good ones,' I replied. 'But do you know which ones I regard as good?'

'You'll have to tell me,' he said.

'I'll try,' I said. 'Your question combined dissimilar cases, however.'

'In what way?' he asked.

'Well, take doctors first. In order for doctors to attain perfect skill, they must not only have learnt their trade. In addition, from childhood onwards, they should have come into contact with as many bodies as they possibly could, in the worst condition they could find; moreover, they themselves should have contracted every single disease there is, and should be con- e stitutionally rather unhealthy. I mean, it's not their bodies they use to treat other people's bodies, of course; if that were the case, it would be out of the question for their bodies to be bad or to get into a bad state. No, it's their minds they use to treat bodies, and it's impossible for a mind which is or has become bad to treat anything well.'

'Right,' he said.

'On the other hand, Glaucon, a legal expert does use his 409a mind to wield authority over other people's minds.* And it's out of the question for a legal expert to be brought up, from childhood onwards, in the company of minds which are in a bad condition, and for his mind to have thoroughly explored the whole arena of immorality until it has become immoral itself and can quickly use itself as a criterion by which to assess the immorality of others' actions (by the analogy of a doctor using his body to assess others' illnesses). Instead, his mind must, while young, have no experience of bad characters, and must not be contaminated by them, if it's to become truly good at assessing the morality of actions in a reliable manner. This also explains why good people are, in their youth, thought by immoral people to be gullible simpletons: they don't contain

b within themselves standards of behaviour which are compatible with anything which is bad.'

'Yes, that's always happening to them,' he said.

'That's why a young man doesn't make a good legal expert,' I said, 'and why advanced age is a prerequisite. A good legal expert must have been slow to learn the nature of immorality, because he's been observing something which is not an inherent quality in his own mind, but an alien quality in other people's minds. He must have trained himself over many years to discern its badness by making use of information, not his own

c experience.'

'At any rate,' he said, 'I suppose the best kind of legal expert is like that.'

'So is a good one,' I said, 'and that was what you were asking about. I mean, it's a good mind that makes someone good. As for that clever paranoiac, who has done wrong himself many times and thinks of himself as smart and unscrupulous: in the company of people similar to himself, his caution—induced by his looking at the standards of behaviour he contains within himself—does make him appear clever. On the other hand, when he associates with good people and older

d people, then his excessive mistrust and his inability to recognize reliability—induced by the fact that he has no standard by which to recognize it—make him appear stupid. Since he more commonly encounters bad people than good people, however, he thinks himself clever rather than stupid, and this opinion is endorsed by others.'

'That's perfectly true,' he said.

'Our search for a good, skilful legal expert had better not end with him, then,' I said, 'but with the type of person we described before, because whereas a bad person can never recognize either goodness or badness, a good person will, with time and education, come to understand both goodness and badness—and therefore it is he, not a bad person, who acquires e skill, in my opinion.'

'And I agree with you,' he said.

'So at the same time as legislating for this type of legal practice in our community, you'll also legislate for the kind of medical practice we described. These two practices will treat the bodies and minds of those of your citizens who are 410a naturally well endowed in these respects; as for the rest, those with a poor physical constitution will be allowed to die, and those with irredeemably rotten minds will be put to death. Right?'

'Yes, we've shown that this is the best course', he said, 'for those at the receiving end of the treatment as well as for the community.'

'And so your young men', I said, 'will obviously be careful about getting themselves into a position where they need legal expertise; they'll rely on that simple cultural training which, as we said, engenders self-discipline.'

'Naturally,' he said.

'And won't anyone culturally trained in this way who follows b the same trail find, if he wants to, the form of physical exercise he's after, with the result that he'll not need doctors at all, except in emergencies?'

'I think so.'

Harking back to the two poles of a guardian's nature (375c–376c), Plato concludes that the primary education whose principles have been outlined in this chapter will produce people in whom the poles of aggressiveness and gentleness have been adequately trained, when neither side is emphasized to the neglect of the other, and they offset each other.

'Now, the goal he aims for even with this physical exercise and effort is the passionate aspect of his nature. This is what he wants to wake up. This, not developing physical strength, will be the goal of his efforts, as distinct from all other athletes, who diet and train for the sake of physical fitness.'

'Definitely,' he said.

'Doesn't it follow, then, Glaucon,' I asked, 'that it's wrong to c think that the people who are making cultural studies and physical exercise the constituents of our educational system are doing so for the purpose of using the one to look after the body and the other to look after the mind?'

'Why is it wrong?' he asked.

'It rather looks as though the mind is the main objective in both cases,' I said.

'I don't understand.'

'Haven't you noticed the psychological effect of people spending their whole lives on physical exercise, but excluding culture,' I asked, 'or the effect of doing the opposite?'

'In what respect do you mean?' he asked.

d 'I mean in respect of the brutality and intractability of the one lot, and the softness and docility of the others,' I replied.

'Yes,' he said, 'I've noticed that people who engage exclusively in physical exercise end up being excessively brutal, while people who engage exclusively in cultural studies end up shamefully soft.'

'Now, brutality is a product of the passionate part of one's nature. With the correct training, this passionate part is brave; but if it is over-stretched, it becomes intractable and unmanageable, as you can imagine.'

'I agree,' he said.

e 'And docility is an attribute of a philosophical temperament. Over-relaxation results in excessive softness, but if a philosophical temperament is properly trained it becomes docile and orderly, doesn't it?'

'Yes.'

'And we said* that our guardians had to possess both characteristics.'

'Yes, they must.'

'So these two features have to fit harmoniously together,* don't they?'

'Of course.'

411a 'If they do, the result is a mind which is self-controlled and courageous, isn't it?'

'Yes.'

'And if they don't, the result is a mind which is timid and insensitive?'

'Yes.'

'So when a person allows the music of culture to charm him and makes his ears a channel for his mind to be flooded with the modes we described not long ago* as enchanting and soft, and the ones we described as plaintive, and spends his whole life humming and entranced by song, then at first he softens his passionate side, like iron in a forge, and makes it useful, instead of useless and intractable; but if he goes on and on, and never b lets up, but is beguiled, then the result is that he dissolves and melts his passionate side, until it becomes completely fluid and he has, so to speak, cut the sinews out of his mind and made himself a "feeble fighter".'*

'Quite,' he said.

'If right from the start he was endowed with a mind which lacked passion,' I went on, 'then it doesn't take long for this to happen; but if he had a passionate mind, then he weakens the passion and destabilizes it, so that even trivial matters make it quickly blaze up and die down again. People like this have exchanged passion for peevishness and irritability, and are c seething with discontent.'

'Absolutely.'

''And what about when someone puts a lot of effort into physical exercise and eats very well, but has nothing to do with culture and philosophy? At first, because he's physically fit, he gets all proud and passionate, and braver than he was before, doesn't he?'

'Yes, exactly.'

'But what if he restricts himself entirely to these activities and has absolutely no contact with the Muse of culture? The intellectual side of his mind is completely starved of intellectual d studies and investigations, and never joins in a discussion or any other cultural activity. Won't it become weak and deaf and blind, because it never receives any stimulation or nourishment and its senses are never purified?'

'Yes.'

'Then this type of person ends up, I suppose, devoid of culture and with a hatred of rationality. He stops relying on the persuasive force of rational argument and instead, like a wild beast, uses brute violence to attain all his ends. He lives his life e in blundering ignorance, lacking elegance or refinement.'

'You're absolutely right,' he said.

'So in my opinion what we find is that, since we have a dual nature, God gave us two corresponding areas of expertise—culture and physical exercise—for our passionate and our philosophical aspects. He didn't give them for the mind and the body, except incidentally; the purpose was for those two 412a aspects of our nature to fit harmoniously together by being stretched and relaxed as much as is appropriate.'

'Yes, that seems to be so,' he said.

'Therefore, it isn't the person who attunes the strings of a lyre to one another, it's the person who makes the best blend of physical exercise and culture, and who applies them to the mind in the right proportions, whom we should really describe as a virtuoso and as having the most harmony in his life.'

'That's hard to deny, Socrates,' he said.

'So, Glaucon, we'll always need someone of this type to oversee our community, if its political system is to remain intact, won't we?'

b 'Yes, that'll be the most important of our requirements.'

Chapter 5

The Guardians' Life and Duties

This chapter covers various topics, which are loosely strung together, in a sketchy form, because Plato is in pursuit of morality, and other features of the community are of less interest to him in this context. Still, important points are made. First, the guardians are divided into guardians proper, who are to rule, and auxiliaries, who are the militia. Selection of full guardians will take years (see also Chapter 10) of checking that they always have the community's best interests at heart. We now have three classes—guardians, auxiliaries, and workers— whom we may call the castes of gold, silver, and copper or iron. The members of the castes have to believe that this is the way God wants them to be, but there is a little room for change.

'So much for our educational principles. I mean, we don't have to describe in detail the guardians' dances, hunts, sporting competitions, and horse-races: it's fairly obvious that these activities must conform to the same principles, and their elucidation shouldn't cause any problems now.'

'No, I suppose they shouldn't,' he said.

'All right,' I said. 'What do we have to decide about next? Shouldn't we decide which members of this particular class will be the rulers and which will be the subjects?'

'Of course.'

'It's obvious that the older ones should be the rulers and the younger ones the subjects, isn't it?'

412c

'Yes.'

'And only the best of the older ones?'

'Yes, that's obvious too.'

'Now, the best farmers are the most accomplished farmers, aren't they?'

'Yes.'

'And in the present case, since we're after the best guardians, they must be those who are particularly good at safeguarding the community, mustn't they?'

'Yes.'

'They not only have to have the intelligence and the competence for the job, but they also have to care for the community, wouldn't you say?'

d   'Yes.'

'Now, you care most for things that happen to be dear to you.'

'Inevitably.'

'And something is particularly dear to you if you regard your interests and its interests as identical, and if you think that your success and failure follow from its success and failure.'*

'Yes,' he said.

'It follows that we should select from among the guardians men who particularly strike us, on investigation, as being the
e type to devote their whole lives to wholeheartedly doing what they regard as advantageous to the community, and to completely refusing to do anything they regard as disadvantageous to it.'

'Yes, they would make suitable rulers,' he said.

'I think we'll have to watch them at every stage of their lives, then, to make sure that they're good at safeguarding this idea and aren't magically or forcibly induced to shed and forget the notion that it's essential to do what's best for the community.'

'What do you mean by this shedding?' he asked.

'I'll explain,' I said. 'It seems to me that the departure of an idea from a person's mind can be either intentional or unintentional. It's intentional if the idea is false and the person
413a learns better, and unintentional whenever the idea is true.'

'I understand intentional loss,' he said, 'but I still don't understand unintentional loss.'

'But don't you think that the loss of good things is unintentional, while the loss of bad things is intentional?' I asked. 'And don't you think that being deceived about the truth is a bad thing, while having a grasp of the truth is good? And don't you think that having a grasp of the truth is having a belief that matches the way things are?'

'Yes, you're right,' he said. 'I agree that the loss of a true belief is unintentional.'

b   'So when this happens, it's the result of robbery, magic, or brute force, wouldn't you say?'

'I don't understand again,' he said.

'I suppose I am talking pompously,' I said. 'When I talk of a person being robbed of a belief, I mean that he's persuaded by an argument to change his mind, or time causes him to forget it: in either case, he doesn't notice the departure of the belief. I should think you understand now, don't you?'

'Yes.'

'And when I talk of a person being forced out of a belief, I mean that pain or suffering makes him change his mind.'

'Yes, I understand that too,' he said, 'and you're right.'

'And I'm sure you'd agree that anyone who changes his mind c because he's been beguiled by pleasure or terrified by threats has had magic used on him.'

'Yes,' he said, 'any deception is a form of magic, I suppose.'

'As I was starting to say a moment ago, then, we must try to discover which of our guardians are particularly good at safe-guarding within themselves the belief that they should only ever pursue courses of action which they think are in the com-munity's best interests. We must watch them from childhood onwards, and set them tasks which maximize the possibility of their forgetting a belief like this and being misled; those who bear the belief in mind and prove hard to mislead are the ones we should select, while excluding the others. Do you agree?' d

'Yes.'

'And we should also set them tough and painful assignments and ordeals, and watch for exactly the same things.'

'Right,' he said.

'Now, we'll have to invent a selection procedure for our third category, magic, as well,' I said, 'and observe how they perform. People test a foal's nervousness by introducing it to noise and commotion, and in the same way we must bring our guardians, while they're young, face to face with fear and then shift them into facing pleasure. People use fire to test gold,* but e our test must be far more thorough, and must show us how well they resist magic and whether they remain graceful what-ever the situation, keep themselves and their cultural education intact, and display rhythm and harmony throughout; if they're capable of doing this, their value to themselves and to the community will be very high. Anyone who emerges without impurities from every single test—as a child, as a young man,

414a and as an adult—should be made a ruler and guardian of our community, and should be honoured in life and in death, in the sense of being awarded the most privileged of funerals and tombs. Anyone who gets corrupted, however, should be excluded. So, Glaucon,' I concluded, 'I think that this is how we should select and appoint our rulers and guardians. These are just guidelines, though: I haven't gone into details.'

'I agree,' he said. 'It must be something like this.'

b 'And we really and truly could hardly go wrong if we reserved the term "guardian" in its fullest sense for these people, who ensure that neither the desire nor the capacity for harming the community arises, whether from external enemies or from internal friends. As for the young men we've been calling guardians up to now, we should strictly call them auxiliaries* and assistants of the guardians and their decision-making, don't you think?'

'Yes, I do,' he said.

'Now,' I said, 'can we devise one of those lies—the kind which crop up as the occasion demands, which we were talking about not long ago*—so that with a single noble lie we can c indoctrinate the rulers themselves, preferably, but at least the rest of the community?'

'What sort of lie?' he asked.

'Nothing too outlandish,' I replied, 'just a tall story* about something which happened all over the place in times past (at least, that's what the poets claim and have persuaded us to believe), but which hasn't happened in our lifetimes and I'm not sure it could, and people would need a great deal of convincing about it.'

'You seem reluctant to tell us the story,' he remarked.

'And you'll see that my reluctance was well founded', I said, 'when I do tell you it.'

'Don't worry,' he said. 'Just talk.'

d 'What I'm saying is . . . I'm not sure where to find the gall or the words to tell the story . . . I'll be trying above all to convince the rulers themselves and the military, and secondarily the rest of the community, that all the nurture and education we provided happened to them in a kind of dream-world; in actual fact, they were at that time being formed and nurtured deep inside the earth, and their weaponry and their equipment in

general were also being made there. When they were finished e
products, the earth,[†] their mother, sent them up above ground;
and now in their policy-making they must regard the country
they find themselves in as their mother and their nurse, they
must defend her against invasion, and they should think of the
rest of the inhabitants of the community as their earth-born
brothers.'

'I'm not surprised you were ashamed to tell us the lie before,'
he remarked.

'I had good reason,' I said. 'All the same, do please listen to 415a
the rest of the story as well. "Although all of you citizens are
brothers," we'll continue the tale by telling them, "nevertheless,
during the kneading phase, God included gold in the mixture
when he was forming those of you who have what it takes to
be rulers (which is why the rulers have the greatest privileges),
silver when he was forming the auxiliaries, and iron and copper
when he was forming the farmers and other workers. Now,
despite the fact that in general your offspring will be similar
in kind to yourselves, nevertheless, because you're all related,
sometimes a silver child might be born to a gold parent, a gold b
one to a silver parent, and so on: any of them might be
produced by any of the others. Therefore, of all his instructions
to the rulers, there is none that God stresses more than this:
there is no aspect of their work as guardians which they shall
be so good at or dedicated to as watching over the admixture
of elements in the minds of the children of the community. If
one of their own children is born with a nature tinged with
copper or iron, they shall at all costs avoid feeling sorry for it:
they shall assign it the status appropriate to its nature and c
banish it to the workers or the farmers. On the other hand, if a
child born to a worker or a farmer has a nature tinged with
gold or silver, they shall honour it and elevate it to the rank of
either guardian or auxiliary, because of an oracle which states
that the community will be destroyed when it has a copper or
iron guardian."[*] Can you think of any tactics to make them
believe this story?'[*]

'No, not for this particular lot, anyway,' he said, 'but I d
can for the immediately succeeding generations and all the
generations to follow.'

'I've got a pretty good idea of what you're getting at,' I said.

'It would help them care even more for the community and for one another. But the future of all this will be decided by popular consensus, not by us.'

Within the community, the guardians and auxiliaries are to live an alert, military life (which resembles that of the Spartans), without owning property, which would corrupt them (by turning them into members of the lower class) and cause the downfall of the community. It is true that they will not be happy in the common, materialistic sense of the term, but arguably they will have the greatest happiness (see Chapter 12). In any case, the happiness of the whole is more important than that of any of its parts.

'What we can do, however, is arm these earth-born men and mobilize them under the leadership of their rulers. They must go and look for the best location within the community for their barracks, a location from where they can control any

e disobedience to the laws on the part of the internal inhabitants, and repel the assault of an external enemy who falls on the community like a wolf on a flock of sheep. When they've occupied the site, they must sacrifice to the appropriate gods and construct shelters, don't you think?'

'Yes,' he said.

'And these shelters should provide adequate protection whatever the weather?'

'Of course,' he said. 'I mean, these are their living-quarters you're talking about, I think.'

'Yes,' I said, 'but military quarters, not places of business.'

416a　'*Now* what distinction are you getting at?' he asked.

'I'll try to explain,' I answered. 'Consider, for example, the dogs which shepherds train to act as their auxiliaries, to help them look after their flocks: there could be nothing more dreadful or despicable than for these dogs, thanks to their nature or thanks to the shepherds' training, to be capable of being influenced by indiscipline or hunger or some other bad habit to try to harm the sheep and behave like wolves rather than sheepdogs.'

'It goes without saying that this would be dreadful,' he said.

b　'So we must do everything possible to guard against the possibility of our auxiliaries treating the inhabitants of our community like that and using their greater power to behave like brutal despots rather than well-intentioned allies.'

'Yes, we must,' he said.

'Wouldn't a really excellent education have equipped them to take the maximum amount of care?'

'But they did receive an excellent education,' he said.

'That's not something we should stake our lives on, my dear Glaucon,' I said. 'But we should stand firmly by our present position, that whatever constitutes a proper education, it is the c chief factor in the guardians' treating themselves and their wards in a civilized fashion.'

'That's right,' he said.

'Now, doesn't it make sense to say that this education isn't all they need? That in addition their living-quarters and their property in general should be designed not to interfere with their carrying out their work as guardians as well as possible or to encourage them to commit crimes against their fellow d citizens?'

'Yes, it does.'

'I wonder if they'd turn out as we want if their lifestyle and living-quarters were somewhat as follows,' I said. 'See what you think. In the first place, none of them is to have any private property, except what is absolutely indispensable. In the second place, none of them is to have living-quarters and storerooms which are not able to be entered by anyone who wants to. Their provisions (which should be suitable in quantity for self-controlled and courageous warriors) are to be their stipend, e paid by their fellow citizens for their guarding, the amount being fixed so that, at the end of a year, there is no excess or shortfall. There will be shared mess-halls for them to go to, and their lives will be communal, as if they were on campaign. We'll tell them that the permanent presence in their minds of divine gold and silver, which they were granted by the gods, means that they have no need of earthly gold and silver as well; and we'll add that it is sacrilegious for them to adulterate and contaminate that heavenly possession by owning the earthly variety, because in the past this earthly variety, which is accepted as currency by the masses, has provoked many acts of desecra- 417a tion, whereas theirs is untainted. So, unlike any of their fellow citizens, they are not permitted to have any contact or involvement with gold and silver: they are not to come under the same roof as gold and silver, or wear them on their bodies, or drink from gold and silver cups. These precepts will guarantee not only their own integrity, but also the integrity of the community which is in their safe keeping. If they do come to own land and homes and money, they will be estate-managers and farmers instead of guardians; they will become despots, and

b enemies rather than allies of the inhabitants of the community; they will spend their lives hating and being hated, plotting and being plotted against; they will have internal enemies to fear more, and more intensely, than their external enemies. With private property, they will be racing ever closer to the ruin of themselves and the whole community. All this confirms the importance of our stated arrangements for the guardians' living-quarters and so on,' I concluded, 'so shall we enshrine them in law, or not?'

'We certainly must,' said Glaucon.

419a Adeimantus came in with an objection: 'Tell me, Socrates,' he said. 'How are you going to reply to the accusation that you're not making these men at all happy, and moreover you're making it their own fault? In a real sense, the community belongs to them, but they don't derive any benefit from the community. Others own estates, build beautiful mansions and stock them with suitable furniture, perform their own special religious rites, entertain, and of course own the items you were just talking about, gold and silver, and everything else without which happiness is, on the usual view, impossible.* Instead of all this, a critic might say, their role in our community really is just like that of auxiliary troops—mercenaries—with nothing

420a to do except maintain a garrison.'

'Yes,' I agreed. 'And they don't even get paid like other auxiliary troops: they get no more than their provisions. Consequently, they can't even take a trip for personal reasons out of town if they want to, or give presents to mistresses, or spend money on anything else they might want to, as so-called happy people can. You're leaving all this out of your accusation, and plenty of other things too.'

'All right,' he said. 'Please assume that the accusation includes them.'

b 'So you're asking how we'll defend ourselves, are you?'

'Yes.'

'I don't think we need to change direction at all to come across a suitable defence,' I said. 'We'll reply that although it wouldn't surprise us in the slightest if in fact there were no people happier than these men, all the same we're not constructing our community with the intention of making one group within it especially happy, but to maximize the happiness of the community as a whole. We thought we'd be most likely to find morality in a community like ours and also immorality in a community with the worst possible management, and that once we'd examined them we'd reach the decision which is the original purpose of our investigation.* What we're doing at the moment, we think, is forming a community which is happy as a whole, without hiving off a few of its members and making them the happy ones; and before long we'll be looking at a community in the opposite condition. c

'Suppose we were painting a statue and someone came up and criticized us for not using the most beautiful paint for the creature's most beautiful features, because the eyes are the most beautiful part and they hadn't been painted purple but black. It would be perfectly reasonable, in our opinion, for us to reply to this critic by saying, "My dear chap, you can't expect us to paint beautiful eyes in a way which stops them looking like eyes, or to do that to the other parts of the body either. Don't you think that if we treat every single part in an appropriate fashion, we're making the creature as a whole beautiful? Likewise, in the present case, please don't force us to graft the sort of happiness on to the guardians which will make them anything but guardians. You see, we know we could dress our farmers in soft clothes and golden jewellery and tell them to work the land only when they have a mind to, and we know we could have our potters lie basking in their kiln-fire's warmth on a formal arrangement of couches,* drinking and feasting with their wheel beside them as a table, and doing pottery only as much as they feel like, and we know we could make everyone else happy in this sort of way, and so have a community which was happy overall; but please don't advise us to do so, because if we follow your recommendation, then our farmers won't be farmers and our potters won't be potters and no one else will retain that aspect of himself which is a constituent of a com- d

e

421a

munity. Now, this isn't so important where the rest of the community is concerned. I mean, if cobblers go to the bad and degenerate and pretend to be other than what they are, it's not catastrophic for a community; but if the people who guard a community and its laws ignore their essence and start to pose, then obviously they're utterly destroying the community, despite the fact that its good management and happiness are crucially in their hands and their hands alone."

b 'Now, if we're creating genuine guardians, who can hardly harm their community, and the originator of that other idea is talking about a certain kind of farmer and people who are, as it were, happy to fill their stomachs on holiday, but aren't members of a community, then he's not talking about a community, but something else. What we have to consider is whether our intention in putting the guardians in place is to maximize their happiness, or whether we ought to make the happiness of the community as a whole our goal and should, by fair means and foul, convince these auxiliaries and guardians

c that their task is to ensure that they, and everyone else as well, are the best at their own jobs. Then, when the community as a whole is flourishing and rests on a fine foundation, we can take it for granted that every group within it will find happiness according to its nature.'*

'I'm sure you're right,' he said.

The continued integrity, unity, and stability of the community require the guardians to prevent the workers neglecting their work by becoming too rich or too poor, and to keep the population from becoming too great. Since they lack the material resources for prolonged warfare, diplomacy and the threat of their military prowess will be the preferred means of resolving conflicts with other states. To save discussing every possible topic, Plato stresses the overall importance of education: good men, with an understanding of principle, will not need endless rules to guide their lives. Once you have a good system of education and a good political system, beware of change and innovation.

'Well, I wonder if a closely related idea of mine will also strike you as sensible,' I said.

'What is it?'

'That there are other factors which corrupt the rest of the d workers and make them bad at their jobs.'

'What factors?'

'Affluence and poverty,' I replied.

'What do you mean?'

'This is what I mean. If a potter gets rich, do you think he'll still be willing to devote himself to his profession?'

'Not at all,' he answered.

'He'll become less hard-working and less conscientious than before, won't he?'

'Considerably less.'

'Then he'll be a worse potter?'

'Again, considerably worse,' he said.

'But if he's so poor that he lacks the means to provide himself with tools and other essentials for his job, then he's going to be turning out inferior products and he'll not be able to provide his sons (or whoever else is apprenticed to him) with e adequate training.'

'Of course.'

'Both affluence and poverty, then, are causes of degeneration in the products and the practitioners of a craft.'

'So it seems.'

'So we've come up with more things which the guardians must at all costs prevent from sneaking into the community without their noticing it.'

'What things?'

'Affluence and poverty,' I said. 'The first brings indulgence, 422a indolence, and innovation; the second entails miserliness and bad workmanship, as well as also bringing innovation.'

'Quite so,' he said. 'But, Socrates, here's a question for you. How will our community be capable of waging war if its coffers are empty, especially if it has to face an enemy who is large and wealthy?'

'Obviously it would be easier to have two such opponents ranged against us than one, relatively speaking,' I said. b

'What are you getting at?' he asked.

'Chiefly this,' I said. 'If they do have to fight, won't it be a case of warriors versus plutocrats?'

'Yes,' he said.

'Well, Adeimantus,' I went on, 'don't you think that a single boxer who has received the best possible training can easily take on two non-boxers who are rich and fat?'

'Maybe not at the same time,' he answered.

c 'Not even if it were possible for him to draw back and then turn around and strike whichever opponent is bearing down on him first?' I asked. 'And what about if he could do this over and over again in the sunshine and stifling heat? Under these circumstances, couldn't he overcome even more opponents of the kind we're postulating?'

'Without a doubt,' he said. 'It wouldn't be at all surprising.'

'Well, don't you think that rich people are better and more experienced boxers than they are soldiers?'

'I do,' he replied.

'Our warriors will, then, in all likelihood, have no difficulty in taking on two or three times the number of rich opponents.'

'I'll concede the point,' he said. 'I think you're right.'

d 'All right, then. Suppose they send a herald to one of the two communities with the following true message: "We have no use for gold and silver; it is taboo for us, though not for you. Side with us in the war, and you can have the other side's assets." Do you think that anyone who received this message would choose the option of fighting tough, lean dogs rather than siding with the dogs against fat, tender sheep?'

'No, I don't. But if all the assets of all the other communities are gathered up by a single community, then don't you think e this situation might entail some danger for our asset-free community?'

'It's naïve of you to think that any community other than the one we're constructing deserves the name,' I said.

'What should I call them?' he asked.

'They should have a more capacious title,' I replied, 'since each of them is not so much a community as a great many communities, as in the game.* Minimally, they contain two warring communities—one consisting of the rich and one of 423a the poor. Then each of these two contains quite a number of further communities. It would be quite wrong to treat this plurality as a unity. However, if you treat them as a plurality and offer one section's assets and power and personnel to another section, then you'll always have a lot of allies and few enemies. And as long as your community's administration retains its discipline and is arranged in accordance with our recent regulations, it will have no equal. I don't mean that it will merely have the reputation of having no equal, but that it really won't, even if its militia numbers no more than a thousand. You'll be hard put to find a community of this size in Greece or abroad which is actually single, though there are plenty of communities which are far larger in size and which b might be thought to be single. Do you agree, or not?'

'I most certainly do,' he said.

'Now, this could also provide our rulers with the best criterion for deciding on the appropriate size for the community,' I said, 'and how much territory they should reserve for a community of this size, without expanding any further.'

'What criterion?' he asked.

'To allow growth as long as growth doesn't jeopardize its unity,' I said, 'but no further. This is the criterion I'm thinking of.'

'It's a good one,' he commented.   c

'So here's another instruction we'll be giving the guardians,' I said. 'They are to do everything possible to guard against the community either being small or merely appearing large, and to ensure that it is just the right size and is a unity.'*

'I suppose you think that's a simple instruction for them to carry out,' he said.

'And here's an even simpler one,' I said, 'which we mentioned earlier as well.* We were talking of the necessity of banishing to the other ranks any inferior child who is born to the guardians, and of having any outstanding child who is born d to the other ranks join the guardians. And the point of this idea was that every single member of the community, from the other ranks as well as any of the guardians, has to dedicate himself to the single job for which he is naturally suited, because this specialization of function will ensure that every person is not a plurality but a unity, and thus that the community as a whole develops as a unity, not a plurality.'

'Oh yes, that's simpler—hardly worth mentioning!' he said.

'As a matter of fact, my dear Adeimantus,' I said, 'the instructions we're giving them are not as numerous or as difficult as they might seem: they're all simple, provided they follow e the saying and "stick to the one thing that's important"—or rather, not important so much as decisive.'

'What is this thing?' he asked.

'Their education and upbringing,' I replied. 'If they receive a good education which makes them moderate, then they'll easily discover everything we're talking about for themselves—and everything we've missed out so far as well, such as what they are to do with their wives, and what to do about marriage and childbirth, and how all these matters have to be dealt with in

424a accordance with the proverbial saying that friends share everything they can.'*

'Yes, that would be best,' he said.

'Now, provided our community's constitution is given a good initial start,' I said, 'then it'll get into a spiral of growth. I mean, a good educational system, if maintained, engenders people of good character; and then people of good character, if they in their turn receive the benefits of an education of this kind, become even better than their predecessors in every respect, but especially—as is the case with other creatures

b too—in that they produce better children.'

'Yes, that seems reasonable,' he said.

'To put it succinctly, then, the government of the community must adhere to this educational system, and make sure that its integrity is not subtly compromised; they should constantly be on their guard against innovations which transgress our regulations about either physical exercise or cultural studies. They should look out for these to the best of their ability, and should worry if they hear the claim that "the most popular song is the one which happens to be on singers' lips at the

c moment",* in case the poet might commonly be taken to be talking not about new songs, but a new type of singing, and might be commended for doing so. This kind of thing should be frowned on, however, and it surely is not what the poet meant. The point is that caution must be taken in adopting an unfamiliar type of music: it is an extremely risky venture, since any change in the musical modes affects the most important laws of a community. This is what Damon claims, and I believe him.'

'You can count me as another convert to this view,' said Adeimantus.

'So now we know where the guardians should build their d lookout post,' I said. 'It's in the field of music and culture.'

'Yes,' he said. 'At any rate, indiscipline can easily creep in here without being noticed.'

'Yes,' I agreed, 'because it's not taken seriously and is assumed to have no harmful effects.'

'That's because it doesn't,' he said, 'except that it gradually establishes itself and then silently seeps into people's mannerisms and habits, which become the basis from which it erupts, now enlarged, into their business dealings with one another, which in turn become the basis from which it assaults the laws and the constitution with gross indecency, Socrates, until it e eventually throws everything into chaos in both the private and the public spheres.'

'Really?' I asked.

'I think so,' he said.

'Our original position* was correct, then: the children of our community must engage in more lawful amusements right from the start, because when pastimes become lawless and children follow suit, it is impossible for them to grow into law-abiding, exemplary adults. Yes?'

425a

'Of course,' he said.

'Therefore, when children play in a proper manner right from the start, and their cultural education introduces them to the orderliness of law, there is the opposite result: lawfulness accompanies them in everything they do, guides their growth, and corrects any aspect of the community which was formerly aberrant.'

'You're right,' he said.

'And they therefore rediscover those apparently trivial rules which their predecessors had completely lost.'

'What rules?'

'For example, that one should be silent in the presence of b people older than oneself. Younger people should also give up their seats for their elders, stand up when they enter the room, and look after their parents. Then there are the rules about hairstyle, clothing, footwear, and in general the way one presents oneself, and so on and so forth. Do you agree?'

'Yes.'

'But in my opinion only an idiot would legislate on these

matters. I don't think these rules come into being, and I don't think they would remain in force either, through being formulated and written down.'

'How could they?'

'Anyway, Adeimantus,' I said, 'education is the factor which
c determines a person's subsequent direction in life. I mean, doesn't like always attract like?'

'Of course.'

'And I suppose we'd say that the final result is a single, dynamic whole, whether or not it's good.'

'Naturally,' he said.

'And that's why I for one wouldn't try to legislate further than we already have done in this area,' I said.

'It makes sense not to,' he remarked.

'Now then,' I said, 'what on earth shall we do about the world of the agora? I mean the commercial deals people make
d with one another and, of course, contracts with labourers, lawsuits for slander and assault, indictments, empanelling juries, the collecting or paying of any money due for renting space in the agora or the port, and any business which concerns the general regulation of the agora or the city or the ports or whatever. Shall we take it on ourselves to make any rules and regulations about these matters?'

'It isn't right to tell truly good men what to do,' he said.
e 'They won't have any difficulty, in the majority of cases, in finding out which matters need legal measures.'

'No, my friend, they won't,' I said, 'as long as, by God's will, the laws we've already discussed are preserved intact.'

'Otherwise,' he said, 'they'll spend their whole lives making rule after rule, and then trying to improve them, in the hope that they'll hit on a successful formula.'

'You mean they'll live like people who are ill, but lack the discipline to give up a way of life that is bad for them,' I said.

'That's it.'

426a 'And what a nice time *they* have! All their treatments get them nowhere (except that they increase the variety and seriousness of their ailments) and they're constantly expecting every medicine they are recommended to make them better.'

'Yes, that's typical of this kind of invalid,' he said.

'And here's another nice feature of theirs,' I said. 'The thing they can abide least of all is someone telling them the truth—

that until they stop getting drunk, stuffing themselves, whoring, and doing no work, no medicine or cautery or surgery, and no b spell or amulet or anything like that either, is going to do them the slightest good.'

'That's not at all nice,' he said. 'There's nothing nice about getting angry at good advice.'

'You don't think highly of this type of person, it seems,' I commented.

'No, I certainly don't.'

'And you also won't think highly of a whole community, then, if it carries on in the equivalent way we mentioned a moment ago. I mean, wouldn't you describe as identical the actions of all those badly governed states which forewarn their citizens not to interfere with the general political system and c threaten with death anyone who does so, while anyone who treats them, despite the condition of their government, in a way which pleases them a great deal, and who gets into their good books by flattering them and anticipating their wishes and by being good at satisfying these wishes, is accounted and acclaimed by them a man of virtue and high skill?'*

'Yes, I think they're doing exactly the same,' he said, 'and I've got nothing good to say about them at all.'

'And what about people who are prepared, and even deter- d mined, to look after such communities? Don't you admire their courage—and their casual attitude?'

'Yes, I do,' he replied, 'except when they're deluded into imagining that they're true statesmen simply because the masses think highly of them.'

'What do you mean?' I asked. 'Don't you feel compassion for them? I mean, do you suppose there's any way in which a man who is incapable of measuring can avoid thinking he's four cubits tall when others (who are just as ignorant) are frequently e telling him he is?'

'No, he can't,' he said.

'Don't be so hard on them, then: they're the nicest of people. They make the kinds of laws we mentioned a short while ago and then try to improve them, and constantly expect the next breach of contract to be the last one, and likewise for the other crimes we mentioned just now, because they are unaware that in fact they're slashing away at a kind of Hydra.'*

'Yes, that's exactly what they're doing,' he said.

427a

'So I wouldn't have thought that in either a badly governed or a well-governed community a genuine legislator need occupy himself with laws and administration of this kind. In the one community they can't help and don't accomplish anything; in the other some of them will be obvious and others will follow automatically from habits the citizens will already have acquired.'

b   'Is there any legislation for us still to see to, then?' he asked.

'Not for us,' I replied, 'but Delphic Apollo still has to make the most important, valuable, and fundamental laws.'

'Which ones?' he asked.

'How to site temples, how to conduct sacrifices, and how in general to worship the gods, deities, and heroes. Then there's the burial of the dead and all the services we have to perform to propitiate those who have gone to the other world. You see, we aren't experts in this area, and in founding our city we won't—

c if we have any sense—trust anyone else's advice or consult any arbiter except our ancestral one. Apollo is, of course, the traditional arbiter in this area for the whole human race, and he performs his function as arbiter from his seat at the earth's navel.'*

'That's a good idea,' he said. 'We must do as you suggest.'

Chapter 6

Inner and Outer Morality

Plato now locates the four presumed elements of goodness in the community he has imagined. The thought and resourcefulness of the guardians, as they take care of the community as a whole, are its wisdom; the lawful bravery of the auxiliaries is its courage; the lower orders tolerating the control of the rulers is its self-discipline; the members of the three classes doing what they are best equipped to do, without usurping the functions of others, is its morality, because (as Plato supposes morality must) it allows the other elements of goodness to exist.

'So there you are, Adeimantus,' I said. 'Your community seems to have been founded. The next thing for you to do is to get 427d hold of a bright enough light and explore the community—you should invite your brother and Polemarchus and the rest of us to join you—to see if we can locate morality and immorality within it, discover how they differ from each other, and find out which of them is a prerequisite for happiness, whether or not its possession is hidden from the eyes of gods and men.'

'Rubbish,' said Glaucon. 'You promised you'd do the investigating, on the grounds that it was sacrilegious for you not to do everything you could to assist morality.'* e

'You're right,' I said. 'Thanks for the reminder. But you should still help me while I do so.'

'We will,' he said.

'I think I know how we'd better conduct the search,' I said. 'I assume that if the community has been founded properly, it has everything it takes to be good.'*

'Necessarily,' he replied.

'Obviously, then, it has wisdom, courage, self-discipline, and morality.'*

'Obviously.'

'And clearly, as we go about our search, we'll discover some of these elements and there'll be some we have yet to discover.'

428a 'Of course.'

'Now, imagine any set of four things, and imagine we're exploring something for one of the four. Either we'd recognize it straight away and that would do the job, or we would recognize the one we're looking for by first recognizing the other three, in the sense that whatever is left is bound to be the one we're looking for.'*

'Right,' he said.

'Well, we're faced with a set of four things here, so the principles of exploration are the same. Yes?'

'Obviously.'

'Now, the first thing which I think is visible here is wisdom.
b And there's a peculiarity in its case.'

'What?' he asked.

'Well, I do think that the community we've described really is wise. I mean, it's resourceful, isn't it?'

'Yes.'

'And this thing, resourcefulness, is obviously a kind of knowledge. I mean, it's not ignorance which makes people resourceful; it's knowledge.'

'Obviously.'

'Now, there are many branches of knowledge in our community, of all different kinds.'

'Naturally.'

'So is it the knowledge its carpenters have which makes the community deserve to be described as wise and resourceful?'

c 'No, that only entitles us to call it good at carpentry,' he replied.

'It shouldn't be called wise, then, because of its knowledge of carpentry and because it is resourceful at ensuring the excellence of its furniture.'

'Certainly not.'

'Because it knows how to make metal implements, then, or anything like that?'

'Definitely not that either,' he said.

'And the fact that it knows how to grow crops only entitles us to describe it as good at agriculture.'

'That's what I think.'

'All right,' I said. 'Is there a branch of knowledge which

134

some of the inhabitants of the community we've just founded have, which enables it to think resourcefully about the whole d community, not just some element of it, and about enhancing the whole community's domestic and foreign policies?'

'There certainly is.'

'What is it?' I asked. 'And which of the citizens have it?'

'It is guardianship,' he replied, 'and the people who have it are those rulers—the ones we not long ago called guardians in the strict sense of the word.'*

'And what description does this branch of knowledge earn the community, in your opinion?'

'Resourceful and genuinely wise,' he answered.

'Now, do you think that in our community metalworkers will outnumber these true guardians, or the other way round?' I e asked.

'There'll be far more metalworkers,' he said.

'And wouldn't these guardians be outnumbered by any of the other acknowledged categories of experts?' I asked.

'Yes, by a long way.'

'So when a community is founded on natural principles, the wisdom it has as a whole is due to the smallest grouping and section within it and to the knowledge possessed by this group, which is the authoritative and ruling section of the community. And we also find that this category, which is naturally the least numerous, is the one which inherently possesses the only 429a branch of knowledge which deserves to be called wisdom.'

'You're absolutely right,' he said.

'So we've somehow stumbled across one of the four qualities we were looking for and found whereabouts in the community it is located.'

'*I* think it's clear enough, anyway,' he said.

'Now, it's not too hard to spot courage and to see which section of the community possesses it and enables the community to be described as courageous.'

'Why?'

'The only feature of a community which might justify b describing it as either cowardly or courageous', I answered, 'is its defensive and military arm.'

'Yes, that's the only one,' he agreed.

'The point is', I went on, 'that whether the rest of its inhabitants are cowardly or brave wouldn't affect the nature of the community either way, I imagine.'

'No, it wouldn't.'

'Again, then, it is a section of a community that earns it the right to be called courageous. This section possesses the ability to retain under all circumstances the notion that the things and

c kinds of things to be feared are precisely those things and kinds of things which during their education the legislator pronounced fearful. Isn't this what you call courage?'

'I haven't understood your point,' he said. 'Please could you repeat it.'

'I'm saying that courage is a sort of retention,' I explained.

'What do you mean, retention?'

'I mean the retention of the notion, which has been inculcated by law through the agency of education, about what things and what kinds of things are to be feared.* And by its retention "under all circumstances" I meant keeping it intact and not

d losing it whether one is under the influence of pain or pleasure, desire or aversion. I can tell you what strikes me as analogous, if you like.'

'Yes, please.'

'Well,' I said, 'you know how when dyers want to dye wool purple, they first select something which is naturally white, rather than any other colour; then they subject it to a lengthy preparatory treatment designed to ensure that the colour will take as well as possible; and when it's in the required con-

e dition, they dye it. Anything dyed in this way holds its colour, and the colour can't be washed out, whether or not one uses solvent. But you know what happens to anything which isn't dyed in this way, when something of another colour is dyed, or when something white is dyed without having been treated first.'

'Yes,' he said. 'The dye washes out and they look ridiculous.'

'So I want you to imagine', I said, 'that we too were doing our best to achieve something similar, when we selected our militia and put them through their cultural and physical edu-

430a cation. You should assume that the educational programme was designed for one purpose only: to indoctrinate them so thoroughly that the laws take in them like a dye, so that their notions about what is to be feared and about everything else

136

hold fast (which requires a suitable character as well as a suitable upbringing), with the dye being incapable of being washed out by those solvents which are so frighteningly good at scouring—pleasure, which is a more efficient cleanser than any soda and lye, and pain and aversion and desire, which outclass any solvent. So this ability to retain under all circumstances a true and lawful notion about what is and is not to be feared is what I'm calling courage. That's how I'll use the term, unless you have an alternative suggestion.'

'No, I don't,' he said. 'I mean, I think your idea is that any true notion about these matters which is formed in an animal or a slave without the benefit of education is not really lawful, and I suppose you'd find some other name for it, not courage.'*

'You're quite right,' I said.

'I accept your definition of courage, then.'

'Accept it by all means,' I said, 'but as a definition of the kind of courage a community has; then your acceptance will be all right. We'll go into the subject more thoroughly later,* if you want; you see, at the moment our quarry is morality, not courage, which I think we've explored enough.'

'That's fine by me,' he said.

'Well, we've still got two qualities to detect in the community,' I said, 'self-discipline and the purpose of the whole enquiry, morality.'

'Quite so.'

'Can we somehow locate morality and not bother any more about self-discipline?'

'I don't know if we can,' he said, 'and anyway I wouldn't like morality to be discovered first if that entails dropping the search for self-discipline. I'd be grateful if you'd look for self-discipline before morality.'

'Then it's my duty to do so, of course,' I said.

'Go on, then,' he said.

'All right,' I said. 'From my point of view, we're faced here with a closer similarity to some kind of harmony and attunement than we were before.'

'Why?'

'To be self-disciplined', I replied, 'is somehow to order and control the pleasures and desires. Hence the opaque expression "self-mastery"; and there are other expressions which hint at its nature. Yes?'

'Absolutely,' he said.

'Isn't the phrase "self-mastery" absurd?* I mean, anyone who is his own master is also his own slave, of course, and vice versa, since it's the same person who is the subject in all these expressions.'

431a

'Of course.'

'What this expression means, I think,' I continued, 'is that there are better and worse elements in a person's mind, and when the part which is naturally better is in control of the worse part, then we use this phrase "self-mastery" (which is, after all, complimentary). But when, as a result of bad upbringing or bad company, the smaller better part is defeated by the superior numbers of the worse part, then we use critical and deprecatory language and describe someone in this state as lacking self-mastery and discipline.'

b

'That sounds plausible,' he said.

'Have a look at our new community, then,' I said, 'and you'll find that the first of these alternatives is attributable to it. I mean, you must admit the justice of describing it as having self-mastery, since anything whose better part rules its worse part should be described as having self-discipline and self-mastery.'

'Yes, I can see the truth of what you're saying,' he said.

'Now, children, women, slaves,* and (among so-called free men) the rabble who constitute the majority of the population are the ones who evidently experience the greatest quantity and variety of forms of desire, pleasure, and pain.'

c

'Yes.'

'Whereas simple and moderate forms, which are guided by the rational mind with its intelligence and true beliefs, are encountered only in those few people who have been endowed with excellence by their nature and their education.'

'True,' he said.

'And is it clear to you that this is a property of your community, where the desires of the common majority are controlled by the desires and the intelligence of the minority of better men?'

d

'It is,' he said.

'So if any community deserves to be described as having

mastered pleasure and desire, and as having self-mastery, it is this one.'

'Without the slightest doubt,' he said.

'So it also deserves to be called self-disciplined, doesn't it?'

'Yes, indeed,' he said.

'Moreover, it is in this community, more than in any other conceivable community, that the rulers and their subjects agree e on who the rulers should be, don't you think?'

'Definitely,' he said.

'In a situation like this, then, is it the rulers or the subjects of the community who, in your opinion, possess self-discipline?'

'Both,' he replied.

'Is it clear to you, then,' I asked, 'that our recent conjecture that self-discipline resembles a kind of attunement wasn't bad?'

'Why?'

'Because unlike courage and wisdom, both of which imbued the community with their respective qualities while being 432a properties of only a part of the community, self-discipline literally spans the whole octaval spread of the community, and makes the weakest, the strongest, and the ones in between all sing in unison, whatever criterion you choose in order to assess their relative strengths—intelligence, physical strength, numerical quantity, wealth, and so on. And the upshot is that we couldn't go wrong if we claimed that self-discipline was this unanimity, a harmony between the naturally worse and naturally better elements of society as to which of them should rule both in a community and in every individual.'*

'I certainly agree,' he said.   b

'All right,' I said. 'We've detected three of the qualities in our community, as far as we can tell. But there's one final way in which a community achieves goodness. What precisely is morality? I mean, morality is this missing type of goodness, clearly.'

'Clearly.'

'We must now imitate hunters surrounding a thicket, Glaucon, and make sure that morality doesn't somehow elude us and disappear into obscurity. I mean, we know it's somewhere round here. Keep your eyes peeled and try to spot it. If c you see it before I do, let me know where it is.'

'I wish I could,' he said. 'But in fact it would be more

realistic of you to regard me as someone who follows in your footsteps and can see things only when they're pointed out to him.'

'Follow me, then,' I said, 'and pray for success.'

'I will,' he said. 'You have only to lead on.'

'Now, we're in a rather rugged and overcast spot, it seems,' I said. 'At any rate, it's gloomy and hunting won't be easy. Still, we must carry on.'

d   'Yes, we must,' he said.

I caught a glimpse of something and shouted, 'Hurray! Glaucon, I believe we're on its trail! I don't think it will get clean away from us.'

'That's good news,' he said.

'What a stupid state to find ourselves in!' I exclaimed.

'What do you mean?'

'It looks as though it's been curled up at our feet all the time, right from the beginning, my friend, and we didn't see it, but just made absolute fools of ourselves. You know how people sometimes go in search of something they're holding in their

e hands all the time? That's what we've been like. We've been looking off into the distance somewhere, instead of at our quarry, and that was why we didn't notice it, I suppose.'

'What do you mean?'

'I'll tell you,' I said. 'I think it's been the subject of our discussion all along and we just didn't appreciate that we were in a sense talking about it.'

'What a long preamble,' he said, 'when I'm so keen to hear what you're getting at!'*

433a 'All right,' I said. 'See if you think there's anything in what I say. From the outset, when we first started to found the community, there's a principle we established as a universal requirement—and this, or some version of it, is in my opinion morality. The principle we established, and then repeated time and again, as you'll remember,* is that every individual has to do just one of the jobs relevant to the community, the one for which his nature has best equipped him.'*

'Yes, that's what we said.'

'Furthermore, the idea that morality is doing one's own job and not intruding elsewhere is commonly voiced, and we our-

b selves have often said it.'*

'Yes, we have.'

'So, Glaucon,' I said, 'it seems likely that this is in a sense what morality is—doing one's own job. Do you know what makes me think so?'

'No,' he answered. 'Please tell me.'

'We've examined self-discipline, courage, and wisdom,' I said, 'and it occurs to me that this principle is what is left in the community, because it is the principle which makes it possible for all those other qualities to arise in the community, and its continued presence allows them to flourish in safety once they have arisen. And we did in fact say* that if we found the other c three, then whatever was left would be morality.'

'Yes, that's necessarily so,' he said.

'But if we had to decide which of these qualities it was whose presence is chiefly responsible for the goodness of the community,' I said, 'it would be hard to decide whether it's the unanimity between rulers and subjects, or the militia's retention of the lawful notion about what is and is not to be feared, or the wise guardianship which is an attribute of the rulers, or the d fact that it is an attribute of every child, woman, slave, free person, artisan, ruler, and subject that each individual does his own job without intruding elsewhere, that is chiefly responsible for making it good.'

'Yes, of course that would be a difficult decision,' he said.

'When it comes to contributing to a community's goodness, then, there's apparently a close contest between the ability of everyone in a community to do their own jobs and its wisdom, self-discipline, and courage.'

'There certainly is,' he said.

'And wouldn't you say that anything which rivals these qualities in contributing towards a community's goodness must be morality?'

'Absolutely.'

'See if you also agree when you look at it from this point of view. Won't you be requiring the rulers to adjudicate when lawsuits occur in the community?'

'Of course.'

'And won't their most important aim in doing so be to ensure that people don't get hold of other people's property and aren't deprived of their own?'

'Yes.'

'Because this is right?'

'Yes.'

'So from this point of view too we are agreed that morality is keeping one's own property and keeping to one's own 434a occupation.'*

'True.'

'See if you agree with me on this as well: if a joiner tried to do a shoemaker's job, or a shoemaker a carpenter's, or if they swapped tools or status, or even if the same person tried to do both jobs, with all the tools and so on of both jobs switched around, do you think that much harm would come to the community?'*

'Not really,' he said.

'On the other hand, when someone whom nature has equipped to be an artisan or to work for money in some b capacity or other gets so puffed up by his wealth or popularity or strength or some such factor that he tries to enter the military class, or when a member of the militia tries to enter the class of policy-makers and guardians when he's not qualified to do so, and they swap tools and status, or when a single person tries to do all these jobs simultaneously, then I'm sure you'll agree that these interchanges and intrusions are disastrous for the community.'

'Absolutely.'

'There's nothing more disastrous for the community, then, than the intrusion of any of the three classes into either of the c other two, and the interchange of roles among them,* and there could be no more correct context for using the term "criminal".'

'Indubitably.'

'And when someone commits the worst crimes against his own community, wouldn't you describe this as immorality?'

'Of course.'

'Then this is what immorality is. Here's an alternative way of putting it. Isn't it the case (to put it the other way round) that when each of the three classes—the one that works for a living, the auxiliaries, and the guardians—performs its proper function and does its own job in the community, then this is morality and makes the community a moral one?'

'Yes, I think that's exactly right,' he said.   d

The existence of conflict within a person's mind proves that there are different 'parts' to the mind. On examination, we can claim that there are three parts. Plato's description of them is rather hard to pin down, and the discussion in this section should be supplemented by reference to 580d–588a, 602c–605c, and Chapter 11 as a whole (and see pp. xxxvi–xxxix). He distinguishes a part which includes our desires or wants or instinctive appetites; our intellect, which uses both pure and applied thinking; and our passionate, assertive, proud, brave side, which (in non-Platonic terms) enhances or defends our 'sense of I'. This is Plato's famous theory of the tripartite mind, which recurs in Phaedrus *and* Timaeus. *Since all three parts have aims and objectives and distinctive pleasures, the most profitable way to think of them is to describe them as forms of desire: instinctive desire; the desire for one's overall good; and the desire for good results based on one's self-image.*

'Let's not be too inflexible about it yet,' I warned. 'If we also conclude that this type of thing constitutes morality in the case of individual human beings as well, then we'll have no reservations. I mean, how could we under those circumstances? However, if we find that it doesn't apply to humans as well, then we'll have to take the enquiry into new areas. So let's now wind up that aspect of the enquiry which is based on the idea we had that it would be easier to detect the nature of morality in an individual human being if we first tried to observe it in something larger and to watch its operation there.† We decided that the larger thing was a community, and so we founded as e good a community as we could, because we were well aware that it would have to be a good community for morality to exist in it. What we have to do now is apply the results we found in the case of the community to an individual. If there's a match, that will be fine; but if we find something different in the case of an individual, then we'll return to the community to test the new result. With luck, the friction of comparing the 435a two cases will enable morality to flare up from these fire-sticks, so to speak, and once it's become visible we'll make it more of a force in our own lives.'

'That's a viable notion,' he said. 'We should do as you suggest.'

'Well,' I said, 'if a single property is predicated of two things of different sizes, then in so far as it's the same predicate, is it in fact dissimilar or similar in the two instances?'*

'Similar,' he said.

b   'So in respect of the actual type of thing morality is, a moral person will be no different from a moral community, but will resemble it.'

'Yes,' he said.

'Now, we decided that a community was moral when each of the three natural classes that exist within it did its own job, and also that certain other states and conditions of the same three classes made it self-disciplined and courageous and wise.'

'True.'

'It follows, my friend, that we should expect an individual to c have the same three classes in himself, and that the same conditions make him liable to the same predicates as the community receives.'

'That's absolutely inevitable,' he said.

'Glaucon,' I said, 'now we're faced with another simple enquiry,* to see whether or not the mind contains these three features.'*

'It hardly seems to me to be a simple one,' he remarked. 'But then it's probably a true saying, Socrates, that anything fine is difficult.'

'I think that's right,' I said. 'In fact, I have to tell you, d Glaucon, that in my opinion we'll never completely understand this issue by relying on the kinds of methods we've employed so far in our discussion: a longer and fuller approach is needed.* Still, we can hope to come up with something which is in keeping with what we've already said in the earlier stages of our enquiry.'

'Shouldn't we be content with that?' he asked. 'I for one would be satisfied with that for the time being.'

'And it'll do perfectly well for me too,' I said.

'No flagging, then,' he said. 'On with the enquiry.'

e   'Well, here's something we're bound to agree on, aren't we?' I asked. 'That we do contain the same kinds of features and characteristics as the community. I mean, where else could it have got them from? When the general population of a community consists of people who are reputedly passionate— Thracians and Scythians, for example, and almost any northerner—it would be absurd to think that passion arises in this community from any other source. And the same goes for love of knowledge, for which our country has a strong reputa- 436a tion; and being mercenary might be claimed to be a particular characteristic of Phoenicians and Egyptians.'*

'Certainly.'

'This is a matter of fact, then,' I said, 'and it wasn't hard to discover.'

'No.'

'But here's a hard one: is there just a single thing which we use for doing everything, or are there three and we use different things for different tasks? Do we learn with one of our aspects, get worked up with another, and with a third desire the pleasures of eating, sex, and so on, or do we use the whole of our mind for every task we actually get going on? These b questions won't be easy to answer satisfactorily.'

'I agree,' he said.

'Well, let's approach an answer by trying to see whether these aspects are the same as one another or are different.'

'How?'

'It's clear that the same one thing cannot simultaneously either act or be acted on in opposite ways in the same respect and in the same context. And consequently, if we find this happening in the case of these aspects of ourselves, we'll know that there are more than one of them.'* c

'All right.'

'What about this, then?'

'What?'

'Is it possible for the same thing to be simultaneously at rest and in motion in the same respect?' I asked.

'Of course not.'

'Let's take a closer look before agreeing, otherwise we'll start arguing later. My assumption is that if someone claims that a person who is standing still, but moving his hands and head, is the same person simultaneously being still and moving, we won't approve of this way of putting it, as opposed to saying that one part of him is still, and another part of him is moving. d Yes?'

'Yes.'

'So even if the advocate of the claim were to get even more

subtle and ingeniously maintain that when a top is spinning round with its peg fixed in place, then this is definitely a case of something simultaneously being still and moving as a whole, or that the same goes for anything else which spins round on one spot, we wouldn't accept this assertion. We'll say that in this
e situation these objects are not still and moving in the same respects. We'll point out that they include an axis and a circumference, and that they may be still in respect of their axes (in the sense that they're not tipping over at all), but they have circular motion in respect of their circumferences; and we'll add that when one of these objects tips its upright to the right or left or front or back while simultaneously spinning round, then it has no stillness in any respect.'

'Yes, that's right,' he said.

'No assertion of this kind will put us off, then, or make us in the slightest inclined to believe that the same thing could ever
437a simultaneously be acted on or exist or act in opposite ways in the same respect and in the same context.'

'I won't be put off, anyway,' he said.

'That's as may be,' I said. 'But let's not feel compelled to have all the bother of going through every single one of these arguments and proving them false. Let's assume that we're right and carry on, with the understanding that if we ever turn out to have been mistaken, all the conclusions we draw on the basis of this assumption will be invalidated.'*

'Yes, that's what we'd better do,' he said.

b 'Wouldn't you count assent and dissent,' I asked, 'seeking and avoidance, and liking and disliking, as all pairs of opposites? It'll make no difference whether you think of them as ways of acting or of being acted on.'

'Yes, they're opposites,' he answered.

'What about thirst and hunger and the desires generally,' I went on, 'and what about wishing and wanting? Wouldn't you say that all these things belong somewhere among the sets
c we've just mentioned? For example, won't you describe the mind of anyone who is in a state of desire as seeking to fulfil his desires, or as liking whatever the desired object is? Or again, to the extent that it wants to get hold of something, don't you think it is internally assenting to this thing, as if in response to a question, and is longing for it to happen?'

'Yes, I do.'

'And what about the states of antipathy, reluctance, or unwillingness? Won't we put these states in the opposite category, which includes dislike and aversion?'

'Of course.'   d

'Under these circumstances, then, won't we say that there is a category which consists of the desires, and that the most conspicuous desires are the ones called thirst and hunger?'

'Yes,' he said.

'And the one is desire for drink, the other desire for food?'

'Yes.'

'Now, is thirst, in itself, the mental desire for anything more than the object we mentioned? For example, is thirst thirst for a hot drink or a cold one, a lot of drink or a little, or in short for any particular kind of drink at all? Doesn't it take heat in addition to thirst to give it the extra feature of being desire for e something cold, and cold to make it desire for something hot? Doesn't it take a thirst which has been aggravated into becoming strong to produce the desire for a lot of drink, and doesn't it take a weak thirst to produce the desire for a little drink? The actual state of being thirsty, however, cannot possibly be desire for anything other than its natural object, which is just drink; and the same goes for hunger and food.'

'Yes,' he said. 'Each desire is for its natural object only, and the desire for an object of this or that type is a result of some addition.'

'It should be quite impossible, then,' I said, 'for anyone to 438a catch us unawares and rattle us with the claim that no one desires drink, but a good drink, and no one desires food, but good food. Everyone desires good, they say, so if thirst is a desire, it must be desire for a good drink or whatever; and so on for the other desires.'

'There might seem to be some plausibility to the claim,' he remarked.

'But there are only two categories of things whose nature it is to be relative,' I said. 'The first category consists, in my opinion, of things which have particular qualities and whose correlates have particular qualities; the second category consists b of things which are just what they are and whose correlates are just what they are.'

'I don't understand,' he said.

'Don't you realize', I said, 'that anything which is greater is greater than something?'

'Yes.'

'Than something smaller?'

'Yes.'

'Whereas anything which is a lot greater is relative to something which is a lot smaller. Agreed?'

'Yes.'

'And anything which was once greater (or will be) is relative to something which was once smaller (or will be), isn't it?'

'Of course,' he said.

c 'And the same goes for more in relation to less, and double in relation to half (and all similar numerical relations); also for heavier in relation to lighter, quicker in relation to slower, and moreover hot in relation to cold, and so on and so forth, don't you think?'

'Yes.'

'And what about the branches of knowledge? Isn't it the same story? Knowledge in itself is knowledge of information in itself (or whatever you choose to call the object of knowledge), but a particular branch of knowledge, knowledge qualified,

d is knowledge of a particular qualified kind of thing. Here's an example: when the knowledge of making houses was developed, didn't it differ from the rest of the branches of knowledge and consequently gain its own name, building?'

'Of course.'

'And didn't it do so by virtue of the fact that it is a particular kind of knowledge, a kind which none of the other branches of knowledge is?'

'Yes.'

'And wasn't it when its object came into being as a particular kind of thing that it too came into being as a particular kind of knowledge? And doesn't the same go for all the other branches of expertise and knowledge?'

'Yes, it does.'

'I wonder if you've grasped my meaning now,' I said. 'You should think of this as the point I was trying to make before, when I said that there are two categories of things whose nature it is to be relative: some are only themselves and are related to objects which are only themselves; others have par-

ticular qualities and are related to objects with particular
qualities. I don't mean to imply that their quality is the same as e
the quality of their objects—that knowledge of health and
illness is itself healthy and ill, and knowledge of evil and good
is itself evil and good. I mean that when knowledge occurs
whose object is not the unqualified object of knowledge, but an
object with a particular quality (say, health and illness), then
the consequence is that the knowledge itself also acquires a
particular quality, and this is why it is no longer called just
plain knowledge: the qualification is added, and it is called
medical knowledge.'

'I do understand,' he said, 'and I agree as well.'

'As for thirst, then,' I said, 'don't you think it finds its 439a
essential place among relative things? And what it essentially is,
of course, is thirst . . .'

'. . . for drink,' he said. 'Yes, I agree.'

'So for drink of a particular kind there is also thirst of a
particular kind; but thirst in itself is not thirst for a lot of drink
or a little drink, or a beneficial drink or a harmful drink, or in
short for drink of any particular kind. Thirst in itself is essentially just thirst for drink in itself.'*

'Absolutely.'

'When someone is thirsty, then, the only thing—in so far as
he is thirsty—that his mind wants is to drink. This is what it
longs for and strives for.'   b

'Clearly.'

'So imagine an occasion when something is making it resist
the pull of its thirst: isn't this bound to be a different part of it
from the thirsty part, which is impelling it towards drink as if it
were an animal? I mean, we've already agreed that the same
one thing cannot thanks to the same part of itself simultaneously
have opposite effects in the same context.'*

'No, it can't.'

'As an analogy, it isn't in my opinion right to say that an
archer's hands are simultaneously pushing the bow away and
pulling it closer. Strictly, one hand is pushing it away and the
other is pulling it close.'

'I quite agree,' he said.   c

'Now, do we know of cases where thirsty people are unwilling
to drink?'

'Certainly,' he said. 'It's a common occurrence.'

'What could be the explanation for these cases?' I asked. 'Don't we have to say that their mind contains a part which is telling them to drink, and a part which is telling them not to drink, and that this is a different part and overcomes the part which is telling them to drink?'

'I think so,' he said.

'And those occasions when thirst and so on are counter-manded occur thanks to rationality, whereas the pulls and impulses occur thanks to afflictions and diseased states, don't they?'*

'I suppose so.'

'So it wouldn't be irrational of us to expect that these are two separate parts,' I said, 'one of which we can describe as rational, and the other as irrational and desirous. The first is responsible for the mind's capacity to think rationally, and the second—which is an ally of certain satisfactions and pleasures*—for its capacity to feel lust, hunger, and thirst, and in general to be stirred by desire.'

'No, it wouldn't be irrational,' he said. 'This would be a perfectly reasonable view for us to hold.'

'Let's have these, then,' I said, 'as two distinct aspects of our minds.* What about the passionate part, however, which is responsible for the mind's capacity for passion? Is it a third part, or might it be interchangeable with one of the other two?'

'I suppose it might be the same as the desirous part,' he said.

'But there's a story I once heard which seems to me to be reliable,' I said, 'about how Leontius the son of Aglaeon was coming up from the Piraeus, outside the North Wall but close to it, when he saw some corpses with the public executioner standing near by.* On the one hand, he experienced the desire to see them, but at the same time he felt disgust and averted his gaze. For a while, he struggled and kept his hands over his eyes, but finally he was overcome by the desire; he opened his eyes wide, ran up to the corpses, and said, "There you are, you wretches! What a lovely sight! I hope you feel satisfied!"'

'Yes, I've heard the story too,' he said.

'Now, what it suggests', I said, 'is that it's possible for anger to be at odds with the desires, as if they were different things.'

'Yes, it does,' he agreed.

'And that's far from being an isolated case, isn't it?' I asked. 'It's not at all uncommon to find a person's desires compelling him to go against his reason, and to see him cursing himself b and venting his passion on the source of the compulsion within him. It's as if there were two warring factions, with passion fighting on the side of reason. But I'm sure you wouldn't claim that you had ever, in yourself or in anyone else, met a case of passion siding with the desires against the rational mind, when the rational mind prohibits resistance.'

'No, I certainly haven't,' he said.

'And what about when you feel you're in the wrong?' I c asked. 'If someone who in your opinion has a right to do so retaliates by inflicting on you hunger and cold and so on, then isn't it the case that, in proportion to your goodness of character, you are incapable of getting angry at this treatment and your passion, as I say, has no inclination to get worked up against him?'

'True,' he said.

'But suppose you feel you're being wronged. Under these circumstances, your passion boils and rages, and fights for what you regard as right. Then hunger, cold, and other sufferings make you stand firm and conquer them,[†] and only success or death can stop it fighting the good fight, unless it is recalled d by your rational mind and calmed down, as a dog is by a shepherd.'

'That's a very good simile,' he said. 'And in fact the part we've got the auxiliaries to play in our community is just like that of dogs, with their masters being the rulers, who are, as it were, the shepherds of the community.'

'Yes, you've got it,' I said. 'That's exactly what I mean. But there's something else here too, and I wonder if you've noticed it as well.'

'What is it?'

'That we're getting the opposite impression of the passionate part from what we did before. Previously, we were thinking that it was an aspect of the desirous part, but now that seems to be way off the mark, and we're saying that when there's mental conflict, it is far more likely to fight alongside reason.'

'Absolutely,' he said.

'Is it different from the rational part, then, or is it a version

of it, in which case there are two, not three, mental categories
—the rational and the desirous? Or will the analogy with
the community hold good? Three classes constituted the
441a community—the one which works for a living, the auxiliaries,
and the policy-makers—so is there in the mind as well a third
part, the passionate part, which is an auxiliary of the rational
part, unless it is corrupted by bad upbringing?'

'It must be a third part,' he said.

'Yes,' I said, '*if* we find that it's as distinct from the rational
part as it is from the desirous part.'

'But that's easy,' he said. 'Just look at children. It's evident
that from the moment of their birth they have a copious supply
of passion, but I'm not convinced that some of them ever
b acquire reason, and it takes quite a time for most of them to do
so.'

'Yes, you've certainly put that well,' I said. 'And animals
provide further evidence of the truth of what you're saying.
Moreover, we can adduce the passage from Homer we quoted
earlier: "He struck his breast and spoke sternly to his heart."*
Clearly, Homer here has one distinct part rebuking another
c distinct part—the part which has thought rationally about
what is better and worse rebuking the part whose passion is
irrationally becoming aroused.'

'You're absolutely right,' he said.

'It's not been easy,' I said, 'but we've made it to the other
shore: we've reached the reasonable conclusion that the constituent categories of a community and of any individual's mind
are identical in nature and number.'

'Yes, they are.'

*Since the three mental parts are precisely analogous to the three social
classes of Plato's community, Plato now analyses individual wisdom,
courage, self-discipline, and morality in ways which precisely parallel
his analysis of their civic manifestations. Morality, then, is an inner
state and has little to do with external appearances. It is harmony
between the parts of a person's mind under the leadership of his or her
intellect; immorality is anarchy and civil war between the parts. For
some discussion of this analysis see pp. xxxix–xlii. The remaining
question, whether morality or immorality is rewarding, is raised, but
then deferred to Chapter 11.*

'Isn't it bound to follow that the manner and cause of a community's and an individual's wisdom are identical?'

'Naturally.'

'And that the manner and cause of a community's and an d individual's courage are identical, and that the same goes for every other factor which contributes in both cases towards goodness?'

'Inevitably.'

'So no doubt, Glaucon, we'll also be claiming that human morality is the same in kind as a community's morality.'

'Yes, that's absolutely inevitable too.'

'We can't have forgotten, however, that a community's morality consists in each of its three constituent classes doing its own job.'

'No, I'm sure we haven't,' he said.

'So we should impress upon our minds the idea that the same goes for human beings as well. Where each of the constituent parts of an individual does its own job, the individual will be e moral and will do *his* own job.'

'Yes, we certainly should do that,' he said.

'Since the rational part is wise and looks out for the whole of the mind, isn't it right for it to rule, and for the passionate part to be its subordinate and its ally?'

'Yes.'

'Now—to repeat*—isn't it the combination of culture and exercise which will make them attuned to each other? The two combined provide fine discussions and studies to stretch and educate the rational part, and music and rhythm to relax, calm, 442a and soothe the passionate part.'

'Absolutely.'

'And once these two parts have received this education and have been trained and conditioned in their true work, then they are to be put in charge of the desirous part, which is the major constituent of an individual's mind and is naturally insatiably greedy for things. So they have to watch over it and make sure that it doesn't get so saturated with physical pleasures (as they are called) that in its bloated and strengthened state it stops doing its own job, and tries to dominate and rule over things b which it is not equipped by its hereditary status to rule over, and so plunges the whole of everyone's life into chaos.'

'Yes, indeed,' he said.

'Moreover, these two are perfect for guarding the entire mind and the body against external enemies, aren't they?' I asked. 'The rational part will do the planning, and the passionate part the fighting. The passionate part will obey the ruling part and employ its courage to carry out the plans.'

'True.'

'I imagine, then, that it is the passionate part of a person c which we are taking into consideration when we describe him as courageous: we're saying that neither pain nor pleasure stops his passionate part retaining the pronouncements of reason about what is and is not to be feared.'

'That's right,' he agreed.

'And the part we take into consideration when we call him wise is that little part—his internal ruler, which made these pronouncements—which knows what is advantageous for each of the three parts and for their joint unity.'

'Yes.'

'And don't we call him self-disciplined when there's concord and attunement between these same parts—that is, when the ruler and its two subjects unanimously agree on the necessity of d the rational part being the ruler and when they don't rebel against it?'

'Yes, that's exactly what self-discipline is, in both a community and an individual,' he said.

'And we're not changing our minds about the manner and cause of morality.'

'Absolutely not.'

'Well,' I said, 'have we blunted the edge of our notion of morality in any way? Do we have any grounds for thinking that our conclusions about its nature in a community don't apply in this context?'

'I don't think so,' he replied.

'If there's still any doubt in our minds,' I said, 'we can e eradicate it completely by checking our conclusion against everyday cases.'

'What cases?'

'Take this community of ours and a person who resembles it by virtue of both his nature and his upbringing, and suppose, for instance, we had to state whether, in our opinion, a person of this type would steal money which had been deposited with him. Is it conceivable to you that anyone would think our man capable of this, rather than any other type of person?'   443a

'No one could think that,' he said.

'And he could have nothing to do with temple-robbery,* theft, and betrayal either of his personal friends or, on a public scale, of his country, could he?'

'No, he couldn't.'

'Moreover, nothing could induce him to break an oath or any other kind of agreement.'

'No, nothing.'

'And he's the last person you'd expect to find committing adultery, neglecting his parents, and failing to worship the gods.'

'Yes, of course,' he said.

'And isn't the reason for all of this the fact that each of his b constituent parts does its own job as ruler or subject?'*

'Yes, that's the only reason.'

'Do you need to look any further for morality, then? Don't you think it can only be the capacity we've come up with, which enables both people and communities to be like this?'

'I for one certainly don't need to look any further,' he said.

'Our dream has finally come true, then. We said* we had a vague impression that we had probably—with the help of some god—stumbled across the origin and some kind of outline of c morality right at the start of our foundation of the community.'

'Absolutely.'

'It turns out, then, Glaucon—and this is why it was so useful†—that the idea that a person who has been equipped by nature to be a shoemaker or a joiner or whatever should make shoes or do joinery or whatever was a dreamt image of morality.'

'So it seems.'

'And we've found that in real life morality is the same kind of property, apparently, though not in the field of external activities. Its sphere is a person's inner activity: it is really a matter of oneself and the parts of oneself. Once he has stopped d his mental constituents doing any job which is not their own or intruding on one another's work;* once he has set his own house in order, which is what he really should be concerned

with; once he is his own ruler, and is well regulated, and has internal concord; once he has treated the three factors as if they were literally the three defining notes of an octave—low, high, and middle—and has created a harmony out of them and however many notes there may be in between; once he has
e bound all the factors together and made himself a perfect unity instead of a plurality, self-disciplined and internally attuned: then and only then does he act—if he acts—to acquire property or look after his body or play a role in government or do some private business. In the course of this activity, it is conduct which preserves and promotes this inner condition of his that he regards as moral and describes as fine,* and it is the knowledge which oversees this conduct that he regards as wisdom; however, it is any conduct which disperses this condition that
444a he regards as immoral, and the thinking which oversees this conduct that he regards as stupidity.'

'You're absolutely right, Socrates,' he said.

'All right,' I said. 'I imagine that we'd regard as no more than the truth the claim that we had found out what it is to be a moral person and a moral community, and had discovered what morality actually is when it occurs in them.'

'Yes, we certainly would,' he said.

'Shall we make the claim, then?'

'Yes.'

'So be it,' I said. 'Next, I suppose, we should consider immorality.'

'Obviously.'

b 'Isn't it bound to involve these three factors being in conflict, intruding into one another's work, and exchanging roles, and one part rebelling against the mind as a whole in an improper attempt to usurp rulership—improper because its natural function is to be dominated unless it belongs to the ruling class?† Our position, I'm sure, will be that it is disruption and disorder of the three parts along these lines that constitutes not only immorality, but also indiscipline, cowardice, and stupidity—in a word, badness of any kind.'

'Precisely,' he said.

c 'Now that morality and immorality are in plain view, doesn't that mean that wrongdoing and immoral conduct, and right conduct too, are as well?' I asked.

'Why?'

'Because their role in the mind happens to be identical to that of healthy or unhealthy factors in the body,' I said.*

'In what sense?'

'Healthy factors engender health, and unhealthy ones illness.'

'Yes.'

'Well, doesn't moral behaviour engender morality, while immoral behaviour engenders immorality?'   d

'Inevitably.'

'But you create health by making the components of a body control and be controlled as nature intended, and you create disease by subverting this natural order.'

'Yes.'

'Doesn't it follow,' I said, 'that you create morality by making the components of a mind control and be controlled as nature intended, and immorality by subverting this natural order?'

'Absolutely,' he said.

'Goodness, then, is apparently a state of mental health, bloom, and vitality; badness is a state of mental sickness, e deformity, and infirmity.'

'That's right.'

'Isn't it the case, therefore, that goodness is a consequence of good conduct, badness of bad conduct?'

'Necessarily.'

'Now we come to what is, I suppose, the final topic. We have to consider whether moral conduct, fine behaviour, and being 445a moral (whether or not the person is known to be moral) are rewarding, or whether it is wrongdoing and being immoral (provided that the immoral person doesn't have to pay for his crimes and doesn't become a better person as a result of being punished).'

'It seems to me that it would be absurd to consider that topic now, Socrates,' he said. 'Life isn't thought to be worth living when the natural constitution of the body is ruined, even if one has all the food and drink and wealth and power in the world. So how could it be worth living when the natural constitution of the very life-force within us is disrupted and ruined? How b could life be worth living if a person's chosen course of action is to avoid the path which will lead him away from badness

and immorality and towards the possession of morality and
goodness, given the evident accuracy of our descriptions of
both of these states?'

'Yes, it is absurd,' I agreed. 'All the same, since we've
reached a point which affords the clearest possible view of the
truth of these matters, we shouldn't give up now.'

'I couldn't agree more,' he said. 'Giving up should be the last
thing on our minds.'

c   'Come and join me here, then,' I said, 'and you'll see, I think,
all the types of badness there are—at least, the ones that are
worth seeing.'

'I'm coming,' he said. 'You have only to tell me.'

'Well,' I said, 'the impression I get from the vantage-point
we've reached at this point of our discussion is that while
there's only one kind of goodness, there are countless types of
badness, of which four are worth mentioning.'

'What do you mean?' he asked.

'There are probably as many types of character,' I said, 'as
there are identifiable forms of political system.'

'And how many is that?'

d   'There are five types of political system,' I replied, 'and five
types of character.'

'Please tell me what they are,' he said.

'All right,' I said. 'One of the forms of political system would
be the one we've described. There are two possible ways of
referring to it, however: if a single outstanding individual arises
within the ruling class, it's called a kingship; but if there is a
plurality of rulers, it's called an aristocracy.'

'True,' he said.

'This is the first of the types of political system I had in
mind,' I said. 'The point is that whether there is a single ruler in
e the community, or whether there are more than one, they won't
disturb any of the community's important laws, since they'll
have been brought up and educated in the manner we've
explained.'

'No, it's implausible to think that they will,' he said.

Chapter 7

Women, Children, and Warfare

The discussion of morality is now interrupted until Chapter 11. However, the intervening chapters are of great importance, and deepen our understanding of some issues already raised. For many readers, these chapters constitute the heart of the book; the metaphysics of Chapters 8–9 is particularly famous, and recurs in several other dialogues. But first we meet Plato's most radical social proposals.

'So that's the kind of community and political system—and the kind of person—I'm calling good and right. Given the rightness of this community, I'm describing all the others as bad and flawed: not only are their political systems wrong, but they also influence individuals' characters incorrectly. And I see them as falling into four categories.'

'What four categories?' he asked.

I was on the point of listing them and explaining how, in my opinion, each in turn evolved out of the preceding one, when Polemarchus (who was sitting just beyond Adeimantus) reached out and got hold of Adeimantus' cloak high up, by his shoulder. He drew Adeimantus towards himself, leaned forward and whispered something with his mouth to his ear, so that all we heard of his words was: 'Shall we let it drop or what?'

'Of course not,' Adeimantus replied—this was out loud.

'What aren't you going to let drop?' I asked.

'You,' he said.

'What have I done?' I asked.

'We think you're being lazy,' he said. 'We think you're doing us out of a whole aspect of the discussion, and a not unimportant aspect at that, so that you don't have to spell out the details. You seem to think you can get away with casually saying, as if it were obvious to everyone, that where wives and children are concerned "friends share".'*

449a

b

c

'But that's right, isn't it, Adeimantus?' I asked.

'Yes,' he replied. 'But it still needs explaining, just as you've explained everything else. What makes this sharing right? I mean, there are all sorts of ways it could happen, so don't leave
d us guessing as to which one you have in mind. For a long time now we've been patiently expecting you to make some mention of their approach to procreation and how they'll bring up their children, and to discuss the whole issue of the sharing of wives and children, which is a subject you raised, because in our opinion, as far as society is concerned, a great deal—no, everything—hinges on whether or not it happens in the right way. That is why, when you were starting to criticize another type of political system before you'd adequately discussed this
450a issue, we made the decision you overheard—not to let you go on until you'd discussed this whole topic as well.'

'You should know that I share his view,' said Glaucon. 'This decision gets my vote too.'

'In fact, you'd better count us as unanimous about this decision, Socrates,' said Thrasymachus.

'If only you knew what you'd done, laying into me like this,' I said. 'You're touching off a huge discussion about the constitution of our community; it'll be like starting again from the beginning. And I was so pleased that I'd finished describing it, and so happy that the description I'd given had been found acceptable and allowed to stand! You've no idea how massive a
b swarm of arguments you're stirring up now with your appeals. It's because I noticed its size that I did nothing about it, to avoid all the bother it would cause us.'*

'Do you think it's gold fever that's brought these people here?' demanded Thrasymachus. 'Don't you suppose they've come to hear arguments?'

'Yes,' I replied, 'but not endless ones.'

'Anyone with any sense lets only death put an end to this kind of discussion,' Glaucon said. 'Please don't spare us a thought: just persevere and explain your views on the matters
c we're asking about. How will our guardians share children and wives? What upbringing will they provide for young children between birth and schooling, which is regarded as the most difficult period? Please try to explain it to us.'

'It's not an easy matter to go into, Glaucon,' I said. 'There are plenty of reasons for misgivings—even more than in the matters we've already discussed. I mean, one might doubt the viability of the proposal, and even granting its viability, there'll be room for doubting whether it's the best course of action. That, my dear friend, is why I'm rather hesitant about addressing the topic: I'm scared of my ideas being thought to d be wishful thinking.'

'Don't worry,' he said. 'You won't be faced with an audience of dunces or sceptics or grumblers.'

'Was that remark supposed to raise my morale, Glaucon?' I asked.

'Yes,' he answered.

'Well, it's having exactly the opposite effect,' I said. 'If I was sure I knew what I was talking about, then your attempt at encouragement would go down well. I mean, there's no danger or uncertainty when someone who knows the truth speaks e among intelligent friends about crucial matters which are close to their hearts, but when someone who is vacillating and who still hasn't formed any definite conclusions does the talking, as I am, it's a cause for alarm and caution. My worry is not that I 451a might make a fool of myself: that would be a childish worry. But I'm frightened of dragging my friends down with me when I stumble and fall short of the truth in matters where uncertainty is the last thing one wants. I humbly beg Nemesis, Glaucon, to pardon what I'm about to say.* You see, I'm sure that deceiving people about customs which are truly good and moral is more of a sin than accidentally killing someone. That is why it's preferable to take this risk when one is in the company of enemies rather than friends—and that's why I really appreciated your encouragement!' b

Glaucon smiled and said, 'Socrates, if anything nasty happens to us as a result of what you say, we'll acquit you of murder, so to speak, and find you free of all taint of deceit. So you can talk with confidence.'

'Well, it's true that in homicide cases there's a law guaranteeing that anyone who has been acquitted is free of the taint of pollution,'* I said, 'so I suppose the same rule applies here too.'

'Then there's nothing to stop you getting on with the discussion,' he said.

Socrates unveils his plans for the equality of female guardians with male guardians. In the first place, their primary education (see Chapter 4) is to be identical. Anyone who finds this idea ludicrous is confusing relevant and irrelevant properties of human nature; the ideas are both feasible and good for the community. Men may be better at most things, but that does not mean they have exclusive rights to those functions. Concern for the welfare of the community should have priority over convention in this context, especially since the convention may be wrong.

c 'We'd better backtrack, then,' I said. 'The proper time for the discussion may have been earlier, but we'll have to have it now. It'll probably be all right this way, though—to proceed with the women's business now that the men's business is completed and done,* especially since that's what you're asking me to do. It is my opinion that there is only one correct way for people with the character and education we've described to have and deal with their children and wives, and that is if they continue in the direction we gave them at the outset. What we tried to do, as you know, was make the men in theory like guardians of a flock.'

'Yes.'

d 'So let's keep to the same path and have the women born and brought up in a closely similar way, and see whether or not it turns out right for us.'

'How?' he asked.

'Well, should female guard-dogs share with the males the guarding and hunting and whatever other duties the males might have, do you think? Or should they stay indoors, incapacitated by their bearing and rearing of whelps, while the males work and do all the overseeing of the flocks?'

e 'They should share in everything,' he said. 'The only qualification is that we're dealing with a physically weaker sex: the males are stronger.'

'Can you employ any two creatures for the same purposes if you haven't given them the same upbringing and education?' I asked.

'No.'

'Therefore, if we're going to use the women for the same purposes as the men, we have to educate them in the same way.'

'Yes.'

'Now, the men were set cultural studies and physical exercise.'

'Yes.'

'So these two subjects had better be set the women too. Then there's the military training: we ought to put them through exactly what we put the men through.'

'That's a reasonable deduction from what you're saying,' he said.

'I suppose a lot of our suggestions would seem ludicrous and outlandish if they became practical realities,' I said.

'No doubt,' he said.

'Which of them do you think would be the most ludicrous?' I asked. 'Isn't it obviously the idea of having women exercising naked in the gymnasia along with the men—and not only young women, but older ones as well? I mean, there are old b men who come to the gymnasia and are still fond of exercise despite their wrinkled flesh and ugly appearance.'

'Good heavens, yes!' he said. 'That would certainly be thought ludicrous, as things stand today.'

'Well,' I said, 'we've chosen the course of our argument, so we shouldn't let sarcastic jibes worry us. People would crack lots of jokes of all kinds if they were faced in practice with changes of this nature in physical and cultural education, let alone in how armour was worn and horses were ridden.' c

'You're right,' he said.

'We've started out on this argument, however, so we must take the legislative rough with the smooth. We'll ask those wits* not to do what they usually do, but to be serious for a change, and we'll remind them that until quite recently the Greeks used to regard it as shocking and ludicrous for *men* to be seen naked—in fact, in most foreign countries this is still the case. The Cretans were the first to exercise naked (followed by the Spartans), and when they started to do so, it was an opportunity for the wags of the day to make fun of it all, don't d you think?'

'Yes.'

'But when experience proved the superiority of nakedness to clothing in all these kinds of contexts, then superficial mockery waned in the light of what reasoned argument revealed to be

best. It was shown to be inane to think anything ludicrous except badness, to try to raise a laugh by regarding as absurd the spectacle of anything except foolishness and badness, and
e also to seriously hold any standard of beauty except goodness.'

'Absolutely,' he said.

'The first thing we have to reach agreement on, then, is whether or not these proposals are viable, isn't it? And shouldn't we allow that there is room for doubting—whether the doubt is expressed humorously or seriously—whether
453a women do have the natural ability to co-operate with men in all their jobs, or in none, or in some but not others (in which case there's the further question of which category warfare belongs to)? Don't you think that this would be the best way for us to make a start and would probably lead to the best conclusion?'

'By far the best,' he said.

'Shall we voice their doubts between ourselves, then, on their behalf,' I asked, 'so that the opposite point of view is not left to fend for itself?'

b 'Why not?' he replied.

'So let's have them say, "You don't need external sceptics, Socrates and Glaucon. You yourselves asserted, right at the start of the founding of your community, that everyone had to do the one job for which his nature had equipped him."'

'Yes, I should say so. Of course we did.'

'"And doesn't a woman's nature differ a great deal from a man's?"'

'Of course it does.'

'"So the members of each sex should properly be assigned different work—work which suits their particular nature—
c shouldn't they?"'

'Of course.'

'"So your current proposal is bound to be incorrect, and you're contradicting yourselves with the claim that men and women should do the same jobs, despite the enormous differences between their natures." Can you defend our proposals against this accusation, Glaucon?'

'Hardly,' he replied, 'not without some preparation. What I'd do is ask *you* to come up with the response for us—so that's what I am doing.'

'I foresaw this accusation a long time ago, Glaucon,' I said, 'and plenty of other similar criticisms too. That's why I was afraid and didn't really want to get involved with regulations d about what to do with wives and how to bring up children.'

'No, it certainly doesn't seem to be an easy task,' he remarked.

'No, it isn't,' I said. 'But it's like this: it makes no difference whether you fall into a little pool or into the middle of the largest ocean—you're still swimming.'

'Yes.'

'So we'd better try swimming to safety out of this sea of argument, hoping for some improbable rescue like a dolphin picking us up.'*

'I suppose so,' he said.   e

'Let's see if we can find a way out, then,' I continued. 'We maintain that different natures should do different work, and that men and women do have different natures; and now we're claiming that these different natures should do the same work. Is this what we're accused of?'

'Exactly.'

'You know, Glaucon, skill at disputation* is a splendid 454 thing,' I said.

'Why?'

'Because a lot of people, I think,' I replied, 'find themselves unconsciously seduced by it: they think they're practising dialectic, not eristic.* The reason for this is their inability to conduct the enquiry by dividing the subject-matter into its various aspects. Instead their goal is the contradiction of statements at the purely verbal level, and they converse with one another eristically, not dialectically.'

'Yes,' he said, 'that's a common phenomenon. But does it have any relevance to our current situation?'

'Nothing could be more relevant,' I answered. 'At any rate, b we're in danger of unconsciously resorting to disputation.'

'How?'

'We're pursuing the idea that different natures should get different occupations with considerable vigour and eristic force at the verbal level, but we haven't spent any time at all enquiring precisely what type of inherent difference and identity we meant when we assigned different occupations to different natures and identical occupations to identical natures, and whether context makes any difference to what we said.'

'No, we haven't looked into that,' he said.

c 'By the same token,' I said, 'we might as well ask ourselves, apparently, whether bald men and men with hair have the same nature or completely different natures. And suppose we agreed that they have completely different natures, then we might have bald shoemakers, and make hair disqualify people from being shoemakers, or vice versa.'

'Which would be absurd,' he said.

'And the reason it would be absurd,' I said, 'is because earlier we weren't talking about identity or difference of nature in any absolute sense. We had in mind only that type of difference or d similarity which is relevant to identity of occupation, didn't we? We meant, for example, that a man with a medical mind and a woman with a medical mind have the same nature. Don't you agree?'

'I do.'

'Whereas a male doctor and a male joiner have different natures?'

'Absolutely.'

'So if either the male or the female gender turns out to be better than the other gender at some profession or occupation, then we'll claim that this is an occupation which ought to be assigned to that gender. But if the only difference turns out to be that females bear offspring, while males mount females, then e we'll say that this doesn't yet bring us any closer at all to proving that men and women are different in the context we're talking about, and we'll continue to think that our guardians and their women should have the same occupations.'

'Right,' he said.

'This is exactly what we'll require our opponent to explain to 455a us next, then—for which of the professions or occupations which bear on the organization of a community are there inherent differences between men and women?'

'Yes, that would be a fair question.'

'And he might well copy what you said a few moments ago, and reply that it's hard to come up with an adequate response on the spur of the moment, but that research would make it easy.'

'Yes, he might.'

'Shall we ask our disputatious friend to accompany us, then, to see if we can prove to him that there is no occupation which bears on the administration of a community which belongs b especially to women or to men?'†

'Yes.'

' "All right, then," we'll say to him, "here's a question for you. When you distinguish people as naturally competent or incompetent in a particular context, don't you mean that some people find it easy to learn that subject, while others find it hard? And that some people start to do their own broadly speaking original work in the subject after only a little study, while others can't even retain what they've learnt after even a lot of study and care? And that some people's bodies are sufficiently subservient to their minds, while others' are obstructive? Aren't these the features—there are more too— which enable you to define some people as naturally competent, c and others as naturally incompetent?" '

'Indisputably,' he said.

' "Well, do you know of any subject on earth in which men do not outclass women in all these respects?" Anyway, do we need to extend the conversation by discussing sewing, looking after pancakes, and boiling vegetables, which women are supposed to be good at, and where defeat makes them the most ridiculous creatures in the world?' d

'You're right,' he said. 'The one gender is far superior to the other in just about every sphere.* It may be that many women are better than many men at many things, but by and large it is as you say.'

'Therefore, my friend, there's no administrative job in a community which belongs to a woman *qua* woman, or to a man *qua* man,' I said. 'Innate qualities have been distributed equally between the two sexes, and women can join in every occupation just as much as men, although they are the weaker e sex in all respects.'

'Yes.'

'So shall we assign the men all the work and leave the women nothing?'

'Definitely not.'

'The point being that some women may be good at medicine

or music, even if others aren't. That's what we'll say, I suppose.'

'Of course.'

456a   'And isn't it the case that some women may be good at sports or warfare, while others aren't?'

'I should say so.'

'And philosophically inclined or disinclined too? And some may be passionate, while others aren't?'

'Again, yes.'

'Some women may make good guardians, then, while others won't, since these were the innate qualities we selected as the marks of men who would make good guardians,* weren't they?'

'They were.'

'Both women and men, then, have the same natural ability for guarding a community, and it's just that women are innately weaker than men.'

'I suppose so.'

b   'These are the women, then, who should be selected to live with the male guardians and to join them in guardianship. They are endowed with the natural ability to do so, and they are from the same stock as the male guardians.'

'Quite.'

'And the same occupations should be assigned to people with the same natures, shouldn't they?'

'Yes.'

'So we've come full circle back to where we were before.* We're agreed that it isn't unnatural for the wives of our guardians to be set cultural studies and physical exercise.'

'Absolutely.'

'Our regulations were viable, then, and weren't just wishful c thinking, since they're compatible with nature. In fact, it is current practice, which contravenes this, which is apparently more likely to be unnatural.'

'So it seems.'

'Now, we were trying to discover whether our proposals were viable and for the best, weren't we?'

'Yes.'

'And we've concluded that they're viable, haven't we?'

'Yes.'

'So next we need to reach agreement on whether they're for the best, don't we?'

'Obviously.'

'Well, in order to make women good at guarding, we won't be providing them with a different education from the one that works for men, will we? After all, it's the same nature the educational system takes on in both cases.'   d

'Yes, it is.'

'Now, I wonder what you think about this idea.'

'Which one?'

'The notion that some men are better than others. Perhaps you think they're all the same?'

'Definitely not.'

'In the community we're founding, then, do you think the guardians or the shoemakers will prove to be the better people, when the guardians have been educated in the way we've described and the shoemakers have been educated in their craft?'

'I'm not going to treat that as a serious question,' he said.

'I see,' I said. 'And what about the rest of the citizen body? Will the guardians be the best?'   e

'By far the best.'

'And won't the women we're talking about be better than all the rest of the women?'

'Again, by a long way,' he said.

'Is anything better for a community than for it to engender women and men who are exceptionally good?'

'No.'

'And this is the effect of cultural studies and physical education when they're employed as we have described, isn't 457a it?'

'Of course.'

'In addition to being viable, then, the regulation we were making for our community was for the best as well.'

'Yes.'

'So the wives of the guardians ought to strip off; they'll be protected by goodness rather than clothes. They'll take part in warfare and whatever else guarding the community involves, and this will be their one and only occupation. However, they will receive lighter duties than the men, because of the

weakness of their sex. Any man who treats the fact that women
b are exercising naked with goodness as their goal as a reason for
laughter is "plucking laughter unripe";*† we now appreciate
that he has no awareness of what he's laughing at or what he's
doing, since it's impossible, and will remain impossible, to
improve on the idea that anything beneficial is commendable,
and anything harmful is deplorable.'

'Absolutely.'

*The guardians will have no family life—or rather, they will regard one
another as all belonging to a vastly extended family. There will be no
formal marriages between them, and their children will be brought up
communally. In the context of maximizing the community's benefit, it
is both morally and eugenically sensible to control sexual pairing (in
the senses of who mates with whom, and when), and to dispose of
unsound children.*

'So may we now claim to have escaped this first wave,* as it
were? We've discussed what legislation to enact where women
are concerned and managed to avoid being completely
swamped while decreeing that our male and female guardians
c have to share all their occupations. In fact, the argument was
internally consistent in its claim that the proposals were both
viable and beneficial.'

'It's a pretty sizeable wave you're escaping,' he remarked.

'You'll be saying it's pretty insignificant when you see the
next one,' I said.

'I won't see it unless you tell me about it,' he said.

'It's legislation which follows from what we've just enacted
and from all the laws we made earlier too, I think,' I said.

'But what is it?'

'That there's to be no such thing as private marriage between
d these women and these men: all the women are to be shared
among all the men. And that the children are also to be shared,
with no parent knowing which child is his, or child knowing
his parent.'*

'This is a far bigger wave than the first one,' he said, 'and its
viability and value are far more likely to be doubted.'

'I don't see how its advantages can be called into question,' I
said. 'If the sharing of wives and children is feasible, it's bound

170

to be extremely valuable. I should think that most of the doubt will be concentrated upon whether or not it's viable.'

'No, there are plenty of reasons to be sceptical about both e aspects,' he said.

'You mean I can't separate the two arguments?' I said. 'I was hoping I'd escape from one of them, by securing your agreement to the idea's advantages, and that I'd only be left with discussing its viability.'

'But you were caught escaping,' he said, 'and you have to justify both aspects.'

'I must pay the penalty,' I said, 'but I ask for a little bit of leniency: please let me indulge in some lazy thinking, as 458a someone out for a solitary stroll might well do. You know how someone like that doesn't bother with the prior question of how to fulfil his desires. He doesn't want to exhaust himself wondering whether or not their fulfilment is viable, so he just imagines that they've been fulfilled and then sorts everything else out and happily details the kinds of things he's going to do when they are realized—and so makes a mind that was already lazy even lazier. Now, I'm feeling enervated myself at the b moment, and I'd like to delay investigating the proposals' viability until later. On the assumption that they are viable, I'll now—with your permission—look into how the rulers will sort them out in practice and prove that nothing could be more advantageous to the community and to the guardians than their enactment. This is what we'll try to investigate together first, if you approve of my suggestion, and then we'll tackle the other issue later.'

'That's all right by me,' he said. 'Go ahead.'

'Well, in my opinion,' I said, 'if the rulers and their auxiliaries live up to their names, then the auxiliaries will be c prepared to carry out instructions, and the rulers will be prepared to give them instructions. These instructions will sometimes be in direct conformity with law, but sometimes— where we've left the possibility—they'll simply reflect our legal principles.'

'That sounds reasonable,' he said.

'Now, you are their legislator,' I said, 'and once the women have been through the same selection procedure as the men, you'll send the ones who match the men's innate qualities as

closely as possible to join them. Since they share living-quarters
and mess-halls and since none of them has any private property
d of this kind, they will coexist and commingle during their
exercises and their educational programme in general, and
consequently their instincts are bound to lure them into having sex with one another. Don't you think that's bound to
happen?'

'I don't think it's logically necessary,' he replied, 'but the
imperative is coming from the sex drive, and I suppose most
people find the proddings of the sex drive far more influential
and compelling than those of logic!'*

'They certainly do,' I said. 'The next point, Glaucon, is that
in a community which is to be happy, undisciplined sex (or
undisciplined anything else, for that matter) is a profanity, and
e the rulers won't allow it.'

'That's because it's wrong,' he said.

'So obviously our next task is to ensure that marriages are as
far removed from profanity as possible—which will happen if
they contribute as much as possible towards the community's
welfare.'

'Absolutely.'

459a 'So we need to ask how to maximize this contribution of
theirs. Now, Glaucon, I've seen lots of hunting dogs and fine
birds* in your house, so I wonder whether you've noticed a
particular aspect of their mating and procreation.'

'What?' he asked.

'The main point is this. Isn't it true that although they're all
pedigree creatures, some of them prove to be exceptionally
good?'

'Yes.'

'So do you breed from all of them indiscriminately, or do you
take care to choose the outstanding ones as much as possible?'

'I choose the outstanding ones.'

b 'And of these, do you choose the youngest ones or the oldest
ones or, wherever feasible, the ones in their prime?'

'The ones in their prime.'

'And wouldn't you expect the result of failure to follow this
breeding programme to be the deterioration of your strain of
birds and dogs?'

'Yes,' he said.

'Does a different principle apply to horses and other creatures, do you think?' I asked.

'It would be odd if it did,' he said.

'My dear Glaucon!' I exclaimed. 'We're going to need really exceptional rulers if the same principle applies to humans too.'

'Well, it does,' he said. 'What do you make of it?'   c

'That they'll be compelled to rely a great deal on medicines,' I said. 'As you know, we regard treating people whose bodies don't require medicine, but who are prepared to follow a diet, as within the competence of a less accomplished doctor; when medicines are called for, however, a more courageous doctor is evidently required.'

'This is true, but what are you driving at?'

'That the rulers will probably have to rely a lot on falsehood and deceit,' I said, 'to help their subjects. You'll remember our claim that lies and so on are useful as a type of medicine.'*   d

'Yes, and there's nothing wrong with using them like that,' he said.

'Well, it occurs to me that this usage is particularly important in the domain of mating and procreation.'

'Why?'

'It follows from our conclusions so far that sex should preferably take place between men and women who are outstandingly good, and should occur as little as possible between men and women of a vastly inferior stamp. It also follows that the offspring of the first group should be brought up, while the offspring of the second group shouldn't. This is how to maximize the potential of our flock. And the fact that e all this is happening should be concealed from everyone except the rulers themselves, if the herd of guardians is to be as free as possible from conflict.'*

'You're quite right,' he said.

'So what we, as legislators, have to do is institute certain holidays and religious ceremonies, during which we'll bring the brides and the grooms together; and we'll have our poets compose suitable wedding-odes for them. We'll leave the 460a quantity of marriages up to the rulers: they'll want to keep the number of men in the community more or less constant, bearing in mind wars and epidemics and so on, so as to do their best to avoid increasing or decreasing the community's size.'

'Right,' he said.

'We'd better set up a subtle lottery, then, so that those inferior men we spoke of blame chance and not the rulers every mating-time.'

'Definitely,' he said.

b 'And the main privilege and reward that any young men who are good at fighting or at some other activity ought to receive is the right to sleep with the women more frequently,* so that as many as possible of the children are fathered by this kind of person, and there is at the same time a plausible reason for this happening.'

'Right.'

'Now, the officials whose job it is to take charge of any children who are born—and they could be men, women, or some of each, since positions of authority are open to both men and women equally, of course . . .'

'Yes.'

c 'Well, I suppose they'll take the children of good parents to the crèche and hand them over to nurses (who live in a separate section of the community); and they'll find some suitable way of hiding away in some secret and secluded spot* the children of worse parents and any handicapped children of good parents.'

'Otherwise our breed of guardians will become tainted,' he said.

'And they'll take care of the children's feeding by bringing the mothers to the crèche when their breasts are full of milk,

d although they'll devise all sorts of stratagems to make sure that no mother recognizes her own child. If the mothers' supply of milk is inadequate, they'll bring in other women to supplement it. They'll take care that the mothers don't breast-feed for too long, and they'll assign sleepless nights and all the hard work to wet-nurses and nannies.'

'You're making child-bearing very easy for the wives of the guardians,' he remarked.

'Which is only right and proper,' I said. 'But let's get on with the next item of our proposals. We said that the children's parents should be in their prime, didn't we?'

'True.'

e 'Do you agree that a woman is in her prime for twenty years or so, and a man for thirty years or so?'

'Which twenty or thirty years?' he asked.

'A woman can serve the community by producing children between the ages of twenty and forty, a man by fathering children from when he passes his peak as a runner* until the age of fifty-five.'

'Yes, in both cases this is the period when they're in their physical and intellectual prime,' he said. 461a

'Therefore, if the production of children for the community is encroached on by anyone too old or too young, we'll say that he has sinned against both gods and men by fathering a child who (if the matter goes unnoticed and the child is born) will not have been affected by the rites and prayers which the priestesses and priests and the whole community pray at each wedding-festival—for every generation of children to improve on their parents' goodness and value—but will instead have been born under the influence of darkness and dire lack of self-control.' b

'Right,' he said.

'And even if a man's age doesn't exclude him from procreation,' I said, 'the same regulation will apply if he has sex with a woman of the right age when a ruler has not paired them. We'll declare the child he's trying to foist on the community a bastard, without standing or sanction.'

'Quite right,' he said.

'When the men and women get past the age for procreation, I imagine we'll release them and allow them the freedom to have sex with anyone they want—except that a man is forbidden to have sex with a daughter and her female offspring, and a c mother and her female precursors, and a woman is forbidden to have sex with a son, a father, and their male descendants and precursors. But before we release them, we'll impress upon them the importance of trying their best to abort absolutely every pregnancy that occurs, and of ensuring that any baby born despite their efforts is not brought up.'*

'Yes, that's a sensible proposal,' he said. 'But how are they to tell who are whose fathers and daughters and so on?' d

'They won't be able to,' I said. 'However, a man will call any child born in the tenth month, and in the seventh month of course,* after he participated in one of the wedding-ceremonies a son (if the child is male) or daughter (if female); they'll call him father and their children will be his grandchildren, who'll regard his generation as grandfathers and grandmothers, and who'll count anyone born in the period when their mothers and fathers were producing children as their sisters and brothers. e The result will be what we were just saying: they'll avoid sex with one another. However, the law will allow brothers and sisters to sleep together, if the lottery turns out that way and the Delphic oracle has no objection.'*

'You're quite right,' he said.

These proposals will prevent conflict and ensure the unity of the community by abolishing from the guardians not only possessions, but the feeling of possessiveness. They will extend the mutual respect and fellow-feeling, typically found within a family, to the whole community.

'So this is how your community's guardians will share women and children, Glaucon. We next need to have the argument confirm that this is basically in keeping with the constitution and that it is by far the best course of action. Isn't that the thing to do?'

462a 'Definitely,' he said.

'Shouldn't we initiate the enquiry by asking ourselves which factor, in our opinion, makes the most important positive contribution towards the organization of a community—and this is the factor a legislator has to aim for when he's making his laws—and which factor does the most harm? Then we should try to see whether these new proposals of ours match the traces of the good factor and not of the harmful one.'

'Absolutely.'

'Could we describe anything as worse for a community, do b you think, than something which tears it apart and destroys its unity? And could we describe anything as better for a community than something which binds it together and unifies it?'

'No, we couldn't.'

'And isn't it the sharing of feelings of pleasure and distress which binds a community together—when (in so far as it is feasible) the whole citizen body feels more or less the same pleasure or distress at the same gains and losses?'

'Absolutely,' he said.

'And isn't it, on the other hand, the non-sharing of these feelings which causes disintegration—when something happens to the community or some of its members and the attendant feelings range from depression to delight?'   c

'Naturally.'

'And doesn't this privatization of feelings happen when the members of a community are out of tune with one another when they use expressions like "mine" and "not mine", and likewise when they identify something as foreign?'

'Absolutely.'

'So the best-run community is the one in which as many people as possible use these expressions, "mine" and "not mine", to refer to the same things in the same respects. Yes?'

'Definitely.'

'And the one which approximates as much as possible to a single human being? I mean, when someone's finger is hurt, the whole federation, which encompasses body and mind in its span and forms a single organized system under its ruling part, is aware of the pain and feels it, as a whole, along with the d injured part, and that's why we say that the person has hurt his finger.* And the same principle applies to any other part of a person, whether it's experiencing the discomfort of pain or the relief of pleasure.'

'Yes, I agree,' he said. 'And, to answer your question, yes— the more closely a community's organization approximates to this situation, the better run that community is.'

'So in this kind of community, any experience—whether good or bad—of any of its members will in all likelihood be regarded as its own experience, and the community as a whole e will share the affected member's feelings of pleasure or pain.'

'Yes, that's bound to be the case in a well-regulated community,' he said.

'Now would be a good time', I said, 'for us to return to our community, and see whether it is the pre-eminent example of a community with the qualities we've just formulated, or whether some other community surpasses it.'

'Yes, we ought to do that,' he said.

'All right. Now, our community—like every community— 463a contains both rulers and commoners, doesn't it?'

'Yes.'

177

'Who all refer to one another as fellow citizens?'

'Of course.'

'But in other communities the commoners call the rulers something else besides "fellow citizens", don't they?'

'Yes, in most communities they call them "masters", and in democracies they call them just that—"rulers".'

'What about in our community? How will the general populace think of the rulers, apart from thinking of them as fellow citizens?'

b 'As their protectors and defenders,' he said.

'And how will *they* regard the general populace?'

'As their paymasters and quartermasters.'

'In other communities how do rulers regard the general populace?'

'As slaves,' he said.

'And one another?'

'As fellow rulers,' he said.

'How do our rulers regard one another?'

'As fellow guardians.'

'Would you say that in other communities a ruler might regard some of his fellow rulers as friends and others as strangers?'

'Yes, that commonly happens.'

'And he regards and describes his friends as belonging to his c circle, and the strangers as nothing to do with him?'

'Yes.'

'What about the guardians in your community? Could any of them regard or refer to a fellow guardian as a stranger?'

'Certainly not,' he said. 'He'll be regarding everyone he meets as a brother or a sister, a father or a mother, a son or a daughter, a grandchild or a grandparent.'

'Excellently put,' I said. 'But here's another question for you. As legislator, will you be obliging them only to label one another relatives, or also to make all their behaviour conform d to these labels? Take their fathers, for instance: will they have to show their fathers all the usual respect and care and obedience due to parents, or else have both gods and men think the worse of them for their unjust and immoral behaviour? Will these be the traditions which every single citizen of your community will din into the ears of the children from their earliest years about the people they are told to regard as fathers and about all their other relatives, or will you have different traditions?'

'No, I'll have the ones you've mentioned,' he said. 'It would e be ridiculous for them only to mouth these family labels without it affecting their behaviour.'

'So there's no community in which it's more likely that, when one of its members does well or badly, people will be in tune with one another in using the expression we mentioned, and will say, "The success is mine" or "The failure is mine."'

'That's absolutely true,' he said.

'Well, didn't we say that when people hold this belief and use 464a this expression they start to share feelings of pleasure and distress?'

'We did, and we were right.'

'Isn't it above all the members of our community, then, who will genuinely share and refer to the same thing as "mine"? And because they share in this way, they'll share feelings of pleasure and distress more than anyone else, won't they?'

'Much more.'

'And, apart from the general constitution of the community, it's the fact that the guardians share their women and children that is responsible for this, isn't it?'

'Yes, that's by far the most important factor,' he said.

'Now, our conclusion was that there is nothing better for a b community than this sharing of feelings. We compared a well-run community to a body, and pointed out what a body does in relation to the pleasure and pain of its parts.'

'Yes, and the conclusion was right,' he said.

'So we've demonstrated that the community's greatest benefit is due to the fact that its defenders share their women and children.'

'We certainly have,' he said.

'Moreover, this conclusion goes with what we were saying earlier. I mean, we did say* that genuine guardians shouldn't own houses or land or anything, but should be given their food c by others, as payment for their guarding, and should all eat together.'

'Right,' he said.

'Isn't it the case, as I say, that both our earlier proposals and

the current ones increase the likelihood of their being genuine
guardians, and prevent them tearing the community apart by
using the expression "mine" to refer not to the same thing, but
to various things? Different people call different things "mine"
when they each have their own houses into which they pull
d anything they can keep out of the hands of others, and when
they each have their own wife and children; and this situation
introduces into the community the personal pleasures and pains
of private individuals. Aren't they more likely to be genuine
guardians if they all regard the same things as within their
circle of interest,* tend in the same direction, and feel pleasure
and pain, as much as possible, under the same circumstances?'

'Absolutely,' he said.

'And won't trials and lawsuits against one another be almost
non-existent, since they'll own nothing except their bodies and
share everything else? And consequently they'll be free of all the
e conflict that arises when people have money or children and
relatives.'

'That's more or less inevitable,' he said.

'Lawsuits for assault or bodily harm won't be part of their
moral code either, because we'll make it a moral obligation for
people in any given age-group to defend themselves against
their peers, which will force them to take care of their bodies.'

'Right,' he said.

465a 'There's something else that makes this regulation right too,'
I said. 'If an angry person satisfies his rage like this, he's less
likely to escalate the matter into a major conflict.'

'Yes.'

'Now, we'll have given older people authority over younger
ones and made them responsible for disciplining them.'

'Obviously.'

'And it's unlikely that younger people will ever try to assault
or strike their elders (unless ordered to do so by the rulers), or
show them disrespect in any other way. There are two
guardians whose presence is enough to stop them—fear and
respect. Respect will stop them laying hands on their parents,
b and they'll be afraid of all the help any victim would get from
people who regard themselves as his sons or brothers or
fathers.'

'Yes, that's what would happen,' he said.

180

'So thanks to our legislation they'll live together in perfect peace, don't you think?'

'Definitely.'

'And because of their freedom from in-fighting, there is no danger of a rift ever forming between them and the rest of the community or within the rest of the community.'*

'No, there isn't.'

'For fear of sounding a discordant note, I hardly like even to mention the trivial mischiefs they'll avoid. There's how poor c people have to flatter the rich; there are all the problems and worries they suffer while they're having their children educated and because in order to support a household they're forced to raise money by borrowing, by refusing to pay back debts, by doing whatever it takes to make an income—only to hand the accumulated money over to their wives and servants to spend on housekeeping. There are a number of different burdens one finds in this context, but they're too obvious and demeaning to be worth mentioning.'

'Yes, even a blind man could see them,' he said. d

'So they'll avoid all these troubles, and they'll live more happily than any Olympic victor.'

'Why?'

'The happiness which people attribute to Olympic victors is due to a tiny fraction of what our guardians have. The guardians' victory is more splendid, and their upkeep by the general populace is more thorough-going. The fruit of their victory is the preservation of the whole community, their prize the maintenance of themselves and their children with food and all of life's essentials. During their lifetimes they are honoured by their community, and when they die they are buried in high e style.'

'These are excellent prizes,' he said.

'Do you remember', I asked, 'that earlier someone or other* criticized us for failing to make the guardians happy because although they could take possession of the property of everyone 466a in the community, they actually had nothing? We said we'd look into the matter later, if it was convenient, and that for the time being we were making our guardians guardians and making our community as happy as we could, and that it wasn't our intention to single out one particular group within the community and devise happiness just for them.'

'I remember,' he said.

'Well, since we now think that our auxiliaries live a far better and more rewarding life than any Olympic victor, we're hardly
b going to place it at the same level as the life of a shoemaker or any of our other urban or rural workers, are we?'

'I don't think so,' he answered.

'Nevertheless, the comment I made at the time is also fair in this context. If a guardian aims for the kind of happiness which is incompatible with his being a guardian—if the moderate, secure, and outstanding lifestyle we've described is not enough for him and, under the influence of some idiotic and immature conception of happiness, he sets about exploiting his power to
c appropriate all the community's assets for himself, he'll start to appreciate how wise Hesiod was when he said that in a sense "half is more than a whole".'*

'I'd recommend him to keep to the guardian's life,' he said.

'Do you agree, then,' I said, 'that the best course is for the men and women to receive the same education, share children, and co-operate in the guarding of the rest of their fellow citizens, as we've described? And do you agree that whether it involves staying within the community or going out to war, the women should help in the guarding and hunting, as female
d dogs do?* They should share in everything as much as they can, and this will not only be the best course of action for them, but is also not incompatible with their nature, as compared with masculinity, and is the kind of partnership which nature intended for the two sexes?'

'Yes, I agree,' he said.

Having decided that these arrangements are for the best, Plato again (see 458b) postpones the issue of their feasibility (until 471c ff.) and turns to warfare instead. Male and female auxiliaries will fight side by side, and young apprentice guardians will observe and participate as much as possible. The prescriptions for punishing cowardice and rewarding bravery, and for how to regard enemies, are all governed by the concern to preserve unity within the community and between natural friends.

'Well, we still have to decide', I said, 'whether in fact, and under what circumstances, this sharing is viable among humans, as it is among other species.'

'I was just about to take you up on that very point,' he said, 'but you got in first.'

'Because it's obvious what they'll do about warfare, I e suppose,' I said.

'What?' he asked.

'Men and women will campaign together, and they'll also take any sturdy children with them to war, so that they see the work they'll have to do when they become adults, just as the children of other kinds of workmen do. But the children won't just watch: they'll also act as apprentices and servants in all 467a aspects of war, and look after their fathers and mothers. I mean, you must have noticed what happens in the case of other occupations—how the children of potters, say, spend a long time as apprentices and observers before getting involved in any actual pottery.'

'Yes, I know.'

'And should potters take more care than the guardians over educating their children by familiarizing them and letting them observe their duties?'

'That would be ridiculous,' he said.

'Moreover, every creature fights better, anyway, when its offspring are around.' b

'True. But Socrates, aren't they running quite a risk? If they fail, which is always a possibility in war, then they'll be responsible for their children being killed as well as themselves, and for the rest of the community finding it impossible to recover.'

'You're right,' I said. 'But the main point is: do you think they should be provided with a risk-free life?'

'Certainly not.'

'Well, if they have to face danger, shouldn't it be when the result of success will be an improvement in their conditions?'

'Obviously.'

'And do you think it hardly matters—not enough to c compensate for the danger—whether or not the children who are to become soldiers when they're adults observe warfare and all it entails?'

'No, it does make a difference, in the sense you're talking about.'

'It'll be best, then, if our primary objective is having the children observe warfare, but we also find ways to keep them safe. Right?'

'Yes.'

'Well, the chief point', I said, 'is that their fathers will know all that can humanly be known about warfare, and will
d therefore be able to distinguish risky military ventures from safe ones.'

'That's likely,' he said.

'So they'll take them to the one kind and steer clear of the others.'

'Right.'

'And they'll not be putting second-rate supervisors in charge of them, but people who thanks to their experience and their age are qualified to act as guides and attendants.'*

'Yes, that's the right thing to do.'

'Still, we're agreed that the unexpected often occurs.'

'Yes.'

'And that is why we'd better equip our children with wings from an early age, my friend, so that they can escape by flying away, if they have to.'
e 'I don't understand,' he said.

'We have to put them on horseback', I explained, 'from the earliest possible age, and they can go and watch campaigns only when they've been taught to ride. The horses they go on won't be excitable or aggressive, but will be the fastest and most manageable ones available. That's the best way for them to take stock of their work, and they'll have no difficulty in following the older people who are their guides to safety if necessary.'

'I think you're right,' he said.
468a 'What about warfare?' I asked. 'What attitudes do you want your soldiers to have towards themselves and towards the enemy? Do you think my ideas are correct or not?'

'Tell me them,' he said.

'Shouldn't anyone who deserts or discards his weapons or does anything cowardly like that be made an artisan or a farmer?' I asked.

'Yes.'

'And anyone who is taken alive by the enemy should be presented to his captors, and they can treat this catch of theirs in any way they choose.'

'Absolutely.'   b

'What about someone who distinguishes himself for outstanding bravery? Shouldn't he first, before returning home from the campaign, be crowned with chaplets by each of his comrades-in-arms—the young men and the children—one by one? Is that a good idea, do you think, or not?'

'I think so.'

'And should they take him by the hand?'

'Yes, that too.'

'But I don't think you'll go so far as to agree with my next idea,' I said.

'What is it?'

'That he should kiss and be kissed by each of his comrades.'

'That's very important indeed,' he said. 'In fact, I'll add a   c
rider to your regulation: for the duration of that campaign, no one he wants to kiss is allowed to refuse. This will make anyone who happens to be in love with a male or female comrade try harder to win the prize for bravery.'

'That's an excellent idea,' I said, 'because we've already said that a good man will be allowed to participate in a greater number of marriage ceremonies than others and that it will invariably be a good man rather than anyone else who is selected for them, so that as many children as possible are fathered by men of this type.'

'Yes, I remember,' he said.

'Moreover, Homer too approved of rewarding young men for their goodness. He said that for distinguishing himself in   d
battle Ajax "was awarded the whole length of the chine"*— this being an appropriate reward for vigour and valour because it's simultaneously a source of strength as well as a reward.'

'You're quite right,' he said.

'We'll let Homer be our guide in this matter, then,' I said. 'I mean, we too will use religious rites and so on as occasions for rewarding anyone who has displayed virtue not only with odes and the privileges we've been talking about, but also "with the seat of honour, with the best cuts of meat, and with goblets full of wine",* so that we simultaneously give our virtuous men and women an opportunity for training as well as a reward.'   e

'That's an exceptionally good idea,' he said.

'All right. Now, what about those who die during the course of a campaign? In the first place, we must count anyone who

185

dies a glorious death as a member of the golden caste,* mustn't we?'

'Definitely.'

469a 'And we'll believe Hesiod when he says that after people of this kind die "they become pure deities attached to the earth, who in their goodness guard mortal men and keep them from harm".* Right?'

'Yes, we will.'

'So won't we consult Apollo to find out how to lay to rest men of superhuman stature and what special things to do, and then bury them in the way he prescribes?'

'Of course.'

'And thereafter we'll regard their tombs as the tombs of b deities, and we'll tend to them and worship there, won't we? And don't you think we should institute the same custom whenever anyone who during his lifetime was acknowledged to be exceptionally good dies of old age or whatever?'

'Yes, that's the right thing to do,' he said.

'Now, what attitude will our soldiers have towards their enemies?'

'In what sense?'

'Take enslavement first. Do you think it's right for communities of Greeks to enslave other Greeks? Shouldn't they do their best to prevent any other community from enslaving Greeks and make it the norm to spare anyone of Greek stock, c for fear of themselves being enslaved by non-Greeks?'*

'It's absolutely crucial that they spare Greeks,' he said.

'Not only should they not own Greek slaves themselves, then, but they should also advise other Greeks to follow their example.'

'Yes,' he said. 'That should encourage them to concentrate on non-Greeks and leave one another alone.'

'And what about the victors despoiling the dead? Taking their weapons is all right, but otherwise is it a good practice? I d mean, doesn't it provide an excuse for cowards not to advance against an enemy who is still fighting, because they can make out that they're doing their duty by poking around among the corpses? This sort of looting has often in the past been the ruin of armies.'

'I quite agree.'

'Plundering corpses seems mean and mercenary, don't you think? And treating the body of a dead person as an enemy, when the hostile element has flown off and only the instrument it once used for fighting remains, seems to indicate a womanly, petty mind. I mean, do you think there's any difference between this behaviour and that of dogs who, if they're hit with stones, get annoyed at the stones, but don't go anywhere near the person who threw them?' e

'That's an absolutely perfect analogy,' he replied.

'So we'd better avoid the practice of plundering corpses and also preventing our opponents from recovering the bodies of their dead, don't you think?'

'Yes, we certainly should,' he said.

'And we won't be taking arms and armour to our temples as trophies either, especially if they came from Greeks, if we're the slightest bit interested in being on good terms with other 470a Greeks. We're more likely to be afraid of the possible pollution involved in robbing our kin of their weapons and taking them to a sacred site, except when the practice is divinely sanctioned.'

'You're quite right,' he said.

'What about devastating the land and burning the homes of Greeks? How will your troops behave towards their enemies?'

'I'd be glad to hear what you have to say about this,' he said.

'Well, I think they'll avoid both practices,' I said, 'and only steal the annual harvest. Shall I tell you why?' b

'Yes, please.'

'I think that the fact that there are these two separate terms, war and conflict, is indicative of the existence of two things with separate distinguishing features. One of the two is an internal affair, within a single domain; the other is an external affair, crossing borders. "Conflict" refers to the hostility of an internal element, "war" to that of an external element.'

'No one could fault what you're saying in the slightest,' he said.

'I wonder if you'll find the next point just as sound. I c maintain that Greeks are bonded to one another by internal ties of blood and kinship, but interact with non-Greeks as people who are foreign and live outside their domain.'

'That's right,' he said.

'When Greeks and non-Greeks fight, then, we'll describe this as warfare, and claim that they are natural enemies and that the term "war" should refer to this type of hostility. But when Greeks get involved in this kind of thing with other Greeks, we'll claim that they are natural friends, and that in a situation like this Greece is diseased and in conflict, and we'll maintain
d that the term "conflict" should refer to this type of hostility.'

'I for one agree with your view,' he said.

'Now that we've agreed what conflict is,' I said, 'imagine it happening, imagine a community divided against itself, and you'll see that, if each side devastates the other side's land and burns their homes, conflict comes across as an abomination and neither side can be regarded as patriotic, since if they were, they would stop short of ravaging their nurse and their mother. However, it seems reasonable for the winners to take the losers'
e crops, and it smacks of aiming for reconciliation rather than perpetual warfare.'

'Yes, there's far more compassion in this aim,' he said.

'Well, this community you're founding is going to be Greek, isn't it?' I asked.

'Of course,' he answered.

'And its members will be good, compassionate people, won't they?'

'Certainly.'

'Won't they feel warmth for their fellow Greeks? Won't they regard Greece as their own land and join all other Greeks in their common religious rites?'

'They certainly will.'

471a 'Then they'll regard any dissension between themselves and Greeks as conflict, since Greeks are their own people, and they won't even use the term "war" in this context, will they?'

'No.'

'So in times of dissension they'll be looking for reconciliation, won't they?'

'Yes.'

'So they won't be motivated by hatred, but by wanting to bring their opponents to their senses. As disciplinarians, then, rather than enemies, they won't punish their opponents with enslavement or death.'

'That's right,' he said.

'And as Greeks, they won't ravage Greece either, or burn homes, or conclude that the whole population of a given community—men, women, and children—is hostile to them, but only those few hostile people who were responsible for the dissension. All these reasons will make them unwilling to b ravage their opponents' land or demolish their houses, since the majority of the population will be their friends; instead, they will see the dispute through until the point is reached when those who are innocent have suffered enough and they force the guilty few to pay for what they've done.'

'I agree that this is the attitude the members of our community ought to have towards their opponents,' he said. 'And they'll reserve for non-Greeks the treatment Greeks currently give one another.'

'Shall we include this rule among our regulations for the guardians, then—that they are not to devastate land or burn c houses?'

'Yes,' he said, 'and let's add that it and our earlier regulations are all good.'

Chapter 8

Philosopher Kings

Plato faces the third wave—the question of the imaginary community's feasibility—and comes up with what is perhaps the most famous (or notorious) proposal a philosopher has ever made: that the only solution to political and personal troubles is for true philosophers to become kings, or for current rulers to become true philosophers. As Plato recognizes, this assertion throws up an urgent need to define what it is to be a true philosopher. A philosopher loves knowledge, but what exactly is knowledge? And then the basic question which will be explored throughout Chapters 8–10, and which connects them to the rest of the book, is the relation between morality and knowledge.

'I get the impression, though, Socrates, that this is the kind of topic where, if no one interrupts you, you'll forget that it is all a digression* from a previous topic—that is, whether this political system is viable, and if so, how. I accept that all these practices, if realized, would be good for any community they were practised in, and I can supplement your account: they are
471d highly likely to fight well against enemy forces, in so far as they are highly unlikely to abandon one another, since they regard one another as brothers, fathers, sons, and call one another by these names; if women joined them on a campaign (whether their task was to fight alongside the men or to support them in the rear), they'd have the effect of terrifying the enemy and could come up as reinforcements in an emergency, and I'm sure this would make our militia completely invincible; and I can see all the domestic benefits they'd bring which you haven't
e mentioned. You can take for granted my agreement that the realization of the constitution would result in all these advantages and innumerable others as well; so you don't have to talk about the actual constitution any more. Let's just try now to convince ourselves that it is viable and to find out how it is viable, and let's not bother with anything else.'

472a 'I wasn't expecting you to ambush my argument like this,' I said. 'Can't you sympathize with my procrastination? Perhaps you don't realize that it was hard enough for me to escape from the first two waves, and now you're invoking the largest and most problematic of the set of three waves. When you see it and hear it, then you'll sympathize with me and see that it was perfectly realistic of me to have misgivings and qualms about proposing such a paradoxical idea for investigation.'

'The more you say this kind of thing,' he said, 'the less likely we are to let you off discussing how this political system might b be realized. Please don't waste any more time: just get on with it.'

'Well, the first thing we have to do,' I said, 'is remember that it's our search for the nature of morality and immorality that has brought us here.'

'All right,' he said. 'So what?'

'Nothing really. It's just that if we do discover what morality is, will we expect a moral man to be indistinguishable from it, and to be a perfect image of morality? Or will we be satisfied if c he resembles it as closely as possible and participates in it more thoroughly than anyone else?'

'Yes, we'll be happy with that,' he said.

'Therefore,' I said, 'it's because we need a paradigm that we're trying to find out what morality is, and are asking whether a perfectly moral man could exist and, if so, what he would be like (and likewise for immorality and an immoral man). We want to be able to look at these men, to see how they stand as regards happiness and misery, and to face the inevitable conclusion about ourselves, that the more we resemble these exemplars, the more our condition will resemble d their condition. In other words, the purpose of our enquiry is not to try to prove that perfect morality or immorality could ever actually exist.'

'True,' he said.

'Do you doubt an artist's competence if he paints a paradigmatically good-looking human being, and portrays everything perfectly well in the painting, but can't prove that a person like that could actually exist?'

'I certainly do not,' he protested.

'Well, aren't we saying that we're trying to construct a theoretical paradigm of a good community?'

e   'Yes.'

'Then do you doubt our competence as theoreticians in this context if we can't prove that a community with our theoretical constitution could actually exist?'

'Of course not,' he said.

'So that's how matters really stand,' I said. 'However, if for your sake I also have to apply myself to proving how and under what circumstances it might get as close as possible to viability,* then although this is a different kind of argument, I must ask you to make the same concession as before.'

'What concession?'

473a   'Is it possible for anything actual to match a theory? Isn't any actual thing bound to have less contact with truth than a theory,* however much people deny it? Do you agree or not?'

'I do,' he said.

'So please don't force me to point to an actual case in the material world which conforms in all respects to our theoretical construct.† If we can discover how a community's administration could come very close to our theory, then let's
b say that we've fulfilled your demands and discovered how it's all viable. I mean, won't you be satisfied if we get that close? I would.'

'I would too,' he said.

'Next, then, I suppose we should try to discover and show what the flaw is in current political systems which stops communities being governed as well as we've described, and what the smallest change is which could enable a community to achieve this type of constitution. By the smallest change, I mean preferably a single change, but if that's impossible, then two changes, or at any rate as few as possible and the least drastic ones possible.'

c   'Absolutely,' he said.

'Well,' I said, 'I think there is a single change which can be shown to bring about the transformation. It's not a small change, however, or easy to achieve, but it is feasible.'

'What is it?' he asked.

'I'm now about to confront the difficulty which, in our image,† is the largest wave,' I said. 'Still, it must be voiced, even if it's going to swamp us, exactly like a wave, with scornful and contemptuous laughter. Are you ready for me to speak?'

'Go ahead,' he said.

'Unless communities have philosophers as kings,' I said, 'or the people who are currently called kings and rulers practise d philosophy with enough integrity—in other words, unless political power and philosophy coincide, and all the people with their diversity of talents who currently head in different directions towards either government or philosophy have those doors shut firmly in their faces—there can be no end to political troubles, my dear Glaucon, or even to human troubles in general, I'd say, and our theoretical constitution will be e stillborn and will never see the light of day. Now you can appreciate what made me hesitate to speak before: I saw how very paradoxical it would sound, since it is difficult to realize that there is no other way for an individual or a community to achieve happiness.'

'What a thing to say, Socrates!' Glaucon said in response. 'This is quite an idea! Now that it's out in the open, you'd better expect hordes of people—and not second-rate people either—to fling off their clothes (so to speak), pick up the 474a nearest weapon, and rush naked at you with enough energy to achieve heroic feats. And if you don't come up with an argument to keep them at bay while you make your escape, then your punishment will be to discover what scorn really is.'

'And it'll all be your fault, won't it?' I said.

'I've no regrets,' he replied. 'But that doesn't mean I'll desert you: I'll defend you to the best of my ability. Goodwill and encouragement are my arsenal, and my answers probably suit you more than someone else's might. You can count on this b assistance, so please try to win the sceptics round to your point of view.'

'You're providing such major support that I must make the effort,' I said. 'Now, in my opinion, we'll never escape from the people you mentioned unless we offer them a definition of a philosopher so that it is clear what we mean by our rash claim that philosophers should have political power. When there's no doubt about what it is to be a philosopher, then a defence becomes possible, if we can show that some people are made to c practise philosophy and to be political leaders, while others shouldn't engage in philosophy and should follow a leader.'

'The definition would be timely,' he remarked.

'All right. I wonder if this route leads to any kind of adequate clarification. Why don't you join me, and we'll see?'

'Lead on,' he said.

'I'm sure you're aware, without me having to remind you,' I said, 'that if the claim that someone loves something* is to be accurate, he must undeniably love that thing as a whole, not just some aspects of it.'

d   'You've got to remind me, apparently,' he said, 'because I don't quite understand.'

'I'd have expected someone else to say that, Glaucon, not you,' I said. 'It's unlike an expert in love to forget that an amorous lover finds some pretext for being smitten and unhinged by every single alluring boy. They all seem to deserve his attention and devotion. I mean, isn't this how you and others like you behave towards good-looking young men? Don't you compliment a snub nose by calling it "pert", describe a hooked nose as "regal", and call one which falls between these two extremes "perfectly proportioned"? Don't you call swarthy young men "virile" and pallid ones "children of the gods"? And who do you think invented the term "honey-coloured"? It could only have been some lover glossing over and making light of a sallow complexion, because its possessor was in the alluring period of adolescence. In short, you come up with every conceivable excuse and all kinds of terms to ensure that you can give your approval to every alluring lad.'

475a   'If you insist on trying out your ideas of how lovers behave on me,' he said, 'you can have my assent, because I don't want to jeopardize the argument.'

'And haven't you seen people who are fond of drinking behave in exactly the same way?' I went on. 'They make all kinds of excuses for their devotion to wine of every kind.'

'Yes.'

'And I'm sure you've noticed that if ambitious people can't get the command of a whole army, they take a company; and if b   they can't win the respect of important and high-powered people, they're happy to be respected by lesser people. It's status in general which they desire.'

'Absolutely.'

'So tell me where you stand on this question. If in our opinion someone desires something, are we to say that he

desires that type of thing as a whole, or only some aspects of
it?'*

'The whole of it,' he replied.

'So the same goes for a philosopher too: we're to say that
what he desires is the whole of knowledge, not just some
aspects of it. True?'

'True.'

'If someone fusses about his lessons, then, especially when
he's still young and without rational understanding of what is   c
and isn't good for him, we can't describe him as a lover of
knowledge, a philosopher, just as we can't describe someone
who is fussing about his food as hungry, as desiring food, and
don't call him a gourmand, but a poor eater.'

'Yes, it would be wrong to call him anything else.'

'On the other hand, if someone is glad to sample every
subject and eagerly sets about his lessons with an insatiable
appetite, then we'd be perfectly justified in calling him a
philosopher, don't you think?'

*In a very important argument (see further pp. xlii–xlv), Plato describes
a philosopher as one who perceives things 'in themselves'. A
philosopher is awake rather than asleep; he has knowledge, while
everyone else has mere belief or opinion, which is fallible and has less
access to reality, because it can see no further than the sensible world,
which is deceptive and deficient. Knowledge is correlated with the
truth of things, which is a property of what each thing is itself, and
which never changes; belief is correlated with the less real aspect of
things, in which they are no more beautiful (say) than ugly.*

'Then a motley crowd of people will be philosophers,'   d
Glaucon said. 'For instance, sightseers all do what they do
because they enjoy learning, I suppose; and it would be very
odd to count theatre-goers as philosophers, when they'd never
go of their own accord to hear a lecture or spend time over
anything like that, but they rush around the festivals of
Dionysus to hear every theatrical troupe, as if they were getting
paid for the use of their ears,* and never miss a single festival,
whether it's being held in town or out of town. Are we to
describe all these people and the disciples of other amusements
as philosophers? And what about students of trivial branches of   e
expertise?'

'No,' I replied, 'they're not philosophers, but they resemble philosophers.'

'Who are the true philosophers you have in mind?' he asked.

'Sightseers of the truth,' I answered.

'That must be right, but what exactly does it mean?' he asked.

'It wouldn't be easy to explain to anyone else,' I said. 'But you'll grant me this, surely.'

'What?'

'Since beautiful is the opposite of ugly, they are two things.'

476a 'Of course.'

'In so far as they are two, each of them is single?'

'Yes.'

'And the same principle applies to moral and immoral, good and bad, and everything of any type: in itself, each of them is single, but each of them has a plurality of manifestations because they appear all over the place, as they become associated with actions and bodies and one another.'

'You're right,' he said.

'Well,' I continued, 'this is what enables me to distinguish the sightseers* (to borrow your term) and the ones who want to acquire some expertise or other and the men of action from the
b people in question, the ones who are philosophers in the true sense of the term.'

'What do you mean?' he asked.

'Theatre-goers and sightseers are devoted to beautiful sounds and colours and shapes, and to works of art which consist of these elements, but their minds are constitutionally incapable of seeing and devoting themselves to beauty itself.'

'Yes, that's certainly right,' he said.

'However, people with the ability to approach beauty itself and see beauty as it actually is are bound to be few and far between, aren't they?'

c 'Definitely.'

'So does someone whose horizon is limited to beautiful things, with no conception of beauty itself, and who is incapable of following guidance as to how to gain knowledge of beauty itself, strike you as living in a dream-world or in the real world? Look at it this way. Isn't dreaming precisely the state, whether one is asleep or awake, of taking something to be the real thing, when it is actually only a likeness?'

'Yes, that's what I'd say dreaming is,' he said.

'And what about someone who does the opposite—who does think that there is such a thing as beauty itself, and has the ability to see it as well as the things which partake in it,* and never gets them muddled up? Do you think he's living in the real world or in a dream-world?' d

'Definitely in the real world,' he said.

'So wouldn't we be right to describe the difference between their mental states by saying that while this person has knowledge, the other one has beliefs?'

'Yes.'

'Now, suppose this other person—the one we're saying has beliefs, not knowledge—were to get cross with us and query the truth of our assertions. Will we be able to calm him down and gently convince him of our point of view, while keeping him in the dark about the poor state of his health?' e

'We really ought to,' he said.

'All right, but what shall we say to him, do you think? Perhaps this is what we should ask him. We'll tell him that we don't resent any knowledge he might have—indeed, we'd be delighted to see that he does know something—and then we'll say, "But can you tell us, please, whether someone with knowledge knows something or nothing?" You'd better answer my questions for him.'

'My answer will be that he knows something,' he said.

'Something real or something unreal?'*

'Real. How could something unreal be known?'* 477a

'We could look at the matter from more angles, but we're happy enough with the idea that something completely real is completely accessible to knowledge, and something utterly unreal is entirely inaccessible to knowledge. Yes?'

'Perfectly happy.'

'All right. But if something is in a state of both reality and unreality, then it falls between that which is perfectly real and that which is utterly unreal, doesn't it?'

'Yes.'

'So since the field of knowledge is reality, and since it must be incomprehension whose field is unreality, then we need to find out if there is in fact something which falls between

b incomprehension and knowledge, whose field is this intermediate, don't we?'

'Yes.'

'Now, we acknowledge the existence of belief, don't we?'

'Of course.'

'Is it a different faculty from knowledge, or is it the same?'

'Different.'

'Every faculty has its own distinctive abilities, so belief and
knowledge must have different domains.'

'Yes.'

'Now, since the natural field of knowledge is reality—its
function is to know reality as reality... Actually, I think
there's something else we need to get clear about first.'

'What?'

c 'Shall we count as a distinct class of things the faculties
which give human beings and all other creatures their abilities?
By "faculties" I mean things like sight and hearing. Do you
understand the type of thing I have in mind?'

'Yes, I do,' he said.

'Let me tell you something that strikes me about them. I can't
distinguish one faculty from another the way I commonly
distinguish other things, by looking at their colours or shapes
or anything like that, because faculties don't have any of those
sorts of qualities for me to look at. The only aspect of a faculty

d I can look at is its field, its effect. This is what enables me to
identify each of them as a particular faculty. Where I find a
single domain and a single effect, I say there is a single faculty;
and I distinguish faculties which have different fields and
different effects. What about you? What do you do?'

'The same as you,' he said.

'Let's go back to where we were before, then, Glaucon,' I
said. 'Do you think that knowledge is a faculty, or does it
belong in your opinion to some other class?'

'I think it belongs to that class,' he said, 'and is the most
powerful of all the faculties.'

e 'And shall we classify belief as a faculty, or what?'

'As a faculty,' he said. 'Belief is precisely that which enables
us to entertain beliefs.'

'Not long ago, however, you agreed that knowledge and
belief were different.'

'Of course,' he said. 'One is infallible and the other is fallible, so anyone with any sense would keep them separate.'

'Good,' I said. 'There can be no doubt of our position: knowledge and belief are different.' 478a

'Yes.'

'Since they're different faculties, then, they have different natural fields, don't they?'

'Necessarily.'

'The field of knowledge is reality, isn't it? Its function is to know the reality of anything real?'

'Yes.'

'And the function of belief, we're saying, is to entertain beliefs?'

'Yes.'

'Does it entertain beliefs about the same thing which knowledge knows? Will what is accessible to knowledge and what is accessible to belief be identical? Or is that out of the question?'

'It's ruled out by what we've already agreed,' he said. 'If different faculties naturally have different fields, and if both knowledge and belief are faculties, and different faculties too, b as we said, then it follows that it is impossible for what is accessible to knowledge and what is accessible to belief to be identical.'

'So if it is reality that is accessible to knowledge, then it is something else, not reality, that is accessible to belief, isn't it?'

'Yes.'

'Does it entertain beliefs about what is unreal? Or is it also impossible for that to happen? Think about this: isn't it the case that someone who is entertaining a belief is bringing his believing mind to bear on something? I mean, is it possible to have a belief, and to be believing nothing?'

'That's impossible.'

'In fact, someone who has a belief has some single thing in mind, doesn't he?'

'Yes.'

'But the most accurate way to refer to something unreal would be to say that it is nothing, not that it is a single thing, c wouldn't it?'

'Yes.'

'Didn't we find ourselves forced to relate incomprehension to unreality and knowledge to reality?'

'That's right,' he said.

'So the field of belief is neither reality nor unreality?'

'No.'

'Belief can't be incomprehension or knowledge, then?'

'So it seems.'

'Well, does it lie beyond their limits? Does it shed more light than knowledge or spread more obscurity than incomprehension?'

'It does neither.'

'Alternatively, does belief strike you as more opaque than knowledge and more lucid than incomprehension?'

'Considerably more,' he said.

d 'It lies within their limits?'

'Yes.'

'Then belief must fall between them.'

'Absolutely.'

'Now, didn't we say earlier that something which is simultaneously real and unreal (were such a thing to be shown to exist) would fall between the perfectly real and the wholly unreal, and wouldn't be the field of either knowledge or incomprehension, but of an intermediate (again, if such a thing were shown to exist) between incomprehension and knowledge?'

'Right.'

'And now we've found that what we call belief is such an intermediate, haven't we?'

'We have.'

e 'So the only thing left for us to discover, apparently, is whether there's anything which partakes of both reality and unreality, and cannot be said to be perfectly real or perfectly unreal. If we were to come across such a thing, we'd be fully justified in describing it as the field of belief, on the principle that extremes belong together, and so do intermediates. Do you agree?'

'Yes.'

'Let's return, on this basis, to the give and take of
479a conversation with that fine fellow who doesn't acknowledge the existence of beauty itself or think that beauty itself has any

permanent and unvarying character,* but takes the plurality of beautiful things as his norm—that sightseer who can't under any circumstances abide the notion that beauty, morality, and so on are each a single entity. What we'll say to him is, "My friend, is there one beautiful thing, in this welter of beautiful things, which won't turn out to be ugly? Is there one moral deed which won't turn out to be immoral? Is there one just act which won't turn out to be unjust?"'

'No, there isn't,' he said. 'It's inevitable for these things to turn out to be both beautiful and ugly, in a sense, and the same goes for all the other qualities you mentioned in your question.'* b

'And there are doubles galore—but they turn out to be halves just as much as doubles, don't they?'

'Yes.'

'And do things which are large, small, light, and heavy deserve these attributes any more than they deserve the opposite attributes?'*

'No, each of them is bound to have both qualities,' he said.

'So isn't it the case, then, that any member of a plurality no more *is* whatever it is said to be than it *is not* whatever it is said to be?'

'This is like those *double entendres* one hears at parties,' he said, 'or the riddle children tell about the eunuch and his hitting a bat—they make a riddle by asking what he hit it with and what it was on*—in the sense that the members of the plurality are also ambiguous: it is impossible to form a stable conception of any of them as either being what it is, or not being what it is, or being both, or being neither.' c

'How are you going to cope with them, then?' I asked. 'Can you find a better place to locate them than between real being and unreality? I mean, they can't turn out to be more opaque and unreal than unreality, or more lucid and real than reality.' d

'True,' he said.

'So there we are. We've discovered that the welter of things which the masses conventionally regard as beautiful and so on mill around somewhere between unreality and perfect reality.'

'Yes, we have.'

'But we have a prior agreement that were such a thing to turn up, we'd have to call it the field of belief, not of knowledge, since the realm which occupies some uncertain intermediate point must be accessible to the intermediate faculty.'

'Yes, we do.'

e   'What shall we say about those spectators, then, who can see a plurality of beautiful things, but not beauty itself, and who are incapable of following if someone else tries to lead them to it, and who can see many moral actions, but not morality itself, and so on? That they only ever entertain beliefs, and do not *know* any of the things they believe?'

'That's what we have to say,' he said.

'As for those who can see each of these things in itself, in its permanent and unvarying nature, we'll say they have knowledge and are not merely entertaining beliefs, won't we?'

'Again, we have to.'

'And won't our position be that they're devoted to and love
480a the domain of knowledge, as opposed to the others, who are devoted to and love the domain of belief? I mean, surely we haven't forgotten our claim that these others love and are spectators of beautiful sounds and colours and so on, but can't abide the idea that there is such a thing as beauty itself?'*

'No, we haven't forgotten.'

'They won't think us nasty if we refer to them as "lovers of belief" rather than as philosophers, who love knowledge, will they? Are they going to get very cross with us if we say that now?'*

'Not if they listen to me,' he replied. 'It's not right to get angry at the truth.'

'But the term "believers" is inappropriate for those who are devoted to everything that is real: they should be called philosophers, shouldn't they?'

'Absolutely.'

A philosopher's inherent virtues are displayed. Though they stem from his or her love of knowledge, they coincide with commonly recognized virtues, and are far from incompatible with rulership.

484a   'It's taken a long and thorough discussion, Glaucon,' I said, 'and it's not been easy, but we've now demonstrated the difference between philosophers and non-philosophers.'

'A short discussion probably wouldn't have been enough,' he replied.

'I suppose you're right,' I said. 'Anyway, I think the conclusion would have been clearer if that had been the only subject we'd had to discuss, and there weren't plenty of topics left for us to cover if we're to see the difference between a moral and an immoral life.' b

'What's the next issue for us to look into?' he asked.

'The next one's the one that follows, of course,' I replied. 'Given that philosophers are those who are capable of apprehending that which is permanent and unvarying, while those who can't, those who wander erratically in the midst of plurality and variety, are not lovers of knowledge, which set of people ought to be rulers of a community?'

'What would be a sensible answer for us to give?' he asked.

'That the position of guardianship should be given to whichever set we find capable of guarding the laws and customs of a community,' I said. c

'Right,' he said.

'I assume it's clear whether someone who's going to guard something should be blind or have good eyesight?' I said.

'Of course it is,' he answered.

'Well, imagine someone who really lacks the ability to recognize any and every real thing and has no paradigm to shed light for his mind's eye. He has nothing absolutely authentic to contemplate, as painters do, and use as a reference-point whenever he needs to, and gain a completely accurate picture d of, before establishing human norms of right, morality, and goodness (if establishing is what is required), and before guarding and protecting the norms that have already been established.* Do you think there's any difference between his condition and blindness?'

'No, there's hardly any difference at all,' he said.

'Is this the type of person you'd prefer us to appoint as guardians? Or shall we appoint those who can recognize every reality, and who not only have just as much practical experience* as the others, but are also at least as good as them in every other respect?'

'If they really are at least equal in every other sphere,' he said, 'and since they are pre-eminent in the sphere you've mentioned, which is just about the most important one there is, then it would be ridiculous to choose anyone else.'

485a 'So what we'd better explain is how a single person can combine both sets of qualities, hadn't we?'

'Yes.'

'Well, right at the beginning of this argument* we said that the first thing we had to grasp was what it is to be a philosopher. I'm sure that if we reached a satisfactory agreement on that point, we'd also agree that despite being a single person, he can combine both sets of qualities, and that philosophers are the only ones who should rule over communities.'

'Why?'

'Let's start by agreeing that it's natural for philosophers to b love every field of study which reveals to them something of that reality which is eternal and is not subject to the vicissitudes of generation and destruction.'*

'All right.'

'Moreover,' I said, 'we can agree that they're in love with reality as a whole, and that therefore their behaviour is just like that of ambitious people and lovers, as we explained before,* in that they won't willingly give up even minor or worthless parts of it.'

'You're right,' he said.

'The next thing for you to think about is whether there's a c further feature they must have, if they're going to live up to our description of them.'

'What feature?'

'Honesty—the inability consciously to tolerate falsehood, rather than loathing it, and loving truth.'

'It makes sense that they should,' he said.

'It doesn't only make sense, my friend: a lover is absolutely bound to love everything which is related and belongs to his beloved.'

'Right,' he said.

'Well, can you conceive of anything more closely related to knowledge than truth?'

'Of course not,' he replied.

'Is it possible, then, for love of knowledge and love of d falsehood to be found in the same nature?'

'Definitely not.'

'Then a genuine lover of knowledge will from his earliest years find nothing more attractive than truth of every kind.'

'Indisputably.'

'And we know that anyone whose predilection tends strongly in a single direction has correspondingly less desire for other things, like a stream whose flow has been diverted into another channel.'

'Of course.'

'So when a person's desires are channelled towards learning and so on, that person is concerned with the pleasure the mind feels of its own accord, and has nothing to do with the pleasures which reach the mind through the agency of the body, if the person is a genuine philosopher, not a fake one.'* e

'Inevitably.'

'He'll be self-disciplined, then, and not mercenary, since he's constitutionally incapable of taking seriously the things which money can buy—at considerable cost—and which cause others to take money seriously.'

'Yes.'

'And here's another point you'd better take into con- 486a sideration, to help you distinguish a philosophical from a non-philosophical character.'

'What?'

'You must watch out for the presence of small-mindedness. Nothing stops a mind constantly striving for an overview of the totality of things human and divine more effectively than involvement in petty details.'

'Very true,' he said.

'When a mind has broadness of vision and contemplates all time and all existence, do you think it can place much importance on human life?'

'Impossible,' he said.

'So it won't find death terrifying either, will it?' b

'Not at all.'

'Then a cowardly and small-minded person is excluded from true philosophy, it seems.'

'I agree.'

'Well now, take a person who's restrained and uninterested in money, and who isn't small-minded or specious or cowardly.

Could he possibly drive hard bargains or act immorally?'

'No.'

'So when you're trying to see whether or not someone has a philosophical mind, you'll watch out for whether, from his earliest years, he shows himself to be moral and well mannered, or antisocial and uncouth.'

'Yes.'

c   'And there's something else you won't forget to look out for as well, I imagine.'

'What?'

'Whether he's quick or slow at learning. I mean, you wouldn't expect someone to be particularly fond of something it hurt him to do and where slight gains were hard to win, would you?'

'I'd never do that.'

'What about if he's incapable of retaining anything he's learnt? Is there any way he can have room for knowledge, when he's full of forgetfulness?'

'Of course not.'

'In the end, don't you think, after all his thankless toil, he's bound to loathe both himself and intellectual activity?'

'Yes.'

d   'So we'd better count forgetfulness as a factor which precludes a mind from being good enough at philosophy. We'd better make a good memory a prerequisite.'

'Absolutely.'

'Now, isn't it the case that lack of culture and grace in someone can only lead him to lack a sense of proportion?'

'Of course.'

'And do you think that truth is closely related to proportion or to its opposite?'

'To proportion.'

'So we need to look for a mind which, in addition to the qualities we've already mentioned, has an inherent sense of proportion and elegance, and which makes a person instinctively inclined towards anything's essential character.'*

'Of course we do.'

e   'All right. Surely you don't think that any of the interconnected qualities we've mentioned are at all inessential for a competent and complete mental grasp of reality?'

'No, they're absolutely essential,' he said. 487a

'Can you find any flaw, then, in an occupation like this, which in order to be competently practised requires the following inherent qualities in a person: a good memory, quickness at learning, broadness of vision, elegance, and love of and affiliation to truth, morality, courage, and self-discipline?'

'Not even Momus* could criticize this occupation,' he replied.

'Now, aren't people who, thanks to their education and their age, have these qualities in full the only ones to whom you would entrust your community?'

To the objection that the popular impression of philosophers is that they are either useless or bad, Socrates replies that the 'useless' ones are so described because people simply fail to understand their value, and the 'bad' ones are either those who have been corrupted by the general populace (and the sophists who pander to the general populace), until they use their natural talents for base ends, or those who try to take up philosophy despite their lack of talent. Both are cases where the 'one man, one job' principle is transgressed; in neither case should we really describe these people as philosophers.

Adeimantus spoke up.* 'Socrates,' he said, 'no one's going to b take you up on this point; but that may be due to the fact that there's a particular experience which people who hear you speak on any occasion always have. They get the impression that, because they lack expertise at the give and take of discussion, they're led a little bit astray by each question, and then when all the little bits are put together at the end of the discussion, they find that they were way off the mark and that they've contradicted their original position. They're like unskilled backgammon players, who end up being shut out by skilled ones and incapable of making a move: they too end up c being shut out and incapable of making an argumentative move in this alternative version of backgammon, which uses words rather than counters, since they feel that this is not necessarily a certain route to the truth. From my point of view, what I'm saying is relevant to our current situation. You see, someone might object that his inability to find the words to challenge you doesn't alter the evident fact that the majority of the people d who take up philosophy and spend more than just their youth on it—who don't get involved in it just for educational purposes and then drop it—turn out to be pretty weird (not to say rotten to the core), and that the effect of this pursuit you're praising even on those of its practitioners who are supposed to be particularly good is that they become incapable of performing any service to their communities.'

I responded by asking, 'Do you think this view is right?'

'I don't know,' he replied. 'But I'd be happy to hear what you have to say on the matter.'

'What you'd hear from me is that I think they're telling the truth.'

e 'Then how can it be right', he said, 'to say that there'll be no end to political troubles until philosophers have power in their communities,* when we agree that philosophers are no use to them?'

'It'll take an analogy to answer your question,' I said.

'And you never use analogies, of course,' he said.

'What?' I exclaimed. 'It's hard enough to prove my point without you making fun of me as well as forcing me to try.

488a Anyway, here's my analogy: now you'll be in a better position to see how inadequate it is. I mean, what society does to the best practitioners of philosophy is so complex that there's no other single phenomenon like it: in order to defend them from criticism, one has to compile an analogy out of lots of different elements, like the goat-stags and other compound creatures painters come up with.

'Imagine the following situation on a fleet of ships, or on a single ship.* The owner has the edge over everyone else on

b board by virtue of his size and strength, but he's rather deaf and short-sighted, and his knowledge of naval matters is just as limited. The sailors are wrangling with one another because each of them thinks that he ought to be the captain, despite the fact that he's never learnt how, and can't name his teacher or specify the period of his apprenticeship. In any case, they all maintain that it isn't something that can be taught, and are ready to butcher anyone who says it is. They're for ever

c crowding closely around the owner, pleading with him and stopping at nothing to get him to entrust the rudder to them. Sometimes, if their pleas are unsuccessful, but others get the job, they kill those others or throw them off the ship, subdue their worthy owner by drugging him or getting him drunk or something, take control of the ship, help themselves to its cargo, and have the kind of drunken and indulgent voyage you'd expect from people like that. And that's not all: they think highly of anyone who contributes towards their gaining power by showing skill at winning over or subduing the owner, and describe him as an accomplished seaman, a true captain, a d naval expert; but they criticize anyone different as useless. They completely fail to understand that any genuine sea-captain has to study the yearly cycle, the seasons, the heavens, the stars and winds, and everything relevant to the job, if he's to be properly equipped to hold a position of authority in a ship. In fact, they think it's impossible to study and acquire expertise at how to steer a ship (leaving aside the question of whether or not people e want you to) and at the same time be a good captain. When this is what's happening on board ships, don't you think that the crew of ships in this state would think of any true captain as nothing but a windbag with his head in the clouds,* of no 489a use to them at all?'

'They definitely would,' Adeimantus replied.

'I'm sure you don't need an analysis of the analogy to see that it's a metaphor for the attitude of society towards true philosophers,' I said. 'I'm sure you take my point.'

'I certainly do,' he said.

'You'd better use it, then, in the first instance, to clarify things for that person who expressed surprise at the disrespect shown to philosophers by society, and try to show him how much more astonishing it would be if they were respected.' b

'All right, I will,' he said.

'And that you're right to say that the best practitioners of philosophy are incapable of performing any public service. But you'd better tell him to blame their uselessness on the others' failure to make use of them, rather than on the fact that they are accomplished philosophers. I mean, it's unnatural for the captain to ask the sailors to accept his authority and it's unnatural for wise men to dance attendance on rich men; this story is misleading.* The truth of the matter is that it makes no difference whether you're rich or poor: if you feel ill, you're bound to dance attendance on a doctor, and if you need to c accept authority, you must dance attendance on someone in authority who is capable of providing it. If he is really to serve any useful purpose, it's not up to him to ask those under him to accept his authority. And you won't be mistaken if you compare present-day political leaders to the sailors in our recent tale, and the ones they call useless airheads to the genuine captain.'

'You're absolutely right,' he said.

'Under these conditions and circumstances, it's not easy for the best of occupations to gain a good reputation, when reputations are in the hands of people whose occupations are
d incompatible with it. But by far the worst and most influential condemnation of philosophy comes about as a result of the people who claim to practise it—the ones the critic of philosophy was talking about, in your report, when he described the majority of the people who take up philosophy as rotten to the core (although the best of them are merely useless). And I agreed that you were telling the truth, didn't I?'

'Yes.'

'Well, we've described the reasons for the uselessness of the good practitioners, haven't we?'

'We certainly have.'

'Shall we next describe why the corruption of most philosophers is inevitable, and try to explain why this shouldn't
e be blamed on philosophy either, if we can?'

'Yes.'

'Let's start our discussion by reminding ourselves of the fundamental points in our description of the kind of character a truly good person will inevitably have. If you remember, above
490a all he was led by truth: if he didn't pursue truth absolutely and wholeheartedly, he was bound to be a specious impostor, with nothing whatsoever to do with true philosophy.'

'That's what we said.'

'Well, that in itself is diametrically opposed to current opinion about philosophers, isn't it?'

'It certainly is,' he said.

'Now, our response will be to point out that a genuine lover of knowledge innately aspires to reality, and doesn't settle on
b all the various things which are assumed to be real, but keeps on, with his love remaining keen and steady, until the nature of

each thing as it really is in itself has been grasped by the appropriate part of his mind—which is to say, the part which is akin to reality. Once he has drawn near this authentic reality and united with it, and thus fathered intellect and truth, then he has knowledge; then he lives a life which is true to himself; then he is nourished; and then, but not before, he finds release from his love-pangs. Would this be a reasonable response for us to make?'

'Nothing could be more reasonable,' he said.

'And will he be the sort of person to love falsehood or will exactly the opposite be the case, and he'll loathe it?'

'He'll loathe it,' he said.   c

'I'm sure we'd insist that no array of evils could follow the leadership of truth.'

'Of course we would.'

'But rather, a character imbued with health and morality, and the self-discipline that accompanies them.'

'Right,' he said.

'Anyway, there's no need for us to have the whole array of the philosopher's characteristics line up all over again. I'm sure you remember how we found that philosophers naturally have courage, broadness of vision, quickness at learning, and a good memory. You interrupted by saying that although our argument was absolutely incontrovertible, it was still possible d for someone to leave arguments out of it and look at the actual people we were talking about, and to conclude that while some philosophers are evidently merely useless, the majority of them are bad through and through. We're trying to uncover the reasons for their bad name, and so we're now up against the question why the majority are bad. That's why we brought the true philosopher's characteristics back in again and felt compelled to provide a clear statement of them.'

'True,' he said.   e

'What we have to do', I said, 'is see how this philosophical nature is corrupted and why it is often completely ruined, while immunity from corruption is rare—and these escapees are the people who get called useless, rather than bad. After that, we'll turn to pseudo-philosophical natures and the kinds of people 491a who take up the occupation which is proper to a philosophical nature, and we'll try to discern what it is in the make-up of their minds which drives them towards an occupation which is too good and too sublime for them, so that they commit a wide variety of offences and make everyone, all over the world, think of philosophy in the way you've mentioned.'

'What sources of corruption do you have in mind?' he asked.

'I'll do my best to explain,' I replied. 'I suppose it's indisputable that a fully philosophical nature—of the kind we've described, with the whole array of qualities we lined up not long ago—is a rare human phenomenon: there aren't going to be very many of them. Don't you agree?'

'Definitely.'

'Well, look how heavily these few people are outnumbered by powerful sources of corruption.'

'What are they, though?'

'The most astounding thing of all is that there isn't one of their commendable characteristics which doesn't ruin a mind which possesses it and cause a rift between it and philosophy. I'm talking about courage, self-discipline, and all the qualities we went through.'

'It's not easy to make sense of this idea,' he said.

c   'And that's not all,' I said. 'Every single one of the acknowledged good things of life is a factor in its corruption and the rift—good looks, affluence, physical fitness, influential family relationships in one's community, and so on and so forth. I've cut the list short, because you can see what I'm saying.'

'I can,' he said. 'And I wouldn't mind hearing a more detailed explanation.'

'If you grasp the general principle of the matter,' I said, 'everything will fall into place and what I've already said will start to make sense.'

'What are you getting at?' he asked.

d   'We know', I said, 'that if any plant or creature, at the stage when it is a seed or a new growth, fails to get the right nourishment or weather or location, then the number of its deficiencies, in respect to properties it should have, is proportionate to its vigour. I mean, bad is the opposite of good, rather than of not-good.'

'Of course.'

'So I suppose it's plausible to think that a very good thing will end up in a worse state than a second-rate thing if the conditions of its nurture are less suited to its nature.'

'Yes.'

'Well, by the same token, Adeimantus,' I asked, 'won't we e claim that if the most gifted minds are subjected to a bad education, they become exceptionally bad? I mean, do you imagine that horrendous crimes and sheer depravity stem from a second-rate nature, rather than from a vigorous one which has been ruined by its upbringing? Could significant benefit or significant harm conceivably proceed from innate weakness?'

'No, you're right,' he said.

'Now, in my opinion, if it receives a suitable education, the 492a philosophical nature we proposed is bound to grow and arrive at perfect goodness. However, if its germination and growth take place in an unsuitable educational environment, then without divine intervention its destination will inevitably be completely the opposite. Or do you follow the masses and believe that there are members of the younger generation who are corrupted by professional teachers, and that there are professional teachers who, despite being private citizens, can be a source of corruption to any degree worth mentioning? Don't you think, rather, that it is the very people who make this claim who are the most influential teachers, and who provide the most thorough education and form men and women of all ages b into any shape they want?'

'When do they do this?' he asked.

'When a lot of them huddle together on seats in the assembly or lawcourt or theatre,' I said, 'or when they convene for military purposes, or when there's any other general public gathering, and the boos and applause of their criticism or praise (excessive in both cases) of whatever is being said or done make a terrible din, and it's not only them—the rocks and their surroundings double the noise of their approval and c disapproval by echoing it. In a situation like this, how do you think a young man's heart, as they say, will be affected? How can the education he received outside of this public arena stand up to it, do you suppose, without being overwhelmed by criticism or praise of this kind and swept away at the mercy of the current? Won't he end up just like them, with the same moral standards and the same habits as them?'

d 'He's bound to, Socrates,' he said.

'And we haven't yet mentioned the most irresistible pressure they bring to bear,' I said.

'What is it?' he asked.

'It's the concrete pressure these consummate professional educators apply when they turn to action, if their words have failed to indoctrinate someone. I mean, surely you're aware that they punish disobedience with forfeiture of rights, and with fines and death?'

'Yes, I'm certainly well aware of that,' he said.

'Can you think of any teacher or any kind of privately received instruction with the strength to hold out against these pressures?'

e 'I think it's impossible,' he said.

'Yes, and it's extremely stupid even to try to be that kind of teacher,' I said. 'You see, it's quite impossible, as the present and the past show, for any educational programme to alter anyone's character, as far as goodness is concerned, contrary to the conditioning he receives in the public arena*—by "anyone" I mean any human, of course, Adeimantus: as the proverb recommends, we'd better make an exception of divinity. I

493a mean, I can tell you that you'd be quite right to see God at work when anything does retain its integrity and fulfil its potential within current political systems.'

'That's what I think too,' he said.

'And I wonder whether you agree with me on a further point as well,' I said.

'What?'

'Even though they call it knowledge, every one of those private fee-charging individuals—the ones who are called sophists* and are regarded as rivals by these educators we've been talking about—teaches nothing but the attitudes the masses form by consensus. Imagine that the keeper of a huge, strong beast notices what makes it angry, what it desires, how

b it has to be approached and handled, the circumstances and conditions under which it becomes particularly fierce or calm, what provokes its typical cries, and what tones of voice make it gentle or wild. Once he's spent enough time in the creature's company to acquire all this information, he calls it knowledge, forms it into a systematic branch of expertise, and starts to teach it, despite total ignorance, in fact, about which of the creature's attitudes and desires is commendable or deplorable, good or bad, moral or immoral. His usage of all these terms c simply conforms to the great beast's attitudes, and he describes things as good or bad according to its likes and dislikes, and can't justify his usage of the terms any further, but describes as right and good things which are merely indispensable, since he hasn't realized and can't explain to anyone else how vast a gulf there is between necessity and goodness.* Wouldn't you really and truly find someone like this implausible as a teacher?'

'Yes, I would,' he said.

'Well, do you think there's anything to choose between him and someone who's noticed what makes the motley masses d collectively angry and happy and thinks he has knowledge— whether it's in the field of painting or music or government? I mean, whenever someone's relationship with the masses consists of displaying his composition (or whatever product it may be) or his political service to them, and giving them power over him—or rather, more power than they need have—then the proverbial necessity of Diomedes* forces him to compose things of which they approve. Sometimes one of the sophists might argue that what the masses like coincides with what is genuinely good and fine, but this argument always comes across as utterly absurd, don't you think?'

'It always has and it always will, in my opinion,' he said. e

'So, against this background, please remember what we were saying before. Is it possible for the masses to accept or conceive of the existence of beauty itself, rather than the plurality of beautiful things? Or anything in itself, rather than the plurality of instances of each thing?' 494a

'Not at all,' he said.

'It's impossible, then, for the masses to love knowledge,' I said.

'Yes, it is.'

'They're bound to run philosophers down, then, as well.'

'That's inevitable.'

'And so are those individuals whose relationship with the masses consists of wanting to please them.'

'Obviously.'

'In this context, can you see how any innate philosopher will

preserve the integrity of his nature, and consequently stay with the occupation and see it through to the end? Look at it in the
b context of what we were saying earlier. We agreed that a philosopher has quickness at learning, a good memory, courage, and broadness of vision.'

'Yes.'

'From his earliest years, then, he'll outclass other children at everything, especially if he's as gifted physically as he is mentally, won't he?'

'Of course,' he answered.

'So when he grows up, his friends and fellow citizens will want to make use of him for their own affairs.'

'Naturally.'

c 'They'll be a constant presence, then, with their requests and courtesies, as they flatter him and try to get him on their side in anticipation of the influence that will one day be his.'

'Yes, that's what invariably happens,' he said.

'What do you imagine he'll do in this situation,' I asked, 'especially if he happens to come from a wealthy and noble family within a powerful state, and is also good-looking and well built? Don't you think he'll be filled with unrealizable hopes, and will expect to be capable one day of managing the affairs not only of Greece, but of the non-Greek world as well?
d In these circumstances, won't he get ideas above his station and puff himself up with affectation and baseless, senseless pride?'

'He certainly will,' he said.

'Now, suppose someone gently approaches him while he's in this frame of mind and tells him the truth—that he's taken leave of his senses and should try to dispel this inanity, but that he won't gain intelligence unless he works like a slave for it—do you think it's going to be easy for the message to penetrate all these pernicious influences and get through to him?'

'No, far from it,' he said.

'And', I went on, 'supposing his innate gifts and his affinity
e with the rationality of what's being said do enable him to pay attention at all, and he is swayed and attracted towards philosophy, what reaction would you expect from those others, when they think they're losing his services and his friendship? Won't they do and say absolutely anything to stop him being

won over? And as for the person who's trying to win him over, won't they come up with all kinds of private schemes and public court-cases to stop him succeeding?'*

'Inevitably,' he said.   495a

'What chance does this young man have of becoming a philosopher?'

'No chance, really.'

'So, as you can see,' I went on, 'we were right to say* that it is, in fact, the actual ingredients of a philosophical nature which are in a sense responsible (given a pernicious educational environment) for someone being deflected from his occupation, and that the acknowledged good things of life—affluence and similar resources—are also responsible. Do you agree?'

'Yes,' he said. 'We were quite right.'

'There we are, then, Adeimantus,' I said. 'Those are the powerful factors which ruin and corrupt anyone who is, by b nature, best suited for the best occupation—and such people are rare anyway, as we said. Moreover, these are the men who have the potential to do the greatest harm to communities and to individuals, and the greatest good too, if that's the course they happen to take. An insignificant person, however, never has any effect of any significance on any individual or society.'

'You're quite right,' he said.

'So that's how the most appropriate people are deflected and desert philosophy, without consummating the relationship. c They end up living a life which is inappropriate for them and which isn't true to their natures, and they leave philosophy, like an orphan with no relatives, to the mercy of others who aren't good enough for her, and who defile her and gain her the kind of tarnished reputation you say her detractors ascribe to her— for going about with people who are either worthless or obnoxious.'

'Yes, that's the usual view,' he said.

'And it's not unreasonable,' I said. 'You see, when the abandonment of this territory is noticed by others—inferior members of the human race—and when they also see how rich it is in renown and status, they behave like escaped convicts d who take sanctuary in temples: they break away from their professions, with no regrets, and encroach on philosophy. In fact, they're the ones who do have some facility at their own

paltry professions, because in spite of this treatment, philosophy still remains more prestigious than other occupations; and this prestige attracts a lot of people—immature people, who have been physically deformed by their
e jobs and work, and are mentally just as warped and stunted by their servile business. Don't you think that's inevitable?'

'It certainly is.'

'Do you think the impression they give', I went on, 'is any different from that of a small, bald metalworker who's come into some money? He's just got himself out of debtors' prison, he's had a bath and is wearing brand-new clothes and a bridegroom's outfit, and he's about to marry his master's daughter because she's hard up and has no one to look after her.'

496a 'No, they're exactly the same, really,' he said.

'What sort of offspring are they likely to father, then? Second-rate half-breeds, don't you think?'

'Inevitably.'

'Now, when people who are unworthy of education force their presumptuous attentions on her, what sorts of ideas and thoughts do they produce, would you say? Isn't it perfectly appropriate to call them sophisms, and to claim that they are all illegitimate and lacking in true intelligence?'*

'Absolutely,' he said.

'That leaves us with only a tiny number of people,
b Adeimantus,' I said, 'who have the right to consort with philosophy. A person of high character and sound education might fortuitously have been exiled, and so have remained true to his nature and faithful to philosophy by being out of the reach of corrupting influences; or occasionally a great mind is born in some backwater of a community and finds the politics petty and beneath him. And I suppose a few, because of their natural gifts, do have the right to find some other occupation demeaning and to turn from it to philosophy. Then there is also the bridle of our friend Theages, which can act as a curb:
c Theages was in all other respects well equipped to be deflected from philosophy, but he had to pamper his physical ailment and so he was curbed and prevented from taking up politics. It's not worth mentioning my own case—the communications I receive from my deity*—because there's either very little or no precedent for the phenomenon.

'When the few members of this band have glimpsed the joy and happiness to be found in mastering philosophy and have also gained a clear enough impression of the madness of the masses; when they've realized that more or less every political action is pernicious and that if someone tries to assist morality there will be no one to back him up and see that he comes out d unscathed, but it would be like an encounter between a human being and wild beasts; since he isn't prepared to join others in their immorality and isn't capable, all alone, of standing up to all those ferocious beasts, but would die before doing his community or his friends any good, and so would be useless to himself and to everyone else—once he has grasped all this with his rational mind, he lies low and does only what he's meant to do. It's as if he's taken shelter under a wall during a storm, with the wind whipping up the dust and rain pelting down; lawlessness infects everyone else he sees, so he is content if he can find a way to live his life here on earth without becoming tainted by immoral or unjust deeds, and to depart from life e confidently, and without anger and bitterness.'

'If he could do that,' he said, 'he'd really have done 497a something with his life.'

Despite the gloomy realism of the previous section, Plato now argues that his imaginary community could, in principle, exist. It would take a correct educational programme, which did not trivialize philosophy but made it the acme of one's life; it would take a correct assessment of the value of philosophy; and it would take radical political changes. However, it is still clear that Plato regards the possibility of all this actually happening as extremely remote; he is more interested in the principle than the practical reality.

'But he could do much more with his life', I replied, 'if he just lived in a suitable political system, which enabled him to develop more and to preserve the integrity of public business as well as his own affairs. Anyway, I think we've said enough about why philosophy has a bad name, and why it doesn't deserve it, unless you've got something to add.'

'No, I've nothing to add on this issue,' he said. 'But which contemporary political system do you think is suitable for philosophy?'

'Not a single one,' I replied. 'That's exactly what I'm critical b of—that no current political system is good enough for a philosophical nature to grow in without getting modified and altered. It's like a seed which has been brought from its native land and planted in foreign soil: its vitality tends to become drained, and the species becomes absorbed into the dominant local variety. In the same way, this type of person can't retain his native qualities, but is deflected and assumes properties that don't really belong to him. If he comes across a political system

c with the same degree of excellence as his character, then the divinity of the philosophical character will become apparent, as distinct from the humanity of all other natures and occupations. Now, your next question is obviously going to be what this political system is.'

'You've got me wrong there,' he said. 'I wasn't going to ask that, but whether the community we're founding and describing is the one you mean, or whether there's another candidate.'

'On the whole, it's our community,' I said. 'But there's an earlier point that needs repeating,* that the community would have to contain an element which understands the rationale of

d the political system and keeps to the same principles which you as legislator followed when you made the laws.'

'Yes, that did come up,' he agreed.

'I didn't make it sufficiently clear, however,' I said, 'because I was worried about the objections you were raising which have shown how long and complicated an argument it takes to prove the point. And what we're still faced with is hardly the easiest part of the account.'

'What is it?'

'How a community can engage in philosophy and survive. I mean, great enterprises are always hazardous, and anything fine really is, as the saying puts it, difficult.'

e 'All the same,' he said, 'the account won't be complete until this point has been cleared up. So we'd better explore it.'

'The only thing that could stop us doing so is lack of ability,' I said. 'It won't be lack of will, and you'll be an eyewitness to my determination. Look at it now, in fact—and how I'm prepared to stick my neck out and say that our community should turn the current approach to philosophy upside down.'

'What do you mean?'

'At the moment,' I said, 'those who actually do engage in it are young men, scarcely out of childhood. In the interval before they take up estate-management and moneymaking, they 498a dabble in the most difficult aspect of philosophy—the bit which has to do with rational argument*—and then they drop it. And they are supposed to be the most advanced philosophers! After that, they count it as no mean achievement actually to accept an invitation to listen to a philosophical debate, since they think that philosophy should be merely an incidental occupation. And in old age they are—with a few exceptions— snuffed out more thoroughly than Heraclitus' sun, since they are never rekindled later.'* b

'Whereas they should do what?' he asked.

'Exactly the opposite. While they're young, they should be educated and should study philosophy in a way which suits their age. Their bodies are growing and developing during this period, and they should concentrate on getting them into a state where they minister to philosophy.* In due course of time, when their minds are beginning to mature, they should put more effort into mental exercise; and when their physical strength starts to wane and they are too old to play a public part in the community or to serve in the militia, they should be c allowed to roam free and graze at will, and to concentrate on philosophy, with everything else being incidental. This is the correct programme for people who are going to live a happy life and guarantee for themselves circumstances in the next world, after their death, which match the life they lived here.'

'You certainly give the impression of being wholehearted about this, Socrates,' he said. 'But I think most of the people who hear you express these views will be even more wholehearted about challenging them, since they won't be convinced in the slightest. And Thrasymachus will take the lead in this, I imagine.'

'Please don't cause trouble between me and Thrasymachus,' I said, 'when we've only just become friends—not that we were d enemies before. I'll spare no effort until I've either won him and everyone else over to my point of view—or at least done something to prepare them in case they ever meet these arguments again in future incarnations!'

'You're thinking in the short term, then!' he remarked.

'It's nothing compared with eternity,' I responded. 'But I'm not at all surprised that most people find what I'm saying incredible: after all, it's never been within their experience.

e They're used to carefully assimilated phrases, rather than hearing words tumbling out without preparation as they are now. And they've never come across even a single case of a man who is, in both his actions and his words, as perfectly identified and assimilated* with goodness as is possible, and

499a who is in a position of authority in an equally good community. Do you think they have?'

'Definitely not.'

'Then again, Adeimantus, they've not been adequately exposed to discussions which aren't dishonourable and mean, but are designed for a thorough and intense quest for the truth, for the sake of knowledge, and which are hardly on nodding terms with those subtleties and eristic tricks whose sole purpose, whether they occur during lawsuits or private conversations, is to increase the speaker's reputation and his chances of winning the argument.'

'No, they haven't,' he said.

'These are the reasons and considerations', I said, 'which led

b me earlier, despite my anxieties—since the truth left me no option—to claim that no community or political system, and by the same token no person either, could ever attain perfection until some accident forced those few philosophers (the ones who are currently called useless, rather than the ones who are called rotten) to take charge of a community whether or not they wanted to, and made the citizens obey them, or alternatively until, thanks to divine providence, either current

c kings and rulers or their sons were gripped by authentic love for authentic philosophy. In my opinion, it's unreasonable to claim that either or both of these alternatives are impossible; if this were so, then we'd deserve to be ridiculed for our empty assertions, our wishful thinking. Don't you agree?'

'Yes.'

'So whether the outstanding practitioners of philosophy were compelled to take charge of a community at some point in the infinity of past time, or whether they are now being compelled to do so in some foreign land which lies far beyond the limits of

d our awareness, or whether they will be compelled to do so in the future, we are prepared to insist that the political system we've described either did or does or will exist, whenever it is that the Muse of philosophy gains control of a community. The point is that the compulsion is feasible, and we aren't talking about unrealizable theories—though we're the first to admit that it wouldn't be easy.'

'I agree,' he said.

'Most people don't, however, wouldn't you say?' I asked.

'I suppose so,' he said.

'Adeimantus,' I said, 'you really shouldn't condemn the masses like that. They'll change their minds if you don't e approach them argumentatively. You mustn't rub them up the wrong way while trying to remove their low opinion of intellectualism. You must show them who you mean by philosophers, and explain (as we did just now) what it takes to be a philosopher and what the pursuit involves, so that they 500a realize that you're not talking about the people they think of as philosophers. I mean, do you think that, even if they see things this way, they won't change their minds and adopt a different position?† Do you think that someone open-minded and even-tempered can get angry unless he's in the presence of anger, or can be resentful unless he's in the presence of resentment? I won't even let you reply before telling you my opinion: this kind of intransigence is a rare phenomenon, and the majority of people don't have it.'

'I agree,' he said, 'without hesitation.'

'Do you also agree that responsibility for the usual b disparagement of philosophy is to be laid at the door of those gate-crashers who barge in where they have no right to be, call one another names, behave offensively, and constantly gossip about people, which is a highly unphilosophical activity?'

'Definitely,' he replied.

'The point is, of course, Adeimantus, that someone whose mind really is fixed on reality has no time to cast his gaze downwards on to the affairs of men and to enter into their c disputes (and so be infected with resentment and malice). His eyes are occupied with the sight of things which are organized, permanent, and unchanging, where wronging and being wronged don't exist, where all is orderly and rational; and he makes this realm the model for his behaviour, and assimilates himself to it as much as is feasible. I mean, don't you think that one's behaviour is bound to resemble anyone or anything whose company one enjoys?'

'Inevitably,' he said.

'So because a philosopher's links are with a realm which is
d divine and orderly, he becomes as divine and orderly as is humanly possible. Even so, he still meets with plenty of criticism from all quarters.'

'Absolutely.'

'Now, if a philosopher were compelled not to restrict his modelling to himself, but to work both publicly and in his private life to stamp men's characters with what he sees in that realm, do you think he'd make a poor artisan of self-discipline, morality, and in general of what it is to be, in ordinary terms, a good person?'

'Not at all,' he answered.

'And if people realize that what we're saying about him is the
e truth, will they still get angry at philosophers? Will they still doubt our claim that there is no way in which a community is going to be happy unless its plan is drawn up by artists who refer to a divine model?'

'No, they won't get angry if they realize that,' he said. 'But
501a how will these artists go about their work?'

'They must treat a community and people's characters like a painting-board,' I said, 'and their first job is to wipe it clean. This isn't a particularly easy thing to do, but you'll appreciate that the main way they differ from everyone else is in refusing to deal with an individual or a community, and not being prepared to sketch out a legal code, until they've either been given a clean slate or have made it so themselves.'

'Yes, and they're right,' he said.

'Next they'll make an outline of the constitution, don't you think?'

'Of course.'

b 'I imagine the next stage would involve their constantly looking this way and that as they work—looking on the one hand towards that which is inherently moral, right, self-disciplined, and so on, and on the other hand towards what they're creating in the human realm.[†] By selecting behaviour-patterns and blending them, they'll produce a composite human likeness, taking as their reference-point that quality which

Homer too called "godly" and "godlike"* in its human manifestation.'

'Right,' he said.

'And I suppose they'd rub bits out and paint them in again, until they've done all they can to create human characters c which stand the best chance of meeting the gods' approval.'

'It should be a very beautiful painting, anyway,' he remarked.

'Well,' I asked, 'are we making any progress towards persuading those energetic opponents of ours, the ones you mentioned,* that this is the kind of painter of constitutions we were recommending to them before? They got angry with him then, because we were putting political power in his hands, but are they rather more mollified now that they've heard our account?'

'They'll be much less upset,' he said, 'if they've got any sense.'

'I mean, how could they have any reservations? Could they d doubt that philosophers are lovers of reality and truth?'

'Hardly,' he said.

'But could they doubt the affiliation of the philosophical nature we described to excellence?'

'No, they couldn't doubt that either.'

'Well, could they argue against the idea that, under the right circumstances, this sort of person is more likely than anyone to become perfectly good and a consummate philosopher? Will our critic maintain that the other lot—the ones we ruled out— are more likely?'

'Of course not.'   e

'Will they stop getting cross at us, then, for saying that until philosophers gain political power, there'll be no end to troubles for communities or their citizens, and our fictional political system will never become a full-fledged reality?'

'They might be less upset,' he said.

'How about if we say that they are completely mollified and utterly convinced,' I suggested, 'rather than that they might be 502a less upset? That should shame them into agreeing with us, if they can't do so for any other reason.'

'All right,' he said.

'Even if we can assume, then, that we've convinced them of

this point,' I said, 'will they still argue that there's no chance of the children of kings or rulers being born with the philosophical characteristics?'

'They couldn't do that,' he said.

'Could they claim that these philosophical children of kings and rulers are absolutely bound to be corrupted? I mean, even we are admitting that it's difficult for them to preserve their b integrity, but is it plausible to argue that, out of all of them, not even a single one could ever, in the entire passage of time, remain unspoilt?'

'Of course not.'

'If even one remains uncorrupted', I said, 'in a community which is prepared to obey him, then that is enough: everything which is now open to doubt would become a full-fledged reality.'

'Yes, one would do,' he agreed.

'Because if he, as ruler, establishes the laws and practices we've described,' I went on, 'then it's surely not inconceivable that the citizens of the community will be prepared to carry them out.'

'Of course it isn't.'

'But is it unimaginable and inconceivable that others might agree with our point of view?'

c   'I don't think so,' he said.

'And our earlier discussion* of the question whether our proposals are for the best (if they are feasible) was, in my opinion, adequate.'

'Yes, it was.'

'So what we've found by now is this, apparently: if our proposed legislation were actually to happen, it would be impossible to improve on it; and its realization may be difficult, but is not impossible.'

'Yes, that's what we've found,' he said.

Chapter 9

The Supremacy of Good

Plato now recommends the 'longer route'—a more thorough approach to morality than that of Chapter 6. Morality will never be understood—nor will it become a reality in the guardians' lives—without knowledge of goodness. After briefly dismissing the equation of goodness with either pleasure or knowledge, Plato stresses the importance of goodness: no one does anything which he does not think is good for him; goodness is a universal goal. Therefore, the analysis of morality which has been accepted up till now must be deepened by understanding its relation to goodness. However, Plato does not actually undertake this longer route himself, and goes on to offer only elusive images and allegories about goodness and its importance.

'Well, it was quite a struggle, but we've completed that topic. Next we'd better go on to the remaining issues. What will it take—what studies and practices—for these preservers of our 502d political system to be a possibility? And at what ages should they undertake the various subjects to be studied?'

'Yes, we ought to discuss these issues,' he agreed.

'So I gained nothing', I said, 'when earlier I cleverly delayed the awkward matter of their marital arrangements, and the topics of procreation and what rulers to appoint. I was aware that the whole truth about what rulers to appoint would arouse resentment and anger. It didn't make any difference, though, because now I'm up against the necessity of discussing these matters anyway. There's nothing more to say about women e and children, but I've got to start all over again, more or less, in exploring the question of the rulers. I'm sure you remember our claim that they have to demonstrate love of their community 503a while being tested in both pleasant and painful circumstances, and make it clear that they won't shed this patriotism whatever ordeals or fears they meet with, or whatever changing

situations they endure. Anyone who is incapable of retaining it is to be excluded, whereas anyone who emerges from every test without impurities (like gold tested in fire) is to be made a ruler and given privileges and rewards in life and in death. We spoke along those lines,* but the discussion was starting to deviate and hide itself, because it was afraid of broaching the matter
b we're now facing.'

'Yes, I remember,' he said. 'You're quite right.'

'I was too scared to make the reckless assertions that have now been expressed,' I said, 'but now the presumptuous statement that if we are to have absolutely authentic guardians, then we must appoint philosophers, is out in the open.'

'Yes, it is,' he said.

'Do you realize how few they'll be, in all likelihood? Consider the nature which, in our account, they have to have and how rare it is for its various parts to coalesce into a single entity: it usually ends up in bits and pieces.'

c 'What do you mean?' he asked.

'People who are quick at learning, have good memories, and are astute and smart and so on, tend—as you know—not to combine both energy and broadness of mental vision with the ability to live an orderly, peaceful, and stable life.† Instead, their quickness carries them this way and that, and stability plays no part at all in their lives.'

'You're right,' he said.

'On the other hand, a sound and stable character, which
d makes people more dependable and slow to respond to frightening situations in battle, also makes them approach their studies in the same way. They're as slow to respond and to learn as if they'd been drugged, and they're constantly dozing off and yawning when they're asked to do anything intellectually arduous.'

'True,' he said.

'But our claim is* that a good and sufficient helping of both sets of qualities is a prerequisite for anyone to be allowed to take part in an authentic educational programme or to be awarded political office and power.'

'Right,' he said.

'So it'll be a rare phenomenon, don't you think?'

'Of course it will.'

'It's not just a matter of testing someone in the ways we've e already mentioned, then—by means of ordeals and fear and pleasure. There's a further point we omitted before, but are including now: we must give him plenty of intellectual exercise as well, so that we can see whether he is capable of enduring fundamental intellectual work, or whether he'll cut and run as cowards do in other spheres.' 504a

'Yes, we certainly ought to try to find that out,' he said. 'But what do you mean by fundamental intellectual work?'

'I'm sure you remember when, as a result of distinguishing three aspects within the mind, we defined morality, self-discipline, courage, and wisdom,' I said.

'If I didn't,' he said, 'then we might as well stop right now.'

'Do you also remember how we prefaced our discussion of those qualities?'

'How?'

'We said* that it would take a different route, a longer one, b to reach the best possible vantage-point and that they would be plainly visible to anyone who went that way, but that it was possible to come up with arguments which were in keeping with the kinds of discussions we'd already been having. You said that would do, and we proceeded at the time on that basis. I think the argument was defective, in terms of precision, but it's up to you to say whether you were happy with it.'

'Yes, I was happy enough with it,' he said, 'and so was everyone else.'

'But in these sorts of matters, my friend,' I said, 'anything c which misses the truth by even a tiny amount is nowhere near "enough". Anything less than perfect is not up to the mark at all, though people occasionally think it's adequate and that they don't need to look any further.'

'Yes, a great many people feel this,' he said, 'because they're lazy.'

'But it's a completely inappropriate feeling for a guardian of a community and its laws to have,' I said.

'I suppose so,' he said.

'Then a guardian had better take the longer route, Adeimantus,' I said, 'and put just as much effort into his d intellectual work as his physical exercise. Otherwise, as we said a moment ago, he'll never see that fundamental field of study through to the end—and it's not just fundamental, but particularly appropriate for him.'

'Are you implying that morality and the other qualities we discussed are not the most important things there are—that there's something even more fundamental than them?' he asked.

'It's not only more fundamental,' I said, 'but it's exactly the kind of thing which requires viewing as a completely finished product, without skimping and looking merely at an outline, as we did just now. I mean, wouldn't it be absurd to devote e extremes of energy and effort to getting as precise and clear a picture as possible of insignificant matters, and then not to think that the most important matters deserve the utmost precision too?'

'An excellent sentiment,'† he said. 'But surely you don't expect to get away without being asked what this fundamental field of study of yours is, and what it is concerned with?'

'No, I don't,' I answered. 'Go ahead and ask your questions. In actual fact, you've not infrequently been told what it is, but it's either slipped your mind for the moment, or you're 505a intending to make trouble for me by attacking my position. I incline towards the latter alternative, since you've often been told that the most important thing to try to understand is the character of goodness, because this is where anything which is moral (or whatever) gets its value and advantages from.* It can hardly have escaped your notice that this is my position, and you must know what I'm going to add: that our knowledge of goodness is inadequate. And you appreciate, I'm sure, that there's absolutely no point in having expert knowledge of everything else, but lacking knowledge of goodness, just as there isn't in having anything else either, unless goodness comes b with it. I mean, do you think there's any advantage in owning everything in the world except good things, or in understanding everything else except goodness, and therefore failing to understand anything worth while and good?'

'I certainly don't,' he said.

'Now, it can't have escaped your notice either that the usual view of goodness is that it's pleasure, while there's also a more ingenious view around, that it's knowledge.'

'Of course it hasn't.'

'As you also know, however, my friend, the people who hold the latter view are incapable of explaining exactly *what* knowledge constitutes goodness, but are forced ultimately to say that it is knowledge of goodness.'*

'And so to make complete fools of themselves,' he remarked.

'Of course they do,' I said. 'First they tell us off for not c knowing what goodness is, then they talk to us as if we did know what it is. I mean, to say it's knowledge of goodness is to assume that we understand what they're saying when they use the term "goodness".'

'You're absolutely right,' he said.

'What about the definition of goodness as pleasure? Aren't its proponents just as thoroughly misguided as the others? I mean, they too are forced to make a concession, in this case that there are bad pleasures, aren't they?'

'Certainly.'

'So their position ends up being that it is possible for a single thing to be both good and bad, doesn't it?'*

'Naturally.' d

'It's clear, therefore, that there's plenty of scope for serious disagreement where goodness is concerned. Yes?'

'Of course.'

'Well, isn't it also clear that whereas (whether it's a matter of doing something, or owning something, or having a certain reputation) people usually prefer the appearance of morality and right,* even if there's no reality involved, yet no one is content with any possession that is only apparently good? It's the reality of goodness they want; no one thinks at all highly of mere appearance in this sphere.'*

'Yes, that's perfectly clear,' he said.

'So here we have something which everyone, whatever their temperament, is after, and which is the goal of all their activities. They have an inkling of its existence, but they're e confused about it and can't adequately grasp its nature or be as certain and as confident about it as they can about other things, and consequently they fail to derive any benefit even from those other activities. When something of this kind and this importance is involved, can we allow the best members of our 506a community, the ones to whom we're going to entrust everything, to be equally in the dark?'

'Certainly not,' he protested.

'Anyway,' I said, 'I imagine that anyone who is ignorant about the goodness of moral and right conduct would make a second-rate guardian of morality and right, and I suspect that no one will fully understand them until he knows about their relation to goodness.'

'Your suspicion is right,' he said.

'So the constitution and organization of our community will
b be perfect only if they are overseen by the kind of guardian who has this knowledge, won't they?'

'Necessarily,' he said. 'But Socrates, do *you* identify goodness with knowledge or pleasure, or with something else?'

'Just listen to him!' I exclaimed. 'It's been perfectly obvious all along that other people's views on the matter weren't going to be enough for you.'

'That's because I don't think it's right, Socrates,' he said, 'for someone who's devoted so much time to the matter to be in a
c position to state others' beliefs, but not his own.'

'But do you think it's right', I responded, 'for someone to talk as if he knew what he doesn't know?'

'Of course not,' he said. 'Not as if he knew, but as if he'd formed opinions—he should be prepared to say what he thinks.'

'But aren't ideas which aren't based on knowledge always defective, in your experience?' I asked. 'The best of them are blind. I mean, don't people who have a correct belief, but no knowledge, strike you as exactly like blind people who happen to be taking the right road?'

'Yes,' he said.

'Well, do you want to see things which are defective, blind, and deformed,' I asked, 'when you could be getting lucid,
d correct views from elsewhere?'

Socrates professes himself incapable of defining goodness and proposes a simile instead. This is the Simile of the Sun, the first of the three great, and justly famous, interconnected images which Plato uses to convey some of his core views. The Sun consists of an extended analogy between the visible and intelligible realms: just as the sun is the source of light and growth, and is responsible for sight and seeing, and is the acme of the visible realm, so goodness is the source of truth

*and reality, and is responsible for knowledge and knowing, and is the
acme of the intelligible realm. Belief, on the other hand, is like partial
sight.*

'Socrates,' said Glaucon, 'please don't back away from the
finishing-line, so to speak. We'd be happy with the kind of
description of goodness that you gave of morality, self-
discipline, and so on.'

'So would I, Glaucon,' I said, 'very happy. But I'm afraid it'll
be more than I can manage,* and that my malformed efforts
will make me ridiculous. What I suggest, my friends, is that we
forget about trying to define goodness itself for the time being. e
You see, I don't at the moment think that our current impulse
is enough to take us to where I'd like to see us go. However, I
am prepared to talk about something which seems to me to be
the child of goodness and to bear a very strong resemblance to
it. Would you like me to do that? If not, we can just forget it.'

'Please do,' he said. 'You can settle your account by
discussing the father another time.'

'I hope I can make the repayment,' I said, 'and you can 507a
recover the debt, rather than just the interest,* as you are now.
Anyway, as interest on your account, here's an account of the
child of goodness. But please be careful that I don't cheat
you—not that I intend to—by giving you a counterfeit
description of the child.'

'We'll watch out for that as best we can,' he replied. 'Just go
ahead, please.'

'First I want to make sure that we're not at cross purposes,' I
said, 'and to remind you of something that came up earlier,
though you've often heard it on other occasions as well.'

'What?' he asked.   b

'As we talk,' I said, 'we mention and differentiate between a
lot of beautiful things and a lot of good things and so on.'

'Yes, we do.'

'And we also talk about beauty itself, goodness itself and so
on. All the things we refer to as a plurality on those occasions
we also conversely count as belonging to a single class by virtue
of the fact that they have a single particular character, and we
say that the x itself is "what really is".'

'True.'

'And we say that the first lot is visible rather than intelligible, whereas characters are intelligible rather than visible.'

'Absolutely.'

c 'With what aspect of ourselves do we see the things we see?'

'With our sight,' he replied.

'And we use hearing for the things we hear, and so on for all the other senses and the things we perceive. Yes?'

'Of course.'

'Well, have you ever stopped to consider', I asked, 'how generous the creator of the senses was when he created the domain of seeing and being seen?'

'No, not really,' he said.

'Look at it this way. Are hearing and sound deficient? Do they need an extra something to make the one hear and the d other be heard—some third thing without which hearing won't hear and sound won't be heard?'

'No,' he answered.

'And in my opinion', I went on, 'the same goes for many other domains, if not all: they don't need anything like this. Or can you point to one that does?'

'*I* can't,' he said.

'But do you realize that sight and the visible realm *are* deficient?'

'How?'

'Even if a person's eyes are capable of sight, and he's trying to use it, and what he's trying to look at is coloured, the sight will see nothing and the colours will remain unseen, surely, e unless there is also present an extra third thing which is made specifically for this purpose.'

'What is this thing you're getting at?' he asked.

'It's what we call light,' I said.

'You're right,' he said.

'So if light has value, then because it links the sense of sight 508a and the ability to be seen, it is far and away the most valuable link there is.'

'Well, it certainly does have value,' he said.

'Which of the heavenly gods would you say is responsible for this? Whose light makes it possible for our sight to see and for the things we see to be seen?'

'My reply will be no different from what yours or anyone

else's would be,' he said. 'I mean, you're obviously expecting the answer, "the sun".'

'Now, there are certain conclusions to be drawn from comparing sight to this god.'

'What?'

'Sight and the sun aren't to be identified: neither the sense itself nor its location—which we call the eye—is the same as b the sun.'

'True.'

'Nevertheless, there's no sense-organ which more closely resembles the sun, in my opinion, than the eye.'*

'The resemblance is striking.'

'Moreover, the eye's ability to see has been bestowed upon it and channelled into it, as it were, by the sun.'

'Yes.'

'So the sun is not to be identified with sight, but is responsible for sight and is itself within the visible realm. Right?'

'Yes,' he said.

'The sun is the child of goodness I was talking about, then,' I said. 'It is a counterpart to its father, goodness. As goodness stands in the intelligible realm to intelligence and the things we c know, so in the visible realm the sun stands to sight and the things we see.'

'I don't understand,' he said. 'I need more detail, please.'

'As you know,' I explained, 'when our eyes are directed towards things whose colours are no longer bathed in daylight, but in artificial light instead, then they're less effective and seem to be virtually blind, as if they didn't even have the potential for seeing clearly.'

'Certainly,' he said.

'But when they're directed towards things which are lit up by d the sun, then they see clearly and obviously do have that potential.'

'Of course.'

'Well, here's how you can think about the mind as well. When its object is something which is lit up by truth and reality, then it has—and obviously has—intelligent awareness and knowledge. However, when its object is permeated with darkness (that is, when its object is something which is subject to generation and decay), then it has beliefs and is less effective, because its beliefs chop and change, and under these circumstances it comes across as devoid of intelligence.'

'Yes, it does.'

e 'Well, what I'm saying is that it's goodness which gives the things we know their truth and makes it possible for people to have knowledge.* It is responsible for knowledge and truth, and you should think of it as being within the intelligible realm, but you shouldn't identify it with knowledge and truth, otherwise you'll be wrong: for all their value, it is even more 509a valuable. In the other realm, it is right to regard light and sight as resembling the sun, but not to identify either of them with the sun; so in this realm it is right to regard knowledge and truth as resembling goodness, but not to identify either of them with goodness, which should be rated even more highly.'

'You're talking about something of inestimable value,' he said, 'if it's not only the source of knowledge and truth, but is also more valuable than them. I mean, you certainly don't seem to be identifying it with pleasure!'

'How could you even think it?' I exclaimed. 'But we can take our analogy even further.'

b 'How?'

'I think you'll agree that the ability to be seen is not the only gift the sun gives to the things we see. It is also the source of their generation, growth, and nourishment, although it isn't actually the process of generation.'

'Of course it isn't.'

'And it isn't only the known-ness of the things we know which is conferred upon them by goodness, but also their reality and their being, although goodness isn't actually the state of being, but surpasses being in majesty and might.'*

c 'It's way beyond human comprehension, all right,' was Glaucon's quite amusing comment.*

'It's your fault for forcing me to express my views on the subject,' I replied.

'Yes, and please don't stop,' he said. 'If you've left anything out of your explanation of the simile of the sun, then the least you could do is continue with it.'

'There are plenty of omissions, in fact,' I said.

'Don't leave any gaps,' he said, 'however small.'

'I think I'll have to leave a lot out,' I said, 'but I'll try to make it as complete as I can at the moment.'

'All right,' he said.

The image of the Line, which now follows, is expressly (509c) supposed to supplement the Sun.

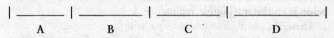

As A stands to B in terms of clarity and opacity, so C stands to D as well. A consists of likenesses, which are identified by conjecture; B consists of the solid things of the material world, which are identified confidently; C and D consist of the types, which are knowable, but the two sections are distinguished because of a difference in methodology. As B stands to A in terms of truth, so C and D together stand to A and B together. A and B together constitute the visible realm, which is the realm of belief; C and D together constitute the intelligible realm, which is the realm of knowledge.

'So bear in mind the two things we've been talking about,' I d said, 'one of which rules over the intelligible realm and its inhabitants, while the other rules over the visible realm—I won't say over the heavens in case you think I'm playing clever word-games.* Anyway, do you understand this distinction between visible things and intelligible things?'

'Yes.'

'Well, picture them as a line cut into two unequal sections and, following the same proportion, subdivide both the section of the visible realm and that of the intelligible realm. Now you can compare the sections in terms of clarity and unclarity. The first section in the visible realm consists of likenesses, by which e I mean a number of things: shadows, reflections (on the surface 510a of water or on anything else which is inherently compact, smooth, and bright), and so on. Do you see what I'm getting at?'

'I do.'

'And you should count the other section of the visible realm as consisting of the things whose likenesses are found in the first section: all the flora and fauna there are in the world, and every kind of artefact too.'

'All right.'

'I wonder whether you'd agree,' I said, 'that truth and lack of truth have been the criteria for distinguishing these sections, and that the image stands to the original as the realm of beliefs* stands to the realm of knowledge?'

b   'Yes,' he said, 'I certainly agree.'

'Now have a look at how to subdivide the section which belongs to the intelligible realm.'

'How?'

'Like this. If the mind wants to explore the first subdivision, it can do so only by using those former originals as likenesses* and by taking things for granted on its journey, which leads it to an end-point, rather than to a starting-point. If it wants to explore the second subdivision, however, it takes things for granted in order to travel to a starting-point where nothing needs to be taken for granted,[†] and it has no involvement with likenesses, as before, but makes its approach by means of types alone, in and of themselves.'

'I don't quite understand what you're saying,' he said.

c   'You will if I repeat it,' I said, 'because this preamble will make it easier to understand. I'm sure you're aware that practitioners of geometry, arithmetic, and so on take for granted things like numerical oddness and evenness, the geometrical figures, the three kinds of angle, and any other things of that sort which are relevant to a given subject.* They act as if they know about these things, treat them as basic, and don't feel any further need to explain them either to themselves or to anyone else, on the grounds that there is nothing unclear about them. They make them the starting-points for their

d subsequent investigations, which end after a coherent chain of reasoning at the point they'd set out to reach in their research.'

'Yes, I'm certainly well aware of this,' he said.

'So you must also be aware that in the course of their discussions they make use of visible forms, despite the fact that they're not interested in visible forms as such, but in the things of which the visible forms are likenesses: that is, their discussions are concerned with what it is to be a square, and with what it is to be a diagonal (and so on), rather than with

e the diagonal (and so on) which occurs in their diagrams. They treat their models and diagrams as likenesses, when these things have likenesses themselves, in fact (that is, shadows and

reflections on water); but they're actually trying to see squares
and so on in themselves, which only thought can see.'*   511a

'You're right,' he said.

'So it was objects of this type that I was describing as
belonging to the intelligible realm, with the rider that the mind
can explore them only by taking things for granted, and that its
goal is not a starting-point, because it is incapable of changing
direction and rising above the things it is taking for granted.
And I went on to say that it used as likenesses those very things
which are themselves the originals of a lower order of
likenesses, and that relative to the likenesses, the originals
command respect and admiration for their distinctness.'

'I see,' he said. 'You're talking about the objects of geometry b
and related occupations.'

'Now, can you see what I mean by the second subdivision of
the intelligible realm? It is what reason grasps by itself, thanks
to its ability to practise dialectic.* When it takes things for
granted, it doesn't treat them as starting-points, but as basic in
the strict sense—as platforms and rungs, for example. These
serve it until it reaches a point where nothing needs to be taken
for granted, and which is the starting-point for everything.*
Once it has grasped this starting-point, it turns around and by a
process of depending on the things which depend from the
starting-point, it descends to an end-point. It makes absolutely
no use of anything perceptible by the senses: it aims for types c
by means of types alone, in and of themselves, and it ends its
journey with types.'*

'I don't quite understand,' he said. 'I mean, you're talking
about crucial matters here, I think. I do understand, however,
that you want to mark off that part of the real and intelligible
realm which is before the eyes of anyone who knows how to
practise dialectic as more clear than the other part, which is
before the eyes of practitioners of the various branches of
expertise, as we call them. The latter make the things they take
for granted their starting-points, and although they inevitably
use thought, not the senses, to observe what they observe, yet
because of their failure to ascend to a starting-point—because d
their enquiries rely on taking things for granted—you're saying
that they don't understand these things, even though they are
intelligible, when related to a starting-point. I take you to be

describing what geometers and so on do as thinking rather than knowing, on the grounds that thinking is the intermediate state between believing and knowing.'

'There's nothing wrong with your understanding,' I said. 'And you should appreciate that there are four states of mind, one for each of the four sections. There's knowledge for the highest section and thought for the second one; and you'd better assign confidence to the third one and conjecture to the final one.* You can make an orderly progression out of them, and you should regard them as possessing as much clarity as their objects possess truth.'

'I see,' he said. 'That's fine with me: I'll order them in the way you suggest.'

The final image, the Allegory of the Cave, is the longest and most famous of the three. It is introduced rather abruptly, but is meant to fit in with the preceding two images (517b–c, 532a–d). Further details of the fit are a matter of dispute, although the broad outlines are clear enough. Like all the great images of the world's greatest literature, Plato's Cave manages simultaneously to appear transparent and yet unexpectedly rich and surprising. Those readers who believe that philosophy is a dry academic pursuit will be surprised at its presentation here as a pursuit which frees us from a terrible slavery; but for Plato and his peers philosophy is a way of life, not just a course of study.

514a 'Next,' I said, 'here's a situation which you can use as an analogy for the human condition—for our education or lack of it. Imagine people living in a cavernous cell down under the ground; at the far end of the cave, a long way off, there's an entrance open to the outside world. They've been there since childhood, with their legs and necks tied up in a way which keeps them in one place and allows them to look only straight ahead, but not to turn their heads. There's firelight burning a long way further up the cave behind them, and up the slope between the fire and the prisoners there's a road, beside which you should imagine a low wall has been built—like the partition which conjurors place between themselves and their audience and above which they show their tricks.'

'All right,' he said.

'Imagine also that there are people on the other side of this wall who are carrying all sorts of artefacts. These artefacts, human statuettes, and animal models carved in stone and wood c and all kinds of materials stick out over the wall; and as you'd 515a expect, some of the people talk as they carry these objects along, while others are silent.'

'This is a strange picture you're painting,' he said, 'with strange prisoners.'

'They're no different from us,'* I said. 'I mean, in the first place, do you think they'd see anything of themselves and one another except the shadows cast by the fire on to the cave wall directly opposite them?'*

'Of course not,' he said. 'They're forced to spend their lives without moving their heads.' b

'And what about the objects which were being carried along? Won't they only see their shadows as well?'

'Naturally.'

'Now, suppose they were able to talk to one another: don't you think they'd assume that their words applied to what they saw passing by in front of them?'*†

'They couldn't think otherwise.'

"And what if sound echoed off the prison wall opposite them? When any of the passers-by spoke, don't you think they'd be bound to assume that the sound came from a passing shadow?'

'I'm absolutely certain of it,' he said.

'All in all, then,' I said, 'the shadows of artefacts would c constitute the only reality people in this situation would recognize.'

'That's absolutely inevitable,' he agreed.

'What do you think would happen, then,' I asked, 'if they were set free from their bonds and cured of their inanity?* What would it be like if they found that happening to them? Imagine that one of them has been set free and is suddenly made to stand up, to turn his head and walk, and to look towards the firelight.* It hurts him to do all this and he's too dazzled to be capable of making out the objects whose shadows he'd formerly been looking at. And suppose someone tells him d that what he's been seeing all this time has no substance, and that he's now closer to reality and is seeing more accurately, because of the greater reality of the things in front of his eyes—what do you imagine his reaction would be? And what do you think he'd say if he were shown any of the passing objects and had to respond to being asked what it was? Don't you think he'd be bewildered and would think that there was more reality in what he'd been seeing before than in what he was being shown now?'

'Far more,' he said.

e 'And if he were forced to look at the actual firelight, don't you think it would hurt his eyes? Don't you think he'd turn away and run back to the things he could make out, and would take the truth of the matter to be that these things are clearer than what he was being shown?'

'Yes,' he agreed.

'And imagine him being dragged forcibly away from there up the rough, steep slope,' I went on, 'without being released until he's been pulled out into the sunlight. Wouldn't this treatment

516a cause him pain and distress? And once he's reached the sunlight, he wouldn't be able to see a single one of the things which are currently taken to be real, would he, because his eyes would be overwhelmed by the sun's beams?'

'No, he wouldn't,' he answered, 'not straight away.'

'He wouldn't be able to see things up on the surface of the earth, I suppose, until he'd got used to his situation. At first, it would be shadows that he could most easily make out, then he'd move on to the reflections of people and so on in water,* and later he'd be able to see the actual things themselves. Next, he'd feast his eyes on the heavenly bodies and the heavens themselves, which would be easier at night: he'd look at the

b light of the stars and the moon, rather than at the sun and sunlight during the daytime.'

'Of course.'

'And at last, I imagine, he'd be able to discern and feast his eyes on the sun—not the displaced image of the sun in water or elsewhere, but the sun on its own, in its proper place.'*

'Yes, he'd inevitably come to that,' he said.

'After that, he'd start to think about the sun and he'd deduce that it is the source of the seasons and the yearly cycle, that the whole of the visible realm is its domain, and that in a sense

c everything which he and his peers used to see is its responsibility.'

'Yes, that would obviously be the next point he'd come to,' he agreed.

'Now, if he recalled the cell where he'd originally lived and what passed for knowledge there and his former fellow prisoners, don't you think he'd feel happy about his own altered circumstances, and sorry for them?'

'Definitely.'

'Suppose that the prisoners used to assign prestige and credit to one another, in the sense that they rewarded speed at recognizing the shadows as they passed, and the ability to remember which ones normally come earlier and later and at the same time as which other ones, and expertise at using this d as a basis for guessing which ones would arrive next. Do you think our former prisoner would covet these honours and would envy the people who had status and power there, or would he much prefer, as Homer describes it, "being a slave labouring for someone else—someone without property",* and would put up with anything at all, in fact, rather than share their beliefs and their life?'

'Yes, I think he'd go through anything rather than live that e way,' he said.

'Here's something else I'd like your opinion about,' I said. 'If he went back underground and sat down again in the same spot, wouldn't the sudden transition from the sunlight mean that his eyes would be overwhelmed by darkness?'

'Certainly,' he replied.

'Now, the process of adjustment would be quite long this time, and suppose that before his eyes had settled down and while he wasn't seeing well, he had once again to compete 517a against those same old prisoners at identifying those shadows. Wouldn't he make a fool of himself? Wouldn't they say that he'd come back from his upward journey with his eyes ruined, and that it wasn't even worth trying to go up there? And wouldn't they—if they could—grab hold of anyone who tried to set them free and take them up there, and kill him?'*

'They certainly would,' he said.

'Well, my dear Glaucon,' I said, 'you should apply this allegory, as a whole, to what we were talking about before. The b region which is accessible to sight should be equated with the prison cell, and the firelight there with the light of the sun. And if you think of the upward journey and the sight of things up on the surface of the earth as the mind's ascent to the intelligible realm, you won't be wrong—at least, *I* don't think you'd be wrong, and it's my impression that you want to hear. Only God knows if it's actually true, however. Anyway, it's my opinion that the last thing to be seen—and it isn't easy to see

c either—in the realm of knowledge is goodness; and the sight of the character of goodness leads one to deduce that it is responsible for everything that is right and fine, whatever the circumstances, and that in the visible realm it is the progenitor of light and of the source of light, and in the intelligible realm it is the source and provider of truth and knowledge. And I also think that the sight of it is a prerequisite for intelligent conduct either of one's own private affairs or of public business.'

'I couldn't agree more,' he said.

'All right, then,' I said. 'I wonder if you also agree with me in not finding it strange that people who've travelled there don't want to engage in human business: there's nowhere else their minds would ever rather be than in the upper region—which is

d hardly surprising, if our allegory has got this aspect right as well.'

'No, it's not surprising,' he agreed.

'Well, what about this?' I asked. 'Imagine someone returning to the human world and all its misery after contemplating the divine realm. Do you think it's surprising if he seems awkward and ridiculous while he's still not seeing well, before he's had time to adjust to the darkness of his situation, and he's forced into a contest (in a lawcourt or wherever) about the shadows of morality or the statuettes which cast the shadows, and into a

e competition whose terms are the conceptions of morality held by people who have never seen morality itself?'

'No, that's not surprising in the slightest,' he said.

518a 'In fact anyone with any sense,' I said, 'would remember that the eyes can become confused in two different ways, as a result of two different sets of circumstances: it can happen in the transition from light to darkness, and also in the transition from darkness to light. If he took the same facts into consideration when he also noticed someone's mind in such a state of confusion that it was incapable of making anything out, his reaction wouldn't be unthinking ridicule. Instead, he'd try to find out whether this person's mind was returning from a mode of existence which involves greater lucidity and had been blinded by the unfamiliar darkness, or whether it was moving from relative ignorance to relative lucidity and had been overwhelmed and dazzled by the increased brightness. Once he'd distinguished between the two conditions and modes of existence, he'd congratulate anyone he found in the second b state, and feel sorry for anyone in the first state. If he did choose to laugh at someone in the second state, his amusement would be less absurd than when laughter is directed at someone returning from the light above.'*

'Yes,' he said, 'you're making a lot of sense.'

Since the Cave was expressly introduced as being relevant to education, its immediate educational implications are now drawn out. We all have the capacity for knowledge (in the Platonic sense, not just information), and education should develop that potential. But since it requires knowledge of goodness to manage a community well, then those who gain such knowledge have to 'return to the cave': paradoxically, those who least want power are the ones who should have it.

'Now, if this is true,' I said, 'we must bear in mind that education is not capable of doing what some people promise. They claim to introduce knowledge into a mind which doesn't have it, as if they were introducing sight into eyes which are c blind.'*

'Yes, they do,' he said.

'An implication of what we're saying at the moment, however,' I pointed out, 'is that the capacity for knowledge is present in everyone's mind. If you can imagine an eye that can turn from darkness to brightness only if the body as a whole turns, then our organ of understanding is like that. Its orientation has to be accompanied by turning the mind as a whole away from the world of becoming, until it becomes capable of bearing the sight of real being and reality at its most bright, which we're saying is goodness. Yes?' d

'Yes.'

'That's what education should be,' I said, 'the art of orientation. Educators should devise the simplest and most effective methods of turning minds around. It shouldn't be the art of implanting sight in the organ, but should proceed on the understanding that the organ already has the capacity, but is improperly aligned and isn't facing the right way.'

'I suppose you're right,' he said.

'So although the mental states which are described as good generally seem to resemble good physical states, in the sense e that habituation and training do in fact implant them where they didn't use to be, yet understanding (as it turns out) is undoubtedly a property of something which is more divine: it never loses its power, and it is useful and beneficial, or useless 519a and harmful, depending on its orientation. For example, surely you've noticed how the petty minds of those who are acknowledged to be bad, but clever, are sharp-eyed and perceptive enough to gain insights into matters they direct their attention towards. It's not as if they weren't sharp-sighted, but their minds are forced to serve evil, and consequently the keener their vision is, the greater the evil they accomplish.'

'Yes, I've noticed this,' he said.

'However,' I went on, 'if this aspect of that kind of person is hammered at from an early age, until the inevitable consequences of incarnation have been knocked off it—the b leaden weights, so to speak, which are grafted on to it as a result of eating and similar pleasures and indulgences and which turn the sight of the mind downwards—if it sheds these weights and is reoriented towards the truth, then (and we're talking about the same organ and the same people) it would see the truth just as clearly as it sees the objects it faces at the moment.'

'Yes, that makes sense,' he said.

'Well, doesn't this make sense as well?' I asked. 'Or rather, isn't it an inevitable consequence of what we've been saying that uneducated people, who have no experience of truth, c would make incompetent administrators of a community, and that the same goes for people who are allowed to spend their whole lives educating themselves? The first group would be no good because their lives lack direction: they've got no single point of reference to guide them in all their affairs, whether private or public.* The second group would be no good because their hearts wouldn't be in the business: they think they've been transported to the Isles of the Blessed even while they're still alive.'*

'True,' he said.

'Our job as founders, then,' I said, 'is to make sure that the best people come to that fundamental field of study (as we called it earlier):* we must have them make the ascent we've been talking about and see goodness. And afterwards, once they've been up there and had a good look, we mustn't let them d get away with what they do at the moment.'

'Which is what?'

'Staying there,' I replied, 'and refusing to come back down again to those prisoners, to share their work and their rewards, no matter whether those rewards are trivial or significant.'

'But in that case,' he protested, 'we'll be wronging them: we'll be making the quality of their lives worse and denying them the better life they could be living, won't we?'

'You're again forgetting, my friend,' I said, 'that the point of e legislation is not to make one section of a community better off than the rest, but to engineer this for the community as a whole.* Legislators should persuade or compel the members of a community to mesh together, should make every individual share with his fellows the benefit which he is capable of 520a contributing to the common welfare, and should ensure that the community does contain people with this capacity; and the purpose of all this is not for legislators to leave people to choose their own directions, but for them to use people to bind the community together.'

'Yes, you're right,' he said. 'I was forgetting.'

'I think you'll also find, Glaucon,' I said, 'that we won't be wronging any philosophers who arise in our community. Our remarks, as we force them to take care of their fellow citizens and be their guardians, will be perfectly fair. We'll tell them that it's reasonable for philosophers who happen to occur in b other communities not to share the work of those communities, since their occurrence was spontaneous, rather than planned by the political system of any of the communities in question, and it's fair for anything which arises spontaneously and doesn't owe its nurture to anyone or anything to have no interest in repaying anyone for having provided its nourishment. "We've bred *you*, however," we'll say, "to act, as it were, as the hive's

leaders and kings, for your own good as well as that of the rest of the community. You've received a better and more thorough education than those other philosophers, and you're more
c capable of playing a part in both spheres. So each of you must, when your time comes, descend to where the rest of the community lives, and get used to looking at things in the dark. The point is that once you become acclimatized, you'll see infinitely better than the others there; your experience of genuine right, morality, and goodness will enable you to identify every one of the images and recognize what it is an image of. And then the administration of our community—ours as well as yours—will be in the hands of people who are awake, as distinct from the norm nowadays of communities being governed by people who shadow-box and fall out with one another in their dreams over who should rule, as if that
d were a highly desirable thing to do. No, the truth of the matter is this: the less keen the would-be rulers of a community are to rule, the better and less divided the administration of that community is bound to be, but where the rulers feel the opposite, the administration is bound to be the opposite."'

'Yes,' he said.

'And do you think our wards will greet these views of ours with scepticism and will refuse to join in the work of government when their time comes, when they can still spend most of their time living with one another in the untainted realm?'
e 'No, they couldn't,' he answered. 'They're fair-minded people, and the instructions we're giving them are fair. However, they'll undoubtedly approach rulership as an inescapable duty—an attitude which is the opposite of the one held by the people who have power in communities at the moment.'*

'You're right, Glaucon,' I said. 'You'll only have a well-
521a governed community if you can come up with a way of life for your prospective rulers that is preferable to ruling! The point is that this is the only kind of community where the rulers will be genuinely well off (not in material terms, but they'll possess the wealth which is a prerequisite of happiness—a life of virtue and intelligence), whereas if government falls into the hands of people who are impoverished and starved of any good things of

their own, and who expect to wrest some good for themselves from political office, a well-governed community is an impossibility. I mean, when rulership becomes something to fight for, a domestic and internal war like this destroys not only the perpetrators, but also the rest of the community.'

'You're absolutely right,' he said.

'Apart from the philosophical life,' I said, 'is there any way b of life, in your opinion, which looks down on political office?'*

'No, definitely not,' he answered.

'In fact, political power should be in the hands of people who aren't enamoured of it. Otherwise their rivals in love will fight them for it.'

'Of course.'

'There's no one you'd rather force to undertake the guarding of your community, then, than those who are experts in the factors which contribute towards the good government of a community, who don't look to politics for their rewards, and whose life is better than the political life. Agreed?'

'Yes,' he said.

Chapter 10

Educating Philosopher Kings

Granted that the rulers need to understand goodness, what kind of education will take them there? This was a delicate subject for Plato. Higher education—intellectual rather than character-building—had been in the hands of the sophists, who also claimed to teach goodness, but whose chameleonic values Plato mistrusted. He first draws a distinction, based on the metaphysics of Chapter 8, between pure and applied subjects. The philosophers will need both, but in the present context Plato stresses the ability of some subjects to lead the mind away from mundane reality and towards the realm at whose apex goodness stands.

521c   'So would you like us to consider next how to produce people of this type in our community, and how to lead them up to the light—like the people we hear about who rise from Hades to dwell among the gods?'*

'Yes, of course I'd like us to do that,' he replied.

'Now, what we're dealing with here, it would seem, is not the spinning of a potsherd,* but the reorientation of a mind from a kind of twilight to true daylight—and this reorientation is an ascent to reality, or in other words true philosophy.'

'Quite so.'

'We ought to try to see which intellectual pursuits can have
d this effect, then, oughtn't we?'

'Of course.'

'What intellectual pursuit, then, Glaucon, might attract a mind away from the realm of becoming and towards reality? Oh, something just occurred to me while I was speaking: we said that in their youth these people had to be warriors, didn't we?'*

'Yes, we did.'

'Therefore, the area of study we're after must have an additional feature.'

'What?'

'It must be of value to men of war.'

'Yes, it certainly must,' he said, 'if possible.'

'Now, the education we've arranged for them so far consists of physical exercise and cultural studies.'   e

'Yes,' he said.

'And physical exercise is concerned with the world of coming into being and passing away, since its domain is physical growth and decay.'

'I suppose so.'

'So it isn't the area of study we're after.'

'No.'   522a

'What about the cultural education we described earlier?'

'But that merely complemented the physical exercise,' he said. 'I'm sure you remember that it trains the guardians by habituation: it doesn't produce knowledge, but harmony in the sphere of music, elegance in the sphere of rhythm, and other allied habits in the field of literature, whether the literature in question is fictional or closer to non-fiction. There's nothing in it which can lead a student towards the kind of goal you're after at the moment.'   b

'Your memory is very accurate,' I said. 'Thanks for reminding me: it's true that there's nothing like that in it. But then, what sort of intellectual pursuit *are* we after? I mean, all the professions seemed servile, somehow.'*

'Of course they did. But if we exclude cultural studies, physical exercise, and the professional occupations, what else is there that anyone could study?'

'Well,' I said, 'if they're all we can take, then let's take something which applies to them all.'

'What?'

'For example, there's that everyday thing—one of the first c things everyone has to learn—which all the modes of expertise, thinking, and knowledge make use of.'

'What are you getting at?' he asked.

'It's nothing special,' I said. 'It's the ability to distinguish one, two, and three—in short, I'm talking about number and counting. I mean, isn't it the case that every branch of expertise and knowledge is bound to have some involvement with numbers and with counting?'

'Definitely,' he said.

'Even military expertise?' I asked.

'Yes, certainly. It has to,' he said.

d 'At any rate, tragedy after tragedy has Palamedes showing up Agamemnon's utterly ridiculous deficiencies as a military commander,'* I said. 'Haven't you noticed how Palamedes claims that, once he'd invented counting, he deployed the troops at Troy and added up the ships and so on? The implication is that previously none of them had been counted, and Agamemnon's inability to count presumably means that he didn't even know how many feet he had. What sort of military commander do you think he was?'

'A peculiar one, I'd say, if there's any truth in this,' he replied.

e 'So our position will be—won't it?—that it's essential for a man of war to learn how to calculate and count,' I asked.

'He absolutely has to,' he said, 'if he's going to know anything at all about deploying troops, or rather, if he's even going to be a human being.'

'Now, there's an idea I have about this subject, and I wonder whether you share it,' I said.

'What is it?'

523a 'It rather looks as though it's one of the subjects we're after, which stimulate a student's intellect. But it also seems likely that no one makes correct use of its consummate ability to attract one towards reality.'

'What do you mean?' he asked.

'I'll try to clarify my point of view,' I said. 'In my mind, I distinguish between things which are and things which are not attractive in the way we're talking about. I'll try to get you to appreciate the distinction as well, and then you can tell me whether or not you agree, so that we can be better placed to see how accurate my hunch is.'

'Yes, do explain,' he said.

'All right,' I said. 'I'm sure you'll see what I mean if I say that at the level of the senses, some things don't encourage the
b intellect to explore further, because the situation can be adequately assessed by the relevant sense, while other things can't help provoking an enquiring attitude, because sense-perception fails to produce a sound result.'

'You're obviously talking about distant impressions and illusory paintings,' he said.

'No, you haven't quite got my point,' I said.

'What are you talking about, then?'

'In order to count as thought-provoking, in my opinion,' I explained, 'they have to produce contradictory sense-impressions at the same time; otherwise, they aren't thought-provoking. The impression sense-perception has to give of an object is that it is no more X than the opposite of X, however close or far away it is when you encounter it. An example will help you understand what I'm getting at. Here are three fingers, we'd say, the little finger, the second one and the middle one.'

'Yes,' he said.

'And please assume that I'm talking about seeing them from close range. Now, here's what I want you to think about.'

'What?'

'Well, each of them equally gives the impression of being a finger. There's no difference between them in this respect, and it doesn't matter whether the finger that's being looked at is in the middle or on either end, pale or dark, thick or thin, and so on and so forth. It's almost inconceivable that anyone's mind would feel impelled in any of these circumstances to think and try to come up with an answer to the question what a finger is, since sight has given the mind no grounds for supposing that the finger is at the same time the opposite of a finger.'

'That's right,' he agreed.

'So it makes sense to say that this situation doesn't provoke or arouse thought,' I said.

'Agreed.'

'What about the bigness or smallness of the fingers, however? Is what sight sees adequate in this case? Does it make no difference to it whether or not the finger it's looking at is in the middle or on either end? And doesn't the same go for touch and the fingers' thickness and thinness or hardness and softness? And the other senses also give inadequate impressions in this kind of situation, don't they? I mean, here's how each sense works: the main point is that the sense into whose domain hardness falls is inevitably also the sense into whose domain softness falls; and the message it passes on to the mind is that, in its perception, the same thing is both hard and soft.* True?'

'True,' he said.

'So isn't what happens in *these* situations that the mind

inevitably feels puzzled about what this sense means by hardness, since it's saying that the same thing is soft as well? And when the sense that perceives weight reports that something heavy is light and that something light is heavy, isn't the mind bound to wonder what lightness and heaviness are?'

b   'Yes,' he said, 'because the messages it's receiving are strange and demand clarification.'

'It makes sense to suppose, then,' I went on, 'that these are the circumstances in which the chief thing the mind does is summon up calculation and thought to help it examine whether in any given case it's being informed about one object or two objects.'

'Of course.'

'And if there turn out to be two objects, then each of them is single and they're different from each other, aren't they?'

'Yes.'

'If each of them is single, then, and it takes two of them to make two, then it'll think about them as two separate objects. I
c   mean, if they were inseparable, it wouldn't be thinking about two objects: it would be thinking about one object.'

'Right.'

'However, in our current example sight sees both big and small as a kind of mixture, not as separate from each other. Yes?'

'Yes.'

'And in order to clarify the situation, the intellect is forced in its turn to look at big and small as distinct entities, not mixed together, which is the opposite of what sight does.'

'True.'

'And this, in outline, is why it occurs to us to ask what in fact bigness and smallness really are, isn't it?'

'Absolutely.'

'And that's how we come to distinguish what we call the intelligible realm from the visible realm.'

d   'You're quite right,' he said.

'So that's what I was getting at just now, when I was saying that some things are thought-provoking, and some things aren't. I define as thought-provoking the things which impinge upon our sense-perception along with their opposites, whereas I describe things which don't do that as incapable of arousing thought.'

'I understand now,' he said, 'and I agree.'

The curriculum is laid out. Trainee philosopher kings must study arithmetic, plane geometry, solid geometry, astronomy, and musicology. In each case, these subjects are interpreted until they reveal an aspect which will help to 'extricate' would-be philosophers from the 'world of becoming'; they also serve to sharpen the mind generally. Mathematics is chosen because it was, in Plato's day, the subject which had been developed furthest towards being laid out along systematic lines (leading within fifty or so years to Euclid's Elements), and Plato wants dialectic to achieve that kind of coherence.

'All right, then. Which of these two categories do you think number—which is to say, oneness*—belongs to?'

'I don't know,' he answered.

'Well, you can work it out from what we've already said,' I replied. 'If oneness is adequately seen (or grasped by any other sense) for what it is, then it doesn't have any power to attract e towards reality—as a finger doesn't, we were saying. However, if it's never seen without its opposite simultaneously being seen, so that the impression it gives is no more of oneness than of the opposite, then evaluation becomes imperative and the mind has no choice but to be puzzled: it sets its thought-processes in motion, and casts about for an answer to the question what oneness itself actually is. And if this is what happens, then oneness is one of those subjects which guide and turn people 525a towards the contemplation of reality.'

'But that's exactly what seeing oneness does, in fact,' he said. 'We see the same thing simultaneously as one and as infinitely many.'*

'And if oneness is like that,' I said, 'then number as a whole is as well.'

'Naturally.'

'Now, calculation and arithmetic are entirely concerned with number.'

'Certainly.'

'And they clearly guide one towards truth.'   b

'Yes, they're exceptionally good at that.'

'Then arithmetic is one of the subjects we're after, apparently. A man of war can't do without it, because he deploys troops, and a philosopher can't do without it, because he has to extricate himself from the world of becoming and make reality his field of operation, or else he'll never be able to reason and calculate.'

'True,' he said.

'And our guardians are, in fact, both warriors and philosophers.'

'Of course.'

'Therefore, Glaucon, we ought to provide for this subject in our legislation, and to persuade the people who are going to undertake our community's most important tasks to take up

c arithmetic. They shouldn't engage in it like dilettantes, but should keep at it until they reach the point where they can see in their mind's eye what numbers really are, and they shouldn't study it as merchants and stallholders do, for commercial reasons, but for the sake of warfare and in order to facilitate the mind's turning away from becoming and towards truth and reality.'

'You're absolutely right,' he said.

'Now that arithmetic has been mentioned,' I said, 'it also

d occurs to me how neatly it fits in the context we're getting at, and how commonly it could be used by anyone who applies himself to it for intellectual rather than commercial purposes.'

'How?' he asked.

'Because it's particularly good at guiding the mind upwards—which is what we've been talking about—and forcing one to discuss numbers in themselves. It excludes the slightest hint, in a discussion, of numbers which have attendant visible or tangible material objects. I mean, I'm sure you're

e aware that the experts in the field pour scorn on any attempt to divide the actual number one and refuse to allow it. If you chop it up, they multiply it; they take steps to preserve one's oneness and to prevent it ever appearing to contain a multiplicity of factors.'*

'You're absolutely right,' he said.

526a 'What do you think they'd say, then, Glaucon, if someone were to ask them, in surprise, "What are these numbers you're talking about? What numbers involve a oneness which fulfils your requirements, where every single unit is equal to every other unit, without even the smallest variation, and without being divisible in the slightest?"'

'I think they'd reply that the numbers they're talking about are only accessible to thought, and cannot be grasped in any other way.'

'So can you see, Glaucon,' I said, 'that it really does seem as though this subject is essential, since it apparently forces the b mind to rely purely on intellectual processes and to aim for truth in itself?'

'Yes,' he said. 'It certainly does do that.'

'Now, have you ever noticed that people who are naturally good at arithmetic are also naturally quick at just about every subject? And that if you make slow-witted people learn and study arithmetic, then without exception they end up quicker than they used to be, even if they gain nothing else from it?'

'That's true,' he said.

'Moreover, I don't suppose it would be easy for you to find c many subjects which require more effort from the student learning them.'

'No.'

'For all these reasons, then, this is a subject we'd better take seriously; we must have our best people study it.'

'I agree,' he said.

'That's the first subject dealt with, then,' I said. 'But in the second place, let's consider whether the subject which follows on its heels suits our purposes.'

'What subject do you mean?' he asked. 'Geometry?'

'Exactly,' I said.

'It obviously suits our purposes,' he said, 'because it has d some military applications. You see, it does make a difference whether or not a person is good at geometry when he comes to organize an encampment, occupy territory, deploy an army over a narrow or wide extent, and form up troops in any other way in the course of a battle or while on the move.'

'Yes,' I said, 'but it hardly takes the whole of geometry and arithmetic to enable someone to cope with that kind of situation. What we have to consider is whether the more advanced aspects of geometry which constitute the bulk of the subject have any relevance in the context of smoothing the way

e towards seeing the character of goodness. And what we're saying is that anything is relevant in this context if it forces the mind to turn towards the realm where the most blessed part of reality is to be found, which the mind should do its utmost to see.'

'You're right,' he said.

'So if it impels the mind to see reality, it suits our purposes; but if it impels the mind to see the world of becoming, it does not.'

'Yes, that's what we're saying.'

527a 'Even people who know very little geometry', I said, 'won't dispute the fact that this branch of knowledge is quite different from how it is described by its practitioners.'

'In what sense?' he asked.

'They have a very absurd, if very inevitable, way of talking about geometry. They talk as if they were actually doing something and as if the point of all their theorems was to have some actual effect: they come up with words like "squaring" and "applying" and "adding" and so on, whereas in fact the

b sole purpose of the subject is knowledge.'

'Absolutely,' he said.

'And there's something else we'd better agree on.'

'What?'

'That this knowledge is of things which exist for ever, rather than of things which come into existence at some time and subsequently pass away.'

'There's no difficulty in agreeing to that,' he said. 'The objects of geometrical knowledge do exist for ever.'

'Therefore, Glaucon, geometry can attract the mind towards truth. It can produce philosophical thought, in the sense that it can reverse the misguided downward tendencies we currently have.'

'It's particularly effective at that,' he agreed.

c 'Then you'd better be particularly effective at telling the inhabitants of your Goodland* to do their utmost not to dismiss geometry,' I told him. 'I mean, its by-products are not unimportant either.'

'What are they?' he asked.

'There are the military ones you mentioned,' I replied, 'and also, as we know, people who've studied geometry are much more receptive than those who haven't to intellectual work in general; it makes absolutely all the difference in the world.'

'Yes, it certainly does,' he said.

'So shall we make this a second subject for the young people of our community to study?'

'Yes,' he said.

'And don't you think the third should be astronomy?'   d

'*I* do, anyway,' he said. 'I mean, it's not only farmers and sailors who need to be sensitive to the seasons, months, and phases of the year: it's just as important for military commanders as well.'

'You seem to be naïvely worried about what people will think of you,' I remarked. 'You don't want them to think you're recommending studies which have no practical benefit. It is, in fact, really hard for people to have confidence in the fact that studying this kind of subject cleans and re-ignites a particular mental organ which everyone has (while other occupations ruin it and blind it), and that this organ is a e thousand times more worth preserving than any eye, since it is the only organ which can see truth. People who acknowledge this fact will be incredibly happy with your ideas, but all those people who are completely unaware of it will in all likelihood think you're talking rubbish, because, as they can see, this kind of study doesn't produce any worthwhile benefit of any other kind. So you'd better hurry up and decide which group of people you're addressing. Alternatively, you're not really 528a addressing either group: you're mainly framing your arguments for your own sake—which is not to say that you'd resent anyone else profiting from them as well.'

'That's what I'd prefer to do—talk, ask questions, and answer them chiefly for my own sake,' he said.

'Well,' I said, 'I'd like you to backtrack a bit. Just now we chose the wrong thing to follow geometry.'

'What do you mean?' he asked.

'We went straight from surfaces to solidity in circular motion,' I said, 'before we'd taken solidity on its own. The b correct procedure is to go from the second dimension to the third—which is, of course, the domain of cubes and anything else with volume.'

'True,' he said. 'But I don't think this domain has been explored yet, Socrates.'

'There are two reasons for that,' I replied. 'First, no society respects it, and therefore its complexity makes people diffident about looking into it. Second, exploration isn't feasible unless the research is conducted under supervision, but a supervisor is unlikely to be found, and moreover, even if one were to be found, the current situation is that the people doing the
c research in the field are so self-assured that they wouldn't listen to him. However, they would listen if a whole community treated the subject with respect and supervised it, and once research was undertaken with continuity and determination, then facts would be discovered. I mean, even under the current circumstances of its general disrespect and depreciation—at the hands of the researchers as well, since they can't explain what good it is—it still manages to be attractive enough to overcome all this opposition and to develop, and I wouldn't be surprised if discoveries were made.'

d 'Yes, it certainly is a particularly attractive subject,' he agreed. 'But please can you explain what you were getting at just now. You referred to geometry as the study of surfaces . . .'

'Yes,' I said.

'. . . and then at first you said that astronomy came next, but later you took this back,' he said.

'I was in a hurry to complete the discussion,' I explained, 'and that was slowing me down. Although investigation of three-dimensionality came next, the research in the field has made the subject so difficult to take seriously that I missed it
e out and put astronomy, which is solidity in motion, after geometry.'

'You're right,' he said.

'So let's make astronomy the fourth subject,' I said, 'on the understanding that, if a community were to underwrite the research, the branch of knowledge we're omitting at the moment would be available.'

'Yes, that sounds reasonable,' he said. 'And since you ticked me off just now for my crude endorsement of astronomy, Socrates, I'll now give it the kind of endorsement you're after. I
529a mean, I can't imagine anyone doubting that it forces the mind to look upwards and guides it from this realm to another realm.'

'It seems as though I'm the only one to doubt it, then,' I said. 'You see, I disagree.'

'On what grounds?' he protested.

'Because I think its current usage, in the hands of those who try to interest people in philosophy,* is guaranteed to make people look downwards.'

'What do you mean?' he asked.

'I get the impression,' I said, 'that your conception of the study of things up on high is rather generous! It looks as though you'd think that the study of decorations on a ceiling by b bending one's neck back, and the acquisition of information that way, makes use of the intellect rather than the eyes! You may be right, and I'm probably being simple-minded, but it's only a field of study which is concerned with immaterial reality that I can regard as making the mind look upwards, and I wouldn't describe the attempt to study perceptible things by gawping upwards or squinting downwards as learning (since there's no knowledge involved in these cases); neither would I say that in these cases the mind is looking upwards rather than c downwards, even if the studying takes place while lying on one's back† on the ground or in the sea.'

'That's a fair comment,' he said. 'You're right to have told me off. But apart from how it's studied at the moment, then, how do you think astronomy should be studied, if studying it is to have some point in the context we're talking about?'

'Like this,' I replied. 'It may be that there's nothing in the visible realm which is more beautiful or less erratic than these decorations in the sky, but even so, since they're within the d visible realm, they should be regarded as considerably inferior to true decorations, in respect of the beauty and precision of the movements which, in the realm of true number and all the true figures, genuine speed and slowness make relative to each other as they transport things which are not accessible to sight, but only to reason and thought.* Don't you agree?'

'Definitely,' he said.

'Therefore,' I continued, 'we should use the heavenly decorations merely as illustrations to help us study the other realm, as we would if we were faced with exceptional geometrical figures drawn in fine detail by Daedalus or some e other artist or painter. On seeing figures of this kind, an expert geometer would think that for all the beauty of their execution,

it would be absurd seriously to expect an examination of them
530a to reveal the truth about equals or doubles or some other ratio.'

'Of course it would be absurd,' he agreed.

'Don't you think that a genuine astronomer feels the same
when he looks at the movements of the heavenly bodies?' I
asked. 'He'll certainly think that the artist of the heavens has
constructed them and all they contain to be as beautiful as such
works could ever possibly be, but what about the ratio between
night and day, between them and a month, between a month
and a year? And what about the relations of the heavenly
b bodies in general to these phenomena or to one another? Don't
you think he'd regard it as ludicrous to suppose that these
things are constant and unvarying, and never change in the
slightest, when they're material and visible, and to devote all
one's energy to discovering the truth about these things?'

'I agree,' he said, 'or anyway, I do when I hear your account.'

'So the way we'll do astronomy will be identical to the way
we do geometry,' I said, 'since in both cases we'll be making
use of matters that require elucidation.* And if we don't ignore
the heavenly bodies, we'll never be engaged in true astronomy,
c and we'll never develop rather than atrophy our mind's innate
intelligence.'

'Your instructions will involve astronomers in a great deal
more work than they're used to at the moment,' he remarked.

'Yes, and I think we'll be issuing further instructions of the
same kind,' I said, 'if our legislation is to do any good. But are
there any other suitable fields of study that you can think of?'

'Not just at the moment,' he replied.

'There are, however, several types of movement, I think,' I
d said. 'An expert would probably be able to give us a complete
list, but even we can easily see two of them.'

'What are they?'

'In addition to the astronomical variety, there's one that
complements it too,' I said.

'Which one do you mean?'

'The eyes are made for astronomy,' I said, 'and by the same
token the ears are presumably made for the type of movement
that constitutes music. If so, these branches of knowledge are
allied to each other. This is what the Pythagoreans claim,* and
we should agree, Glaucon, don't you think?'

'Yes,' he said.

'Music is a difficult subject,' I said, 'so we'll consult the e Pythagoreans to find out their views, and to see if they've anything to add. But throughout we'll be looking after our own agenda.'

'Which is what?'

'To make sure that our wards don't set about learning any pointless aspects of music—any aspect which doesn't unfailingly fetch up at the place which (as we were just saying in the case of astronomy) ought to be the destination of all these subjects. Don't you realize that people get music wrong 531a too? They laboriously measure the interrelations between audible concords and sounds, which is as useless an activity as anything astronomers get up to.'

'Yes, they really make fools of themselves,' he said. 'They talk about "concentrations"* and bring their ears close to the source of the sound—as if they were trying to hear what the people next door were saying! And then some of them claim to be able to detect a further intermediate resonance and maintain that they've found the smallest possible interval, which should be used as the basis of measurement, while others dispute all this and claim that the notes in question are to all intents and purposes identical. But both camps rate their ears above their b intellect.'

'You're talking', I said, 'about those excellent characters who make life hard for strings and torture them by twisting them on pegs.* I don't want to push the image too far and mention how they strike the strings with a plectrum and challenge them, and how the strings refuse to talk and come up with specious pleas. So I'll drop the image and tell you that I wasn't thinking of those people, but the ones we were saying just now would explain music to us, because they act in the same way that astronomers do. They limit their research to the numbers they c can find within audible concords, but they fail to come up with general matters for elucidation, such as which numbers form concords together and which don't, and why some do and some don't.'

'That's a superhuman task you're talking about,' he remarked.

'But a useful one,' I said, 'if it serves the aim of trying to understand what morality and goodness are. In any other context, however, it's a pointless pursuit.'

'I suppose so,' he said.

'What I'd say', I continued, 'is that engaging in all the d subjects we've been discussing has some relevance to our purposes, and all that effort isn't wasted, if the work takes one to the common ground of affinity between the subjects, and enables one to work out how they are all related to one another; otherwise it's a waste of time.'*

'I suspect you're right,' he said. 'But you're talking about an awful lot of hard work, Socrates.'

Following the course in the mathematical sciences, the crowning part of the curriculum is dialectic, which gives one the ability to understand things as they are in themselves, and therefore to understand their relation to goodness. Without dialectic, we are condemned to the semi-conscious level of belief.

'What?' I asked. 'The prelude is hard, you say? Don't you realize that this is all just the prelude to the main theme, which is the important subject? I mean, you surely don't think that being accomplished in these subjects makes one good at e dialectic.'

'No, certainly not,' he answered, 'although it does happen sometimes—very occasionally—in my experience.'

'But don't you think the inability to explain anything, and to understand explanations, rules out the possibility of knowing any of the things we're saying are important?' I asked.

'Yes, I agree with you on this too,' he replied.

532a 'And isn't this exactly the theme which dialectic develops, Glaucon?' I asked. 'It may be an intelligible theme, but sight can be said to reflect it, when, as we were saying,* it sets about looking at actual creatures, at the heavenly bodies themselves, and finally at the sun itself. Just as, in this case, a person ends up at the supreme point of the visible realm, so the summit of the intelligible realm is reached when, by means of dialectic and without relying on anything perceptible, a person perseveres in b using rational argument to approach the true reality of things until he has grasped with his intellect the reality of goodness itself.'

'Absolutely,' he said.

'And this is the journey a practitioner of dialectic makes, wouldn't you say?'

'Of course.'

'And the prisoners' release from their bonds,' I went on, 'their reorientation away from shadows and towards figurines and firelight, their ascent out from under the ground into sunlight, their lingering inability to look in the upper world at creatures and plants and the light of the sun, rather than gazing[†] at reflections in water and at shadows (shadows, that c is, of real things, not the shadows of figurines cast by a light which, relative to the sun, is of the same order as the figurines)—just as, in this case, the most lucid part of the body is taken up to see the most lucid part of the material, visible realm, so the whole business of studying the areas of expertise we've been discussing has the ability to guide the best part of the mind upwards until it sees the best part of reality.'[*] d

'I'm happy with that,' he said, 'despite the fact that acceptance and rejection both seem to me to be problematic, from different points of view. However, we shouldn't let this be just a one-off discussion today, but should often return to the issue. So let's assume that our ideas are correct, and get on with discussing the actual main theme in as much detail as we did the prelude. So please tell us the ins and outs of the ability to do dialectic, and how many different types of it there are, and e what methods it employs, since they'd presumably be the means of approaching that place which, once reached, is travellers' rest and journey's end.'

'You won't be able to follow me there, my dear Glaucon,' I 533a said, 'which is a pity, because there'd be no shortage of determination from me, and what you'd see there wouldn't be an image of what we're talking about:[*] you'd see the truth itself—or that's what I think, anyway. I may be right, and I may be wrong—that's not for us to insist on at the moment; but we can state with confidence that there'd be something of the kind to be seen, don't you think?'

'Of course.'

'And what about the idea that dialectic alone can elucidate these matters, to someone with experience in the subjects we've discussed, and that otherwise it's impossible?'

'Yes, we should state that confidently too,' he said.

b   'Anyway, what is indisputable in what we're saying', I said, 'is that dialectic is the only field of enquiry which sets out methodically to grasp the reality of any and every thing. All the other areas of expertise, on the other hand, are either concerned with fulfilling people's beliefs and desires, or are directed towards generation and manufacture or looking after things while they're being generated and manufactured. Even any that are left—geometry and so on, which we were saying do grasp reality to some extent—are evidently dreaming about reality.

c There's no chance of their having a conscious glimpse of reality as long as they refuse to disturb the things they take for granted and remain incapable of explaining them. For if your starting-point is unknown, and your end-point and intermediate stages are woven together out of unknown material, there may be coherence, but knowledge is completely out of the question.'*

'Yes, it is,' he agreed.

'So dialectic is the only field of enquiry', I went on, 'whose quest for certainty causes it to uproot the things it takes for granted in the course of its journey, which takes it towards an

d actual starting-point. When the mind's eye is literally buried deep in mud,* far from home, dialectic gently extracts it and guides it upwards, and for this reorientation it draws on the assistance of those areas of expertise we discussed. It's true that we've often called them branches of *knowledge* in the past, but that's only a habit and they really need a different word, which implies a higher degree of clarity than belief has, and a higher degree of opacity than knowledge has. Earlier, we used the term "thought".* But I don't suppose we'll quarrel about

e terminology when we're faced with matters as important as the ones we're looking into at the moment.'

'No, we won't,' he said, 'just so long as whatever term is used expresses the state of mental clarity.'†

'So the terms we used earlier will do,' I said. 'We'll call the first section knowledge, the second thought, the third

534a confidence, and the fourth conjecture; and the first pair constitute intellect (which is concerned with real being), the second pair belief (which is concerned with becoming). As being stands to becoming, so intellect stands to belief; and as intellect stands to belief, so knowledge stands to confidence and thought to conjecture.* However, we'd better pass over the proportionate relations between the objects of intellect and belief, Glaucon, and the twofold division of each of the two realms—the domain of belief and the domain of intellect—if we want to avoid getting entangled in an argument which would be many times as long as the ones our discussion has already thrown up.'

'Well, I agree with everything else you've said, in so far as I b can follow it,' he said.

'And don't you think that the ability to understand what it is to be any given thing, when someone else explains it, is indicative of a dialectician? And wouldn't you say that, in so far as anyone who lacks this ability is incapable of explaining anything to himself or to anyone else either, then he doesn't know anything?'

'Of course I would,' he answered.

'The same principle applies to goodness, then, as well. If someone is incapable of arguing for the separation and distinction of the character of goodness from everything else, and cannot, so to speak, fight all the objections one by one and c refute them (responding to them resolutely by referring to the reality of things, rather than to people's beliefs), and can't see it all through to the end without his position suffering a fall—if you find someone to be in this state, you'll deny that he has knowledge of goodness itself or, in general, of anything good at all.* Instead, if he does somehow manage to make contact with a reflection of goodness, you'll claim that the contact is due to belief, not knowledge. He dreams his current life away in a state of semi-consciousness, you'll say, and he'll never wake up here: he'll go to Hades, the place of total sleep, d first. Agreed?'

'Yes, definitely,' he said. 'I'll certainly be making all of these claims.'

'Now, suppose your theoretical upbringing and education of your younger generation were to become a reality. I imagine you'd deny them power and crucial responsibility in the community if they were as irrational as surds.'*

'Yes, I would,' he said.

'Will you include in your legislation, then, the ruling that a major part of the education they engage in must be the subject

267

which will enable them to acquire particular expertise at the give and take of discussion?'

e   'I will,' he replied, 'if you join me.'

'Don't you think', I asked, 'that dialectic occupies the highest position and forms, as it were, the copestone of the curriculum? And that, if so, there's no subject which ought to occupy a higher position, and therefore it completes our educational

535a programme?'

'Yes, I agree,' he answered.

Plato repeats (from Chapter 8) the qualities potential philosopher kings must have, stressing in this context their enthusiasm for intellectual pursuits. The main educational stages are allotted to ages: the primary education of Chapter 4 goes up to about 17 or 18; there will follow a couple of years of intense military training; then ten years spent with the mathematical sciences; then five years of solid dialectic. Trainees who are found to be unsuited to each successive stage will be weeded out. Those who make it through to the end will now become executives and teachers for fifteen years, until finally they understand goodness and are allowed to alternate periods of contemplative philosophy with periods of rulership. Now that we have seen (a) what it is to be a true philosopher, and (b) how to produce true philosophers, we can see the truth of the proposal that the imaginary community will be feasible (if at all) only when philosophers are kings.

'All that remains for you to do,' I said, 'is distribute the subjects: to whom, and on what basis, shall we assign them?'

'Yes, that's obviously what we're left with,' he said.

'Well, do you remember what kind of people we chose as rulers, when we made our choice earlier?'*

'Of course I do,' he answered.

'Now, on the whole,' I went on, 'the characteristics we should favour ought to remain the same, I suggest. I mean, we should prefer people with a high degree of reliability and courage, and also, within reason, people who are very good-

b looking.* In addition, however, to being good and solid, we must also look for people with a natural talent for these studies.'

'What special qualities do you have in mind?'

'They must be sharp and quick at learning, Glaucon,' I said. 'You see, physical exercise is far less appalling to the mind than intense intellectual work, since intellectual work is more exclusively mental. It belongs to the mind, rather than being shared with the body.'

'True,' he said.

'And we should also look for people who have good c memories, are tenacious, and enjoy all kinds of work. Otherwise, there's no way that they'll be prepared to complete such a long course of intellectual study over and above all the hard work of the physical programme.'

'That's right,' he said. 'That'll take all the advantages nature can provide.'

'The problem nowadays, anyway,' I said, 'and the reason why philosophy has become devalued, is (to repeat ourselves)* that its practitioners are people who aren't good enough for it. It should be practised by men of true pedigree, not by bastards.'

'What do you mean?' he asked.

'The main thing', I explained, 'is that the practitioner must d not be hamstrung in his enjoyment of work, with half of him enjoying it and half of him not. That's what you get when someone enjoys exercising and hunting and all kinds of physical work, but doesn't enjoy using his mind or listening to lectures or undertaking research, and instead loathes working in all these contexts. Then there are also people who are hamstrung in their enjoyment of work by having the opposite attitude.'

'You're absolutely right,' he said.

'By the same token,' I continued, 'we'll call a mind handicapped in the context of truth if, while loathing conscious e lying (in that it not only finds it hard to stomach from itself, but also gets highly irritated when others do it), it happily puts up with unconscious lying* and doesn't get irritated when its ignorance is exposed, but wallows in ignorance as cheerfully as any pig.'

'Absolutely,' he said.   536a

'And the same goes for self-control, courage, broadness of vision, and all the other aspects of virtue,' I said. 'It's particularly important to distinguish men of true pedigree from bastards in all these contexts. The inability to look at these qualities from every possible angle leads people and

269

communities to use crippled bastards for some purpose or other—as their friends, maybe, or as their rulers.'

'Very true,' he said.

'It's important for us to take precautions against all traps of
b this kind,' I said. 'If we bring people who are in perfect physical and mental condition to this lengthy study programme and course of training, and educate them in it, we'll have done nothing wrong even by the strictest standards of moral behaviour, and we'll be preserving the integrity of our community and political system. However, if we introduce people of any other kind to it, we'll not only achieve the opposite results, but we'll also increase the flood of ridicule which pours down on philosophy.'

'That would be disgraceful,' he said.

'Yes, it would,' I agreed. 'But it looks as though I'm open to ridicule myself at the moment.'

'In what respect?' he asked.

c 'I forgot that our tone has been light-hearted,' I answered, 'and I spoke with rather too much intensity. You see, while I was speaking, I looked at philosophy and saw how unjustly it has been dragged in the gutter. That made me cross, and I suppose I used the over-serious tone that I did because I felt a kind of rage.'

'Well, from my point of view as a member of the audience,' he said, 'it didn't strike me as excessive.'

'But from my point of view as the speaker,' I said, 'it did. Anyway, we should bear in mind that although our earlier selection procedure favoured old men, our present one rules
d them out.* I mean, we shouldn't let Solon convince us that while growing old there is still plenty of scope for learning:* in fact, there's more scope for running than for learning! In any given sphere, it's up to young people to work long and hard.'

'That's necessarily true,' he said.

'So it's while they're young that we should set them arithmetic, geometry, and the rest of the studies which are the essential preliminaries before taking up dialectic. But we shouldn't present the work as compulsory.'

'Why not?'

e 'Because an autonomous person should never learn a subject in a slavish fashion,' I explained. 'It's true that if physical work is performed under compulsion, the body isn't impaired, but compulsory intellectual work never remains in the mind.'

'True,' he said.

'So the educational environment in which you foster your younger generation, Glaucon,' I said, 'should be light-hearted 537a rather than authoritarian. This will also help you to see what natural abilities every one of them has.'

'That's plausible,' he said.

'And do you remember', I continued, 'our assertion that the children should be taken on horseback to observe warfare* and, if they can do so safely, should also be taken up to the front and given a taste of blood, as young dogs are?'

'Yes, I do,' he replied.

'Well, any of them who demonstrates a high degree of proficiency in his exercising, studying, and facing fear should be enrolled in a special unit,' I said.

'At what age, do you mean?' he asked.   b

'When they've finished with the basics of physical exercise,' I said. 'The point is that it's out of the question for them to do anything else during the period in question, which may last for two or three years, because exertion and exhaustion don't mix with intellectual work. Also, one of the crucial ways we'll be testing them will be by seeing what impression each of them gives during the period when they're concentrating on physical exercise.'*

'Of course,' he said.

'After this period', I went on, 'a select group of the twenty-year-olds will receive promotion above the rest, and will be required to consolidate the subjects they were taught unsystematically as children until they gain an overview of the c relationships these subjects have to one another and to reality.'

'Yes,' he said, 'it's only when this has occurred that one's learning has a secure foundation.'

'And it's also the main way of testing whether or not someone is naturally suited for dialectic,' I said, 'since the ability to take an overview is the distinguishing mark of a dialectician.'

'I agree,' he said.

'What you'll have to do, then,' I said, 'is look out for this quality and try to see which of your people are particularly d capable in this respect, and have staying power in their intellectual work, in warfare, and in their other duties. These are the ones who, once they're past the age of thirty, you must select from among the select and promote even further; and you must subject them to dialectical training, to try to see which of them is capable of letting go of vision and of sense-perception in general, and can proceed to the realm of truth and reality itself. But you have to be very careful at this point, Glaucon.'

'Why?' he asked.

e 'Don't you realize how much harm occurs in the way dialectic is practised nowadays?' I said.

'What harm?' he asked.

'People become thoroughly rebellious,' I answered.

'They certainly do,' he said.

'Well, it's not a surprising state for them to get into, is it, do you think?' I asked. 'Can't you forgive them?'

'Why should I?' he asked.

'Here's an analogy,' I said. 'Suppose an illegitimate child is
538a brought up in affluent circumstances, in the midst of a large, powerful family with hordes of flatterers;* and suppose that, when he grows up, he becomes aware that he isn't the child of his self-styled parents, but can't find out who his real parents are. Can you guess what his attitude would be towards the flatterers and towards his surrogate parents when he didn't know that this wasn't his rightful place, and then when he learnt the truth? Or shall I tell you what I suspect?'

'Please do,' he said.

'I suspect', I said, 'that, before he learnt the truth, he'd be
b more inclined to respect his father and mother and the rest of the people he'd presumed to be his relatives than he would the flatterers, and less inclined to turn a blind eye to any need of theirs, and to do or say anything rebellious to them, and to disobey them in any important respect.'

'That's likely,' he said.

'However, once he'd become aware of the true state of affairs, I suspect he'd leave off giving them his respect and concern, and transfer his attention to the flatterers instead. He'd listen to them more than he did before, model his lifestyle
c on theirs, openly spend time with them, and not have the

slightest interest in that father of his and the rest of his pseudo-family—unless he's inherently a person of high principles.'

'Yes, that's exactly what would happen,' he agreed. 'But how does this analogy apply to people who are exposed to rational arguments?'

'Like this. From childhood, we've held certain views about moral and right conduct. These views formed the environment of our upbringing, we are subject to them as we are to our parents, and we obey them and respect them.'

'True.'

'Now, there are also enjoyable practices which run counter d to this moral code. These practices flatter and tempt our minds, but anyone with even a scrap of restraint doesn't give in, and continues instead to respect and obey those traditional views.'

'True.'

'Well, suppose', I went on, 'that the kind of person we're imagining is faced with a question like "What is right?" He answers that it consists in the conduct enjoined by the originator of his society's code, but the argument proves him wrong, and proves him wrong again and again, until he's battered into thinking that this code is no more right than wrong. Then the same happens with morality and goodness e and all the qualities he used particularly to respect.* What do you think the consequences of this are on his behaviour? What will happen to his respect and obedience?'

'He'll inevitably become more disrespectful and disobedient than he was before,' he said.

'Now, when he's changed his mind about what to respect and about his former familiar code,' I said, 'and at the same time can't discover the truth, where can he turn? Doesn't it only make sense to think of him being seduced by the tempting 539a lifestyle?'

'Yes,' he said.

'So he'll stop being law-abiding and become rebellious.'

'Inevitably.'

'People who are exposed to rational arguments, then,' I said, 'are quite likely to rebel and, as I suggested a moment ago, we should forgive them, don't you think?'

'Yes, and feel sorry for them,' he added.

'So if you want to avoid having to feel sorry for your thirty-year-olds, then you must handle rational arguments with the utmost circumspection, mustn't you?'

'Yes, definitely,' he said.

b   'And one important precaution you can take is not to let them get wind of rational arguments when they're young, don't you think? I mean, I'm sure you've noticed how when adolescents get their first taste of argumentation, they abuse it and treat it like a game. They can't find any other use for it except disputation;* they use knock-down arguments which they borrow from others to demolish people's positions. Like puppies, they love to tug away at anyone they come across and to tear his argument to shreds with theirs.'

'Yes, it's incredible,' he said.

'So before long—once they've demolished a lot of arguments
c and often had their own demolished as well—they find they've radically changed their minds about everything. And the result of this is that people take a dim view of them, and of philosophy in general.'

'You're absolutely right,' he said.

'An older person, however,' I went on, 'is hardly likely to succumb to this insanity: he'd sooner resemble someone who's willing to practise dialectic and look for the truth, than someone who trivializes everything with his game-playing and disputatiousness. His own behaviour will be more moderate,
d and he'll increase, rather than decrease, dialectic's reputation.'

'Right,' he said.

'And hasn't the point of what we've been saying been to get rid of the current practice of letting absolutely anyone, even when entirely unsuitable, come to rational argumentation, and to ensure that it is only orderly and stable people who get involved in it?'

'Yes,' he said.

'Suppose, in order to complement the way physical exercise was approached, someone were to study, with constancy and concentration, nothing but rational argumentation for twice as many years as he devoted to physical exercise. Would that do?'

e   'Do you mean six years or four years?'* he asked.

'Why don't you just make it five?' I suggested. 'You see, the next thing you have to do is make them go back down into that cave and force them to take charge of warfare and whatever other areas young people should be responsible for, so that they gain just as much practical experience as everyone else. Moreover, while they hold these positions of responsibility, you'd better test them to see whether they remain unmoved by all the various temptations they're exposed to, or whether they 540a go astray.'

'How long do you suggest for this?' he asked.

'Fifteen years,' I replied. 'Not all of them will reach their fiftieth year unscathed and with absolutely outstanding performances in every task they undertook and branch of knowledge they studied, but you can guide those who do to the climax of their lives. You must make them open up the beam of their minds and look at the all-embracing source of light, which is goodness itself.* Once they've seen it, they must use it as a reference-point and spend the rest of their lives ordering the b community, its members, and themselves. They take turns at this: they spend most of their time doing philosophy, but when their turn comes, then for the community's sake they become involved in its affairs and slog away at them as rulers. This is something they do as an obligation, not as a privilege. Because they have this attitude, they're constantly training others to follow suit, and once they've completed this process and have bequeathed guardianship of the community to others in their place, they depart for a new home in the Isles of the Blessed.* And the community constructs public memorials and establishes ceremonies in their honour, and treats them (if the Delphic oracle gives its blessing) as deities,* or otherwise as c happy and godlike men.'

'You've created an image of the rulers which makes them as thoroughly attractive as a master sculptor makes his statues, Socrates,' he remarked.

'And there are female rulers too,* Glaucon,' I said. 'Please don't think that what I've been saying doesn't apply equally to any women in the community with the required natural abilities.'

'That's right,' he said. 'Men and women will share everything equally, as we explained.'

'Well then, do you agree that our community and political d system weren't just wishful thinking?' I said. 'The community may be difficult to realize, but it's feasible; the essential

275

prerequisite, as we've insisted, is that genuine philosophers—
one or more of them—wield power. They have to be born in a
community, but grow up to regard the political rewards
currently available to them as despicable, as mean and
worthless. Instead, they have to find nothing more valuable
e than integrity and its rewards, and nothing more important and
essential than morality, which they serve and foster as they take
in hand every detail of their community.'

'How do they go about this?' he asked.

'First, they banish everyone over the age of ten into the
541a countryside,' I answered. 'Then they take charge of the
community's children and make sure that they're beyond the
reach of existing conventions, which their parents adhere to,
and bring them up under their own customs and laws, which
are similar to the ones we were describing before. That's the
quickest and simplest way* for the community and political
system we've been discussing to be established, to attain
happiness, and to benefit the people among whom they occur.'

'Yes, definitely,' he said. 'And I think you've given an
b excellent explanation of how our community would be realized,
if it ever were.'

'So is that it, then?' I asked. 'Have we finished discussing this
community of ours and its human counterpart? I mean, I
suppose it's obvious what kind of person we'll claim he has to
be.'

'Yes, it is,' he said. 'And, to answer your question, yes, I
think we've finished.'

Chapter 11

Warped Minds, Warped Societies

Plato now returns to the question of morality, apparently interrupted since the end of Chapter 6. He has said what it is, but he has yet to show that it benefits its possessor. Since the best form of society and type of individual have already been described, he proposes to describe debased versions, and to slant the descriptions so that the question of their relative happiness may become clear. This will involve some rather schematic and simplistic psychology based on the analogy between communities and types of individual, but also some brilliant and much-admired vignettes of these individuals.

'All right, Glaucon. Now, we concluded that the best 543a
government of a community depends on sharing women,
children, and education in all its aspects, and by the same token
on peacetime and wartime functions being performed by
women as well as by men, and on their kings being those who
have proved outstanding at philosophy and warfare.'

'Yes, we did,' he agreed.

'And we also agreed that, once they're in office, the rulers are b
to take the militia and settle them in the kind of quarters we
described earlier—that is, where nothing is exclusive to any
individual, but everything is shared. Furthermore, apart from
their quarters being like this, we also drew some conclusions
about their possession of property, as you may remember.'

'I do,' he said. 'We thought that, contrary to current practice,
none of them should own any property, but that as warriors
and guardians they should be paid by everyone else an annual
stipend for their guarding, consisting of the provisions c
appropriate to their duties, and that they should look after the
community as a whole, as well as themselves.'

'That's right,' I said. 'But now that we've finished with all
that, let's try to resume our journey by recalling where we were
when we took the side-turning that led us here.'

'That's no problem,' he said. 'You were talking, much as you are now, as if your discussion of our community were complete. You were saying that you'd call good the kind of community you'd described at that point, and its human

d counterpart—even though, as it turns out, you were in a position to describe an even better community and an even

544a better person.* Anyway, you claimed that, given the rightness of our community, all the rest were flawed, and you said, if my memory serves me well, that of these remaining political systems, four types would be worth mentioning, and that we ought to see where they and their human counterparts go wrong, so that we can decide whether or not the best person is also the happiest person, and the worst the unhappiest, which we can only do once we've seen all these types of human being and reached agreement as to which is best and which is worst. I had just asked which four political systems you had in mind,

b when Polemarchus and Adeimantus interrupted. You responded to them, and that's how the discussion reached this point.'

'Your memory is spot on,' I said.

'Why don't you resume your stance, then, as if you were a wrestler? I'll ask the same question, and you can have a go at saying what you were poised to say then.'

'I'll try,' I said.

'In fact, speaking for myself, I really would like to hear which four political systems you had in mind,' he said.

c 'I should be able to tell you that without any difficulty,' I said, 'since the ones I mean are recognized political systems with names. There's that popular favourite,* the Cretan and Spartan system; the second one, which is also the second most popular, is the thoroughly rotten system known as oligarchy; then next there's democracy, oligarchy's adversary; and the fourth, the ultimate political disease, which leaves all the rest behind, is noble dictatorship. Can you think of any other type of political system which counts as a distinct variety? I mean,

d there are autocracies and monarchies which can be bought, and other political systems (to be found among both Greeks and non-Greeks) which equally fall somewhere among the ones I've mentioned.'*

'Yes, there are all sorts of odd systems one hears about,' he remarked.

'Well, do you appreciate that there are bound to be as many types of human being as there are of political system?' I asked. 'Or do you imagine that political systems somehow come into being from oak or from rock,* rather than from the characters of the communities' inhabitants? If one type of character outweighs the rest, so to speak, then don't you think it draws all the other types with it?'   e

'Yes, that's the only possible way in which political systems arise,' he agreed.

'So if there are five types of society, then any given individual should also have one of five kinds of mental trait.'

'Naturally.'

'Now, we've already described the individual counterpart to aristocracy,* and no one could fault our claim that it's a person of goodness and morality.'

'Yes, we have.'   545a

'So next we'd better describe the inferior kinds of person— the competitive and ambitious person who corresponds to the Spartan system, then the oligarchic, democratic, and dictatorial types. This will enable us to see which of them is the least moral; we can then contrast him with the most moral type, and that will complete our enquiry into how absolute morality compares with absolute immorality in respect of the happiness or unhappiness they entail for people who possess them. Then we'll be in a position either to follow Thrasymachus and pursue immorality, or to follow the argument which is developing at the moment and pursue morality. Do you think that's what   b we'd better do?'

'Yes, most definitely,' he said.

'Well, we started off by looking at characteristics as they manifested in societies, before turning to individuals, on the grounds that this would make it easier for us to see them. So we'd better continue by looking first at the "ambitious" political system—I can't think of another familiar word for it: perhaps we should call it "timocracy" or "timarchy".* We'll examine its human counterpart, by comparing him with it; then oligarchy and an oligarchic person; next we'll look at   c democracy and try to form an impression of a democratic person; and in the fourth place we'll turn our attention to dictatorial government of a community and then we'll look at a dictatorial temperament. Don't you think this is how we should try to gain the competence to assess the matter before us?'

'Yes, that's a perfectly reasonable way to go about the investigation and the assessment,' he replied.

Time and again, Plato has stressed the stability of his 'aristocratic' community, in such a way as to make its degeneration seem unlikely. But nothing in this world is permanent, and the rulers of the aristocracy will, sooner or later, be less than perfect. 'Timarchy' will take the place of 'aristocracy'. Timarchy is rule by people governed by the passionate part of the mind, who value military ideals and success, but have begun to be corrupted by money. The degeneration will begin when the community ceases to be a unity and ceases to keep to the Principle of Specialization. The behaviour of the corresponding timarchic individual is based on the fact that he is torn between the highest and lowest parts of his mind, and so compromises on the intermediate part.

'All right, then,' I said. 'Let's try to account for the transition from aristocracy to timocracy. I suppose this much is straightforward—that all political change is due to the actual
d power-possessing members of society themselves, when conflict arises among them. Even if there are very few of them, instability is out of the question as long as they're of one mind.* Yes?'

'Yes.'

'How, then, Glaucon,' I asked, 'will change become a feature of our community? How will conflict arise between and among the auxiliaries and the rulers? Perhaps you'd like us to imitate Homer and pray for the Muses to tell us "how conflict first
e occurred",* and to have them speak in a pompous and highfalutin fashion, using the kind of semi-serious tone one uses when teasing and making fun of children.'

'What do you mean?'

546a 'Something like this. Hard though it may be for a community with this structure to undergo change, yet everything that is born must die, and so even this kind of structure will not last for ever, but will fall apart. This is how it will happen. Fertility and infertility are not restricted to plants: surface-dwelling creatures also periodically experience both mental and physical fertility and infertility, each time their cycles complete a revolution. Short-lived creatures have short cycles, long-lived ones the opposite. Where the human species is concerned, despite the cleverness of the people you've trained to be in charge of your community, they'll still fail to catch the times of fertility and barrenness, although they supplement the evidence of their senses with rationality. They'll mistime things and produce children when they shouldn't.

'Now, a divine creature's cycle is defined by a perfect number;* but a human creature's number is the smallest one in which increases entailing potential and realized potential gain three intervals and four terms from among the causes of similarity and dissimilarity, and from among the things that increase and decrease, and so make everything mutually conformable and rational. The base numbers involved—3 in c relation to 4, along with 5—produce two harmonies when they are increased three times. One harmony is made up of a factor squared, times a hundred times itself; the other harmony is in a sense made up of equal factors, but in a sense of unequal factors—one factor being 100 of the numbers from the rational diagonals of 5, each diminished by 1 (or 100 of the numbers from the irrational diagonals of 5, each diminished by 2), and the other factor being 100 of the cubes of 3.*

'The geometrical number* produced is responsible for this area—for the quality of children born—and when your guardians are unaware of this, they pair men and women d sexually on the wrong occasions,* and the resulting children will not be naturally gifted or fortunate. It may be that the preceding generation will choose only the best of these children for office, but all the same they won't be as good as they should be, and when they in turn inherit their fathers' positions of authority, despite being guardians they'll begin to neglect us: they'll underrate the importance of cultural studies, and then of physical exercise, and consequently the young people of your community will become rather uncultured. As a result, the next generation of rulers to be appointed will not be particularly good at guarding, in the sense that they won't be so good at assessing those castes of Hesiod's and yours*—the castes of e gold and silver, of copper and iron. Iron will get all mixed up 547a with silver, copper with gold; discrepancy and discordant incongruity will occur, and they always breed hostility and antagonism, wherever they occur. It has to be admitted that "this is the lineage"* of conflict, whatever the circumstances of its occurrence on any given occasion.'

'Yes, we'll endorse their opinion,' he said.

'We have to,' I said. 'They are the Muses, after all.'

b   'What are they going to say next?' he asked.

'Once conflict has been born,' I said, 'the two castes start to pull in different directions. The iron and copper caste incline towards business and want to possess land, houses, gold, and silver. The gold and silver caste, on the other hand, don't feel in need of money: thanks to their innate wealth, they tend to be temperamentally attracted towards goodness and the traditional ways. Because of the tension and antipathy between them, they compromise by agreeing to assign themselves land

c and houses for private ownership,* and at the same time they subjugate their former friends and wards, whom they used to guard, and make them their dependants and slaves,* while they take responsibility for warfare and for guarding themselves against them.'

'Yes, I think that's the cause of the transition,' he agreed.

'And wouldn't this political system fall between aristocracy and oligarchy?' I asked.

'Yes.'

'Anyway, that's how the transition will take place. But once it has taken place, how will the community be governed?

d Perhaps the answer's obvious: won't it in some respects take after both oligarchy and the system which preceded it (since it falls between them), and in other respects have its own distinctive features?'

'Yes,' he answered.

'Now, there'll be respect for the rulers, and its militia won't get involved in any businesses like farming and manufacture, but will have arranged common mess-halls for themselves and will devote themselves to physical exercise and to training for war. In all these respects, it'll reflect the political system which preceded it, won't it?'

'Yes.'

e   'On the other hand, there'll be reluctance to choose men of knowledge for political office, since the only intellectuals within the community by then will be complex characters, lacking in robust directness. The community will incline towards the greater directness of passionate types, who are by their natures more suited for war than for peace; it will value the ruses and stratagems which war entails, and will spend all its time on 548a warfare. Most of these sorts of features will be peculiar to it, won't they?'

'Yes.'

'Furthermore,' I went on, 'the members of this kind of community will share with people under oligarchies a craving for money. They'll have a fanatical respect for gold and silver—but a furtive respect, because they'll have storerooms and vaults in their homes where they can put them and hide them away, and they'll also have surrounded their homes with walls, for all the world as if their houses were private dens within whose confines they can extravagantly spend their money on their b wives and anyone else they choose.'

'True,' he said.

'But because they value money and aren't open about possessing it, they'll actually be mean about it—although they'll be happy to satisfy their craving by spending other people's money. They'll pluck their pleasures in secret, hiding away from the law like children running and hiding from their father. The background to all this will be the fact that their education will have been forced on them, rather than finding willing ears, and this will be due to their neglect of the authentic Muse—and of her companions, reason and philosophy—and to their placing more value on physical c exercise than on cultural studies.'

'You're talking about a political system which is a thorough mixture of good and bad,' he remarked.

'Yes, it is a mixture,' I agreed, 'but thanks to the predominance of the passionate element, there's only one aspect which particularly stands out—all its competitiveness and ambition.'

'Yes, that's extremely noticeable,' he said.

'So much, then,' I said, 'for the origin and nature of this political system. I assume that a verbal sketch of the outline of the system will do, rather than filling in all the details, since d even a sketch will enable us to see where the extremes of human morality and immorality lie, and it would take for ever to go through every possible political system and human characteristic in minute detail.'

'Yes, that's right,' he said.

'What about the person who corresponds to this political system, then? What's his background? And what's he like?'

'I think he'd approximate pretty closely to Glaucon here,' said Adeimantus, 'with his competitiveness.'*

e   'Maybe he would in this respect,' I said, 'but there are traits he has which do not resemble any of Glaucon's, I think.'

'Which ones?'

'He's bound to be more obstinate,' I said, 'and to have spent less time on cultural studies. He'll approve of culture, however, and he'll enjoy listening to lectures, even though he won't be

549a any good at speaking himself. This kind of person will treat slaves harshly (rather than finding them beneath consideration, which is the attitude of a properly educated person), but he'll be gentle with those he likes. He'll be excessively submissive to authority, and ambitiously eager for authority himself. He'll regard military achievements as qualifying someone for political office, rather than ability at speaking and so on, and he'll be fond of sports and hunting.'

'Yes,' he said, 'because these are the characteristics of the political system we've been describing.'

'Now, as a young man,' I continued, 'a person of this type

b will disdain money, but the older he gets, the more he'll welcome it at every opportunity, don't you think? This is because his mercenary side will have come to the fore, and because his attitude towards goodness will be tainted, thanks to his lack of the best guardian.'

'What guardian is that?' asked Adeimantus.

'A mind which combines reason and culture,' I replied. 'It's only when this resides in someone throughout his life that his goodness is kept intact.'

'You're right,' he said.

'So that's what a timocratic person is like in his youth,' I said. 'And he is the counterpart to the kind of community we've been talking about.'

c 'Yes.'

'As for his background,' I went on, 'it's something like this.

284

As a young man, he's the son of a father who is good, but who lives in a badly governed community and therefore steers clear of status and office, and lawsuits and all that kind of involvement in public affairs, and is happy to be discounted and consequently to avoid all the nuisance of involvement.'

'Yes, but how does this produce a timocratic type?' he asked.

'It all starts', I explained, 'when he hears his mother* complaining that her husband doesn't have political power, and that this is why she is snubbed by all the other women. Then d she sees that he isn't especially interested in money, and plays no part in the fighting and mud-slinging that occur in private lawsuits or in political situations, and doesn't get worked up about all that kind of thing; she also notices that he's always minding his own business, and doesn't overrate her (not that he underrates her either). All this makes her cross and she tells him that his father isn't a real man, and that he's too nonchalant, and goes on and on with all the usual complaints women routinely come up with in these kinds of circumstances.'   e

'Yes, there are plenty of these typical complaints,' said Adeimantus.

'As you know, then,' I continued, 'even the supposedly loyal servants of this sort of man whisper the same kinds of things to his sons, and if the servants notice that a young man's father is failing to prosecute someone who owes him some money or is wronging him in some other way, they encourage the son to make sure that he gets even with all these people when he's an adult, and to be more of a man than his father. Outside of the 550a house, the young man hears and sees more of the same sort: he notices that people who mind their own business are regarded by the rest of the community as stupid and are despised, while those who don't are respected and admired. So, when the young man hears and sees all this, and also listens to what his father has to say, and sees his way of life from close quarters and compares it with the alternative, he is pulled in two directions: his father irrigates and nurtures his rational mind, b while everyone else nurtures the desirous and passionate parts of his mind. Now, he isn't a bad person, but he's been exposed to some bad influences, so he resolves these contrary impulses by reaching a compromise: he transfers authority within himself to the intermediate part of himself—the competitive and passionate part—and so he becomes a supercilious, ambitious man.'

'I think you've described his background perfectly,' he said.

c 'So there's our second political system and our second type of person,' I said.

'Yes,' he agreed.

After timarchy, oligarchy. This is not described neutrally as 'the rule of the few', otherwise Plato's aristocracy would be an oligarchy. It is rule by the wealthy few (i.e. plutocracy), who value money over goodness, and do not necessarily have the expertise rulership requires. They are governed by the third, acquisitive part of the mind. Even more than timarchy, oligarchy transgresses the two fundamental principles of the ideal state: it lacks unity, its members are not restricted to a single occupation, and they do not all contribute to the good of the whole. In fact, some of its members may lack any occupation at all. It is a society of 'drones'. There is a strong criminal element, which is barely suppressed. The psychology of the corresponding individual is an exact introjected counterpart to this oligarchic society.

'Next, to paraphrase Aeschylus, shall we "tell who else has been deployed, to stand before which community"*—or rather, shall we keep to our plan and speak of the community first?'

'Yes,' he said.

'I think that oligarchy would follow the kind of political system we've described.'

'But what kind of constitution do you mean by oligarchy?' he asked.

'A political system which is based on property value,' I

d replied, 'so that the rich have political power, and the poor are excluded from government.'

'I see,' he said.

'Hadn't we better explain the initial transition from timarchy to oligarchy?'

'Yes.'

'But even a blind man could see how it happens,' I said.

'How?'

'The downfall of timarchy is brought about by trying to keep that storeroom we spoke of—the one people have for their gold—full up. You see, first people invent ways to spend their money and they subvert the laws for this purpose, in the sense that they and their wives refuse to obey them.'

'That makes sense,' he said.

'Next, I suppose, everyone starts to look at everyone else e with envy, and that becomes the normal attitude.'

'That's likely.'

'And then', I said, 'they get more and more involved in making money; and the higher they rate money, the lower they rate goodness. I mean, isn't the difference between wealth and goodness analogous to them each lying in one of the pans of a pair of scales and constantly tending in opposite directions?'

'It certainly is,' he said.

'So if wealth and wealthy people are admired in a 551a community, then goodness and good people are despised there.'

'Obviously.'

'Now, you cultivate what you admire, whatever it may be, and ignore what you despise.'

'Yes.'

'So eventually they stop being competitive and ambitious, and become acquisitive and mercenary instead. They acclaim and admire anyone rich, and make it easy for him to gain political power, but they despise anyone poor.'

'Yes.'

'They then enact the legislation which is the distinctive feature of an oligarchic political system, in which they ordain a certain amount of money—a larger amount if the oligarchy is b more of an oligarchy, a smaller amount if it is less of one—and announce that only those whose property attains the ordained value shall play a part in government. They either use force of arms to get this legislation passed, or they've already used fear to make this kind of constitution a *fait accompli*. Do you agree?'

'Yes.'

'So that's more or less how it comes to be established.'

'Yes,' he said, 'but what kind of system is it? We said it was flawed*—what are these flaws?'   c

'You should start by thinking about its distinctive feature,' I said. 'I mean, what do you think it would be like if ships' captains were appointed in this way, because of the value of their property, and poverty ruled someone out even if he was a better captain?'

'Then people would have terrible voyages,' he said.

'And does the same go for positions of authority in other spheres?'

'I'd say so.'

'Except political power?' I asked. 'Or does it also apply to political power?'

'It applies there above all,' he said, 'because it's the most difficult and important kind of power there is.'

d 'That's the first major mistake oligarchy makes, then, apparently.'

'So it seems.'

'Well, here's another flaw, and I wonder if it's any less serious.'

'What is it?'

'That a community of this kind can't be single:* it's inevitably divided into the haves and the have-nots. They may live in the same place, but they're constantly plotting against one another.'

'No, that's certainly just as serious a flaw,' he said.

'Another deplorable feature is that they'd probably be incapable of going to war against an enemy. They could either arm the populace at large, in order to use them in the war—but

e that would inevitably give them more cause for fear than the enemy; or they could avoid using the populace, and then, when it came to actual fighting, they'd be revealed as true oligarchs!* At the same time their mercenary nature makes them unwilling to levy a war-tax.'

'That's no good.'

'Then there's something we've been expressing disapproval of all along—the fact that in this kind of political system

552a people won't stick to a single occupation, but will be farmers, businessmen, and soldiers at the same time. Do you think that's the right way to go about things?'

'No, I certainly don't.'

'Now, would you agree that this is the first political system to admit the ultimate evil?'

'What are you getting at?'

'It's possible for someone to sell everything (and for someone else to acquire his property) and continue to live in the community without being one of its limbs*—without being a businessman or a manufacturer, or in the cavalry or the heavy infantry. He'd be classified instead as impoverished and destitute.'

'Yes, this is the first system it could happen in,' he agreed.   b

'Anyway, that kind of thing isn't ruled out by an oligarchy, otherwise we wouldn't find both excessive affluence and utter poverty at the same time.'

'Right.'

'Now what do you think about this? Did the person we're imagining actually benefit his community in the respects we're considering* while he was well off and was spending his money? Or is it true to say that he was only a pseudo-ruler, and that in reality he didn't rule over the community or serve it in any capacity, but merely consumed whatever he could lay his hands on?'

'Yes, that's right,' he said. 'He wasn't an authentic ruler: he   c
was nothing but a consumer.'

'Shall we describe him as a drone, then?' I asked. 'His home is equivalent to the cell in a honeycomb where a drone is born, and he becomes the bane of his community as a drone becomes the bane of the hive.'

'I like that idea, Socrates,' he said.

'Now, the first variety of drones, Adeimantus—the ones with wings—have been denied stings by God. The second variety, however—the ones that go on foot—fall into two categories: some of them are stingless, but some have terrifying stings, don't they? The stingless ones end up in their old age as beggars, while everyone who's designated a criminal started life as one of the drones with stings. Yes?'   d

'True,' he said.

'It obviously follows,' I said, 'that any community where you can find beggars also has thieves, pickpockets, temple-robbers,* and perpetrators of similar crimes concealed somewhere about the place.'

'Yes, obviously,' he agreed.

'Well, don't you find beggars in communities which are governed by oligarchies?'

'Yes,' he said, 'just about everyone except for the rulers!'

e   'Isn't the implication of what we're saying that these communities also contain plenty of criminals with stings,' I asked, 'who are deliberately and forcibly repressed by the authorities?'

'Yes, it is,' he said.

'And we're claiming that the presence of these criminals is a direct result of lack of education, bad upbringing, and a bad political system?'

'We are.'

'There you are, then. That's what a community is like when it's governed by an oligarchy, and those are its major flaws—though there may be more.'

'That all sounds about right,' he said.

553a   'So much, then,' I concluded, 'for our description of the kind of political system which uses property value as a criterion for rulership, and which is called "oligarchy". Next, we'd better look at the background and nature of its human counterpart.'

'Yes.'

'The transition from a timocratic person to an oligarchic one invariably happens as follows, wouldn't you say?'

'How?'

'When a child is born to a timocratic man, he initially looks up to his father and follows in his footsteps. Later, however, he

b   sees him suddenly wrecked on some political reef, and watches as his father and all his property are washed overboard. His father might have been a military commander or held some other important position, and then have ended up in court as a result of sycophants* making trouble for him,† and been put to death or exiled or deprived of his citizenship and had all his property confiscated.'

'Yes, that's not at all impossible,' he said.

'The effect of seeing and experiencing all this, Adeimantus, and of losing his property, is (I should think) that the son gets

c   afraid and immediately tosses ambition and his passionate side headlong from the throne they'd been occupying in his mind. Laid low by poverty, he turns to tawdry commercial activities, and gradually accumulates wealth by thrift and hard work. Don't you think that under these circumstances he'd install his desirous and mercenary side on that throne? Don't you think he'd make it his internal equivalent of the Persian king, and deck it out with tiaras and necklaces and scimitars?'*

'I do,' he said.

'While his rational and passionate aspects, I imagine, are d made to sit on the ground on either side of the king's feet in abject servitude. The only calculations and researches he allows his rational mind to make are concerned with how to start with a little money and increase it, the only admiration and respect he allows his passionate side to feel are for wealth and wealthy people, and he restricts his ambition to the acquisition of money and to any means towards that end.'

'There's no transition so quick or so complete in its effects', he remarked, 'as when a young person becomes mercenary instead of ambitious.'

'So do you think we've found our oligarchic type?' I asked. e

'Well, he does evolve from the type who corresponds to the political system from which oligarchy evolves.'

'Let's see if he has similar characteristics, then.'

'All right.' 554a

'The first point of similarity is the supreme value he places on money, wouldn't you say?'

'Of course.'

'Then there's the fact that he's thrifty and hard-working. He satisfies only those of his desires which are essential, and suppresses all the rest (he thinks they're pointless), so as not to incur any further expenses.'

'Yes.'

'He's rather ascetic,' I said. 'He tries to make a profit out of every situation, and he's a hoarder—an attribute which is commonly admired in people. Aren't these the characteristics of the person who corresponds to the political system we've been b describing?'

'I'd say so,' he said. 'At any rate, money is the be-all and end-all for that community as well as for him.'

'It's because he never bothered about his education, I suppose,' I said.

'Yes, I think so,' he replied. 'Otherwise, he wouldn't have thought so highly of a blind person and made him the leader of his troupe.'*

'Good point,' I said. 'Now, what about this? Don't you think we should say that his lack of education engenders within him

drone-like desires—some in the beggarly mode, some in the
c criminal mode—which are forcibly and deliberately repressed,
on the whole?'

'I certainly do,' he replied.

'Do you know where you'll find these people behaving like
criminals?' I asked.

'Where?' he asked.

'When they're entrusted with the guardianship of orphans,
and when similar easy opportunities for wrongdoing come their
way.'*

'True.'

'This makes it clear that it's only because some remnant of
decency makes them forcibly repress their evil desires that they
have a reputation for fair dealing in other contexts. And they
d repress these desires not because they're convinced that they
should, or because they've used reason to tame them, but
because they have no choice and because they're afraid—afraid
for the rest of their property. Do you agree?'

'Yes, definitely,' he said.

'But when it's a case of them spending someone else's money,
Adeimantus,' I went on, 'then, I swear, the drone-like desires
most of them contain will be exposed.'

'Yes,' he said, 'I couldn't agree more.'

'So internal conflict will characterize this kind of person: he
isn't single, he's divided into two. His condition is simply that
e his better desires by and large control his worse ones.'

'True.'

'That is why, in my opinion, although this sort of person
gives a better impression than lots of people do, he still comes
nowhere near true goodness, which requires mental unity and
harmony.'

'I agree.'

'Moreover, because he's mean about money, he doesn't put
himself personally on the line and strive to win some political
555a victory or generally to gain public recognition for good deeds.
He's reluctant to spend money for the sake of prestige or for
anything else like that which involves rivalry against others,
because he's afraid of waking up desires which would require
him to spend money and of summoning up their assistance in a
competitive situation. So he fights in true oligarchic fashion,

with just a few parts of himself,* and he's usually defeated—but rich.'

'That's right,' he said.

'So we have no reason now to doubt the correspondence between a community governed by an oligarchy and a mean, mercenary type of person, do we?' I asked.   b

'None at all,' he said.

After oligarchy, democracy. Plato is obviously thinking to some extent of the system familiar to him from the Athens of his day. The brutality of oligarchy leads (usually) to a violent revolution and the establishment of democracy, which is a kind of free-for-all. It does not correspond to rule by any of the three divisions of the mind: it is disarray, the rule of none of the parts of the mind, or of different parts at different times. The community has no unity, and anyone can do any job he likes—even govern without the required expertise. The psychology of the democratic individual is characterized by a similar lack of discipline. Each passing whim is indulged, just as in a democracy leaders come and go.

'Next, I suppose, we'd better try to see how democracy starts, and what its characteristics are once it exists. That will help us identify the corresponding individual, and then we can assess his merits, relative to those of the other types.'

'Yes, that would be in keeping with what we've been doing so far,' he said.

'Don't you think,' I said, 'that the transition from oligarchy to democracy is a result of people being insatiably greedy for what they've come to accept as good—that they ought to get as rich as they possibly can?'

'In what sense?'

'The way I see it is that because political power within the   c
community depends on the possession of wealth, the rulers aren't disposed to curb by legal means the undisciplined elements of the younger generation, to prevent them from spending their money and ruining their estates, because this enables them to buy up those estates and to loan money at interest, and so get even richer and gain even more public standing.'

'That's extremely plausible.'

'We need no further evidence, then, for the impossibility of

the citizen body of a community simultaneously rating affluence highly and being adequately self-disciplined:* they are bound
d to neglect either one or the other.'

'Yes, that's clear enough,' he said.

'Now, the negligent sanctioning of indiscipline which occurs within oligarchies has been known in the past to reduce men of some calibre to poverty.'

'It certainly has.'

'There they squat in the community, I imagine, equipped with their stings—and with weapons. Some are in debt, some have lost their citizenship, some are enduring both these hardships. In their hatred of the people who have acquired their property, they long for revolution, and plot against them and
e everyone else as well.'

'True.'

'But their targets, stooped businessmen that they are, appear not to notice. They continue to inject the venom of money into any remaining member of the community who submits to them, they continue to collect compound rates of interest, the offspring of the loan,* and they continue to fill the community
556a with drones and beggars.'

'Of course they do,' he said.

'Nor do they show any inclination to extinguish the blaze of this kind of trouble', I went on, 'by banning indiscriminate usage of one's assets or by some alternative legislation which gets rid of behaviour of that sort.'

'What alternative legislation?'

'It's not as effective as the first option, but it does force the members of a community to cultivate goodness. I mean, if there were a rule to the effect that most categories of voluntary
b contract should be entered upon at the lender's own risk, then the pursuit of money within the community would become less shameless, and fewer evils of the kind we've been talking about would develop.'

'Considerably fewer,' he said.

'As things are, however,' I said, 'it's thanks to the rulers of the community—for all the kinds of reasons we've been describing—that their subjects are in the state they're in. Meanwhile, they make themselves and their families ... well, their children never know what it's like to work, physically or

mentally, so they become spoilt and too soft and lazy to resist c
pleasure and pain, don't they?'

'Of course.'

'And they themselves ignore everything except making
money: there's nothing to tell between them and the poor in
terms of how little attention they pay to goodness, is there?'

'No, there isn't.'

'So this is the basis on which the rulers and their subjects
meet one another, as they walk in the streets or come together
under any circumstances—for a show, say, or as fellow sailors
or fellow soldiers on a campaign. Even in the teeth of danger,
they eye one another; but there's no way that the poor are d
despised by the rich in this situation. Poor people tend to be
lean and sun-tanned, and when they stand in the battle-line
next to the rich with their indoor pallor and plentiful extra
flesh, they notice their breathlessness and utter ineptitude.
Don't you think they'll conclude that it's their own cowardice
that has allowed the rich to get rich, and they'll get together in
private and tell one another, "They're ours for the taking.
There's nothing to them"?'

'I'm sure that's what they do,' he said.

'Now, it takes only a slight external influence to push an
unhealthy body towards illness, and sometimes nothing
external need be involved at all for the body's elements to start
fighting one another. Likewise, a community which is in a
similarly unhealthy state needs only a slight pretext—one party
might bring in reinforcements from an external oligarchy, or
the other from an external democracy—to fall ill and start
fighting with itself, and sometimes no external influence at all is
needed for conflict to begin. Do you agree?'

'Definitely.'   557a

'So democracy starts, in my opinion, when the poor members
of the community are victorious. They kill some of the rich,
they expel others, and they give everyone who's left equal social
and political rights: in a democratic system governmental posts
are usually decided by lot.'

'Yes,' he said, 'that's how democracy is founded, but it might
not involve force of arms: fear might have been used to drive
their enemies away.'

'All right,' I said, 'but what kind of constitution is it? What's b a democratic political system actually like? I mean, this is how we'll learn about the corresponding democratic individual, obviously.'

'Obviously,' he agreed.

'Well, in the first place, the members of the community are autonomous, aren't they? The community is informed by independence and freedom of speech, and everyone has the right to do as he chooses, doesn't he?'

'That's the claim, anyway,' he answered.

'And given this right, then clearly every individual can make for himself the kind of life which suits him.'

'Clearly.'

c 'I should think, then, that there'd be a wider variety of types of people in this society than in any other.'

'Of course there would.'

'It's probably the most gorgeous political system there is,' I continued. 'Its beauty comes from the fact that it is adorned with every species of human trait, as a cloak might be adorned with every species of flower. And I suppose', I added, 'that plenty of people would find it highly attractive, just as women and children are attracted by the sight of colourful variety.'

'Yes, a great many would,' he said.

d 'It's a good place to look for a constitution, Adeimantus, as well,' I said.

'Why?'

'Because it's so open that it contains every type of political system there is. For anyone wanting to construct a community, as we were a short while ago, a visit to a democratically governed community is essential, to help him choose the kind he likes. It's a sort of general store for political systems: you can visit it, make your choice, and then found your community.'

e 'Yes, I suppose it would be easy to find samples,' he said.

'You're not forced to hold political office in this kind of community,' I said, 'even if you'd be good at it; you're not forced to be a subject either, unless you want to. You don't have to go to war when there's a war on, or to keep the peace when everyone else is, if peace isn't to your liking. Then again, even if you're legally forbidden to play a part in governmental 558a or judicial procedures, you can still do both, if you feel like it.

296

Isn't this an extraordinarily pleasant way to spend one's life, in the short term?'

'Yes, probably,' he said, 'but not in the long term.'

'And what about the exquisite calmness of some condemned criminals? I'm sure it's within your experience of this kind of society how people who've been sentenced to death or exile still stay on and go about their daily business in full view of everyone. No one cares or notices as they roam around, as invisible as the dead.'

'Yes, this is not uncommon,' he said.

'One could hardly call this system's attitude towards the b
principles we took seriously when we were founding our community pedantic—"flexible" and "high-handed" would be more accurate. We said that no one could be good (short of having been born with really exceptional talents), unless even his childhood games had taken place within a good environment and his way of life had been the same. This political system, however, arrogantly spurns all of that, and doesn't care what kinds of provenance people had before coming to government; as long as someone claims to be sympathetic to the general populace, he is honoured within this c
political system.'*

'A very vulgar way of going about things,' he commented.

'So these are democracy's features—these and others like them,' I said. 'It looks as though it's an enjoyable, lax, and variegated kind of political system, which treats everyone as equal, whether or not they are.'*

'Yes, this is all perfectly familiar,' he said.

'Now, what do you think the corresponding private individual is like?' I asked. 'I suppose we'd better start by considering his background, as we did in the case of the political system.'

'Yes,' he said.

'Here's my idea. Any son born to that mean, oligarchic character would, I imagine, be brought up by his father to d
behave in the same way.'

'Naturally.'

'So he too would forcibly control his desires for any pleasures which involve spending money rather than making it—that is, for the pleasures which have been classified as unnecessary.'

'Obviously he would,' he agreed.

'Shall we start by defining what we mean by necessary and unnecessary desires, then?' I asked. 'We don't want our conversation to be shrouded in obscurity.'

'Yes, let's,' he replied.

e 'Wouldn't it be right to describe as necessary any desires which we're incapable of stopping, and any whose satisfaction is beneficial to us? I mean, both these categories of desire* are essential to human nature, wouldn't you say?'

'Definitely.'

559a 'We'd be right to think of them in terms of necessity, then.'

'Yes.'

'What about desires which can be dispensed with (given training from childhood onwards) and whose presence certainly does no good, and may even do harm? Wouldn't we be right to call them unnecessary?'

'Yes, we would.'

'Shall we find an example of each type, so that we can get a rough idea of their nature?'

'We'd better.'

'Don't you think the desire for eating (provided it doesn't go beyond what's required for a healthy physical condition), the

b desire simply for bread and savouries,* is a necessary one?'

'Yes, I do.'

'In fact, the desire for bread is necessary in both senses: it's beneficial, and it's impossible for a living creature to stop it.'†

'Yes.'

'Whereas the desire for savouries is necessary only as an aid towards physical fitness.'

'Yes.'

'What about the desire for more food than this, however, or for a varied diet? It can usually be eliminated by the habit of restraint, learnt young in life, and it's harmful to both the body and the mind (in the context of intelligence and self-discipline),

c so we wouldn't be wrong to call it unnecessary, would we?'

'No, that would be perfectly correct.'

'Shall we say that unnecessary desires involve spending money, while necessary desires help one work and therefore make money?'

'Of course.'

'And doesn't the same principle apply to the desire for sex, and desire in general?'

'Yes.'

'So, to put this in the context of a distinction we drew earlier, the type of person we've been calling a drone is overflowing with these pleasures and desires, and is ruled by the unnecessary ones, whereas the mean, oligarchic type is ruled by the necessary ones. Right?' d

'No doubt about it.'

'Let's return, then, to the transition from the oligarchic type to the democratic one,' I said. 'It seems to me that it invariably happens as follows.'

'How?'

'When a young person, whose upbringing has been as uncultured and mean as we were saying a short while ago, tastes the drones' honey and starts to associate with ferocious, dangerous beasts who are capable of arranging for him pleasures of every conceivable kind, form, and description— that, I suggest, is how the transition begins from an internal e oligarchic state to a democratic one.'[†]

'It's almost inevitable,' he said.

'Now, we found that the transition occurs at a political level when one party is helped by like-minded reinforcements from outside. In the same way, doesn't our young man change when one of his aspects is supported from outside by desires of the same persuasion and breed?'

'Absolutely.'

'And if his oligarchic aspect is reinforced in response to this threat, as a result of his being scolded and ticked off by his father or by the rest of his relatives, I should think the upshot 560a would be conflict and counter-conflict, an internal civil war.'

'Of course it would.'

'Sometimes, I imagine, the democratic aspect is routed by the oligarchic aspect, and some of his desires are killed or expelled. This happens when inhibitions are implanted in the young man's mind, and he puts his life in order again.'

'Yes, that sometimes happens,' he said.

'Then later, I suppose, the father's ignorance of how to bring up his child leads to other desires, of the same breed as the b exiled ones, growing up and becoming plentiful and powerful.'

'Yes, that tends to happen,' he said.

'They draw him back to his old associates, and these secret liaisons result in the birth of a horde of them.'

'Of course.'

'In the end, I suppose, they seize the fortress in the young man's mind and find it deserted: it holds no information of value, no sound habits and true ideas—none of the sentinels and guardians which best protect the minds of men who find favour in God's sight.'

c 'Yes, they are by far the best,' he agreed.

'So false and specious ideas and thoughts charge up the hill and occupy the young man's fortress instead of these sentinels.'

'I'm sure you're right,' he said.

'Then he returns to those lotus-eaters* and lives with them openly. If his relatives send reinforcements for the mean part of his mind, those specious ideas shut the gates of the royal fortress within him. Not only do they not let these reinforcements in, but they also refuse to accept any mediation

d by older people from outside the family. Once they've won the war, they denounce inhibition as simple-mindedness, deprive it of rights, and send it out into exile; they call self-control "cowardice", drag its name in the gutter, and then expel it; they perpetuate the view that moderation shows lack of style and that frugality is stinginess, and then, with the help of a horde of futile desires, they banish them beyond their borders.'

'They certainly do.'

'Once they've taken over the mind of the neophyte, and

e purged and purified it for the great mysteries, they next waste no time before recalling from exile insubordination, disorder, extravagance, and uninhibitedness. They parade them in glory, with chaplets on their heads and with a full complement of attendants. They sing the praises of these qualities and gloss over their true nature: they call insubordination "erudition", disorder "freedom", extravagance "magnificence", and

561a uninhibitedness "courage". Isn't this', I asked, 'more or less how a young person exchanges conditioning by necessary desires for the permissiveness and laxity of unnecessary, futile pleasures?'

'Yes, you've explained it very well,' he said.

'From then on, I imagine, he spends as much money, effort,

and time in his life on unnecessary pleasures as on necessary ones. With luck, however—and if he doesn't overdo the high life—and if, when he's older and the main disturbance has passed, he allows the exiles back to some extent and doesn't b succumb utterly to the invaders, then he finds a way of life which involves a balance of pleasures. He submits to every passing pleasure as its turn comes to hold office, as it were, until it has been satisfied, and then submits to the next one, and so on. He doesn't deprive any pleasure of its rights, but tends all of them equally.'

'Yes.'

'And', I continued, 'he refuses to listen to—to let into his fortress—the truth of the idea that there are differences between pleasures. Some are the result of fine, good desires, c and these are worth cultivating and valuing; but some are the result of bad desires, and these are to be curbed and kept down. He denies this, however, and insists that they are all alike and of equal value.'*

'Yes, I quite agree,' he said. 'That's his attitude, and that's what he does.'

'So that's how he lives,' I said. 'He indulges in every passing desire that each day brings. One day he gets drunk at a party, the next day he's sipping water and trying to lose weight; then again, he sometimes takes exercise, sometimes takes things easy d without a care in the world, and sometimes he's apparently a student of philosophy. At frequent intervals, he gets involved in community affairs, and his public speaking and other duties keep him leaping around here, there, and everywhere. If military types arouse his admiration, he inclines towards the military life; if it's businessmen, he's all for business. His lifestyle has no rhyme or reason, but he thinks it enjoyable, free, and enviable and he never dispenses with it.'

'You've given a perfect description of an egalitarian,' he said. e

'Yes,' I said, 'and I think he's also multi-hued and multi-faceted, as gorgeous and varied a patchwork as that community is. His way of life can be admired by many men and women, because he contains examples of so many political systems and walks of life.'*

'Yes, he does,' he agreed.

'I suggest, then, that we designate this type of individual the 562a

301

counterpart to democracy and assume that we'd be correct to call him the democratic type.'

'I agree,' he said.

After democracy, dictatorship. If democracy is the idle indulgence and satisfaction of every kind of pleasure, the dictatorial type is driven by insatiable, base pleasures alone. He is so extreme that he cannot be equated with one of the three divisions of the mind: he is a criminal, beyond social castes. The three layers of Plato's imaginary community find a vague reflection in the fact that a democratic society consists of wealthy people, demagogues, and the general populace. The demagogues side with the people, so it is basically a case of rich versus poor—and again there is no unity. The poor find themselves a champion, who acquires a taste for power and gradually becomes an autocratic, bloodthirsty dictator, who is surrounded by a bodyguard of ex-slaves and mercenaries, loathed by anyone with any goodness, and whose subjects can only be described as slaves.

'All that's left for us to do, then,' I said, 'is describe the political system and the individual which are the ultimate in excellence—dictatorship and the dictator.'

'Exactly,' he said.

'All right, then. How does dictatorship begin, Adeimantus? I mean, apart from the fact that we can be pretty certain that it evolves out of democracy.'

'Yes, that's clear.'

'I wonder whether dictatorship evolves out of democracy in
b more or less the same way that democracy evolves out of oligarchy.'

'How is that?'

'There is something', I said, 'which the members of an oligarchy have come to accept as good, and which is the *raison d'être* of oligarchy. This is wealth, isn't it?'

'Yes.'

'And it is insatiable greed for wealth—being too busy making money to pay attention to anything else—which causes its downfall, we found.'

'True,' he said.

'So what I'm wondering is whether democracy's downfall is also brought about by insatiable greed for what it defines as good.'

'What's that, do you think?'

'Freedom,' I replied. 'I'm sure you've been in a community with a democratic government and heard them claim that there is nothing finer than freedom, and that this is why democracy is c the only suitable environment for a free man.'

'Yes, one hears the claim repeatedly,' he said.

'So, to complete the question I was about to ask a moment ago,' I said, 'is it insatiable greed for freedom and neglect of everything else which causes this political system to change and creates the need for dictatorship?'

'How would it do that?' he asked.

'In its thirst for freedom, a democratically governed community might get leaders who aren't any good at serving d wine. It gets drunk on excessive quantities of undiluted freedom,* and then, I suppose, unless the rulers are very lenient and keep it provided with plenty of freedom, it accuses them of being foul oligarchs and punishes them.'

'Yes,' he agreed, 'that's what it does.'

'Then those who obey authority have abuse heaped on them,' I said, 'and are described as voluntary slaves, nonentities; admiration and respect are given to people who, in both their private life and in public, behave like subjects if they're rulers, and behave like rulers if they're subjects. Isn't it inevitable that a community of this kind will take freedom as far as it can go?' e

'Of course.'

'Equally inevitably, my friend,' I said, 'lawlessness seeps into everyone's homes; ultimately, even animals are infected.'

'Can you explain this for us?' he asked.

'For instance,' I said, 'the pursuit of freedom makes it increasingly normal for fathers and sons to swap places: fathers are afraid of their sons, and sons no longer feel shame before their parents or stand in awe of them. And it starts to make no difference whether one is a citizen or a resident alien, or even a visitor from abroad: everyone is at the same level.'   563a

'Yes, that happens,' he said.

'Those are the most important cases,' I said, 'but there are others. In these circumstances, for example, teachers are afraid of their pupils and curry favour with them, while pupils despise their teachers and their attendants as well.* In short, the younger generation starts to look like the older generation, and

they turn any conversation or action into a trial of strength with their elders; meanwhile, the older members of the community adapt themselves to the younger ones, ooze frivolity
b and charm, and model their behaviour on that of the young, because they don't want to be thought disagreeable tyrants.'

'Right,' he said.

'The peak of popular freedom for this community is reached', I continued, 'when male and female slaves have as much freedom as the people who bought them. And I almost forgot to mention the extent to which men and women meet as autonomous equals.'

c 'Why don't we just do what Aeschylus suggests,' he said, 'when he asks, "Shall we voice what we were poised to say?"'*

'All right,' I said. 'This is what I have to say. If you hadn't seen it, you'd never believe how much more freedom pets have in this community compared with any other. The dogs really do start to resemble their mistresses, as the proverb says, but so do horses and donkeys as well, in the way they learn to strut about with absolute freedom, bumping into anyone they meet on the road who doesn't get out of the way. And everything else is just
d as saturated with freedom.'

'You're telling me my own dream,'* he said. 'I often experience just that on my way out of town.'

'Taking all this into consideration,' I said, 'the long and short of it is that the minds of the citizens of a democracy become so sensitive that they get angry and annoyed at the slightest hint of enslavement. Do you know what I mean? And they're so worried about the possibility of anyone having authority over them that they end up, as I'm sure you're aware, taking no
e notice of the laws either, whether written or unwritten.'

'Yes, I'm well aware of that,' he said.

'So there, I think,' I said, 'you have the fine, vigorous shoot from which dictatorship grows.'

'No one could deny its vigour,' he said. 'But what's the next stage?'

'The same sickness that infected oligarchy and caused its demise', I said, 'erupts in democracy too, but in a more widespread and virulent form, because of its openness, and reduces it to slavery. In fact, it's a general principle that overdoing anything leads to a huge compensatory shift towards

the opposite: seasons, plants, and bodily health are all subject
to this principle, and political systems are particularly good 564a
examples of it.'

'That sounds plausible,' he said.

'In other words, it's plausible to claim that excessive
freedom, at both the individual and the political level, can only
change into excessive slavery.'

'Exactly.'

'It makes sense, then,' I continued, 'to say that dictatorship is
bound to arise out of democracy—from what, I take it, is the
peak of freedom to the most severe and savage form of slavery.'

'Yes, it does,' he agreed.

'But that wasn't the point of your question, I think,' I said.
'You wanted to know what the sickness is which proliferates in
a democracy as well as in an oligarchy, and reduces it to b
slavery.'

'That's right,' he said.

'Well,' I said, 'I've already mentioned that breed of lazy,
extravagant people and how they're divided into leaders or
followers, depending on the degree to which they possess
courage. They're the ones we said were like drones—the
leaders with stings, the followers stingless.'

'Yes, that's right,' he said.

'Well, the presence of these two kinds of drone,' I said,
'throws any political system into chaos, as phlegm and bile do
in the case of the body.* The ability to look a long way ahead
and take precautions against them is a sign of a good doctor
and legislator, just as much as it is a sign of a skilful bee- c
keeper. Ideally, they should try to prevent their birth; but if
they've already been born, they should try to eradicate them as
quickly as possible, cells and all.'

'Yes, you're absolutely right,' he said.

'Now, we'll never be in a position to make the assessment we
want without a clear enough view,' I said. 'Here's a move
that'll help.'

'What move?'

'Let's assume that there are three distinct components to a
democratically governed community—as in fact there are. First, d
its openness allows the drone element to develop within it, and
in this respect it resembles an oligarchy.'

'True.'

'But this element is far more vigorous in a democracy than an oligarchy.'

'Why?'

'In an oligarchy it isn't given any respect and is excluded from political office, so it never gets a chance to flex its muscles and become strong. In almost all democracies, however, it is the leading element: its most vigorous members make speeches and do things, while the rest settle in a buzzing swarm around the rostra and prevent anyone presenting alternative points of e view, and consequently the government of a democratic community is almost entirely in the hands of this element.'

'Yes, indeed,' he said.

'Now, the second element is constantly being propagated by the inhabitants.'

'What is it?'

'Although everyone is trying to make money, it's invariably the most disciplined people who do best financially.'

'That's likely.'

'They're a rich source of honey for the drones, I should think: it's very easy for them to siphon[†] it off from there.'

'Well, it's hardly possible to siphon it from the have-nots,' he remarked.

'And this element, the drones' fodder, is called the moneyed class.'

'That sounds about right,' he said.

565a 'The third element would be the general populace—the smallholders, who don't spend all their time on politics and don't have a great deal of property. They form the largest section of the population, and when they gather in one spot they are the most authoritative group in a democracy.'

'True,' he said. 'But they tend not to gather very often, unless there's honey to be gained.'

'And they always get it,' I said. 'Those champions of theirs do their very best to rob the rich and distribute the trivial amounts they don't keep for themselves to the general populace.'

b 'Yes, that's how they get their honey,' he said.

'Their victims are forced to defend themselves, I suppose, by making speeches to the people and acting wherever possible.'

'Of course.'

'And then they're accused by the democratic leaders of plotting against the people and of being oligarchs, even if revolution is the last thing on their minds.'

'Of course.'

'Ultimately, when they realize that the populace at large is out to wrong them, not because it really wants to, but because in its ignorance it's been misled by the lies and slanders of their opponents, then—and only then—they do in fact willy-nilly become oligarchs. It's not that they really want to, but the drones' stings inject this poison into their systems as well, to grow inside them.'

'That's undeniable.'

'And the result is that the two sides turn to arraignments, lawsuits, and trials about each other's conduct.'

'Yes.'

'And aren't the people always given to setting up a particular individual as their special champion, who under their caring nurture grows to a prodigious size?'

'Yes, they do tend to do that.'

'It's clear, then,' I said, 'that this champion is the only possible root from which any dictatorial shoot that appears is bound to have grown.'

'Perfectly clear.'

'So what makes a champion change into a dictator? Isn't it obviously when a champion starts to behave in the same way as what the stories tell us happens to people in the sanctuary of Zeus Lycaeus in Arcadia?'*

'What's that?' he asked.

'That anyone who tastes even a single morsel of human entrails mixed in among those of other sacrificial offerings is bound to become a wolf. Haven't you heard this story?'

'Yes, I have.'

'Doesn't the same thing happen to a champion of the people? Suppose the masses are more or less totally under his thumb and he feels no compunction about shedding the blood of a fellow citizen; suppose he trumps up the usual charges against someone, takes him to court, and murders him, thereby eliminating a human life; suppose on his tongue and in his unholy mouth is the taste of the blood of a kinsman, and he

566a turns to demanding banishment and death, and to hinting at the cancellation of debts and the reassignment of land. Isn't it unalterably inevitable that this man will next either be assassinated by his enemies or change into a wolf instead of a human being—that is, become a dictator?'

'It's absolutely inevitable,' he agreed.

'And he's the one who stirs up conflict against the propertied class.'

'Yes.'

'Now, he might be exiled and return to his home country in spite of his enemies. If so, then he comes back as a complete dictator, doesn't he?'

'Obviously.'

b 'Alternatively, his enemies might not be able to arouse enough hostility against him to have him exiled or executed, so they start to try to find a secret way to assassinate him.'

'Yes, that's the usual course of events,' he said.

'And then, at this stage, every dictator comes up with the notorious and typical demand: he asks the people for bodyguards to protect him, the people's defender.'

'Yes,' he agreed.

'And because they're afraid for his safety, and at the same time optimistic about their own future, they give him his bodyguards, I'm sure.'

c 'That's right.'

'This is when anyone wealthy, whose wealth has made him suspected of being opposed to democracy, acts in accordance with the oracle given to Croesus and "flees beside the pebbly Hermus without delay and without worrying about cowardice".'*

'Yes, because he won't get a second chance to worry,' he said.

'And if he's caught, he'll be put to death,' I added.

'Inevitably.'

'Now, that champion obviously doesn't "lie sprawled in his d vastness over a vast area", but topples numerous others and stands firm on the chariot of the state,* a complete dictator now, instead of a champion.'

'That's bound to be the case,' he said.

'How happy do you think he is?' I asked. 'And how happy is

308

the community which contains a creature of this sort? Shall we talk about this?'

'Yes, let's,' he said.

'In the early days,' I said, 'in the first period of his supremacy, he greets everyone he meets with a smile. He claims not to be a dictator, makes a lot of promises to his close e associates and in his public speeches, rescinds debts, gives land to the people and to his supporters, and poses as an altogether amiable and gentle person, doesn't he?'

'Inevitably,' he said.

'Meanwhile he is, I imagine, settling his differences with some of his exiled enemies, and killing others. Once that threat is a thing of the past, he turns to provoking warfare, so as to keep the people in need of a leader.'

'Yes, that's likely.'

'And also, wouldn't you say, so as to tax them* and make 567a them poor, so that they're forced to concentrate on their daily business and have less time to plot against him?'

'Obviously.'

'And also, I think, to find a plausible way of killing people he suspects of entertaining notions of freedom, and of consequently being likely to resist his authority: he simply makes sure that the enemy get their hands on them. Don't you agree? All of these reasons guarantee that a dictator must constantly be provoking wars, mustn't he?'

'He has to.'

'Now, these actions of his will probably be resented by the citizens of his community, won't they?' b

'Of course they will.'

'And some—they'll have to be the bravest—of those who helped him on his way and who are in positions of power will speak their minds to him, as well as to one another, and will criticize what's going on, won't they?'

'I should think so.'

'So a dictator has to eliminate the lot of them—or else relinquish power—until there's no one of any value left among either his friends or his enemies.'

'Obviously.'

'He has to keep a sharp eye out, then, for anyone with courage, self-confidence, intelligence, or wealth. He has no c choice in the matter: he's bound to treat them as enemies and to intrigue against them, until he's purged the community of them. That's the nature of his happy state.'

'A fine purge that is,' he remarked.

'Yes,' I said, 'and quite different from a medical purge of the body. Doctors remove the worst and leave the best; he does the opposite.'

'He has to, if he's to retain power, apparently,' he said.

d 'He's caught in an enviable dilemma, then,' I said, 'which requires him to choose between sharing his life with people who are, on the whole, second-rate, and who hate him, or not living at all.'

'That's right,' he said.

'Now, the greater the resentment felt by the citizens of his community at his conduct, the larger and more reliable his bodyguard will have to be, won't it?'

'Of course.'

'Well, who can he rely on? Where will he get his soldiers from?'

'Swarms of them will wing their way to him as if by magic,' he said, 'if he offers them the payment they want.'

'You wouldn't be talking about drones, by any chance, e would you?' I asked. 'Drones of all different shapes and sizes from abroad?'

'You've understood me perfectly,' he said.

'But who can he rely on from his own community? Do you think he'd . . . ?'

'What?'

'. . . steal slaves from his citizens, emancipate them, and include them among his bodyguard?'

'He undoubtedly would,' he replied. 'He could surely rely on them more than on anyone else.'

'Dictatorship is certainly an enviable thing, then,' I said. 568a 'Look at the friends he has and the people he can depend on, once he's killed all his previous associates.'

'Yes, well, that *is* the kind of person he keeps company with,' he said.

'These companions of his, these newly created citizens, form his circle of admiring friends, while decent people avoid him like the plague, don't they?'

'Of course they do.'

'It's not surprising', I said, 'that tragedy in general is thought to be a clever affair and Euripides is taken to be the most outstanding tragic playwright.'

'Why?'

'Because with his penetrating mind he's already expressed this idea: "Dictators are clever because of the clever company b they keep,"* he says. He was obviously referring to the clever people we've been saying form a dictator's circle.'

'He also eulogizes dictatorship in a number of ways,' he added, 'by calling it "godlike", for instance.* And he's joined in this by all the other poets.'

'And it's precisely because tragic poets are clever', I said, 'that they'll forgive us (and others with a similar political system) for refusing to allow them into our society, on the grounds that they sing the praises of dictatorship.'

'I expect the gifted ones will forgive us, anyway,' he said. c

'They can tour around other communities instead, where they'll attract huge audiences and use the beauty, carrying-power, and persuasiveness of the voices of the actors they hire to convert them to dictatorship or democracy.'

'Yes.'

'And that's not all. They'll be paid and acclaimed for doing this. They'll get the most from dictatorships, and somewhat less from democracies; and then the higher up our scale of political systems they go, the more the acclaim will die away, as if it d were short of breath and unable to continue.'

'Yes.'

'But we digress,' I said. 'We'd better return to that army which a dictator possesses, in all its splendour, size, variety, and inconstancy, and discuss how he'll maintain it.'

'He'll obviously use up any wealth the community's temples have,' he said, 'whenever his victims' money runs out,† so that he won't have to tax the people too much.'

'What about when there's no longer enough in the temples?' e

'He and all the men and women who hobnob with him will obviously be maintained by his father's wealth,' he said.

'I see,' I said. 'You're implying that the general populace, which is the dictator's father, will keep him and his companions.'

'They'll have little choice in the matter,' he said.

'What do you mean?' I said. 'Suppose the people get annoyed with him and tell him it's wrong for a son in his prime to be kept by a father, and that, on the contrary, the son should be keeping the father; suppose they tell him that the purpose of 569a their giving him life and power was not for them to be dominated, now that he's grown up, by their own slaves and for them to support him and their slaves and all the rest of the riff-raff, but so that he could be their champion in freeing them from the dominion of the rich and the so-called gentlemen of their community; suppose they now behave like a father throwing his son out of the home, along with his freeloading friends, and they order him to leave the community, and to take his companions with him. What would happen then, do you think?'

'Then it'll certainly take hardly any time for the people to find out what sort of creature they've fathered, cared for, and b nurtured to maturity,' he said. 'And they'll soon see that the people they're trying to expel are the stronger party.'

'What?' I exclaimed. 'Do you mean that the dictator will be unscrupulous enough to lay hands on his father—to respond to a difference of opinion with physical violence?'

'Yes,' he said, 'once he's deprived his father of his weapons.'

'In other words,' I said, 'a dictator is guilty of the crime of father-beating, and is no comfort to his father in his old age.* This, it turns out, is what dictatorship is and would be acknowledged to be. And, as the saying goes, the people would escape the smoke of being the slaves of free men only to fall c into the fire of having slaves as their masters. They exchange considerable, and even excessive, freedom for the worst and harshest kind of enslavement—enslavement to slaves.'

'Yes, this is exactly what happens,' he agreed.

'In that case,' I said, 'it would be reasonable for us to claim that we've done enough to explain how dictatorship evolves out of democracy, and what it's like as a fully fledged entity. Yes?'

'Yes, we've certainly done enough,' he said.

571a 'All there is left for us to do', I said, 'is study an actual dictatorial person, to try to see how he evolves out of the democratic type, what he's like once he does exist, and whether his life is happy or unhappy.'

'Yes, that's right,' he said.

'Well, there's still a deficiency to remedy, I think,' I said.

'What?'

'I don't think we've finished distinguishing the various kinds of desires or finding out how many different kinds there are.* And as long as this job remains unfinished, our enquiry will be veiled in obscurity.'   b

'But it's not too late, is it?' he asked.

'No. The thing about them I want to have out in the open is that some of the unnecessary pleasures and desires strike me as lawless. We probably all contain these pleasures and desires, but they can be kept under control by convention and by the co-operation of reason and the better desires. Some people, in fact, control them so well that they get rid of them altogether or leave only a few of them in a weakened state, but they remain stronger and more numerous in others.'   c

'What pleasures and desires are you thinking of?' he asked.

'The ones that wake up while we're asleep,' I replied. 'When all the rest of the mind—the rational, regulated, controlling part—is asleep, then if the wild, unruly part is glutted with food or drink, it springs up and longs to banish sleep and go and satisfy its own instincts. I'm sure you're aware of how in these circumstances nothing is too outrageous: a person acts as if he were totally lacking in moral principle and unhampered by intelligence. In his dreams, he doesn't stop at trying to have sex with his mother and with anyone or anything else—man, beast, d or god; he's ready to slaughter anything; there's nothing he wouldn't eat. In short, he doesn't hold back from anything, however bizarre or disgusting.'

'You're quite right,' he said.

'On the other hand, I imagine, when someone who's self-disciplined and who keeps himself healthy goes to sleep, he's made sure that his rational mind is awake and has eaten its fill of fine ideas and arguments, which he's brought to an agreed conclusion within himself. Since he hasn't either starved or over-indulged his desirous part, it can settle down to sleep and e not bother the best part of him with its feelings of pleasure or pain, and consequently the best part is free to get on with the 572a enquiries it carries out all by itself, when it is secluded and untarnished by anything else, and to try to fulfil its impulse for perceiving something in the past or present or future that it doesn't know. He's also calmed down his passionate part and doesn't go to bed in an emotionally disturbed state because he's been angry with someone. In other words, he's quietened down two aspects of himself, but woken up the third—the one in which intelligence resides—and that's how he takes his rest; and, as you know, in this state he can maximize his contact with the truth and minimize the lawlessness of the visions he b sees in his dreams.'

'I'm sure you're absolutely right,' he said.

'Now, we've wandered rather far from the main course of the argument, but the point I'm trying to get across is this: every one of us—even someone who seems very restrained— contains desires which are terrible, wild, and lawless, and this category of desire becomes manifest during sleep. Do you agree? Do you think I have a point?'

'Yes, I do agree.'

'Well, remember the nature of the democratic man, as we c described him: his formative childhood upbringing was by a skinflint of a father who valued only desires which helped him make money, and despised all the unnecessary ones with their frivolity and frippery, wasn't it?'

'Yes.'

'But then he fell in with a more elegant crowd, consisting of people who indulge in the desires we've just been describing, and his dislike of his father's meanness drove him to all kinds of outrageous behaviour, and to modelling himself on them. However, he was essentially better than these corrupters of his, and since he was being pulled in both directions, he found between the two ways of life a compromise in which he drew d on each of them to a reasonable extent, in his opinion, and lived a life which wasn't miserly, but at the same time wasn't lawless either. And that's how he made the transition from being oligarchic to being democratic.'

'Yes, that's what we thought earlier, and it still seems valid,' he said.

'Now imagine', I said, 'that our democratic type has grown older and has a son who's been brought up, in his turn, in his father's ways.'

'All right.'

'And imagine that the same thing happens to him as happened to his father: he's attracted by complete lawlessness (although the people who are advertising it to him call it e complete freedom), his father and his family in general reinforce the desires he settled on as a compromise, and others reinforce his lawless side. When these black magicians, these creators of dictators, realize that there's only one way they're going to gain control of the young man, they arrange matters until they implant in him a particular lust, to champion the rest of his desires which are too idle to do more than share out anything that readily comes their way. And don't you think this 573a kind of lust is exactly like a great, winged drone?'

'Yes, that seems to me to be a perfect description of it,' he said.

'Then the rest of the desires buzz in a swarm around their champion, reeking of incense and perfumes, laden with garlands, overflowing with wine, and offering all the indulgent pleasures that go with that kind of social life. Under their caring nurture, he grows to his fullest extent and gains a sting whose poison is unfulfilled longing. This inner champion now takes frenzy for his bodyguard and runs amok. If he finds that b the person contains any apparently good beliefs or desires which still cause him to feel shame, he kills them and banishes them, until he's purged the person of self-discipline and imported frenzy in its place.'

'That's a perfect description of a dictatorial type's evolution,' he said.

'And isn't this also the kind of reason why lust is traditionally called a dictator?' I asked.*

'I suppose so,' he said.

'Now, there's something dictatorial about a drunken person's arrogance too, isn't there, Adeimantus?' I asked. c

'Yes, there is.'

'And people who are insane and mentally disturbed try to dominate the gods, let alone other human beings, and expect to be able to do so.'

'Yes,' he agreed.

'So strictly speaking, Adeimantus,' I said, 'the dictatorial type is the result of someone's nature or conditioning—or both— making him a drunken, lustful maniac.'

'Absolutely.'

'So that's how the dictatorial type evolves, apparently. Now, what's his life like?'

d 'At the risk of sounding like a tease,' he said, 'it's you who'll have to tell me.'

'All right,' I said. 'I think he proceeds to give himself over to feasting and revelry, parties and prostitutes, and all the activities which typically indicate that the dictator lust has taken up residence within a person and is in complete control of his mind.'

'Yes, that's bound to happen,' he agreed.

'Every day and every night, terrible desires with prodigious appetites branch out in large numbers from the main stem, don't they?'

'Yes, they do.'

'So his income is soon exhausted.'

'Of course.'

e 'And then he starts borrowing and working his way through his estate.'

'Naturally.'

'And when there's nothing left, his young brood of desires is bound to clamour long and loud. He's driven by the stinging swarm of his desires (and especially by lust, the captain of the bodyguard the others form) to run amok—to see if there's 574a anyone he can steal anything from by deceit or by force. Yes?'

'Definitely,' he said.

'He has no choice: he can either filch from every available source, or be racked with agonizing pains.'

'Agreed.'

'Now, every passing pleasant sensation he feels takes precedence over the ones which are in the past and steals from them, so by the same token he expects to take precedence over his parents, despite being younger than them, and to steal from them, in the sense of appropriating his father's property once he's exhausted his own. Yes?'

'Of course,' he agreed.

b 'And if his parents refused to hand it over to him, he'd initially resort to obtaining money from them on false pretences, wouldn't he?'

'Absolutely.'

'And if that didn't work, he'd turn to robbery with violence?'

'I think so,' he said.

'If his elderly parents resisted and fought back, Adeimantus, do you think he'd be circumspect and hesitant about doing anything dictatorial?'

'No, I don't hold out much hope for the parents of someone like this,' he said.

'Would he really beat up his mother, who's cared for him for years, Adeimantus, and whom he could never have lived without, for the sake of his latest dispensable girlfriend, whom he's just fallen in love with? Would he really beat up his aged, c indispensable father, who may not be much to look at any more, but whose affection has lasted for so many years, for the sake of his latest alluring, but dispensable, boyfriend? Would he honestly let his parents be dominated by them, if he had them all living together in the same house?'

'Yes, he certainly would,' he said.

'What a happy thing it is, then,' I exclaimed, 'to be the parent of a dictator!'

'That's right,' he agreed.

'What happens when there's none of his parents' property d left, but a large number of pleasures have gathered together in a swarm within him? Won't he first turn his hand to a bit of burglary or to mugging travellers late at night, and then try emptying out a temple?* At the same time a gang of beliefs which had until recently been suppressed, but now form lust's bodyguard, come to his assistance to enable him to overpower all the views about good and bad behaviour he'd been brought up to hold and which he'd assumed to comprise morality. This gang consists of attitudes which had formerly—during the period when there was still a democratic government within him, and he was still subject to the laws and to his father— e broken free only at night, while he was asleep. Once he's under the dictatorship of lust, however, his constant waking state is one that was formerly rare and restricted to dreams: there's no form of murder, however vile, that he isn't willing to commit; there's nothing he won't eat, no deed he isn't ready to perform. Lust lives within him like a dictator, with no regard for law and 575a convention. It uses its absolute power to influence the person in whom it lives, as an autocrat influences his community, to stop at nothing as long as the result is the perpetuation of itself and the pandemonium it generates. Some of this pandemonium is the result of bad company, and has therefore been introduced from outside; the rest is the result of the person's own practice of the same bad habits, and so has been released and set free internally. Don't you think this is how he lives?'

'Yes,' he said.

b 'Now, if people of this kind form a small proportion of a community's population, while the rest are self-disciplined,' I said, 'then they leave and serve in the bodyguard of a dictator somewhere else, or as mercenaries in some war or other. But if they occur in a time of peace and stability, they stay in their community and commit lots of trivial crimes.'

'What sort of crimes do you mean?'

'They're thieves, burglars, pickpockets, muggers, temple-robbers, kidnappers; if they have any ability at public speaking, they might be sycophants,* and they're the kind of people who commit perjury in court and take bribes.'

c 'Yes, these are trivial crimes, as long as there aren't many people committing them,' he said.

'Anything trivial is only trivial in comparison with something important,' I went on, 'and all these crimes are (as the saying goes) well wide of the mark of dictatorship in the effect they have on how rotten and unhappy a community is. In fact, it's when these people and their followers start to form a significant proportion of a community's population, and realize how many there are of them, that they—assisted by the folly of the people—become the ones to whom the dictator we discussed owes his origin: he is simply whichever one of them has the

d greatest and most thriving dictator in his own mind.'*

'Yes, that's likely,' he agreed. 'Dictatorship would come most naturally to him.'

'There's no problem if they're happy to defer to him, but if the community refuses to submit, then, if he can, it'll be his fatherland's turn for the same punishment he inflicted on his mother and father before. He'll bring new friends in from abroad and, for all her long-standing care, he'll make sure that his motherland (as the Cretans call their country) and fatherland are kept and maintained—in a state of enslavement to these new friends of his. After all, that's how the desire of this sort of person is fulfilled.'

e 'Yes, it is, absolutely,' he said.

'Now, don't people of this sort behave like dictators in their private lives even before they gain political power?' I asked. 'Take their relationships with others, for instance. They either go about with people who flatter them and are ready to carry out their every whim, or they're deferential themselves, if they want something from someone. As long as that's the case, there's nothing they wouldn't do to make him believe they're 576a his friends, but once they've got what they want, they're distant again.'

'Definitely.'

'They never have any friends, then, throughout their lives: they can only be masters or slaves. Dictatorial people can never experience freedom and true friendship.'

'No.'

'We couldn't exactly call them reliable, could we?'

'Of course not.'

'And, assuming that our earlier conclusions about the nature of morality were correct,* we'd have to say that there's no one b more immoral than them.'

'Well, our earlier conclusions *are* right,' he said.

'In short, then,' I said, 'the worst type of person is one whose waking life resembles the dreams we discussed.'

'Yes.'

'He's the product of absolute power falling into the hands of an inherently dictatorial person, and the longer he spends as a dictator, the worse he becomes.'

Glaucon took over the job of talking with me, and said, 'Yes, that's bound to happen.'

Chapter 12

Happiness and Unhappiness

Plato now declares himself to be in a position to adjudicate the relative happiness or unhappiness of the five types of individual. As usual, he starts by looking at the equivalent communities. Happiness is circumscribed by a number of properties—freedom, lack of need, lack of fear—and it is concluded that a community ruled by a dictator, and a dictatorial person (especially if he becomes an actual dictator), are in the most miserable condition. On the weak basis of the fact that in the previous chapter the five types were presented as a series of degenerations, with the dictator at the bottom, the happiness and unhappiness of the five types are now ranked according to the order of degeneration.

'Now,' I continued, 'won't we find that the worst person is
576c also the unhappiest person? And won't we find—whatever most people think—that it's the most enduring and thorough dictator who has the most enduring and thorough un-happiness?'

'Yes,' he said, 'that's inevitable.'

'Now, isn't it the case', I asked, 'that a dictatorial person is the counterpart of a community which is ruled by a dictator, and a democratic person corresponds to a community with a democratic government, and so on for the rest?'

'Of course.'

'So we can compare the state of goodness and the happiness of one type of community with another and apply the results to their corresponding human types, can we?'

d   'Of course.'

'How does the state of goodness of a community which is ruled by a dictator compare, then, with that of the one we described first, with its kings?'

'They're at opposite ends of the scale,' he answered. 'One is the best type of community, the other is the worst.'

'I don't need to ask which is which,' I said, 'because it's

obvious. But now what about their happiness and un-happiness?* Would you come up with the same estimate, or a different one? We shouldn't be rushed into a decision by our impressions of just one person, the dictator himself, or by the few people who constitute his immediate circle. We should visit the community and see all the sights, immerse ourselves e thoroughly in it and look everywhere, and then express an opinion.'

'That's a good suggestion,' he said. 'And everyone would see that a community under a dictator is as unhappy as any community can be, while a community under kingship is the happiest one possible.'

'And suppose I were to make the same suggestion as regards their human equivalents too,' I said. 'Would that be a good 577a suggestion? I'd be expecting someone to come up with his assessment of their happiness and unhappiness only if he has the ability to gain insights into a person by using his mind to take on that person's characteristics. Rather than childishly looking from the outside and being won over by the ostentatious façade a dictator presents to the outside world, he should be capable of insight. Suppose we found someone who's not only this good at assessment, but who has also lived in close proximity with a dictator, and has been an eyewitness to what goes on inside a dictator's house and how he treats the various members of his household, because these are the best circumstances for seeing a dictator stripped of his pompous b clothing; and suppose he'd also seen how a dictator reacts to the risks involved in political life.* Would I be right to claim that we should all listen to what this person has to say? Should we ask him to draw on all this firsthand experience to tell us how a dictator fares, as regards happiness and unhappiness, compared with our other types?'

'Yes, that would be a very good idea as well,' he said.

'Shall we pretend, then', I said, 'that *we* are expert assessors, and have in the past met dictators?* Otherwise, there'll be no one to answer our questions for us.'

'Yes, let's.'

'All right, then,' I said, 'here's how you'd better proceed with c the enquiry. You should bear in mind the equivalence between community and individual and submit them one after another to a detailed examination; then you'll be in a position to describe the attributes either or both of them have.'

'What attributes?' he asked.

'Starting with a community,' I said, 'do you think a community which is ruled by a dictator is free or oppressed?'

'It's impossible to imagine a more complete state of oppression,' he replied.

'But some of its members are evidently free and are doing the oppressing.'

'Yes,' he said, 'but they're the minority. Wretched servitude, with no civil rights, is pretty much the universal condition of the citizen body—certainly of the truly good elements.'

d 'Given the correspondence between individual and community,' I said, 'then isn't his structure necessarily identical? Oppression and servitude must pervade his mind, with the truly good parts of it being oppressed, and an evil, crazed minority doing the oppressing.'

'Necessarily,' he agreed.

'Well, do you think a mind in this condition is free or enslaved?'

'Enslaved, I'd say—definitely.'

'Then again, a community which is enslaved and ruled by a dictator is hardly ever free to do what it wants, is it?'

'I quite agree.'

e 'What about a mind which is ruled by an inner dictator, then? Treating the mind as a single whole, it'll hardly ever be free to do what it wants, will it? It'll constantly be subject to the overpowering whims of its lust, and this will make it highly inconsistent and fickle.'

'Of course.'

'And would a community under a dictator be poor or well off?'

'Poor.'

578a 'So a person with a dictatorial mind is bound to be in a constant state of poverty and need.'

'Yes,' he agreed.

'Now, isn't fear ever-present in communities and individuals of this sort?'

'It certainly is.'

'Is there any other community, do you think, where you'd

come across more moaning, complaining, grievances, and hardships?'

'No, definitely not.'

'Would you come across more of them in any other type of individual, do you think? Or has the limit been reached with this dictatorial type and the frenzy caused by his desires and lusts?'

'Of course it has,' he said.

'I imagine all this was the kind of evidence which led you to b conclude that the community is as unhappy as any community can be.'

'Do you disagree?' he asked.

'Not at all,' I replied. 'But what does the same evidence lead you to think about a dictatorial person?'

'That he is far unhappier than any of the other types,' he answered.

'Now you've made a claim I *do* disagree with,' I said.

'Why?' he asked.

'I don't think he's that outstandingly unhappy,' I said.

'Who is, then?'

'I should think you'd agree that here's an even more miserable person than the one we've been discussing.'

'Who?'

'A dictatorial person who can't remain a private citizen all c his life,' I said, 'but has the misfortune to end up, by force of circumstance, as an actual dictator.'

'If I'm to be consistent with our earlier argument,'* he said, 'I have to admit that you're right.'

'Yes,' I said, 'but it's important for us not to rely on assumptions in these sorts of cases. We're looking into the most important issue there is—which kind of life is good, and which is bad—so we must conduct a really thorough investigation, and I think I see how to proceed.'

'You're quite right,' he said.

'Well, I wonder what you'll make of my idea that we should start the investigation by bearing in mind the following points.' d

'Which ones?'

'Every single wealthy citizen in a community owns a lot of slaves. In this respect—that they have a number of people under their control—they resemble dictators; the only difference is that dictators control larger numbers of people.'

'That's right.'

'Well, do you appreciate that these slave-owners aren't in a state of fear? They aren't afraid of their slaves, are they?'

'What reason would they have to be?'

'None,' I answered. 'But do you realize why?'

'Yes. It's because behind every single citizen is the community as a whole.'

e 'Exactly,' I said. 'Now, imagine that a man who owns fifty or more slaves is plucked by some god from his community—wife, children, and all—and deposited in some isolated spot along with all his property, especially his slaves. There are no other free men around to help him. Would he be afraid of his slaves killing him and his family? And if so, how frightened do you think he'd be?'

'He'd be absolutely terrified, I expect,' he replied.

579a 'What he'd have to do, then, despite their being his slaves, is immediately get on the right side of some of them, make them extravagant promises, and give them their freedom, whatever misgivings he may have. In fact, he'd end up being dependent on the goodwill of his servants, wouldn't he?'

'It's either that or be killed,' he said, 'so he doesn't really have a choice.'

'And what do you think would happen if this god also surrounded him with a lot of neighbours in nearby settlements, and these neighbours of his couldn't abide anyone presuming to be anyone else's master, and punished with extreme severity any case they came across of this kind of oppression?'

b 'He'd be in an even worse trap,' he said, 'with all those enemies hemming him in on every side.'

'Well, is there any difference between this and the prison a dictator finds himself in, because of all the fears and lusts his nature, as we've described it, makes him liable to? He may be greedy for new experiences, but he's the only person in the community who can't travel abroad or see all the sights every other free man longs to see. Instead, he lives like a woman, buried indoors most of the time, resenting any of his fellow

c citizens who go abroad and see something worth while.'

'Absolutely,' he said.

'So these are the kinds of troubles which swell the harvest of evils reaped by the individual who, in your recent assessment, is as unhappy as anyone can be—the dictatorial type, whose bad government is restricted to himself—when he can't remain a private citizen all his life, but is forced by some misfortune to take on the government of others, despite his inability to control even himself. This is like someone ill with spastic paralysis being forced to enter the public arena and spend his life competing as an athlete against others or fighting in wars.' d

'That's a perfect analogy, Socrates,' he said. 'You're quite right.'

'There's nothing but misery in a dictator's life, then, is there, Glaucon?' I asked. 'You thought you'd identified the worst life possible, but there's even more hardship in his, isn't there?'

'Definitely,' he said.

'The truth of the matter, then, even if people deny it, is that a real dictator is actually a real slave—judging by the extent of his obsequiousness and servitude—and a flatterer of the worst kinds of people. His desires are completely insatiable as well: e any expert observer of the totality of the mind can see that a dictator is actually never fulfilled and is therefore poor. Moreover, fear pervades his whole life, and he's convulsed with constant pains. This is what he's like, if his condition resembles that of the community he rules over—and it does, doesn't it?'

'Yes, it does,' he agreed.

'And we haven't finished with his attributes yet: there are 580a also all the ones we mentioned earlier,* which he's not only bound to have, but bound to have even more thoroughly than before because of being in office. He's resentful, unreliable, immoral, friendless, and unjust; and he gives room and board to every vice. And the result of all this is not just the extreme wretchedness of his own condition: these attributes of his also rub off on people who come near him.'

'That's beyond all reasonable doubt,' he said.

'All right, then,' I continued. 'Now is the time for you to play the part of the judge with overall authority* and reveal your b verdict. Of the five types—regal,* timocratic, oligarchic, democratic, and dictatorial—which comes first, in your opinion, in the contest of happiness? Which comes second? You'd better grade all five of them.'

'It's an easy decision to make,' he said, 'because the order in which they made their entrance, like troupes of dancers on a stage, corresponds to how I rate them. That's my estimate of where they come on the scale of goodness and badness, and of happiness and unhappiness.'

'Shall we hire a town crier, then,' I asked, 'or shall I be the one to proclaim that the son of Ariston* has judged the happiest person to be the best and most moral person—that is,

c the person who possesses the highest degree of regal qualities and who rules as king over himself? And that he has also judged the unhappiest person to be the worst and most immoral person—that is, the person who possesses the highest degree of dictatorial qualities and rules as completely as possible as a dictator over himself and his community?'

'*You* make the announcement,' he said.

'And can I add a rider that this is so whether or not their condition is hidden from the eyes of gods and men?'* I asked.

'You can,' he said.

A second proof of the philosopher's happiness proceeds on the basis of the threefold division of the human mind (Chapter 6) and the corresponding types of individual—philosophical, competitive, avaricious. Each enjoys different things, and each claims that what he or she enjoys is best. However, the philosopher's claim is the most authoritative since he has the experience and intelligence to decide the issue.

'All right, then,' I said. 'That's the first proof, but I wonder

d how the second one strikes you.'

'What is it?'

'I think the correspondence between the three classes into which the community was divided and the threefold division of everyone's mind provides the basis for a further argument,' I said.

'What argument?'

'It seems to me that each of the three mental categories has its own particular pleasure, so that there are three kinds of pleasure as well.* The same would also go for desires and motivations.'

'What do you mean?' he said.

'We found that one part is the intellectual part of a person,

326

another is the passionate part, and the third has so many manifestations that we couldn't give it a single label which applied to it and it alone, so we named it after its most prevalent and powerful aspect: we called it the desirous part, because of the intensity of our desires for food, drink, sex, and so on, and we also referred to it as the mercenary part,* because desires of this kind invariably need money for their fulfilment.'

e

581a

'And we were right,' he said.

'What if we said that what it enjoys, what it cares for, is profit? This would be the best way for us to clarify the issue for ourselves: we could keep our references to this part of the mind concise, and call it mercenary and avaricious. Would that description hit the mark?'

'I think so,' he said.

'And isn't our position that the passionate part always has its sights set wholly on power, success, and fame?'

'Yes.'

b

'So it would be fair for us to call it competitive and ambitious, wouldn't it?'

'Perfectly fair.'

'And it's patently obvious that our intellectual part is entirely directed at every moment towards knowing the truth of things, and isn't interested in the slightest in money and reputation.'

'Certainly.'

'So we'd be right to call it intellectual and philosophical, wouldn't we?'

'Of course.'

'Now, sometimes this intellectual part is the motivating aspect of one's mind; sometimes—as circumstances dictate— it's one of the other two. Yes?'

c

'Yes,' he said.

'Which is why we're also claiming that there are three basic human types—the philosophical, the competitive, and the avaricious.'*

'Exactly.'

'And it also explains why there are three kinds of pleasure as well, one for each of the human types, doesn't it?'

'Yes.'

'Now, I'm sure you're aware', I said, 'that if you were to

327

approach representatives of these three types one by one and ask them which of these ways of life was the most enjoyable, they'd each swear by their own way of life, wouldn't they? A
d money-minded person wouldn't think that respect or learning, and their pleasures, were anywhere near as important as making money, unless there was also a profit to be made out of them, would he?'

'True,' he said.

'Then again, an ambitious person would regard enjoyment of money as vulgar,' I continued, 'and would think that only some concomitant respect could redeem enjoyment of intellectual activities from being an impractical waste of time, wouldn't he?'

'Yes,' he agreed.

'What about a philosopher?' I asked. 'How do you think he
e rates other pleasures compared with knowing the truth of things and with constantly employing his intellect and feeling that kind of pleasure?[†] Doesn't he think they miss the mark by a long way? Doesn't he describe them as necessary, in the strict sense that, apart from intellectual pleasures, he needs only those which are unavoidable?'

'We can be perfectly certain about that,'[†] he replied.

'Now, when people are arguing about the various pleasures which accompany aspects of themselves,' I said, 'and even about the kind of life one should lead, and when the only criterion they're using is where a way of life comes on the scale of pleasure and distress, rather than on the scales of right and
582a wrong or good and bad, then how can we know who has truth on his side?'

'I really couldn't tell you,' he said.

'Well, look at it this way. What does it take to make a good decision? Doesn't it take experience, intelligence, and rationality? Aren't these the best means of reaching a decision?'

'Of course,' he said.

'All right, then. Which of the three men has had the greatest exposure to all the pleasures we've mentioned? Do you think the avaricious type understands the truth of things and has therefore had more experience of intellectual pleasure than a
b philosopher has of the pleasure of moneymaking?'

'There's a world of difference,' he replied. 'From his earliest years onwards a philosopher has inevitably experienced both the other kinds of pleasure; there's never been any reason, however, for an avaricious person to experience the sweetness of intellectual pleasure and it remains unfamiliar to him—in fact, even if he wanted to get a taste of it, he'd find it difficult.'*

'In other words,' I commented, 'a philosopher's experience of both intellectual and moneymaking pleasures puts him in a better position than an avaricious person, anyway.'

'A far better position.'   c

'And how does he compare with an ambitious person? Is he more familiar with the enjoyment of respect than an ambitious person is with the enjoyment of intelligence?'

'But anyone can get respect: it's a result of attaining one's objective,' he said. 'Respect is showered on people for their wealth, their courage, and their intelligence: all three types are familiar with what it's like to enjoy being respected, at any rate. But only a philosopher can have found out by experience what it's like to enjoy contemplating reality.'

'As far as experience is concerned, then,' I said, 'it's a   d philosopher who's in the best position to make a decision.'

'By far the best position,' he agreed.

'And he's the only one who'll be in a position to combine experience and intelligence.'

'Naturally.'

'Moreover, the resources for making a decision are available only to a philosopher, not to an avaricious or an ambitious person.'

'What resources?'

'We did say that decisions require rational argumentation, didn't we?'

'Yes.'

'And rational argumentation is a particularly important resource in this context.'

'Of course.'

'Now, if money and wealth were the best means of making decisions, then the likes and dislikes of the avaricious type e would necessarily be closest to the truth.'*

'Yes.'

'And if prestige, success, and courage were best, it would be the likes and dislikes of the ambitious, competitive type. Yes?'

'Obviously.'

'But since it takes experience, intelligence and rationality . . . ?'

'Then it's the philosophical type, with his appreciation of rationality, whose tastes are closest to the truth,' he said.

583a 'Of the three kinds of pleasure, the most enjoyable, then, is that which belongs to the intellectual part of the mind; one's life becomes most enjoyable when this part of the mind is one's motivating force.'

'Of course,' he said. 'I mean, when a thoughtful person recommends his own way of life, he ought to be taken seriously.'*

'Which way of life—which pleasure—comes second, in his assessment?'

'Obviously the pleasure which accompanies the military, ambitious life, since it differs less from his own way of life than the moneymaking one does.'

'Apparently, then, the way of life pursued by the avaricious type comes last, in his estimate. Yes?'

'Of course,' he said.

The third proof of the philosopher's happiness is again concerned with pleasure. In a suggestive fashion, Plato distinguishes between true (genuine) pleasures and false (illusory) pleasures. The vast majority of so-called pleasures are actually only relief from pain—a state intermediate between pleasure and pain. Genuine pleasures are pure, unsullied by pain in this way. They are, above all, the pleasures of the mind, since the things of the rational mind, being more real, offer more real or genuine satisfaction. Since only the philosopher is familiar with these mental pleasures, then only he has true pleasure. Since morality is the rule of the rational mind, then a moral life is far happier and more desirable—involves far more true pleasure—than the immoral life of a dictator. In fact, one could say that a philosopher was 729 times happier than a dictator!

b 'That makes it two, then, one after another: immorality has twice been defeated by morality. In Olympic fashion, here's the third round—for Zeus the Saviour and Zeus of Olympus.* I wonder whether you agree that only the philosopher's pleasure is true and pure, while the others are illusory; I seem to remember having heard some clever fellow or other expressing this idea.* And in fact this would be the most important and serious fall of the whole competition.'

'It certainly would. But what are you getting at?'

'I'll find out, if you'll help my investigation by answering my c questions,' I said.

'Go ahead,' he said.

'All right,' I said. 'Pain is the opposite of pleasure, wouldn't you say?'

'Yes.'

'And is there a state which involves no pleasure or pain?'

'Yes, there certainly is.'

'It's an intermediate state in which the mind isn't active in either of these ways, isn't it? What do you think?'

'I agree,' he said.

'Now, can you remember what people say when they're ill?' I asked.

'What?'

'They claim that health really is the most pleasant thing in the world, but that they didn't appreciate the fact until they got d ill.'

'Yes, that's familiar,' he said.

'And you're aware that when people are in great pain they say that the most pleasant thing in the world would be for the pain to end.'

'Yes.'

'And you've come across all sorts of other situations, I should think, in which people are feeling pain and claim that there is nothing more pleasant than the remission and absence of pain. It's not pleasure whose praises they sing in these situations.'

'That's because under these circumstances remission does become pleasant and desirable, I suppose,' he remarked.

'And it follows that when someone stops feeling pleasure, the e remission of pleasure will be painful.'

'I suppose so,' he said.

'So the intermediate state, as we called it a moment ago—the state of inactivity—will at different times be both pleasure and pain.'

'So it seems.'

'Is it possible for anything to be both of two things if it is neither of those two things?'

'I don't think so.'

'Now, the mental feelings of pleasure and pain are both activities, aren't they?'

'Yes.'

584a 'And didn't we just find that the state which involves no pain or pleasure is actually a state of *in*activity which falls between the two?'

'Yes, we did.'

'How can it be right, then, to regard absence of pain as pleasant, or absence of pleasure as painful?'

'It can't be.'

'There's no reality here, then, just some superficial effect,' I said. 'Inactivity merely appears pleasant and painful on those occasions, because it's being contrasted respectively with pain and with pleasure. These appearances aren't reliable in the slightest: they're a kind of deception.'

'Yes, that *is* what the argument suggests,' he said.

b 'Well, I'd like to show you pleasures which aren't products of pain,' I said. 'I'm worried about the possibility of your currently regarding all pleasure as the cessation of pain, and all pain as the cessation of pleasure, and thinking that this is how things are.'

'Where shall I look?' he asked. 'What pleasures are you talking about?'

'If you'd care to consider the enjoyment of smells,' I replied, 'you'd see particularly clear examples, though there are plenty of other cases too.* The point is that there's no preceding feeling of pain, and yet you can suddenly get an incredibly intense pleasure at a scent, which also leaves no distress behind when it's over.'

'That's true,' he said.

c 'So we'd better resist the notion that pure pleasure is escape from pain, and pure pain is escape from pleasure.'

'Yes.'

'All the same,' I went on, 'I dare say that most so-called pleasures—the most intense ones, anyway—which reach the mind through the body* are of this kind: in some way or other they involve escape from pain.'

'True.'

'And doesn't the same go for anticipatory pleasure and

distress, which happen before the event as a result of expectations?'*

'Yes.'

'Do you know what they're like—what the best analogy for d them is?' I asked.

'What?' he answered.

'You know how things can be high, low, or in between?' I asked.

'Yes.'

'Well, someone moving from the bottom of anything to the middle is bound to get an impression of upward motion, isn't he? And once he's standing at the halfway point and looking down to where he travelled from, then if he hasn't seen the true heights, he's bound to think he's reached the top, isn't he?'

'Yes, I'd certainly have to agree with that,' he said.

'And if he retraced his steps, he'd think—rightly—that he e was travelling downwards, wouldn't he?' I asked.

'Of course.'

'And all these experiences of his would be due to his ignorance of the true nature of high, middle, and low, wouldn't they?'

'Obviously.'

'So would you think it odd for people who have never experienced truth, and who therefore have unreliable views about a great many subjects, to be in the same position where pleasure, pain, and the intermediate state are concerned? They not only hold the correct opinion that they are feeling pain, and 585a do in fact feel pain, when they move into a state of pain, but they're also certain about the satisfaction and pleasure they feel when they move away from pain and into the intermediate state. But they're being misled:* there's no difference between people who've never experienced pleasure comparing pain with absence of pain, and people who've never experienced white comparing black with grey.'

'No, I don't find this at all odd,' he replied. 'In fact, I'd be far more surprised if it didn't happen.'

'Here's something for you to think about,' I said. 'Aren't hunger, thirst, and so on states in which the body is lacking b something?'

'Naturally.'

'While stupidity and unintelligence are states in which the mind is lacking something?'

'Yes.'

'So food and intelligence are the sources of satisfaction in these cases?'

'Of course.'

'Is it the case that the more real something is, the more it can be a source of true satisfaction? Or is it the less real it is?'

'Obviously it's the more real it is.'

'Well, is reality present in a purer form in things like bread, drink, savouries, and food in general, do you think, or in things like true belief, knowledge, intelligence, and in short in all the
c things that constitute goodness? Here's another issue to help you decide. There are objects which never alter, never perish, and are never deceptive, and which are not only like that in themselves, but are found in an environment which is also like that; on the other hand, there are objects which are constantly altering and are perishable, and which are not only like that in themselves, but are found in an environment which is also like that. Which class of objects, do you think, contains a higher degree of reality?'

'The class of objects which never alter is far superior in this respect,' he replied.

'And isn't the reality of that which never alters just as knowable as it is real?'

'Yes.'

'And just as true?'

'Again, yes.'

'If it were less true, it would be less real as well, wouldn't it?'

'Necessarily.'

d 'To sum up, then, the kinds of things which tend to the body are less true and less real than the kinds of things which tend to the mind. Yes?'

'Yes, certainly.'

'And don't you think the same goes for the body, compared to the mind?'

'I do.'

'Is it the case, then, that an object which is satisfied by more real things, and which is itself more real, is more really satisfied

334

than an object which is satisfied by less real things, and which is itself less real?'

'Of course.'

'Therefore, assuming that being satisfied by things which accord with one's nature is pleasant, an object which is really satisfied more (that is, by more real things) would be enabled more really and truly to feel true pleasure, while an object e which comes by less real things would be less truly and steadily satisfied and would come by a less dependable and less true version of pleasure.'*

'That's absolutely inevitable,' he agreed.

'It turns out, then, that people to whom intelligence and 586a goodness* are unfamiliar, whose only interest is self-indulgence and so on, spend their lives moving aimlessly to and fro between the bottom and the halfway point, which is as far as they reach. But they never travel any further towards the true heights: they've never even looked up there, let alone gone there; they aren't really satisfied by anything real; they don't experience steady, pure pleasure. They're no different from cattle: they spend their lives grazing, with their eyes turned down and heads bowed towards the ground and their tables. Food and sex are their only concerns, and their insatiable greed for more and more drives them to kick and butt one another to b death with their horns and hoofs of iron, killing one another because they're seeking satisfaction in unreal things for a part of themselves which is also unreal—a leaky vessel they're trying to fill.'*

'Socrates,' Glaucon declared, 'you've given an inspired and perfect description of the life most people lead.'

'Isn't it also inevitable that the pleasures they're involved with are, in fact, combinations of pleasure and pain, mere effigies of true pleasure? Like those illusory paintings, the pleasure and pain are vivid only because of the contrast c between them, and their intensity is therefore no more than apparent. They impregnate people with an insane lust for the pleasure they offer, and these fools fight over them, as the Trojans in Stesichorus' story, out of ignorance of the truth, fought over the mere apparition of Helen.'*

'Yes, something like that's bound to be the case,' he said.

'What about the passionate part of the mind? Won't the

situation be more or less the same for anyone who brings its desires to a successful conclusion? He's either ambitious, in which case he's motivated by resentment and seeks satisfaction in status; or he's competitive, in which case he relies on force and seeks satisfaction in success; or he's bad-tempered, in
d which case he resorts to anger and seeks satisfaction in an angry outburst. But none of these involve reason and intelligence.'*

'Again, yes, something like that's bound to be the case,' he said.

'All right, then,' I said. 'Shall we confidently state that, where avarice and competitiveness are concerned, any desire which succeeds in attaining its objective will get the truest pleasure available to it when it is guided by truth, which is to say when it follows the leadership of knowledge and reason in its quest
e for those pleasures to which intelligence directs it? And shall we add that the pleasures it gets will also be the ones which are particularly suitable for it—that is, if suitability and benefit coincide?'

'Well, they do coincide,' he said.

'It follows that when the whole mind accepts the leadership of the philosophical part, and there's no internal conflict, then each part can do its own job and be moral* in everything it does, and in particular can enjoy its own pleasures, and thus
587a reap as much benefit and truth from pleasure as is possible for it.'

'Exactly.'

'When one of the other two parts is in control, however, it not only fails to attain its own pleasure, but it also forces the other parts to go after unsuitable, false pleasures.'

'Right,' he agreed.

'Now, the further removed something is from philosophy and reason, the more it'll have an effect of this kind.'

'Certainly.'

'And aren't things separated from law and order to the same extent that they're separated from reason?'

'Obviously.'

'And didn't we find that it's the lustful, dictatorial desires
b which are the furthest removed from law and order?'

'We certainly did.'

336

'While the regal, restrained desires are closest to them?'

'Yes.'

'The more of a dictator a person is, then, the greater the distance between him and pleasure which is both true and suitable; the more of a king a person is, the shorter the distance.'

'Necessarily.'

'It follows that there is no life less enjoyable than a dictator's, and no life more enjoyable than a king's.'

'No doubt about it.'

'Do you know, in fact, how much less enjoyable a dictator's life is than a king's?' I asked.

'No. Please tell me,' he replied.

'There are three kinds of pleasure, apparently, and one of them is genuine, while two are spurious. A dictator, in his flight from law and reason, crosses over into the land beyond the c spurious pleasures and settles down with his bodyguard of slavish pleasures.* Perhaps the best way to describe the extent of his degeneration, which isn't all that easy to describe, is as follows.'

'How?' he asked.

'The dictator occupies the third place in the series which starts with the oligarchic type, since the democratic type comes in between them.'

'Yes.'

'So the pleasure he beds down with is also, assuming the truth of our earlier conclusions,* a reflection three places away from oligarchic pleasure. Yes?'

'Yes.'

'Moreover, counting from the regal type (and assuming that aristocracy and kingship belong to the same category),* it's the d oligarchic type's turn to come third.'

'Yes.'

'It follows', I said, 'that a dictator's distance from true pleasure is, in numerical terms, triple a triple.'

'I suppose so.'

'So it appears', I said, 'that the reflection which constitutes a dictator's pleasure is a plane number based on the quantity of the linear number.'

'Yes, definitely.'

'And the extent of the distance can be expressed as a square and a cube.'

'It can by a mathematician, anyway,' he said.

e 'So suppose you wanted to put it the other way round and state how far a king is from a dictator in terms of the truth of pleasure, the completed multiplication would show that his life is 729 times more pleasant than a dictator's. And a dictator is that much more wretched than a king.'*

588a 'You've had to spout some complex mathematics,' he remarked, 'to describe the difference, in terms of pleasure and distress, between the two men—the moral one and the immoral one.'

'Yes, but I'm right,' I said, 'and it's a number which suits lives, assuming that days, nights, months, and years are related to lives.'*

'Well, they certainly are,' he said.

'Now, if this is how decisive a victory a good, moral person wins over a bad, immoral one on the field of pleasure, just think how infinitely more resounding his victory will be on the field of elegance and propriety of life, and of goodness.'

'Yes, that's absolutely right,' he said.

Plato concludes that he has responded to the challenge of Chapter 2: he has demonstrated that morality is intrinsically rewarding and desirable. He rounds this off with a graphic image of the tripartite mind as consisting of three creatures: a human being (reason), a lion (passion), and a mutable monster (desire). Morality feeds the human being, tames the lion, and subdues the monster; immorality— especially if it goes undiscovered—makes one a monster. Self- discipline (as a result of the educational programme of Chapters 4 and 10) is best, but the externally imposed discipline of law and convention is a good second best. One must use the imaginary community as a paradigm on which to model one's own inner constitution.

b 'All right,' I said. 'At this point in the argument, let's remind ourselves of the original assertion which started us off on our journey here. Wasn't it someone saying that immorality was rewarding if you were a consummate criminal who gave an impression of morality? Wasn't that the assertion?'*

'Yes, it was.'

'Well, now that we've decided what effect moral and immoral conduct have,' I said, 'we can engage him in conversation.'

'What shall we say?' he asked.

'Let's construct a theoretical model of the mind, to help him see what kind of idea he's come up with.'

'What sort of model?' he asked.   c

'Something along the lines of those creatures who throng the ancient myths,' I said, 'like the Chimera, Scylla, Cerberus, and so on, whose form is a composite of the features of more than one creature.'*

'Yes, that's how they're described,' he said.

'Make a model, then, of a creature with a single—if varied and many-headed—form, arrayed all around with the heads of both wild and tame animals, and possessing the ability to change over to a different set of heads and to generate all these new bits from its own body.'

'That would take some skilful modelling,' he remarked, 'but d since words are a more plastic material than wax and so on, you may consider the model constructed.'

'A lion and a man are the next two models to make, then. The first of the models, however, is to be by far the largest, and the second the second largest.'

'That's an easier job,' he said. 'It's done.'

'Now join the three of them together until they become one, as it were.'

'All right,' he said.

'And for the final coat, give them the external appearance of a single entity. Make them look like a person, so that anyone incapable of seeing what's inside, who can see only the external husk, will see a single creature, a human being.'   e

'It's done,' he said.

'Now, we'd better respond to the idea that this person gains from doing wrong, and loses from doing right, by pointing out to its proponent that this is tantamount to saying that we're rewarded if we indulge and strengthen the many-sided beast and the lion with all its aspects, but starve and weaken the 589a man, until he's subject to the whims of the others, and can't promote familiarity and compatibility between the other two, but lets them bite each other, fight, and try to eat each other.'

'Yes, that's undoubtedly what a supporter of immorality would have to say,' he agreed.

'So the alternative position, that morality is profitable, is equivalent to saying that our words and behaviour should be
b designed to maximize the control the inner man has within us, and should enable him to secure the help of the leonine quality and then tend to the many-headed beast as a farmer tends to his crops—by nurturing and cultivating its tame aspects, and by stopping the wild ones growing.* Then he can ensure that they're all compatible with one another, and with himself, and can look after them all equally, without favouritism.'

'Yes, that's exactly what a supporter of morality has to say,' he agreed.

'Whichever way you look at it, then, a supporter of morality
c is telling the truth, and a supporter of immorality is wrong. Whether your criterion is pleasure, reputation, or benefit, a supporter of morality is right, and a critic of morality is unreliable and doesn't know what he's talking about.'

'I quite agree: he doesn't in the slightest,' he said.

'But he doesn't mean to make a mistake, so let's be gentle with him. Here's a question we can ask him, to try to win him over: "My friend, don't you think that this is also what accounts for conventional standards of what is and is not acceptable? Things are acceptable when they subject the bestial
d aspects of our nature to the human—or it might be more accurate to say the divine—part of ourselves, but they're objectionable when they cause the oppression of our tame side under the savage side."* Will he agree, do you think?'

'Well, I'll be recommending him to,' he answered.

'So what follows from this argument? Can there be any profit in the immoral acquisition of money, if this entails the enslavement of the best part of oneself to the worst part? The
e point is, if there's no profit in someone selling his son or daughter into slavery—slavery under savage and evil men—for even a great deal of money, then what happens if he cruelly enslaves the most divine part of himself to the vilest, most godless part? Isn't unhappiness the result? Isn't the deadly business he's being paid for far more terrible than what
590a Eriphyle did when she accepted the necklace as the price for her husband's death?'

'Yes, by a long way,' Glaucon said. 'I mean, I'll answer on behalf of our supporter of immorality.'

'Now, do you think the reason for the traditional condemnation of licentiousness is the same—because it allows that fiend, that huge and many-faceted creature, greater freedom than it should have?'

'Obviously,' he said.

'And aren't obstinacy and bad temper considered bad because they distend and invigorate our leonine, serpentine* b side to a disproportionate extent?'

'Yes.'

'Whereas a spoilt, soft way of life is considered bad because it makes this part of us so slack and loose that it's incapable of facing hardship?'

'Of course.'

'And why are lack of independence and autonomy despised? Isn't it still to do with the passionate part, because we have to subordinate it to the unruly beast and, from our earliest years, get the lion used to being insulted and to becoming a monkey instead of a lion—and all for the sake of money and to satisfy our greed?'

'Yes.' c

'What about mundane, manual labour? Why do you think it has a bad name? Isn't it precisely because there's an inherent weakness in the truly good part of the person which makes him incapable of controlling his internal beasts, so that all he does is pander to them, and all he can learn is their whims?'*

'I suppose that's right,' he said.

'The question is, how can a person in this condition become subject to the kind of rulership which is available to a truly good person? By being the slave, we suggest, of a truly good person, whose divine element rules within him.* But we're not d suggesting, as Thrasymachus did about subjects,* that his status as a subject should do him harm; we're saying that subjection to the principle of divine intelligence is to everyone's advantage. It's best if this principle is part of a person's own nature, but if it isn't, it can be imposed from outside, to foster as much unanimity and compatibility between us as might be possible when we're all governed by the same principle.'

'You're right,' he said.

e   'It's also clear', I continued, 'that this is the function of law: this is why every member of a community has the law to fall back on. And it explains why we keep children under control and don't allow them their freedom until we've formed a government within them, as we would in a community. What

591a we do is use what is best in ourselves to cultivate the equivalent aspect of a child, and then we let him go free once the equivalent part within him has been established as his guardian and ruler.'

'Yes, that's clear,' he said.

'Is there any conceivable argument, then, Glaucon, which will enable us to claim that immorality or licentiousness is rewarding, when the result of any kind of shameful behaviour may be a richer or otherwise more powerful person, but is certainly a worse person?'

'No, there isn't,' he replied.

'And how can it be profitable for a person's immorality to go

b unnoticed and unpunished?* The consequence of a criminal getting away with his crimes is that he becomes a worse person. If he's found out and punished, however, then his bestial side is tamed and pacified, his tame side is liberated, and in short his mental state becomes as good as it can be. And, in so far as the mind is a more valuable asset than the body, it's more important for the mind to acquire self-discipline, morality, and intelligence than it is for the body to become fit, attractive, and healthy.'

'You're absolutely right,' he said.

c   'Then anyone with any sense will put all his energies, throughout his life, into achieving this goal. In the first place, he'll value only those intellectual pursuits which have the effect we've described on the mind, and regard any others as trivial, won't he?'

'Obviously,' he said.

'In the second place,' I went on, 'there's more to his attitude towards the care and condition of his body than simply the fact that he won't give himself over to bestial and irrational pleasure and make that the whole point of his life. He won't, in fact, be interested in physical health and he won't take the pursuit of physical fitness, health, and beauty seriously unless they also

d lead to self-discipline. We'll find him, throughout his life, attuning his body in order to make music with his mind.'

'Yes, that's exactly what it takes to be a true virtuoso,' he said.*

'And won't the same attunement and harmony guide his acquisition of money? He's hardly going to be swayed by the usual standards of happiness and amass an inexhaustible pile of money, along with its inexhaustible troubles, is he?'

'I don't think so,' he said.

'What he'll do, however,' I said, 'is keep an eye on his own e inner society and watch out for trouble brewing among its members, caused by his having either too much or too little property.* He'll stick to this guiding principle as much as possible, and increase and decrease his assets accordingly.'

'Exactly,' he agreed.

'And the same consideration will also guide his attitude 592a towards honours. He won't hesitate to accept and experience those which will, in his view, make him a better person, but in his private life as well as in public life he'll avoid those which he thinks would cause the downfall of his established constitution.'*

'If that's what's important to him,' he said, 'he's unlikely to have anything to do with government.'

'Actually,' I said, 'he certainly will, in his own community. But I agree that he probably won't in the country of his birth, short of divine intervention.'

'I see,' he said. 'You mean that he will in the community we've just been founding and describing, which can't be accommodated anywhere in the world, and therefore rests at the level of ideas.'   b

'It may be, however,' I replied, 'that it is retained in heaven as a paradigm for those who desire to see it and, through seeing it, to return from exile. In fact, it doesn't make the slightest bit of difference whether it exists or will exist anywhere: it's still the only community in whose government he could play a part.'

'Yes, I suppose so,' he said.

Chapter 13

Poetry and Unreality

Plato now launches his notorious attack on poetry (with painting introduced in a supporting role); the critique is supplementary to that of Chapter 4. On the whole issue, see also pp. xxix–xxxiii. The attack begins with the claim that artistic products are two stages removed from reality and truth, and that they represent things as they appear to be, not as they are. It is easy to be a master of representing appearances, since it involves no understanding of any of the things represented, no penetration beyond the surface of things to its function or to whether or not it serves some moral purpose.

595a   'You know,' I said, 'the issue of poetry is the main consideration—among many others—which convinces me that the way we were trying to found our community was along absolutely the right lines.'*

'What are you thinking of?' he asked.

'That we flatly refused to admit any representational poetry.* I mean, its total unacceptability is even clearer, in my opinion, b now that we've distinguished the different aspects of the mind.'

'How is it clearer?'

'Well, this is just between ourselves: please don't denounce me to the tragic playwrights and all the other representational poets. But it looks as though this whole genre of poetry deforms its audience's minds,* unless they have the antidote, which is recognition of what this kind of poetry is actually like.'

'What do you mean? What do you have in mind?' he asked.

'It's fairly clear', I said, 'that all these fine tragedians trace their lineage back to Homer: they're Homer's students and disciples, ultimately. And this makes it difficult for me to say c what I have to say, because I've had a kind of fascinated admiration for Homer ever since I was young. Still, we should value truth more than we value any person, so, as I say, I'd better speak out.'

'Yes,' he said.

'And you'll listen to what I have to say, or rather respond to any questions I ask?'

'Yes. Go ahead and ask them.'

'Can you tell me what representation basically is? You see, I don't quite understand its point myself.'

'And I suppose I do!' he said.

'It wouldn't surprise me if you did,' I said. 'Just because a person can't see very well, it doesn't mean that he won't often 596a see things before people with better eyesight than him.'

'That's true,' he said. 'All the same, I'd be too shy to explain any views I did have in front of you, so please try to come up with an answer yourself.'

'All right. Shall we get the enquiry going by drawing on familiar ideas? Our usual position is, as you know, that any given plurality of things which have a single name constitutes a single specific type.* Is that clear to you?'

'Yes.'

'So now let's take any plurality you want. Would it be all right with you if we said that there were, for instance, lots of b beds and tables?'

'Of course.'

'But these items of furniture comprise only two types—the type of bed and the type of table.'

'Yes.'

'Now, we also invariably claim that the manufacture of either of these items of furniture involves the craftsman looking to the type and then making the beds or tables (or whatever) which we use.* The point is that the type itself is not manufactured by any craftsman. How could it be?'

'It couldn't.'

'There's another kind of craftsman too. I wonder what you think of him.'

'What kind?' c

'He makes everything—all the items which every single manufacturer makes.'

'He must be extraordinarily gifted.'

'Wait: you haven't heard the half of it yet. It's not just a case of his being able to manufacture all the artefacts there are: every plant too, every creature (himself included), the earth, the heavens, gods, and everything in the heavens and in Hades under the earth—all these are made and created by this one man!'

d   'He really must be extraordinarily clever,' he said.

'Don't you believe me?' I asked. 'Tell me, do you doubt that this kind of craftsman could exist under any circumstances, or do you admit the possibility that a person could—in one sense, at least—create all these things? I mean, don't you realize that you yourself could, under certain circumstances, create all these things?'

'What circumstances?' he asked.

'I'm not talking about anything complicated or rare,' I said. 'It doesn't take long to create the circumstances. The quickest method, I suppose, is to get hold of a mirror and carry it e   around with you everywhere. You'll soon be creating everything I mentioned a moment ago—the sun and the heavenly bodies, the earth, yourself, and all other creatures, plants, and so on.'

'Yes, but I'd be creating appearances, not actual real things,' he said.

'That's a good point,' I said. 'You've arrived just in time to save the argument. I mean, that's presumably the kind of craftsman a painter is.* Yes?'

'Of course.'

'His creations aren't real, according to you; but do you agree that all the same there's a sense in which even a painter creates a bed?'

'Yes,' he said, 'he's another one who creates an apparent bed.'

597a   'What about a joiner who specializes in making beds? Weren't we saying a short while ago that what he makes is a particular bed, not the type, which is (on our view) the real bed?'

'Yes, we were.'

'So if there's no reality to his creation, then it isn't real; it's similar to something real, but it isn't actually real. It looks as though it's wrong to attribute full reality to a joiner's or any artisan's product, doesn't it?'

'Yes,' he said, 'any serious student of this kind of argument would agree with you.'

'It shouldn't surprise us, then, if we find that even these products are obscure when compared with the truth.'

'No, it shouldn't.'   b

'Now, what about this representer we're trying to understand? Shall we see if these examples help us?' I asked.

'That's fine by me,' he said.

'Well, we've got these three beds. First, there's the real one, and we'd say, I imagine, that it is the product of divine craftsmanship. I mean, who else could have made it?'*

'No one, surely.'

'Then there's the one the joiner makes.'

'Yes,' he said.

'And then there's the one the painter makes. Yes?'

'Yes, agreed.'

'These three, then—painter, joiner, God—are responsible for three different kinds of bed.'

'Yes, that's right.'

'Now, God has produced only that one real bed.* The   c restriction to only one might have been his own choice, or it might just be impossible for him to make more than one. But God never has, and never could, create two or more such beds.'

'Why not?' he asked.

'Even if he were to make only two such beds,' I said, 'an extra one would emerge, and both the other two would be of that one's type.* It, and not the two beds, would be the real bed.'

'Right,' he said.

'God realized this, I'm sure. He didn't want to be a kind of   d joiner, making a particular bed: he wanted to be a genuine creator and make a genuine bed. That's why he created a single real one.'

'I suppose that's right.'

'Shall we call him its progenitor, then, or something like that?'

'Yes, he deserves the name,' he said, 'since he's the maker of this and every other reality.'

'What about a joiner? Shall we call him a manufacturer of beds?'

'Yes.'

'And shall we also call a painter a manufacturer and maker of beds and so on?'

'No, definitely not.'

'What do you think he does with beds, then?'

e   'I think the most suitable thing to call him would be a representer of the others' creations,' he said.

'Well, in that case', I said, 'you're using the term "representer" for someone who deals with things which are, in fact, two generations away from reality, aren't you?'

'Yes,' he said.

'The same goes for tragic playwrights, then, since they're representers: they're two generations away from the throne of truth, and so are all other representers.'*

'I suppose so.'

'Well, in the context of what we're now saying about representation, I've got a further question about painters. Is it, 598a in any given instance, the actual reality that they try to represent, or is it the craftsmen's products?'

'The craftsmen's products,' he said.

'Here's another distinction you'd better make: do they try to represent them as they are, or as they appear to be?'

'What do you mean?' he asked.

'I'll tell you. Whether you look at a bed from the side or straight on or whatever, it's still just as much a bed as it ever was, isn't it? I mean, it doesn't actually alter it at all: it just *appears* to be different, doesn't it? And the same goes for anything else you can mention. Yes?'

'Yes,' he agreed. 'It seems different, but isn't actually.'

b   'So I want you to consider carefully which of these two alternatives painting is designed for in any and every instance. Is it designed to represent the facts of the real world or appearances? Does it represent appearance or truth?'*

'Appearance,' he said.

'It follows that representation and truth are a considerable distance apart, and a representer is capable of making every product there is only because his contact with things is slight and is restricted to how they look. Consider what a painter does, for instance: we're saying that he doesn't have a clue about shoemaking or joinery, but he'll still paint pictures of c   artisans working at these and all other areas of expertise, and if

348

he's good at painting he might paint a joiner, have people look at it from far away, and deceive them—if they're children or stupid adults—by making it look as though the joiner were real.'*

'Naturally.'

'I think the important thing to bear in mind about cases like this, Glaucon, is that when people tell us they've met someone who's mastered every craft, and is the world's leading expert in absolutely every branch of human knowledge,* we should reply d that they're being rather silly. They seem to have met the kind of illusionist who's expert at representation and, thanks to their own inability to evaluate knowledge, ignorance, and representation, to have been so thoroughly taken in as to believe in his omniscience.'

'You're absolutely right,' he said.

'Now, we'd better investigate tragedy next,' I said, 'and its guru, Homer, because one does come across the claim* that there's no area of expertise, and nothing relevant to human e goodness and badness either—and nothing to do with the gods even—that these poets don't understand. It is said that a good poet must understand the issues he writes about, if his writing is to be successful, and that if he didn't understand them, he wouldn't be able to write about them. So we'd better try to decide between the alternatives. Either the people who come across these representational poets are being taken in and are failing to appreciate, when they see their products, that these products are two steps away from reality and that it certainly 599a doesn't take knowledge of the truth to create them (since what they're creating are appearances, not reality); or this view is valid, and in fact good poets are authorities on the subjects most people are convinced they're good at writing about.'

'Yes, this definitely needs looking into,' he said.

'Well, do you think that anyone who was capable of producing both originals and images would devote his energy to making images, and would make out that this is the best thing he's done with his life?' b

'No, I don't.'

'I'm sure that if he really knew about the things he was copying in his representations, he'd put far more effort into producing real objects than he would into representations, and would try to leave behind a lot of fine products for people to remember him by, and would dedicate himself to being the recipient rather than the bestower of praise.'*

'I agree,' he said. 'He'd gain a lot more prestige and do himself a great deal more good.'

'Well, let's concentrate our interrogation of Homer (or any c other poet you like) on a single area. Let's not ask him whether he can tell us of any patients cured by any poet in ancient or modern times, as Asclepius cured his patients, or of any students any of them left to continue his work, as Asclepius left his sons. And even these questions grant the possibility that a poet might have had some medical knowledge, instead of merely representing medical terminology. No, let's not bother to ask him about any other areas of expertise either. But we do have a right to ask Homer about the most important and glorious areas he undertakes to expound—warfare, tactics, d politics, and human education. Let's ask him, politely, "Homer, maybe you aren't two steps away from knowing the truth about goodness; maybe you aren't involved in the manufacture of images (which is what we called representation). Perhaps you're actually only one step away, and you do have the ability to recognize which practices—in their private or their public lives—improve people and which ones impair them. But in that case, just as Sparta has its Lycurgus and communities of all different sizes have their various reformers, please tell us which community has you to thank for improvements to its e government. Which community attributes the benefits of its good legal code to you? Italy and Sicily name Charondas in this respect, we Athenians name Solon. Which country names you?" Will he have any reply to make?'

'I don't think so,' said Glaucon. 'Even the Homeridae* themselves don't make that claim.'

600a 'Well, does history record that there was any war fought in Homer's time whose success depended on his leadership or advice?'

'No.'

'Well then, are a lot of ingenious inventions attributed to him, as they are to Thales of Miletus and Anacharsis of Scythia? I mean the kinds of inventions which have practical applications in the arts and crafts and elsewhere. He is, after all, supposed to be good at creating things.'

'No, there's not the slightest hint of that sort of thing.'

'All right, so there's no evidence of his having been a public benefactor, but what about in private? Is there any evidence that, during his lifetime, he was a mentor to people, and that they used to value him for his teaching and then handed down b to their successors a particular Homeric way of life? This is what happened to Pythagoras: he wasn't only held in extremely high regard for his teaching during his lifetime, but his successors even now call their way of life Pythagorean and somehow seem to stand out from all other people.'

'No, there's no hint of that sort of thing either,' he said. 'I mean, Homer's associate Creophylus' cultural attainments would turn out to be even more derisory than his name suggests they are,* Socrates, if the stories about Homer are true. You see, Creophylus is said to have more or less disregarded Homer during his lifetime.'† c

'Yes, that *is* what we're told,' I agreed. 'But, Glaucon, if Homer really had been an educational expert whose products were better people—which is to say, if he had knowledge in this sphere and his abilities were not limited to representation—don't you think he'd have been surrounded by hordes of associates, who would have admired him and valued his company highly? Look at Protagoras of Abdera, Prodicus of Ceos, and all the rest of them: they can use their exclusive tuition to make their contemporaries believe that without them in charge of their education they won't be capable of managing their own estates, let alone their communities, and they're so d appreciated for this expertise of theirs that their associates almost carry them around on their heads.* So if Homer or Hesiod had been able to help people's moral development, would their contemporaries have allowed them to go from town to town reciting their poems? Wouldn't they have kept a tighter grip on them than on their money, and tried to force them to stay with them in their homes? And if they couldn't persuade them to do that, wouldn't they have danced e attendance on them wherever they went, until they'd gained as much from their teaching as they could?'

'I don't think anyone could disagree with you, Socrates,' he said.

'So shall we classify all poets, from Homer onwards, as representers of images of goodness (and of everything else which occurs in their poetry), and claim that they don't have any contact with the truth? The facts are as we said a short while ago: a painter creates an illusory shoemaker, when not 601a only does he not understand anything about shoemaking, but his audience doesn't either. They just base their conclusions on the colours and shapes they can see.'

'Yes.'

'And I should think we'll say that the same goes for a poet as well: he uses words and phrases to block in some of the colours of each area of expertise, although all he understands is how to represent things in a way which makes other superficial people, who base their conclusions on the words they can hear, think that he's written a really good poem about shoemaking or military command or whatever else it is that he's set to metre, rhythm, and music. It only takes these features to cast this b powerful a spell: that's what they're for. But when the poets' work is stripped of its musical hues* and expressed in plain words, I think you've seen what kind of impression it gives, so you know what I'm talking about.'

'I do,' he said.

'Isn't it', I asked, 'like what noticeably happens when a young man has alluring features, without actually being good-looking, and then this charm of his deserts him?'

'Exactly,' he said.

'Now, here's another point to consider. An image-maker, a representer, understands only appearance, while reality is c beyond him. Isn't that our position?'

'Yes.'

'Let's not leave the job half done: let's give this idea the consideration it deserves.'

'Go on,' he said.

'What a painter does, we're saying, is paint a picture of a horse's reins and a bit. Yes?'

'Yes.'

'While they're made by a saddler and a smith, aren't they?'

'Yes.'

'Does a painter know what the reins and the bit have to be

like? Surely even their makers, the smith and the saddler, don't know this, do they? Only the horseman does, because he's the one who knows how to make use of them.'

'You're quite right.'

'In fact, won't we claim that it's a general principle?'

'What?'

'That whatever the object, there are three areas of expertise: d usage, manufacture, and representation.'

'Yes.'

'Now, is there any other standard by which one assesses the goodness, fineness, and rightness of anything (whether it's a piece of equipment or a creature or an activity) than the use for which it was made, by man or by nature?'

'No.'

'It's absolutely inevitable, then, that no one knows the ins and outs of any object more than the person who makes use of it. He has to be the one to tell the manufacturer how well or badly the object he's using fares in actual usage. A pipe-player, for example, tells a pipe-maker which of his pipes do what they're supposed to do when actually played, and goes on to e instruct him in what kinds of pipes to make, and the pipe-maker does what he's told.'

'Of course.'

'So as far as good and bad pipes are concerned, it's a knowledgeable person who gives the orders, while the other obeys the orders and does the manufacturing. Right?'

'Yes.'

'Justified confidence, then, is what a pipe-maker has about goodness and badness (as a result of spending time with a knowledgeable person and having to listen to him), while knowledge is the province of the person who makes use of the 602a pipes.'*

'Yes.'

'Which of these two categories does our representer belong to? Does he acquire knowledge about whether or not what he's painting is good or right from making use of the object, or does he acquire true belief because of having to spend time with a knowledgeable person and being told what to paint?'

'He doesn't fit either case.'

353

'As far as goodness and badness are concerned, then, a representer doesn't have either knowledge or true beliefs about whatever it is he's representing.'

'Apparently not.'

'How nicely placed a poetic representer is, then, to know what he's writing about!'

'Not really.'

b   'No, because all the same, despite his ignorance of the good and bad aspects of things, he'll go on representing them. But what he'll be representing, apparently, is whatever appeals to a large, if ignorant, audience.'

'Naturally.'

'Here are the points we seem to have reached a reasonable measure of agreement on, then: a representer knows nothing of value about the things he represents; representation is a kind of game, and shouldn't be taken seriously; and those who compose tragedies in iambic and epic verse* are, without exception, outstanding examples of representers.'

'Yes.'

Since poetry deals with appearances, it appeals to—and fattens up— the lower part of the mind, not the rational part. It makes us indulge in emotional feelings which hamper reason, even when we would not normally sanction those feelings. Reason uses measurement to combat some illusory appearances, and calculation of benefit to combat unnecessary feelings. In short, poetry does nothing to establish an ordered, moral inner constitution, and if one is already established, it threatens to subvert it. Until or unless it can be proven that feelings foster philosophy, rather than hinder it, we must be extremely wary of them.

c   'So the province of representation is indeed two steps removed from truth, isn't it?' I said.

'Yes.'

'But on which of the many aspects of a person does it exert its influence?'

'What are you getting at?'

'Something like this. One and the same object appears to vary in size depending on whether we're looking at it from close up or far away.'

'Yes.'

'And the same objects look both bent and straight depending on whether we look at them when they're in water or out of it, and both concave and convex because sight gets misled by colouring.* Our mind obviously contains the potential for every single kind of confusion like this. It's because illusory d painting aims at this affliction in our natures that it can only be described as sorcery; and the same goes for conjuring and all trickery of that sort.'

'True.'

'Now, methods have evolved of combating this—measuring, counting, and weighing are the most elegant of them—and consequently of ending the reign within us of apparent size, number, and weight, and replacing them with something which calculates and measures, or even weighs. Right?'

'Of course.'

'And this, of course, is the job of the rational part of the e mind, which is capable of performing calculations.'

'Yes.'

'Now, it's not uncommon for the mind to have made its measurements, and to be reporting that x is larger than y (or smaller than it, or the same size as it), but still to be receiving an impression which contradicts its measurements of these very objects.'

'Yes.'

'Well, didn't we say that it's impossible for a single thing to hold contradictory beliefs at the same time about the same objects?'*

'Yes, we did, and we were right.'

'So the part of the mind whose views run counter to the 603a measurements must be different from the part whose views fall in with the measurements.'*

'Yes.'

'But it's the best part of the mind which accepts measurements and calculations.'

'Of course.'

'The part which opposes them, therefore, must be a low-grade part of the mind.'

'Necessarily.'

'Well, all that I've been saying has been intended to bring us

355

to the point where we can agree that not only does painting—
or rather representation in general—produce a product which
is far from truth, but it also forms a close, warm, affectionate
relationship with a part of us which is, in its turn, far from
b intelligence. And nothing healthy or authentic can emerge from
this relationship.'

'Absolutely,' he said.

'A low-grade mother like representation, then, and an equally
low-grade father produce low-grade children.'

'I suppose that's right.'

'Does this apply only to visual representation,' I asked, 'or to
aural representation as well—in other words, to poetry?'

'I suppose it applies to poetry as well,' he said.

'Well, we'd better not rely on mere suppositions based on
painting,' I said. 'Let's also get close enough to that part of the
c mind which poetic representation consorts with to see whether
it's of low or high quality.'

'Yes, we should.'

'We'd better start by having certain ideas out in the open.
We'd say that representational poetry represents people doing
things, willingly or unwillingly, and afterwards thinking that
they've been successful or unsuccessful, and throughout feeling
distressed or happy.* Have I missed anything out?'

'No, nothing.'

'Well, does a person remain internally unanimous
d throughout all this? We found that, in the case of sight, there's
conflict and people have contradictory views within themselves
at the same time about the same objects. Is it like that when
one is doing things too? Is there internal conflict and dissent?
But it occurs to me that there's really no need for us to decide
where we stand on this issue now, because we've already done
so, perfectly adequately, in an earlier phase of the discussion,*
when we concluded that, at any given moment, our minds are
teeming with countless thousands of these kinds of
contradictions.'

'That's right,' he said.

'Yes,' I said. 'But that earlier discussion of ours was
e incomplete, and I think it's crucial that we finish it off now.'

'What have we left out?' he asked.

'If a good man meets with a misfortune such as losing a son

or something else he values very highly, we've already said, as you know, that he'll endure this better than anyone else.'*

'Yes.'

'But here's something for us to think about. Will he feel no grief, or is that impossible? If it's impossible, is it just that he somehow keeps his pain within moderate bounds?'

'The second alternative is closer to the truth,' he said.

'But now I've got another question for you about him. Do 604a you think he'll be more likely to fight and resist his distress when his peers can see him, or when he's all alone by himself in some secluded spot?'

'He'll endure pain far better when there are people who can see him, of course,' he said.

'When he's all alone, however, I imagine he won't stop himself expressing a lot of things he'd be ashamed of anyone hearing, and doing a lot of things he'd hate anyone to see him do.'

'That's right,' he agreed.

'Isn't it the case that reason and convention recommend resistance, while the actual event pushes him towards distress?' b

'True.'

'When a person is simultaneously pulled in opposite directions in response to a single object, we're bound to conclude that he has two sides.'†

'Of course.'

'One of which is prepared to let convention dictate the proper course of action, isn't it?'

'Can you explain how?'

'Convention tells us, as you know, that it's best to remain as unruffled as possible when disaster strikes and not to get upset, on the grounds that it's never clear whether an incident of this nature is good or bad, that nothing positive is gained by taking it badly, that no aspect of human life is worth bothering about a great deal, and that grief blocks our access to the very thing c we need to have available as quickly as possible in these circumstances.'

'What do you have in mind?' he asked.

'The ability to think about the incident', I replied, 'and, under the guidance of reason, to make the best possible use of one's situation, as one would in a game of dice when faced with how the dice had fallen. When children bump into things, they clutch the hurt spot and spend time crying; instead of behaving like that, we should constantly be training our minds

d to waste no time before trying to heal anything which is unwell, and help anything which has fallen get up from the floor—to banish mourning by means of medicine.'

'Yes, that's the best way to deal with misfortune,' he said.

'Now, our position is that the best part of our minds is perfectly happy to be guided by reason like this.'

'That goes without saying.'

'Whereas there's another part of our minds which urges us to remember the bad times and to express our grief, and which is insatiably greedy for tears. What can we say about it? That it's incapable of listening to reason, that it can't face hard work, that it goes hand in hand with being frightened of hardship?'

'Yes, that's right.'

e 'Now, although the petulant part of us is rich in a variety of representable possibilities, the intelligent and calm side of our characters is pretty well constant and unchanging. This makes it not only difficult to represent, but also difficult to understand when it is represented, particularly when the audience is the kind of motley crowd you find crammed into a theatre, because they're simply not acquainted with the experience that's being represented to them.'

605a 'Absolutely.'

'Evidently, then, a representational poet has nothing to do with this part of the mind: his skill isn't made for its pleasure, because otherwise he'd lose his popular appeal. He's concerned with the petulant and varied side of our characters, because it's easy to represent.'

'Obviously.'

'So we're now in a position to see that we'd be perfectly justified in taking hold of him and placing him in the same category as a painter.* He resembles a painter because his creations fall short of truth, and a further point of resemblance

b is that the part of the mind he communicates with is not the best part, but something else. Now we can see how right we'd be to refuse him admission into any community which is going to respect convention, because now we know which part of the mind he wakes up. He destroys the rational part by feeding and fattening up this other part, and this is equivalent to someone destroying the more civilized members of a community by presenting ruffians with political power. There's no difference, we'll claim, between this and what a representational poet does: at a personal level, he establishes a bad system of government in people's minds by gratifying their irrational side, which can't even recognize what size things are—an object c which at one moment it calls big, it might call small the next moment*—by creating images, and by being far removed from truth.'

'Yes.'

'However, we haven't yet made the most serious allegation against representational poetry. It has a terrifying capacity for deforming even good people. Only a very few escape.'

'Yes, that *is* terrifying. Does it really do that?'

'Here's my evidence: you can make up your own mind.* When Homer or another tragedian represents the grief of one of the heroes, they have him deliver a lengthy speech of d lamentation or even have him sing a dirge and beat his breast; and when we listen to all this, even the best of us, as I'm sure you're aware, feels pleasure. We surrender ourselves, let ourselves be carried along, and share the hero's pain; and then we enthuse about the skill of any poet who makes us feel particularly strong feelings.'

'Yes, I'm aware of this, of course.'

'However, you also appreciate that when we're afflicted by trouble in our own lives, then we take pride in the opposite—in our ability to endure pain without being upset. We think that this is manly behaviour, and that only women behave in the e way we were sanctioning earlier.'

'I realize that,' he said.

'So,' I said, 'instead of being repulsed by the sight of the kind of person we'd regret and deplore being ourselves, we enjoy the spectacle and sanction it. Is this a proper way to behave?'

'No, it certainly isn't,' he said. 'It's pretty unreasonable, I'd say.'

'I agree,' I said, 'and here's even more evidence.' 606a

'What?'

'Consider this. What a poet satisfies and gratifies on these occasions is an aspect of ourselves which we forcibly restrain when tragedy strikes our own lives—an aspect which hungers after tears and the satisfaction of having cried until one can cry no more, since that is what it is in its nature to want to do. When the part of us which is inherently good has been inadequately trained in habits enjoined by reason, it relaxes its guard over this other part, the part which feels sad. Other

b people, not ourselves, are feeling these feelings, we tell ourselves, and it's no disgrace for us to sanction such behaviour and feel sorry for someone who, even while claiming to be good, is over-indulging in grief; and, we think, we are at least profiting from the pleasure, and there's no point in throwing away the pleasure by spurning the whole poem or play. You see, few people have the ability to work out that we ourselves are bound to store the harvest we reap from others: these occasions feed the feeling of sadness until it is too strong for us easily to restrain it when hardship occurs in our own lives.'

c 'You're absolutely right,' he said.

'And doesn't the same go for humour as well? If there are amusing things which you'd be ashamed to do yourself, but which give you a great deal of pleasure when you see them in a comic representation or hear about them in private company— when you don't find them loathsome and repulsive*—then isn't this exactly the same kind of behaviour as we uncovered when talking about feeling sad? There's a part of you which wants to make people laugh, but your reason restrains it, because you're afraid of being thought a vulgar clown. Nevertheless, you let it have its way on those other occasions, and you don't realize that the almost inevitable result of giving it energy in this other context is that you become a comedian in your own life.'

'Yes, that's very true,' he said.

d 'And the same goes for sex, anger, and all the desires and feelings of pleasure and distress which, we're saying,* accompany everything we do: poetic representation has the same effect in all these cases too. It irrigates and tends to these things when they should be left to wither, and it makes them our rulers when they should be our subjects, because otherwise we won't live better and happier lives, but quite the opposite.'

'I can't deny the truth of what you're saying,' he said.

e 'Therefore, Glaucon,' I went on, 'when you come across

people praising Homer and saying that he is the poet who has educated Greece,* that he's a good source for people to learn how to manage their affairs and gain culture in their lives, and that one should structure the whole of one's life in accordance with his precepts, you ought to be kind and considerate: after 607a all, they're doing the best they can. You should concede that Homer is a supreme poet and the original tragedian, but you should also recognize that the only poems we can admit into our community are hymns to the gods and eulogies of virtuous men.* If you admit the entertaining Muse of lyric and epic poetry, then instead of law and the shared acceptance of reason as the best guide, the kings of your community will be pleasure and pain.'

'You're quite right,' he agreed.

'So,' I said, 'since we've been giving poetry another hearing, b there's our defence: given its nature, we had good grounds for banishing it earlier from our community. No rational person could have done any different. However, poetry might accuse us of insensitivity and lack of culture, so we'd better also tell her that there's an ancient quarrel between poetry and philosophy. There are countless pieces of evidence for this enmity between them, but here are just a few: there's that "bitch yelping and baying at her master";* there's "featuring prominently in the idle chatter of fools"; there's "control by a c crowd of know-alls"; there are those whose "subtle notions" lead them to realize that they do indeed have "notional incomes". All the same, we ought to point out that if the kinds of poetry and representation which are designed merely to give pleasure can come up with a rational argument for their inclusion in a well-governed community, we'd be delighted— short of compromising the truth as we see it, which wouldn't be right—to bring them back from exile: after all, we know from our own experience all about their spell. I mean, haven't *you* ever fallen under the spell of poetry, Glaucon, especially when the spectacle is provided by Homer?' d

'I certainly have.'

'Under these circumstances, then, if our allegations met a poetic rebuttal in lyric verse or whatever, would we be justified in letting poetry return?'

'Yes.'

'And I suppose we'd also allow people who champion poetry because they like it, even though they can't compose it, to speak on its behalf in prose, and to try to prove that there's more to poetry than mere pleasure—that it also has a beneficial effect on society and on human life in general. And we won't

e listen in a hostile frame of mind, because we'll be the winners if poetry turns out to be beneficial as well as enjoyable.'

'Of course we will,' he agreed.

'And if it doesn't, Glaucon, then we'll do what a lover does when he thinks that a love affair he's involved in is no good for him: he reluctantly detaches himself. Similarly, since we've been conditioned by our wonderful societies until we have a deep-

608a seated love for this kind of poetry, we'll be delighted if there proves to be nothing better and closer to the truth than it. As long as it is incapable of rebutting our allegations, however, then while we listen to poetry we'll be chanting these allegations of ours to ourselves as a precautionary incantation against being caught once more by that childish and pervasive love. Our message will be that the commitment appropriate for an important matter with access to the truth shouldn't be given to this kind of poetry. People should, instead, be worried about the possible effects, on one's own inner political system, of

b listening to it and should tread cautiously; and they should let our arguments guide their attitude towards poetry.'

'I couldn't agree more,' he said.

'You see, my dear Glaucon,' I said, 'what's in the balance here is absolutely crucial—far more so than people think. It's whether one becomes a good or a bad person, and consequently has the calibre not to be distracted by prestige, wealth, political power, or even poetry from applying oneself to morality and whatever else goodness involves.'

'Looking back over our discussion,' he said, 'I can only agree with you. And I think anyone else would do the same as well.'

Chapter 14

Rewards Now and Hereafter

Plato has argued that morality is intrinsically rewarding, in that it is the vital component of individual happiness. He now allows himself to claim that it also brings external advantages: the discussion moves from 'being moral' to 'appearing moral'. The brevity and dogmatism of the claim show that Plato thought this to be by far the less interesting and important part of the response to the challenge formulated in Chapter 2. First, however, to pave the way for the aspect of the claim which depends on the doctrine of reincarnation, we get an unusual (and rather dense) argument for the mind's immortality: everything has a specific affliction which is the only thing that can destroy it; the mind's specific affliction—immorality—cannot destroy it; therefore the mind is indestructible and immortal.

'But, you know,' I said, 'we haven't discussed the most 608c substantial rewards and wages which goodness entails.'

'You mean there's more?' he said. 'They must be stupendous, if they're bigger than the ones we've already talked about.'*

'How can anything grow big in a short span of time?' I asked. 'I mean, a complete lifetime, from childhood to old age, is tiny compared with the whole of time.'

'It's nothing at all,' he agreed.

'Well then, don't you think that anything immortal should concern itself with the whole of time, rather than with such a d short extent?'

'Yes, I do,' he said. 'But what are you getting at?'

'Don't you realize that our mind is immortal and never dies?' I asked.*

He looked straight at me in surprise and said, 'No, I certainly don't. Are *you* in a position to claim that it is?'

'Certainly,' I said. 'So are you, I'd say. I mean, it's a relatively straightforward subject.'

'Not to me, it isn't,' he replied. 'But I'd be glad to hear what you have to say on this "relatively straightforward subject"!'

'All right,' I said.

'Go on, then,' he said.

'You acknowledge the existence of good and bad, don't you?' I asked.

'Yes.'

e   'I wonder if your conception of them is the same as mine.'

'What is that?'

'Badness always manifests in destruction and corruption, while goodness always manifests in preservation and benefit.'

'I agree,' he said.

'Now, would you say that there are things which are good and bad for a given object? For example, ophthalmia is bad for 609a eyes, illness for the body as a whole, blight for corn, rot for wood, rust for bronze and iron—as I say, nearly every object has some specific thing to afflict it, which is bad for it.'

'I agree,' he said.

'Isn't it the case that whenever one of these objects is afflicted by its affliction, it deteriorates, and ultimately decomposes and perishes?'

'Of course.'

'Therefore, any given object is destroyed by its specific affliction and defect; apart from this, there's nothing else that b can destroy it, because goodness is never destructive, and neither is anything which is intermediate between good and bad.'

'Of course,' he said.

'Suppose that we come across something, then, which is certainly subject to the degenerative action of its defect, but which cannot be decomposed and destroyed by it. Won't we immediately realize that we're faced with something which, by its very nature, is indestructible?'

'I should think we would,' he replied.

'Now, is there anything which makes a mind bad?' I asked.

'Yes, definitely,' he said. 'All the things which have cropped up in the course of our discussion—immorality, lack of self-c control, cowardice, and ignorance.'*

'Well, do any of these defects cause it to decompose and perish? Be careful now: we don't want to fall into the trap of thinking that when an immoral person is stupid enough to have his crimes found out, this is an instance of his being destroyed

364

by his mental defect—in this case, by his immorality.* No, here's how to proceed. You know how illness, which is a body's defect, wastes and ruins a body, until it is actually annihilated; and you know how all the objects we mentioned a moment ago are brought to a state of annihilation when they're taken over and afflicted by their specific defect, with its d destructive power. Yes?'

'Yes.'

'All right, let's apply the same line of argument to the mind. When immorality (or some other kind of defect) occupies a person's mind, does its presence and occupancy cause his mind to deteriorate and decay, and does it eventually bring his mind to death and cause it to separate from the body?'

'No, it doesn't do that,' he said.

'On the other hand,' I said, 'it doesn't make sense to think that anything could be destroyed by some other object's defect, rather than by its own.'

'No, it doesn't.'

'You see, Glaucon,' I continued, 'I want you to appreciate e that a body does not, in our view, have to be destroyed by some defect or other in its food—staleness or mouldiness or whatever. No, we'll explain any instance of bad food making a body deteriorate by saying that the *cause* of the body's destruction was its specific defect, illness, and that the food was the *reason* it became ill. But since a body and food are quite different from each other, we'd better resist the temptation to 610a say that a body is destroyed by bad food—that is, by something else's defect—unless it engenders the body's specific defect.'

'You're quite right,' he said.

'By the same token,' I went on, 'if a bad physical state can't cause a bad mental state, we'd better not claim that a person's mind is destroyed (unless its own special defect is present) by a defect from elsewhere: that would be an instance of one thing being destroyed by something else's defect.'

'Yes, that makes sense,' he agreed.

'We've got a choice, then. We can either prove this idea of ours wrong, or (in the absence of such proof) we have to say b that no fever, no illness of any kind, and no injury either—not even chopping the whole body up into the tiniest possible

pieces—has the slightest destructive effect on the mind. In order for us to accept that it does, someone would have to demonstrate that these physical afflictions cause an increase in immorality and injustice in the mind. But we should refuse to accept the assertion that the mind or anything else is destroyed if its own specific defect doesn't occur, and it's just a case of
c one thing providing an environment for something else's defect to occur.'

'But no one will ever prove that death makes a dead person's mind more immoral,' he said.

'Someone might venture to tackle our argument head on, however,' I said, 'and might try to avoid having to concede the mind's immortality by claiming that a dying person degenerates and becomes less moral.* In that case, I suppose, if our opponent was right, we'd have to deny our current claim that the *cause* of death for immoral people is other people administering justice, while immorality is the *reason* they do so. Instead, we'd have to claim that immorality is as fatal as a disease for anyone
d who possesses it; that people who contract it die of it, because it is in its nature to kill; and that the speed at which it kills them depends on the extent of their immorality!'

'Yes, and if immorality is fatal to its possessor,' he added, 'then it obviously gives him no cause for alarm,* since it'll put an end to all his troubles. No, I'm sure we're more likely to find
e that, on the contrary, immorality kills other people, if it can, not its possessor. In fact, an immoral person even gains quite a lot of vitality from it, and restless vigour as well. In other words, the impression it gives is that it's found a billet a long way from being fatal.'

'You're right,' I said. 'Now, since we've found that the mind can't be exterminated by its specific defect and destroyed by its specific affliction, it's hardly likely that a defect which is designed for the destruction of something else is going to destroy the mind—or anything else, for that matter, except whatever it's designed for.'

'Yes, that's hardly likely,' he agreed.
611a 'It cannot be destroyed, then, by any defect specific to itself, or any defect specific to anything else. It plainly follows that it must exist for ever. And if it exists for ever, then it is immortal.'

366

'Yes, inevitably,' he agreed.

'So much for that, then,' I said. 'Now, if this is so, you'll appreciate that there must always be the same minds in existence.* None of them can be destroyed, so their number cannot decrease; and it can't increase either, because any additional immortal entity of any kind would have to come, as I'm sure you realize, from a mortal entity, and therefore everything would eventually become immortal.'

'You're right.'

'But that's too implausible an idea for us to believe,' I said. 'And we'll also find it hard to believe that, in essence, the mind is the kind of thing to be pervaded by internal diversity, inconsistency, and dissension.'

'What do you mean?' he asked.

'That something is unlikely to be immortal if it's a compound, formed imperfectly from diverse parts,' I replied. 'But that's what we found the mind to be not long ago.'*

'Yes, that would make immortality improbable.'

'Well, the immortality of the mind would seem to have been conclusively proved by the argument we've just been through, and by our other arguments as well.* What we have to do, however, is try to see what the mind is really and truly like, when it's not deformed by its association with the body and with other evils (which is how we've been looking at it so far). We should try to see what it's like when it's untainted, and we'll have to rely on reason to get a clear enough view of that. You'll find that its beauty is greatly enhanced, and you'll gain far more insight into cases of morality and immorality, and all the qualities we've been discussing.* Our current ideas about the mind are true, in so far as they correspond to what we can see of it at the moment; but the condition in which we're observing it is like that of Glaucus the sea-deity. If people were to see Glaucus, it would be hard for them to discern his original state any more, because some of the original parts of his body have been knocked off, some have been worn away and generally deformed by the waves, and other things—shells, seaweed, and stones—have grown on him, so that his appearance is quite different from what it used to be, and he looks altogether more like a monster. Similarly, when we look at the mind too, its condition, as we see it, is the result of

367

countless malign influences. What we have to do, Glaucon, is look in a different direction.'

'Where?' he asked.

e   'We should take note of the fact that it is attracted towards wisdom, and consider what it is related to and the affiliations it desires, given that it is of the same order as the divine, immortal, and eternal realm. And we should consider what would happen to the mind if the *whole* of it* allowed this realm to dictate its direction, and if this impulse carried it out of its current underwater location, and all the stones and shells

612a   were broken off—all the accretions of earth and rock (since earth is its food) which currently grow uncontrollably in large numbers all over it because it indulges in the pleasures which men say bring happiness. Then we'd be able to see what it's really like—whether it is manifold or uniform, or what its true nature and condition is. Anyway, I think we've given a reasonable account of what happens to it and the forms it assumes in human life.'

'Definitely,' he said.

A recurrent problem in Greek popular ethics was why immoral people's external affairs often appeared to prosper, while those of moral people suffered. Plato's response here is to insist that a moral person must be in the gods' favour and therefore, even if he does not prosper at first, he will eventually, while an immoral person will sooner or later suffer catastrophe.

'Now,' I said, 'haven't we succeeded in refuting all the charges that were mentioned? In particular, haven't we avoided

b   praising the respects in which morality is rewarding and enhances a person's reputation, which is what you all said Hesiod and Homer did,* and discovered that, when morality and the mind are both taken just in themselves, there's nothing better for the mind than morality, and that a person ought to behave morally whether or not he owns Gyges' ring, and whether or not he owns Hades' helmet as well a magical ring?'*

'You're quite right,' he said.

'Surely, then, Glaucon,' I said, 'no one will mind if, as an appendix, we now go on to assign rewards to morality and

virtue in general, and describe all the various ways in which c
men and gods remunerate morality during a person's lifetime
and after his death?'

'Of course they won't,' he said.

'Now, you incurred a debt in the course of our discussion.
Are you going to pay me back?'

'What debt?'

'I allowed you a moral man with a reputation for immorality,
and an immoral man with a reputation for morality. You were
asking for this concession to be made, for the sake of argument,
because even though it might in fact be impossible for the true
state of affairs not to be known by gods and men, you thought
it would still help us compare and assess morality and
immorality on their own terms. Do you remember?'*   d

'Of course I do,' he said.

'Well, our assessment *has* been made,' I said, 'and so I am
now, on behalf of morality, asking you for a favour in return: I
want us to agree, along with everyone else, that morality does
have the reputation it enjoys among gods and men. We've
found that actually being moral entails benefits, and that those
in whom morality is genuinely present are not gaining a false
impression of morality, so if you grant me this favour, morality
can also collect the prize for its reputation and gain the benefits
it bestows on its possessors.'

'It's a fair request,' he said.   e

'Well, the first idea I want to redeem from you', I said, 'is
that the gods don't notice what these two characters are like.
All right?'

'Yes, we'll repay that debt,' he said.

'Now, if they're both known to the gods, then the one must
be in the gods' favour and the other must be their enemy, as we
agreed at the beginning too.'*

'True.'

'Now, I'm sure we'll agree that everything the gods have to
give will happen, in as beneficial a way as possible, to the   613a
person who's in their favour (unless he's already owed some
unavoidable harm as a result of a former misdemeanour).'

'Yes.'

'If a moral person appears to be in a bad way, then, we're
bound to assume that his poverty or illness or whatever will

eventually be good for him, whether this happens during his lifetime or after it.* The point is that the gods never neglect anyone who is prepared to devote himself to becoming moral and, by practising virtue, to assimilate himself to God as much

b as is humanly possible.'

'Yes, it doesn't seem likely that he'd be neglected by God, when he resembles him,' he remarked.*

'Now, we have to suppose that an immoral person is in the opposite situation, don't we?'

'Definitely.'

'Anyway, these are the kinds of prizes that a moral person would get from the gods.'

'That's what I think, at any rate,' he said.

'What about from men?' I asked. 'In all honesty, isn't it true that clever criminals are exactly like those runners who do well on the way up the track, and then flag on the way back?* They sprint away at the beginning, but end up being jeered off the

c track, and have to beat a hasty retreat with their ears on their shoulders* and without winning any chaplets. Genuine runners, however, complete the course and earn themselves rewards as well as chaplets.* Isn't that the usual outcome in the case of moral people? Aren't they acclaimed, and rewarded as well, at the end of every activity and transaction they're involved in, and at the end of their lives?'

'Yes, they certainly are.'

'You're not in a position to object if I make the same claims about moral people that *you* made about immoral people,*

d then, are you? I'm going to claim that moral people can, in later life, have political power in their own communities if they want, can marry women from any families they want, can have their children marry whomever they want, and so on. Everything you said about immoral people I am now claiming applies to moral people. On the other hand, my position as regards immoral people is that, even if they get away with it when they're young, at the end of the race they're found out. Their old age is made miserable by the jeering insults of strangers and countrymen alike; they're flogged and they

e undergo the punishments you rightly described as coarse* . . . and then they'll be tortured on the rack, and they'll have their eyes burnt out . . . well, you'd better imagine that I've given you the whole list of the torments they suffer. Anyway, as I say, please see if you have any objections to all this.'

'No, I don't,' he said. 'What you're saying is perfectly fair.'

Finally, morality also brings rewards after death. By means of a myth which interweaves traditional and mystical eschatology, and Greek and Near Eastern notions, Plato depicts the horrors of the punishments which await an immoral person in Hades. A moral person avoids these, and can also remain conscious and rational enough to choose his next incarnation with care. Plato also offers a stupendous rationalistic vision of the universe. The myth as a whole emphasizes the orderliness of things, under necessity, and underscores the importance of having order in one's mind, which is morality. There can be no possible grounds for doubting that Plato believed in all the ingredients of the myth: he uses this literary form because he accepts that they are not susceptible of reasoned proof.

'So in addition to the benefits which stem from morality in itself,' I said, 'those are the kinds of prizes and rewards and trophies which a moral person comes by during his lifetime from gods and men.' 614a

'They're wonderful,' he said, 'and well founded.'

'Actually they're nothing,' I said. 'They are few and insubstantial compared with what our two characters will meet after their death. I'd better explain: we owe it to both of them to do so, and if I don't, the debt won't be repaid in full.'

'Please do,' he said. 'There's hardly anything I'd rather hear a b description of.'

'Well, I'm not going to tell you the kind of saga Alcinous had to endure,'* I said. 'Endurance will be my theme, however— that of brave Er the son of Armenius, who was a Pamphylian by birth. Once upon a time, he was killed in battle, and by the time the corpses were collected, ten days later, they had all putrefied except his, which was still in good shape. He was taken home and, twelve days after his death, just as his funeral was about to start and he was lying on the pyre, he came back to life. Then he told people what he'd seen in the other world.

'He said that his soul* left his body and went on a journey, with lots of other souls as his companions. They came to an c awesome place, where they found two openings next to each other in the earth, and two others directly opposite them up in the sky. There were judges* sitting between the openings who made their assessment and then told the moral ones to take the right-hand route which went up and through the sky, and gave them tokens to wear on their fronts to show what behaviour they'd been assessed for, but told the immoral ones to take the left-hand, downward route. These people also had tokens, but on their backs, to show all their past deeds. When Er

d approached, however, the judges said that he had to report back to mankind about what goes on there, and they told him to listen and observe everything that happened in the place.

'From where he was, he could see souls leaving, once they'd been judged, by one or the other of the two openings in the sky and in the earth, and he noticed how the other two openings were used too: one was for certain souls, caked in grime and dust, to arise out of the earth, while the other was for other,

e clean souls to come down out of the sky. They arrived periodically, and he gained the impression that it had taken a long journey for them to get there; they were grateful to turn aside into the meadow* and find a place to settle down. The scene resembled a festival. Old acquaintances greeted one another; those who'd come out of the earth asked those from the heavens what had happened to them there, and were asked the same question in return. The tales of the one group were

615a accompanied by groans and tears, as they recalled all the awful things they'd experienced and seen in the course of their underworld journey (which takes a thousand years),* while the souls from heaven had only wonderful experiences and incredibly beautiful sights to recount.

'It would take ages to tell you a substantial proportion of their tales, Glaucon, but here's a brief outline of what Er said. Each individual had been punished—for every single crime he'd ever committed, and for every person he'd ever wronged—ten times, which is to say once every hundred years (assuming that

b the span of human life is a hundred years), to ensure that the penalty he paid was ten times worse than the crime.* Take people who had caused a great many deaths, by betraying a country or an army, and people who had enslaved others or been responsible for inflicting misery in some other way: for every single person they had hurt, they received back ten times the amount of pain. Conversely, the same principle applied to the rewards people received for their good deeds, their morality and justice. Things are different, however, for those who die at c birth or shortly afterwards, but what he told me about them isn't worth mentioning.* However, he did tell a story about the even greater rewards and penalties for observance and non-observance of the proper behaviour towards gods and one's parents, and for murder with one's own hand.

'He said that he overheard someone asking someone else where Ardiaeus the Great was. (A thousand years earlier, this Ardiaeus had been the dictator of a certain city-state in Pamphylia, and is said to have committed a great many abominable crimes, including killing his aged father and his elder brother.) The person who'd been asked the question d replied, "He's not here, and he never will be. One of the terrible sights we saw was when we were near the exit. At last, after all we'd been through, we were about to come up from underground, when we suddenly caught sight of Ardiaeus. There were others with him, the vast majority of whom had been dictators, while the rest had committed awful non-political crimes. They were under the impression that they were e on the point of leaving, but the exit refused to take them. Whenever anyone whose wickedness couldn't be redeemed tried to go up, or anyone who hadn't been punished enough, it made bellowing sounds. Fierce, fiery-looking men were standing there," he went on, "and they could make sense of the sounds. These men simply grabbed hold of some of the criminals and took them away, but they placed fetters on Ardiaeus' wrists, ankles, and neck, and others got the same 616a treatment; then they threw their prisoners to the ground and flayed them, and finally dragged them away along the roadside, tearing them to pieces on the thorny shrubs. They told any passers-by that they were taking them away to hurl them into Tartarus,* and explained why as well."

'He added that of all the various terrors they experienced there, the worst was the fear they each felt that, as they started their ascent, they'd encounter the bellowing sound, and that there was nothing more gratifying than hearing no sound and making the ascent.

'So much for Er's description of the penalties and punishments, and the equivalent rewards. They spent seven b

373

days in the meadow, and on the eighth day they had to leave
and go elsewhere. On the fourth day after that they reached a
place from where they could see a straight shaft of light
stretching from on high through the heavens and the earth; the
light was like a pillar, and it was just like a rainbow in colour,
except that it was brighter and clearer. It took another day's
travelling to reach the light, and when they got there they were
at the mid-point of the light and they could see, stretching away
c out of the heavens, the extremities of the bonds of the heavens
(for this light binds the heavens together, and as the girth that
underpins a trireme holds a trireme together, so this light holds
the whole rotation together),* while stretching down from the
extremities was the spindle of Necessity, which causes the
circular motion of all the separate rotations.

'The spindle's stem and hook are made of adamant, while its
whorl consists of various substances, including adamant. In
d appearance, the whorl basically looks like whorls here on earth,
but, given Er's description, one is bound to picture it as if there
was first a large hollow whorl, with its insides completely
scooped out, and with a second, smaller one lying snugly inside
it (like those jars which fit into one another), and then, on the
same arrangement, a third whorl, a fourth one, and finally four
others. For he said that there were eight concentric whorls in
e all, and that their circular rims, looked at from above, formed a
solid surface, as if there were just a single whorl attached to the
stem, which was driven right through the middle of the eighth
whorl.*

'The circle which constituted the rim of the first whorl, the
one on the outside, was the broadest; next broadest was the
rim of the sixth whorl; third was the rim of the fourth whorl;
fourth was the rim of the eighth whorl; fifth was the rim of the
seventh whorl; sixth was the rim of the fifth whorl; seventh was
the rim of the third whorl; and eighth was the rim of the
second whorl.* The rim of the largest whorl was spangled; the
rim of the seventh whorl was brightest; the rim of the eighth
617a whorl gained its colour by reflecting the light of the seventh
one; the rims of the second and fifth whorls were more yellow
than the rest, and were almost identical in hue; the third was
the whitest; the fourth was reddish; the sixth was white, but
not as white as the third.*

'Now, although the rotation of the spindle as a whole was uniform, nevertheless within the motion of the whole the seven inner circles moved, at regular speeds, in orbits which ran counter to the direction of the whole.* The seven inner circles varied in speed: the eighth was the fastest; then second fastest were, all at once, the seventh, sixth, and fifth;* the third fastest b seemed to them (Er said) to be the fourth, which was in retrograde motion;* the fourth fastest was the third, and the fifth fastest was the second. The spindle was turning in the lap of Lady Necessity. Each of the spindle's circles acted as the vehicle for a Siren. Each Siren, as she stood on one of the circles, sounded a single note, and all eight notes together made a single harmonious sound.

'Three other women were also sitting on thrones which were c evenly spaced around the spindle. They were the Fates, the daughters of Necessity, robed in white, with garlands on their heads; they were Lachesis, Clotho, and Atropos, accompanying the Sirens' song, with Lachesis singing of the past, Clotho of the present, and Atropos of the future. Clotho periodically laid her right hand on the outer circle of the spindle and helped to turn it; Atropos did the same with her left hand to the inner circles; and Lachesis alternately helped the outer circle and the inner circles on their way with one hand after the other. d

'As soon as the souls arrived, they had to approach Lachesis. An intermediary arranged them in rows and then, once he'd taken from Lachesis' lap lottery tokens and sample lives, stepped up on to a high rostrum and said, "Hear the words of Lady Lachesis, daughter of Necessity. You souls condemned to impermanence,* the cycle of birth followed by death is beginning again for you. No deity will be assigned to you: you will pick your own deities.* The order of gaining tokens e decides the order of choosing lives, which will be irrevocably yours. Goodness makes its own rules: each of you will be good to the extent that you value it. Responsibility lies with the chooser, not with God."

'After this announcement, he threw the tokens into the crowd, and everybody (except Er, who wasn't allowed to) picked up the token that fell beside him. Each soul's position in the lottery was clear once he'd picked up his token. Next, the intermediary placed on the ground in front of them the sample 618a

lives, of which there were far more than there were souls in the crowd; every single kind of human and animal life was included among the samples. For instance, there were dictatorships (some lifelong, others collapsing before their time and ending in poverty, exile, and begging), and also male and female versions of lives of fame for one's physique, good looks, and general
b strength and athleticism, or for one's lineage and the excellence of one's ancestors; and there were lives which lacked these distinctions as well. Temperament wasn't included, however, since that inevitably varies according to the life chosen; but otherwise there was every possible combination of qualities with one another and with factors like wealth, poverty, sickness, and health, in extreme or moderate amounts.

'Now, it looks as though this is an absolutely critical point for a person, my dear Glaucon. And that is why every single
c one of us has to give his undivided attention—to the detriment of all other areas of study—to trying to track down and discover whether there is anyone he can discover and unearth anywhere who can give him the competence and knowledge to distinguish a good life from a bad one, and to choose the better life from among all the possibilities that surround him at any given moment.* He has to weigh up all the things we've been talking about, so as to know what bearing they have, in combination and in isolation, on living a good life. What are the good or bad results of mixing good looks with poverty or
d with wealth, in conjunction with such-and-such a mental condition? What are the effects of the various combinations of innate and acquired characteristics such as high and low birth, involvement and lack of involvement in politics, physical strength and frailty, cleverness and stupidity, and so on? He has to be able to take into consideration the nature of the mind and so make a rational choice, from among all the alternatives, between a better and a worse life. He has to be in a position to
e think of a life which leads his mind towards a state of increasing immorality as worse, and consider one which leads in the opposite direction as better. There's no other factor he'll regard as important: we've already seen that this is the cardinal decision anyone has to make, whether he does so during his lifetime or after he's died. By the time he reaches Hades, then,
619a this belief must be absolutely unassailable in him, so that there too he can resist the lure of afflictions such as wealth, and

won't be trapped into dictatorship or any other activity which would cause him to commit a number of foul crimes, and to suffer even worse torments himself. Instead, he must know how to choose a life which occupies the middle ground, and how to avoid either extreme, as much as possible, in this world and throughout the next. For this is how a person guarantees happiness for himself.

'Anyway, according to the report the messenger from the other world delivered on the occasion I'm talking about, the intermediary continued: "Even the last to come forward will find an acceptable life, not a pernicious one, if he chooses wisely and exerts himself during his lifetime. The first to choose should take care, and the last need not despair."

'Er said that no sooner had the intermediary fallen silent than the person whose turn was first stepped up and chose the most powerful dictatorship available. His stupidity and greed* made him choose this life without inspecting it thoroughly and in sufficient detail, so he didn't notice that it included the fate of eating his own children* and committing other horrible crimes. When he took the time to examine his choice, he beat his breast and wept, but he didn't comply with the intermediary's earlier words, because he didn't hold himself responsible for his afflictions; instead he blamed fortune, the gods, and anything rather than himself. He was one of those who had come out of the heavens, since he'd spent his previous life in a well-regulated community, and so had been good to a certain extent, even though it was habituation rather than philosophy that had made him so. In fact, those who had come from the heavens fell into this trap more or less as often as the others, since they hadn't learnt how to cope with difficult situations, whereas the majority of those who had come out of the earth didn't rush into their decisions, because they knew about suffering from their own experiences as well as from observing others. That was one of the main reasons—another being the unpredictability of the lottery—that most of the souls met with a reversal, from good to bad or vice versa. The point is this: if during his lifetime in this world a person practises philosophy with integrity, and if it so happens, as a result of the lottery, that he's not one of the last to choose, then the report brought back from that other world makes it plausible to expect not only that he'd be happy here, but also that he'd travel from here to there and back again on the smooth roads of the heavens, rather than on rough underground trails.

'It was well worth seeing, Er said, how particular souls chose
620a their lives; the sight was by turns sad, amusing, and astonishing.* Their choice was invariably dictated by conditioning gained in their former incarnation. For instance, he said he saw the soul which had once belonged to Orpheus choose the life of a swan; because women had killed him, he hated everything female, and wanted to avoid a female incarnation.* He saw Thamyras choose a nightingale's life, while a swan and other songbirds opted for change and chose
b to live as human beings. The soul which was twentieth in line picked the life of a lion; it was Ajax the son of Telamon, and he didn't want a human incarnation because he was unable to forget the decision that had been made about the armour.* The next soul was that of Agamemnon: again, his sufferings had embittered him against humanity, and he chose instead to be reborn as an eagle. About halfway through, it was the turn of Atalanta's soul, and she caught sight of a male athlete's life: when she noticed how well rewarded it was, she couldn't walk on by, and she took it. After Atalanta, Er saw the soul of
c Epeius the son of Panopeus becoming a craftswoman; and later, towards the end, he saw the soul of Thersites the funny man taking on a monkey's form. As the luck of the lottery had it, Odysseus' soul was the very last to come forward and choose. The memory of all the hardship he had previously endured had caused his ambition to subside, so he walked around for a long time, looking for a life as a non-political private citizen. At last he found one lying somewhere,
d disregarded by everyone else. When he saw it, he happily took it, saying that he'd have done exactly the same even if he'd been the first to choose. And the same kind of thorough exchange and shuffling of roles occurred in the case of animals too, as they became men or other animals—wild ones if they'd been immoral, tame ones otherwise.

'When the souls had all finished choosing their lives, they approached Lachesis in the order the lottery had assigned them. She gave each of them the personal deity they'd selected, to accompany them throughout their lives, as their guardians and
e to fulfil the choices they had made. Each deity first led its soul

to Clotho, to pass under her hand and under the revolving orbit of the spindle, and so to ratify the destiny the soul had chosen in the lottery. Then, once a connection had been made with her, the deity led the soul to Atropos and her spinning, to make the web woven by Clotho fixed and unalterable.* Afterwards, the soul set a fixed course for Lady Necessity's throne and passed under it; once it was on the other side, and when 621a everyone else had joined it there, they all travelled through terrible, stifling heat (since no trees or plants grew in that place) to the Plain of Oblivion.* Since the day was now drawing to a close, they camped there by the River of Neglect, whose waters no vessel can contain.

'Now, they were all required to drink a certain amount of water, but some were too stupid to look after themselves properly and drank more than the required amount.* As each person drank, he forgot everything. They lay down to sleep, b and in the middle of the night there was thunder and an earthquake. All of a sudden, they were lifted up from where they were, and they darted like shooting stars* away in various directions for rebirth. As for Er, although he hadn't been allowed to drink any of the water he had no idea what direction he took, or how he got back to his body, but he suddenly opened his eyes and found that it was early in the morning and that he was lying on the funeral pyre.*

'There you are, then, Glaucon. The story has made it safely through to the end,* without perishing on the way. And it might save us too, if we take it to heart, and so successfully c cross the River of Oblivion without defiling our souls. Anyway, my recommendation would be for us to regard the soul as immortal and as capable of surviving a great deal of suffering, just as it survives all the good times. We should always keep to the upward path, and we should use every means at our disposal to act morally and with intelligence, so that we may gain our own and the gods' approval, not only during our stay here on earth, but also when we collect the prizes our morality has earned us, which will be just as extensive as the rewards victorious athletes receive from all quarters.* And then, both d here and during the thousand-year journey of our story,* all will be well with us.'

EXPLANATORY NOTES

Chapter 1

327a *the goddess*: worship of the Thracian goddess Bendis had recently been introduced into Athens; since in function and form of worship she was similar to Artemis (whose temple was prominent in the Piraeus, Athens' seaport about five miles south-west of the city), the Athenians inaugurated a joint festival.

327a *its first performance*: unfortunately, we cannot date the introduction of Bendis into Athens. Other references in the book to external events and figures make a dramatic date of about 420 BC seem most plausible for the dialogue, although all the relevant indications are so slight as to make certainty impossible. Socrates is not too old (328d–e; he was born in 469), and Damon may still be alive (400b; he was born about 500). Poulydamas the pancratiast (338c) became prominent when he won at the Olympic Games in 408, but he may have been well known locally already. The battle of Megara mentioned at 368a, however, is unlikely to have been that of 424, since Glaucon and Adeimantus would probably not have been old enough to have taken part; it is more likely to have been that of 409, with a consequent anachronism. Ismenias' misdeeds (336a) are not datable with certainty; Herodicus seems to be dead (406a–b), but we do not know when he died; other references to contemporaries such as Euripides and Sophocles are no help in this context, because they give us no indication as to whether or not they are still alive. While Plato is often concerned to make his dialogues lifelike portraits of conversations that might have taken place, he is rarely interested in fixing the dramatic dates with certainty and without anachronisms.

328a *worth seeing*: since it would involve singing and dancing.

328a *talking to*: Socrates' predilection for talking to young men was notorious.

328c *in the courtyard*: the daily offering to Zeus the Protector of the Household, whose altar stood in the courtyard.

328d *enjoyment of conversation*: Cephalus enunciates a curious anticipation of the important psychological principle of 485d.

328e *on the threshold of old age*: a traditional phrase occurring several times in Homer (e.g. *Iliad* 22. 60; *Odyssey* 15. 246) and elsewhere.

Since the impression we are given of Cephalus is that he is quite ancient, then the Greeks clearly thought of the threshold as something you crossed on leaving, as well as on entering, so that the phrase is a polite way of saying that he is not far off death.

329a *vindicate the ancient proverb*: the proverb or cliché is, in its minimal form, 'People enjoy the company of others their own age'; it may have continued by singling out old people as particularly prone to this.

329e *Themistocles*: for a slightly different version of this story see Herodotus 8. 125.

330b *I inherited*: Plato's readers would know that the family was ruined only a few years after the dramatic date of the dialogue. Cephalus is being portrayed as rather complacent.

331a *Pindar*: fragment 214 Snell.

331b *context*: the context of the afterlife is more fully and vividly described in the closing stages of *Republic*—by which time, however, we also know that morality is an inner state, and does not consist merely in the performance of a few conventional duties (as Cephalus is saying) or, more generally, in the acceptance from outside of ethical standards (as Polemarchus will say).

331c *doing right*: or 'morality'—the topic of the dialogue is introduced. The adjective *dikaios* is translated 'moral' or 'right', and the cognate abstract nouns 'morality' or 'doing right'.

331d *the ceremony*: he was probably a priest, with a role to play in the day's ceremonial proceedings.

331e *fine remark*: but it does not occur in our extant fragments of Simonides. However, Simonides was a traditional Greek sage, and the saying may have become attributed to him because of his prestige. However fine a remark it is, though, it is an example of moral behaviour rather than a definition of morality; and Socrates notoriously makes short work of interlocutors who give him examples instead of definitions: examples are liable to counter-examples, whereas a definition must hold true under any circumstances. 'He wants not a list of [moral] actions, but a criterion for inclusion in or exclusion from such a list' (MacIntyre, 33).

332b *something bad*: this was a perfectly normal aspect of Greek, pre-Christian, popular ethics. Consider how revolutionary, then, Socrates is being in casting doubt on it (and see also 615a–b).

334a *stealing it*: this is clearly intended as a *reductio ad absurdum*, and so Plato is not committed to it as a conclusion. Nevertheless, because he consistently portrays Socrates as wedded to intellectualism and to comparing morality to arts and crafts, it is not clear that we are being invited to consider the craft analogy as in some way defective (perhaps because it ignores the obvious alternative account, which is to distinguish between character and capacity and say that a moral person's character will prevent him from stealing, even if he has the capacity to do so). It is more likely (as Penner argues) that the artificiality of the argument is due to its suppression of other aspects of Socrates' thought, which would have salvaged it. At any rate, we *are* supposed to think that something is wrong, not only with this argument, but with all the arguments of Chapter 1—otherwise, there would have been no need for thirteen other chapters on the subject.

334b *at theft and perjury*: *Odyssey* 19. 396. Two lines earlier Autolycus is described as 'good', and elsewhere in Homer gains other commendatory epithets.

334c *for enemies*: whereas nowadays we think of friends primarily as those we like or feel affection for, the less sentimental Greeks thought of them as those who do you good. Friendship involved ties of loyalty as much as of warmth.

335b *I asked*: in what follows Plato exploits an ambiguity in the notion of harming. Polemarchus uses it to mean 'deprive someone of something—his goods, even his life'; Socrates uses it to mean 'make someone worse'. The equivocation between the functional and the moral senses of 'good' is particularly blatant.

335c *unmusical*: it was first pointed out only recently (A. Jeffrey, 'Polemarchus and Socrates on Justice and Harm', *Phronesis*, 24 (1979), 54–69) that the argument is flawed at this point too. If Socrates wants to maintain that experts can only pass on their expertise, then the parallel with Polemarchus' position must be that a Polemarchan moral expert makes his enemies good at benefiting friends and harming enemies; since these enemies by definition include the moral expert, then a Polemarchan moral expert would, on Socrates' argument, do himself harm! Socrates is wrong to infer from a few cases of experts passing on their expertise that the same must go for the Polemarchan moral expert.

335d *to make people bad*: the last sentence could have been translated, 'Can people who are good at something use what they are good at to make people bad at that thing?' The argument is a particularly clear case of the Socratic belief that, in several respects, morality is like a skill or a craft.

336a   *vastly powerful*: the irony is especially heavy here, since the first three people mentioned *were* powerful in conventional terms: they were rulers of countries and, in Xerxes' case, an empire too; see the Index of Names.

336d   *unable to speak*: in Greek superstition, if a wolf spotted you before you spotted it, you were struck dumb.

337d   *What penalty would you expect?*: under Athenian law a defendant in some cases had the right either to accept the penalty proposed by the court or to propose an alternative penalty. Thrasymachus is inviting Socrates to propose his own penalty. The most notorious such counter-proposal in Athenian legal history was made by Socrates himself (see Plato, *Apology* 36b ff.): instead of a lesser penalty, Socrates proposed that he be kept at public expense, like a victorious athlete.

337d   *the money*: as a matter of fact, Socrates cannot have been too badly off, since he was assessed as rich enough to serve as a hoplite in the Athenian army; but his lack of concern about money was translated into poverty, and became a theme among the several Socratic writers after his death. Anyway, the sophists tended to charge exorbitant fees for their teaching.

338c   *applauding*: the sophists went in for startling statements and audience approval, rather than logical consistency and moral worth. This gets Thrasymachus into trouble, because his statement here is actually an incomplete version of his thesis, which emerges under pressure from Socrates in the next section as 'Morality is the promotion of someone else's good, and is therefore bad.'

338c   *the pancratiast*: pancration was a brutal combination of wrestling and boxing; the word literally means 'all-powerful'. Extra poignancy is added to this exchange since it is quite possible that Thrasymachus himself had, historically, drawn on pancratiastic imagery in his writing. This would be one of a number of similarly subtle features of this chapter which mock the sophist; the whole matter is skilfully argued by J. H. Quincey, 'Another Purpose for Plato, *Republic* I', *Hermes*, 109 (1981), 300–15.

339b   *some kind of advantage*: in Plato's early dialogues Socrates is portrayed as a moral egoist. He thinks that morality is good for one's own soul.

340c   *he protested*: Thrasymachus rejects this option because it emphasizes the trivial aspect of his position (that morality is obedience to the rulers' rules), whereas he has a far more robust view to defend (see note on 338c).

340d **bully**: the Greek word is *sukophantēs*, which has no precise English equivalent, though it led through several changes to our 'sycophant'. Under Athenian law, any citizen could prosecute any other. If a conviction was gained, the prosecutor might well get a proportion of the fine. Some people, therefore, made a living out of such actions and the out-of-court settlements gained by the threat of them: these bullies were 'sycophants'.

341c **shave a lion**: proverbial for an all-but-impossible task.

341d **he answered**: Thrasymachus is thinking of procuring the interests of the captain or ruler in each instance; Socrates is thinking of procuring the interests of the subject. It is, of course, easy for Socrates to argue that any branch of expertise is concerned with its objects; but it does not follow from this that it looks out for their interests.

342a **branch of expertise**: that is, medicine, which looks after eyes and ears as well as the whole body.

342b **nothing more and nothing less**: for example, as long as medicine is just medicine, not moneymaking as well (see 341c).

343b **real rulers**: as opposed to the analogous ruling of Socrates' ship's captain.

343d **tax on property**: in Athens there was no regular system of taxation. Instead, wealthy people financed public projects like the theatre or the navy, and in times of war were liable to a property tax.

343e **political office**: every male Athenian citizen might be elected to some public office at some time in his life.

344b **temple-robbers**: temples often served, like modern banks, as treasuries of private and public funds.

345d **as we know**: from 341e–342b.

346b **moneymaking**: but, of course, earning money is deliberate, whereas getting healthy during a sea-voyage is accidental.

347c **occasionally**: but only occasionally. Plato's pessimism about politics in the real world pervades *Republic*.

347d **to avoid power**: for this feature of Plato's imagined community see especially 519c ff.

348e **how to respond to it**: Socrates' particular difficulty is that Thrasymachus is directly attacking Socrates' own typical assumptions. In Plato's early dialogues—as in the discussion with Polemarchus—the assumptions that a given virtue is good and that it is some kind of knowledge are what regularly enable Socrates to find inconsistencies in his interlocutors' positions, once they too admit that they share these assumptions. Thrasymachus, however, is making Socratic claims about *im*morality!

348e *as others do*: for example, Polus in *Gorgias* 474c ff.

350d *red-faced Thrasymachus*: Socrates chooses to interpret Thrasymachus' flushing as due to humiliation in the argument rather than to the weather.

350d *the claim*: 349a; cf. 344c.

351d *better chance of success*: all that Socrates can demonstrate from this line of argument, strictly speaking, is that morality within the gang is necessary for effective action, not that they need be moral to anyone else.

352d *postponed*: from 348b.

353d *a function of the mind*: Socrates' question could also be translated 'And what about life?' The Greek word for mind, *psukhē*, is also the word for soul or life-force. Thus Plato's concept of mind is rather closer in broadness to the Buddhist than to the rationalist Western usage.

353e *we agreed*: not in so many words, but see 335c, 350d.

354c *unhappy or happy*: the claim that you have to know or understand *x* before you can know any of its attributes, or even behave in an *x* fashion, is familiar from other dialogues. But it does not preclude acting on one's beliefs about *x*, or having beliefs about *x*'s attributes; it is, rather, a call for more precise knowledge than belief can supply.

Chapter 2

358a *and for its consequences*: in fact Plato spends very little time on morality's consequences, which are introduced only at 612b, as a kind of appendix. The whole of the rest of the book is concerned with morality 'for its own sake' (which I take to include non-external, intrinsic concomitants such as pleasure and happiness). Plato argues that morality, properly understood, fulfils one's true nature and therefore brings true pleasure and happiness. The Kantian or deontological objection that Plato takes too much account of the consequences of morality, and the utilitarian objection that he takes too little account, are both red herrings: they want morality to be located respectively in the first and the third categories. Plato wants it in the second.

358b *they might have*: it follows from the previous note that there is no substantial conflict between Glaucon's challenge to Socrates to praise morality in isolation and Adeimantus' request (367d) for praise of morality's benefits: 'benefits' should be read as another term for what I have called 'intrinsic concomitants' (previous note). For a delicate scholarly interpretation of this near inconsistency see C. A. Kirwan, 'Glaucon's Challenge', *Phronesis*, 10 (1965), 162–73; see also N. P. White, 'The Classification of Goods in Plato's *Republic*', *Journal of the History of Philosophy*, 22 (1984), 393–421.

359b *and so on*: Glaucon's account resonates with the fifth-century distinction (associated particularly with the sophistic movement) between nature and convention, and the preference for the competitive values of natural law rather than the co-operative values of conventional law. The cynicism of claiming that obedience to law is involuntary, rather than being precisely what we choose in forming and remaining in a society, is familiar in modern times. Glaucon's views are interestingly discussed and developed by R. E. Allen, 'The Speech of Glaucon: On Contract and the Common Good', in S. Panagiotou (ed.), *Justice, Law and Method in Plato and Aristotle* (Edmonton: Academic Printing & Publishing, 1987), 51–62.

359d *an ancestor of Gyges of Lydia*: this is the reading of the manuscripts, and it is confirmed by Proclus (a Platonist of the fifth century AD). Curiously, though, in Herodotus (1. 8–13) we read how Gyges himself took power by seducing the king's wife; and later sources assign Plato's ring story to Gyges, not some ancestor. To add to the confusion, Plato himself calls it simply 'Gyges' ring' at 612b. It looks as though there were two versions of the story, involving either an ancestor of Gyges or Gyges himself. Others prefer to emend the text: see most recently S. R. Slings, 'Critical Notes on Plato's *Politeia* II', *Mnemosyne*, 42 (1989), 380–97.

359d *to a certain extent*: in Greek science of Plato's time and earlier water—and heavy rainfall in particular—was thought to cause earthquakes (see Aristotle, *Meteorologica* 365^a–369^a). The association was pre-scientific, however: Poseidon was the god of both water and earthquakes.

361b *aura of goodness*: see Aeschylus, *Seven against Thebes* 592.

362b *deep furrow*: Aeschylus, *Seven against Thebes* 593–4—i.e. the two lines which follow the one paraphrased above.

363a *Hesiod says*: *Works and Days* 232–4.

363b *similar claims*: *Odyssey* 19. 109–13, minus 110.

363c *Musaeus and his son*: Eumolpus, legendary founder of the Eleusinian mysteries, was on one genealogy the son of Musaeus, an equally legendary bard and colleague of Orpheus. In associating the Orphic and Eleusinian mysteries with this phrase, Plato means little more than just 'the mystics'.

363d *Others*: the Delphic oracle given to Glaucus in Herodotus 6. 86, and Hesiod, *Works and Days* 285, both offer this reward specifically for avoiding perjury. But the trans-generational effects of both virtue and vice were common themes in Greek thought.

363d *a kind of mud*: evidence elsewhere too suggests that this was a feature of Orphic eschatology.

363d *water in sieves*: one of several familiar punishments by futile and endlessly repeated action which we find in Greek myth. This one was also attributed especially to the daughters of Danaus, for murdering their husbands on their wedding-night.

364b *the other type of person*: one explanation of this phenomenon, which is often remarked on by the Greek poets (e.g. Solon 4. 9 Diehl), is that good men are being punished by the gods for some misdeed committed by an ancestor. Hence the sequence of thought of this paragraph.

364d *in the way of goodness*: Hesiod, *Works and Days* 287–9.

364d *he too said*: Iliad 9. 497–501, minus 498.

365a *initiations*: the Greek preserves a piece of Orphic etymologizing which is impossible to capture in meaningful English: 'initiation' (*teletē*) is associated with 'death' (*teleutē*).

365b *follow Pindar*: part of fragment 213 Bergk.

365c *Appearance overpowers reality*: Simonides, fragment 76 Bergk.

365c *Archilochus*: cf. fragments 86–9 Bergk.

365d *clubs and pressure-groups*: a feature of Athenian politics towards the end of the fifth century. Since these cliques often restricted membership to the rich, they were (in a political context) largely designed to look after the interests of a ruling oligarchy, or to plan for such a government.

365d *overpower them*: Adeimantus continues with his series of imaginary objections and responses.

365e *their lineage*: especially Hesiod, in his *Theogony*.

367a *to add*: Adeimantus, like Glaucon (358b), claims to be supporting Thrasymachus. But they also both disclaim sincere adherence to Thrasymachus' position. This will make them more amenable interlocutors for Socrates: see second note on 368a.

367b *as Glaucon suggested*: at 361b–c. Since the brothers' challenge is
what Socrates responds to in the rest of the dialogue, it is worth
noticing how peculiar it is, in a way. They have urged a strong
distinction between being moral and appearing moral; they have
asked Socrates to explain morality as an inner psychological state,
with no reference to its consequences. But this distinction is rather
artificial, one may think. Since morality (as commonly understood)
involves the performance and non-performance of certain actions,
and since actions take place in the external world, then how can
morality sensibly be discussed without *any* reference to the external
world? Plato wants to talk about the psychological disposition for
morality, rather than what is commonly understood by morality.
For these and similar reflections see L. W. Beals, 'On Appearing
Just and Being Unjust', *Journal of Philosophy*, 49 (1952), 607–14.

Chapter 3

368a *eminent sire*: the battle of Megara referred to took place in 409;
therefore, since the dialogue is probably set *c.*420 (see note on
327a), Plato is allowing himself a slight anachronism, in order to
josh his brothers. It is not known who Glaucon's lover was, but the
word is masculine: homosexuality was an accepted aspect of life in
upper-class levels of Athenian society at the time. See K. J. Dover,
Greek Homosexuality (London: Duckworth, 1978).

368a *better than morality*: it is always important for Socratic
argumentation to identify a tension such as this one. What follows
in the next few chapters can then be seen as an extended piece of
Socratic dialectic: you are claiming *x* and you are claiming *y*; but
they clash; which of *x* and *y* will you drop?

368d *really identical*: 'If you have some letters set out at a distance from
you just barely too great for them to be read, and you then have
larger versions of the same letters set out at the same distance, you
will discover that you suddenly can actually *see* what the smaller
letters are … I do not know the explanation of this
phenomenon' (White, *Companion*, 83).

368e *individuals*: the assumption that use of a single term points to a
significant single something is open to criticism, but underpins
Socrates' search for definitions, and Plato's theory of types. See also
435b and, more abstractly, 475e–476a, 507b, and 596a.

369a *wouldn't it?*: speculations about the origins of society and
civilization were familiar from the fifth century. See G. B. Kerferd,

The Sophistic Movement (Cambridge: Cambridge University Press, 1981), ch. 12.

369c *in exchange*: the principle affirmed in Socrates' last three contributions—that societies are formed because we are not self-sufficient and we have needs which others can satisfy—is quite general and need not apply only to the materialist needs of the first community, but to any community at all (J. R. S. Wilson, 'The Basis of Plato's Society', *Philosophy*, 52 (1977), 313–20). The selfishness of the first community lies not in its adherence to this principle, but in its restriction to physical needs—to equivalence to the desirous part of the mind.

370b *in only one*: compare the function argument of 352d ff. The idea of a *natural* function or talent is opaque, but never argued for by Plato, despite its importance later in the book. The idea here is that each of us has a particular contribution we ought to make towards the welfare of the whole. The notion that each of us has only one talent, at which we must work exclusively, is restrictive and artificial; the notion that we would be content to spend our whole lives within this kind of limitation is absurd. However, as throughout the book, Plato is developing political ideas with an eye on psychological implications: the notion that there are discrete mental faculties is plausible.

372c *or war*: because, as Plato is shortly to suggest, the cause of war is overpopulation.

372c *savouries*: Greek fare usually consisted of bread (the two main types of which—barley-cakes and wheat-cakes—have just been mentioned) plus something to give it taste, such as cheese, olives, fish, vegetables, and more rarely meat. These were collectively called *opson*, translated here as 'savouries'.

372e *in communities*: since morality is going to be found, by the end of Chapter 6, to be the control of desire and passion by reason, Plato needs to imagine a community where desires tend towards excess and therefore need controlling.

372e *the one we've described*: in calling this 'community fit for pigs' an ideal, Plato is only partly being ironic. Of course, it cannot be his ideal, since it consists of people satisfying their selfish desires, and there is no room in it for the ideal of the philosopher king. On the other hand, it represents the limited ideal of restrained desire, rather than desires which have got out of hand (see 399e).

373b *hunters and imitators*: a list of 'imitators' follows; a short list of 'hunters' is given at *Euthydemus* 290b–c. This was clearly a

familiar classification of occupations in Platonic circles. Hunters
'discover what's already there' (*Euthydemus*); imitators presumably
copy what's already there: both are therefore dependent on what's
already there and are not original or essential.

373b *rhapsodes*: professional public reciters (by heart) of epic poems,
especially Homer's.

373c *attendants*: here and elsewhere this is used to translate *paidagōgos*.
The institution of the *paidagōgos* is, however, peculiarly Greek: he
was a slave whose job it was to take children to and from school,
and at the same time to supervise certain aspects of their moral
education.

375e *love of knowledge*: notice how Plato assimilates the contrast
between passion and gentleness to that between passion and a
philosophic nature: the assimilation will be justified at the end of
the argument (410c ff.). Plato also conflates the love of *knowing*,
which we automatically associate with a philosopher, with a dog's
love of *the known*: again, the conflation is justifiable in the light of
the portrait of the philosopher at 474c ff. as a kind of omnivore of
knowledge.

376c *strong*: 'This passage contains in tight bud much of what will
unfold into flower as the talk proceeds, when its full import will
appear. Briefly, it implies that the perfect guardian is the perfect
man, for his character must be a delicate balance of what will later
be described in detail, the three main types of impulse in the
psyche' (Guthrie, 450).

Chapter 4

376c *bring these people up*: 'these people' clearly refers to the guardians
(more strictly, auxiliaries: see note on 414b). They are the sole
focus of the discussion from beginning to end: they are mentioned
at 378c, 383b, 387c, 388a, 394e, 395b–c, 398e, 401c, 402c, 403e,
410e, and 415d. Whenever the educational programme of this
chapter is referred back to (as at 423e), it is clear that the guardians
are being talked about. It has worried some commentators that
there is no provision for educating the lowest class. But it is not
clear that even in Athens, despite widespread literacy, there was
widespread schooling: schoolteachers charged for their services, so
most poorer children received the rudiments of education at home,
before being apprenticed to a craft, usually their father's (see 456d).
So if Plato does not provide for their education, he is not being
outrageously élitist. It is commonly argued that Plato must have

allowed the workers to be educated, as a means for the guardians to spot which ones deserved promotion to other classes (415a–c). It emerges, however, that promotion and demotion are only remote possibilities (see note on 459e). Other contexts, such as warfare, would enable the guardians to decide when they are called for.

376e *for the mind*: nowadays we think of education, especially school education, in terms of information and skills above all. But it is important to realize that the kind of education Plato is offering here, which is primarily education of character (though reading, writing, and elementary arithmetic (see 536d) would be covered by the *grammatistēs*, the teacher responsible for literature, as it was in Athens), is *all* the education a contemporary Athenian child could expect: he would be taught by a *grammatistēs*, a *kitharistēs* (music and lyric poetry), and a *paidotribēs* (physical exercise). Higher (i.e. intellectual) education of any kind was a novelty, introduced by the sophists.

376e *true and false*: or 'non-fiction and fiction'.

377c *reject the others*: on the issue of censorship, see pp. xxiii–xxxiii.

377c *form their bodies*: see *Laws* 789d–e for the view that massaging infants strengthens and shapes their bodies.

378a *Cronus' revenge on Uranus*: cf. Hesiod, *Theogony* 154–210. Uranus (Heaven) hated his children and kept them packed in their mother Earth's womb, to her agony. One of the children, Cronus, was persuaded by Earth to castrate his father when he came to have sex with Earth. Cronus then became lord of creation.

378a *his son did to him*: cf. Hesiod, *Theogony* 453 ff. Cronus wanted to remain king, so he swallowed all his children in case one of them might take over some day. Their mother Rhea, however, hid one of them away on Crete and gave Cronus a rock to swallow instead. In due course the child, Zeus, overthrew Cronus and established himself as king of the gods.

378a *no mere piglet*: a pig or piglet was a standard small sacrifice and was usual before initiation into the Eleusinian mysteries.

378c *gods and giants*: e.g. Zeus' war against the Titans, who were his father's siblings; or Athena killing her father, the giant Pallas, for trying to rape her; or all the gods (with Heracles' help) repelling the invasion of the giants sent by Earth to overthrow them. This last episode was prominent on a ceremonial robe presented to the statue of Athena every year during her main festival in Athens: this gives particular point to Plato's mention of 'pictures', though it was no doubt a common theme for all kinds of artists.

378d *allegorical*: allegorical interpretation of Homer was popular; for a few small Platonic examples see *Theaetetus* 152e, 153c–d, 194c. Epicharmus and Pindar had apparently retold a legend of Hephaestus tying his mother Hera to her throne; for Zeus hurling Hephaestus off Olympus see Homer, *Iliad* 1. 586–94; for further divine internal warfare, verbal or physical, see e.g. *Iliad* 1. 536–70, 20. 1–74 (continued at 21. 328–513).

378e *once again to be asked*: as at 377e.

379a *as he really is*: the Greek philosophers tend to talk equally of 'God' and 'the gods': there is a single Divine of which the gods are various manifestations.

379d *wretched destinies*: these lines and the next two quotes are taken, with alterations caused by misremembering, from Homer, *Iliad* 24. 527–32.

379e *dispenser of both good and evil*: a half-line of unknown origin.

379e *Athena and Zeus*: Homer, *Iliad* 4. 20 ff.

380a *Themis and Zeus*: perhaps *Iliad* 20. 1–74 or 15. 12–217.

380a *Aeschylus*: fragment 160 Nauck, from *Niobe*.

380a *descendants of Pelops*: i.e. the ill-starred Atreus, Agamemnon, Orestes, and Electra: see especially Aeschylus' Oresteian trilogy.

381d *visitors from other lands*: Homer, *Odyssey* 17. 485–6.

381d *Proteus and Thetis*: shape-shifting sea-deities.

381d *river Inachus*: Aeschylus, fragment 168 Nauck, from *Xantriae*. The children are presumably his tributaries, with their 'life-giving' water.

383a *Agamemnon*: *Iliad* 2. 1 ff. Zeus sends a lying dream to Agamemnon, that the capture of Troy is imminent. Notice that Plato is not denying the existence of omens and portents, only that they can be false or that false ones can be sent by the gods; it is we who misinterpret the gods' messages.

383a *Aeschylus*: fragment 350 Nauck; it is not certain from which lost play the lines come.

383c *chorus*: Athenian dramatists had to apply to the state for a chorus, which would be awarded to a select number per year, and each play would be financed by a wealthy citizen.

386c *spirits of the dead*: Homer, *Odyssey* 11. 489–91 (Achilles' ghost to Odysseus). The next six quotes are: *Iliad* 20. 64–5; *Iliad* 23. 103–4; *Odyssey* 10. 495; *Iliad* 16. 856–7; *Iliad* 23. 100–1; *Odyssey* 24. 6–9.

387c *Cocytus and Styx*: two of the rivers of Hades—Lamentation and Hateful.

388a *goddess*: Thetis. The six following Homeric paraphrases or quotes are: *Iliad* 24. 10–13 (with the last line differing a great deal from the received text); *Iliad* 18. 23–4; *Iliad* 22. 414–15; *Iliad* 18. 54 (Thetis on the inevitability of Achilles' death); *Iliad* 22. 168–9 (Zeus speaking of Hector); *Iliad* 16. 433–4.

388b *gods by birth*: Priam was descended from Zeus.

388e *laughter either*: on both grief and laughter see also 605c–606d.

389a *about the gods*: *Iliad* 1. 599–600.

389b *a short while ago*: 382c–e.

389d *or carpenter*: Homer, *Odyssey* 17. 383–4.

389e *Diomedes say*: *Iliad* 4. 412. The next quote is a combination of *Iliad* 3. 8 and 4. 431.

389e *heart of a deer*: *Iliad* 1. 225. Achilles is insulting his leader, Agamemnon, by calling him a lecherous, cowardly drunk.

390b *into the cups*: *Odyssey* 9. 8–10 (Odysseus speaking).

390b *fate to face*: *Odyssey* 12. 342. The point is that this sentiment encouraged Odysseus' men to steal the Sun-god's cattle.

390b *the passage*: *Iliad* 14. 294–351 (the quote is from 296).

390c *for them to hear*: the story is told in *Odyssey* 8. 266–366.

390d *the lines*: *Odyssey* 20. 17–18, spoken by Odysseus.

390e *magnificent kings*: a proverb, possibly originating with Hesiod.

390e *wrath*: Plato uses the archaic word which was famous as the first word of the *Iliad*. Phoenix's advice to Achilles is in *Iliad* 9. 515–605.

391a *a ransom*: Achilles accepts Agamemnon's gifts at *Iliad* 19. 278–81; Priam brings him gifts to release Hector's body at *Iliad* 24. 470 ff.

391a *to Apollo*: *Iliad* 22. 15 and 20.

391b *ready to fight him*: the river Scamander in *Iliad* 21. 211 ff.

391b *take it with him*: *Iliad* 23. 151. The river was supposed to guarantee Achilles' safe return from the war; because it has failed to do so, Achilles tells it off and bitterly re-dedicates his hair to his dead companion Patroclus. It was a primitive Greek practice to dedicate your hair to a river; the fact that hair grows makes it an external manifestation of one's life-force, so in dedicating your hair, you are dedicating yourself.

391b *funeral pyre*: *Iliad* 24. 14–18; 23. 175–7.

391c *for gods and men*: avarice requires others for its fulfilment; hence it is opposed to disdain, which would keep Achilles aloof from others.

391c *Peirithous*: see the Index of Names.

391e *but also false*: see 377d ff., especially 379b–c and 380b–c.

391e *still fresh*: both quotes are combined as Aeschylus, fragment 162 Nauck (from the *Niobe*). Niobe is talking about her father Tantalus, a notorious criminal whose father was Zeus.

392a *and the dead*: that is, all kinds of supernatural beings.

392b *of the enquiry*: that is, the expediency of morality.

392c *impression of morality*: it has been suggested that the promise to discuss what kinds of stories about human beings can be told is fulfilled in Chapter 13. This is an attractive suggestion (especially since it would make Chapter 13 less of an afterthought), but it is untenable. Chapter 13 does not discuss that topic (except, at the most, in an extremely oblique way) and Plato never signals that he is there fulfilling this or any other promise. In fact, the promise is never fulfilled, nor need it be: by the time the discussion of morality is over, it would be mere repetition to say what kinds of people can be portrayed in poetry.

393a *his god*: Chryses was a priest of Apollo.

393a *the lines*: Iliad 1. 15–16.

393e *garlands*: he carried a staff wreathed with Apollo's sacred laurel.

394c *dithyrambic poetry*: or lyric poetry in general. Dithyrambic was simply the form of lyric poetry most commonly composed and performed in Socrates' and Plato's time. Originally composed in celebration of Dionysus, by Socrates' time the form had degenerated into artificiality of language and music.

394e *single role*: it is important to appreciate that Plato is not talking about acting on a stage so much as the unconscious assimilation of roles to which we are all subject.

395a *rhapsodes*: see note on 373b.

395e *grief and sorrow*: Plato clearly has particular tragic or comic stage roles in mind, but they are not now identifiable with certainty. Note that in classical times all actors were male.

396b *and so forth*: the implication is not that actors made the sounds of rivers splashing and so on: the context is Homeric, and Plato is thinking of onomatopoeia in poetry. See W. B. Stanford, 'Onomatopoeic Mimesis in Plato, *Republic* 396b–397c', *Journal of Hellenic Studies*, 93 (1973), 185–91.

397c *variation*: representational poetry leaps, for example, from imitation of a woman, to imitation of a man, to a slave, and so on; on the other hand, speaking always in one's own name guarantees uniformity.

398a *chaplet of wool*: that is, treated him like a statue of a god or some other sacred object. Note that Plato does not intend a blanket ban on all poets and poetry: incidental remarks such as 460a and 468d show that some poets, even Homer, are acceptable if they conform to Plato's requirements.

398b *principles*: as discussed at 379a–392a.

398d *we said*: at 387d ff.

398e *musical modes*: Plato mentions several Greek musical modes or octaves, each of which differed in sequence of intervals and started from different notes:

> Mixed Lydian: b–c–d–e–f–g–a–b
> Taut Lydian: a–b–c–d–e–f–g–a
> Loose Lydian: f–g–a–b–c–d–e–f
> Loose Ionian: g–a–b–c–d–e–f–g
> Dorian: e–f–g–a–b–c–d–e
> Phrygian: d–e–f–g–a–b–c–d

On the modes see S. Michaelides, *The Music of Ancient Greece: An Encyclopaedia* (London: Faber and Faber, 1978), s.v. *tonos*. For an excellent brief essay on all aspects of Greek music see the article 'Music' in the *Oxford Classical Dictionary*. 'Mode' translates the Greek *harmonia*, which elsewhere has to be translated 'music' or 'harmony'.

399c *he said*: the Dorian mode was regarded as tight and controlled (like a warrior), the Phrygian as open (like a man of peace).

399e *Marsyas and his kind of instrument*: on Marsyas see the Index of Names. Note that all English translations, rather than transliterations, of Greek musical instruments are somewhat inaccurate. For accurate information the reader is referred to the various articles, under transliterated titles, in Michaelides (see note on 398e): *aulos* (reed-pipe); *kithara* (cithara); *lyra* (lyre); *pektis* (harp); *salpinx* (trumpet); *syrinx* (wind-pipe); *trigōnon* (psaltery).

399e *a while back*: 372e, to be precise. Note that since Plato is aiming for a conception of morality as the control, by reason, of other mental faculties, he creates the 'inflamed' community (372e) precisely so that he can demonstrate the necessity of keeping in check the excess of emotion it encourages.

400a *all the musical modes*: it is disputed what these four basic constituents of music are. However, the three elements of rhythm were expressed by mathematical ratios as 2:2 (i.e. short–short:short–short, or long:long, or long:short–short, or short–short:long), 3:2 (long–short:long), and 2:1 (long:short) or 1:2 (short:long). The best guess for the musical elements, then, is that they are the four primary musical ratios—2:1, 3:2, 4:3, and 9:8 (or for Pythagoreans 4:2).

400b *its rise and its fall*: the dactyl or 'finger' is 'martial' and 'heroic' because it is the basis of the hexameters in which Greek epic verse was composed; it is a 'compound' because it is made up of two halves, the first consisting of a long syllable, the second of two short syllables; two short syllables count the same as one long syllable, so it is 'equal in its rise and its fall'. In the terms of the previous note, it is a 2:2 rhythm. It is called a 'finger' because the distance between your first and second knuckles is (roughly, at least) equal to the two shorter lengths remaining.

400b *trochee too*: an iamb, as Plato says, is short:long; a trochee is long:short.

400e *goodness of character*: the Greek term *euētheia* was used for both 'goodness of character' and, euphemistically, 'mental simplicity'. See the clever pun at 348c–d: Thrasymachus uses the word to mean 'simplicity', Socrates pretends to understand him as meaning 'goodness of character'.

401b *edifices*: the importance of a pleasing architectural environment has been rediscovered in the modern world, forced upon our attention by the damage done to the psyches of people living in grim tower blocks. On the subject in general see H. Skolimowski, *Living Philosophy* (Harmondsworth: Penguin Arkana, 1992), ch. 7.

401d *the beauty of reason*: in this sentence (and again at 412a) Plato adumbrates the broader role of the guardians—or some section of them—as those who know goodness and can model a society along its lines: see Chapters 8–10.

402a *when it did arrive*: Plato (in common with normal Greek views) did not regard very young children as rational or capable of discrimination. Note that he obviously does not expect the arrival of reason to promote criticism, but to reinforce the values inculcated by the education. Plato's opponents would say that his citizens have been so indoctrinated into uniformity of belief that they are incapable of criticizing the system. Be that as it may, since morality is psychic harmony under the rule of reason (441d–e), then it is clear from what is said here that the educational programme is supposed to prepare a mind for becoming moral. Thus the blend of reason and passion (410b–412a) is said at 441e–442a to become morality when these two parts take control of the desirous part.

403e *we've already said*: 398e.

403e *greatest contest of all*: that is, war.

404d *Syracusan rations*: these were proverbially luxurious, just as Corinthian prostitutes were notorious and Attic pastries were famously rich.

405b *most of one's life*: the Athenian lawcourts were an essential part of their direct democracy: every male citizen could act as a juror, prosecute another person, or be prosecuted. Plato's condemnation of lawyers here should be compared especially with *Theaetetus* 172b–177b.

405d *Asclepiadae*: the people who continued Asclepius' medical work called themselves the Asclepiadae, or 'sons of Asclepius'. Since Asclepius became revered as the divine founder of medicine, the term means just 'doctors'.

405d *as the names of diseases*: the words had familiar, non-medical meanings—'gust of wind' and 'downflow'.

405e *wounded at Troy*: a confusion of *Iliad* 11. 624 ff. (Hecamede makes a refreshing potion of Pramnian wine) with *Iliad* 11. 836 ff. and 15. 390–94 (Patroclus treats Eurypylus' wound). It is important to remember that Plato would have been quoting from memory: texts were available only on cumbersome rolls, not in handy books.

407a *unrewarding*: the implication is that anyone who does not contribute to the welfare of Plato's community is to be denied medical attention. This is, I think, a case of the external political provisions being driven by the psychological layer of the book: would one foster within one's mind an aspect of it which did one no good?

407c *philosophy*: note that here, as occasionally elsewhere in the book, 'philosophy' means not so much the pursuit of virtue as higher education in general.

408a *soothing medicines*: a loose recollection of *Iliad* 4. 218.

408c *struck by lightning*: Pindar, *Pythian Odes* 3. 55–8; Aeschylus, *Agamemnon* 1022 ff.; Euripides, *Alcestis* 3–4.

408c *wasn't the son of a god*: see 390d ff.

409a *other people's minds*: by oratory.

410e *we said*: at 375c.

410e *fit harmoniously together*: that is, they have to be attuned by being stretched and relaxed like the strings of a lyre: see 412a as well. The talk of psychic harmony anticipates 441c–444a.

411a *not long ago*: 398d–e.

411b *feeble fighter*: said of Menelaus at *Iliad* 17. 588.

Chapter 5

412d *success and failure*: see pp. lvi–lviii on Plato's 'moral egoism': good for me coincides with good for others.

413e *to test gold*: the purity of a lump of gold was tested by melting it until the impurities could be separated off, and pure gold produced. Since invariably only a small quantity of pure gold would remain, the analogy is peculiarly apt to Plato's purposes.

414b *auxiliaries*: the translation is traditional and the best available, but the Greek word means, all at once, 'assistant and military ally in charge of policing and defence'. 'Executives' might be a passable translation, if it did not nowadays conjure up an image of men in business suits. It is important to note that we are here instructed to think of *all* the people who have so far been called 'guardians' as 'auxiliaries', as distinct from guardians proper. In other words, the differentiation of guardians from auxiliaries is promissory, in the sense that we do not yet know who the real guardians are. All we know is that they are to be discovered by a series of tests. Echoes of this testing at the end of Chapter 10 (540a) suggest that these tests are part of the higher education of philosophers. At 521e–522b the educational programme of Chapter 4 is expressly distinguished from the higher education of philosophers. Looking back over Chapter 4, it seems clear that it takes a 'guardian' up to the stage of being an 'auxiliary'. They have true beliefs, not knowledge (429b–430a, and notice the stress on belief here in 412e ff.), and the emphasis throughout has been on military training and the passionate virtues (we will soon be told that the auxiliaries correspond to the passionate part of the mind): this is especially clear in Plato's concern to tone down their innate fierceness (375b–c) by combining it with enough rationality to moderate it (410b–412a, 416c), and in the explicit references to them as the militia at 398b, 399a, and 403e. They are supposed, by the end of the curriculum, to be able to *act* on true beliefs—but not necessarily to know why it is good to act in this way. Having the community's best interests at heart is here said to be a property of the guardians proper, rather than the auxiliaries.

414b *not long ago*: 389b–c.

414c *a tall story*: literally, 'a Phoenician lie'—the Phoenicians proverbially told tall stories.

415c *copper or iron guardian*: so at 546a ff. Plato analyses the state's decline as due to the presence of inferior guardians.

415c *this story*: Plato is commonly criticized for using the story as propaganda to keep the lower orders in their place. This is over-simplistic. He believes that all the citizens of his community will agree to the system, because they appreciate that it is for the greater good (e.g. 433c). That may be politically naïve, but in this light the story is little more than a way of putting things simply. It was very common for ancient cities to have a foundation myth: the tale of Romulus and Remus and the founding of Rome is probably the best known today.

419a *impossible*: despite this feature of the imaginary state, Plato's critics still charge him with treating the lower class as underdogs and 'human cattle' (Popper). Yet they are the ones with all the good things of life.

420c *original purpose of our investigation*: the expediency of morality.

420e *formal arrangement of couches*: literally, 'reclining from right to left': by protocol, at the most formal dinner-parties, the relative importance of the guests was indicated by this anticlockwise movement from the head couch.

421c *according to its nature*: the issue of the happiness of the rulers and the happiness of the community is returned to in an important passage, 519d–521b.

422e *as in the game*: there was apparently a board-game called 'Communities'. As with most ancient Greek games, the rules are now uncertain; however, it is tempting here to think of the Far Eastern game 'Go', where the territory one controls (one's community?) may consist of several discrete areas (communities?).

423c *is a unity*: we hear later (458d ff.) how the guardians will oversee the procreation of other guardians, but we are given no details about how they will limit the size of the population as a whole.

423c *earlier as well*: see 415a–b.

424a *everything they can*: on women, marriage, and children see Chapter 7.

424c *at the moment*: Homer, *Odyssey* 1. 351–2, with variations.

424e *our original position*: see 377a, perhaps, but more particularly 424a.

426c *high skill*: see also 488a ff.

426e *Hydra*: a many-headed beast which had a famous battle with Heracles. Since every time a head was chopped off it grew two in its place, it was proverbially impossible for even Heracles to defeat it single-handedly.

427c *earth's navel*: Plato's community is assumed to be Greek. Apollo was the traditional arbiter of crucial issues for all Greeks, by the method of consulting his oracle at Delphi. A particular spot in Delphi was considered to be the exact centre, or navel, of the earth.

Chapter 6

427e *assist morality*: see 368b–c.

427e *to be good*: this is an important premiss in the argument, but it is not argued for. What allows Plato to assume that his imaginary community is good? It is presumably because it is a good example of a community: it has unity and the ability, engendered by the educational programme, to remain as it is.

427e *and morality*: this is a fairly standard list of Greek cardinal virtues, reflected also in the discussion of the effects of literature at 386a ff. But even so, Plato is merely assuming that morality is good; and this makes his position less of a response to Thrasymachus, who denied that morality was good (see especially Socrates' comment at 348e), than to Glaucon and Adeimantus (see the comment at 368a). It may be that Chapter 1 originally formed a separate work; but it was Plato who stitched the whole book together, so he should, strictly, have argued for this assumption. It is, in fact, not difficult to construct a better argument based largely on the features of Plato's own argument:

1. Our community is good.
2. Therefore it contains all the elements of goodness, whatever they may be.
3. The fact that everyone does his own job is an element of the community's goodness.
4. Everyone doing his own job is commonly acknowledged to be morality.
5. Therefore morality is good.

The chief difference between this and Plato's own argument is the abstractness of step 2. Plato's error, then, is to have immediately specified morality as an element of goodness. He does so because he is looking ahead: morality will be defined by means of the Principle of Specialization, with its three components (see note on 433a), and Plato already knows that the community does its job perfectly.

428a *looking for*: although Plato calls on this method at 433b–c to support his case, it has obvious weaknesses: it will work only if it is known exactly how many elements there are, and if there is nothing more to the goodness of a community than what is provided by the four elements Plato specifies. Plato is content with it because he is sure that the three parts of the mind/community define the three domains in which morality manifests as the 'left-over' virtue: intellect channelled by concentrating on its own role is wisdom; passion channelled is courage; desire channelled is self-discipline.

428d *in the strict sense of the word*: see 414b. The notion that in the community only the rulers can think beyond self-interest is clearly motivated by Plato's dominant interest in individual psychology, since he will shortly claim that our psychological make-up consists of three parts, only one of which is capable of reasoning about the good of the whole. 'Note that strictly speaking the presence of this knowledge in the rulers is not the only structural condition for wisdom . . . There might be a *polis* in which those by nature fitted to rule had the appropriate knowledge, but in which they were not allowed to rule. Such a *polis* would not be wise' (Wilson, 'The Argument of *Republic* IV', 117). And the same goes, *mutatis mutandis*, for the other three virtues: each has a task, a function to perform.

429c *to be feared*: for instance, that loss of freedom is more to be feared than death (386a ff.).

430b *not courage*: rashness, for example, or mere daring: see *Protagoras* 349b–351b, *Laches* 196d ff.

430c *later*: presumably 442b–c, though this hardly deserves to be called a more thorough treatment.

430e *absurd*: this seems strange: why should the phrase be absurd? Given the analogy between community and individual, we already suspect that the individual will turn out to have 'parts' as the community has its classes. Plato's comment here is only explicable on the understanding that he is implicitly modifying the Socratic view that an individual was somehow unified by his desire and pursuit of what he perceived as his own good (see especially *Protagoras* 352a–357e).

431b *slaves*: it is only from asides like this (see also 433d) that we know
that Plato's community is (like all other Greek states) to contain
slaves; we could also have inferred from 469c that non-Greek
prisoners of war would become slaves in the community.

432a *in every individual*: there is an important ambivalence in Plato's
account of community self-discipline, which also affects how he
regards desire in an individual. He is trying simultaneously to say
that the workers/desires need tight control (431c) *and* that they
acquiesce in the control (432a). It is likely that the conflict would
have appeared less harsh to a Greek, because it was a Greek
commonplace to describe rational persuasion as a form of
compulsion: one can acquiesce for good reasons which one finds
compelling (see also note on 443b). Still, it is extremely naïve of
Plato to expect the lower orders of his community to acquiesce in
having little control over their own lives: I take this to be further
evidence of Plato's lack of interest in external politics. Put at its
bluntest, how can Plato expect a community with a caste system to
be a unified community? Yet he not only expects it, he even claims
that the caste system is an important factor in its unity (e.g. 431c–
432a, 434a–c).

432e *getting at*: all this by-play is due to Plato's awareness of the
somewhat anti-climactic nature of what he is to say about morality.

433a *as you'll remember*: from passages such as 370a–c, 374a–d,
394e–395b, 397d–e, 423d.

433a *best equipped him*: normal thinking about morality would be likely
to talk about one's relationship with others (372a), and Plato has
often been criticized for his weak attempts, in what follows, to
bring an unorthodox theory of his more into line with normal
thinking. In fact, however, the 'one man, one job' principle of
specialization has three components: first, do only one job, without
interfering with others' jobs; second, do the job you are best
equipped to do; third, do the job through which you best
contribute to the welfare of the whole. Plato's theory can
immediately be seen to be less unorthodox, more of a theory of
social morality. If I stick to my own function, I am contributing to
the welfare of the whole, and I am not inclined to *pleonexia*—to
usurping more than my fair share. See also 589cff. for Plato's
alignment of his own version of morality with common morality,
and pp. xxxix–xlii for discussion.

433b *often said it*: that is, in everyday conversation, not in this or in any
other dialogue. Plato is probably referring to popular sayings like:
'It's not right to poke your nose into other people's business.'

433c *we did in fact say*: at 427e–428a.

434a *one's own occupation*: as it stands, this is a singularly bad argument, since it relies merely on vague verbal similarity. Popper sneers (p. 98), 'This is how the greatest philosopher of all time tries to convince us that he has discovered the true nature of justice.' But Plato's argument could be extended by means of either the first or the third component of the 'one man, one job' principle (see note on 433a), to bring the verbal formulae into some substantial relation with each other. Note also the extra insurance that the guardians will be moral in this sense: they are to have no property at all (416d ff.).

434a *to the community*: so, in effect, the principle of 'one man, one job' has come to mean keeping within one's caste, rather than keeping to one's particular profession. This is why morality is said at 433a to be 'some version of' the principle.

434c *roles among them*: sentences like this make it rather hard to distinguish self-discipline from morality, as they are both described. Self-discipline is (like the Christian virtue of humility, properly understood) neither overestimating nor underestimating one's abilities and role; morality is keeping to one's role, for good and sufficient reasons. Morality is, as it were, what makes self-discipline, courage, and wisdom virtues rather than mere abilities (433b). If each class in the community does its own job (which is morality), then the community can be wise (because that is the rulers doing their job), courageous (because that is the militia doing its job), and self-disciplined (because that is the third class doing its job of falling in with the other two classes doing their jobs).

435a *in the two instances*: the principle that usage of the same predicate points to the sharing of a real something by the things which are given the predicate is a vital underpinning of Plato's metaphysics. Compare also 436b–c and 596a.

435c *another simple enquiry*: see 423c.

435c *features*: Plato refers to these features as 'parts' rather rarely (although the necessities of translation make it seem less rare). Quite what he means by a part has exercised scholars; but Plato distinguishes and separates various impulses and traits within us, and the word 'part' is appropriate for an enterprise of distinguishing and separating. By approaching the desirous part, for instance, from different angles throughout the book, we end up with a reasonably clear notion of what it is and how it differs from other 'parts'.

435d *is needed*: at 504b–e Plato says that this 'longer approach' would involve the full further-educational programme of Chapter 10. Then one could see the mind as it is, rather than when it is deformed by association with the body (611cff.).

436a *Phoenicians and Egyptians*: the three ethnic groups correspond to the three parts of the mind we are about to meet: they are respectively passionate, rational, and desirous or mercenary (Egyptians and Phoenicians are so characterized presumably because they were the main traders in the Mediterranean). This is not a coincidence. Plato is suggesting that these three impulses can only occur in a community as a result of their presence in the inhabitants. This is what motivates him, ostensibly (436a), to look for the same impulses within individuals that he has found in his imaginary community, exemplified in the three classes.

The claim that traders form trading communities (or that people who prefer democracy form democratic communities—544d–e) is not the stronger claim that *all* properties of communities are due *only* to the properties of its dominant members: it is no more than the claim that the interests of the dominant class in a society form that society's interests (see J. P. Maguire, 'The Individual and the Class in Plato's *Republic*', *Classical Journal*, 60 (1965), 145–50). The stronger claim would be inconsistent with the community–individual analogy of Chapter 3 (of which we have just been reminded at 434d–435b), because it would make the individual prior to the state, whereas the analogy claims that they are isomorphic. For a discussion, and an alternative view, see B. A. O. Williams, 'The Analogy of City and Soul in Plato's *Republic*', in E. N. Lee *et al.* (eds.), *Exegesis and Argument* (*Phronesis* suppl. 1, 1973), 196–206.

436c *more than one of them*: strict application of this principle to the issue of dividing the mind into parts would result in infinite parts of the mind—as many as there are conflicting whims (defined by the objects they desire). Plato uses it, however, to point to conflicting sources and types of motivation, rather than conflicts between objects.

437a *invalidated*: Plato's hesitancy here may be due to the idea, expressed at 611b–612a, that the mind is essentially unitary. But the idea as expressed there does not contradict the doctrine of the tripartite mind, which also recurs in other dialogues.

439a *drink in itself*: Plato has to say that thirst is desire for just drink, rather than for good drink, because it is arguably reason which adds attributes like 'good', and Plato is trying to drive a wedge between desire and reason. Elsewhere, however (in Chapter 11 especially), it is clear that the desirous part is rational, at least in the sense that it can work out how to achieve its aims (553d), which it describes as good (562b). But this apparent inconsistency is easily resolved: Plato is using thirst here as a clear example, and is making it wholly unreasoning in order to drive as wide a wedge as possible between these two parts of the mind. The wedge, more fully spelt out, is that the other parts seek their own good, whereas only reason seeks what is good for the whole person (see also note on 443b, and pp. xxxvi–xxxix).

439b *in the same context*: so Plato is claiming that wanting to drink and not wanting to drink are opposites, such that it is impossible for the same part of my mind to have both desires at the same time. A sophisticated critic might claim that it is possible to want and not want the same thing under different descriptions: Oedipus wants to marry Jocasta, but does not want to marry his own mother. But Plato is talking about real, non-opaque objects of want, such as the drink on the table in front of me. And then, given the stringency of the conditions Plato sets up, it is hard to refute his argument. Apparent counter-examples turn out to violate the conditions in some respect: they are not 'wanting and not wanting' exactly the same thing, or at exactly the same time.

439d *don't they?*: the kind of situation Plato is thinking of is one where the rational mind knows it would be better for the body, because of the particular illness it has, not to receive liquid.

439d *certain satisfactions and pleasures*: but not all: some pleasures are purely rational (see 585a ff.; *Philebus* 51b–52b).

439e *aspects of our minds*: Plato has been criticized for making a redundant move. If what he is wanting to explain is how I desire *x*, then has he gained anything by referring us to a desirous part? One can still ask how the desirous part desires *x*, and so on *ad infinitum*, potentially. In fact, however, since 'I' am more complex than just 'I-desiring', then as long as the desirous part is simpler than the whole, it does serve an explanatory function. The three parts are not themselves significantly subdivisible: they have only specialist roles to play. Another problem: if I contain these three parts, in what sense am I still a single person (apart from the fact that I have a single body)? Moline suggests, with some plausibility (pp. 77–8), 'Plato's answer is suggested in his famous hydraulic simile at *Republic* 485d–e. The parts of the psyche are like channels or tubes into which the flow of a single stream is divided. The total flowage is constant, so that what goes into one tube or channel is lost to the others (*Republic* 485d, borne out at 588e–589b). Both the *Republic* and the *Symposium* suggest that this single source is *eros*, a primordial energy source powering not simply the stereotypically erotic activities, but all human activities whatever ... The parts of the psyche are one psyche in that they are but different ways of channeling one finite, personal stream of energy or desire.'

439e *near by*: the North and South Walls (completed *c*.455) formed a secure corridor between Athens and her vital seaport. Leontius' route would have taken him past the ravine where criminals' corpses were thrown by the executioner.

441b *sternly to his heart*: *Odyssey* 20. 17, previously quoted at 390d.

441e *to repeat*: see 411e–412a. However, the idea that psychic harmony is a result of the educational programme is somewhat promissory, since it is clear enough that the education so far—which is education by habituation (522a)—has been concerned predominantly with the passionate part of the mind (see note on 414b), rather than the rational part, whose training is described in Chapter 10. But then it is not clear how the education of Chapter 10, which is rigorously intellectual, equips the rational mind to look after the mind as a whole, which is the claim made here and again at (for instance) 586d–587a and 589a–b (see also notes on 484d and 520e). There are in fact different objectives for the two educational programmes. The later one is for philosophers, to enable them to work with the 'types' (which are never mentioned in Chapter 4) and ultimately to understand goodness; the one in Chapter 4 is for auxiliaries, to inculcate true belief (see e.g. 429b ff.). Philosophers gain knowledge of absolute goodness; auxiliaries work with what is good for themselves (442c).

443a *temple-robbery*: see note on 344b.

443b *as ruler or subject*: the implication is that it is our desirous part which impels us towards immoral acts (see also 571a ff., and 590a–c), and that in a moral person reason controls these desires. As the book progresses, we learn more about why it is correct and important for reason to rule, and wrong for either of the other parts to rule. In the first place, the other parts use coercion to direct the mind towards their ends (442a–b, 554a) and the rest of the mind is enslaved to them (553d, 573d), whereas reason uses education (548b–c, 554d) and achieves a harmonious mind in which there is agreement that it should rule (441e–442a, 442c–d, 443d–e). In the second place, only reason aims at the good of the whole and of each of the parts, rather than selfishly and divisively aiming for its own good alone (442c, 586c–d, 590c–e).

443b *We said*: see 432b ff., probably.

443d *one another's work*: there is an important gap in Plato's theory here, which we can fill by reference to passages later in the book. Mere formal marshalling of the mental parts may be necessary, but is not also sufficient for morality: an immoral person could marshal his parts to be a more effective criminal. In other words, the mere leadership and resourcefulness of the rational mind does not guarantee morality. However, we will later find that reason also inherently loves truth and goodness, and tries to realize such qualities. It then becomes more plausible to suggest that the rule of reason is morality.

443e *describes as fine*: Plato seems to be asserting (and no more than that, unfortunately) that actions commonly recognized as moral promote the mental harmony he is describing as morality—that is, as well as offering an analysis of inner morality, he is also implying an analysis of 'moral' as applied to actions (see also 590a–c). Since we are given no argument for this, there are important grey areas. Do all conventionally moral actions promote mental harmony, even when those actions are the result of luck or habit (as at 619c–d)? Are all conventionally moral actions the result of mental harmony (either as a permanent state or as temporarily acquired)? See further pp. xxxix–xlii.

444c *I said*: contemporary theories of health stressed the notion of balance or harmony between the bodily elements or humours; so for a Greek of the time the analogy between this and Plato's account of morality would have seemed natural. Since health belongs in the second category of goods (357c), which Socrates was challenged to show morality belonged to as well, then the analogy with health is tacitly forcing the issue (445a–b). Another tacit move is buried in Plato's emphasis here on morality as natural: Glaucon had claimed that it repressed human nature (Chapter 2). On the pervasiveness of the analogy with health, and more of its consequences, see Kenny.

Chapter 7

449c *friends share*: see 424a.

450b *cause us*: it is a bit unfair of Plato to have Socrates pretend that he had the proposals of this chapter in mind all along: during the last chapter he presented morality against the background of a normal social system, which he now dispenses with altogether (in the case of the guardians).

451a *I'm about to say*: he fully expects to be punished for voicing an opinion when he shouldn't, so he somewhat formulaically prays for this to be averted.

451b *pollution*: that is, he is not tainted in the religious sense, requiring ritual purification for himself or his community. On pollution and purification see A. W. H. Adkins, *Merit and Responsibility* (London: Oxford University Press, 1960), ch. 5; W. Burkert, *Greek Religion* (Oxford: Basil Blackwell, 1985), 75–84.

451c *completed and done*: if there is any external source for the contrast between men's and women's 'business' (*drama*), it may be the mimes of Sophron (a Syracusan of the fifth century about whose work we know little else except that it dealt alternately with men and women), or the Eleusinian mysteries.

452c *those wits*: there is certainly a reference to Aristophanes' comic masterpiece *Ecclesiazousae*, which imagines women with political power proposing laws similar to Plato's here: see especially *Ecclesiazousae* 588 ff.

453d *a dolphin picking us up*: the Greeks knew that dolphins occasionally helped humans in distress. Plutarch, *Moralia* 160 F–163 D, tells a number of such tales.

454a *disputation*: literally 'antilogic', defined by G. B. Kerferd (*The Sophistic Movement* (note on 369a), 61) as 'causing the same thing to be seen by the same people now as possessing one predicate, and now as possessing the opposite or contradictory predicate'. In other words, it is deceptive and sophistic. Plato's dialogue *Euthydemus* ridicules a couple of sophists and their eristic practice of antilogic, and contains some fine examples. For some reflections on the issue see A. Nehamas, 'Eristic, Antilogic, Sophistic, Dialectic: Plato's Demarcation of Philosophy from Sophistry', *History of Philosophy Quarterly*, 7 (1990), 3–16.

454a *not eristic*: dialectic is philosophical discussion whose goal is the truth and the improvement of life; the interlocutor is seen by its chief practitioner, Socrates, as a fellow-traveller. Eristic's goal is the confusion and refutation of an interlocutor who is seen as an opponent. On dialectic see also notes on 510c ff.

455d *every sphere*: Plato regards men as not just physically stronger than women (451e), but better in most if not all respects; he is interested only in the equality of female guardians, not in that of all women in the community; he displays a high-handed attitude of ownership at 451c, 453d, and elsewhere; he lets slip casual remarks such as those in 388a, 398e, 431c, 469d, 557c, 563b, and 605e, which reveal that he retains the usual Greek attitude towards women; all this shows that Plato is very far from counting as a true feminist. He is not interested in women's rights, only in ensuring the unity of the community, and in applying the principle that all people should perform the function for which they are best equipped by nature. But whatever one makes of the ideas, their revolutionary nature in a social context should not be underestimated. In short, although he clearly believed that at least some of the resources available to contemporary societies were being misused, it is not clear that he thought they were being abused. Good discussions of the issues are those by Annas (*Philosophy*, 51 (1976)), Calvert (*Phoenix*, 29 (1975)), Fortenbaugh (*Apeiron*, 9 (1975)), Jacobs (*Apeiron*, 12 (1978)), Lesser (*Philosophy*, 54 (1979)), Okin (*Philosophy and Public Affairs*, 6 (1976–7)), and Wender (*Arethusa*, 6 (1973)).

456a *good guardians*: see 375a ff.

456b *where we were before*: 425a.

457b *plucking laughter unripe*: a parody of Pindar, fragment 209 Bergk, which reads 'Plucking wisdom unripe'.

457b *first wave*: harking back to 453d. The second wave immediately follows, and the third wave—proverbially the largest—starts at 471c.

457d *knowing his parent*: Plato's proposals about children would inevitably have reminded his contemporary readers to some extent of Sparta, where male children were removed from their families at an early age and brought up communally as trainee soldiers. Another Spartan feature in this chapter is women exercising alongside men, with both sexes naked.

458d *than those of logic*: actually, the Greeks spoke of geometrical necessity where we speak of logical necessity.

459a *birds*: probably cocks and quails, which were bred for fighting.

459d *a type of medicine*: see 382c–d, 389b, and 414b; see also 535e. On the whole topic of lying in *Republic* see C. Page, 'The Truth about Lies in Plato's *Republic*', *Ancient Philosophy*, 11 (1991), 1–33. The puzzle is, of course, how guardians, with their love of truth (486c–d, 490b), can lie in these ways. But for Plato a conscious lie was not a true lie (382b), since one is not self-deceived. To a friend who has gone mad and is demanding the return of his axe (331c) I *should* lie: 'I'm sorry, I haven't got your axe any more.'

459e *from conflict*: not only will Plato's eugenic proposals and stock-breeding vocabulary disgust many people, but they also sit awkwardly with his earlier claim (412c) that the only criterion for rulership is intelligence. It now appears (and see 424a) that he wishes to breed for rulership, so that the kind of flexibility envisaged at 415a–c and 423c–d will be very rare.

460b *more frequently*: since the timing of sexual intercourse is crucial (545d ff.), this does not mean they can have sex outside the allotted times—the 'holidays'; so it must mean that the lottery is more commonly fixed in their favour.

460c *secluded spot*: the Greek is deliberately ambiguous: it could refer to the deadly exposure of unwanted children, and there are similar hints at 459d–e and 461b–c. Nearly all Greek states, as far as we know, regarded excess population as undesirable, and took steps, including such exposure, to avoid it. On the other hand, at *Timaeus* 19a (where Plato is summarizing some of *Republic*), he says: 'We said that the children of good parents ought to be brought up, while those of bad parents should be secretly distributed throughout the rest of the community.' (But this need only be a reference to 415a–b and 423c–d.) In any case, one should always remember that the outer politics of *Republic* is driven by the inner politics—the analogy with an individual's mind. Therefore, the primary meaning of these passages has to do with the rejection of unwanted ideas, and Plato leaves us in the dark as to his real views (if he had formed them) about infanticide. There is a very good discussion of the issue of infanticide in C. Patterson, ' "Not Worth the Rearing": The Causes of Infant Exposure in Ancient Greece', *Transactions of the American Philological Association*, 115 (1985), 103–23. She finds four causes: deformity, illegitimacy, the poverty of the parents, and unwanted female children. If Plato is recommending the practice, then, it is because of the first two of these causes, which accounted for the majority of cases in the Greek world.

460e *his peak as a runner*: possibly a Pythagorean definition for the end of one of the seven-year periods of life: compare pseudo-Hippocrates, *De hebdomadibus* 5; and for a slightly fuller statement pseudo-Iamblichus, *Theologoumena arithmeticae* 66. 13–18 (de Falco), though he places the peak of physical prowess at 35 rather than around 28. (For a translation see p. 95 of my *The Theology of Arithmetic* (Grand Rapids: Phanes Press, 1988).)

461c *not brought up*: with our knowledge of genetics, we would doubt that it makes any difference whether a child is born to parents who are 'past their prime' or to those same parents when younger: the child has the same genetic make-up. But Plato clearly believed that being in one's prime added a certain vitality to one's child (there were contemporary theories which allowed for weakening of the sperm in men and loss of vital generative heat in women). And it remains true that certain kinds of deformity are more likely to be present in the children of older parents.

461d *the seventh month of course*: Plato is reckoning in lunar months. By Greek embryological lore (which was closely allied with arithmology or number-mysticism) these two months were when an embryo was most likely to be born alive.

461e *no objection*: a guardian's 'family' would be extensive, but would not include *all* other members of the guardian class, only those covered by the regulations of this paragraph. This is also the implication of 465a–b—that some will be a person's relatives, but not all. Therefore, Glaucon's remarks at 463c and 471c–d are an inoffensive exaggeration. See G. M. A. Grube, 'Marriage Laws in Plato's *Republic*', *Classical Quarterly*, 21 (1927), 95–9.

462d *hurt his finger*: rather than just saying that the finger is hurt.

464b *we did say*: at 416d ff.

464d *circle of interest*: compare 412d ff.

465b *rest of the community*: why does Plato assume that unity among the guardians causes unity in the whole community (see also 434a–b and 545c–d)? Mainly because he is assuming that they are the only effective force in the community, so they are all he needs to take into consideration in questions like this. I doubt he is thinking that the threat of their military prowess will, if they present a united front, cow the working class into submission.

465e *someone or other*: it was Adeimantus, at 419a.

466c *half is more than a whole*: Hesiod, *Works and Days* 40.

466d *as female dogs do?*: a reference to 451d.

467d *attendants*: see note on 373c.

468d *the chine*: *Iliad* 7. 321. The chine is the backbone, with its choice meat.

468d *full of wine*: *Iliad* 8. 162.

468e *golden caste*: see 415a ff.

469a *keep them from harm*: *Works and Days* 122–3. Hesiod was speaking of a golden race of men in the distant past.

469c *by non-Greeks*: that is (cf. *Laws* 693a), in case Greece should become divided and easy prey for foreigners.

Chapter 8

471c *a digression*: see 466d.

472e *to viability*: Plato vacillates on this issue: sometimes he effectively admits the impossibility of the imaginary community ever becoming actualized (472a–e, 592b); sometimes he assumes that it could happen (502c, 540d–541b; and this is the pretext for the whole argument of Chapters 8–10). Yet if Plato was interested in external politics, he would have made up his mind on this issue above all. The issue is, in short, not important for Plato: as he has just argued, he only has to show that the community is possible in principle, and that will (it is to be hoped) act as a paradigm to spur us to be more moral ourselves.

473a *than a theory*: a gnomic and, on the face of it, rather implausible idea, which is allowed to stand as if it were a matter of common agreement. It must, therefore, refer to the kind of gloomy view of the world which is colloquially called (in the UK these days) Murphy's Law: 'Anything that can go wrong will go wrong.' The world is imperfect, but we can fantasize perfection.

474c *loves something*: this is not an abrupt new topic: a philosopher is literally a 'lover of wisdom' or 'lover of knowledge'.

475b *some aspects of it*: but is a 'true' collector one who collects everything in a given area indiscrimately, or one who specializes? Plato is thinking of an alcoholic rather than a wine-lover, a sex maniac rather than someone with an ordinary sex drive. Note, then, that philosophy, as Plato understands it, is not a dry academic pursuit, but a lifelong overwhelming passion. For a valiant attempt to resurrect this notion of philosophy in modern times see J. Needleman, *The Heart of Philosophy* (London: Routledge & Kegan Paul, 1982).

475d *use of their ears*: theatre-going counts as use of ears rather than eyes because that was the emphasis in Greek theatre. At one of the really big theatres, like that of Epidaurus, from the back seats the actors would appear tiny. Festivals of Dionysus were the occasions of dramatic performances.

476a *sightseers*: literally, 'lovers of spectacles'. There has been controversy over whether 'the many beautifuls' (the literal translation) that this class of people is said to recognize are beautiful things or conceptions of beauty (see, for instance, the exchanges between J. C. B. Gosling and F. C. White in *Phronesis*, 1960, *Canadian Journal of Philosophy*, 1977, and *Phronesis*, 1978). Plato is usually, however, concerned to contrast types with the things of this world. In fact, I am not sure the distinction between particulars and conceptions would have interested Plato much in this context, since his primary distinction is between an unchanging realm and a changing one, whatever its inhabitants. Thus at 479d he does suddenly mention conventional views about beauty. Adherence to convention is, in its way, just as unreliable a guide to the truth as adherence to sense-impressions, since convention is equally subject to alteration.

476d *partake in it*: this is one of the metaphors Plato tries out for the relation between 'things in themselves' or 'types' or 'characters' (see note on 479a) and their instances. Other metaphors are that the type 'is present in' the instances, and that the instances 'imitate' the type (imitation has just occurred at 476c, and is prominent in Chapters 9 and 13, for instance). The difficulty is the difficulty of explaining how a single thing can appear all over the place and yet remain single.

476e *something unreal*: the Greek is, literally, 'Something which is or something which is not?' This is ambiguous. According to which of the relevant senses of the Greek verb *einai* ('to be') is preferred, 'what is' could mean 'what exists' or 'what is true' or (where X is some predicate) 'what is X'. I have tried to retain at least some of this ambiguity throughout the following argument, and yet provide a smooth translation, by turning 'what is' into 'what is real' or 'what really is' or even just 'reality'. As a matter of fact, the predicative sense of the verb provides the most coherent and straightforward way of reading the argument: 'what is real' is 'what really is what it is'; 'what both is and is not real' is 'what both does and does not securely possess its attributes'. For discussion, see pp. xlii–xlvii. At the same time, the translation also captures an important subsidiary implication—that of dependability. Something is reliable, and therefore a suitable object of knowledge, if it genuinely is what it is.

477a *be known*: as commonly interpreted, Plato is thinking of knowing as a kind of direct apprehension of an object, as in 'I know Joan.' He is therefore overlooking the other main kind of knowing— propositional knowledge, as in 'I know that two and two make four'—because it is far from clear that talk of reality and unreality makes any sense in this case: is a 'that . . .' clause real or unreal?

However, whether or not Plato was aware of these distinctions (he almost certainly was not), there is still plenty of value in the discussion. There is nothing to prevent one thinking along the following lines: whatever knowledge (of any kind) encompasses is

real in the senses that (a) it fills me with certainty; (b) it allows me
to give a coherent account of it; (c) its features which enable me to
be certain about it are unchanging features. I could not be said to
know that two and two make four, if they occasionally made some
other number; and I could not be said to *know Joan*, if she even
occasionally resembled someone else; and I could not be said to
know how to mend cars if their structure was unstable. However,
even if all these things were unstable, I could believe that two and
two make four, that the person I am seeing is Joan, and that this
bolt goes in that hole. In other words, it is a sufficient
interpretation of the passage to see that Plato is working with a
portmanteau conception of knowledge, which covers aspects of all
the various subspecies of knowledge.

479a *permanent and unvarying character*: Plato's technical usages of the
Greek word *idea* and its cognate *eidos* are usually nowadays
translated 'Form'—as in Plato's famous Theory of Forms. This is
unsatisfactory, however: the word 'form' is opaque in contexts like
'the form of beauty'; and it implies physical appearance alone,
whereas the Greek word implies 'what enables us to identify
something', which is far broader than just physical appearance.
There is no finally satisfying translation; I use 'character' for *idea*,
and 'type' for *eidos*. The following definitions of 'type' from my
dictionary are relevant: 'a distinguishing mark; a foreshadowing;
an exemplar; a model or pattern; a kind; the general character of a
class.' The philosophical type–token distinction is also useful: in
the word 'aardvark' there is one type of the letter 'a', but three
tokens (see 402c, for instance). The words have occurred in
Republic before this, the first clearly technical usage: they have
most commonly been translated 'category' (or synonyms), as at
357c, or 'appearance', as at 380d. As often as possible, 'type' has
been used as a synonym of 'category', because that points up the
evolutionary background of the technical term: 'type' in the
technical metaphysical sense is originally a short form for 'type of
thing' (see especially 435b and 476a, where the familiar sense of
the word almost breaks through into the technical sense). The
connection between these various senses of the words can easily be
seen by thinking about *identification*: a physical thing's
'appearance' enables us to identify it, and it is things of a certain
'type' or 'character' that we put together into a single set and
identify as belonging together.

479b *in your question*: since this is the main point of contrast between
particular things and the reality of the types, then Plato is
committed to thinking that the type is a kind of super-particular: it

really and unalterably is beautiful (or whatever), whereas nothing else is absolutely beautiful (or whatever). This is Plato's notorious 'self-predication assumption' which (as he came to see by the time he wrote *Parmenides*) may lead to a vicious regress: if the type of beauty is itself beautiful, and if the presence of beauty in anything is to be explained as the presence of a type, then the beauty of the type of beauty itself must be explained by a further type of beauty, and so on.

Recent intense study of self-predication has revealed a number of senses in which Plato *might* have said that 'F-ness is an F thing' (to use the convenient jargon); however, most of them are not without their difficulties (Malcolm, *Self-predication*; Heinaman). And the only sense that survives (as in the above paragraph) seems absurd. In the famous words of R. E. Allen (in Allen (ed.), *Studies in Plato's Metaphysics*, 43), 'Oddness is not odd; Justice is not just; Equality is equal to nothing at all. No one can curl up for a nap in the Divine Bedsteadity; not even God can scratch Doghood behind the Ears.' It seems that Plato had not thought through all the implications of what he was saying. One must always remember that he does not really have a *theory* of types: types are introduced from time to time, in different contexts, but they are never expounded and explained. They are a theme, not a theory. Therefore, there seems to me to be little point in asking what exactly Plato meant by statements implying that F-ness is F: if Plato had been interested in the subject, he might have told us. Personally, I think that he would have inclined towards Nehamas's interpretation of the statement: 'F-ness is what it is to be F' (see the papers by Nehamas cited in the Select Bibliography).

479b *opposite attributes*: it is important to understand how Plato envisages things as deserving opposite attributes; otherwise, one might think he has transgressed the principle enunciated at 436b and 436e–437a. There is no transgression, because particulars here bear opposite predicates in different respects: Helen of Troy may appear beautiful to me, but not to you; she may be beautiful compared with a face that launches only a hundred ships, but she is not compared with Aphrodite; and so on. A later passage (522c–524d) is worth comparing on these 'incomplete' (evaluative or relational) predicates, although the idea that they are somehow puzzling does not play a part here. For further discussion see (apart from works in the bibliography) pp. xlii–lii, and C. A. Kirwan, 'Plato and Relativity', *Phronesis*, 19 (1974), 112–29.

479c *what it was on*: the riddle is: 'A man who was not a man hit a bird which was not a bird with a stone which was not a stone as it was sitting on a twig which was not a twig.' The solution is: 'A eunuch hit a bat with a pumice-stone as it was sitting on a reed.'

480a *beauty itself*: Plato believes that our usual view of things is unsatisfactory because it makes them no more F (where F is some predicate such as 'big') than not-F. He has argued for this, but he merely assumes the next step—that there must therefore be something which is perfectly F. The assumption seems natural to him because the underlying issue is one of identification (see note on 479a): there must be something which is securely F, otherwise I would not have a paradigm to enable me to recognize even unsatisfactorily F things as F.

480a *if we say that now*: see 476d.

484d *established*: there is an implied reference back to 412c, where it was argued that the best rulers are the best guardians of a community. The concern of philosophers with paradigms is effectively the main theme of Chapters 9 and 10.

484d *practical experience*: because philosophers do not live in some other world, even if their concerns sometimes seem other-worldly. It has in fact been assumed so far that philosophic intelligence is practical intelligence, of the kind that might be required for ruling a community (428b–429a; see also 488a–489a). Later, however, when it has been argued that philosophers are really interested in abstract thinking (e.g. 500b), we will find that they have to be *forced* to gain practical experience (e.g. 539e–540a; but on this conceit see pp. lvi–lviii). 'In Plato's educational theory, as in his own life, there is a certain wavering between the ideal of action and that of contemplation' (Barker, 203). See also notes on 441e and 520e.

485a *the beginning of this argument*: 474b.

485b *vicissitudes of generation and destruction*: very literally, 'and does not wander as a result of coming-to-be and ceasing-to-be'. By 508d Plato feels he can characterize the whole of the visible world as subject to these processes. Since the things of the visible world do not bear their predicates reliably, Plato is hesitant to say that they *are* big or beautiful or whatever; he says instead that they *come to be* or *become* big etc. for some person in some respect. In shorthand, he talks of the world of 'becoming' or 'coming-to-be' or 'generation'.

485b *explained before*: 474c–475b. The idea that philosophers are intellectual omnivores paves the way for the transition (see note on 484d) from practical wisdom to theoretical knowledge.

485e *not a fake one*: this (with an equivalent passage at 588e–589b) is a very important paragraph. It has already been referred to in the note on 439e. It enables us to go some way towards reconciling a conflict, and at the same time to see an important way in which these central chapters of the book deepen Plato's views on morality. The conflict is the one mentioned in the note on 432a, between whether Plato expects the desires/workers to need controlling or to acquiesce in being ruled. The answer is that the more energy is diverted into the activities of the rational mind (the more the philosophers' role in the community is valued), the less actual heavy-handed control of one's baser desires (the workers) will be required, and the more the situation is describable as acquiescence.

486d *essential character*: see note on 479a. Since the type of anything is its truest feature, and since proportion and truth are related (in plain terms, a truthful person doesn't exaggerate, but sees things as they are), then the sequence of thought of this sentence becomes clear.

487a *Momus*: the personification of criticism.

487b *spoke up*: the topic Socrates raised is now delayed until 497b.

487e *in their communities*: see 473c–d.

488a *single ship*: the image is not applicable to all kinds of constitution (as it strictly should be, in this context): Plato has in mind the Athenian democratic system. The passage is in fact typical of his (and Socrates') attitude towards Athenian democracy.

489a *clouds*: there may be a slight reference to the comic poet Aristophanes' portrait of Socrates in *Clouds*; but the image of the star-gazing philosopher failing to notice what is right before his eyes had already entered popular lore.

489b *misleading*: according to Diogenes Laertius (2. 69), Dionysius, the tyrant of Syracuse, was teasing Aristippus by asking why philosophers dance attendance on rich men rather than rich men on philosophers. Aristippus quipped in reply, 'Because philosophers know what they want and the others don't.' But the author of the story is unknown.

492e *public arena*: how thorough is Plato's pessimism on this point? Does he mean that even the educational programme he outlines in Chapter 10 would be ineffective? I doubt that this is his meaning: all the pessimism of this section of the book is about current practice in the real world (see 497a).

493a *sophists*: the same word was recently translated 'professional teachers' (492a,d), but here it clearly carries some of the pejorative connotations it came to acquire. The sophists were literally just professional teachers, offering (at a price) an education to supplement what was conventionally available. They came to be regarded as subversive of traditional morals, as teachers of alternative standards of excellence from the conventional norms. By far the best general account of their work can be found in Kerferd, *The Sophistic Movement* (note on 369a). Plato's point here—that the sophists only pander to the values of the societies they teach in—is very ironic, since they clearly saw themselves as important, and even revolutionary. The basic point is that they charged for their services: if people are to want a product, then the product has to fit into their existing frames of reference.

493c *necessity and goodness*: true goodness requires free will and rational choice, rather than blind adherence to any standards. This is always the message of Socratic work: see my *Xenophon: Conversations of Socrates* (Harmondsworth: Penguin, 1990), 63–6.

493d *necessity of Diomedes*: the origin of the proverb is unclear. Of the many stories we know about the hero Diomedes, none is the obvious provenance and several could be.

494e *to stop him succeeding*: this argument has undoubtedly been based on Socrates' relationship with the brilliant young Alcibiades. The best account—because by a master story-teller—is Plutarch's, in his *Life of Alcibiades* 4–7.

495a *right to say*: at 491b–c.

496a *in true intelligence*: another category of second-rate practitioner of philosophy is mentioned at 539b–c, after the reintroduction of the image of bastardy at 535c.

496c *from my deity*: Plato held the view (perhaps Pythagorean in origin in the West) that everyone had a personal deity: in *Republic*, see 617e and 620d. Socrates could somehow know some things in advance: above all, when something bad was going to happen, he would know it and avoid it. He attributed this warning function to his deity; the phenomenon is frequently mentioned in both Plato's and Xenophon's Socratic works. For ancient speculation on the phenomenon see Plutarch's essay 'On Socrates' Personal Deity', *Moralia* 579 F–582 C and 588 B–589 F. The particular point of its mention here is that it apparently forbade him to take much part in Athens' political life (Plato, *Apology* 31d).

497c *needs repeating*: the closest Plato gets to this earlier is at 412a–b, 423e, and 458c.

498a *rational argument*: note that 'philosophy' often means little more than 'higher education' or 'intellectual work', as opposed to what we call philosophy, which is what Plato here calls 'rational argument'. So we can retranslate Plato's words here as: '...the most difficult aspect of intellectual work—i.e. philosophy ...'

498b *never rekindled later*: as opposed to Heraclitus' sun, which was a bowl filled with fire: exhalations from the earth extinguished it every night, and it was rekindled at dawn.

498b *minister to philosophy*: particularly by not interrupting it with physical demands. See 518b, but especially *Phaedo* 66b ff.

498e *identified and assimilated*: Plato is punning: the two words used also had technical meanings within rhetoric. The first, *parisōsis*, refers to the technique of composing clauses of equal length; the second, *homoiōsis*, to all kinds of rhetorical assimilation, especially assonance. On the ideal of assimilation to goodness, and to God, see also 500c–d and 613b.

501b *"godly" and "godlike"*: Plato uses two epithets which Homer used of his heroes.

501c *you mentioned*: 474a.

502c *our earlier discussion*: 450c–466d.

Chapter 9

503a *along those lines*: there are verbal echoes of 412c–d and 413d–414a. The question of the education of would-be guardians had just been concluded at 412a; Plato is now saying that they should have continued with the issue.

503d *our claim is*: 485a ff. Self-discipline and courage are examples of what are here called 'stable' qualities.

504b *We said*: see 435c–d.

505a *gets its value and advantages from*: however, Plato will shortly ascribe different kinds of importance to goodness as well: he will declare it to be responsible for the knowability and truth of everything that is knowable and true.

505b *knowledge of goodness*: we must imagine Socrates questioning them along the lines of 428b–c.

505c *doesn't it?*: and if goodness can be an attribute of certain pleasures, it cannot be equated with pleasure *tout court*. Note also that to deny that pleasure is the good is not to deny that some pleasures are good; then see Chapter 12.

505d *morality and right*: see Chapter 2.

505d *in this sphere*: the distinction between apparent good and real good
needs some restriction. What is an apparent good? That sixth
cocktail? If so, at the time I presumably *did* want it (however much
I regret it the next morning), so Plato's talk of not wanting
apparent goods would be dubious. He must mean something like:
'No one wants a lawnmower that looks good, but (as far as they
know) doesn't actually cut grass.' Notice again the Platonic
assumption of univocality (see e.g. 596a): in the context of a
discussion about moral good, he talks equally about goodness in
the sense of benefit. The ambiguity of 'good' was (in the guise of
the analogy between morality and the crafts) the main recurrent
difficulty with the arguments against Thrasymachus in Chapter 1.

506d *more than I can manage*: it may also be worth remembering that
Plato's thoughts on goodness were notoriously obscure. He once
gave a public lecture on the subject, which was so concerned with
mathematics (and arithmology?) that it left the audience baffled
and disappointed.

507a *interest*: the Greek word also means 'child'—a debt bears interest
as a parent bears a child. But the pun is untranslatable. The pun in
the next line is not Plato's, but is meant to capture the tone of the
interchange for an English reader.

508b *than the eye*: the eye was commonly regarded as containing a good
proportion of fire—it flashes and twinkles. Moreover, since it takes
like to see like (see also note on 613b) and we need light to see,
then the eye must contain light.

508e *people to have knowledge*: what is the meaning of the assertion
that goodness is responsible for truth and knowledge? (Truth
means little more than just knowability here: see also 585c.) It
cannot be merely that to know a thing is to know in what way it is
good, because Plato envisages knowable types of immorality and
evil (476a); nevertheless, this does seem to be part of his point—the
rulers must be able to relate morality to goodness. But we have also
seen that the types are perfect examples (notes on 476e, 479b), so
Plato's general meaning may well be that each type is good in this
sense: it is a good example of what it is. (See also the connection at
380d–381b between being a good case of something and
permanence: we know that the types are permanently what they
are.) This also makes sense of the idea that they are fully knowable
because they fully are what they are. Still, there is the usual
equivocation of 'good', as meaning 'morally good' or 'beneficial' or
'skilful' or (now) 'good of its kind'.

Note too that knowledge and goodness are also related in Plato's mind in less metaphysical ways than in this passage. It is only where there is room for improvement that a branch of knowledge is developed, to work for its objects' improvement (342d ff., 346e).

509b *majesty and might*: goodness is responsible for the 'being' of the types in the same sense that it is responsible for their knowability (note on 508e). Things are knowable as true if they are perfectly and permanently what they are; this is also their being and their reality. The notion that goodness 'surpasses being' is hyperbole: it does not mean that we cannot talk of goodness 'being' and have to think of it as somehow beyond the intelligible realm of types (otherwise we would have to think of the sun as beyond the visible realm); it just stresses the exalted status of goodness within the intelligible realm.

509c *quite amusing comment*: the joke lies, of course, in whether Glaucon is commenting on the condition of goodness, or on Socrates' argument. Socrates plays along by responding as if Glaucon had meant the latter alternative.

509d *word-games*: However, at *Cratylus* 396b–c Plato succumbs to the temptation and derives *ouranos* ('heavens') from *horan anō* ('look upwards'). *Horan* is cognate with *horatos*, 'visible'.

510a *realm of beliefs*: the shift from talk of sense-perception to talk of belief is startling, but not outrageous, given the background of 475e–480a, where again belief and sensible objects were correlated (and where we learnt that 'belief' was a portmanteau word for 'unreliable thinking or apprehension'). Plato appreciates that all identification is due to the mind: the sense-impression is, so to speak, passed on to the mind for identification (see *Philebus* 38c–39c).

510b *originals as likenesses*: it is important to notice that here and at 510d–e we are told that things within the material world are within the purview of the mathematical sciences. We already know that things of the material world are the contents of section B of the line: they are also the contents of section C (and note also the necessary equality of sections B and C, given Plato's instructions for dividing and subdividing the line). Therefore, the Line is not based on a fourfold division of objects: there are three kinds of object—shadows and so on, actual things, and types; and there are four mental states. The Line is merely a convenient tool, to pull together a number of points under the headings of the fourfold division of mental states. These differ in clarity or access to truth, but it should be noted that they do not represent any kind of gradual mental development: no one starts life with his sole objects of perception being reflections in puddles, before moving on to solid objects.

510c *a given subject*: this proves that 'taking things for granted' does not mean quite 'assuming', since there is nothing tentative about the existence of odd and even numbers, for instance: it is a given, a fact. Plato is delineating—in a highly condensed fashion—a certain approach to facts, which uses them deductively, to reach conclusions, and does not form them into coherent abstract systems, but takes each fact (or proposition, or concept) as a separate starting-point in a separate argument. This will shortly be contrasted with the approach of dialectic, which refers factual propositions upwards to ever higher principles, until any lingering unclarity in the facts is altogether eliminated: they are ultimately referred to something self-evident, 'where nothing needs to be taken for granted', and formed into coherent systems, each part of which may be taken to be true given the self-evident truth of the starting-point. This interpretation, apart from making good sense of the text here (and fitting in with 531d ff. and 537e ff.), has the advantage of being in accord with Plato's use of the term 'dialectic' in the early dialogues (see note on 511b) and even in late dialogues, like *Sophist*, which concentrate on the systems of types.

511a *only thought can see*: this paragraph should not be read (as it often is) as *criticizing* geometers for drawing diagrams: that would be an idiotic criticism. Plato is only pointing out that, despite geometry's use of diagrams, it is properly seen as concerned with the intelligible realm (this is exactly the point Plato claims in the next paragraph to have made). No criticism is intended: it is just that use of diagrams obscures the mathematical sciences' true domain. For further examples of this obscuring see 527a–531c (where Plato *is* critical, because in these cases the scientists themselves have forgotten their true domain).

511b *dialectic*: dialectic (see also second note on 454a) means philosophical discussion (with others or with oneself) whose goal is knowledge and truth. It is the name given to Socrates' philosophical method, as exemplified particularly in Plato's early dialogues such as *Laches* and *Charmides*. But what has what Plato is saying here (see note on 510c) to do with Socratic practice? It is, in fact, a perfect condensed outline of Socratic dialectic. Socrates asks, for instance, 'What is courage?' He is given the reply, 'Courage is endurance in the face of danger.' This proposition is then tested by being referred to other propositions. Sooner or later, a supposedly self-evident general proposition is formulated, such as 'Courage is good.' In order to prove or disprove 'Courage is endurance in the face of danger', then, Socrates only has to test it (and/or its consequences) in the light of the self-evident proposition. If it survives the test, it forms part of a coherent system under the self-evident proposition; if it fails, it is rejected.

511b *starting-point for everything*: the generality of this kind of statement, and the contrast with the method of mathematics, has led some commentators to believe that Plato means that knowledge of goodness (which it is reasonable to suppose is the most ultimate starting-point possible) enables someone to deduce mathematical truths from it. But this is absurd. We should distinguish between the common properties which all types have (permanence, everlastingness, singleness, etc.) and the peculiar properties which particular types have (circularity is circular, and so on): Plato may mean that the former set of properties are deducible from goodness (see notes on 508e and 509b), but not the latter.

511c *types*: why has dialectic as outlined (notes on 510c and 511b) to do with types? Because it relies entirely on abstract statements, and never 'descends' to examples like 'repaying gifts' (see note on 331e). It works with propositions like 'morality is good', even before checking whether everything we can properly identify as belonging to the class or type of morality is good.

511e *to the final one*: conjecture is assigned to shadows and reflections because we have to be hesitant before identifying what the likeness is of, and because the details will be far from clear (remember that ancient Greek mirrors were nowhere near as good as ours!). Confidence is the mental state appropriate for the material world: as 505e shows, it is the state in which I assume unreflectively that I know all there is to know about something. Because the material world is clear to our senses, we do have this confidence.

515a *no different from us*: this statement is unequivocal evidence that the Cave is an *allegory*. The prisoners are said to be like us, but we do not spend our lives literally gazing at shadows of artefacts. Although there are almost as many interpretations of the relation between the Cave and the Line as there are writers on it, this consideration rules out one common set of interpretations, which tries to find an exact correspondence between the four main objects in the Cave (shadows on the wall, artefacts in the cave, reflections outside the cave, real things outside the cave) and the four divisions of the Line. However, as we have seen, the Line is not a figure for mental development, as the Cave is, and in any case there are only three sets of objects in the Line (see note on 510b). Nor is it at all clear that the Cave settles on four stages: 506a–b alone could be seen as talking of five 'stages' outside the cave. In short, it is probably better to see the Cave as illustrating and expanding certain aspects of what has gone before, rather than looking for exact fits.

515a *opposite them*: the crucial factor for interpreting the Cave is to see that the shadows are cast by things which are themselves effigies of real things. We know from 517b that real things outside the cave stand for types. Therefore the effigies are reflections of types, and the shadows are reflections of reflections of types. (One's mind jumps to 596a ff. and the castigation of artistic products as copies of copies of types; but this is correct only in so far as there is an equivalence of delusion.) But what kinds of things are reflections of reflections of types? They should be things within our everyday experience, since the prisoners symbolize the common human condition. I argue on pp. li–lii that in *Republic* Plato is taking for granted two different kinds of types: one kind ('bed', 'finger') is perfectly instantiated directly in the physical world, with hardly any need for dispute and doubt about their identification; the other kind (described by incomplete predicates such as 'big' and 'moral') has to be mediated by our minds, in the sense that we have to think about what objects deserve these predicates. The Cave is concerned (as Plato usually is, but particularly here in the context of determining what knowledge philosopher kings need) with this latter variety: the effigies are my mental impressions or thoughts of morality and so on; the shadows on the wall are moral actions, big rocks, and all the physical things of the world. Thus the bearers of the effigies behind the wall may be the 'doubles' of the chained prisoners, or may be the poets, politicians, and so on who have formed the prisoners' views about morality and similar matters.

515b *in front of them*: in Platonic terms, this shows the extent of the prisoners' delusion, since our words really refer to types (596a).

515c *inanity*: the kind of reorientation Plato envisages here is later typified, in an educational curriculum, by the effect of the mathematical sciences (521d ff.). But we need not suppose that mathematics is the *only* thing which can reorient one to break out of the shackles (see note on 532d).

515c *towards the firelight*: we are undoubtedly meant to remember the 'artificial lights' of 508c. On my interpretation of the Cave, the effect of firelight may, in a moral and political context, be convention or the views of others (the bearers of the effigies).

Seeing the dependence of one's cherished views on convention blinds one to things in the sense of 537e–539a: having seen that they were merely conventional, one is tempted to dismiss and despise them, or (the alternative stressed here) to run back to the safety of not challenging them.

516a *in water*: the stage of looking at reflections and so on outside the cave does not differ in terms of objects from the stage of looking at the effigies in the cave (compare the identity of objects in sections B and C of the Line—see note on 510b). But it differs in that it is now more difficult for one to return to the safety of convention (see note on 515c).

516b *in its proper place*: the sun in the allegory is, of course, goodness, as it was in the Sun.

516d *without property*: *Odyssey* 11. 489, also quoted at 386c.

517a *and kill him*: as Socrates was killed.

518b *the light above*: because (as *Theaetetus* 175b–d shows) he finds the antics of those unfamiliar with the upper regions somewhat amusing.

518c *which are blind*: many commentators have seen here a hint of the famous theory of recollection, according to which all so-called learning is in fact recollection of knowledge acquired before one's present incarnation. If that is the case, nothing is made of it in *Republic*. And in Socrates' next sentence he mentions only the 'capacity' for knowledge, which is quite different from how the theory is presented in *Meno* and *Phaedo*.

519c *private or public*: on the importance of a reference-point or paradigm see also 484c–d. The single point of reference mentioned here is clearly goodness. Compare the unifying power of reason in one's life at e.g. 442c ff., 590d.

519c *still alive*: the Isles of the Blessed were that part of the underworld reserved for people, after their death, who had lived particularly virtuous lives.

519c *earlier*: 504d ff.

519e *as a whole*: see 419a–421c, and 465d–466d.

520e *at the moment*: Plato never makes completely clear what will induce the philosophers to take up politics: he obscures the issue under the conceit of himself and his fellow interlocutors forcing them to do so. The compulsion is probably a combination of (*a*) the fact that the rulers have been specifically chosen from among those who feel that their own good and the good of the community as a whole coincide (412c ff.), and like everyone else they want to see their own good happen (505d–e); (b) horror at the prospect of worse people than themselves gaining power (347a–d; in the ideal state, however, they themselves will take turns at ruling (540b), so this motivation will be excluded); (c) understanding the importance of debt-repayment (520d–e). Of these, (a) is by far the most important, and it raises the question as to *why* philosophers should think that their good and that of the community as a whole coincide: see pp. lvi–lviii.

Plato has to talk of compulsion now, because he has made contemplation of types seem so attractive that it is unclear why the philosophers should want to end it. This is related to an important issue (already noted at 441e and 484d). He has driven a huge wedge between the philosopher's experiences and knowledge and everyday life. Yet he is still maintaining that philosophic contemplation is to be of practical benefit to the community. What is the relation between the practical work of reason and its contemplation of unchanging types? Plato does not tell us in so many words, but the gap can be closed to some extent: see pp. liii–liv and the next note.

521b *political office*: 'Philosophizing is essential to ruling because it is the activity that is preferable to ruling, and so the activity that the ruler *must* have *available* to him if he is to wish *not* to rule, where wishing not to rule is, paradoxically, what makes it possible for him to rule well. Thus the total task of ruling, properly construed, must *include* the activity of philosophy, both as a lure from the practical side of actually managing the affairs of the city, and as a source of that knowledge by which the managing is guided. The upshot is that philosophizing is not thought of by Plato as a task somehow additional to that of ruling, but as an essential part of effective ruling' (White, *Companion*, 190).

Chapter 10

521c *among the gods*: people like Heracles were said to be deified after death, but this is not quite the same as arising from the underworld to heaven. What Plato says best fits Amphiaraus, a healing deity who was swallowed up into the underworld, but later rose up to become a god (Pausanias 1. 34; for this interpretation see I. M. Linforth in *Classical Philology*, 17 (1922), 141–2). Moreover, it was probably a Pythagorean tradition that after death one was judged in the underworld, and if untainted went to join the gods.

521c *potsherd*: the Greeks spun a piece of broken pottery, with one side painted white and the other black, as we might spin a coin for heads or tails. If the white side landed uppermost, 'day' had defeated 'night'—an appropriate image for Plato's metaphorical journey from darkness to light.

521d *didn't we?*: see 404a, 416d, 422b.

522b *seemed servile, somehow*: the reference is to 495d–e.

522d *military commander*: the Palamedes myth of a wronged innocent had been boosted in the fifth century by plays by all the major playwrights, and a rhetorical defence by the sophist Gorgias of Leontini. It sounds as though Plato thought Palamedes was in danger of overexposure. The playwrights were also unanimous in crediting Palamedes with the invention of counting.

524a *both hard and soft*: because nothing in this world is absolutely hard and soft. So, according to Plato, the mind asks, 'What is hardness? How do I know there is such a thing as hardness, when there's no such thing, strictly speaking, in the world of the senses?' We are meant to remember the claim at 478e–479a that each of the plurality of material things 'both is and is not'. Note that Plato's spelling out of that idea here as 'both is and is not hard' supports the interpretation that 'is' in the earlier passage is the 'is' of predication (see note on 476e).

524d *which is to say, oneness*: because all number is simply the accumulation of onenesses.

525a *infinitely many*: for instance, as one thing with many actual or theoretical parts; or as one thing with many different qualities.

525e *multiplicity of factors*: fractions were not recognized in the mathematics of Plato's day, so $1/n$ was not seen as the division of 1 into n parts, but as a relation between integers, and therefore as the production of n. Concretely, if I divide an apple in half, I have multiplied one thing into two things.

527c *Goodland*: Plato says 'Callipolis', which was the name of known Greek cities, but means literally 'Fair City'. Many English-language settlements used to apply the same custom, but Goodland (Kansas, USA) seems the closest equivalent for translation.

529a *those who try to interest people in philosophy*: astronomy, like any science at the time, was considered to be part of 'philosophy', which often means little more than 'higher education'.

529d *reason and thought*: in brief, the astronomical model of the universe Plato is taking for granted consists of a number of concentric spheres which move at various speeds around the earth and transport the heavenly bodies: one sphere might be the vehicle for Venus, for instance, and another for the fixed stars. (The spheres consisted of transparent matter, so that only the body they transport is visible.) In this obscure paragraph Plato abstracts this model into an ideal counterpart, with abstract speed and slowness instead of the various actual speeds of the spheres; and with immaterial loads, in place of the heavenly bodies, being transported with perfect beauty and precision.

530b *matters that require elucidation*: diagrams in geometry, the heavenly bodies and their movements in astronomy. Therefore, Plato's condemnation of physical rather than mathematical astronomy is not total: physical astronomy is still necessary to give us the material for higher astronomy. See also G. E. R. Lloyd, 'Plato as a Natural Scientist', *Journal of Hellenic Studies*, 88 (1968), 78–92.

530d *Pythagoreans claim*: for the Pythagoreans, the distances between the planets formed a harmonic proportion, and the heavenly bodies, as they whirled around, produced a harmonious sound (which is inaudible to us because it has been with us since we were born). This is the famous theory of the Harmony of the Spheres.

531a *concentrations*: a 'concentration' was a series of notes with intervals of less than a semitone.

531b *twisting them on pegs*: to make them taut enough to give a clear note, or to tune the string to a different note.

531d *waste of time*: the sciences are not to be pursued for their own sake, because that would turn one's sight down towards their material objects; consideration of their affinity would 'reorient' the mind, since it is a higher aspect. Note that this consideration is not said to be the job of dialectic (which is what commentators invariably assume): it is simply the attitude of mind with which we should study the sciences. The sciences themselves serve the greater aim of understanding the rational orderliness and goodness of the universe: that is why they form such an important part of the philosopher's curriculum. Dialectic *is* synoptic, but the sciences train this ability in the budding dialectician (537c).

532a *as we were saying*: see 516a ff.

532d *best part of reality*: notice (see first note on 515c) that there is no implication that the mathematical sciences are the *only* means of reorientation. They are just the only ones which can be encompassed in an educational curriculum. And notice also that what Plato says here again (see first note on 515a) shows that the parallelism between Cave and Line is not exact. The *whole* reorientation of the mind out of the cave is the work of the mathematical sciences, which belong to section C alone of the Line. It is true that 517b says that 'the region which is accessible to sight should be equated with the prison cell'; but we already know (note on 510b) that mathematics employs diagrams which fall within the visible region. The implication of 517b is simply that the reorienting effect of mathematics (and similar extracurricular activities) takes one out of the cave, where dialectic takes over and guides one gradually to perception of goodness.

533a *what we're talking about*: the reference is to the image of the Sun at 507a ff. At 506e it was again doubt about the audience's ability to perceive the absolute truth (coupled, there, with doubt about Socrates' ability to describe it) which made it necessary to use an image. Plato has been criticized for leaving no clear clues as to the nature of goodness, since he always pulls back from defining or even describing it; but he obviously thinks that anyone who perceived it would be in no doubt that it *was* goodness he had perceived.

533c *out of the question*: there are echoes in the last two sentences of 510b ff.

533d *deep in mud*: an Orphic afterlife punishment (see 363d).

533d *the term "thought"*: 511d etc.

534a *thought to conjecture*: knowledge and confidence involve certainty; thought and conjecture are not fully reliable.

534c *anything good at all*: although the dreaming/waking metaphor and the constant terminology of sight suggest that perceiving goodness is some kind of illuminative insight, it is also clear that one has to tie down and test the insight by hard thinking and argument. This is presumably the kind of argument to a conclusion Plato envisages at 511b–c. The insight alone does not guarantee the kind of understanding a dialectician has to have, which also involves the ability to explain matters (531e, 534b, and see 510c).

534d *irrational as surds*: a surd is an irrational number—one which is not commensurable with natural numbers. The Greek literally says 'while they are irrational like lines', because arithmetic was strongly influenced by geometry in Plato's day, and the archetypal irrational line was the diagonal of a square with sides 1 in length: the diagonal is $\sqrt{2}$.

535a *choice earlier*: 375a ff., 412b ff., 485a ff., 503c.

535b *good-looking*: the Greeks naturally (given their language) supposed that a *kalos* (good-looking) person was a *kalos* (good) person— that is, they tended to assume that good looks were a reflection of inner worth.

535c *to repeat ourselves*: from 495cff.

535e *unconscious lying*: for example, vanity, false estimation of one's abilities, and perhaps also those defensive lies which slip out almost before we realize it.

536d *rules them out*: there is no real contradiction with 412c, since by the time they come to rule (after the educational programme) they will be describable as 'old'. Even at 414a it was clear that they would be old by the time they had finished the series of tests.

536d *scope for learning*: a paraphrase of Solon, fragment 18 Bergk (= fragment 22. 7 Diehl): 'As I grow old, I constantly find there's plenty to learn.'

537a *to observe warfare*: see 467a–e. The terrifying assumption in these passages (and at 539e, for instance) is that the community will always be involved in some war somewhere for the trainee guardians to observe. Although warfare was common in the Greek world, it is still an odd assumption to make. Moreover, it sits awkwardly with the fact that at 422a–423b the community was to avoid war as much as possible, especially against rich states. Perhaps we should remember the possibility that on one reading of the psychology of the book (see p. xix) 'warfare' means no more than 'impinging on others'—i.e. everyday interaction.

537b *physical exercise*: Plato doesn't specify what these late teenagers will do in this two- or three-year period. Plato's original audience would have been aware that in Athens there was compulsory military service between the ages of 17 or 18 and 20. Then 539e confirms that something of the kind is what Plato has in mind.

538a *flatterers*: the phenomenon of 'flattery' of the rich and powerful is distinctively Greek and Roman. The term refers to a wide variety of dependency, from what we would call flattery to being a client of a patron. See Plutarch's essay 'How to Distinguish a Flatterer from a Friend', *Moralia* 48 E–74 E.

538e *particularly to respect*: this is an accurate summary of what happens in the dialectic of a Socratic discussion, as portrayed in Plato's early 'Socratic' dialogues. However, we need not think that Plato is criticizing Socrates' practice; he is talking about abuse of it by people who use it superficially and destructively, and without the kind of foundation Plato is here proposing.

539b *disputation*: see 454a–b with notes.

539e *six years or four years*: since at 537b Plato had prescribed 'two or three years' for (as it transpires: see note on 537b) advanced physical exercise.

540a *goodness itself*: since it is clear from e.g. 532a–b that the vision of goodness is a result of dialectic, then we must suppose that they continue with dialectic beyond the five years mentioned in 539d and during their period as teachers (539e–540a). In other words, we are to understand the five-year period as when they study dialectic *exclusively*.

540b *Isles of the Blessed*: see second note on 519c.

540c *as deities*: for the notion that certain outstanding people could become 'deities' (a state between humanity and godhood) see also 469a.

540c *female rulers too*: throughout the book masculine forms of word have been used to indicate both exclusively male objects and (as was Greek linguistic practice) whole classes of objects, even when the class contains some female members. So Glaucon here used the masculine form of the word for 'rulers' for the whole class; Socrates chooses to be pedantic and to pretend that Glaucon meant exclusively the male rulers.

541a *simplest way*: but not seriously intended by Plato. It just shows how remote he thinks the possibility is of his imaginary community ever being realized. Even if it were possible (which is not an issue he is concerned with: see note on 472e), it would take a move this drastic. The implausibility of the move is simply the culmination of a series of implausible moves—above all, the unattainable ideal of the philosopher king. In his latest work (*Laws* 739a–e) Plato himself remarks on the unattainability of the community he outlines in *Republic*. In our book he is concerned with paradigms, on which we can model ourselves here and now. Note also the implication of the present passage that it is no part of Plato's programme to reform existing communities: his ideal would (counterfactually) make a clean break with the past.

Chapter 11

544a *even better person*: that is, a community run not just by guardians, but by philosophers who have seen goodness, as described in the 'digression' of Chapters 7–10. This helps to give us some insight into the rough architecture of the book (see also note on 414b).

There is an implied progression from the first community of Chapter 3—the community fit for pigs—with its correspondence to the psychological level of desire (see note on 372e), to the community outlined in Chapters 4–7, which values the passionate part's virtues as much as those of the rational mind and inculcates true beliefs (see note on 441e), to the community run by philosopher kings with their knowledge. But this 'architecture' is not fully elaborated by Plato; it is certainly not as clear as has been claimed (M. Ostwald, 'The Two States in Plato's *Republic*', in J. P. Anton and G. L. Kustas (eds.), *Essays in Ancient Greek Philosophy* (Albany: State University of New York Press, 1972), 316–27).

544c *popular favourite*: this is heavily ironic, since the 'Creto-Spartan' system was very far from acknowledging popular rights.

544d *ones I've mentioned*: see Aristotle, *Politics* 4, for a survey and discussion of different types of oligarchy and democracy and so on.

544d *from oak or from rock*: the phrase is common, occurs even in the earliest Greek literature, and was used in a variety of contexts: in the context of birth (as here), or of insensitivity, for example. See M. L. West, *Hesiod:* Theogony (Oxford: Oxford University Press, 1966), 165–7.

544e *aristocracy*: the word means literally 'rule by the best', so Plato uses it for the political system he's been describing, where philosophers rule.

545b *"timocracy" or "timarchy"*: 'Ambition' translates *philotimia* (literally 'love of status'); so Plato coins these words from the root *tim-*.

545d *of one mind*: again (see 434a–b and 465b with note), disunity among the guardians is taken to be enough to destroy the unity of the community as a whole.

545e *first occurred*: a paraphrase of *Iliad* 16. 113: Homer has 'fire' where Plato has 'conflict'.

546b *perfect number*: a perfect number is, in strict arithmology, one which is equal to the sum of its factors: $6(1 + 2 + 3)$, $28(1 + 2 + 4 + 7 + 14)$, 496, 8128, etc. There is no certainty as to the length of the 'Great Year' after which the universe—the 'divine creature'—would perish, according to Plato (see the end of the next note, however). He may even be using the term 'perfect' in a less strict sense. All he is really saying here is 'Whatever the divine creature's number, it must be perfect.' At *Timaeus* 39d the Great Year is defined, equally vaguely, as the length of time it takes for *all* the heavenly bodies to return to the same positions relative to one another (cf. the Babylonian Saros cycle, after which the sun, moon, and earth are in the same positions relative to one another; the fifth-century Pythagorean Philolaus seems to have been aware of this Saros cycle).

546c *cubes of 3*: Plato's 'nuptial number' (as it is known) was already proverbially incomprehensible by Cicero's time (first century BC). Let's start with what is certain. The number referred to at the end of this paragraph is $4,800 \times 2,700 = 12,960,000$. (2,700 is a hundred of the cubes of 3; 4,800 is $100 \times (49 - 1)$, or $100 \times (50 - 2)$; the 'diagonal of 5' is $\sqrt{50}$, the diagonal of a square whose sides are 5; the 'numbers from' the diagonal of 5 are squares based on the diagonal; the 'rational diagonal of 5' is the nearest whole number to $\sqrt{50}$, i.e. $\sqrt{(50 - 1)}$; the 'irrational diagonal of 5' is $\sqrt{50}$.) These figures, 4,800 and 2,700, are 'harmonies' because they stand in rational proportion to each other.

Working backwards through the paragraph, the 'first harmony' is probably $36^2 \times 100^2 = 12,960,000$. This figure is also produced when $(3 \times 4 \times 5)$ is 'increased three times', if we understand the latter phrase to mean 'raised to the power of 4'—i.e. involving three dimensional increases beyond the first dimension: if this is correct, then $(3 \times 4 \times 5)^4 = 12,960,000$.

The difficult previous sentence appears to give general instructions, of which the calculations that follow are applications. 'Potential and realized potential' is recognizable Greek mathematical language for 'roots and powers'—as in the calculations $(3 \times 4 \times 5)$ is a root and it is raised to the fourth power. The formula $(3 \times 4 \times 5) \times (3 \times 4 \times 5) \times (3 \times 4 \times 5) \times (3 \times 4 \times 5)$ then gives us four 'terms' (i.e. the bracketed items) and three 'intervals' (represented by the multiplication signs between the brackets). The 'causes of similarity and dissimilarity' are respectively the odd and even numbers: it was standard Greek arithmology that odd numbers cause similarity and even numbers dissimilarity (see Aristotle, *Physics* 203ª13–15; T. L. Heath, *A History of Greek Mathematics*, i (London: Oxford University Press, 1921), 77, 82–3). 'From among the causes of similarity and dissimilarity' therefore just means that the terms are numerical: both odd and even numbers are involved. More obscurely, one must presume that 'and from among the things that increase and decrease' is also a reference to numbers in general. A great deal of the obscurity of the passage is due to the fact that Plato is deliberately using language with implications and applications beyond the merely mathematical, as if to suggest that number imbues all things with its laws.

If the number in question is 12,960,000, we are left with the problem as to why on earth this is the 'number of the human creature' and why it 'makes everything mutually conformable and rational'. The ancient commentators are little help here, and we have to resort to guesswork. My own guess is that Plato means it to be the number which ties up all the arithmologically significant aspects of human life (makes them conformable). There are 100 years in human life (*Republic* 615b); there are 360 days in a year (*Laws* 758b); and there are 360 degrees to the sun's passage around the earth, which (astrologically speaking—and Plato believed in astrology) would provide the smallest significant moments of a person's life. (However, the evidence that the Greeks of Plato's time knew of the 360 degrees of a circle is controversial.) The product of these numbers is 12,960,000, and they cover the smallest to the largest time-spans of human life. It is the number of significant 'moments' in a person's life. I do not rule out the possibility that 12,960,000 is *also* the number of days in the Platonic Great Year (cf. Adam ad loc.): this just means that a human moment is equivalent to a macrocosmic day. Scholars nowadays largely ignore the passage; a recent exception (with bibliography) is E. Ehrhardt, 'The Word of the Muses (Plato, *Rep.* 8.546)', *Classical Quarterly*, 36 (1986), 407–20; her interpretation differs from mine.

546c *geometrical number*: it is geometrical because, as the previous paragraph shows, arithmetic and geometry were closely allied in Plato's day. The nuptial number has been produced by multiplying numbers which are seen as the sides of squares or oblongs.

546d *wrong occasions*: Plato seems to envisage the guardians drawing on arithmological and/or astrological lore to pick the auspicious times, within the 12,960,000 'moments' of a lifetime, for conception to occur. They would also, of course, bear in mind the parameters laid down at 460d ff.

546e *Hesiod's and yours*: see 415a–c, and Hesiod, *Works and Days* 110 ff., where he traces the degeneration of mankind from a golden race to silver, copper, heroic, and finally to the present grim iron race.

547a *this is the lineage*: Homer, *Iliad* 6. 211.

547c *private ownership*: this is how they abandon the principle of 'one man, one job', since according to Plato's strict reading of that principle (345e ff., 417a–b), you cannot be both a guardian and a property-owner.

547c *dependants and slaves*: there are a few implicit references to Sparta, here and in what follows. The word translated 'dependants' was the technical term for the inhabitants of towns and villages subject to Sparta.

548d *competitiveness*: there is quite a nice portrait of Glaucon, compatible with this brotherly remark, in Xenophon, *Memorabilia* 3. 6.

549c *his mother*: so the 'communism' of the aristocratic community (Chapter 7) has also been abandoned. But this sort of note is also partly irrelevant: Plato is writing universal character sketches, which are not supposed to be limited to the particular context of this book.

550c *before which community*: the verse paraphrases Aeschylus, *Seven Against Thebes* 451 ('Tell me who else has been selected, to stand before which gate'), with 'deployed' possibly remembered from line 570 of the same play and *polei* ('community') punning for *pulais* ('gate').

551c *flawed*: see 544c.

551d *can't be single*: see 422–423a, 462b ff.

551e *true oligarchs*: 'oligarchy' means literally 'rule of the few', or 'minority rule'. So there would be few of them to face the enemy!

552a *limbs*: Plato has in mind the organic unity of his ideal community, graphically described at 462b ff.; see also 423a–b.

552b *we're considering*: that is, as a businessman etc. (see a few lines above) or—Plato adds now—as a ruler.

552d *temple-robbers*: see note on 344b.

553b *sycophants*: see note on 340d.

553c *scimitars*: eastern kings—especially the Persian king—had the reputation among the Greeks of having absolute sovereignty (and a great deal of wealth).

554b *troupe*: in Greek art, Wealth personified was often portrayed as blind (because it was indiscriminate: bad people were just as likely to make money as good people).

554c *come their way*: such as embezzlement. Plato is thinking of criminal monetary gain (in keeping with this type's obsession with money). It was far from unknown for Athenian guardians to squander their wards' estates.

555a *few parts of himself*: see note on 551e. Plato's analogy between oligarchy and the oligarchic type is particularly exact.

555c *self-disciplined*: he is referring back to the point made at 550e.

555e *offspring of the loan*: see note on 507a.

558c *this political system*: Athenian democracy was non-representational: every male citizen had the right to participate directly in political procedure in various ways—and to elevate demagogues of his choice to positions of authority—despite their lack of expertise (as Plato saw it).

558c *whether or not they are*: this was certainly *not* the case in ancient Athens. Women were chattels, and slaves even more so (*pace* 563b); intellectuals were often suspected of religious unorthodoxy (for an excellent, balanced view of this issue see K. J. Dover, 'The Freedom of the Intellectual in Greek Society', *Talanta*, 7 (1976), 24–54).

558e *categories of desire*: in fact, the distinction between these two categories is rather artificial, since it emerges that in practice they coincide.

559b *bread and savouries*: the staple items of Greek diet: see note on 372c. So this phrase means 'the desire simply for food'.

560c *lotus-eaters*: for the original lotus-eaters see Homer, *Odyssey* 9. 82–104. Eating 'lotus' makes you forget your past and live only for the pleasures of the moment.

561c *of equal value*: as Protarchus does at the beginning of *Philebus*. On pleasure in *Republic* see also 505c and especially 580d ff. On the whole subject see J. C. B. Gosling and C. C. W. Taylor, *The Greeks on Pleasure* (Oxford: Oxford University Press, 1982).

561e *walks of life*: because Plato portrays democracy as a pluralist free-for-all, he inadvertently stretches the premiss of the whole argument. He wants to maintain that a society has the character it has because of its dominant members (544d–e). This works more or less well for the other kinds of degenerate communities, but he is portraying democracy as a society where *nothing* is dominant. Conversely (taking the analogy between state and individual the other way round), his portrait of the democratic individual as weak-willed and so on becomes unfair: it does not follow merely from the pluralist nature of a democracy.

562d *undiluted freedom*: the Greeks generally took their wine diluted with water.

563a *attendants as well*: see note on 373c.

563c *poised to say*: Aeschylus, fragment 351 Nauck.

563d *my own dream*: proverbial for trying to tell someone what he already knows.

564b *the body*: phlegm and bile occur in several of the medical treatises current in Plato's day as opposed bodily elements (respectively, hot and cold) and, in imbalance, as causes of illness. See, for instance, G. E. R. Lloyd, *Hippocratic Writings* (Harmondsworth: Penguin, 1978), in the index under these two headings.

565d *in Arcadia*: Zeus Lycaeus was Zeus in wolf's form, worshipped particularly in the mountains of Arcadia in the central Peloponnese. From what little we know about the cult, it looks as though a primitive shamanistic wolf-cult was taken over by worship of Zeus, but retained magical elements into historical times.

566c *about cowardice*: the Hermus was the main river of Lydia, of which Croesus was king (560–546 BC). This oracle also occurs at Herodotus 1. 55, where we gain another one and a half lines. Croesus had asked whether his reign would be long. The reply was: 'When a mule is king of the Medes, that is the time, gentle Lydian, for you to flee...' Cyrus the Great (who counts as a mule because he was half Persian, half Mede) later defeated Croesus.

566d *chariot of the state*: in Homer, *Iliad* 16. 731 ff., Hector and Patroclus meet in battle. Hector's charioteer Cabriones is toppled from his chariot (742–3) and 'lay sprawled in his vastness over a vast area' (776).

567a *to tax them*: see note on 343d.

568b *company they keep*: the line is also attributed to Sophocles (fragment 13 Nauck). Its context is unknown, but it is more likely to refer to the Greek tyrants' practice of trying to turn their states into cultural centres by inviting 'clever' people there, rather than to have had the ironical twist Plato gives it here.

568b *for instance*: *Trojan Women* 1169.

569b *in his old age*: Plato uses the poetic word from the Pindar fragment quoted at 331a.

571a *how many different kinds there are*: the discussion was begun at 558d ff.

573b *I asked*: we are inevitably reminded of Cephalus' remarks in 329c–d.

574d *temple*: see note on 344b. Again, Plato's portrait of the dictatorial type is particularly close to that of the dictatorial society: see 568d ff.

575b *sycophants*: see note on 340d.

575d *in his own mind*: so far, Plato has been trying to make the dictatorial type parallel to the dictatorial community: both are ruled by a dictator (lust in the case of the individual). However, he now tries to equate the dictatorial type with an actual political dictator, which is an illegitimate and unconvincing shift. Any dictator who was utterly controlled by lust would be incapable of ruling and thus of deserving the name 'dictator'. And Plato is well aware of the ineffectiveness of the lust-controlled person (577e, 579c–d). All this makes it very unclear why Plato chose lust to characterize the dictator (except for the formal reason that it allows him to join his denigration of the dictator on to the denigration of the other types). I think we have to conclude that, as usual in *Republic*, he is less interested in external politics than in psychology.

576b *correct*: the reference is to 441d–444e. However, on the view that morality is psychic harmony, the democratic type ought perhaps to be the least moral, since his mind is chaotic and far from harmonious. I suppose Plato's meaning is that the dictator is immoral because he is topsy-turvy: his desirous part is a king when it ought to be a slave (but that is also true of the oligarch). And since lust is only capable of pursuing its own agenda, there is no morality in it, because morality involves the ability of reason to take thought for the whole, and satisfy the necessary desires of *all* the parts of the mind (586e–587a). But he also seems to be appealing to common conceptions of morality: the dictator is immoral because he breaks the law, and so on. This is only fair if there is a strong coincidence between common conceptions of morality and the Platonic conception of morality as psychic harmony: see pp. xxxix–xlii on this topic.

Chapter 12

576d *unhappiness*: 'The question of which of these two men has the happier life is so heavily loaded by the description given of each as to become pointless' (Cross and Woozley, 264).

577b *in political life*: dictators react with bloodthirsty violence, as we know.

577b *met dictators*: Plato himself had lived for a few months in the palace of Dionysius I of Syracuse, probably in 388 BC.

578c *our earlier argument*: presumably the description of the misery of the dictator at 566d ff. See also the shift (noted at 575d) from the dictatorial type to the actual dictator. The considerations mentioned in that note severely weaken Plato's argument here. He is supposed to be responding to Thrasymachus' and Glaucon's portrait of the dictator (344a–c, 360e–361b) as someone who is successful at controlling a community. This, as we have seen, would be impossible for Plato's dictator. This is an important phase of the main argument, the argument about morality, but Plato wins it by rhetoric rather than by hard argument.

580a *mentioned earlier*: 571a–576b.

580b *overall authority*: the reference is probably to some obscure function performed by one of the judges of the annual dramatic contests in Athens.

580b *regal*: see 445d: Plato's ideal political system is called a kingship if it is ruled by a single person, an aristocracy if it is ruled by more than one.

580b *son of Ariston*: Plato himself was, of course, also a son of Ariston.

580c *hidden from the eyes of gods and men*: the formula recalls Adeimantus' challenge to Socrates in Chapter 2. See 366e and 367e, and Socrates' use of the phrase at 427d.

580d *pleasure as well*: it is interesting to note Plato's assumption that *happiness* can be assessed by means of *pleasure*. In earlier dialogues he had vacillated between thinking that pleasure was, in some sense, such a criterion and condemning pleasure as base and bodily. But his position here does not make him a hedonist (in the normal sense of the term, according to which any and all pleasures are desirable), since he is careful to distinguish acceptable from non-acceptable pleasures. It is the model of pleasure as replenishment (585a–b) which allows him to make this distinction and therefore to mediate between outright hedonism and outright condemnation of pleasure. Plato has not infrequently been criticized for introducing pleasure into a discussion of happiness, but in my view he is merely being realistic: a life devoid of any pleasure is surely not worth living.

580e *mercenary part*: the word has indeed occurred several times, but not explicitly as another name for the desirous part of the mind—436a, 549b, and 551b are closest.

581c *the avaricious*: it is relevant to note that these three words are all *philo-* words, meaning respectively 'lover of wisdom', 'lover of success', and 'lover of money'. Thus they express the types' motivations. Closely similar words to the last two have already occurred at 347b, where Socrates and Glaucon agreed that they were insulting.

582b *find it difficult*: there are evident weaknesses in this phase of the argument. It is assumed that the philosopher knows as much about the pleasures of eating as anyone else because he does, after all, not live in some other world. But does he really know as much about them as a gourmet, say? At 519a–b we hear that philosophers should escape the things of this world as quickly as possible—so does a philosopher have even adequate experience of these pleasures? The tension is even more acute in the case of the pleasures of ambition, where it is less plausible to assume that, just because a philosopher is alive in this world, he knows enough about ambition to be an authoritative judge. Plato would have done better to de-emphasize the philosopher's personal experience and (in the mode of 409a–c) argue the possibility of his assessing other kinds of pleasure by recognizing their effects on others: we do not have to have experienced heroin addiction personally to be in a position to deplore it.

582e *closest to the truth*: I take this to be a casual way of saying 'whose claims about what is pleasant are closest to the truth', rather than actually predicating truth of the philosopher's pleasures, which would anticipate the next argument. Note, by the way, that the premiss that 'it takes experience, intelligence, and rationality' has biased the argument from the start in favour of the philosopher. Others might well argue that personal taste is a better judge of what is pleasant than philosophic reason. It is true that, by and large, the argument has been concerned with the pleasantness of a life as a whole, rather than that of any particular pleasure, and appeals to experience and intelligence are more plausible in this wide context; but this at best still only entitles the philosopher to judge the worth of a life, not the degree of its pleasantness. The third argument of this chapter, however, will contend that a philosopher's pleasures are actually in some sense more pleasant, and therefore could be seen as trying to remedy this defect of the second argument.

583a *taken seriously*: Plato merely assumes without argument that an intelligent person will, *qua* intelligent, prefer the philosophic life to, say, a life of political ambition or business; and he assumes that this preference is not deluded. The missing argument may be taken to be the cumulative weight of Chapters 8–11.

583b *Zeus of Olympus*: there are several allusions buried in this sentence. The first part refers to the fact that in a wrestling match— the one at the Olympic Games being the most prestigious—a third fall indicated defeat; the reference to Zeus the Saviour is due to the fact that the third libation at a dinner-party was dedicated to him; and Zeus of Olympus enters simply because this was Zeus' most important manifestation, and Plato is stressing the importance of this third argument.

583b *expressing this idea*: it is impossible to know for certain who the 'clever fellow' referred to is. Since there is a high degree of coincidence between the ideas expressed in this section and those of *Philebus* (which I think, controversially, was written soon after *Republic*: see my article in *Phronesis*, 25 (1980), 270–305), then it is most tempting to think that Plato himself was the 'clever fellow', and that he was already sounding these ideas out within the Academy.

584b *other cases too*: the pure pleasures of smell (such as the sudden scent of wild honeysuckle in a Cornish hedgerow) recur at *Philebus* 51b, and *Timaeus* 65a adds a 'scientific' reason for their purity, based on the fineness of the particles involved. *Philebus* 51b–52b mentions other cases: seeing pure colours; seeing simple geometrical figures; hearing simple musical sounds; learning new information. Notice that since a number of these pleasures are physical, Plato cannot argue that they are peculiarly philosophic pleasures: that is why we get the second, metaphysical phase of the argument, that only mental pleasures are really satisfying. However, we are surely supposed to think that even these physical true pleasures belong more properly to the philosopher, since in order to be true they must not be followed by any regret at their departure, and that kind of dispassion is a result of a philosopher's training.

584c *through the body*: Plato thought that the body was, in itself, an inert and insensitive lump of matter; it is the mind which feels, thinks, provides impulse, imagines, senses, remembers, etc.; and the mind is also the life-force and is subject to reincarnation.

584c *expectations*: granted that (most) physical pleasures are relief from distress (= satisfaction of desire), why should an anticipated pleasure be regarded in the same light? 'People may anticipate with pleasure the prospect of downing a draught of cool beer later in the afternoon after a game of tennis. They are not presently in distress, nor anticipating with dread their future thirst' (Gosling and Taylor, *The Greeks on Pleasure* (note on 561c), 116). Plato is using 'anticipation' in a narrower sense, I suggest, according to which I would not now anticipate the pleasure of the beer if I was not also now feeling thirsty.

585a *misled*: the chief difficulty with Plato's argument in this section has been taken to be that even if we allow that some external observer might want to call certain pleasures false, yet pleasure is a feeling, and it does not follow that the pleasure I feel is any the less real. In fact, however, we do not need to understand Plato to be denying the reality of any feeling of pleasure: he is trying to provide criteria for distinguishing better and worse feelings. In terms of the simile of 584d ff., every pleasure is an upward movement, but where does the movement start from and where does it end? The answer to that question, Plato is saying, provides objective criteria for assessing the reality of feelings.

585e *version of pleasure*: all the talk of 'reality' is clearly supposed to remind us of 475e–480a, but the fit is not quite perfect. Of the two main implications of 'real being' there, the subsidiary sense of dependability is here more prominent than the main predicative sense of 'really being what it is' (see note on 476e). For it does not make sense to claim that the mind really is the mind, in contrast with the body not really being the body.

586a *intelligence and goodness*: it is worth remembering that although intellectual pleasures are the best, and the philosopher is the happiest person, yet knowledge is not goodness (505b–c). Goodness, in the Sun image, makes things knowable: it guarantees that there are things for the philosopher to know. It is therefore, as it were, the prerequisite of happiness.

586b *trying to fill*: but if pleasure is the satisfaction of need (which is what we have been led to suppose so far), it is unclear why some pleasures are to be described as insatiable. Plato is saying that they are insatiable because they are never really satisfied, which is to say that they are not real pleasures; but this would imply that a philosopher's pleasures are real because they fully satisfy some need. Yet Plato has been at pains to show that true pleasures involve no (perceived) prior need (584b). Alternatively, then, one might think that insatiable pleasures are so pleasant that one just wants to repeat them: one is addicted. The pleasure ends and leaves one with a greater sense of lack than was felt before. This idea avoids the difficulty mentioned above, but is further removed from Plato's text here, which is in some sense concerned with all physical pleasures, not just those of the addict. One could follow clues from *Philebus* to argue that all physical pleasures are more or less addictive, but we are not given the premisses of such an argument in *Republic*.

586c *apparition of Helen*: see the Index of Names, s.v. 'Stesichorus'.

586d *reason and intelligence*: this is a bit of an exaggeration. Someone ruled by the passionate part can calculate how to achieve his aims, and use reason to a limited extent (see 553d). Plato means that he lacks philosophic reason.

586e *be moral*: remember that at 433a ff. doing one's own job and being moral were identified.

587c *slavish pleasures*: see 573a ff. The dictator is beyond the spurious
pleasures because only the first three types correspond to the three
parts of the mind (intellectual, competitive, and mercenary), the last
two of which entail spurious pleasures, as Plato has argued.

587c *earlier conclusions*: that is, assuming that each descending pleasure
is a reflection of—is less true than—the one above it.

587d *same category*: see note on 580b.

587e *than a king*: although this arithmological passage is only semi-
serious, it would undoubtedly have been more redolent with
meaning to a Pythagorean of the time. First, Plato divides the
five-term series (king, timocrat, oligarch, democrat, dictator) into
two conjunct three-term series; this involves taking the oligarch
twice, as the conclusion of one series and the beginning of the
other. Then we are told that the total distance involved is 'triple a
triple'. This, I take it, is a condensed way of saying that the three
terms in one series are to be multiplied by the three terms in the
other series. Since we know that the final product is to be 729, then
the sum must be $729 = (27 \times 27) = (3 \times 3 \times 3) \times (3 \times 3 \times 3)$.
The basic number used is 3 because, I suppose, in Greek
arithmology 3 symbolized completion of process, and the lives
under discussion here are processes.

Socrates' next two sentences state certain properties of 729. It is
a 'plane number based on the quantity of the linear number'—i.e. it
is the square (which is a plane number in Greek mathematical
terminology) of a side 27 in length; and it is both a square and a
cube. Precisely why these properties should be significant is
obscure. In the sequence of triples (1, 3, 9, 27, 81, 243, 729),
however, the Pythagoreans used to stress that 729 was the first
actual square-and-cube (they took 1 to be number in potential, not
an actual number); so perhaps it represents some kind of ultimate,
as the king's and the dictator's lives are ultimates.

588a *related to lives*: why should Plato's number, 729, have anything to
do with time-measurement? The simplest answer is to assume that
Plato knew of the draconitic or nodical lunar cycle of 27 days, since
27 is stressed as the root of 729. However, it is not certain that the
nodical cycle was known in Plato's time.

Alternatively, the following calculations had been made by
Plato's time. The smallest whole number of years to contain a
whole number of lunar months is 59: there are 730 lunar months
of 29.5 days in 59 years of 360 days (with 10 intercalary months).
All these numbers nicely interconnect: $730 = (360 \times 2) + 10$; $59
= 29.5 \times 2$. It is true that 729 is not exactly 730, but then 29.5 is

not exactly the length of a lunar month; for the purposes of his pleasantry, precision need not have worried Plato.

588b *the assertion*: made by Glaucon himself, at 360e ff. See also Glaucon's little joke at 590a, where he says he will answer on behalf of the unnamed supporter of immorality—which is to say, on behalf of himself.

588c *more than one creature*: the Chimera was a combination of goat, lion, and snake; Scylla's top half was that of a beautiful young woman, but the lower half of her body had a fish-tail and her waist was ringed by the heads of snakes and canine monsters; Cerberus was the three-headed dog which guarded Hades, and whose lower half was serpentine.

589b *the wild ones growing*: the distinction between the wild and tame aspects of the monster is, of course, an image for the necessary and unnecessary pleasures and desires discussed earlier (558d–559d, 571a–572b): the distinction is solely within the desirous part of the mind. It is worth noting that the rule of reason which Plato advocates is not as ascetic an ideal as it might at first seem: here the necessary pleasures are assumed to be acceptable (see *Philebus* 63e for a fuller statement), and at 442c it is said to be the job of wisdom to provide what is best for all the parts (i.e. including the desirous part).

589d *savage side*: here and at 590a–591a we again (see 443e with note) find Plato aligning his specialized view of morality as psychic harmony with common morality. See pp. xxxix–xlii.

590b *serpentine*: there has been no previous mention of this, but it clearly represents some inferior manifestation of passion; cf. 'the lion with all its aspects' at 588e.

590c *their whims*: this is the internal equivalent, of course, of the situation described at 493a–c.

590d *rules within him*: at 463a–b and 547c it is asserted that in Plato's imaginary community the relation between rulers and ruled is *not* that of masters and slaves. But the metaphor of slavery or submission to a good master is recurrent in Plato's works, and is perfectly clear: it would be petty to charge him with inconsistency on this point. The metaphor is no more than another way of expressing the agreement of the lower orders to the rule of reason (432a, 442c). Plato uses it here for the emotive force of describing 'slaves' as their masters' friends: this would have struck his contemporaries as almost paradoxical.

590d *as Thrasymachus did about subjects*: at 343b ff.

591b *unpunished*: Chapter 14 adds that there is really no such thing as undiscovered and unpunished morality. Thrasymachus and Glaucon had claimed that happiness is unpunished immoral behaviour.

591d *he said*: see the 'virtuoso' of 412a, and compare 432a and 443d–e.

591e *too much or too little property*: see 422a for this feature on the macrocosmic scale of the state.

592a *established constitution*: this makes Plato's moral person sound very introverted (see also 443e), which (*a*) weakens the plausibility of his assertion that such a person will behave in ways we commonly recognize as moral (note on 443e), since we commonly assume that morality involves relating to other people; and (*b*) makes the self-sacrifice of the philosophers in returning to the cave (519cff.) less comprehensible (or perhaps an exaggeration). What Plato must mean is that the state of one's 'inner constitution' is a kind of yardstick that is referred to prior to engaging in any action, to assess the action's morality; he clearly believes that what is good for me is also good for others.

Chapter 13

595a *the right lines*: the myth which constitutes the bulk of Chapter 14 makes a stunning conclusion to the book. Plato did not want to spoil the effect by placing his afterthoughts on poetry at the end of the book. They are awkward here, since they interrupt the discussion of the rewards of morality; they might have been better after Chapter 10 (which is the earliest they could have appeared). But an interesting effect is obtained by juxtaposing an attack on the poet's art with the artistry of the myth; and these afterthoughts have been triggered by the renewed mention, a page earlier, of our 'inner constitutions' (592a). The basic message of Chapter 13 is that poetry threatens our inner constitution (605b, 608a–b)—and we are to remember that an orderly inner state is morality.

595a *representational poetry*: actually, representation of good characteristics was previously allowed and even encouraged (396c–e, 398b; see also 500c); and 'there is much to commend in Homer' (383a). Moreover, 'representation' is a broader term here than it was in Chapter 4, where it meant 'impersonation': thus at 394c epic poetry is only partially representational, whereas here it is entirely representational (602b, 607a), as is all poetry (600e). In short, the fit with Chapter 4 is not as exact as Plato implies. 'Representation' (the word also means 'imitation') here in Chapter

13 has the metaphysical sense of 'removed from reality'. Plato has not fixed his technical vocabulary in this sphere, and this makes for these inconsistencies. His main target in this chapter is tragedy (and Homeric epic as a kind of tragedy), and he remembers that in Chapter 4, at 394b–d, tragedy was described as entirely representational: it is this 'entirely representational poetry' that he is pleased to have banished.

595b *audience's minds*: poetry deforms minds in the sense that it feeds our lower mind (602c ff.) and, by virtue of the fact that its domain is appearance, does not feed that inner organ (518c) which can perceive truth and reality.

596a *single specific type*: see 435a–b, 475e–476a, 507b.

596b *which we use*: as opposed to a painter, who (we are shortly to be told) copies the craftsman's products. All this is somewhat artificial, of course: there is nothing to stop a craftsman using a particular bed as his model, and nothing to stop a painter painting from a bed he perceives in his mind's eye. Plato's underlying point has to do, I believe, with something like degrees of freedom: the more a thing is fixed in form, the less potential for change it has. A craftsman can fashion beds in a wide variety of shapes and sizes, and they will still count as 'beds' as long as they satisfy certain structural requirements, which he takes as his model. However, if a painter wants his audience to recognize what he has painted as a bed, he has to work within a more restricted compass, limited by his audience's expectations of what a bed looks like. A painter, then, is less creative—has less room for manoeuvre—than a craftsman.

596e *kind of craftsman a painter is*: this should not be interpreted as implying that a painter's work is as trivial as holding a mirror up to things. A painter is like a mirror-holder metaphysically speaking. To say that a painter deals with superficial aspects of things is not necessarily to say that his or her work is trivial. In fact, it is a premiss of Plato's attack on poetry that poets are non-trivial and dangerous.

597b *could have made it?*: scholars have worried unnecessarily about the fact that elsewhere in Plato the types are eternal, not made. (In *Timaeus* 28a ff. they are even pre-existent patterns which God looks to in order to create the world; but that only makes them pre-existent to creation, not to God.) The concept of eternity is like that of infinity: within infinite time, one eternal being (God) can create other eternal beings (types), without our having to conclude that the types must therefore not be eternal. To think that this act of creation interrupts infinite time and therefore makes it finite is to think of eternity as having duration, as everyday passing time does; but Plato might be thinking of eternity as timeless time. On all such issues see R. Sorabji, *Time, Creation and the Continuum* (London: Duckworth, 1983), ch. 8, 'Is Eternity Timelessness?'

597c *one real bed*: because of the kinds of difficulties mentioned in the previous note, and more particularly because the evidence for Plato's commitment to 'types' of artefacts (such as beds and tables) is slim (but see pp. l–lii), some commentators have tried to explain these difficulties away by arguing either that the whole chapter is an interpolation, written by Plato at some other time and carelessly inserted into *Republic*, or even that the passage is some kind of joke. The trouble with all these interpretations is that Plato does not mark the passage as such a caricature or whatever.

597c *that one's type*: since it is a requirement of Plato's metaphysics that it is the presence of a type which allows us to recognize the respect(s) in which things are identical, then the type must exhibit perfect identity; since two things cannot, by definition, be perfectly identical (at the very least, they are two, not one), then there cannot be more than one type (see 596a and further references in the note there).

597e *all other representers*: actually, it is hard to see how the concept of representation as mirroring reality applies to poets.

598b *appearance or truth*: it is bound to strike us as very odd, and even misguided, to *criticize* painting for depicting things in perspective and from only one angle. But the criticism is of a piece with the imperfection of things in Plato's metaphysical scheme: see pp. xlii–l.

598c *the joiner were real*: the exaggeration in this paragraph runs the risk of obscuring the important point. If art is seen as imitation of reality, then perfect art perfectly imitates reality and obliterates Plato's vital epistemological distinction between reason and sensation. Art is an impostor, which fulfils the human need for knowledge with illusory fare: in the terms of 583c ff., there is no *real* satisfaction to be gained from art.

598d *human knowledge*: the sophist Hippias of Elis used to make extravagant claims like this (Plato, *Hippias Minor* 368b ff.).

598d *come across the claim*: especially (for us today) by reading Plato's *Ion*.

599b *bestower of praise*: a poet bestows praise by recording the deeds of famous people. On the theme of the priority of action to words see especially Plutarch's essay 'Whether Military or Intellectual Exploits Have Brought Athens More Fame', *Moralia* 345 C–351 B.

599e *the Homeridae*: the 'guild' of people who claimed descent from Homer, in the sense of maintaining and perpetuating his poems (as the Asclepiadae did for Asclepius: 405e–406a, 407e–408b, 599c), also claimed inside knowledge of all aspects of the poet's life and perpetuated a lot of apocryphal tales about him.

600b *suggests they are*: his name means literally 'meat-kin'. Glaucon's meaning is that meat was a more important part of a coarse athlete's diet than a cultured intellectual's; and it would have been a sign of culture on Creophylus' part not to have neglected his mentor.

600d *on their heads*: as (I suspect) effigies and images of the gods were carried through the streets during a ritual procession.

601b *musical hues*: nowadays, however, we would be inclined to say either that the beauty of a work of art is an end in itself, or (more subtly) that it engages and educates parts of oneself that other forms cannot engage. In this latter sense, art may even gain an ethical function; but more importantly, art would be allowed a place and purpose of its own, rather than being an impostor which attempts to usurp the place and purpose of philosophy.

602a *use of the pipes*: in this sentence Plato echoes the terminology of the Divided Line (especially 511d–e). It is clear that he means the threesome using/making/imitating to reflect the threesome type/instance/representation. But nothing in the text asks us to make the fit between the two threesomes exact, which is just as well, since it is difficult to make sense of *using* a type. Plato is simply making use of a kind of knowledge—know-how or expertise—to illustrate a point about knowledge in general: that it grasps the truth of things.

602b *iambic and epic verse*: the iambic metre was the chief metre in which tragedies were written; Homer is as usual the main target among the epic poets.

602c *misled by colouring*: is this a picture of a frying-pan seen from the top (in which case it is concave) or from the bottom (convex)?

602e *about the same objects*: see 436b and 439b with the whole discussion in which these passages are embedded.

603a *measurements*: in this chapter Plato works with a straightforward division of the mind into rational and irrational parts, rather than the more complex threefold division of Chapter 6. Passion is here lumped along with the desires as irrational. But this does not mean that Plato has abandoned the tripartite model: even if the arguments in Chapter 6 for the separation of passion are somewhat weak, we have recently met the timocratic man as a personification of passion, so Plato is clearly committed to the tripartite model.

603c *distressed or happy*: compare 399a–c.

603d *phase of the discussion*: 439c–441b.

603e *than anyone else*: 387d–e.

605a *category as a painter*: earlier in the argument (see note on 597e) it became hard to see how Plato meant a point about painting to apply to poetry. Here the converse is true: granted that poetry appeals to the emotions, it is difficult to see how the kind of *trompe l'œil* painting Plato has in mind has any emotional impact at all.

605c *the next moment*: the same object appears smaller in the distance than close to. As far as mere sensation is concerned, this is a variation in the actual size of the same object; thought and measurement would reveal the truth.

605c *your own mind*: compare 387d–389b on grief and laughter.

606c *repulsive*: it is important to remember in this paragraph that Greek Old Comedy (of which Aristophanes is our only surviving representative) relied extremely heavily on very crude sexual humour.

606d *we're saying*: 603c.

606e *educated Greece*: as Herodotus said (2. 53) that Homer and Hesiod had described the form and function of the gods for the Greeks. In general, Homer was still in Plato's day considered an essential part of one's education, not only as poetry, but as a source of wisdom, morality, and all kinds of information. This is the background to Plato's attack.

607a *eulogies of virtuous men*: in the sense of 'representation' employed earlier in the chapter (see second note on 595a), even these eulogies would be representational. They are legitimate, however, because they would tell the truth and portray morality in a way—a boring way, we post-Romantics might well think—that did not appeal to the lower, emotional parts of the mind. It is in this sense that poetry can predispose the mind for philosophy (401c–402a).

607b *at her master*: we know the author of none of these snatches of verse. Since all the quotes are poetic, the target in every case is presumably philosophy, and *Laws* 967c also suggests that the bitch, with her useless noises, is philosophy. The poverty of philosophers was a traditional theme. For the other side, Plato could have quoted Xenophanes, fragment 11 ('Homer and Hesiod have attributed to the gods every form of objectionable human behaviour—stealing, adultery, deceiving one another ...'), or Heraclitus, fragment 42 ('Rhapsodes should exclude Homer and Archilochus from their competitions and beat them with their staffs').

Chapter 14

608c *talked about*: this appears to be a reference to 576b–588a, in the chapter before last. The abruptness of the start of this section supports the idea that Chapter 13 is a kind of afterthought: see first note on 595a.

608d *I asked*: I have retained the translation 'mind' for *psukhē*, even though 'soul' would sound rather more natural during this argument. However, the word has been translated 'mind' throughout the book; and we have already noted (especially on 584c) that Plato's concept of mind is very large: he amalgamates several functions which are more commonly, in the West, separated. Glaucon's surprise at the notion of the mind's immortality reflects the majority view in ancient Greece: *Phaedo* 77b speaks of 'the ordinary man's fear that the mind may disintegrate at the moment of death'. In other words, it was common to regard the Homeric belief in an afterlife as either fictional or a religious doctrine to which one paid no more than lip-service.

609c *and ignorance*: that is, the opposites of the four cardinal virtues of 427e ff. See also 444c–e for a brief argument that these things harm the mind, and 353e for morality as the specific goodness of the mind.

609c *his immorality*: that is, simply because he is found out and executed (see 610d). Plato is distinguishing physical death (which is separation of the soul from the body) from the possibility that the soul itself dies, at the point of physical death or at any other time. However, this points up the major weakness of his argument: it is implicitly circular. There is no reason to suppose that physical death and psychic death are not identical, or that what destroys bodies does not also destroy minds, unless one already believes that the mind is different in substance from the body. But Greeks would have been less likely to question this assumption.

610c *becomes less moral*: it is very unclear precisely what this notional opponent's position is supposed to be. Any guess is as good as another. In any case, Socrates' response is (I take it) an implicit *reductio ad absurdum*: 'Your position makes immorality like a deadly disease, but this is absurd: why then do we see immoral people living for so many years?'

610d *cause for alarm*: see Cephalus' speech, at 330d–e.

611a *in existence*: Plato does not here consider the possibility of a common pool, as it were, out of which souls are drawn for incarnation. The idea of a fixed number of souls is slightly odd, given the fact that some souls (such as that of Ardiaeus in 615c–616a) remain for ever in Tartarus (see also *Phaedo* 113e); and, at the opposite extreme, other dialogues show that a true philosopher could escape the round of reincarnation so that his soul would remain for ever in some blessed place. But perhaps Plato thought that these extreme cases were so rare that they would not significantly deplete the stock of souls.

611b *not long ago*: 435b ff.

611b *other arguments as well*: such as those in *Meno* and *Phaedo*.

611c *we've been discussing*: that is, you would actually be able to *see* the inner workings of the mind as it behaves morally and immorally, etc. This would, at a stroke, solve the problems raised by Glaucon and Adeimantus at the beginning of Chapter 2. The claim that the mind is essentially unified, and that it is incarnation which makes it tripartite, is of course a matter of faith rather than argument, since it is only within incarnation that we can normally perceive the workings of the mind and so have a basis for arguing about its nature; but it is certainly implicit in earlier phases of the book that it becomes more unified the more moral it is (see the note on 439e for the soul as a single 'energy-body'). It follows from Plato's description of the unitary mind that the philosopher is closest to this ideal state and has therefore detached himself most from the consequences of incarnation: this is no more than one would expect, given passages such as 519b. He also probably has in mind the disruptive effects of immorality on the mind (see especially Chapter 11).

611e *the whole of it*: that is, all three parts (as opposed to the usual situation of at least the lowest, acquisitive part dragging it downwards). Careless reading of this passage has often led commentators to claim that Plato is conceiving of the mind here as unitary, and is therefore implicitly denying the earlier tripartition of the mind. But the single word 'whole' disproves this reading. The statements at 611b therefore refer to a disunited mind—an immoral one, where the three parts pull in different directions; and the present paragraph refers to a unified mind, the closest approximation to which on earth (see the previous note) is the moral mind of Chapter 6, in which the three parts are in harmony. Plato is saying that the mind is always a three-in-one: conflict may obscure this, but it does not destroy it. Immorality tends to obscure it, but morality is (like physical health) a natural state. Other than this, the passage has suffered from over-interpretation, and the conservative approach of R. A. Shiner is best ('Soul in *Republic* X, 611', *Apeiron*, 6 (1972), 23–30).

612b *Homer did*: Adeimantus, at 363a ff.

612b *magical ring*: Gyges' ring makes its appearance at 359c–360d (but see the note on 359d). Hades' helmet was another magical instrument of invisibility.

612d *Do you remember?*: 360e–361d.

612e *the beginning too*: 352b. This back reference is presumably what makes Plato feel entitled to produce such a cursory argument in this section.

613a *or after it*: compare 379a–380c.

613b *he remarked*: it was a common Greek philosophical belief that perception of all kinds works by the principle of 'like to like': we can see *x* because in some sense we have some *x* in our eyes. So Plato stresses (as at 611e–612a) that the mind is of the same order as the types which it ideally perceives. Here we have a religious application of the same principle: God must perceive a person who is like him. On morality as assimilation to God see also 500b–d and *Theaetetus* 176b–177a; the principle runs directly counter to the usual Greek view that it is hubris to aspire to resemble God. On the idea that you become like what you spend time with see (for instance) 395d and 606b, where it forms part of the reason for condemning representational poetry.

613b *on the way back*: a Greek track event called a *diaulos* consisted of running once up the track and once back.

613c *ears on their shoulders*: like a dejected donkey. We would say, of course, 'With their tails between their legs.'

613c *as well as chaplets*: a chaplet was the official prize, but a successful athlete would be well rewarded by his home town as well (see 621c).

613c *about immoral people*: 362b–c.

613e *coarse*: see 361e for Glaucon's use of the word and his list of tortures.

614b *Alcinous had to endure*: Odysseus' account of his adventures, told to Alcinous, occupies all of books 9–12 of Homer's *Odyssey*. There is a slight but untranslatable pun in the Greek: Er is described as *alkimos* ('brave')—a poetic word chosen for its cognate similarity to Alcinous' name. My 'endure...endurance' at least goes some way towards capturing the light tone. As a piece of moral literature, the myth that now follows should just be read and enjoyed; the best critical and philosophical account is that of J. Annas, 'Plato's Myths of Judgement', *Phronesis*, 27 (1982), 119–43.

614b *soul*: see note on 608d: it is now impossible to resist the translation 'soul', so the reader should be aware that it is the same word which has previously been translated 'mind'. This makes the anthropomorphic features of the souls' afterlife experiences slightly less odd.

614c *judges*: traditional figures of an indeterminate number, but three became prominent—Minos, Rhadamanthys, and Aeacus. Belief in afterlife judgement (and therefore in some kind of crossroads in the underworld) was widespread in Greece.

614e *meadow*: the asphodel meadow of Homer's *Odyssey* 11. 539, which entered tradition as part of the geography of the underworld.

615a *a thousand years*: note how Plato plays with multiples of the Pythagorean sacred number 10 throughout the myth; there are other Pythagorean and Orphic features in the myth, interwoven with tradition and Plato's invention. Plato's eschatological myths at the ends of *Gorgias* and of *Phaedo* are also well worth reading for comparison. The souls' time in the underworld is described as a journey because specific punishments for specific crimes were located in different regions of the underworld, so the souls would have gone from region to region before being allowed back.

615b *than the crime*: in other words, in the afterlife you relive your life ten times.

615c *isn't worth mentioning*: possibly they entered a kind of limbo, as Virgil records (*Aeneid* 6. 426–9): this is irrelevant to Plato's present purposes, for which he must stress rewards and punishments. This is his reason for not discussing their fate: I very much doubt that he is motivated by guilt (as some commentators have suggested) over his ambiguous suggestions about exposing unwanted children (460c, 461c).

616a *Tartarus*: the lowest and ghastliest region of Hades.

616c *the whole rotation together*: we know that Er is on the surface of the earth (614c ff.)—it may, however, be the 'real earth' of which the concluding myth of *Phaedo* speaks, in so far as it is not our familiar earth. He is taken on a journey to the centre of the universe; in Plato's geocentric view, this coincides with the centre of the earth. He approaches the shaft of light—soon to be called the spindle of Necessity too—which forms the central axis of the universe. Looking up, he can see that the ends of the outer rim of the universe join on to the shaft of light and stretch away from it:

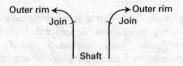

Notice how the shape resembles the top of a pillar, to which Plato has just likened the shaft. The shaft extends into a kind of strap which pulls the two halves of the universe together, and so the shaft maintains the integrity of the universe. (The naval simile refers, I think, to the cables which ran under a trireme, from one side to the other, ending in a tightening apparatus, and thus helped to keep the planks of wood together.)

616e *of the eighth whorl*: here is an ancient Greek spindle:

The spindle hung freely. The wool, drawn from the distaff, passed under the hook (to keep the spindle upright) and was wound round the stem. The whorl helped rotation and balance.

616e *of the second whorl*: the concentric whorls, viewed from above, would have looked something like this:

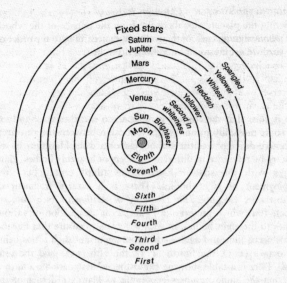

(Note that Plato here transposes Venus and Mercury.) Why do the 'rims' vary in broadness? And why in this way? It is difficult to say that the differing widths represent Plato's views on the distances between the planets, since at *Timaeus* 36d we meet an entirely different system for the distances between planets, and our passage seems to concern size rather than distance: distance is not really taken into account, since all the whorls fit 'snugly' inside one another.

In the *Timaeus* passage, as well as here, Plato is undoubtedly imagining the planets as being related to one another in terms of precise and meaningful mathematical ratios. In short, he is not trying to explain actual astronomical phenomena; he is concerned with arithmological theories like the Pythagorean Harmony of the Spheres (617b).

Although Plato chose not to assign actual values to the various widths in our passage (since his purpose is to impress the orderliness of the universe on our minds without boring us with minutiae), it is impossible to escape the impression that he did have particular values in mind. Given Plato's silence, informed guesswork is the best one can do; but it is worth noting, as justification for the attempt, that the assignment of different widths is certainly not as random as it may appear (see J. Cook Wilson,

'Plato, *Republic* 616e', *Classical Review*, 16 (1902), 292–3). Ordering the planets alphabetically from the outside of the whorl, and then assigning each of them a number according to the order of rim-size, we get clusters of additions up to 9:

$$\begin{array}{cccccccc} A & B & C & D & E & F & G & H \\ 1 & 8 & 7 & 3 & 6 & 2 & 5 & 4 \end{array}$$

It is clear that the context is musical; so it makes sense to look for some musically meaningful relationship between the rim-sizes. Although different ancient authors elaborated the Harmony of the Spheres by reference to different numbers of heavenly bodies, Plato shares with the scholar Eratosthenes (third century BC) the employment of eight bodies. There is a bizarre fragment of Eratosthenes (see my *The Theology of Arithmetic* (see note on 460e), 104) which preserves a Pythagorean assignation of various values to the eight bodies, in such a way as to ensure that musical ratios occur time and again—the most important such ratios being the octave (2:1), the fourth (4:3), the fifth (3:2) and the tone (9:8). Here is a table showing Eratosthenes' assignations, and then ordering the same numbers according to Plato's ordering of the rim-sizes:

Fixed Stars	♄	♃	♂	☿	♀	☉	☽
A	B	C	D	E	F	G	H
Eratosthenes 36	32	24	21	12	16	18	9
Plato? 36	9	12	24	16	32	18	21

It would be more than foolish to claim that these values are at all certain, since Plato leaves no clues. However, this is the *kind* of thing he was up to. And note, in passing, that on this system the Harmony of the Spheres is a triple octave (36:9).

617a *not as white as the third*: these colours are clearly assigned on the basis of observation, plus the theoretical knowledge—gained originally from the Presocratic philosopher Parmenides of Elea (fl. *c.*475), as far as we know—that the moon reflects the sun's light.

617a *the direction of the whole*: from a geocentric point of view, the planets appear to travel from west to east, while the diurnal movement of the whole heaven is from east to west.

617b *and fifth*: from the geocentric point of view, the sun, Venus, and Mercury all take about a year to circle the earth; the moon takes some 29.5 days; Mars takes 687 days; Jupiter takes about twelve years; Saturn takes about 29.5 years.

617b *retrograde motion*: of course, all the planets periodically appear retrograde from a geocentric perspective; Plato's mention of the phenomenon in the case of Mars is a mere embellishment of his narrative.

617d *condemned to impermanence*: this must refer to the impermanence of repeated incarnations, since the souls themselves are immortal.

617e *your own deities*: that is, the *genius* or guardian spirit of your life—which, ultimately, makes you the particular individual you are, with your predilections and life-pattern. It steered you, in Greek thought, subconsciously (see 620e); but a particularly advanced individual such as Socrates could consciously hear its voice (see note on 496c).

618c *at any given moment*: so our prenatal choice of life does not determine our destiny once and for all time. We can reinforce or change that choice at every instant of our lives (within a predetermined framework: see note on 620e). This elusive sentence invites us to read the myth as not only concerned with a time between incarnations, but also as allegorical for a 'time' when one is in an altered state of consciousness within one's own lifetime: famous examples of such revelatory mystical visions include those of Muhammad and St Teresa of Avila.

619b *stupidity and greed*: it is odd to find the soul, which has just been said to be tripartite only because of its involvement with the physical world (611b–612a), liable after death to the kinds of base motives we have come to associate with the lower parts of the mind/soul. It may be that even after a thousand years of purgation traces remain of one's previous incarnation: this is the implication of 619c–d.

619c *eating his own children*: as legendary dictators such as Thyestes had done.

620a *amusing, and astonishing*: in other words, it aroused precisely the emotions Plato expressed disapproval of in 603e–606d. It is arguable that the myth is meant to be an example of the kind of story-telling Plato finds acceptable. It is in prose, and it tells a moral tale. Another clue to the same reading of the myth lies in the predominance of the heroes of the Homeric poems and fifth-century tragedies.

620a *a female incarnation*: the Greeks regarded all swans as male. Swans were famous for their 'swansong' at the approach of death; hence Plato will shortly classify them as songbirds, and it makes a suitable incarnation for the musician Orpheus, as (more obviously) the nightingale does for Thamyras.

620b *about the armour*: after Achilles' death, Ajax laid claim to his armour—symbolically to his status as supreme Greek champion. To Ajax's chagrin, however, it was awarded to Odysseus: in consequence, Ajax killed himself. Nevertheless, Ajax's prowess matches that of a lion, as Agamemnon's nobility does that of an eagle.

620e *unalterable*: perhaps we are to imagine one of them spinning the warp, and the other the woof, of a person's life. There are clear astrological connotations to the passage: the word translated 'destiny' also means (or came to mean) 'degree on the zodiacal circle'; 'ratify' is cognate with the rulership of a planet. In short, as well as setting an individual's destiny in a more abstract sense, the Fates do so according to the positions of the planets (Atropos) and the zodiacal signs (Clotho). Note that, despite Plato's use of the word 'unalterable' (and see also 618b on temperament), it is only the broad framework which is fixed; the whole of Plato's philosophy leaves room for self-improvement within that framework. Annas, 'Plato's Myths of Judgement' (note on 614b), overstresses the predetermination and downplays the element of moment-by-moment choice. She also finds the myth incompatible with the rest of the book in that it portrays a universe in which there is an overall balance of good and bad, such that my personal contribution cannot make any difference. On this see p. lv. And in other dialogues Plato holds out the prospect of breaking free of the cycles of incarnation, as a result of unmitigated goodness; the myth of *Republic* is surprisingly silent on this score, but it is not incompatible with his vision here, and there seems to be an oblique reference to it at 498c.

621a *the Plain of Oblivion*: a familiar geographical feature of the underworld in Greek thought, as is a variously named river to make one forget. The lack of shelter from the heat appears to be a Platonic invention—perhaps to explain the souls' instinctive willingness to drink from the river.

621a *the required amount*: presumably those who drink less can be more conscious in their next incarnation: they stand a better chance of recollection, perhaps (see note on 518c). Plato does call philosophers awake or conscious (as at 476c and 520c). It is odd that we are supposed to choose a life and *then* forget; but it is a common religious notion that each of us is here on earth for some particular purpose which is preordained in some way and which we have to work to uncover.

458

621b *shooting stars*: there is a not uncommon belief that on death people's souls become stars. Plato probably got the idea from the Middle East.

621b *funeral pyre*: see 614b.

621b *to the end*: a traditional phrase for ending a story.

621d *from all quarters*: for the athletic imagery see especially 465d ff. and 613b ff.

621d *of our story*: see 615a.

TEXTUAL NOTES

I have translated the Greek of J. Burnet's Oxford Classical Text, *Platonis Opera*, vol. iv (Oxford University Press, 1903), except at the following points, indicated in the text by an obelisk. Line-references are to the OCT.

344e1 Reading ἀλλ' οὐ with the better MSS.

345c3 Reading ποιμαίνειν with the majority of the MSS.

352e9 Retaining ἄν with the MSS and reading φαῖμεν (Stephanus).

359d8–e1 Reading ἔχειν οὐδὲν ... ὄν ... with the majority of the MSS.

363d3 Reading φασὶν ἀμείνους κατόπισθεν (Waterfield): καὶ γένος is an easy corruption from contexts like Tyrtaeus 9. 30 Diehl.

367d2 Reading ὀνήσιμα (Waterfield).

380d3 Retaining καί with the best MSS.

387c2 Omitting ὡς οἴεται (Hertz).

399d4 Reading πάντα τὰ παναρμόνια (Waterfield).

400b5 Reading δακτυλικόν, after a suggestion of Jackson's.

400b7–8 I transpose εἰς βραχύ τε καὶ μακρὸν γιγνόμενον to after ἴαμβον (cf. Adam's note ad loc.).

400e2 Retaining ὡς εὐήθειαν with the MSS.

414e2 Omitting καί before ἡ γῆ (Ast).

434d7 Omitting Burnet's added ἤ.

440c8–d1 Reading καὶ διὰ τὸ πεινῆν καὶ τὸ ῥιγοῦν καὶ πάντα τὰ τοιαῦτα πάσχειν ὑπομένει καὶ νικᾷ (Waterfield).

443c4 Reading ὠφέλει (Ast).

444b5 Reading δουλεύειν τῷ τοῦ [δουλεύειν] ἀρχικοῦ γένους ὄντι (Waterfield).

455b2 Reading γυναικὶ ἢ ἀνδρί (Waterfield).

457b2 Omitting σοφίας (Schneider).

473a6 Bywater's ἄν is unnecessary.

473c6 I follow all the best MSS in reading ἐπ' αὐτὸ ... εἶμι ... προσεικάζομεν.

500a2–4 Burnet's excision of this whole sentence is far too drastic. Baiter's τ' οὐ instead of τοι, with the sentence read as a question, is an easy solution.

501b3–4 Reading πρὸς ἐκεῖνο αὖ ὃ ἐν τοῖς ἀνθρώποις ἐμποιοῖεν (Adam).

503c4 Transposing καί from before νεανικοί to before οἷοι (Heindorf).

504e4 Retaining the transmitted text ἄξιον τὸ διανόημα.

510b6–7 Omitting τό before ἐπ' ἀρχήν (Ast), and altering Burnet's punctuation accordingly.

515b4–5 Reading οὐ ταῦτα ἡγῇ ἂν τὰ παριόντα αὐτοὺς νομίζειν ὀνομάζειν ἅπερ ὁρῷεν with the best MSS and recent editors.

529c2 Marindin's ἐξυπτιασμένος seems obviously correct.

532c1 Reading θέα (Ast, Apelt).

533e4–5 Reading (as part of Glaucon's reply): ἀλλ' ὃ ἂν μόνον δηλοῖ πρὸς τὴν ἕξιν σαφηνείας πῶς ἔχει ἐν ψυχῇ (Waterfield), and omitting Burnet's additions.

553b4 Retaining βλαπτόμενον with the MSS.

559b4 Reading τε παῦσαι ζῶντα οὐ δυνατή (Hermann).

559e1–2 The text seems undeniably corrupt. I suggest reading μεταβολῆς ἐξ ὀλιγαρχικῆς ⟨κατασκευῆς⟩ τῆς ἐν ἑαυτῷ εἰς δημοκρατικήν. This at least has the virtue of raising the possibility of haplography.

564e10 Reading βλίττειν (Adam).

568d8–9 Reading ὅποι ποτὲ ἂν μὴ ἐξαρκῇ τὰ τῶν ἀπολομένων (Waterfield).

581e2 Retaining τῆς ἡδονῆς with the MSS and reading it as a genitive of measure after ἐν τοιούτῳ τινί (Adam).

581e5 It is surely a misprint in the OCT to read this as a question.

600c1 Reading ὑπ' αὐτοῦ ἐκείνου (Ast).

604b4 Reading αὐτῷ ἀναγκαῖον with the best MSS.

Cleitophon

I append a translation of this fragmentary dialogue first because it is very rarely read or translated, although it is enjoyable, and second because it has considerable interest and value as an appendix to Republic. Although it is preserved in the corpus of Platonic works, it is unlikely to be by Plato himself: stylistic reasons seem to rule that out. Nevertheless, there is no reason to doubt that it was written in the fourth century. Since it lifts characters and themes from the first chapter of Republic, do we have here a fragment of work from one of Plato's students at the Academy? Was he trying to respond to what Plato had written in Republic? I imagine it being read out loud to provoke debate within the Academy.

Initially, we meet some over-brief paraphrases of themes and ideas from earlier Platonic dialogues: bits of Protagoras and Euthydemus are particularly evident. But soon Republic starts to form the background. The central criticism of the piece is that it is all very well making grandiose claims about morality and about how important it is for all of us, but what exactly does it do? What is its product? These questions are raised not only concerning the kinds of ideas about morality which are floated in the first chapter of Republic, but also concerning an 'elegant' definition of morality as 'friendship within communities' (which seems to reflect the definition of social morality in Chapter 6, although it does also occur at 351d) and as knowledge (which seems to reflect Chapters 8–10). And they are questions many readers of Republic have asked themselves. In the Introduction (pp. lii–lxii) I have suggested that ultimately Plato sees the 'product' of morality as the spread of rational order.

406a SOCRATES. Someone's just been telling me that Cleitophon the son of Aristonymus, in conversation with Lysias, was critical of Socrates' discourses and highly complimentary about Thrasymachus' company and teaching.

CLEITOPHON. In that case, Socrates, he didn't give you an accurate report of my conversation with Lysias. I had both good things and bad things to say about you. Now, however much you might pretend not to be bothered, I can see you're cross with me, so why don't I tell you myself what I said? There's no one else here besides the two of us, and I'd love to tell you, so that you'll be less inclined to think I'm running you down. I mean, you probably haven't had an accurate account, because if you had, you wouldn't be as angry with me as you seem to be. If you'll let me speak freely, I'd relish the opportunity and I'd like to explain.

SOCRATES. It would be shocking of me not to submit to your 407a critique, when you're so keen to do me this favour. I call it a favour because obviously, once I'm aware of my good and bad aspects, I'll do my best to cultivate and pursue the good aspects and avoid the bad ones.

CLEITOPHON. All right, then. Now, I've spent a lot of time in your company, Socrates, and I've found what you say very impressive. I don't think that anyone has anything more valuable to say than you when you tell people off, like a god in a dramatic contraption,* and constantly ask them, 'Where are you off to? You don't know what it's right to do. You devote b all your energy to making money, but you don't try to find teachers of morality for your sons, to whom you're going to pass on all this money, to enable them to know how to use it for moral purposes—that is, if morality is teachable: if it's a matter of training and practice, then you ought to be looking for people to give them adequate training and practice. Moreover, you've never spent time looking after yourselves in the same way. But since you can see that all the education you and your children have had in reading and writing, music and c physical exercise (which you regard as a complete education in goodness), hasn't made the slightest difference to the badness of your behaviour when you're faced with money, why don't you despise the current educational system and try to find people to rid you of this coarseness? After all, the discordant clash of brothers falling out with one another and countries going to war doesn't arise over some discord between feet and music; the d extremes of action and suffering that war brings are a result of people clashing over morality, and of people not bothering to pay attention to the matter. You claim that immorality isn't a result of lack of education or ignorance—that immoral people choose to be immoral; but on the other hand you *do* admit that immorality is wrong and loathed by the gods, and in that case how could anyone deliberately *choose* something that bad? Because he can't resist pleasure, you reply. But if resistance is

---

* Asterisks refer to the notes below, p. 468.

deliberate, is failure to resist not deliberate? Whichever way you look at it, the argument proves that immorality is not deliberately chosen, and from this it follows that every
e individual and every country should pay more attention to the matter.'

So when I hear you going on and on like this, Socrates, I'm full of admiration and I praise you to the skies. The same goes for when you add that people who cultivate their bodies but neglect their minds are behaving badly: they're neglecting the ruler and cultivating the subject. And when you claim that if people don't know how to make use of a thing, it's better for them not to have anything to do with it. So if someone doesn't know how to make proper use of his eyes or ears or his body in general, then rather than using them at all, it's better for him not to hear or see or use his body for anything. And the same
408a goes for expertise. Anyone who doesn't know how to use his own lyre obviously doesn't know how to use his neighbour's lyre either, and anyone who doesn't know how to use others' lyres doesn't know how to use his own either, and so on for all his other implements and possessions.* You draw a good conclusion from all this, that anyone who doesn't know how to use his mind is better off leaving the mind alone and not living,* rather than living without its influence on his behaviour. Alternatively, if he really has to live, then it's better for him
b actually to spend his life as a slave rather than as a free man— to behave like someone handing over the rudder of the ship of his mind to someone else, someone who has learnt how to steer human affairs, which is how you often describe political expertise, Socrates, which you also say is the same as expertise in law and morality.

I've never said a word against all these excellent arguments, and others like them, about how goodness can be learnt and
c how everyone should look after himself above all. And I doubt I ever will say anything against them: I think they're very inspirational* and beneficial, and literally wake us up from a kind of sleep.

So I was anxious to hear what came next. I didn't ask *you* at first, Socrates, but some of your contemporaries and some of those who share your interests—your companions, or whatever you'd like me to call them. I first questioned the ones who are highly regarded by you and asked them what you went on to say next. My interrogation of them resembled one of yours! d 'My friends,' I said, 'Socrates inspires us to be good, but how do we understand the inspiration he offers? Is this all there is, even though it isn't the kind of thing you can just go out and get all at once? Is this to be our lifelong task, to inspire those who have not yet been inspired, and to inspire them to inspire others? Or should we ask Socrates and one another what comes next: on the understanding that it's possible for people to pursue good- e ness, then what? What do we say is the proper place to begin learning about morality?

'Suppose someone inspired us to take care of our bodies, because he saw that, like children, we didn't have the slightest awareness of the existence of the arts of physical exercise and of medicine; and suppose he then told us off and said that it was wrong to devote all our attention to wheat, barley, vines, and all the things we cultivate and acquire for the sake of our bodies, and not to try to find the art or means of maximizing the body's welfare—which is to say, the arts I've mentioned. And suppose we asked this person, "What are these arts you're 409a talking about?" He'd presumably reply that they are the arts of physical exercise and of medicine. So my question is this: which art is it, in our opinion, whose domain is the goodness of the mind? What's your answer?'

Well, the most formidable-looking of the people I spoke to like this replied, 'The art you're asking about is the one you hear Socrates talking about—that is, morality.' So I said, 'Don't only tell me its name; I need an answer along the following lines. Take the art called the art of medicine: it has two results. b One is that doctors, in addition to being doctors, can always make others doctors, and the other is health. Neither of these on its own actually constitutes the art, and what we call health is the product of the art, which both teaches and is the subject taught. The same goes for building: the product is a house, while building is the theory. So let's say, on the same principle, that it's the job of morality to make people moral, just as it's the job of each of the arts to create artisans. But what about the other result? What *product* are we to say a moral person produces? Can you answer this?' c

Now, I think it was the person I was addressing who replied

that the product was advantage, while from others I received different answers—duty, benefit, and profit.* I started up again and said, 'These names are also applicable within every art: they *all* involve correct action, profit, benefit, and so on. And every art will also lay claim to the underlying point of profit, benefit, and so on. For example, building will lay claim to goodness, fineness, and appropriateness in the context of producing

d wooden objects—i.e. things which are not identical with the art. Can you also say what the product of morality is as well?'

Eventually, Socrates, one of your companions gave me an answer which seemed very elegant. He said that the particular product of morality, which none of the other arts produced, was friendship within communities. On being questioned, he went on to say that friendship was good and never bad, and on being questioned further he said that although we use the same term in referring to pederasty and bestiality, he didn't accept that they were kinds of friendship.* Then it turned out that

e there are more harmful kinds of friendship than there are good ones. He tried to escape from these difficulties by denying that any harmful ones were in fact kinds of friendship and by claiming that anyone who used the term in this way was using it wrongly. Authentic and genuine friendship was obviously, he said, unanimity. When he was asked whether he'd define unanimity as identity of belief or as knowledge, he said that mere identity of belief didn't deserve to be called friendship, since people commonly hold the same *harmful* beliefs, whereas his position was that friendship was good in all respects, and was the product of morality, and that was why he claimed that it was unanimity and that unanimity was knowledge, not belief. At this point in the conversation, then, we reached an impasse,

410a since he was in the company of people who could caustically point out that his argument had come round in a circle to the same place it started from.* And I said, 'The art of medicine too is a kind of unanimity,* and so are all the arts, and they too are capable of giving an account of their domains.* But the objective of this morality or unanimity of yours has escaped us: it's unclear what its product is.'

Eventually, then, Socrates, I came to you yourself with my questions, and you told me that it was the job of morality to

b harm one's enemies and help one's friends. Later, however, it transpired that a moral person never harms anyone,* since everything he does to anyone is for that person's good. I stood my ground and persistently—not just once or twice—tried to resist thinking that although there's no one better than you at inspiring people to attend to goodness, nevertheless there are two possibilities.

First, perhaps you were only capable of so much and no more, which is what one might find in the case of any other art. One can conceive, for instance, of someone who isn't a helmsman concentrating on how to praise the respects in which helmsmanship is valuable to people; and the same thing is c possible for all the other arts. So you might perhaps be liable to the same charge in the case of morality—of not being particularly knowledgeable about morality, because you eulogize it so well.*

Not that this was the case, as far as I was concerned; still, there are the two possibilities—either you're ignorant, or you're keeping morality from me. That's why I think I'll go to Thrasymachus and anywhere else I can—because I'm stuck, unless you're prepared to put an end to the inspirational talk d now. For instance, if you'd been inspiring me to physical exercise and saying that I oughtn't to neglect my body, you might follow your inspirational argument by next describing what kind of thing the body is and, given its nature, what kind of attention it requires. I'd appreciate the same thing happening now. You can count Cleitophon as agreeing to the absurdity of paying attention to other things and yet neglecting the mind, when the mind is what we cultivate those other things for. And e please assume that I've also just said the same about all the subsequent topics—the ones I just went through, in fact.*

I beg you to carry out my wishes, to stop me doing what I do at the moment, which is praise you to Lysias and others in some respects, but criticize you in others. Otherwise I'll have to say, Socrates, that while your value to someone who has not been inspired is inestimable, yet when someone has already been inspired you are not far off actually impeding his attainment of complete goodness and of happiness.

Notes

407a *dramatic contraption*: actors playing the parts of gods in Greek plays were often raised to a higher level than the mundane stage by means of a piece of machinery. Hence, if a god intervened from there he was (in the Latin phrase which has entered the English language) a *deus ex machina*.

408a *implements and possessions*: the point of the argument must be political: anyone who does not wield knowledge in his own life should not have control over others' lives.

408a *and not living*: remember that the mind (*psukhē*) is also the life-force.

408c *inspirational*: 'inspire' and its cognates translate the Greek *protrepein* and its cognates. To *protrepein* someone, in a philosophical context, was to convert him to a life of philosophy.

409c *duty, benefit, and profit*: see *Republic* 336d.

409d *friendship*: philia, the Greek word translated 'friendship', covered a range of emotions and activities, including friendship, loyalty, and love.

410a *started from*: to define morality as friendship begged the question as to what kind of friendship; to define it as knowledge begs the question as to what kind of knowledge. All the other party (Plato?) appears to be able to say is that it is good kinds of friendship and knowledge.

410a *kind of unanimity*: the ideal of any science lies in establishing a fixed body of knowledge on which no further advances can be made. Ideally knowledgeable doctors would agree about their diagnoses, prognoses, treatments, and so on.

410a *their domains*: notice the assumption that knowledge can be defined by the ability to give an account: see *Republic* 531e and 534b.

410b *never harms anyone*: see *Republic* 335b–d. In *Republic*, however, it is certainly not Socrates who claims that morality lies in helping friends and harming enemies.

410c *eulogize it so well*: the point has not been clearly made. He means that one might exhaust one's limited resources on *either* becoming an expert *or* in learning how to eulogize a subject, but not have the capacity for both.

410e *went through, in fact*: the eyes, ears, and lyres argument (407e–408b).

INDEX OF NAMES

death and glory of the Trojan War, while his *Odyssey* recounts the fanciful and marvellous adventures of one hero, Odysseus, returning from the war to his home on Ithaca.

HOMERIDAE, a guild consisting of the 'descendants of Homer', not in the literal sense, but in that they felt they were continuing and preserving his work and his name.

ISMENIAS, a Theban democrat at the end of the fifth and beginning of the fourth centuries who was known to accept bribes.

LACHESIS, one of the three Fates; her name means 'she who allots'.

LEONTIUS, an Athenian who illustrates an important philosophical and psychological point at 439e–440a; curiously, in this context, a contemporary comic fragment says that he was sexually attracted to young men who were as pale as corpses.

LYCURGUS, the semi-legendary founder of Sparta's constitution.

LYSANIAS, Cephalus' father.

LYSIAS, *c*.459–380, son of Cephalus; silently present throughout the dialogue; subsequent to the dramatic date of *Republic*, he was to become one of the most famous writers of political and legal speeches, and was highly admired for his simple, straightforward style.

MARSYAS, inventor of the reed-pipe in myth; challenged Apollo to a musical contest, but Apollo with his cithara won and Marsyas was flayed to death for his presumption.

MENELAUS, king of Sparta and brother of Agamemnon at the time of the Trojan War; it was the rape of his wife Helen by Paris that started the war.

MIDAS, legendary king of Phrygia; one of the famous stories about him has him turning everything he touches into gold—a talent he soon comes to regret.

MUSAEUS, legendary bard and founder of the Eleusinian mysteries, often closely associated with Orpheus.

NICERATUS, son of the eminent Athenian general Nicias; silently present throughout the dialogue; recurs in a Socratic context in Xenophon's *Symposium*; killed during the oligarchic reign of terror in Athens in 404 BC.

NIOBE, in Greek myth the archetype of grief; she boasted that, because she had borne twelve children, she was better than Leto, who had only borne two; but those two were the gods Apollo and Artemis, who then killed all her children; in her grief Niobe was turned into a weeping rock, which was a famous spectacle.

ODYSSEUS, the resourceful hero of Homer's *Iliad* and (especially) *Odyssey*, which tells the stories of his arduous journey home from the Trojan War, plagued by the hatred of the god Poseidon.

ORPHEUS, legendary bard and founder of a mystic sect originating in

Thrace; he was supposed to have been killed and dismembered by maenads, female followers of Dionysus.

PALAMEDES, a Greek hero at the time of the Trojan War, best known for his various inventions (the alphabet, counting, backgammon); he found out that Odysseus had tried to avoid military service, and in revenge Odysseus forged a letter which made Palamedes seem a traitor and caused him to be executed.

PANDARUS, a Trojan archer who broke a truce between the Greeks and the Trojans by shooting at and wounding Menelaus; in Homer's account (*Iliad* 4. 20 ff.) Zeus, Hera, and Athena are as much to blame as Pandarus himself.

PATROCLUS, Achilles' inseparable companion in Homer's *Iliad*, whose death finally spurs Achilles out of his injured pride and back into battle.

PEIRITHOUS, son of Zeus and Dia; all his most famous adventures are undertaken with Theseus; together they fought the centaurs and the Amazons, abducted Helen (the same Helen whom Paris was later to abduct more permanently), and braved Hades in an attempt to abduct Persephone.

PELEUS, grandson of Zeus; proverbially self-disciplined in resisting the sexual advances of Astydameia, wife of his host Acastus in Iolcus; for his virtue he was awarded Thetis as his wife.

PELOPS, started life badly by being chopped up by his father Tantalus and served to the gods (who then put him back together again, except for a shoulder which Demeter had eaten); later cursed by Myrtilus, whom he treacherously killed out of jealousy; the curse ran through several generations.

PERDICCAS, king of Macedon *c*.450–413; probably regarded as treacherous by Athenians, because he (*a*) weakened their hold on his lands, (*b*) kept entering into and breaking alliances with them; but he succeeded in establishing Macedon as a unified kingdom—and a future power-base for Alexander the Great.

PERIANDER, tyrant of Corinth *c*.625–575; under his rule Corinth became a rich and powerful commercial centre; he is sometimes counted as one of the Seven Sages (see e.g. Solon).

PHOCYLIDES, fl. *c*.540; lyric poet from Miletus, only a few fragments of whose work survive.

PHOEBUS, another name for Apollo.

PINDAR, 518–438, from Cynoscephalae, arguably the greatest of the Greek lyric poets.

PITTACUS, fl. *c*.600, from Mytilene in Asia Minor; with Solon, Bias, and Thales, he is one of the constant members in the varying lists of the Seven Sages, famed chiefly for their practical wisdom.

POLEMARCHUS, son of Cephalus, interlocutor in Chapter 1; we may infer from *Phaedrus* 257b that he became a disciple of Socrates; he was executed during the oligarchic reign of terror in Athens in 404 BC.

POSEIDON, brother of Zeus and Hades; lord of the surface of the earth (hence mainly of the sea), as Zeus is of the upper air and Hades is of the underworld.

POULYDAMAS, a well-built Athenian pancratiast; winner at the Olympic Games of 408 BC.

PRIAM, king of Troy at the time of the legendary Trojan War of the Homeric poems; father of Hector, Paris, etc., and grandson or great-grandson of Zeus.

PRODICUS, a contemporary of Socrates from the island of Ceos, and one of the leading lights of the sophistic movement.

PROTAGORAS, fl. *c.*450; from Abdera, the first and greatest of the sophists; his views are discussed extensively by Plato in his *Protagoras* and *Theaetetus*.

PROTEUS, mythical shape-shifting sea-deity from Egypt.

PYTHAGORAS, fl. *c.*530, mystical philosopher from Samos and southern Italy; especially famous for his arithmology (rather than his arithmetic).

PYTHAGOREANS, there were two main schools in the fifth century, both owing their origin to Pythagoras: one group concentrated on the sciences, especially mathematics; the other perpetuated their teacher's mystical and moral teaching. Plato seems not to think highly of the first lot (531c), but respects the others (600b).

SARPEDON, from Lycia, an ally of Troy during the legendary Trojan War; a favourite of Zeus, who was his father.

SIMONIDES, fl. *c.*500, famous lyric poet from the island of Ceos; many fragments survive.

SIRENS, although in Homer they were wicked women whose charming singing lured sailors to their death, by Plato's time they were well on their way (largely through Pythagorean influence) to becoming virtual demigods of song, and singers of universal harmony.

SOLON, fl. *c.*590, Athenian statesman and lyric poet; one of the constant members of the varying lists of Seven Sages of Greece; considered in Athenian popular history as the founding father of their democracy.

SOPHOCLES, *c.*495–406, with Aeschylus and Euripides, the second of the three great Athenian tragedians.

STESICHORUS, fl. *c.*585, lyric poet; famous for his vivid embellishments of myth and legend; became blind after composing a poem which insulted Helen, and so composed a palinode which claimed that she was innocent of causing the Trojan War—that she never even left home, and Paris eloped with her mere apparition! Since we have few fragments of Stesichorus' work, the story survives best for us through Euripides' *Helen*.

THALES, fl. *c.*575, from Miletus in Asia Minor; with Bias, Solon, and

Pittacus, one of the constant members in the varying lists of the Seven Sages, famed for their practical wisdom; also became an archetypal philosopher, and is reckoned, with some justification, to be the first of the so-called Presocratic philosophers, or proto-scientists.

THAMYRAS, a legendary bard, who thought he was a better singer than the Muses and was struck dumb for his presumption.

THEAGES, a companion of Socrates; the precise medical nature of the 'bridle of Theages' (which later became proverbial for bad health) of 496b is unknown; a possibly spurious Platonic dialogue is named after him.

THEMIS, originally an earth-goddess, and the patron of the oracle of Delphi before Apollo; her name means 'religiously sanctioned behaviour', so she later became a mere personification of this.

THEMISTOCLES, c.530–462; great Athenian military commander during the Persian Wars, and the statesman chiefly responsible for establishing Athens' potential for greatness after the wars.

THERSITES, the only non-aristocrat to have a speaking part in Homer's *Iliad* (2. 212 ff.); it is not a favourable part, however, and he became the archetype of a non-hero or a buffoon.

THESEUS, son of Poseidon; legendary early king, and national hero, of Athens; a great many tales were told about his various adventures.

THETIS, sea-nymph who mainly achieves prominence in Homer's *Iliad* as Achilles' mother; as with many sea-deities, she was a shape-shifter.

THRASYMACHUS, sophist from Chalcedon, an important trading town at the mouth of the Black Sea, on the Turkish side; Socrates' main interlocutor in Chapter 1; a well-known figure in Athens, where he lived for some time in the late fifth century.

URANUS, chief deity before Cronus (his name means 'Heaven'); the story of his castration by Cronus is vividly told in Hesiod, *Theogony* 154–210.

XERXES, king of Persia 486–465; notorious in Greece for his invasion in 480, which was at first highly successful but later defeated; the historian Herodotus is our main source.

ZEUS, chief god of the Olympian pantheon; god of the skies; brother of Hades and Poseidon; husband and brother of Hera.

	Classical Literary Criticism
	Greek Lyric Poetry
	Myths from Mesopotamia
APOLLODORUS	**The Library of Greek Mythology**
APOLLONIUS OF RHODES	**Jason and the Golden Fleece**
APULEIUS	**The Golden Ass**
ARISTOTLE	**The Nicomachean Ethics** **Physics** **Politics**
CAESAR	**The Civil War** **The Gallic War**
CATULLUS	**The Poems of Catullus**
CICERO	**The Nature of the Gods**
EURIPIDES	**Medea, Hippolytus, Electra, and Helen**
GALEN	**Selected Works**
HERODOTUS	**The Histories**
HESIOD	**Theogony and Works and Days**
HOMER	**The Iliad** **The Odyssey**
HORACE	**The Complete Odes and Epodes**
JUVENAL	**The Satires**
LIVY	**The Rise of Rome**
LUCAN	**The Civil War**
MARCUS AURELIUS	**The Meditations**
OVID	**The Love Poems** **Metamorphoses** **Sorrows of an Exile**

THOMAS AQUINAS	**Selected Philosophical Writings**
GEORGE BERKELEY	**Principles of Human Knowledge and Three Dialogues**
EDMUND BURKE	**A Philosophical Enquiry into the Origin of Our Ideas of the Sublime and Beautiful** **Reflections on the Revolution in France**
THOMAS CARLYLE	**The French Revolution**
CONFUCIUS	**The Analects**
FRIEDRICH ENGELS	**The Condition of the Working Class in England**
JAMES GEORGE FRAZER	**The Golden Bough**
THOMAS HOBBES	**Human Nature and De Corpore Politico** **Leviathan**
JOHN HUME	**Dialogues Concerning Natural Religion and The Natural History of Religion** **Selected Essays**
THOMAS MALTHUS	**An Essay on the Principle of Population**
KARL MARX	**Capital** **The Communist Manifesto**
J. S. MILL	**On Liberty and Other Essays** **Principles of Economy and Chapters on Socialism**
FRIEDRICH NIETZSCHE	**On the Genealogy of Morals** **Twilight of the Idols**
THOMAS PAINE	**Rights of Man, Common Sense, and Other Political Writings**
JEAN-JACQUES ROUSSEAU	**Discourse on Political Economy and The Social Contract** **Discourse on the Origin of Inequality**
SIMA QIAN	**Historical Records**
ADAM SMITH	**An Inquiry into the Nature and Causes of the Wealth of Nations**
MARY WOLLSTONECRAFT	**Political Writings**

The Bhagavad Gita

The Bible Authorized King James Version
  With Apocrypha

The Koran

The Pañcatantra

Upaniṣads

AUGUSTINE   **The Confessions**
                On Christian Teaching

BEDE   **The Ecclesiastical History**

HEMACANDRA   **The Lives of the Jain Elders**

ŚĀNTIDEVA   **The Bodhicaryàvatàra**

	Oriental Tales
WILLIAM BECKFORD	**Vathek**
JAMES BOSWELL	**Boswell's Life of Johnson**
FRANCES BURNEY	**Camilla** **Cecilia** **Evelina** **The Wanderer**
LORD CHESTERFIELD	**Lord Chesterfield's Letters**
JOHN CLELAND	**Memoirs of a Woman of Pleasure**
DANIEL DEFOE	**Captain Singleton** **A Journal of the Plague Year** **Memoirs of a Cavalier** **Moll Flanders** **Robinson Crusoe** **Roxana**
HENRY FIELDING	**Joseph Andrews and Shamela** **A Journey from This World to the Next and** **The Journal of a Voyage to Lisbon** **Tom Jones** **The Adventures of David Simple**
WILLIAM GODWIN	**Caleb Williams** **St Leon**
OLIVER GOLDSMITH	**The Vicar of Wakefield**
MARY HAYS	**Memoirs of Emma Courtney**
ELIZABETH HAYWOOD	**The History of Miss Betsy Thoughtless**
ELIZABETH INCHBALD	**A Simple Story**
SAMUEL JOHNSON	**The History of Rasselas**
CHARLOTTE LENNOX	**The Female Quixote**
MATTHEW LEWIS	**The Monk**

ANN RADCLIFFE	The Castles of Athlin and Dunbayne
	The Italian
	The Mysteries of Udolpho
	The Romance of the Forest
	A Sicilian Romance
FRANCES SHERIDAN	Memoirs of Miss Sidney Bidulph
TOBIAS SMOLLETT	The Adventures of Roderick Random
	The Expedition of Humphry Clinker
	Travels through France and Italy
LAURENCE STERNE	The Life and Opinions of Tristram Shandy, Gentleman
	A Sentimental Journey
JONATHAN SWIFT	Gulliver's Travels
	A Tale of a Tub and Other Works
HORACE WALPOLE	The Castle of Otranto
GILBERT WHITE	The Natural History of Selborne
MARY WOLLSTONECRAFT	Mary and The Wrongs of Woman

The
Oxford
World's
Classics
Website

www.worldsclassics.co.uk

- Information about new titles
- Explore the full range of Oxford World's Classics
- Links to other literary sites and the main OUP webpage
- Imaginative competitions, with bookish prizes
- Peruse *Compass*, the Oxford World's Classics magazine
- Articles by editors
- Extracts from Introductions
- A forum for discussion and feedback on the series
- Special information for teachers and lecturers

www.worldsclassics.co.uk

American Literature

British and Irish Literature

Children's Literature

Classics and Ancient Literature

Colonial Literature

Eastern Literature

European Literature

History

Medieval Literature

Oxford English Drama

Poetry

Philosophy

Politics

Religion

The Oxford Shakespeare

A complete list of Oxford Paperbacks, including Oxford World's Classics, OPUS, Past Masters, Oxford Authors, Oxford Shakespeare, Oxford Drama, and Oxford Paperback Reference, is available in the UK from the Academic Division Publicity Department, Oxford University Press, Great Clarendon Street, Oxford OX2 6DP.

In the USA, complete lists are available from the Paperbacks Marketing Manager, Oxford University Press, 198 Madison Avenue, New York, NY 10016.

Oxford Paperbacks are available from all good bookshops. In case of difficulty, customers in the UK can order direct from Oxford University Press Bookshop, Freepost, 116 High Street, Oxford OX1 4BR, enclosing full payment. Please add 10 per cent of published price for postage and packing.